THE OXFORD HANDBOOK OF

NATURAL
THEOLOGY

THE OXFORD HANDBOOK OF

NATURAL THEOLOGY

Edited by

RUSSELL RE MANNING

Consultant Editors

JOHN HEDLEY BROOKE & FRASER WATTS

OXFORD
UNIVERSITY PRESS

OXFORD

UNIVERSITY PRESS

Great Clarendon Street, Oxford, OX2 6DP,
United Kingdom

Oxford University Press is a department of the University of Oxford.
It furthers the University's objective of excellence in research, scholarship,
and education by publishing worldwide. Oxford is a registered trade mark of
Oxford University Press in the UK and in certain other countries

British Library Cataloguing in Publication Data

Data available

Library of Congress Cataloging in Publication Data

Data available

ISBN 978-0-19-955693-9

Printed in Great Britain by
MPG Books Group, Bodmin and King's Lynn

ACKNOWLEDGEMENTS

Putting together a Handbook such as this is a collaborative enterprise and I am primarily grateful to all those who have contributed chapters to the book. It has been an absolute pleasure to work with such a distinguished set of contributors, all of whom have added more to the volume that simply their respective chapters. I was fortunate to be able to reliable upon the expertise and guidance of my two Consultant Editors, especially in the early stages as the project emerged from a proposal into reality. I have learnt much from both John and Fraser—in the course of this project and more widely—and it has been a privilege to work with them.

This project began in Cambridge and bears the marks of my initial engagement with the varieties of natural theology whilst combining teaching in the Philosophy of Religion with being a part of Fraser Watts' Psychology and Religion Research Group. I am grateful, amongst others, to Douglas Hedley, Liz Gulliford, Vittorio Montemaggi, Léon Turner, and Louise Hickman. To the Master and Fellows of St Edmund's College, Cambridge I owe a great debt for their warm and generous collegiality—and for allowing me keys to the cellar! What was begun in Cambridge has been brought to fruition in Aberdeen, where I am lucky enough, as Lord Gifford Fellow, to have an official mandate to 'promote, advance, teach and diffuse the study of natural theology in the widest sense of that term'. I am grateful, amongst others to Phil Ziegler, John Webster, Tom Greggs, Chris Brittain, Catherine Wilson, Bob Plant, and Nate Jezzi for the warmth of their welcome to the Silver City. As always, I have learnt much from my students as well as testing their patience with my reluctance to settle on a definition of natural theology!

The most patience, however, has been demonstrated by Lizzie Robottom and Tom Perridge at Oxford University Press. I am truly grateful for their support throughout the development of this book. I also want to thank the anonymous readers, whose reports encouraged me to take the book on; I hope the final result lives up to their expectations.

Finally, of course, I thank my family, friends, and Francesca. The book is dedicated to Edmund, with love and wonder.

13 March 2012
The Old Brewery
Old Aberdeen

CONTENTS

PART I HISTORICAL PERSPECTIVES ON NATURAL THEOLOGY

PART II THEOLOGICAL PERSPECTIVES ON NATURAL THEOLOGY

PART III PHILOSOPHICAL PERSPECTIVES ON NATURAL THEOLOGY

PART IV SCIENTIFIC PERSPECTIVES ON NATURAL THEOLOGY

PART V PERSPECTIVES ON NATURAL THEOLOGY FROM THE ARTS

List of Illustrations

LIST OF CONTRIBUTORS

Pamela Sue Anderson, Reader in Philosophy of Religion at the University of Oxford.

Jeremy S. Begbie, Thomas A. Langford Research Professor of Theology at Duke Divinity School.

Guy Bennett-Hunter, Research Fellow, Emergence: From Biology to Theology, at the University of Aberdeen.

John Hedley Brooke, Emeritus Andreas Idreos Professor of Science and Religion and former Director of the Ian Ramsey Centre at the University of Oxford.

Frank Burch Brown, Frederick Doyle Kershner Professor of Religion and the Arts at Christian Theological Seminary and Alexander Campbell Visiting Professor of Religion and the Arts at the Divinity School at the University of Chicago.

Stephen R. L. Clark, Emeritus Professor of Philosophy at the University of Liverpool.

Philip Clayton, Dean and Ingraham Professor of Theology at Claremont School of Theology.

Clayton Crockett, Associate Professor of Philosophy and Religion at the University of Central Arkansas.

Matthew D. Eddy, Senior Lecturer in the History of Science and Culture at the University of Durham.

Denis Edwards, Lecturer in Historical and Systematic Theology at Flinders University.

Paul Ewart, Professor of Atomic and Laser Physics at the University of Oxford.

Richard K. Fenn, Maxwell M. Upson Professor of Christianity and Society and Princeton Theological Seminary.

Daniel H. Frank, Professor of Philosophy at Purdue University.

Jessica Frazier, Lecturer in Religious Studies at the University of Kent.

David Ray Griffin, Emeritus Professor of Philosophy at the Centre for Process Studies at the Claremont School of Theology.

Alexander W. Hall, Associate Professor of Philosophy at Clayton State University.

Wayne Hankey, Carnegie Professor of Classics at Dalhousie University.

Douglas Hedley, Reader in Hermeneutics and Metaphysics at the University of Cambridge.

Rodney D. Holder, Course Director of the Faraday Institute, St Edmund's College, Cambridge.

Robert K. Johnston, Professor of Theology and Culture at Fuller Theological Seminary.

Christopher C. Knight, Executive Secretary of the International Society for Science and Religion, St Edmund's College, Cambridge.

David Knight, Emeritus Professor of the History and Philosophy of Science at the University of Durham.

Scott Mandelbrote, Official Fellow and Director of Studies in History at Peterhouse, Cambridge.

Neil A. Manson, Associate Professor of Philosophy at the University of Mississippi.

Andrew Moore, Fellow of the Centre for Christianity and Culture, Regent's Park College, University of Oxford.

Robert G. Morrison, Associate Professor of Religion at Bowdoin College.

Kristóf Nyíri, Professor of Philosophy at Budapest University of Technology and Economics.

Keith M. Parsons, Professor of Philosophy at the University of Houston–Clear Lake.

John Polkinghorne, Past President of Queens' College, Cambridge and former Professor of Mathematical Physics at the University of Cambridge.

Russell Re Manning, Lord Gifford Fellow in the School of Divinity, History, and Philosophy at the University of Aberdeen.

Christopher Rowland, Dean Ireland Professor of the Exegesis of Holy Scripture at the University of Oxford.

Michael Ruse, Lucyle T. Werkmeister Professor of Philosophy at Florida State University.

William Schweiker, Edward L. Ryerson Distinguished Service Professor of Theological Ethics in the Divinity School at the University of Chicago.

Christopher Southgate, Research Fellow in Theology at the University of Exeter.

Charles Taliaferro, Professor of Philosophy at St Olaf College.

Fraser Watts, Starbridge Reader in Science and Religion at the University of Cambridge.

Wesley J. Wildman, Professor of Theology and Ethics at Boston University.

Mark Wynn, Professor of Philosophy and Religion at the University of Leeds.

INTRODUCTION

RUSSELL RE MANNING

WHAT is natural theology? There is no easy answer to this question; indeed it is one of the primary aims of this *Handbook* to highlight the rich diversity of approaches to, and definitions of, natural theology. The lack of a fixed consensus on the definition of natural theology is due, in part, to its inherently interdisciplinary character and the inevitable limitations on definitions that belong firmly within particular disciplines. By opening up various different 'perspectives' on natural theology, this *Handbook* hopes to enrich reflection on the topic and to provoke engagement with the new varieties of natural theology emerging in a range of contexts—from historical and religious studies, constructive theology, philosophy of religion, science-and-religion research, cultural theories, and the arts. Throughout this *Handbook* individual contributors give their own definitions of natural theology and there has been no editorial attempt to impose consistency; rather the various approaches adopted by the contributors reflect the plurality of contexts within which the study of natural theology must be situated. The result, hopefully, is that the complexity of natural theology is allowed to emerge, in contrast to the dominant tendency within existing accounts of natural theology towards universal 'one size fits all' definitions and the temptation to restrict it to one context or another.

Beyond testifying to the complex diversity of natural theology, the chapters in this *Handbook* also bear witness to its ongoing significance for a wide range of contemporary disciplines. The vitality of natural theology centres on several key issues that emerge as leading themes in many of the chapters:

- an awareness of the significance of natural theology in the history of ideas, both in terms of the links between philosophical and religious thought and of the importance of natural theology in the development of modern science;
- the importance of natural theological themes in contemporary theology, both for religious reflection on the relations between reason and revelation and for the contemporary concerns of inter-religious dialogue, the environment, and secularization;

- philosophical topics, ranging from the traditional arguments for the existence of God to the impact of recent developments in philosophy (post-modernism and feminism, for example) on the question of ultimate reality;
- the extent to which scientific investigation of the natural world relates to the claims of natural theology, both in terms of specific hot-topics, such as evolution and fine-tuning, and in terms of the potential and limitations for natural theology in different scientific disciplines;
- aesthetic engagement with the natural world and the complex relations between theology and the arts, both in terms of the apparently theological aspirations of some art and of the role of the imagination.

It is important to stress that throughout the *Handbook* the aim is to present natural theology as a topic of serious academic and intellectual consideration (from a variety of perspectives: historical, theological, philosophical, scientific, and aesthetic), not to present an apology for natural theology or a case for its revival. What is undeniable, however, is that interest in natural theology—and the issues it is concerned with—is very much at the centre of contemporary thought, be it in the retrieval of the complexity of the relations between science and religion in recent historical scholarship, the increasingly prominent place of the arts in theological teaching and research, the rise of science and religion as a field of study, and the particularly vibrant state of philosophical reflection on the question of God, not to mention the wide popular appeal of recent 'new atheist' critiques of natural theology.

To assert the contemporary vitality of natural theology is to cut against a widely accepted and deeply ingrained standard narrative of the rise and fall of natural theology, a simplified story of the historical and intellectual trajectory of natural theology that still dominates most assessments of the topic. As the chapters in this *Handbook* collectively demonstrate, however, this standard story is a myth, and one that deserves nothing so much as a decent burial. According to the accepted narrative, natural theology, which is primarily and definitively contrasted to 'revealed theology', had a brief, if significant, flourishing at a kind of interim point of the scientific revolution and culminated in William Paley's 1802 book, *Natural Theology*, before being fatally undermined by the combined effects of a three-pronged philosophical, scientific, and theological critique (albeit not before having secured the triumph of Newtonianism and sown the seeds of modern atheism). Between them, so the story goes, Hume, Darwin, and Barth pulled the rug out from underneath the pretentions of natural theology to any philosophical, scientific, or theological legitimacy, such that the enterprise was forced to retreat beyond the pale of intellectual respectability, showing up only in some of the more suspect speculations of so-called Intelligent Design creationism (even if the Intelligent Design theorists themselves reject the label). Richard Dawkins is a prominent exponent of such an account of natural theology, but it is hardly restricted to natural theology's atheistic opponents, with many of those who are sympathetic to it, in some form or another, similarly repeating more or less wholesale this canonical narrative.

No matter how widely accepted it is, it is now time to put the lie to this myth once and for all, point by point:

- As many of the contributions in this *Handbook* emphasize, the 'natural' vs 'revealed' characterization of natural theology is frequently hard to sustain and serves only to obscure or distort the real concerns and issues at the heart of natural theological thinking. Likewise, clunky either/or oppositions between Athens and Jerusalem are rarely helpful when considering the subtleties of natural theological thinking, in particular when considered in the light of perspectives from different religions, as well as from different Christian traditions.
- This history of natural theology manifestly extends beyond Anselm's 'ontological argument' and Aquinas' 'Five Ways' and the complexities behind the emergence of a distinctive form of modern scientific natural theology are well-illustrated by the variety of types of natural theology in the seventeenth and eighteenth centuries—an insight that helps to put Paley's particular work in context.
- The persistence of natural theology within the nineteenth and twentieth centuries refutes the supposition of its eclipse with the rise of distinctly modern science (as opposed to 'natural philosophy'); indeed there is a strong case, it seems, that it is the nineteenth century that is the true heyday of natural theology.
- Hume's philosophical criticisms of the arguments of natural theology have been rightly influential and remain the cornerstone of much recent philosophy of religion; an insight that in itself serves to question the finality of Hume's alleged demolition of natural theological arguments, and the design argument in particular. The vitality of much recent work in the philosophy of religion—both in and beyond the framework of analytic philosophy of religion—is ample testimony to the ongoing philosophical import of such arguments.
- The story is often told of Darwin's love of Paley's works as a student and the anxiety he felt as it became clear that his theory of evolution by natural selection destroyed the inference to design by providing a natural mechanism for the apparent design of the natural world. The personal story of Darwin's religious life is a fascinating one; however, it is problematic when taken as representative of the wider scientific discrediting of natural theology, as unavoidably trading on scientific ignorance to invoke the 'God of the gaps'. Indeed, as recent historical work has convincingly demonstrated, the story of the reception of Darwin's works is far from the simple either/or of the famous Oxford University debate between Huxley and Wilberforce. Indeed, it has been one of the central features of recent work on the history of the relations between science and religion that the conflict model quite clearly reflects certain ideological assumptions rather than the complexities of the historical record.
- Likewise, it is striking that much of the contemporary revival of interest in natural theology is spurred by work in the science-and-religion field that has moved beyond the restrictive typological categorizations of the relations between science and religion, such as those developed by Ian Barbour to suggest new forms of

scientific natural theology sensitive to the particularities of different scientific disciplines.

- The importance of Karl Barth for the theological reception of natural theology in the twentieth century cannot be underestimated. However, it is far less clear that his particular 'Nein!' justifies the resistance to all forms of natural theology and indeed it is striking just how much natural theology has, in fact, persevered in the twentieth century, even in those traditions most decisively influenced by Barth.
- Finally, as should be clear from the above, the proponents of Intelligent Design Theory are correct in distancing themselves from the enterprise of natural theology (albeit not for the right reasons); however it is that natural theology is to be defined it is as far from Intelligent Design creationism as it is from Dawkin's 'new atheism'!

This revisionary account of the character and history of natural theology is long overdue and it is to be hoped that this *Handbook* will go some way towards renewing engagement with natural theology from a variety of different perspectives—historical, theological, philosophical, scientific, and cultural/aesthetic. Clearly, such a multi-faceted topic requires a collaborative approach and a pluralist editorial policy. Even within this context, however, there are some perspectives that it has not been possible to include and hard decisions have had to be made. In each of the Parts, there are additional perspectives that could be engaged with. For instance, in Part I additional work might consider the place of natural theology in the Reformation period and develop perspectives on natural theology within Continental Europe and the United States, as well as the impact of empire on natural theology and the importance of the material contexts of natural theological texts. Part II could further be extended to engage perspectives from Chinese religious traditions and indigenous animist traditions, with their subtle accounts of relations between nature and the divine(s), as well as exploring the place of natural theology in Nonconformist Christianity and the complex (and controversial) situation of natural theology in American evangelical Christian theology. Clearly, Part III only scratches the surface of natural theology within analytic philosophy and there is certainly room for further engagement with, for instance, the critique of natural theology within Reformed Epistemology; likewise the differentiations between natural theology and 'religious naturalism' clearly merit further consideration, as well as the questions raised by a comparative approach to natural theology. The range of scientific engagements with natural theology is as wide as the range of the scientific disciplines themselves and further interesting perspectives could be explored by a discussion of the (mainly historical) relations between the earth sciences and natural theology, as well as the new sciences of information and the contemporary debates in the philosophy of science about altruism, emergence, and the laws of nature. Finally, the cultural/aesthetic perspectives of Part V might be expanded to include not only additional art forms, such as sculpture and poetry, but also to explore further the interrelations between natural theology and the development of the modern novel and the intersections between natural and cultural theologies.

The above list of additional perspectives is not meant simply to pre-empt reviewers looking for omissions, but rather to highlight, as if it needed to be stated, that this *Handbook* hardly represents the final word on natural theology! As the wide variety of perspectives included in this volume and those gestured to above shows, the future for work in this area is bright and might, finally, be able to get beyond the debilitating myths towards multi-perspectival and interdisciplinary engagements with the rich diversity of theological thinking rooted in human nature and the environments that we find ourselves in.

PART I

HISTORICAL PERSPECTIVES ON NATURAL THEOLOGY

CHAPTER 1

....

THE CLASSICAL ORIGINS
OF NATURAL THEOLOGY

....

STEPHEN R. L. CLARK

OUT OF CHAOS

....

> Verily at the first Chaos came to be, but next wide-bosomed Earth, the
> ever-sure foundations of all the deathless ones who hold the peaks of
> snowy Olympus, and dim Tartarus in the depth of the wide-pathed Earth,
> and Eros (Love), fairest among the deathless gods, who unnerves the
> limbs and overcomes the mind and wise counsels of all gods and all men
> within them.... And Earth first bare starry Heaven, equal to herself, to
> cover her on every side, and to be an ever-sure abiding-place for the
> blessed gods.... She bare also the fruitless deep with his raging swell,
> Pontus, without sweet union of love. But afterwards she lay with Heaven
> and bare deep-swirling Oceanus, Coeus and Crius and Hyperion and
> Iapetus, Theia and Rhea, Themis and Mnemosyne and gold-crowned
> Phoebe and lovely Tethys. After them was born Cronos the wily, youngest
> and most terrible of her children, and he hated his lusty sire.

[Hesiod 1914: 116–38]

So begins the first 'classical' account of the deathless ones, the gods, as recounted to Hesiod
of Boeotia in the late eighth century BC by the nine daughters of Mnemosyne (which is
Memory). The genealogy continues with increasing complexity and darker implications,
occasionally dipping into narratives about selected gods, especially the line from Ouranos
(Heaven) to Cronos to Zeus. The defining character of 'gods' is that they are deathless—
and glorious. But their glory is usually not kindly, and their kin are often terrible: Typhoeus,
another son of Earth, for example, in whose contest with Zeus for the kingship 'the whole
earth seethed, and sky and sea: and the long waves raged along the beaches round and
about, at the rush of the deathless gods: and there arose an endless shaking'. The message of
Hesiod's *Theogony* is that there are deathless and unageing powers, both glorious and

terrible, and that mortals had better be content with the peace—such as it is—imposed by Zeus. He is not kind—but the alternative is worse. The volcanic eruption that demolished the island of Thera has, probably, left its mark in folklore as a monstrous rebellion, finally contained (Greene 2000: 46–72). Earth's survival, and ours, gives reason to think that 'it is not possible to deceive or go beyond the will of Zeus' (Hesiod 1914: 613).

Hesiod's story is both like and unlike those of other Mediterranean nations. In Egyptian thought Atum emerges out of Nothing, and generates Shu and Tefnut, from whom in turn more gods derive, culminating in the story of Isis, Osiris, and Set, their enemy. In Babylon Apsu plots against the younger gods and is destroyed by Ea, who in turn gives way to Marduk who fights with his grandmother Tiamat and her new off-spring. In each case complexity and personality gradually emerge from Chaos (which is not confusion, but a void), younger gods inherit power from the older, and peace is established after some catastrophe. Or rather, Law is established: 'Peace' is projected back into the rule of Cronos, or of Osiris before his murder.

Those stories were told by priests. There seems to have been no priestly caste in Greece, nor any grand revelation—except perhaps in the poems of a greater poet than Hesiod, Homer. In *Iliad* and *Odyssey* and the *Homeric Hymns*, the Olympian gods are on display, all with mature personalities and family histories. Satirists have usually supposed these gods to be simply superhuman, and their histories nothing more than gossip. But the gods were more than this: first, as for Hesiod, they were *deathless*, and unavoidable. They were more than personalities: they were whole worlds of meaning. Aphrodite, for exam-ple, is the mind-beguiling charm of sexual desire, born—mythologically—from Heaven's severed phallus (and so the last born of the Titans), but also conceived as the child of Zeus and the goddess Dione. Similarly Athena, daughter of Zeus and Metis, is born from Zeus's head (Zeus having swallowed her mother, on being warned that any male child born to her was bound to surpass his father), and Dionysus, son of Zeus and Semele, is reborn from Zeus's thigh after his mother has been burnt up by Zeus's self-revelation. In each case what might have been an independent power is given a place in the order maintained by Zeus: the overarching sky from which lightning strikes down the mighty. Zeus also holds men to their oaths, defends the laws of hospitality, and forbids the eating of people. It is this last offence which brings down the Flood. Though the gods aren't *kind*, and owe us nothing, they do demand some minimal morality from mortals. Sometimes some gods have favourites: Athena, for instance, strongly favours the much-tried Odysseus. But she cannot always save him from the malice of another god, and even Zeus's favour-ites can't escape from Fate. Indeed, being *Zeus's* favourite guarantees his wife's hostility!

These tales were told in many variants, constantly rewritten to serve some new dramatic or political purpose. What remains throughout—at least until they became entirely the butt of satirists—is a sense that the world has many faces, that our task as mortals can only be to keep our balance among competing powers, that we should not imagine ourselves exempt from justice. 'Lay up these things within your heart and listen now to right, ceasing altogether to think of violence. For the son of Cronos has ordained this law for men, that fishes and beasts and winged fowls should devour one another, for right is not in them; but to mankind he gave right which proves far the best.' (Hesiod 2008: 274–6). The Olympians are bound, like us, to keep their promises. But they are also glorious, and offer occasional brightness to their devotees. 'A shadow in a dream is man, but when God sheds a brightness, shining light is on earth and life is as sweet as honey' (Pindar 1998: 8.95 f.). That brightness *is* the god.

PARMENIDEAN AND EMPEDOCLEAN MUSES

Out of emptiness, diversity. Hesiod's Muses told him that there was only Chaos, Emptiness, at first. Earth, Tartarus under Earth, and Eros (Love) came next, and after them Night and Day. Manifold abstractions followed (Death, Blame, Toil, Strife and Forgetfulness, for example), and at last the world-defining powers under whose whim we live. Hornung summarizes the Egyptian story: 'from the one emerges the duality of "two things", and the diversity of the "millions" of created forms.... Creation is division.' (Hornung 1996: 253). The One from which things emerge, he comments, is the non-existent, that to which no single label can apply, and within which there is no division. It is a theme that returns in the later days of the classical imagination—and one relevant to the next Muse-inspired theologian, namely Parmenides, for whom diversity could only be delusion.

Parmenides of Elea (early fifth century BC) has a good claim to be the father of Western philosophy, who chose to *reason* his way to his conclusions. Only what can be thought without contradiction can be true. Neither our senses nor our imagination can show us more than delusion. Nonetheless, the obvious fact about Parmenides' own writing is that he claimed, like Hesiod, to be Muse-inspired:

> The Goddess greeted me kindly, and took my right hand in hers, and addressed me with these words: 'Young man, you who come to my house in the company of immortal charioteers with the mares which bear you, greetings. No ill fate has sent you to travel this road—far indeed does it lie from the steps of men—but right and justice. It is proper that you should learn all things, both the unshaken heart of well-rounded truth, and the opinions of mortals, in which there is no true reliance.' [Kirk, Raven, and Schofield 1983: 242]

This is to cast doubt from the beginning on the easy distinction between 'natural' and 'revealed' theology. Hesiod, Homer, and Parmenides are witnesses to a revelation, as openly as Isaiah—and Parmenides' revelation is more shocking, less in line with common sense and practice, than was Hesiod's. Maybe this introduction to Parmenidean thought was only a literary conceit? But this is to insist that we know better than Parmenides what brought him to his conviction: even if he 'reasoned' his way, the experience of this reasoning was alien to ordinary thought. Realizing that the way things *seem* to us need not be how they *are* is, emotionally and intellectually, a revelation. And why should we care for that reality unless it is somehow brighter, better, more worth knowing and living by, than the worlds with which we are comfortably familiar?

Does 'Reason' differ from 'Revelation' at least in this, that we all have access directly to the former, if we choose? Hesiod might be a liar, or be deceived, and his audience must form an impression of his character and wit before they can rely on his 'revelation'. The force of Parmenides' argument, perhaps, is independent of his character and intelligence. Hesiod could reasonably reply that his advice to his erring brother is backed both by revelation and by everyday experience: 'Be careful to avoid the anger of the deathless gods. Do not make a friend equal to a brother; but if you do, do not wrong him first.... But if he wrongs you first, offending either in word or in deed, remember to repay him double; but if he ask you to be his friend again and be ready to give you satisfaction, welcome him' (Hesiod 2008: 706–13). The strategy is now called Tit-for-Tat, and reckoned mathematically the best available. Parmenides, it seems, hoped for an argument that need not rely on any such experience, but rather be—as we later came to say—entirely 'a priori', but not therefore obvious.

So what was the argument the goddess (or his reason) showed him?

> I will tell you the only ways of enquiry that are to be thought of. The one, that it is, and that it is impossible for it not to be, is the path of Persuasion (for she attends upon Truth); the other, that it is not and that it is needful that it not be, that I declare to you is an altogether indiscernible track; for you could not know what is not. [Kirk, Raven, Schofield 1983: 245]

There cannot be anything whose essence is simply not to be. Nothing, Non-being, Absolute Emptiness is, precisely, not. So Hesiod and the Egyptians were mistaken: things do not arise from Emptiness, since there is no such thing. Indeed, there can be no *arising* or *departing*: 'It never was nor will be, since it is now, all together, one, continuous' (249). Nor can there be any *differences*, nor any gaps between one thing and another. 'It all exists alike; nor is it more here and less there, which would prevent it holding together, but it is all full of being' (250–1).

How Parmenides or his goddess went on to describe the world we see is uncertain. Do mortals live and conceive a lie? But there can be no *lies*, no falsehoods, no thought of what is not. Do they somehow encounter the only truth there is? But they imagine that there are really differences, distances, passings away, and comings into being (falsely). The One Truth is simultaneously diverse and single: a sphere no part of which is further from the centre than any other (252). Both distance and time's passage are but ways of speaking.

Later logicians sought to disentangle the different ways in which 'not being' can be said and thought. Falsehood depends on saying what is not: but this is not saying nothing (and so not saying anything at all). Difference is being other than *such-and-such*, but this is not the same as being nothing at all. The world of common life is vindicated: we can coherently insist that day is something else than night, that phantoms—though they are real phantoms—are not tangible people, that it is possible to tell and believe a lie. But this is not entirely to reject Parmenides' insight. Absence, falsehood, and negation are functions of our thought. Really, there is only *positive* reality, and nothing lies outside that reality (which is to say, it includes all things, both tangible and imaginable). Nowhere is distant (which is to say, here/now is everywhere). Nothing, it seems to follow, can be mortal.

So the father of philosophy, who put his trust in reason, is also the father of mystical theology, riding his intuition to the same conclusion as Empedocles of Acragas (*c.*495–435 BC):

Of all mortal things none has birth, nor any end in accursed death, but only mingling and interchange of what is mingled – birth is the name given to these by men.... Fools, since they think that what before did not exist comes into being, or that a thing dies and is completely destroyed.... For it is impossible for anything to come to be from what is not, and it cannot be brought about or heard of that what is should be utterly destroyed; for wherever one may ever set it, there indeed it will always be. [291–2]

Empedocles—to our eyes—seems schizophrenic: on the one hand, he avows that he 'has been a bush, and a bird, and a boy and a girl, and a dumb fish in the sea' (Diogenes Laertius in Kirk, Raven, and Schofield 1983: 319), and is an immortal god, confined here for some primordial, cannibalistic sin, 'an exile from the gods and a wanderer, having put my trust in raving Strife' (315). On the other, he invents a simple evolutionary theory, that the creatures first emerging from the play of fire, water, earth, and air (under the influence of Love and Strife) were elementary parts and random composites. Only some survived to breed: 'wherever everything turned out as it would have if it were happening for a purpose, there the creatures survived, being accidentally compounded in a suitable way; but where this did not happen, the creatures perished and are perishing still, as Empedocles says of his "man-faced ox-progeny"' (Aristotle in Kirk, Raven, and Schofield 1983: 304). But there is no contradiction. This whole world is run by Strife, and 'we' are embedded in it, by our cannibalistic error, very much as Hesiod's gods may be condemned to lie frozen by the Styx when they break their oath (Hesiod 1914: 775–806). Zuntz's aphorism is almost correct: 'the banished god described by Hesiod is—Man' (Zuntz 1971: 267). Almost correct, but not exactly: for Empedocles' point is that the banished god *is not* human, even if it is born among humans 'as prophets, bards, doctors and princes' (Kirk, Raven, Schofield 1983: 317)—and among beasts as lions, or laurels amongst trees. Our collective sin is cannibalism: 'will you not cease from the din of slaughter? Do you not see that you are devouring each other in the heedlessness of your minds?' (Sextus Empiricus in Kirk, Raven, and Schofield 1983: 319).

Here in the world of our present perception competitive diversity rules: at once the occasion of our sin, and its penalty. But reality is 'the Sphere', in which all parts are equal, and none further from the centre than the rest. In affirming our consanguinity, and rejecting common-sense divisions, he seemed to himself to be pursuing 'Reason'. In realizing our imprisonment he was able to present himself as 'an immortal god, mortal no more' (Diogenes Laertius in Kirk, Raven, and Schofield 1983: 313).

WHETHER THE GODS ARE GOOD

Xenophanes of Colophon (*c*.570–*c*.475 BC), said Aristotle, was the first of the Eleatic tribe 'to postulate a unity (for Parmenides is said to have been his pupil), [but] made nothing clear' (Aristotle in Kirk, Raven, and Schofield 1983: 165). His place in the history of natural theology is assured for another reason: 'if cattle and horses or lions had hands, or were able to draw with their hands and do the works that men do, horses would draw the forms of the gods like horses, and cattle like cattle' (169). Homer and Hesiod were especially at fault, in saying that the gods stole, slept around, and lied. Really, the gods are nothing like us in bodily form or mind, and could not misbehave in the ways that Hesiod or Homer said, not because they were too *good* to do so, but because they had neither the opportunity, the impulse, nor the organs. The gods weren't *human*, and their ways, their thoughts, weren't ours (Sextus Empiricus in Long and Sedley 1987: 143).

Xenophanes may have missed the point. That Cronos swallowed his children meant, to a later Neoplatonic ear, that the Intellect (*Nous*) was filled up (*koros*) with intelligible reality, and that the Soul (*Zeus*, after *zen*, to live) emerges from that fullness (see Plotinus *Ennead* V.1 [10].4, 8 after Plato (1926) *Cratylus* 396b). Even the literal stories may not have been so shameful: Zeus wasn't simply sleeping around with goddesses, nymphs, and mortals—but begetting gods and heroes. And why should the gods obey *our* rules? Their power is such that it is mad to defy them. Their glory is such that defiance is also vulgar. But only the foolish *imitate* them: their ways aren't ours, and (*pace* Empedocles) we are mortal. We had better ourselves be kind to one another, because the gods won't be. Does that mean it is wrong to worship them? Is it wrong to be impressed, amazed, by a killer whale, a tiger, a lightning storm, or the sun? Why not admire the gods (from a safe distance, and with no wish to be one)? Why might not this admiration motivate us to be kindly, temperate, pious, and courageous, precisely because they have no need to be? Homer, perhaps, showed better sense than Plato: Odysseus can admire the nymph Calypso's beauty, and her promise of immortality, but still pines for home and Penelope. Precisely because the world is *not* being run to suit us, we can appreciate virtues that the gods do not need—though even they are bound to keep their oaths, and bound by their natures to defend the world against the jealous anger of an earlier brood.

The gods are not to be imitated, but obeyed. Unfortunately, their commands are inconsistent—and that is what demands our aid. So Aeschylus proposed in his *Oresteia* that Orestes' misfortune—that he must do wrong (by one command) in order to do right (by another) and so be damned whatever he did or failed to do—can only be resolved in a human court, the Areopagus. Neither the Furies (who seek revenge for a mother's blood) nor Apollo (who had commanded that Orestes avenge his father) are permitted to be the only law: Athena casts her vote, in the end, 'for the father', but accommodates the Furies in Athenian civil order. Voting 'for the father' is not merely patriarchalist: it amounts to a vote for Zeus, the overarching sky, who demands that oaths be kept *and suppliants pitied*. The gods, to us, seem heartless and inconsistent, but it does not follow that the Greeks condemned them for it. It is *because* the gods are heartless that we must ourselves be kind; because they are in conflict that we must learn to think.

Plato's response is different. He is remembered nowadays for arguing that the gods do not make the 'moral law'. Either they command it *because* it is right, or their command might as easily have been a prohibition, obeyed only from fear (and not any *moral* reason). Surely, we are to suppose, God or the gods can't make it right to murder or steal or sleep around merely by telling us so? They can only, at best, be witnesses to what is already right or wrong, and we ought to obey that law, not them. The argument is drawn from his *Euthyphro*, with some additional pointers from *The Republic*, and is still frequently repeated even by those who have read neither text.

Actually, if they had read the texts, it might be harder to think that this is what Plato argued (Clark 2010)! He does not deny that our duty is to please God or the gods, and that they have laid down the natural conditions which identify what is best for us. They are what we should imitate: 'we ought to fly away from earth to heaven as quickly as we can; and to fly away means to become like God, as far as this is possible; and to become like him, means to become holy, just, and wise' (Plato 1949: 176b). And how are we to do this?

> God ought to be to us the measure of all things, and not man, as men commonly say: the words are far more true of Him. And he who would be dear to God must, as far as is possible, be like Him and such as He is. Wherefore the temperate man is the friend of God, for he is like Him; and the intemperate or unjust man is unlike Him. [Plato 2000a: 4.716c ff.]

So 'God' and 'the gods', for Plato, identify the best: to be imitated, not just respected. So also Aristotle, who declared that our final duty was *ton theon theorein kai therapeuein*, 'to love and serve the Lord' (Aristotle 1992a: 8.1249b20), by seeking to live as far as possible as gods:

> We must not follow those who advise us, being men, to think of human things, and, being mortal, of mortal things, but must, so far as we can, make ourselves immortal, and strain every nerve to live in accordance with the best thing in us. [Aristotle 1999: 10.1177b30 ff.]

What is the life gods live? Certainly not, so Aristotle insisted, a merely 'moral' life. The gods aren't 'morally' good: praising them as such is vulgar (10.1178b8 ff.). We must not think that the active moral life is the best life: a truly courageous person (say) would not want to exercise courage—since that depends on there being wrongs to resist or even wars to fight—'as if a physician were to wish that nobody needed his skill' (Plotinus 1966–8: VI.8 [39].5, 13–21). The best life is the practice of *theoria*—and that life *is* God.

Neither Aristotle nor his successors are clear about what *theoria* involves, but it does at least include a delight in beauty, *to kalon*. We serve the gods, so Euthyphro concluded, by doing or making *kala*, fine and noble things. But this making is dependent on our seeing *to kalon*, in even the smallest and basest creature (Aristotle 1992b: 1.645a15 f.), and chiefly in the ordered passage of the heavens, and in 'beautiful works, not those which the arts produce, but the works of men who have a name for goodness' (Plotinus 1966–8: I.6 [1].9, 4 ff.).

Aristotle's gods, and especially his 'Unmoved Mover', do not act to defend the innocent or openly rebuke the wicked. Nor does he suggest that we as bodily beings are anything but mortal. But something in us, the immortal *Nous*, is God or a god, a *daimon*. Sharing His life is the core of *eudaimonia*, the life well-lived: the term itself carries the implication, being—etymologically—'having a good *daimon*' (Sextus Empiricus in Long and Sedley 1987: 1:143):

Nous is our king. But we too are kings when we are in accord with it; we can be in accord with it in two ways, either by having something like its writing written in us like laws, or by being as if filled with it and able to see it and be aware of it as present. [Plotinus 1966–8: V.3.3, 46 ff.]

Those who live in the consciousness of that divinity will also be righteous, both because any vicious desires they had would get in the way of the practice, and because the god-filled have no desire or need for any of the usual goods to tempt them.

WHETHER AND HOW GOD RULES THE WORLD

The poets suggested that the gods might intervene, for their own purposes, in human and other lives, but not that the world existed 'because God wished it', nor that the world was governed by any purpose. And yet Aristotle easily mocked the Empedoclean story that separate limbs and organs once emerged 'of themselves' and only later found some viable combinations. All living organisms must have been viable wholes from the beginning, not patched together, by chance, from previously non-viable bits. Living organisms also reproduce themselves, passing 'the same form' down generations, modified by the material it influenced, and the environment in which it grew. Aristotle thought that such 'formal causes' were immanent in the world, and that we were equipped to see them. We could also see such forms at work in the heavens, in the cycles of the fixed stars and the planets (including sun and moon). Formal and final cause cohere: the 'final cause' of anything is to complete and maintain, as far as possible, the form of its own being.

For Plato the forms were themselves eternal. Only they, indeed, could truly be said to be, since every tangible reality existed only in flux; all claims about tangible realities were only sometimes, and in some ways, true. Only mathematical and 'formal' truths were permanent, and so only they could strictly be 'known'. In a late dialogue, *Timaeus*, Plato proposed that the tangible world was made (or else is being made, perpetually) by a Craftsman copying the eternal world, the world of forms. His successors did not agree whether he meant this as a partly 'literal' creation story, or only meant to show how the tangible world can be understood in the light of eternal principles.

One direction in which the story was developed suited Christian thought: this tangible world was a copy—and a fallen, faulty copy—of the original. Maybe we could hope, by God's grace, to awaken into that better world when we have served our time—as Plato himself suggests, in the *Phaedo* and elsewhere. Another development was also significant. Plato himself offered no definite doctrine about the *ontology* of the Forms, what sort of being they were, and where. Even the divine creator was confronted by them, so that there were at least two independent and eternal sorts of thing: the Forms and the creative God (or gods). A solution to this oddity seems to have emerged quite early, on the back of Aristotle's suggestions about the 'Unmoved Mover'.

That Mover was the reason why the heavens—and so the whole superlunary and sublunary world—were always in motion: they were seeking to share, as best they could, in the eternity of the Thinker. What could the Thinker be thinking? What else but itself (Aristotle 1998: 12.1072b16 ff.)? Or rather, the objects of its thought must be internal: if they were *external* to its thinking it would be in the same distress as us, unable to compare the copies with reality. Reality must be contained in the single Intellect, which knows everything that is eternally, necessarily, true. The Forms, that is, are the thoughts of God, or better still, the structure of the divine intellect, which also illuminates *our* minds. In understanding the laws that govern tangible reality, we are attuned to God. Only so can 'the laws of nature' be an explanation of what happens: they aren't tangible realities, of a sort that could *push* their subjects. And neither are they abstractions, summary accounts of what happens. They are what God intends for all and each of us.

In the revolving heavens and the reproduction of living species, the thought of God is continually re-embodied. If we take each moment or segment separately we miss its significance. Only by remembering, imagining, realizing to ourselves the whole in which we live, shall we discover truth. Anything less is a failure, a living by sensation like beasts or savages. Philosophers may see this as something like Spinoza's vision, but we should also remember the *ceremonial* year. Why do the heavens rotate? Perhaps the story is not so far from the biblical version, in which the stars are signs: we are attuned to the divine by sharing in ceremonial, not only by filling ourselves with 'scientific knowledge', as though it were only the speculative physicist who could know 'the mind of God':

> General opinion makes the Hours goddesses and the Month a god, and their worship has been handed on to us: we say also that the Day and the Night are deities, and the gods themselves have taught us how to call upon them. [Proclus *In Timaeum* 248d in Cumont 1960: 61]

That the world is governed, in some sense, by 'intelligence' is an axiom of any proper science: if it were not so, we could not hope for an intelligent, or scientific, grasp of what goes on. Wherever we look, from the largest to the smallest scale, we find mathematical beauty. Only, it sometimes seems, at the *human* scale do we discover instead confusion, ignorance, injustice, evil. Maybe, if we saw things straight, with the eyes of eternity, the human would also be beautiful—as beautiful, at any rate, as tigers or ants or viruses. Or maybe we would conclude, with Empedocles and others, that the human world is out of step with the real; that we are condemned, like Hesiod's gods, to a time of trouble. In either account there may be gods on whom we can call, gods with at least some thought to spare for us. Neither Plato nor Aristotle expressly denied this. Both, indeed, seem to have assumed that at least some stories about the divine were true, and that the life of the gods could spill over into ours, or our lives be taken up by them. Even a lucky chance was, in a way, a god. It does not follow that everything we do will work out for the best, let alone for what we foolishly imagine is best. God or the gods don't take such care for us as to prevent our doing things for ourselves—or to ourselves. It is, perhaps, enough that the world goes on, as a partial, shifting, image of an eternal beauty, and that nothing real is ever lost forever.

But what does that permanence imply? During the Hellenistic Era Stoic philosophers proposed that the whole world order, animated by a single divine principle, would repeat itself. Enlightenment lay in realizing that everything that happened was what *had* to happen, and that it would happen 'again' in an unending cycle. The traditional gods were assumed to be allegorical: standing for different elements and forces, but all subsumed in the single animating spirit. In their anthropocentric moments, the Stoics insisted that God and Nature engineered our good: even bed-bugs had their function, in helping us get up! A less anthropocentric version insisted rather that it was the good of the whole world that mattered. 'Man himself has come to be in order to contemplate and imitate the world, being by no means perfect, but a tiny constituent of that which is perfect' (Cicero in Long and Sedley 1987: 1:326). Either way, the intelligence that ruled was providential, and every moment is forever.

In opposition to this, the followers of Epicurus revived the Democritean atomic theory. Everything was composed of tiny unbreakable (literally, a-tomic) bits that bounced and clung to each other in an unlimited space, and over unlimited time. There were no limits on what could happen somewhere. In fact, the Epicureans thought that everything we could imagine—including the gods—was real: the very fact that we received their images was reason to think they existed. 'There are gods', Epicurus said: 'the knowledge of them is self-evident' (Epicurus in Long and Sedley 1987: 1:140). We might, if we choose, admire them—but they had nothing to do with us, for good or ill.

The Epicurean vision is usually now considered atheistical, and it is true that they denounced 'religion'—that is, the assumption that the gods demanded sacrifice, and that we would suffer in an afterlife for offending them. But even Epicureans had their prayers to make, hoping that the goddess of love would help engender peace (Lucretius 1992: Book 1), and praising Epicurus as the source of their salvation. That there were gods was self-evident; that they didn't care for us, also. Enlightenment lies in realizing that there are no destinations, and no travellers, but only the fall of atoms through an unending void. Epicureans, like Buddhists, sought refuge in their Saviour, in his doctrine, in the community of friends, and the fourfold remedy: 'God presents no fears, death no worries. And while good is readily attainable, evil is readily endurable' (Long and Sedley 1987: 1:156).

Stoics and Epicureans were more alike than they supposed, especially in the moral advice they gave. Both agreed that the corporeal world was all there was, and that our 'selves' were no real entities: for the Epicurean we were only aggregates; for the Stoic we were segments of a continuous, determined whole. Stoics supposed that what didn't happen anywhere must be impossible; Epicureans that everything possible happened somewhere. The claims are logically equivalent, though the Epicurean reality is larger. The Stoics conceived that there was a single God, whom only the wise could love. Epicureans did not believe in a universal providence, but were as certain as the Stoics that the wise would accept what happened without complaint.

OUT OF THE WORLD

Either God or the gods aren't kind, or else their power is limited. Neither conclusion affects most classical religion. We may still hope for help from them, and must in any case admire their glory. But there is that other option, adopted by Empedocles and perhaps by Plato: that this is a fallen world, or we are fallen into it. In its extreme form this account suggests that this world was made by a lesser spirit as a trap for other immortals. We need to discover an exit, and owe the present powers no worship. Whatever seems most 'natural' to us is likeliest to be delusion, and the gods of our usual worship are no more than demons—in a new and deadly sense. Patriotic pride and anger excite the emotions that tie us to this world—and so do erotic love, parental feeling, curiosity, hunger, artistry.

Is there an exit? The commonest classical response was that there was not. Why should we suppose there should be? Do we have a *right*, somehow, to more than the little successes we can achieve here and now? Better bow down before the powers, even knowing that they will betray us when they please. Rebellion only amuses them, a little. Nor can we expect to trick them by engaging in 'unnatural practices', doing whatever we think is most unlike what they would have us do—as some later 'Gnostics' perhaps proposed. Those who starve themselves to death leave few descendants. Those who won't procreate leave none! Nor is it easy to suppose that such purists really awaken back in the real original world.

Pagan Platonists and Christians in the later antique centuries resisted these extremes. Both insisted that the world and its creator deserved respect, even though we should not involve ourselves too deeply in worldly affairs. Even if this world is a nightmare, or a prison cell, it still bears the imprint of the real and glorious world to which we hope to ascend (in orthodox Christian terms) or return (in pagan). It was only in this context that the argument widely attributed, but mistakenly, to Epicurus makes much sense: God must either be unable or unwilling to eliminate human evil, and so could not be both omnipotent and kind (Sextus Empiricus 2000: 1.175). It was a strange argument directed against Stoics, who typically denied that anything at all *was* evil; and also strange when directed against less philosophical devotees of one god or another (who did not suppose that their gods had any universal sympathies or powers). The argument only affects those who suppose that God intends the good of all His creatures, and has all the power that He needs to accomplish His design. Even they might respond that there were no natural evils: the fact that we dislike things doesn't prove that they are evil. True, malice and ignorance are *moral* evils, and will in the end be dealt with: we may be grateful that they haven't been dealt with yet! And maybe even if God is, in His own way, 'kind', and so desires that His creatures themselves feel 'happy', it does not follow that He will therefore obliterate all unhappiness. That would, after all, amount to obliterating, rather than reforming (redeeming, rescuing) us. Pagan and Christian philosophers in the late antique era could agree that God and the gods had power to help us, and also the will. Whether we always like being helped is not so easy.

There were real disagreements between Pagan and Christian. When Justinian issued his edict in 543 AD against the errors of Origen (185–254 AD), he blamed them on the pagan Platonic tradition. Christians were not to agree that our souls had been imprisoned in bodies as a punishment, nor that they might have several incarnations. They were not to agree that the stars themselves were living, nor that our resurrection bodies were ball-shaped (that is to say, that we could expect to rise as stars). It was our present selves, our souls and bodies, that Christ came to save. But Christians and pagan philosophers alike expected new 'spiritual bodies' in another, better world. All alike admired and sought to imitate the 'holy', those who had abandoned this-worldly passions and possessions in pursuit of the divine. The pagans, perhaps, were more easily persuaded that they could 'reason' their way to understanding, without need of revelation, but they agreed that 'theurgy' was better than 'theology': the ritual invocation of divine assistance was our most reliable route away from this world here. Even Plotinus (204–70 AD), who seems to have paid less attention to public ritual, lived in hope of that assistance. His chief disciple and editor, Porphyry of Tyre, said that that 'it seems that the gods often set him straight when he was going on a crooked course "sending down a solid shaft of light", which means that he wrote what he wrote under their inspection and supervision' (Porphyry in Plotinus 1966–68: 1:70):

> Plotinus recognized truths which we, whether we will or not, must call revelations, which are entirely strange to the modern consciousness and even excite the highest degree of indignation. And now the main point: when Plotinus had to decide between 'revealed' and 'natural' truths, he unhesitatingly took the side of the former; *ha gar hegeitai tis einai malista, tauta malista ouk esti* (that which appears most real to common consciousness has the least existence) (Shestov 1975: Pt 3 'Plotinus's Ecstasies', citing *Ennead* V.5 [32].11).

Late antique Platonism inherited a millennium of classical philosophy, from Hesiod to the Stoics, but read it in the light of Plato's insight. Hesiod was not wrong to suppose that all things arose from Emptiness, from the 'non-existent One' of Egypt, for the origin of all things wasn't itself 'a thing'. Even the patricidal tales of Ouranos, Cronos, and Zeus are allegories for the One, the Intellect, and the Soul. Parmenides' One, in Plato's dialogue *Parmenides*, turns out to be, first, the One of which we can say nothing, which also features in Plato as the Good, 'beyond being and thought' (Plato 2000b: 509b); secondly, the One and Many, which is the Intellect and its manifold, complex objects; thirdly, the One in Many, which is Soul, whose essence it is to exist in multiple points of view, to be stuck in linear time. Empedocles was correct to understand himself, and us, as fallen deities, discontented with being all together, and each seeking 'his own':

> Even before this coming to be we were there, men who were different, and some of us even gods, pure souls and intellect united with the whole of reality; we were parts of the intelligible, not marked off or cut off but belonging to the whole; and we are not cut off even now. [Plotinus 1966–8: VI.4 [22].14, 18 ff.]

The divine Intellect, the first 'emanation' of the One, contains the real form of all things, including our real selves, and its being is Love: lover, beloved, and the love between (VI.8 [39].15). Returning to that company is possible for those who remember how to love—in fact, 'to become love' (VI.7 [38].22). Our exile here is not entirely a mistake: we were inspired to assist the World Soul in creating a lovely image of the eternal, but have foolishly forgotten that the world is not just *ours*. Aristotle was almost right in his study of the composite beings we are. Plato was right to insist that we belong 'elsewhere', and that the journey 'back' is one which requires us to find another way of seeing (I.6 [1].8, 23). Even the Stoics were right to think that we are part of a glorious, cross-connected cosmos, though wrong to suppose that we, as individuals, have nothing to contribute. Even the Epicureans were right: we can choose our future. This world here is not what a kindly god would wish, and neither are the rewards the world can offer ones that we should wish. Finding our way in the world is hard, but we can manage it if we look towards the One:

> It is like a choral dance: in the order of its singing the choir keeps round its conductor but may sometimes turn away so that he is out of their sight, but when it turns back to him it sings beautifully and is truly with him; so we are always around him— and if we were not, we should be totally dissolved and no longer exist—but not always turned towards him; but when we do look to him, then we are at our goal and at rest and do not sing out of tune as we truly dance our god-inspired dance around him. [VI.9 [9].8, 38 ff.]

Philosophy, and chiefly Neoplatonic philosophy, has left theologians both images and problems worth exploring, from the utterly incomprehensible One (the source and explanation of all things, which we can 'know' only by love, and not by understanding (VI.7 [38].35)), to the difficulty of seeing how we, as individuals, can contribute to the workings of a single coherent cosmos whose real being is eternal. How this tradition has helped or hampered Jews, Christians (Catholic or Orthodox), and Muslims in understanding their own doctrines is another, larger story.

There is one last classical contributor to natural theology: the Roman senator Boethius (480–524 AD), who composed the *Consolation of Philosophy* in a prison cell. The chief argument remembered from this work is a demonstration that God's omniscience, His knowledge of all human history, is not incompatible with human freedom. God does not know what we will do and suffer because He sees what causes us to act: He knows what we do and suffer, by our own decisions, because He sees the whole of history. The less abstract conclusion, familiar to pagan philosophers and thinkers from the beginning, is that Fortune rules this world, and that her gifts of riches, power, or glory (or poverty, weakness, and public shame) are all a sham. All fortune is, in a way, *good* fortune: 'since every fortune, welcome and unwelcome alike, has for its object the reward or trial of the good, and the punishing or amending of the bad, every fortune must be good, since it is either just or useful' (Boethius 1973: 4.7). The happiness we seek, Boethius tells us—or rather his Muse, Philosophy herself, tells us—is God: not that God is happy, but that He is happiness (3.10), as earlier philosophers and theologians had said that He was *theoria*, or success, or love, or luck.

REFERENCES

Aristotle (1992a). *Eudemian Ethics. Books I, II and VIII.* Translated from Greek by Michael J. Woods. Oxford: Oxford University Press.

—— (1992b). *De Partibus Animalium I and De Generatione Animalium I with passages from II 1–3.* Revi. edn. Translated from Greek by D. M. Balme. Oxford: Clarendon Press.

—— (1998). *Metaphysics.* Translated from Greek by Hugh Lawson-Tancred. Harmondsworth: Penguin.

—— (1999). *Nicomachean Ethics.* Translated from Greek by T. H. Irwin. Indianapolis: Hackett.

Boethius (1973). *Theological Tractates. The Consolation of Philosophy.* Translated from Latin by H. F. Stewart, E. K. Rand, and S. J. Tester. Loeb Classical Library. Cambridge, MA: Harvard University Press.

Clark, Stephen (2010). 'Theory and Therapy Reconstructed: Plato and his Successors' in *Philosophy as Therapeia.* Edited by Clare Carlisle and Jonardon Ganeri. Cambridge: Cambridge University Press: pp. 1–20.

Cumont, Franz (1960 [1912]). *Astrology and Religion among the Greeks and Romans.* New York: Dover.

Greene, Mott T. (2000). *Natural Knowledge in Preclassical Antiquity.* 2nd edn. Baltimore: Johns Hopkins University Press.

Hesiod (1914). *Theogony.* Translated from Greek by Hugh G. Evelyn-White. Loeb Classical Library. London: Heinemann.

—— (2008). *Hesiod: Theogony and Works and Days.* Translated from Greek by M. L. West. Oxford: Oxford University Press.

Hornung, Erik (1996). *Conceptions of God in Ancient Egypt: The One and the Many.* Translated from German by J. Baines. Ithaca, NY: Cornell University Press.

Kirk, G. S., J. E. Raven and M. Schofield, eds. (1983). *The Presocratic Philosophers.* 2nd edn. Cambridge: Cambridge University Press.

Long, A. A. and D. N. Sedley, eds. (1987). *The Hellenistic Philosophers.* Vol. I. Cambridge: Cambridge University Press.

Lucretius (1992). *On the Nature of Things.* Translated from Latin by W. H. Rouse. Loeb Classical Library. Cambridge, MA: Harvard University Press.

Pindar (1998). *Odes and Selected Fragments.* Translated from Greek by G. S. Conway. London: Orion.

Plato (1926). *Plato: Cratylus, Parmenides, Greater Hippias, Lesser Hippias.* Loeb Classical Library. Cambridge, MA: Harvard University Press.

—— (1949). *Theaetetus.* Translated from Greek by Benjamin Jowett. Indianapolis: The Library of Liberal Arts.

—— (2000a). *The Laws.* Translated from Greek by Benjamin Jowett. Amherst, NY: Prometheus Books.

—— (2000b). *The Republic.* Translated from Greek by T. Griffith. Cambridge: Cambridge University Press.

Plotinus (1966–8). *Enneads.* 6 vols. Translated from Greek by A. H. Armstrong. Loeb Classical Library. Cambridge, MA: Harvard University Press.

Sextus Empiricus (2000). *Sextus Empiricus I. Outlines of Phyrronism.* Translated from Latin by R. G. Bury. Loeb Classical Library. Cambridge, MA: Harvard University Press.

Shestov, Lev (1975 [1932]). *In Job's Balances.* Edited by Bernard Martin. Translated from Russian by Camilla Coventry and C. A. Macartney. Ohio: Ohio University Press.

Zuntz, Günter (1971). *Persephone: Three Essays on Religion and Thought in Magna Graecia.* Oxford: Clarendon Press.

CHAPTER 2

....

NATURAL THEOLOGY AND THE CHRISTIAN BIBLE

....

CHRISTOPHER ROWLAND

THE opening chapters of 1 Corinthians and its stark contrast between human and divine wisdom seem to anticipate Karl Barth's rejection of natural theology, and Barth haunts James Barr's major work on the Bible and natural theology, *Biblical Faith and Natural Theology* (1994), which represents a sustained attack on Karl Barth's suspicion of natural theology. Barr is right to remind us that all theology (including Barth's) is a product of human culture. Whatever their protests about human wisdom and the transcendence of God over the natural world, biblical writers were attempting to understand God through analogies with the natural world or through the culture of which they were a part.

In this chapter, I am deliberately playing with several approaches to the meaning of nature and natural, including both the explicit statements in the Bible about the natural world as a witness to the divine but also the ways in which human relations, culture, and convention inform the biblical writings and the importance of the material world as the arena of salvation history (Bockmuehl 2000). Notwithstanding the attempts to distinguish between revealed theology and natural theology, the 'signs' of God's activity come through nature in all its diversity mediated and understood by human minds, however much those minds might be viewed as enlightened by the divine.

I first of all consider how the biblical authors write about nature and God's relationship to it and then look at the function of nature and the natural world in the Bible, and their peculiar role in apprehending the divine. This reveals the centrality of nature, in particular human nature, as the key mode of theological understanding. Whatever the biblical writers may have said about their relationship between themselves as the people of God and nature and culture, they were deeply immersed in the culture of their day, albeit articulating a distinctive approach. In particular, I will consider the early Christian conviction about the way in which God 'spoke' through a human being (to paraphrase the opening of the Letter to the Hebrews), and is believed to be present in particular patterns of human relating. Also, in the process of interpretation, we can discern the way in which nascent Christian theology, for example, in the parables of Jesus uses analogy between nature and human affairs. The other issue considered in the second part of the chapter is the central part the material world plays in biblical eschatology.

WHAT THE BIBLICAL WRITERS SAY ABOUT NATURE

While in the collection of literature loosely described as the Wisdom Literature (e.g. Proverbs in the Bible and Ecclesiasticus and Wisdom of Solomon in the Apocrypha) experience and consideration of the way of the world serve as a basis for determining human behaviour and relationship with God, elsewhere in the Bible there is a widespread suspicion of nature as a vehicle of divine revelation. Such suspicion is rooted in the reaction of emerging Judaism to surrounding culture. The Jews were apprehensive of the idolatry that results when nature is identified with the divine (Isaiah 40:18–20; 44:9–20). In the New Testament Paul exhorts the Galatians not to be taken in by beings which are not by nature gods:

> Formerly, when you did not know God, you were in bondage to beings that by nature (*physis*) are no gods; but now that you have come to know God, or rather to be known by God, how can you turn back again to the weak and beggarly elemental spirits, whose slaves you want to be once more? You observe days, and months, and seasons, and years! [Galatians 4:8–10]

Paul's words suggest that there is a qualitative difference between God the creator and other parts of the creation, whether spiritual, animal, or material. This is a theme that runs throughout the Hebrew Bible's repudiation of idolatry: Israel should not be taken in by the urbane religion of Canaan, firmly rooted in a sophisticated way of life and in the habits and genius of a particular place. By contrast, the rudimentary Hebrew religion is attached neither to place nor image. 'I am who I am' goes before a group of refugees, appears to refuse to sanctify arrangements in surrounding society, and is not to be identified with nature. Yet the pantheon of Canaanite gods and the religious practices of surrounding cultures permeated Israel's life, however much the biblical writers came to repudiate it. Moreover, as we can see from the Psalms, and the mythological language elsewhere, links between God and nature are frequent, with storms and other extraordinary phenomena of nature being construed as vehicles of divine revelation—though occasionally, not, as is the case with Elijah in 1 Kings 19:12: not in the wind or earthquake or fire, but in 'a sound of sheer silence' as the NRSV puts it!

The creation account in Genesis 1 presents God as the one who brings order out of chaos and thus offers a blueprint for the distinctions and sense of holiness which are endemic in biblical religion. Psalms 104 and 19 demonstrate Jewish interest in the creation as a sign of divine providence and in the witness of nature to the divine creator. Psalm 104 lauds God as sustainer of the universe, and the provider of the animal and human world with food:

> You set the earth on its foundations, so that it shall never be shaken. You cover it with the deep as with a garment; the waters stood above the mountains... You set a boundary that they may not pass, so that they might not again cover the earth.... You cause the grass to grow for the cattle, and plants for people to use, to bring forth food from the earth, and wine to gladden the human heart.... The young lions roar for their prey, seeking their food from God...O LORD, how manifold are your works! In wisdom you have made them all; the earth is full of your creatures. [Psalm 104:5–24]

In Psalm 19 the psalmist writes that there is no need of words to laud God's glory, as the creation is itself a living testimony to it:

> The heavens are telling the glory of God; and the firmament proclaims his handiwork. Day to day pours forth speech, and night to night declares knowledge. There is no speech, nor are there words; their voice is not heard; yet their voice goes out through all the earth, and their words to the end of the world. In the heavens he has set a tent for the sun, which comes out like a bridegroom from his wedding canopy, and like a strong man runs its course with joy. Its rising is from the end of the heavens, and its circuit to the end of them; and nothing is hid from its heat. The law of the LORD is perfect, reviving the soul; the decrees of the LORD are sure, making wise the simple.... More to be desired are they than gold, even much fine gold; sweeter also than honey, and drippings of the honeycomb. Moreover by them is your servant warned; in keeping them there is great reward. [Psalm 19:1–11]

Yet Psalm 19 is not simply about the creation as witness to the divine glory. Precise observation of the created world is a key part not only of the learned tradition of the wise but is also essential for Jewish piety, with the calculation of the new moon and Sabbath being central to the regulating of life and the celebration of divinely sanctioned feasts—something else which is reflected in the opening text of the Book of Genesis. Psalm 19 is not only about the creation as a witness to the divine glory: its abrupt move to discussion of the law of the Lord as the centre of life of the righteous is a juxtaposition which is crucial to much in the Bible. Thus, it is no accident that Sabbath observance is central to Genesis 1, and obedience to the divine command central to the story of Adam and Eve in the Garden of Eden. Meditation on creation is never an end in itself. Indeed, probing questions posed by nature and experience, as we find in Job and 2 Esdras, lead to only one theological answer: the inability of the human mind to understand the divine purposes or to comprehend the discrete elements of the world and to move from this to some kind of coherent theology. The Book of Job is testimony to the limitations of natural theology, and, as is evident in both Job and 2 Esdras, the human attempts to gain understanding have to be complemented by divine or angelic revelations which serve to stress the incomprehensibility of the divine and the poverty of the human intellect (Job 38–42:6), the ultimate triumph of the divine promises (2 Esdras 11–13), and the validation of obedience rather than knowledge as the necessary response of humanity.

Chapter 13 of the Wisdom of Solomon, written just before the Common Era, describes the ease with which humans ignorant of God misinterpreted the evidence of nature and 'deemed either fire, or wind, or the swift air, or the circle of the stars, or the violent water, or the lights of heaven, to be the gods which govern the world' (Wisdom 13:2). Thereby, they worship the created rather than the creator. The author of Wisdom admits that they may err, but do so in their search for God, though that is not an excuse:

> For all men who were ignorant of God were foolish by nature; and they were unable from the good things that are seen to know him who exists, nor did they recognize the craftsman while paying heed to his works; but they supposed that either fire or wind or swift air, or the circle of the stars, or turbulent water, or the luminaries of heaven were the gods that rule the world. If through delight in the beauty of these things men assumed them to be gods, let them know how much better than these is their Lord, for the author of beauty created them. And if men were amazed at their power and working, let them perceive from them how much more powerful is he who formed them. For from the greatness and beauty of created things comes a corresponding perception of their Creator. Yet these men are little to be blamed, for perhaps they go astray while seeking God and desiring to find him. For as they live among his works they keep searching, and they trust in what they see, because the things that are seen are beautiful. Yet again, not even they are to be excused; for if they had the power to know so much that they could investigate the world, how did they fail to find sooner the Lord of these things? But miserable, with their hopes set on dead things, are the men who give the name 'gods' to the works of men's hands, gold and silver fashioned with skill, and likenesses of animals, or a useless stone, the work of an ancient hand. [Wisdom 13:1–10]

Following these lines and echoing a similar passage in Isaiah (44:9–20), there comes a sarcastic critique of idolatry.

We also find this kind of polemic against idolatry in the New Testament. Thus the Paul of Acts in Acts 17 sets out to explain to the Athenians their underlying desire for the divine: 'Athenians, I see how extremely religious you are in every way. For as I went through the city and looked carefully at the objects of your worship, I found among them an altar with the inscription, "To an unknown god." What therefore you worship as unknown, this I proclaim to you' (Acts 17:22–3). This is an apologetic strategy which would flourish in the second century, and beyond, as early Christian apologists explored the unseen activity of God in humankind and in culture outside the history of Israel. Similar arguments to these are found in the opening chapter of Romans. Paul's Hellenistic-Jewish background suggests there is a degree of human knowledge of God, albeit imperfect and capable of being misdirected in its goals. Such knowledge is not reserved for some elect but is the fulfilment of the divine promises for the whole of humanity.

The Greek word *physis* is little used in the New Testament, and many commentators think that this might be a deliberate rejection of the natural theology of the Hellenistic tradition. Nevertheless, there are appeals to nature as the teacher of right conduct, a form of argument which has been central to much natural theology. In Romans 1 'unnatural' sexual relations are seen as a sign of divine judgement on an idolatrous world: 'For this reason God gave them up to dishonourable passions. Their women exchanged natural relations [*physiken chresin*] for unnatural [*para physin*]' (Romans 1:26). In Romans 2:14 in the context of his argument to demonstrate the need of all humanity for messianic redemption, Paul refers to the righteous Gentiles who though they do not have the Law 'do by nature what the Law requires':

> When Gentiles who have not the Law do by nature [*physis*] what the law requires, they are a law to themselves, even though they do not have the law. They show that what the Law requires is written on their hearts, while their conscience also bears witness and their conflicting thoughts accuse or perhaps excuse them on that day when, according to my gospel, God judges the secrets of men by Christ Jesus. [Romans 2:14–16]

Elsewhere in the Pauline corpus, Paul characterizes 'conscience' as an important part of the human ability to discern right conduct, however much that conscience needs to be informed (1 Corinthians 8:7, 12). Paul's argument in Romans 1–3, demonstrating the extent of human culpability, is based on the assumption that, whether or not humanity has the Torah, men and women have the innate capability to know what is required of them. Indeed, Paul even uses language reminiscent of Jeremiah 31:31–34 and calls it a law written on the heart. All this is a reminder of the importance of that strand in both Jewish and Christian theology which suggests that man and woman created in God's image are not devoid of moral sensibility. So, though Moses legislated 'because of the hardness of human hearts' (Mark 10:5) the Law was given not to totally uncomprehending humanity but to men and women in whom the light of the divine image could burn strongly (a theme which was taken up and used in early Christian apologetics by means of the Logos doctrine).

In 1 Corinthians 11:14 in the middle of Paul's argument in favour of sexual differentiation and male superiority he appeals to nature: 'does not nature itself teach you that if a man wears long hair, it brings dishonour to him, but if a woman wears long hair it is her pride'. This is then backed up by biblical support, by reference to a hierarchy of mimesis:

> Any man who prays or prophesies with something on his head disgraces his head, but any woman who prays or prophesies with her head unveiled disgraces her head—it is one and the same. . . . For a man ought not to have his head veiled, since he is the image and reflection of God; but woman is the reflection of man . . . Judge for yourselves; is it proper for a woman to pray to God with her head unveiled? Does not nature [*physis*] itself teach you that for a man to wear long hair is degrading to him, but if a woman has long hair, it is her glory? [1 Corinthians 11:4–7, 14–15]

Perhaps, more surprisingly, given his tirade against the wisdom of the world at the beginning of the letter, Paul is appealing here to what is in effect cultural convention, just as in 1 Corinthians 5, when it serves his interests, he appeals to pagan culture as well as nature in a situation where he wants to shame his opponents.

Throughout the Bible there is a recognition that human reason can find in the natural world signs of the glory of God. Observation of nature, along with observations of human relating, the pitfalls and advantages of different patterns of behaviour, offer a paradigm for understanding providence and what makes for the providential ordering of the world and people in it. This recognition is particularly evident in the Book of Proverbs and the Wisdom of Jesus ben Sirach, or Ecclesiasticus, in the Apocrypha. Of course, this was particularly linked with the fear of God whose expectations of humans are outlined in the Law of Moses. Thus, good order in society and the revealed wisdom to Moses coincide. But alongside this overlap of reason and revelation, there is throughout the Bible what the writers regard as a prophetic charisma, an ability to speak in a way which contrasts with convention and brings insight into situations, whether personal or political. As we shall see in the case of Amos and Jeremiah, ordinary objects and events can be invested with significance which many may miss.

Theological Discourse and human Relating, Visionary Imagination, and Eschatology

Biblical writings rarely offer an argument for God's existence based on appeal to the natural world. There are passages about the natural world in relation to God (as in Genesis 1) but never as part of a sustained argument to demonstrate the probability of God's existence. Even as regards those passages we have examined which use the natural world as evidence for God's existence, as in Wisdom of Solomon 13 and Romans 1–2, these are part of the apologetic tradition which serves to demonstrate the inadequacies of human epistemology and warns against the human tendency to worship 'nature not the God of nature'.

What we find in the Bible is the story of a tiny segment of humanity, and the account of their relations with God in history. That emphasis is important. Biblical writings testify to the divine being discerned through the ordinary course of nature, whether that be the physical world, or human intercourse and the various modes of human engagement. The focus of attention in the Bible is the human in the midst of the natural world, human life together, and how and why it is that fallible human beings need to begin over and over again the process of discerning what makes for their peace.

The Bible's different literary genres, whether in terms of complete texts or individual sentences, are rooted in human speech patterns, and evince ways of subverting the outlook of humans, whose capacity for habit and domestication require such subversion because they fail to understand and act aright. The biblical texts are *effective* texts, therefore. They persuade, disturb, and elicit praise, a sense of awe or injustice, guilt as well as confidence. Their purpose is to awaken people to life reflecting the divine image, by drawing readers into the dynamic of communication as to what that might mean. The Bible is full of analogies to nature and human life, and there is much use of familiar tropes, in order to enable the formation of people who may better reflect the nature of God. Ironically, it is those very chapters of 1 Corinthians advocating the superiority of the divine wisdom which contain some of the most obvious examples of human wisdom. Paul uses various rhetorical devices, techniques of persuasion, sarcasm, irony, and, in general, exploits the whole panoply of rhetorical devices to make sure his words have their full effect (Betz 1979; Mitchell 1991, 2010). They are techniques widespread in the rhetorical conventions of his day.

The understanding of God, especially in the synoptic Gospels, is rarely given in speculations about the nature of divinity, but frequently in familiar stories from everyday life. The Sermon on the Mount is full of appeals to nature, about the rain falling on the just and unjust (Matthew 5:45), about the beauty of the flowers, the provision for the birds, dealing with anxiety (Matthew 6:26–33), and the appeal to common sense in settling disputes (Matthew 5:23–26; Luke 14:28–33). The origin of Christian theology lies less with grand themes and systems than with analogies from nature and human life. A recurring theme of the synoptic Gospels is the Kingdom of God, but once we have read the Gospels we are left in as much uncertainty about exactly what is meant by this phrase. The critical consensus concerning its meaning is that it relates to the imminence of a future 'this-worldly' state of affairs which contrasts with the present time and which will be characterized by the fulfilment of the divine purposes. But nowhere do we find any neat encapsulation of this in the form of a utopian programme. Indeed, at the heart of the major theological texts of Christianity we find not exposition but resort to analogy requiring hearers and readers to make sense of the juxtaposition of various different kinds of ancient circumstances to help grasp what the Kingdom of God is like.

Parables are less frequent in the Gospel of John but we find a similar attempt to involve the reader or hearer in a process of epistemological transformation, which disorientates before it illumines and leads to an act of faith. That is a commitment to engagement with the ambiguity of the words, persistence with the interpretation of which may enable another way of seeing, and point to other levels of reality and ways of being. The riddling sayings and discourses of Jesus either captivate and open the eyes or otherwise drive people away in puzzlement. Nicodemus becomes typical as readers of the Gospel share his sense of bewilderment (Meeks 1972). The natural image of birth is a way of comparing the evolution of comprehension and ethical transformation. Nicodemus is a teacher of the Jews (John 3:1). To use Blake's words he needs the 'door of his perception cleansed' by the riddles and puzzles with which he is confronted to discern the Infinite embodied in his midst (cf. Blake 1988: *The Marriage of Heaven and Hell*, 14). This will enable him to begin to move from bemusement to a better grasp of the nature of things.

Encounter with God and with that which merits the epithet 'theological' in the Bible are a mixture of intellectual and practical engagements involving both the theologically freighted significance of certain persons and actions, and the use of rhetorical and other literary devices to enable a transformation of perception of that which has been received.

THEOLOGICAL DISCOURSE
AND HUMAN RELATING

Whatever the metaphysical expositions of Christian theology as it has developed, the ordinary (literally and metaphorically) has mediated understanding of God. Thus, even when we consider central tenets of Christianity (and indeed of Judaism) they are focussed on beliefs about ordinary lives, bodies, and events in the material world. To come face to face with God, said the author of the Gospel of John, meant meeting an apparently ordinary human person. 'Is this not Joseph's son?', the crowd asks in John 6:42. This is what the doctrine of the incarnation is about, not about some overwhelming supernatural revelation. To see the human Jesus is to see God and, derived from that, reading about him is to be enabled to meet that figure so central for early Christian experience (John 14:9; 1:18). Understanding more about that figure meant telling of his actions as signifiers, called *semeia* rather than merely recounting supernatural *thaumasia* ('miracles' or 'wonders', a word only rarely used in the New Testament). Those signs may be a first step (John 10:38 and 14:11) but are not in themselves the proof. God speaks through a human being and through agents of that human being. Faith in an ordinary human person, not sight of a supernatural being or event, is what counts: 'blessed are those who have not seen and yet have believed' (John 20:29).

Many of the central tenets of Christianity are not based on a supernatural revelation mediated by an angel, or other divine being to a privileged individual, even though, say, in the Book of Revelation, in the New Testament, we have a mode of revelation which is, at first sight, similar to the kind of claim made about Muḥammad's reception of the *Qur'ān*. 'At first sight' because John's words in the Apocalypse express what he had seen; he is not a channel of divine speech (the letters to the angels of seven churches apart). He bears witness to what lies *beyond* the text, therefore, as the divine is borne witness to approximately in fallible human words describing his visionary experience (of which more below). In Jewish tradition too, Moses was regarded both as a legislator inspired by God, and a channel of the oracles of God whose personal contribution was kept to a minimum (Lierman 2004). The Jewish tradition, however, never set these words in themselves as special and the debates about the content of religion in the rabbinic tradition did not focus on the words, so much as the ongoing ability to move beyond them to discern through the words the nature of the obligation in the present ever new contexts of life.

One of the things that emerges out of the New Testament, therefore, is that words are not the only, or even the prime, theological medium. Of course, the New Testament consists of words but they are words which bear witness to God's communication in the form of a person. That sense of the divine being borne witness to, through human action and appropriate mutual engagement, is found in several places, and is, arguably, central to the issue that Paul would have the Corinthians face up to. In 1 Corinthians Paul seems to be addressing groups who regarded themselves as elite because of their knowledge, their language, or other claims to status, and who ignored what it meant to be embodied persons relating one to another. In one of the most famous passages in the New Testament he explicitly contrasts a community which prizes skills in language, which ends up fragmenting, with a community based on charity, which is the very bond of peace: 'Though I speak with the tongues of men and angels and yet have no love, I were even as sounding brass: and as a tinkling cymbal' (1 Corinthians 13:1, in William Tyndale's translation). Paul deals with the issue of dissension by underlining the way in which the practice of human relating is the test of any talk about, or to, God. Paul demands that attention is given to the way in which language is used and subordinates this to the practice of charity as the necessary context and presupposition of theology. Language shaped by the practice of love and vulnerability is a very good commentary on what Paul writes in 1 Corinthians. Or, in the words of 1 John, theology is not just in word and speech but deed and truth also (1 John 3:18). It is a very natural activity, and none more so than that described in 1 John where relating to God means relating to one's brother (or sister): 'the one who does not love a brother whom he has seen cannot love God whom he has not seen' (1 John 4:20). The stuff of ordinary life is the necessary vehicle of the understanding of, and practice of theology. It is natural human life lived (and even died) and transformed by God that reveals who God is. If we are looking for God, therefore, the focus is on the human as the peculiar vehicle of the divine.

Nowhere is this better exemplified than in two passages in the Gospel of Matthew, 18:15–20 and 25:31–45. Matthew 18 is the paradigmatic passage in the Gospels dealing with forgiveness of sins. 18:15 is about addressing conflict, expressing it rather than concealing it. It is in this kind of activity that God is present, and something of divine significance takes place within such reconciling work: 'Again, truly I tell you, if two of you agree on earth about anything you ask, it will be done for you by my Father in heaven. For where two or three are gathered in my name, I am there among them' (Matthew 18:19–20). The practice is paralleled in the line in the Lord's Prayer 'Forgive us our debts as we forgive those who sin against us.' The process of conflict resolution, a natural way of relating, therefore, according to this passage, guarantees the divine presence.

It is of a piece with what we find elsewhere in the Gospel of Matthew—the divine being encountered in specific actions. At the climax of the eschatological discourse the Last Judgement is described (Matthew 25:31–45), and compared to a shepherd separating the sheep from the goats. The criteria of judgement, to the surprise of both those who turn out to be righteous and those who turn out to be wicked, are not theological but ethical: 'inasmuch as you have done it to one of the least of these my brethren you have done it to me' (Matthew 25:40). We need not worry now about the identity of the brethren (is it a reference to Christian disciples or is it all the poor, the naked, and the destitute?). The point is that acts of charity done to the 'least of these' turn out to be of ultimate theological significance, and the divide between the natural and supernatural is not as great as one might have thought. Similarly, echoing Genesis 18:2, Hebrews 13:2 commends friendship to strangers, for one may thereby entertain angels unawares.

Relating to, and experience of, God also were believed to come through interpreta-tion and the application of words, especially the interpretation of the Bible. There is a famous passage in an early collection of rabbinic sayings, *Pirke Aboth*, 3:9 in which we read:

> R. Chalaftha of Kaphar-Chananiah said, When ten sit and are occupied in words of Torah the Shekinah is among them, for it is said, God standeth in the congregation of the mighty. [Psa. lxxxii. 1]

This parallels the sentiments of Jesus from Matthew 18:20 already mentioned.

Visionary Imagination

What it means to be occupied in studying the words of Torah is beautifully evoked by the writer of Ecclesiasticus:

> He who devotes himself to the study of the law of the Most High will seek out the wisdom of all the ancients, and will be concerned with prophecies; he will preserve the discourse of notable men and penetrate the subtleties of parables; he will seek out the hidden meanings of proverbs and be at home with the obscurities of para-bles. [39:1–3]

Here the possibility of new insight as a result of knowledge of the past is acknowledged. Penetrating scriptural subtleties often involves an exercise of imagination, and it is the exercise of imagination which best helps us understand those charismatic moments described in the Bible as supernatural events when prophets and seers discern deeper things about the world through dreams, visions, and moments of insight, when connec-tions are made between objects in the natural world and the human situation. So, related to this process of exercising the imagination are the dreams, auditions, and visions that offer another way of unsettling the complacent, pointing them to different kinds of reali-ties and behaviours. Jeremiah saw the branch of an almond tree and a boiling cauldron (Jeremiah 1:11–13), and Amos, among other things, a plumb line and basket of fruit (Amos), and all become vehicles of God's prophetic word. Mary Carruthers has shown how in antique and medieval readings of the Bible there was a creative process of imagi-native engagement. Such meditative practice, she argues, was a craft of imagination which opened up the possibility of an interweaving of biblical allusions and personal context to effect an engagement with scripture which yielded new meaning by a process of spontaneous interconnection, through meditative recall and visualization (Carruthers 1990, 1998).

A neat separation between exegesis and experience cannot do justice to what was going on in antiquity, where the reading of the Bible may have involved, as in the case of the interpretation of some prophetic passages like the opening chapter of Ezekiel, an empathetic identification and replication of the earlier prophet's experience:

In the thirtieth year, in the fourth month, on the fifth day of the month, as I was among the exiles by the river Chebar, the heavens were opened, and I saw visions of God.... As I looked, a stormy wind came out of the north: a great cloud with brightness around it and fire flashing forth continually, and in the middle of the fire, something like gleaming amber. In the middle of it was something like four living creatures.... Over the heads of the living creatures there was something like a dome, shining like crystal, spread out above their heads... And above the dome over their heads there was something like a throne, in appearance like sapphire; and seated above the likeness of a throne was something that seemed like a human form.... Like the bow in a cloud on a rainy day, such was the appearance of the splendour all around. This was the appearance of the likeness of the glory of the LORD. [Ezekiel 1:1–28]

For John of the Book of Revelation, and his visionary predecessors and contemporaries, the exegesis of a prophetic text such as Ezekiel was probably not just the subject of learned debate but also the catalyst for visionary experience through imaginative engagement (Halperin 1988; Rowland 1982, 2011; Scholem 1955; Rowland and Morray-Jones 2009). This is what we find in the tradition of visionary interpretation of Ezekiel, loosely referred to as 'merkabah mysticism'.

ESCHATOLOGY: THE NATURAL WORLD AS THE ARENA FOR THE FULFILMENT OF THE DIVINE PURPOSES

We have just mentioned the major apocalyptic text of the New Testament, the Book of Revelation, and suggested that the apocalyptic is about visionary insight. Yes, included in this is insight into the future of the cosmos and the nature of its institutions, but there is also the link between apocalypse and catastrophe. The Book of Revelation, in common with the rest of the Bible, is not about the description of the end of the world but its catharsis and its future as the arena of God's saving activity (Finamore 2009). The New Testament in particular has gained the reputation of being world-denying because of its eschatology. There is some truth in the world-denying elements, in the sense that there were strong counter-cultural elements at work, as there were in Judaism, but the idea that early Christians expected the winding up of human history and were not interested in the natural world is a view that flies in the face of the evidence of Christian texts down to the third century.

In the Johannine literature the cosmos is the object of God's love (John 3:16); it is the place to which the divine Logos came and where those who would follow the divine Logos are to carry on their work. But the cosmos can be the place which is under the domination of the ruler of this world (cf. 2 Corinthians 4:4), as well as being the arena of God's saving activity. Existence in the cosmos is marked by ambivalence: the disciples of Jesus are to be in the world but not of it (John 17:14–15). The present order of the cosmos is not an unambiguous demonstration of the divine will, therefore. That which may constitute activity acceptable to God cannot merely mirror that of the cosmos and its culture. Rather, as we find in the Gospel of John, there is need for a change in both perspective and action; the biblical texts set out to redefine the cosmos's ideas of the way things are. So, for example, with kingship. Jesus' kingship is not of this world (John 18:36). It does not reflect what is presumed to be the natural order of things where kings exercise authority, dominate, and fight. Here is a king who washes feet. He exercises a kingship not of this world, in the sense that it is defined by other criteria.

The form of the cosmos is not what it might be. As far as the author of 1 John is concerned, 'we are already children of God, but it is not yet apparent what we shall be'. When the Messiah appears we shall be like him, because we shall see him as he is (1 John 3:2). Paul can write of seeing in a glass darkly with only glimpses of the perfection still awaited (1 Corinthians 13:12). Meanwhile the advice is not to be taken in by the cosmos as it is, especially, in its desires for property, status, and wealth (1 John 2:16 f.). But it is important to stress that in saying that early Christianity was ambivalent about the cosmos it was not because Christians believed that the end of the world was imminent. Rather its arrangements would be changed. Meanwhile in the midst of its present disorder it was important not to be conformed to the world as it was. Early Christian hopes for the future, for the first century and a half of Christianity's existence (and to which much of the New Testament bears witness), involved the coming of God's kingdom *on earth*, this world, this nature, not some otherworldly realm.

Ambivalence about the present arrangements, however, certainly did lead to negative words about God's destruction of the world and many of those in it, and yet there are also hints of an awareness of another dimension to the importance of creation. Thus, in the book of Revelation, in the midst of the torrent of images of upheaval, there emerges the comment that responsibility for the ecological disaster lies at the door of humanity: 'The time has come for judgement on the destroyers of the earth' (Revelation 11:18). This brief hint is a reminder that Revelation offers one of the best examples of a neglected theme in biblical theology which is particularly pertinent to the theme of this chapter: the divine covenant with the cosmos and not just with humans, or even one small group of humans, within it (Rowland 1998).

There are hints of covenant language in the imagery of Revelation 4:3 and 4 (cf. Exodus 19:16). This may not be the Sinai covenant, for, in addition, to the covenant theme related to Sinai, however, there is evidence for a parallel belief, a covenant between God and creation as a whole, not just a fraction of the world's population (Murray 1992). The opening chapter of Genesis depicts a harmonious order of the cosmos after the divine subjugation of natural and supernatural forces. A covenant is made with Noah after the flood signified with the 'bow in the clouds on the day of rain', to use Ezekiel's words (Genesis 9–16; Isaiah 54:9 f.). In Hosea the whole of the created world is linked to God's covenant:

> I will make for you a covenant on that day with the wild animals, the birds of the air, and the creeping things of the ground; and I will abolish the bow, the sword, and war from the land; and I will make you lie down in safety. [Hosea 2:18–20]

The breach of what Robert Murray terms this 'cosmic covenant' is stated in Isaiah:

> The earth dries up and withers,
> the world languishes and withers;
> the heavens languish together with the earth.
> The earth lies polluted
> under its inhabitants;
> for they have transgressed laws,
> violated the statutes,
> broken the everlasting covenant. [Isaiah 24:4–5]

The effect of the breach is that 'The land mourns' (Hosea 4:1–3; Jeremiah 12:4; Joel 1:18–20). Right order in the world brings about prosperity (Isaiah 32:17: Joel 2:19–29; cf. Haggai 1:10–11), and right order in the human world reflects, and runs in parallel with, order in the cosmos. A just social order embracing the whole world, humans and animals is the vision of Isaiah 11. The messiah is a key figure in maintaining the stability of that order (Psalm 72 and 89). As the mediator between God and the people God's anointed one had a key role in mediating *shalom*. The apocalyptic imagery of Revelation evoking upheaval might be seen as a consequence of the fracture of the cosmic covenant, the repair of which is, it seems to me, the storyline of Revelation, as upheaval precedes heaven coming down to earth and the Paradise of God existing in the New Jerusalem in this world (Finamore 2009).

It is occasionally hinted that the followers of Jesus might have a special role in sharing the affliction and healing of the cosmos. In Romans 8, with its imagery of gestation and birth, the followers of the Messiah share the anguish of creation in travail, awaiting that moment when the divine purposes come to birth:

> For the creation waits with eager longing for the revealing of the children of God...We know that the whole creation has been groaning in labour pains until now; and not only the creation, but we ourselves, who have the first fruits of the Spirit, groan inwardly while we wait for adoption, the redemption of our bodies. [Romans 8:19–23]

Those in Christ cannot shut themselves off from the natural world, therefore. Indeed, in some respects those who belong to Christ might be especially aware of the suffering and in some special way contribute to the birth of a new creation (Matthew 19:28–30; Colossians 1:24). In what are at best tantalizing glimpses, which lack coherent exposition, we find no miraculous escape from the world, nor a mystical identification with nature, but a perception of a threat to the cosmic order and a longing for it to be redeemed.

CONCLUSION

Paul writes of Satan hindering him (1 Thessalonians 2:18), or buffeting him, when he probably referred to missing a boat across the Aegean or suffering some physical or psychological ailment (2 Corinthians 12:7). Jeremiah saw branches of an almond tree and

Amos a basket of fruit, both of which were vehicles of God's word. This may recall William Blake's point about the ability of the person of imagination to see angels in the sunshine, or 'To see a World in a Grain of Sand / And a Heaven in a Wild Flower' (1988: 'Auguries of Innocence'). Here the natural is a signifier for the theological. William Blake was a younger contemporary of William Paley. At first sight Blake seems to be an implacable opponent of natural theology. Yet, in many ways his theology was every bit as 'natural' as William Paley's and encapsulates some of the major themes of this chapter. Blake is an example of a writer who held to a strong belief in the traces of the divine in humanity and indeed the whole of existence which became a signifier of the divine in a way akin to what Paul writes of in Romans 1. He did not neglect to note human fallibility in clouding the ability to discern the divine in the human nor the way humans prioritize sense experience at the expense of the imaginative. Blake anticipated much in modern theology in his insistence that human psychology and relating was the way in which one might speak meaningfully of God. Nature and the natural, with humanity as the means of understanding its significance, were for Blake the key to any language about God, nevertheless with this caveat: 'Nature Teaches nothing of Spiritual Life but only of Natural Life' (1988: *Annotations to Boyd's Historical Notes on Dante*). So, Blake was no romantic about nature: 'Where man is not nature is barren' (1988: *The Marriage of Heaven and Hell* Plate 10). It is his fascination with men and women at the centre of the natural, the complexity of their psychologies, and the political processes which can both degrade and offer hope, that he sought to interpret in words and images. Like the biblical writers who exerted such a powerful influence on him, Blake was a keen supporter of extending human knowing to include the poetic and the imaginative and not allowing preoccupation with sense experience to be given a hegemonic place (1988: *There is No Natural Religion* version B; Rowland 2010: 6, 28, 52–5). The divine discerned through the imagination was less for him an outside, 'supernatural' influence, than a neglected dimension of human experience, and it is the key to the understanding of the image of God in humanity, as he put it in these deceptively simple words:

'The Divine Image'

To Mercy Pity Peace and Love,
All pray in their distress:
And to these virtues of delight
Return their thankfulness.

For Mercy Pity Peace and Love,
Is God our father dear:
And Mercy Pity Peace and Love,
Is Man his child and care.

For Mercy has a human heart
Pity, a human face:
And Love, the human form divine,
And Peace, the human dress.

Then every man of every clime,
That prays in his distress,
Prays to the human form divine
Love Mercy Pity Peace.

And all must love the human form,
In heathen, turk or jew.
Where Mercy, Love & Pity dwell,
There God is dwelling too. [Blake 1988: 12–13]

REFERENCES

Barr, James (1994). *Biblical Faith and Natural Theology*. The Gifford Lectures for 1991. Oxford: Oxford University Press.

Betz, H. D. (1979). *Galatians: A Commentary on Paul's Letter to the Churches in Galatia*. Philadelphia: Fortress Press.

Blake, William (1988). *The Complete Poetry and Prose of William Blake*. Edited by David V. Erdman. New York: Random House.

Bockmuehl, Marcus N. A. (2000). *Jewish Law in Gentile Churches: Halakhah and the Beginning of Christian Public Ethics*. Edinburgh: T&T Clark.

Carruthers, M. (1990). *The Book of Memory: A Study of Memory in Medieval Culture*. Cambridge: Cambridge University Press.

—— (1998). *The Craft of Thought: Meditation, Rhetoric, and the Making of Images, 400–1200*. Cambridge: Cambridge University Press.

Finamore, S. (2009). *God, Order and Chaos: René Girard and the Apocalypse*. Carlisle: Paternoster.

Halperin, D. (1988). *The Faces of the Chariot*. Tübingen: Mohr.

Lierman, J. (2004). *The New Testament Moses: Christian Conceptions of Moses and Israel in the Setting of Jewish Religion*. WUNT 137. Tübingen: Mohr Siebeck.

Meeks, W. (1972). 'The Man from Heaven in Johannine Sectarianism'. *Journal of Biblical Literature* 91: 44–72.

Mitchell, M. (1991). *Paul and the Rhetoric of Reconciliation: An Exegetical Investigation of the Language and Composition of 1 Corinthians*. Tübingen: Mohr.

Mitchell, M. M. (2010). *Paul, the Corinthians, and the Birth of Christian Hermeneutics*. Cambridge: Cambridge University Press.

Murray, R. (1992). *The Cosmic Covenant*. London: Sheed and Ward.

Rowland, C. (1982). *Open Heaven. Study of the Apocalyptic in Judaism and Early Christianity*. London: SPCK.

—— (1998). 'Revelation' in *The New Interpreters' Bible*. Vol. XII. Nashville: Abingdon.

—— (2010). *Blake and the Bible*. London: Yale University Press.

Rowland C. and C. Morray-Jones (2009). *The Mystery of God: Early Jewish Mysticism and the New Testament*. Leiden: Brill.

Scholem, G. (1955). *Major Trends in Jewish Mysticism*. London: Thames & Hudson.

CHAPTER 3

....

NATURAL THEOLOGY IN THE PATRISTIC PERIOD

....

WAYNE HANKEY

THE centrality of natural theology in this period and its inescapable formation of what succeeds are indicated by the multiple forms it takes in Hellenic, Jewish, and Christian philosophies, religious practices, and theologies. Commonly, the term, as used to refer to an apologetic or instrument presupposed by or leading to revealed religion and theology, makes no distinction between the forms of philosophy. Moreover, when those listed as 'philosophers' in our histories touch on theological or religious matters, they are usually treated as if what they wrote was all 'natural', in the sense of coming from inherent human capacity, as opposed to what is inspired or gracious. Packing the natural theology of what we are calling 'the Patristic Period' into such crudely undifferentiated lumps moulded by later binary schematizing destroys what it most distinctively accomplished. It not only produced the new language of metaphysics and the supernatural, but also thought through how nature and what is beyond it interpenetrated one another (de Lubac 1946: 323–428; Brisson 1999; Harrington 2004: 121–3).

The Hellenic, Jewish, and Christian philosophers and theologians of the period, themselves frequently bridging the natural/supernatural divide in their 'divine' miracle working or at least consecrated persons, took what was diversely established within classical antiquity to build hierarchically connected levels and kinds within wholes. Physical and metaphysical, fate and providence, sensible and supersensible, the immanent and the transcendent, being and non-being (both excessive and deficient in respect to being), the rational and what was below and above it, the natural and the supernatural, what was in human power and what was a gift from without, profane and holy, what theory could reach and what required practical cooperation with the divine, what was open to all and what required initiation, were all distinguished, sometimes opposed, and always related. In leading humans to the gods and even beyond, after instilling communal, religious, and moral virtues, philosophers, often consecrated at least by their lineage as successors handing on sacred traditions, shepherded their disciples not only up the long difficult ladder of philosophy's hierarchy, but also to what before, accompanying, and beyond this required worldly practice and its frustration, myth, mystery, prayer, magic, inspiration, prophesy, madness, hymn, symbol, theurgy, sacrament, the breaking in of the divine, the violation of the self, and, finally, yielding and silence. Evidently, in these situations, 'natural' as well as 'theology' became polyvalent.

I shall not manage to set out and explain all this extravagant diversity, especially because understanding one term requires thinking its pairs. To get some sense of these diverse significations, and recollecting that the study of nature in antiquity may serve as spiritual exercise, the striking use of physics as theological foundation for Epicurean and Stoic ways of life, and how Plato's *Timaeus* as philosophical genesis reaches across religious differences to dominate the Patristic Period, we may begin with the Stoic Middle Platonism of Philo Judaeus and Josephus. With Philo, uniting Plato's and Moses' genesis, and thus connecting God, the cosmos, and the human in the opposite way to the one taken by Lucretius in his *De Rerum Natura*, we encounter most of the forms natural theology took in the period. We discover not only that there is no operation of pure nature abstracted from the divine activity but also that physics leads to theology and that nature, the human, and community depend on gifts given beyond them from above.

PHILO: NATURAL THEOLOGY
AS *PHYSIOLOGIA*

Philo, when commenting on a text from Numbers which makes every day a feast, writes that the Law 'accommodates itself to the blameless life of righteous men who follow nature' (Philo 1937: II.42). After noting the practice of civil and moral virtue by these righteous Greeks and Barbarians in training for wisdom, he makes them 'the best contemplators of nature and everything found in her'. So, while their bodies are below, their souls take wing and they know the ethereal powers, 'as befits true cosmopolitans' (Philo 1937: II.42). The cosmos is the city of these acute physiologues; their associates are the wise in the universal commonwealth ruled by virtue. They themselves keep above passions and do not buckle under the blows of fate.

Physics does not only lead to Stoic *apatheia*, it opens the human to prophecy. According to Philo in another context, connection to the natural elements made the authors of the *Septuagint* open to revelation; they became not translators but 'hierophants and prophets'. After prayer, to which God assented so that the human race might be led to a better life by using the 'philosophical and truly beautiful ordinances' of the Jewish Law, secluded on the island of Pharos with 'nothing except the elements of nature: earth, water, air, heaven, the genesis of which was to be the first theme of their sacred revelation—for the production of the cosmos is the principle of the laws—like men inspired, they prophesied'. In consequence, without conferring with one another 'they found words corresponding to the things'. In arriving at the very realities which had been revealed through Moses, and expressing them in Greek, their minds went along with the purest of spirits (Philo 1935: II.36–40). The Mosaic Law understood in union with nature, and as both philosophical and revealed, is now available to teach all humankind.

For Josephus, who depended upon and shared the mentality, Jewish history is written by starting with Genesis as normative *physiologia*: 'first we must study the nature of God and, then, having contemplated his works with the eye of reason, we can go on to imitate in our own deeds, so far as possible, the work of God, the best of all models, and endeavour to follow it'. For Josephus, all things told in his history are 'in accord with the harmony in the nature of the whole' (Josephus 1930: I.4). God always acts so as to maintain the cosmic order eternally founded in his very nature. Philo not only shows God doing this but also explains how the divine, human, cosmic interconnection is known and maintained.

Philo was 'the first thinker to associate the goodness of Plato's demiurge with the Judaeo-Christian conception of God the creator' (Runia 1986: 135). God is the all good and desires to share that goodness as much as possible. He is continually creative (Philo 1929a: I.18) in an activity with two stages; the first, his image eternally formed in his mind, is *ex nihilo*. The physical world, made according to the incorporeal model, has presuppositions. Philo explains how the cosmos is both created and eternal in language which reminds us of Aristotle, *De Anima* III.5:

> in all existing things there must be an active cause, and a passive subject; the active cause is the intellect of the universe, thoroughly unadulterated and thoroughly unmixed, superior to virtue and superior to science, superior even to abstract good or abstract beauty; while the passive subject is something inanimate and incapable of motion by any intrinsic power of its own, but having been set in motion, and fashioned, and endowed with life by the intellect, became transformed into that most perfect work, this cosmos. [Philo 1929a: 8–9]

The account of the education and offices of Moses, the mediator between God and the cosmos, depends on differentiating between what is innate and belongs to philosophical labour, on the one hand, and what is from without and above, on the other. By the union of both, Moses acquires the capacities of the philosopher-king, legislator, high priest, and prophet who establishes the cosmic priesthood of Israel. While he receives a complete education, including symbolic philosophy, from all kinds of masters employed from Egypt, the adjacent countries, and Greece, his innate genius meant that he was recollecting rather than learning and was improving upon what his teachers gave (Philo 1935: I.18–24). This grounding of his human labours in the nature given to him indicates the principle at work in Philo's treatment of the unique bridge between the divine and the human, one with both sides. While Philo is careful to differentiate the offices Moses holds and the diverse capacities by which he exercises each, the foundation of them all is both a moment in his history and activities and is also its underlying source, namely his union with the divine Logos in the mystical darkness. There is a reciprocity by which, in return for his labours, virtues, and giving up all personal possessions, he receives from God. The gift, however, is out of all proportion to the human work and power. Moses, as the friend of God and his heir, is given as recompense the wealth of the whole earth, sea, and rivers, and of all the other elements and their combinations; 'therefore, every one of the elements obeyed him as its master, changing the power which it had by nature and submitting to his command' (Philo 1935: 155–6). Moses is, of course, a citizen of the cosmos, but far more he has the names of God: 'For he also was called the god and king of the whole nation, and he is said to have entered into the darkness where God was, into the unseen, invisible, incorporeal, archetypal essence of all beings. There he beheld things invisible to mortal nature.' He becomes the middle between the divine and the human to be imitated by us (Philo 1935: 157–9). When he is about to die, the Father changes Moses from 'a double being, composed of soul and body, so that his whole nature is that of a monad without elements, thus transforming him wholly and entirely into a most sun-like mind' (Philo 1935: II.288; Parker 2010).

This reciprocity is extended to all. Grace and nature are two sides of the same coin—a principle which will be common also to pagans and Christians in the period, despite some tendencies associated with an aspect of Augustine's thought. While Philo tells us that the creature should be conscious of his own 'nothingness' when approaching his Maker, God is 'one who loves to give', his gifts are boundless and without end (Philo 1932: 31; see also Iamblichus 1966: I.15, 47, 17; and Feichtinger 2003: 136). He is the 'saviour' of those who cry to him. Philosophy has never been anything else except the desire to see the Existent, his image the Logos, and, after these, his perfect work, the cosmos, truly according to our diverse capacities; Moses is given to lead the way (Philo 1932: 92–7). Although many forces push us down, none are powerful against the soul suspended from God, who, with a greater strength, draws it to himself (Philo 1935: 59).

The human is the image of God, and the human mind stands to the rest in the way that God stands to the cosmos as a whole. They are connected in mutual support through the priesthood. Having presented the dress of the High Priest as visible representation of the cosmos, Philo explains that this is, first, so that by constantly contemplating 'the image of the all', the life of the High Priest will be worthy of the nature of the whole. Secondly, the cosmos will become his co-ministrant in his sacred rites: 'It is very right and fit that he who is consecrated to the service of the Father of the cosmos should bring the Father's son, the all, to the service of the creator and begetter' (Philo 1937: I.95–6). Finally, in contrast to the priests of other nations, the High Priest of the Jews offers his prayers and sacrifices 'not only on behalf of the whole human race, but also for the parts of nature: earth, water, air, fire; for he looks upon the cosmos (as indeed it really is) as his country' (Philo 1937: I.97).

Philo's influence was not primarily within his own religious community, where, after the Roman destruction of the Second Temple, although Hellenic Judaism persisted, there was a turn against the kind of identification with Greco-Roman culture of which his corpus was the acme. Nonetheless, Philo shares the common theology out of which the Wisdom of Solomon, and great parts of the New Testament—most notably the Epistle to the Hebrews, the Pauline corpus, and the Gospels of Luke and John emerge

(Siegert 2009). This will facilitate his gigantic influence among the Christian Fathers, underestimated because substantially unacknowledged by them. Clement of Alexandria, and the Catechetical School there, continued Philo's unification of philosophy and scriptural revelation in his home city, and Clement's works contain massive reiterations of both content and methods. In Alexandria, Origen also came into the heritage and made a hugely important contribution to its dissemination when he carried the Philonic corpus to Palestine when he moved. There, among other uses, his *Life of Moses* came to underlie the ideology of the Byzantine Empire through Bishop Eusebius of Caesarea's modelling of Constantine on it, and beyond the Christian Empire, even into the understanding of the philosopher-king, legislator, prophet, and religious leader in an Islamic philosopher like al-Farabi (O'Meara 2003). However, no one has traced what we owe to him outside the Fathers with the barest adequacy; not only the Islamic but also the pagan philosophical reception are neglected. Philo's natural theology certainly massively provided content and method for the philosophical interpretation of Christian scripture generally and of Genesis and Moses especially, which we may indicate by mentioning the works entitled *Hexamaeron* of Bishops Basil of Caesarea, Gregory of Nyssa, Ambrose of Milan, and the multiple interpretations of Genesis by Augustine; there are also the *De Vita Moysis* and *De Hominis Opificio* of Gregory, to mark the most obvious (Runia 2009; Pelikan 1995 and 1997). John Scottus Eriugena translated Gregory's *On the Creation of Humankind* and (probably) Basil's *Hexamaeron* into Latin. Their content passed into his *Periphyseon*.

The ways Philo and his philosophical sources are taken up illumine how physics, cosmogony, theology, metaphysics, 'true gnosticism', and the vision of those initiated into the mysteries are connected in our period. Thus, for example, Clement in his *Stromata*, when passing to 'the *physiologia* truly gnostic', speaks of those initiated into the mysteries, moving from the lesser to the greater as distinguished in the *Gorgias* (Clement 2001: IV.3.1; cf. Plato 1959: 497C; and Philo 1929b: 62). For him, *physiologia* is a gnosis conformed to the canon of truth—or, better, the contemplation belonging to the highest degree of initiation into the mysteries (*epopteia*) which reposes on the discussion of cosmogony. From this we are elevated to theology. Appropriately, he says, after philosophical *physiologia*, he will go on to consider the prophetic Genesis (Clement 2001: IV.3.2–3).

Basil of Caesarea took up the anagogy in Plato's *Symposium* which both differentiated and linked the contemplation of physical and intelligible beauties. Above sensible eros, Diotima had spoken of the highest mysteries of revelation and contemplation (Plato 1901: 210A). For Basil, someone who for a long time had been among the physiologues but desired to follow the command to seek God's face would go beyond this level of reality to place himself closer to God. The seeker would then be turned to the truly beautiful and desirable, reserved for the pure in heart, and, passing from *physiologia* to the greater beauty beyond nature (*meta physin*), would join those initiated into the supreme contemplation (Basil 1999: V.162; cf. Brisson 1999: 38–40). Determined pagans in this period also made metaphysical contemplation into spiritual exercise. Proclus organized the Academy as a kind of monastery. Its programme of study initiated its members step by step into contemplation within a context of prayer. The philosophy of Plato was 'mystagogy', an 'initiation into the holy mysteries themselves... installed, for eternity, in the home of the gods on High' (Saffrey 1984: 182 quoting Proclus 1968: I.1; cf. Saffrey 1997). His own *Elements of Theology* may be considered 'metaphysics as spiritual exercise' (O'Meara 2000: 279–90). In this view of philosophy, Plato becomes a theologian, his dialogues sacred scripture to be interpreted appropriately. This helps explain the greater antipathy towards Platonism by the Christian authorities and why it was increasingly passed on by Neoplatonists through commentary on Aristotle's comparatively more secular writings.

Boethius: The Consolations of Natural Theology

Two heirs of Proclus, Boethius and his contemporary Dionysius the Areopagite, exhibited none of the polemical antipathy to philosophy which marks Augustine's deeply ambiguous relation to what enabled his return to his Christian beginnings. When writing out the philosophical concord in late antiquity which consoled his imprisonment awaiting execution by torture, the Christian Boethius not only repeated many times and in various ways and metres the contemplation of nature which Philo promised would be efficacious against the blows of fate, but also had Lady Philosophy imitate the *Timaeus* by praying (Plato 1902a: 27B–C; Boethius 1973: III.ix; cf. I.v, V.ii). At the exact centre of the *Consolation*, in a beautiful poem fashioned from elements of the Platonic genesis, Philosophy prays to the 'creator of heaven and earth'. The concord by which the *Consolation* purges, illumines, and converts the prisoner to meet the gaze of God with hope bridges the pagan–Christian divide. The *Consolation* makes no explicit reference to anything distinctively Christian, although allusions are plentiful for those who seek, and there is very little or nothing taught by Lady Philosophy which stands against Christian doctrine—the reference of the *Timaeus* to an existence of the world before time is interpreted so that the interminable life of the world does not share God's simple eternity of motionless infinite possession (Boethius 1973: V.vi). The prayer converts the prisoner towards that simplicity by turning him from reason which divides what is one (Boethius 1973: III.ix). He moves to the perspective of the One in which the mind is led through intellectual deduction from unity to goodness to God, so as to explain why 'every happy man is a god' (Boethius 1973: III.x).

Many features of the natural theology of our period appear in the *Consolation*: the study of nature as spiritual exercise; a conciliating synthesis of philosophies; Lady Philosophy's preference for a Platonism which has assimilated Aristotle, together with her use of the cathartic spiritual exercises and techniques for self-care of the Sceptics, Stoics, Epicureans, and Cynics, while their philosophies are rejected as partial or false; philosophy's use and need of religious acts, myth, hymn, poetry, rhetoric; allegorical interpretation of myth; arguments for the necessity and possibility of prayer; her medicinal and salvific work; the identity of philosophy and religion; the differentiation of higher and lower forms of apprehension; her anagogy of the fallen soul, so that, ultimately, divine and human intuition meet; the subordination of fate to providence. The last helps us to understand how nature and grace interpenetrate in this period.

In the *Laws* Plato taught that the divine goodness involved a universal and particular providential care: 'The gods perceive, see, and hear everything' (Plato 1907: 901D) and these gods 'are more, not less, careful for small things than for great' (900D). For Philo, Moses, in agreement with Plato, taught 'that God exerts his providence for the benefit of the cosmos' (Philo 1929a: 172). Defending the Platonic doctrine requires dealing with the flat-out denial essential to Epicurean enlightened religion, and the Peripatetic limitation which denies that providence is for the sake of individuals and intervenes for or against them (Alexander of Aphrodisias 1983: XXX–XXXI). Plotinus undertakes this defence, by using Alexander of Aphrodisias' refutation of the Stoic determinism which would make prayer pointless and by employing the Middle Platonic distinction between higher providence and lower fate, which we saw in Philo. He writes: 'One thing results from all, and there is one providence; but it is fate beginning from the lower level; the upper is providence alone' (Plotinus 1967: III.3.5). Iamblichus, for whom the gods contain and employ the material for the sake of human souls altogether descended into it, has a sense of the integrity of nature, how it is connected, and how it serves justice. Because, following Plotinus, physical movements depend upon immaterial intellectual activities, and secondary causes on primary ones, the 'divine' Iamblichus writes to a correspondent: 'Fate is enmeshed with providence and exists by virtue of the existence of providence' (Iamblichus 2009: To Macedonius, On Fate, Fr. 4, p. 23). Systematizing, the 'divine' Proclus, successor of Plato, divides and connects for the sake of anagogy. In the distinction within the order, fate is on the side of movement, multiplicity, and the corporeal, but 'providence precedes fate, and everything that comes about according to fate comes about far more according to providence.... [M]any things escape fate, but nothing providence' (Proclus 2007: §3). Fate connects things, but providence directs them to the good. 'Providence is per se god, whereas fate is something divine, but not god' (Proclus 2007: §14).

Boethius brings all of this into *Philosophy's Consolation*, so that fate and providence become two different perspectives on the same plan: 'When this plan is thought of in terms of the purity of God's own understanding, it is called providence. When this same plan is thought of in terms of the manifold different movements which are the life of individual things, it is called fate by the ancients' (Boethius 1973: IV.vi). Perspective is creative, as Eriugena will demonstrate most thoroughly, but Boethius anticipates some of his principles. Reiterating a theme we encountered in Philo, he works out how, by changing their perspective, by turning from sense and imagination to reason, and from reason to intellect and intuition, humans free themselves from the chains of fate and come under God's beneficent providence. We become what we know and love; ultimately this will carry us out of ourselves.

For Plotinus, union with the First is a breaking in or a bringing to birth where there is a 'sudden reception of a light' compelling the soul 'to believe' that 'it is from Him, it is

Him'. With this arrival of the 'true end of the soul', it 'contemplates the light by which it sees', but it is no longer operating by a power over which it has control. Augustine shared with Plotinus the experience that, when united with the First, the soul moves beyond thinking about itself and discovered that the attempt to grasp its goal results in failure (Plotinus 1984: V.3.17, 1988: VI.9.7; VI.9.11; Augustine 1981: 7.16.22; 9.10.24–5; 1968: 15.25). Thus the soul passes here beyond philosophy into the realm of grace. Despite systematic differences, Proclus has an analogous view of that to which the providence of the gods leads and how it comes. Real freedom for humans requires their help because they possess the virtue we desire. Slavery to them is our greatest freedom: 'by serving those who have power over all, we become similar to them, so that we govern the whole world' (Proclus 2007: §24). Knowledge beyond intellect, divine madness, involves arousing 'what is called the "one of the soul" ... and to connect it with the One itself'. Then the soul loves to be quiet and becomes speechless in internal silence. The acme of liberation is 'the life of the gods and that of the souls who dance above fate and follow providence' (Proclus 2007: §§31–4).

These representations of the conclusion beyond philosophy of philosophy's *itinerarium* are well beyond anything found in the sober Boethius, but they bring us back to his contemporary who claimed to inherit the fruit of St Paul's blinding encounter with a heavenly light 'beyond the brightness of the sun' (Acts 26.13). Dionysius interpreted this through what descended to him from Philo on Moses in the divine darkness, Plotinus, Proclus, and Damascius. *The Mystical Theology* prays for union with the good beyond thought and being for which Plato's analogy was the sun, a brilliantly shining darkness and a trumpeting silence, where soul and mind are left behind (Plato 1902b: 509B–C).

Dionysius, concluding beyond negation and affirmation a journey begun with a sensuous affirmative symbolic theology, shows that the Neoplatonism which became the natural theology of the Fathers, and their successors Christian and Islamic, surpasses matter/spirit, body/soul, sense/reason, evil/good dualisms by way of the ineffable First. He, joined in the Latin West by Boethius, is the main source of a Christianized rendition of Proclus' doctrine of the non-being of evil, the one most representative of Neoplatonism, which became the authoritative common teaching of the scholastics. Dionysius reproduces great parts of Proclus' *On the Subsistence of Evil* in *On the Divine Names* so literally that it is used to restore the lost Greek text of Proclus' treatise.

Plotinus had been clear that defending the Platonic doctrine of providence required dealing with evil and injustice, but his theodicy made matter evil and its cause (Plotinus 1967: III.2.2; 1966: I.8). Proclus' *De malorum subsistentia* is directed not only against the Plotinian treatment of the nature of evil and its cause, but also against everything which would give evil substantiality. For Proclus, matter is directly caused by the Good. Matter is not evil, and, as the means of the complete explication of the Good, is, at least indirectly, good. In consequence, the Good can have no contrary and evil no single cause. Proclus, and Dionysius in his wake, warn us against giving evil strength by magnifying its reality. Evil comes from particular weaknesses, is parasitic on good, and can only get such power as it has from goodness (Proclus 2003:§§7–9, §§30–8, §§47–54; Dionysius 1990: Ch. 4). In the *Consolation*, evil is 'nothing' (Boethius 1973: III.xii). Doing evil makes humans powerless and drags them down towards non-being. 'The divine nature is such that to it even evils are good, since by a suitable use of them God draws out as a result some good' (Boethius 1973: IV.vi).

Before leaving the sixth century, a little must be said about a Hellenic concordantist and Christian who began in that tradition but moved against it for the sake of defending the positions which separated his faith from the philosophical consensus.

THEOLOGICAL CONCORD AND DISSENT: SIMPLICIUS AND THE BEGINNINGS OF DIALECTICAL THEOLOGY

Bringing Plato and Aristotle into concord long predates Boethius. From the beginning of the Platonic school fundamental Aristotelian ideas like activity and potentiality were adopted by Platonists and his criticism of the existence of the Forms outside thinking was accepted. We have witnessed the result in Philo. Exchange between Peripatetics and Platonists intensified in our period, and, beyond this, despite reciprocal criticisms and rivalries, the harmony of the two philosophies was asserted and demonstrating it became a Neoplatonic project. Tracing the history of this concordism is outside our purpose and is complicated by the inevitable endeavour of the later enthusiasts to push back the harmony as early as Pythagoras. Nonetheless, a word about motives and results is necessary.

Porphyry is clearly engaged in philosophical harmonization, but, with Iamblichus and those in his wake, the project widens to embrace reconciling revelations, including religious practices and myths, to one another and to philosophy, which is regarded as having revelation at its origins. Thus, for example, Iamblichus writes as if he were an Egyptian priest defending the ancient mysteries and Hierocles of Alexandria turns Homer into a Platonist. Iamblichus fixes the curriculum of the Platonic schools, giving the sciences of Aristotle an essential, if secondary, place. With Proclus, following Iamblichus, philosophy itself is explicitly only a preparation. It is given a role comparable to that of purifications, rites of ablution and expiation in the Mysteries, so that 'philosophy constitutes a preliminary purification and a preparation for self-knowledge and the immediate contemplation of our own essence' (Proclus 1984: proem). The motive of the concord is twofold. One aim is to draw all spiritual activities together into a hierarchical and differentiated leading of the soul upward to the gods, thus showing that nothing escapes their mastery. The other is to give authority to the Hellenic tradition as both inclusive and consistent—it is not a morass of contradictory squabbling sects. The primary technique beyond distinguishing, classifying, and hierarchical ordering was that used by Philo, allegorizing, but now this includes texts of philosophy, certainly Plato's. One influential result, both with the Islamic philosophers and Latin medievals, was the reconciliation of Plato and Aristotle on creation.

The harmonizers want to draw together the *Timaeus*, and its Demiurge, with Aristotle's *Physics*, and his Unmoved Mover. To do this they need to reconcile Aristotle's eternal universe with that in the *Timaeus*, which is generated and corruptible, though perpetual because it is held in being by the divine will. The diverse positions of his Platonic and Peripatetic predecessors are treated by Simplicius. The following is an example of the result:

> [T]he truly marvellous Aristotle brings his instruction about the principles of nature to culmination in theology, which is above nature, and proves that the entire corporeal structure of nature is dependent on the incorporeal intellective goodness that is above nature and unrelated—here too following Plato. But it was from the very existence of the body of the world that Plato discovered the intellective god who is the creator of the world ... Aristotle too proceeds from motion and change and from the subsistence of bodies, which is finite and has extension, to the unmoved, unchangeable, unintermittent cause. [Simplicius 2001: 1359, 5–1359, 10]

A little further on, when he is showing how both Plato and Aristotle make god the efficient and final cause of creation, Simplicius reveals a source, a determined conciliator and pupil of Proclus. He writes of his teacher, who also taught his adversary, the Monophysite Christian John Philoponus, that: 'Ammonius has written an entire book which provides many proofs of the fact that Aristotle considers god to be also the efficient cause of the entire world, and I have here taken over some points sufficiently for my present purposes' (Simplicius 2001:1363, 8–1363, 12).

Simplicius explains how a commentator on Aristotle ought to work. When there are apparent disagreements between Plato and Aristotle, the good exegete 'must ... not convict the philosophers of discordance by looking only at the letter of what [Aristotle] says against Plato; but he must look towards the spirit, and track down the harmony which reigns between them on the majority of points' (Simplicius 2003: 7, 30–2). Commenting on Aristotle's *On the Heavens,* where Aristotle and his Peripatetic followers are unrelenting in their criticism of Plato, Simplicius complains repeatedly about literalism which does not understand that Plato speaks metaphorically in the manner of theologians. The gods speak through him: his words in the *Timaeus* 'are those of the Creator of all these things, whose thoughts and deeds Plato revealed as a prophet' (Simplicius 2006: 106, 5–6).

Although Boethius was determined both to hand on the translated works of Plato and Aristotle to a barbarian age and to present them as harmonious, his caution about interpreting the *Timaeus* on the eternity of the world hinted that some Christians might have problems with the Neoplatonic conciliation on creation. This is confirmed in Simplicius on the *De Caelo* which is full of mean-spirited polemic against John Philoponus because of his dissent. Whatever the outcome of their disputes at the time, Simplicius' attacks helped Philoponus by preserving his arguments, thus the reconstruction of his *Against Aristotle on the Eternity of the World* draws all except one of its Greek fragments from Simplicius (Philoponus 1987). Philoponus also wrote against Proclus on the same question. However, what is most interesting to us is that Philoponus, who must represent here many others, not only opposed the philosophic consensus on particular matters but began the unravelling of the project as a whole. This makes him, as Moses Maimonides discerned, a leader in a new relation of philosophy to religion, that of dialectical theology. Maimonides, who denounced these '*Mutakallimūn*' and the '*kalam*', sees the dialectical theologians rising first from among Greeks who had adopted Christianity, and then within Islam and Judaism, as unconcerned for philosophical truth in itself and wanting to use philosophical arguments as persuasions to predetermined dogmatic positions (Maimonides 1963: I, 71). Whether or not this is fair to Philoponus whose arguments were entirely philosophical, what Maimonides condemns was not at all the mode of the Carolingian figure who stands at the end of Patristic natural theology, namely John the Scot, Irish born.

ERIUGENA: PHYSICS AS THE COMPLETE THEOLOGY

Having arrived at Boethius and his sixth-century contemporaries, we have the elements which will enable us to conclude our consideration of theology as physics with its acme, the *Periphyseon* of John Scottus Eriugena. Because, by gathering all within a single system, Eriugena does in Latin what Origen had undertaken six centuries earlier in Alexandria with his *On First Principles*, the first Christian theological system, and because Eriugena's is a *physiologia*, predating the methods and divisions of the medieval scholastics, and because Eriugena derives his philosophy almost entirely from the Christian Fathers, he provides a terminus.

Eriugena 'reinvented the greater part of the theses of Neoplatonism', by his time largely forgotten in the Latin West (Trouillard 1983: 331). His authentic repossession and radical reworking of pagan Platonism illuminates how it served as natural theology. By discovering his Neoplatonic principles mostly in Christian theological writings, Eriugena showed the overwhelming degree to which Patristic Christian theologians had assimilated them. Noting a few outstanding features of his work displays something of what that philosophical theology gave to Christian (and, indeed, to Islamic and Jewish) philosophy and theology. Moreover, his is another concordism with a new dimension exhibiting a further use of philosophy by theologians.

After Boethius, Eriugena was the first to unite the Greek and Latin Platonisms of late antiquity; this enabled his reconciliation of Latin and Greek Christian theologies. His beginnings are with the Latin Fathers—pre-eminently Augustine, crucially Boethius, and importantly Ambrose. In *Periphyseon* they are contained within a single system with the Greek Fathers of whom he made translations, beginning with the Dionysian corpus. Eriugena's reconciliation of East and West was accomplished by extending the primarily Plotinian and Porphyrian Platonism of the Latin Fathers in the direction of notions from Iamblichus, Syrianus, Proclus, and Damascius transmitted by the Greeks. As generally when the earlier Platonism of Augustine met the later, most authoritatively conveyed by Dionysius, the later determined the systematic structure. It was to it that Eriugena also owed his conceptions both of nature and the supernatural.

Eriugena gave his masterwork a Greek title, *Peri physeōn, Concerning Nature*; it is a *physiologia* (Eriugena 1996–2003: IV PL441C), a term he found in Gregory of Nyssa's *De hominis opificio*. Physics includes all, because, as Plato had taught, genesis embraces 'what is and what is not' (Eriugena 1996–2003: I PL441A) and the divine superessential nothingness of the Neoplatonists, the infinite fullness beyond all things which are and are not, is the principle of his completely inclusive theology. In his system, nature is completely divided logically, and returns to itself according to the same logic: 'first, into that which creates and is not created, second into that which is created and creates, third into that which is created and does not create, fourth, that which neither creates nor is created' (Eriugena 1996–2003: I PL441D). These divisions produce four subjects: (1) God as creator; (2) the primary causes; (3) what is subject to generation in place and time, i.e. the labours of the *hexamaeron*, including the human—the work of the sixth day—and its Fall; as the terminus of the procession, it becomes the point of departure for the return into (4) God as end, the final object of investigation. This fundamental Neoplatonic movement he discerned in Dionysius: *monē* (remaining), *proodos* (going-out), *epistrophē* (return); it enabled a mutual assimilation to one another of philosophical and biblical structures.

In the pagan Neoplatonists, soul mediates between supersensible and the sensible. Christians tend to give this role to the human. Eriugena found the human as the immediate connection of God and the all in Augustine and radicalized it. Drawing upon Gregory of Nyssa, he came to understand human nature in such a way, that, more than being 'that in which all things could be found', it became 'that in which all things are created' (Zier 1992: 80; cf. Eriugena 1996–2003: II PL531AB; III PL733B; IV PL807A; V PL893BC). The medium through which God creates himself and the universe of beings out of his own nothingness is the human, because, uniquely among beings, it possesses all the forms of knowing and ignorance, including sensation and because the human mind shares the divine nothingness and self-ignorance. There are no absolute objects, because everything is through the diverse human perceptions. As with the Middle and Neo Platonists, the Platonic forms have become not only thoughts, but types of apprehension in various kinds of subject; as Plotinus puts it, 'all things come from contemplations and are contemplations' (Plotinus 1967: III.8.7). Like Neoplatonic systems generally, *Periphyseon* is an interplay of diverse subjectivities.

The notion of a divine self-creation takes up and transmutes another feature of Neoplatonism essential to understanding how nature and grace are related in this period, namely the complementarity of extreme transcendence and immanence. Because the First is beyond thought and being, is nothing, and comes into being only in what derives from it, the First is immanent in the finite without compromise either to its own transcendence or to the existence of beings. Plotinus teaches this (e.g. 1984: V.1.7), but it is developed more radically by successors like Iamblichus and Proclus. It enables the incarnational and sacramental aspects of Iamblichan thought where the gods include the material and cooperate in its use so as to draw to themselves humans immersed in genesis—features inherited by Dionysius. Jean Trouillard exposits what characterized Proclus' universe:

> it is traversed by a series of vertical lines, which like rays diverge from the same universal center and refer back to it the furthermost and the most diverse appearances. These chains tend to absorb the hierarchical ordering of the levels and to link them all directly to the One.... Thus, a stone is itself able to participate in the divine power to purify. [Trouillard 1965: 23–5].

Eriugena's first work was commissioned to solve a local theological controversy, originating in a literal reading of Augustine so that he taught double predestination—the doctrine that God wills both the damnation of the reprobate and the salvation of the elect, with the consequent destruction of human free will. In the event, his *On Divine Predestination* increased the theological troubles and made him part of them; nonetheless, it displays important features of natural theology.

Following Boethius, Eriugena attempted to maintain divine predestination and grace together with human freedom. Through Boethius, his solution is located at the end of a line of Platonic treatises and commentaries which start from a principle stated by Porphyry that everything is accommodated to the substance of each knower (Porphyry 1975: 10). In order to save *both* human freedom *and* divine providence, Iamblichus, Ammonius, Proclus, and Boethius distinguished between the mode of the knower and the mode of the thing known. Eriugena, by emphasizing the difference between the eternal mode of the divine being and the temporal mode of the human, concludes that the problem in our reasoning arises when 'foreknowledge and predestination are transferred to God by likening him to temporal things' (Eriugena 1978: XI.7 PL393B). When we make this transferral, we place God's operations within the process of time where they must predetermine our acts in such a way as to make them unfree.

Eriugena rejected double predestination on the strictly philosophical ground that it is inconsistent with the goodness and unity of God. His simplicity is such that predestination and God are one: 'the one eternal predestination of God is God' (Eriugena 1978: E.3 PL438C; cf. Proclus 2007: §14). Eriugena insisted that the means by which he had arrived at this flinty solution were essential to theology, asserting that correctly interpreting Scripture requires the liberal arts—for him the rhetorical trivium and the mathematical quadrivium. The theological errors on predestination had grown out of 'an ignorance of the liberal arts' and 'of the Greek writings in which the interpretation of predestination generates no fog of ambiguity' (Eriugena 1978: XVIII.1 PL430C–D). His determination to interpret Augustine through the Greek Fathers reminds us that their thought never fell into the kind of opposition of nature and grace which emerged out of Augustine's controversy with Pelagius and had the consequences for the understanding of predestination of which Eriugena was unhappily conscious.

Eriugena also serves to remind us of a theme as old as the apologists of the Apostolic age, Christianity as philosophy, because his conclusion brought his readers back to his first chapter and its assertion that, 'true philosophy is true religion and, conversely, true religion is true philosophy'. This formula reproduced, but also intensified, Augustine, whom he had just quoted, so that philosophy and theology form a dialectical unity (Eriugena 1978: I.1 PL358A; Augustine 1962: V.8). The mutual transformation of philosophical ideas and religious images which Eriugena would accomplish in *Periphyseon* was only suggested here, but he was on his way to a 'coinherence of *recta ratio* and biblical *auctoritas* that forestalls real conflict between the two and therefore denies any meaningful distinction between philosophy and theology' (McGinn 1996: 65). However, Eriugena is concerned about more here than a hermeneutical procedure; the practice of the liberal arts brings immortality. Eriugena comments that Martianus, one of his few pagan sources, 'openly teaches that the study of wisdom makes the soul immortal . . . all the arts which the rational soul employs are naturally present in all men whether [or not] they make good use of them . . . and, for this reason, every human soul is made immortal by the study of wisdom which is innate in itself' (Eriugena 1939: 17.12; cf. 171.10).

This understanding of the study of wisdom, or philosophy, when taken with the interplay between it and religion asserted in *On Divine Predestination*, renders comprehensible his notorious comment: 'No one enters heaven unless through philosophy, the seed of splendours' (Eriugena 1939: 57.15). The gloss concerns 'a certain woman who speaks of Philosophy'. She has the virtues and the arts at her disposition and brings to mind the *Consolation* of Boethius, which inspired the solution in *On Divine Predestination* (Crouse 2004: 108–9). In the *Consolation*, Lady Philosophy opens the door of heaven in virtue of her capacity to be earthy, human, and heavenly, and even to pierce through the heavens.

Gone with Boethius, Dionysius, and Eriugena is the confrontation between Christian and pagan philosophy. For Eriugena, philosophy is neither pagan, as opposed to Christian, nor mundane, as opposed to theology. Dialectic, mystical interpretation, and the itinerarium towards union with God, all belong to its work which is to give us the mind of Christ, for 'the perfect human is Christ' (Eriugena 1996–2003: IV PL543B).

NATURE AND GRACE IN AUGUSTINE

I am placing the discussion of nature and grace in Augustine at the end in the hope that the foregoing will provide context. If we reify nature and grace, separating them ontologically in a medieval scholastic or modern way, Platonic philosophy becomes a preliminary natural theology through which and from which Augustine passed to a Christian life governed by grace. However, in fact, he lived and thought within the patterns we have considered and they prevent such a separation. The Platonism to which he comes, and within which he lives his Christianity, will not allow nature to set itself up against what comes from above and within as the substance and power of its existence. When an attempt is made to establish it independently in this way, Augustine produces the assertions of the nullity of nature and the totality of grace which characterize his anti-Pelagian writings. Plotinus, were he forced to speak in such a framework, would produce something analogous, as his equation of the fall of the human soul and our desire for independence shows. Moreover, he would agree with Augustine that, although this is not our natural, in the sense of proper, position, humans are born into a fallen state (cf. Augustine 1966: 3, 33, 69, 75; 1981: 6.16.16 and Plotinus 1984: V.1.1).

Natural theology takes many forms in Augustine. We have already noted that, in his Genesis commentaries, he followed Philo, the Greek Fathers, and Ambrose in hexamaeral *physiologia*. Indeed, surpassing them, in the *Confessions*, he places the autobiographical account of his Christian return to his Beginning (Books I–IX) within an allegorical interpretation of Genesis (Books XII–XIII). His fall and redemption belong within the cosmic becoming; both are a 'running back to you the One' (Augustine 1981: 12.28.38). In the same work he repeatedly ascends to the metaphysical by way of the physical, most notably when he depicts the natural world as testifying that it was not the object of his love and that God made it (Augustine 1981: 10.6.9).

The *Confessions* is overall a search for love and Augustine recounts there how he first learned to love God properly. Because, as also later in the crucial conversion to Platonism at the centre of the work, he is taught this love by a pagan, it might seem to belong to natural theology. However, what happens is not theoretical abstraction. Augustine tells us that in reading Cicero's *Hortensius*, an exhortation to philosophy, his feelings were changed. It changed his experience, religious practice, values, and desires in respect to God himself: 'It altered my prayers, and created in me different purposes and desires.' Inflamed by philosophy, Augustine repented his vain hopes; in their place, he writes: 'I lusted for the immortality of wisdom with an incredible ardour of the heart.' Now his conversion begins, and he represents it, in language Neoplatonists use, as the return to the divine source: 'I began to rise up to return to you' (Augustine 1981: 3.4.7–8). This philosophical love of God remained religiously determinative for Augustine.

The method of his treatise *On the Trinity* seems to require natural theology in a standard form. It unites philosophical arguments with what comes from the authority of Scripture and the Church to arrive at an understanding of faith. However, as when philosophy taught him the true love of God, it is never discarded. The *De Trinitate* is a metaphysical spiritual exercise, a step-by-step deepening of the understanding that we are essentially rational, what this means, what it makes possible, and what it requires. When Augustine finally reaches the consideration of the inner and superior reason and the image of the Trinity which belongs to it, he makes his principle explicit. The image of the Trinity has been impaired by sin but not lost: 'Behold! the mind . . . remembers itself, understands itself, and loves itself; if we perceive this, we perceive a Trinity, not yet God indeed, but now finally an image of God' (Augustine 1968: 14.11). If the essential incorporeal rationality of the human soul could be denied, nothing in the whole *itinerarium* to beatitude in the contemplation of God would work and the ascent itself would have no purpose. On this account, Augustine returns, in the final book of the *De Trinitate* (15.21), to the philosophical refutation of the Sceptics, a project to which he had devoted himself when preparing for baptism, because now he needs a mirror in which to see the divine Trinity. This is natural theology which will not go away.

Augustine's greatest telling of how Neoplatonism brought him back to God is the fulcrum point of the *Confessions*. Books again, this time Platonic ones, admonished him now to return into himself. They were the means of God's own guidance. What he saw on that interior journey, described in Plotinus' language, finally gave him the positive conception of incorporeal substance which he required to move beyond Scepticism to Christianity. He encountered immutable light. That is to say, unchanging and unchangeable knowing was both the means and the content of the vision he describes. The identity of knowing and being gave true knowledge of the incorporeal, eternal, and immutable God, and, consequently, of himself, as immortal, incorporeal, but mutable soul. He discovers that the divine life is a triad in one substance: 'Eternal truth and true love and beloved eternity'. All else is created by God and is therefore good. The Platonic hierarchy of being enables solving the problem of evil in what we recognize as a Proclean, rather than in a Manichean or Plotinian, way—it is a consequence of choosing the lesser good against the higher. Augustine also learns that, through His Word, God provides grace sustaining us and drawing us to himself (Augustine 1981: 7.8.12–7.15.21).

Of course, Augustine also finds differences between Platonism and Christian teaching. However, of the many things he learned from the Platonist books and will retain, one came to define Augustinian reason and certainly determined something essential in his interpersonal experience of Christ, namely the doctrine of illumination. It is pure Platonism but, when, in Book X, he obeys the Delphic '*Gnothi seauton*', the idea that he knows and judges through contact with the immutable light above and within enables him to ask: 'Truth, when did you ever fail to walk with me, teaching me what to avoid and what to seek after . . . ?' (Augustine 1981: 10.40.65) Is such a theology only natural?

REFERENCES

Alexander of Aphrodisias (1983). *On Fate*. Edited and translated from Greek by R. W. Sharples. London: Duckworth.

Augustine of Hippo (1962). *De vera religione*. Edited by K. Daur. *Corpus Christianorum, Series Latina* 32. Turnhout: Brepols.

—— (1966). *De Natura et Gratia*. In *La Crise pélagienne I*. Edited by G. de Plinval and J. de la Tullaye. Œuvres de Saint Augustin, 21. Paris: Desclée de Brouwer.

—— (1968). *De trinitate*. Edited by W. J. Mountain et F. Glorie. *Corpus Christianorum, Series Latina* 50. Turnhout: Brepols. (Abbreviated as *Trin.*)

—— (1981). *Confessiones*. Edited by L. Verheijen. *Corpus Christianorum, Series Latina* 27. Turnhout: Brepols.

Basil of Caesarea (1999). *Commentaire sur Isaïe* V.162. In Brisson 1999, Annexe 1: 55–7.

Boethius, A. N. S. (1973). *Consolatio philosophiae*. Latin text edited by E. K. Rand. Loeb Classical Library. Cambridge, MA: Harvard University Press; London: William Heinemann.

Brisson, L. (1999). 'Un si long Anonymat' in *La Métaphysique: son histoire, sa critique, ses enjeux*. Edited by L. Langlois and J.-M. Narbonne. Collection Zêtêsis. Paris : Vrin; Québec: Presses de l'Université Laval: pp. 37–60.

Clement of Alexandria (2001). *Stromate IV*. Edited and translated from Greek by A. van den Hoek. Sources chrétiennes 463. Paris: Cerf.

Crouse, R. (2004). 'St. Augustine, Semi-Pelagianism and the *Consolation* of Boethius'. *Dionysius* 22: 95–110.

Dionysius the Areopagite (1990). *De divinis nominibus* in *Corpus Dionysiacum* I. Edited by B. R. Suchla. Berlin: de Gruyter.

Eriugena, John Scottus (1853). *Opera quae supersunt omnia*. Edited by H. J. Floss. In *Patrologia Latina*. Edited by J. P. Migne. Vol. CXXII, coll. 439–1022. Paris: Migne. (abbreviated as PL).

—— (1939). *Annotationes in Marcianum*. Edited C. Lutz. Cambridge, MA: Mediaeval Academy of America.

—— (1965). Translation (into Latin) of Gregory of Nyssa, *De Hominis Opificio*. In M. Cappuyns. 'Le *De imagine* de Grégoire de Nysse traduit par Jean Scot Erigène'. *Recherches de théologie ancienne et médiévale* 32: 205–62.

—— (1978). *De divina praedestinatione liber*. Edited by G. Madec. Corpus Christianorum Continuatio Mediaevalis 50. Turnhout: Brepols.

—— (1996–2003). *Periphyseon: Editionem nouam a suppositiciis quidem additamentis purgatam, ditatam uero appendice in qua uicissitudines operis synoptice exhibentur*. Liber Primus, Liber Secundus, Liber Tertius, Liber Quartus, Liber Quintus. Edited by É. Jeauneau. Corpus Christianorum Continuatio Mediaevalis 161, 162, 163, 164, 165. Turnhout: Brepols.

Feichtinger, H. (2003). '*Oudeneia* and *humilitas*: Nature and Function of Humility in Iamblichus and Augustine'. *Dionysius* 21: 123–60.

Gregory of Nyssa (1952–). *Opera*. Edited by W. Jaeger. Leiden: E. J. Brill.

Harrington, L. (2004). *Sacred Place in Early Medieval Neoplatonism*. New York and Houndmills, England: Palgrave.

Iamblichus of Chalcis (1966). *Les Mystères d'Égypte*. Edited and translated from Latin by É. des Places. Paris: Les Belles Lettres.

—— (2009). *The Letters*. Translated by J. M. Dillon and W. Polleichter. Atlanta: Society of Biblical Literature.

Josephus (1930). *Jewish Antiquities*. Edited and translated from Greek by H. Thackeray. Loeb Classical Library. Cambridge, MA; London: Harvard University Press; William Heinemann.

Lubac, Henri de (1946). *Surnaturel. Études historiques*. Paris: Desclée de Brouwer.

Lucretius (1921). *De Rerum Natura*. Edited by C. Bailey. Oxford Classical Texts. Oxford: Clarendon Press.

McGinn, B. (1996). 'The Originality of Eriugena's Spiritual Exegesis' in *Iahannes Scottus Eriugena, The Bible and Hermeneutics*. Edited by Riel, G. Van, C. Steel, and J. McEvoy. Leuven: Leuven University Press.

Maimonides, Moses (1963). *The Guide of the Perplexed*. Translated from Arabic by S. Pines. Chicago: University of Chicago Press.

O'Meara, D. J. (2000). 'La Science métaphysique (ou théologie) de Proclus comme exercice spirituel' in *Proclus et la Théologie Platonicienne. Actes du Colloque International de Louvain (13–16 mai 1998) en l'honneur de H.D. Saffrey et L.G. Westerink*. Edited by A. Segonds and C. Steel. Leuven: Leuven University Press; Paris: Les Belles Lettres: pp. 279–90.

—— (2003). *Platonopolis*. Oxford: Oxford University Press.

Origen (1973). *On First Principles*. Translated from Greek by G. W. Butterworth. Gloucester, MA: Peter Smith.

Parker, E. (2010). 'Swiftly Runs the Word: Philo's Doctrine of Mediation in *De Vita Mosis*'. Unpublished MA Thesis. Dalhousie University Department of Classics, Halifax.

Pelikan, J. (1995). *Christianity and Classical Culture: The Metamorphosis of Natural Theology in the Christian Encounter with Hellenism*. Gifford Lectures at Aberdeen, 1992–1993. New Haven and London: Yale University Press.

—— (1997). *What Has Athens to Do with Jerusalem? "Timaeus" and "Genesis" in Counterpoint*. Ann Arbor: University of Michigan Press.

Philo of Alexandria (1929a). *De Opificio Mundi* and *Legum allegoriae*. Edited and translated by F. H. Colson and G. H. Whitaker. Loeb Classical Library. Cambridge, MA: Harvard University Press; London: William Heinemann.

—— (1929b). *De Sacrificiis Abelis et Caini*. Edited and translated by F. H. Colson and G. H. Whitaker. Loeb Classical Library. Cambridge, MA: Harvard University Press; London: William Heinemann.

—— (1932). *Quis Rerum Divinarum Heres* and *De Confusione Linguarum*. Edited and translated by F. H. Colson and G. H. Whitaker. Loeb Classical Library. Cambridge, MA: Harvard University Press; London: William Heinemann.

—— (1935). *De Vita Mosis* and *De Abrahamo*. Edited and translated by F. H. Colson. Loeb Classical Library. Cambridge, MA: Harvard University Press; London: William Heinemann.

—— (1937). *De Specialibus Legibus*. Edited and translated by F. H. Colson. Loeb Classical Library. Cambridge, MA: Harvard University Press; London: William Heinemann.

Philoponus (1987). *Against Aristotle on the Eternity of the World*. Translated from Greek by C. Wildberg. The Ancient Commentators on Aristotle. Ithaca, NY: Cornell University Press.

Plato (1901). *Symposium*. Edited by J. Burnet. Oxford Classical Texts. Oxford: Clarendon Press.

—— (1902a). *Timaeus*. Edited by J. Burnet. Oxford Classical Texts. Oxford: Clarendon Press.

—— (1902b). *Republic*. Edited by J. Burnet. Oxford Classical Texts. Oxford: Clarendon Press.

—— (1907). *Leges*. Edited by J. Burnet. Oxford Classical Texts. Oxford: Clarendon Press.

—— (1959). *Gorgias: A Revised Text with Introduction and Commentary*. Edited by E. R. Dodds. Oxford: Clarendon Press.

Plotinus (1967). *Enneads* III. 1–9. Edited and translated from Greek by A. H. Armstrong. Loeb Classical Library. Cambridge, MA: Harvard University Press; London: William Heinemann.

—— (1984). *Enneads* V. 1–9. Edited and translated from Greek by A. H. Armstrong. Loeb Classical Library. Cambridge, MA: Harvard University Press; London: William Heinemann.

—— (1988). *Enneads* VI. 6–9. Edited and translated from Greek by A. H. Armstrong. Loeb Classical Library. Cambridge, MA: Harvard University Press; London: William Heinemann.

Porphyry (1975). *Sententiae ad Intelligibilia Ducentes*. Edited by E. Lamberz. Leipzig: Teubner.

Proclus (1968). *Théologie platonicienne*, Livre I. Edited and translated from Latin by H.-D. Saffrey and L. G. Westerink. Paris: Les Belles Lettres.

—— (1984) *Sur le Premier Alcibiade de Platon*. Edited and translated from Latin by A. Ph. Segonds. Vol. I. Paris: Les Belles Lettres.

—— (2003). *On the Existence of Evils*. Translated from Latin by J. Opsomer and C. Steel. Ancient Commentators on Aristotle. Ithaca, NY: Cornell University Press.

—— (2007). *On Providence*. Translated from Latin by C. Steel. Ancient Commentators on Aristotle. London: Duckworth.

Runia, D. T. (1986). *Philo of Alexandria and the* Timaeus *of Plato*. Leiden: E. J. Brill.

—— (2009). 'Philo and the Early Christian Fathers' in *The Cambridge Companion to Philo*. Edited by A. Kamesar. Cambridge: Cambridge University Press: 210–30.

Saffrey, H.-D. (1984). 'Quelques aspects de la spiritualité des philosophes néoplatoniciens de Jamblique à Proclus et Damascius'. *Revue des sciences philosophiques et théologiques* 68/2: 169–82.

—— (1997). 'Theology as Science (3rd–6th Centuries)'. Edited by E. A. Livingstone. Translated by W. J. Hankey. *Studia Patristica* 29. Leuven: Peeters: pp. 321–39.

Siegert, F. (2009). 'Philo and the New Testament' in *The Cambridge Companion to Philo*. Edited by A. Kamesar. Cambridge: Cambridge University Press: 175–207.

Simplicius (2001). *On Aristotle's 'Physics 8.6–10'*. Translated by R. McKirahan. Ancient Commentators on Aristotle. Ithaca, NY: Cornell University Press.

—— (2003). *On Aristotle's 'Categories 1–4'*. Translated by Michael Chase. Ancient Commentators on Aristotle. Ithaca, NY: Cornell University Press.

—— (2006). *On Aristotle's 'On the Heavens 1.10.–12'*. Translated by R. J. Hankinson. Ancient Commentators on Aristotle. Ithaca, NY: Cornell University Press.

Trouillard, J. ed. and trans. (1965). *Proclus, Éléments de théologie*. Bibliothèque philosophique. Paris: Aubier.

—— (1983). 'La "Virtus Gnostica" selon Jean Scot Érigène'. *Revue de théologie et de philosophie* 115: 331–54.

Zier, M. (1992). 'The Growth of an Idea' in *From Athens to Chartres: Neoplatonism and Medieval Thought. Studies in Honour of Édouard Jeauneau*. Edited by H. Westra. Leiden: E. J. Brill: pp. 71–83.

CHAPTER 4

NATURAL THEOLOGY IN THE MIDDLE AGES

ALEXANDER W. HALL

INTRODUCTION

MEDIEVALS were familiar with the expression 'natural theology' from Augustine's (350–430) discussion of the *Antiquities of Human and Divine Things* by the noted Roman scholar and satirist Marcus Terrentius Varro (116–27). Following the Stoics, Varro describes natural theology as the type of theology that 'philosophers have in many books', in their discussions of

> what gods there are, where they are, of what kind they are, of what quality, for how long they existed, whether they have always existed...and other things which the ears can more easily endure inside the walls of a school than outside in the forum. [Varro 1998: 6.5]

Yet, it appears that it was not until the publication of Raymonde of Sabunde's posthumously titled *Natural Theology* in 1485 that the expression comes to denote the branch of Christian theology whose deliberations concerning the essence and existence of God and other related matters forego premises drawn from Scripture, dating, perhaps, to the work of Christian apologists during the fourth-century reign of Constantine (on this period see Bosley and Tweedale 1997: xv). These apologists and other natural theologians in the medieval, Abrahamic tradition generally believe that: (1) absent revelation, knowledge of God can be difficult to acquire (hence they often discuss the need for some type of divine illumination); (2) since creation is a divine artefact, the Book of Nature signifies something of God's essence; and (3) the articles of faith are indemonstrable and reason fallible, thus philosophy is ancillary to theology.

By the late seventeenth century, mechanism begins to eclipse spiritual (i.e. allegorical, anagogical, and moral) accounts of nature (Harrison 2006), and thinkers such as Spinoza urge the separation of philosophy and theology:

> Every man is in duty bound to adapt… religious dogmas to his own understanding
> and to interpret them for himself… [Since] between faith and theology on the one
> side and philosophy on the other there is no relation and no affinity. [Spinoza 1991:
> 225–6]

Medievals, by contrast, believed that the natural world in some way represents the divine
essence and insisted that Scripture sets the agenda for and fixes the parameters of natural theology. As these beliefs fall out of style in the seventeenth century, the influence of
theologians in this tradition wanes (as we shall see was the case with Yves of Paris).
Accordingly, the type of natural theology that we are considering continued from the
fourth century to the seventeenth, outside the generally accepted dating according to
which the Middle Ages begin with the fall of Rome in 476 and give way in the early 1500s
to the High Renaissance.

Especially important to the development of medieval natural theology was the rebirth
that Western Europe experienced beginning in the 1000s owing to the emergence of stable
monarchies and consequent reconquest of the Iberian peninsula (Lindberg 1992: Ch. 9).
This expansion gave scholars access to the vast libraries of scientific and philosophical literature held in Arabic cultural centres, libraries that contained Aristotelian works on natural, ethical, and metaphysical sciences, which had for centuries been lost to the Latin West.
The new texts fed the growth of universities, where secular interests helped shape the curriculum, as the centre of intellectual gravity shifted from the monastery to the town, and
theologians responded to the influx of pagan learning with a re-evaluation of certain principles expressed in the three aforementioned shared sets of beliefs.

We will study figures representative of various moments in the medieval tradition,
during and after these developments. Anselm and Abelard immediately predate the universities and recovery of Aristotle. Aquinas and Scotus write on either side of the
Condemnations of 1277 (see below). Raymonde's work first applies the expression 'natural theology' to Christian practice, and Yves seeks late into the seventeenth century to
revitalize this project. Since, however, Augustine's earlier treatment of the principles
expressed in (1)–(3) was authoritative for these thinkers, we begin with a brief discussion of his thought and influence.

AUGUSTINE AND THE PRINCIPLES
OF MEDIEVAL NATURAL THEOLOGY

On the Scope of Reason

Augustine credits Plato with discovering that God is 'the author of all created things, the
light by which things are known, and the good for the sake of which things are done'
(Augustine 1998: 8.1). Yet such is Augustine's mistrust of reason that he speculates that
Plato's success may have been due to contact with Egyptian sages who had access to

Hebrew Scripture (Augustine 1998: 8.11). Indeed, Augustine believes that most philosophers exhaust 'their ingenuity and zeal in seeking the causes of things and the right way to learn and to live'. On the other hand:

> A Christian man instructed only in the literature of the Church...knows that it is from the one true and supremely good God that we receive the nature with which we are made in His image, and the doctrine by which we know Him and ourselves, and the grace through which, cleaving to Him, we are blessed. [Augustine 1998: 8.10]

Similar considerations would lead Aquinas to state that:

> Beneficially, therefore, did the divine Mercy provide that it should instruct us to hold by faith even those truths that the human reason is able to investigate. In this way, all men would easily be able to have a share in the knowledge of God, and this without uncertainty and error. [Aquinas 1975: 1.4.6]

The Book of Nature

> Some people read books in order to find God. Yet there is a great book, the very appearance of created things. Look above you; look below you! Note it; read it! God, whom you wish to find, never wrote that book with ink. Instead, He set before your eyes the things that He had made. [Augustine 1974: 123]

Following St Paul who writes that 'God's eternal power and divinity have become visible, recognized through the things he has made' (Romans 1.20), medievals think of the world as a divine artefact that reflects the nature and intentions of its maker. However, 'now we see indistinctly, as in a mirror' (1 Corinthians 13.12), since, absent an extraordinary illumination, we must infer divine perfections from imperfect, creaturely limitations thereof.

Philosophy as Handmaiden

Augustine allows that philosophers have acquired some knowledge of God; and he values history, anatomy, the mechanical arts, rhetoric, and mathematics (Augustine 1948: 661–2). Again, he recognizes the importance to Christians of keeping abreast of scientific findings, lest biblical literalists appear foolish to learned pagans (Augustine 1982: 42–3, 131); and he welcomes truth, whatever its source:

> If those who are called philosophers...have said things which are indeed true and are well accommodated to our faith, they should not be feared; rather, what they have said should be taken from them as from unjust possessors and converted to our use. [Augustine 1958: 54]

Nonetheless, faith in the authority of Scripture is prerequisite for the proper use of reason: 'authority demands faith, and prepares man for reason' (Augustine 1974: 31); and

Augustine repeatedly warns against the 'wondrous vanity' of the philosophers, who 'have wished … to achieve blessedness by their own efforts' (Augustine 1998: 19.4).

ANSELM: THE MIND'S ENDOWED UNDERSTANDING

Anselm (1033–1109) predates the rise of the universities in the second half of the twelfth century and the translation into Latin of the nearly complete Aristotelian corpus; thus his access to Aristotle was limited to the 'old logic', comprising Boethius' translations of *Categories* and *De interpretatione*, along with Porphyry's *Isagoge*. Prior to his archbishopric, Anselm lived thirty years at the abbey at Bec, where he wrote primarily for his brethren (though the works were later circulated widely). Even his critics, such as Gaunilo of the abbey at Marmoutier, generally share Anselm's orthodoxy, and the foundations were not as yet in place to support debates such as those which unfolded in the mid-thirteenth century over supposed theological implications of Aristotelian ontology (see below).

Anselm's *Monologion* is a 'model meditation' keeping to a form specified by the monks of Bec:

> Nothing whatsoever to be argued on the basis of the authority of Scripture, but the constraints of reason concisely to prove, and the clarity of truth clearly to show, in the plain style, with everyday arguments, and down-to-earth dialect, the conclusions of distinct investigations. [Anselm 1998a: Prologue]

What follows deduces the existence of a supremely good entity from that of innumerable entities that are good 'through that same one thing, through which all good things necessarily are good' (Anselm 1998a: Ch. 1); and, from the existence of contingent entities, Anselm deduces 'some one thing through which all existing things exist' (Anselm 1998a: Ch. 3). Again, as a composite owes its being to some other, God is simple (Anselm 1998a: Ch. 17); and thus the persons of the Trinity exist as one essence (Anselm 1998a: Ch. 53).

Monologion avoids proofs that depend on Scripture, employing 'a connected chain of many arguments' (Anselm 1998c: Preface). After reflection, Anselm 'began to wonder if perhaps it might be possible to find one single argument that … by itself would suffice to prove that God really exists … and also … whatever we believe about the Divine Being' (Anselm 1998c: Preface). Anselm's 'single argument' may refer to a particular demonstration or rather to the notion of God as that than which a greater cannot be thought, adduced repeatedly to prove God's existence and perfections (Holopainen 2007). At any rate, Anselm argues God must exist on the grounds that the term 'God' brings to mind the notion of that than which a greater cannot be thought, which would not be a notion of that than which a greater cannot be thought unless the notion refers to an extra-mental entity:

For if it exists solely in the mind, it can be thought to exist in reality also, which is greater. If then that than which a greater cannot be thought exists in the mind alone, this same that than which a greater cannot be thought is that than which a greater can be thought. But this is obviously impossible. Therefore... something than which a greater cannot be thought exists in the mind and in reality. [Anselm 1998c: Ch. 2]

Yet Anselm introduces the proof with the claim that one must believe in order to understand:

I do not seek to understand so that I may believe; but I believe so that I may understand. For I believe this also, that 'unless I believe, I shall not understand' (Isa. 7:9). [Anselm 1998c: Ch. 1]

Indeed, critics such as Aquinas claim Anselm's proof cannot work without pre-existent faith in God:

Nor can it be argued that [that than which a greater cannot be thought]... exists in reality unless it were granted that there exists in reality something than which a greater cannot be thought, which would not be granted by those who deny that God exists. [Aquinas 2006: 1a.2.1, ad 2]

Does the *Proslogion* proof of God's existence presuppose faith and thereby break with the methodological limitations spelled out in *Monologion*? Anselm would likely deny this. He claims that his demonstration is sufficient to compel the assent even of one who does not want to believe in the existence of God:

What I believed before through Your free gift I now so understand through Your illumination, that if I did not want to believe that You existed, I should nevertheless be unable not to understand it. [Anselm 1998c: Ch. 4]

Admittedly, a Christian may want not to believe and Anselm may have in mind only the opinion of the reluctant faithful (as opposed to the non-believer) when gauging the force of his claims. Nevertheless, since Anselm's argument rests on the necessity of an inference rather than Scripture, his comment that he believes in order to understand should be seen not as a break with the methodology of the *Monologion*, but, rather, as a reflection of Anselm's subscription to the then generally accepted (aforementioned) principle that it is difficult to acquire knowledge of God independently of Scripture. The passage just cited suggests that he thinks we need an illumination to receive this knowledge; but this is not to say that the proof cannot compel assent absent faith. Hence, faith is not needed to understand that God exists, but, rather, to establish parameters of investigation for the benefit of reason, which is apt to go astray:

The mind's endowed understanding is... sometimes taken away, and faith itself subverted, when upright conscience is neglected... Therefore, no one should rashly plunge into the complex things involved in questions about God unless the person first have a solid faith... lest a persistent falsity ensnare the person who runs with careless levity through many little diverting sophisms. [Anselm 1998b: Ch. 1]

ABELARD: UNDERSTOOD INSTEAD
OF JUST MOUTHED

Abelard (1079–1142) studied philosophy under the controversial nominalist Roscelin of Compiègne in the 1090s and then, around 1100, with the realist William of Champeaux. By 1102, Abelard had broken with William to establish schools at Melun and Corbeil. Abelard returns to Paris in 1108 where he secures his reputation by humiliating William in debate. In 1113 Abelard studies theology with Anselm of Laon, soon departing on bad terms. Abelard's subsequent career as master of the school of Notre Dame terminates in 1117, when his affair with Heloise ends with his castration. Abelard next joins the Benedictine order. Ultimately embracing this new role, he composes his *Theology* (subtitled after its opening line 'On the highest good'); but students of Anselm of Laon conspire to have the work condemned in 1121. Abelard resumes teaching at Paris in 1133, until Bernard of Clairvaux and others arrange for the condemnation of nineteen propositions taken from Abelard's revised *Theology* (subtitled 'In the schools') in 1140, resulting in Abelard's temporary excommunication and then retirement.

At the root of Abelard's theology is his unwavering belief that enquiry and reasoned consent are necessary to a mature faith:

> Someone who looks at Scripture without understanding is like a blind man holding up a mirror to his eyes. He does not have the means to see who he is and does not seek to learn what Scripture teaches…He cannot enter God's word through his own understanding or use another's teaching to break his way in. [Abelard 2007c: 243–4]

Mary's pondering the words of the magi is cast as paradigmatic of the philosophical attitude one should adopt towards Scripture. 'The matchless bride of God' ponders in her heart their words, 'arguing every one, weighing each against the other, to determine how they might all be consistent' (Abelard 2007c: 254–5).

Abelard places such value on the importance to faith of enquiry that he contends that Christians should be termed 'philosophers' and 'logicians':

> Since Christ is the very wisdom of God and the Greeks call wisdom '*sophia*', I affirm that no people are more rightly called philosophers than those who live as lovers of this highest and perfect wisdom…We call Christ alone 'God's Word'—which the Greeks call *logon*…All those who cling to this…word…should truly be called logicians (*logici*) as well as philosophers, and no discipline ought more truly to be called 'logic (*logica*)' than Christian doctrine. [Abelard 1984: 892–3]

Indeed, it was his students' desire for a philosophical account of the Trinity that led Abelard to compose his first *Theology*:

> My students…kept asking for rational arguments, demanding things that could be understood instead of just mouthed…They said that words were pointless if

understanding did not follow, that nothing can be believed if it is not first understood. [Abelard 2007b: 22]

Yet, despite this inversion of the Anselmian formula, Abelard acknowledges that certain truths surpass human reason:

> It should be a clear matter of reason that God far exceeds what can come under human discussion or the powers of human intelligence. Hence he cannot be seized upon in any particular place or be comprehended by the human mind. It would be a great slight to the faithful if God proclaimed Himself as accessible to petty human arguments or as definable in mere mortal words. [Abelard 1948: 68]

The writings of Aristotle that would by 1200 inundate the Latin West were trickling in during Abelard's lifetime, fuelling the growth of the nascent universities. Abelard was very much a man of (if not ahead of) his times, but conservative thinkers such as Bernard, conspicuous for his dedication to the earlier, monastic tradition, were uncomfortable in this shifting landscape. In his correspondences, Bernard complains that 'the faith of the simple is being ridiculed, the secrets of God are being torn to pieces, questions concerning the highest things are being recklessly discussed in the open' (Bernard of Claivaux 1993b: 24). Abelard is singled out as representative of the new, corrupt dialectician, who:

> transgresses the boundaries placed by our Fathers in disputing and writing about faith...He changes each thing according to his wish, adding to it or taking from it...He...oversteps his capacity, by the wisdom of his words evacuating the virtue of the cross. [Bernard of Clairvaux 1993a: 22]

Bernard's reaction is perhaps inevitable, given Abelard's pugnacious derision of uninformed assent. Nonetheless, if Abelard insists we subject Scripture to philosophical scrutiny, he carefully relegates philosophy to handmaiden status:

> I would not be the philosopher who would challenge Paul; I would not be the Aristotle who is barred from Christ, for there is no other name under heaven in whom I must be saved. [Abelard 2007a: 60]

Ancillary to theology, philosophy can assist in resolving seeming conflicts between religious authorities. The prologue of Abelard's *Yes and No* remarks that when such conflicts arise:

> One should not make a rash judgment...[but instead] carefully consider what the author is aiming at...For consistent or frequent questioning is defined as the first key to wisdom...For by doubting we come to enquiry, and by enquiry we perceive the truth. [Abelard 1992: 87–99]

Peter of Lombard (*c.*1100–*c.*1164) likely found in *Yes and No* the inspiration for his *Sentences*, the Middle Ages' most widely read and commented-upon theological textbook, which presents 'the sentences [i.e. opinions] of the Fathers in a brief volume, with their appropriate testimonies', lest enemies misrepresent its teachings in order to turn 'the Church into something hateful to God' (Lombard, 2006: Prologue). The *Sentences*' structure and method of enquiry were central to the efforts of thirteenth-century theologians to synthesize Christian and pagan authorities.

AQUINAS: REASON AND REVELATION WILL NOT CONTRADICT

Aquinas (1225–74) was born into a noble family but joined the mendicant Dominican Order in 1244. He completed his studies in theology at the University of Paris in 1256, where he remained as regent master until 1259. In 1268, Aquinas was recalled to the Parisian regency to check the spread of Aristotelian naturalism in the form of Latin Averroism (see below), to allay the concerns of conservative theologians who objected to the integration of Aristotle at every level of the curriculum, and to combat secular masters hostile to the growing influence of the mendicant orders at the university (Torrell 1996: Ch. 10). Aquinas departed Paris for Naples in 1272 and died in 1274, two months after a religious vision had convinced him of the relative worthlessness of his writings and left him wishing to die.

By 1200, Latin editions of nearly all of Aristotle's writings had appeared at Paris and Oxford. Owing to charges emerging from the graduate faculty of theology that Parisian arts masters (responsible for undergraduate education) were inspired by Aristotle to teach pantheism, a council of bishops meeting at Paris in 1210 forbade the Parisian arts masters to teach Aristotelian natural philosophy. After some three decades the decree lost its force and masters lectured freely on all of Aristotle's writings.

Western thinkers used Arabic commentators to help understand Aristotle, first Avicenna (980–1037) and later Averroes (1126–1198), whose writings inspired the Aristotelian naturalism of Siger of Brabant (c.1240–81/4) and other Parisian arts masters. Known collectively as Latin Averroists, these scholars drew from Aristotle propositions that contradicted certain tenets of faith concerning matters such as the eternality of the universe, Providence, human freedom, and personal immortality. Siger advanced his claims as true only according to philosophy (acknowledging the fallibility of human reason) and his later writings tend towards orthodoxy, but the Averroistic controversy nonetheless stirred fears that philosophy and theology might arrive at different, equally valid truths.

Throughout his career, Aquinas insisted that since reason and revelation both proceed from God, valid arguments will never contradict Scripture:

> What is divinely taught to us by faith cannot be contrary to what we are endowed with by nature. One or the other would have to be false, and since we have both of them from God, he would be the cause of our error, which is impossible. [Aquinas 1987: 2.3c]

Moreover, some revealed truths are accessible to reason operating independently of revelation:

> There are some truths which the natural reason...is able to reach. Such are that God exists, that He is one, and the like. [Aquinas 1975: 1.3.2]

Thus during his second regency Aquinas produces a variety of works with the purpose of showing that Aristotelianism need not threaten Christianity. Even so, three years after Aquinas' death, continuing Averroist pressure precipitated the Condemnations of 1277, initiated by Stephen Tempier, bishop of Paris and drafted with the help of Henry of Ghent, who went on to become a leading scholar of his generation. Seven years prior, Stephen had condemned thirteen propositions comprising the main tenets of Latin Averroism. The Condemnations of 1277, by contrast, were of 219 articles in theology and natural philosophy. The Condemnations were effective at Paris throughout the four-teenth century and cited as authoritative in England by scholars such as Scotus and Ockham (Grant 1979).

The Condemnations emphasized God's absolute power to do whatever he wills absent violation of the principle of non-contradiction. Article 17 (following the numbering in Mandonnet 1908) explicitly condemned the view that God cannot bring about what is impossible according to nature:

> What is impossible absolutely speaking cannot be brought about by God or by another agent.—This [proposition] is erroneous if we mean what is impossible according to nature. [Tempier 1973: 586]

The result was to undermine naturalism and encourage counterfactual reasoning; God was free to alter natural law.

For his part, Aquinas believes that we can prove that God exists by means of scientific demonstrations that trace phenomena such as motion to their ultimate source in God (Aquinas 2006: 1a.2.3c). A scientific demonstration is a syllogism whose middle desig-nates *either* an essential feature of the subject *or* a property for which the subject's exist-ence is a necessary condition (Aristotle 1984a: 1.4). In both cases, 'the cause of what belongs to a subject is the subject itself or something pertaining to the subject' (Aquinas 2007: 1.10). We lack the unmediated access to God that would acquaint us with what is essential to the divine essence, hence Aquinas' demonstrations reason from creation viewed as an effect.

An effect bears a likeness to its cause, for 'it belongs to the nature of action that an agent produces its like' (Aquinas 1975: 1.29.2). Hence, creatures bear likenesses to the creator by which we can learn of God. However, the resemblance between God and crea-tures is imperfect, at the very least in as much as divine simplicity entails that the mani-fold and diverse perfections of creatures correspond to 'one and the same power' in the divine essence (Aquinas 1975: 1.31.2). Viewed in this light, the perfections and attributes of creatures represent God in an incomplete, fragmented manner. Theological discourse must recognize this gap between God's essence and our conception of God's essence, which is taken from creatures; hence, Aquinas stipulates that terms significative of God and creatures are analogical, meaning that these terms signify differently in different con-texts, like the term 'healthy', which can signify one's health or the medicine by which one is healthy. So too, terms such as 'good' may signify God as the cause of goodness in creatures.

However, Aquinas holds that when we say that God is good, we intend to say more than that God is the cause of goodness in creatures. Hence the medicine–patient model is somewhat misleading:

> When we say 'God is good,' it does not mean that God is the cause of goodness or that God is not bad; rather, this means that what we call good in creatures pre-exists in God, albeit in a higher mode. From this it does not follow that it belongs to God to be good insofar as God is the cause of goodness, but rather just the opposite: that because God is good, God diffuses goodness to things. [Aquinas 2006: 1.13.2c]

The type of analogy described here is that of attribution (Aquinas offers no systematic treatment of analogy; rather, he variously employs different types in different contexts). By analogy of attribution, any predicate 'F' said of God signifies God as: (1) the cause of other things less properly termed F, (2) wholly identical with Fness, and (3) most eminently denominable with respect to Fness (that is, possessed of Fness in the highest possible degree). Since, then, theological discourse is analogical, a complete account of Aquinas' various proofs of God's existence should, it seems, seek in the case of each proof to accommodate his language to the type of analogy at play in the text (Hall 2007b).

As reason and revelation will not contradict, it is fitting theologians take up natural theology to clarify and demonstrate certain revealed truths. Nonetheless, Aquinas believes that theologians have an advantage over philosophers, as the latter lack principles of faith that would contextualize their findings in light of our supernatural end (Bradley 1981). On Aquinas' Aristotelian understanding of science, subaltern sciences receive their axioms from superaltern sciences, as optics receives its principles from geometry (Aristotle 1984: 1.2, 71^{b}872^{a}8). Theology (or sacred teaching) is accordingly conceived to be a subaltern science, receiving its axioms from revelation:

> Thus the truths we hold on faith are, as it were, our principles in this science, and the others become, as it were, conclusions. From this it is evident that this science is nobler than the divine science taught by the philosophers, proceeding as it does from more sublime principles. [Aquinas 1987: 2.2c]

Scotus: Metaphysics as Natural Theology

John Duns Scotus (1265/6–1308) was a Franciscan theologian writing after the Condemnations of 1277. Scotus famously contended that some theological discourse is univocal, meaning that certain terms signify concepts that apply equally well to God and creatures, 'so that to affirm and deny [such a concept] ... of one and the same thing would be a contradiction' (Scotus 1987: 20). Scotus makes this claim because he believes that the perfections and attributes of creatures disclose something of the essence of the creator. Absent an extraordinary illumination, our knowledge of God is restricted to concepts derived from creatures. Hence, unless creation can give rise to ideas that truly represent God, 'we would have no more reason to conclude that God is...wise from the notion of wisdom derived from creatures than we would have reason to conclude that God is...a stone' (Scotus 1987: 25). Scotus' move to univocity follows his rejection of Henry of Ghent's theory of analogy (other criticisms Scotus levels against Henry's account, criticisms not addressed in this study, pertain as well to Aquinas').

Henry taught that concepts of God are analogous. Acquired through illumination, Henry believes that these concepts pertain to but are not of God's essence. Scotus rejects Henry's account on the grounds that it degrades our intellect and entails apophaticism. First, there is Henry's reliance on illumination. Scotus believes that were the human mind so weak as to require an illumination to know God, then such knowledge would soon be lost absent divine interference (Scotus 1987: 104). As regards apophaticism, we cannot acquire a concept of an attribute that pertains to but is not of God's essence; for knowledge of an attribute proper to God is knowledge of God, in whom the attribute exists (Scotus 1987: 16–17). Hence, for Scotus, Henry's account of analogy is incoherent. Besides, if Henry is correct and analogical concepts of God tell us nothing of God's essence, Scotus holds that 'a disconcerting consequence ensues; namely that from the proper notion of anything found in creatures nothing at all can be inferred about God' (Scotus 1987: 25).

Yet, despite his belief that we prize from creatures some knowledge of God's essence, Scotus calls into question the capacity of reason (construed along Aristotelian lines) with a distinction between experiential and unqualified scientific knowledge (Scotus 1987: 105–6). Experiential scientific knowledge depends on the principle that like causes generally produce like effects, and is therefore less certain than unqualified scientific knowledge, which is of propositions true by definition. This Humean distinction between matters of fact and relations among ideas emerges after the Condemnations of 1277, which emphasized divine omnipotence at the expense of Aristotelian naturalism and thus cast lasting suspicion on proofs from the natural order (such as Aquinas' proof from motion). William of Ockham (c.1287–1347), for instance, adduces self-moving souls as a counter-example to the principle that 'whatever moves is moved by some other agent' and concludes that the principle 'is not self-evident, nor is it deduced from self-evident propositions, and consequently it is not a demonstrative principle' (Ockham 1938: 188–92). Again, some two and a half centuries later, reasoning nearly identical to Ockham's leads the Jesuit theologian Francisco Suárez (1546–1617) to conclude that God's existence cannot be demonstrated 'by the aid of [such] uncertain principles' (Suárez 1993: 362).

Scotus holds that it belongs to the metaphysician rather than the natural philosopher to show that God exists. Following Avicenna, Scotus defines metaphysics as the science of 'being as being and its properties' (Scotus 1995: 19). As such, metaphysics studies the attributes and perfections that pertain to entities simply by virtue of their existence. Scotus, a realist, takes from Aristotle a belief that diverse categories of being correspond to diverse types of entities. For instance, accidents are mere modes of substances, yet both substances and their accidents are said to exist. Hence, substance and accident make up diverse categories. Since they are trans-categorial, the aforementioned attributes and perfections are termed 'transcendentals'. Scotus recognizes three types of transcendentals: (1) the proper attributes of being that are coextensive with being, viz. unity, truth, and goodness; (2) exhaustive disjunctions that are likewise coextensive with being, e.g. 'possible-or-necessary'; and (3) pure perfections, defined as perfections that are absolutely and without qualification better than anything incompatible with them (hence, for any being, it would be better to possess than not to possess a pure perfection, though some beings are naturally incapable of possessing certain pure perfections—a tree, for instance, cannot acquire wisdom). Scotus' strategy is to demonstrate God's existence by means of transcendental disjunctions such as 'necessary-contingent':

> As a universal rule by positing the less noble extreme of some being we can conclude that the more noble extreme is realized in some other being. Thus...if some being is contingent, then some being is necessary. For...it is not possible for the more imperfect extreme of the disjunction to be existentially predicated of being particularly taken, unless the more perfect extreme be existentially verified of some other being upon which it depends. [Scotus 1987: 8, for the complete proof, with commentary, see Scotus 1995: 40–107]

Since the metaphysician describes God as a necessary being, he offers a more immediate and perfect image of God than the natural philosopher, who simply identifies God with the first mover (Scotus 1950– : 131). Accordingly, when Scotus reflects on the proof from motion, he mainly raises objections such as those made later by Ockham and Suárez.

The transcendentals pertain to all beings and thus we refer them to both God and creatures. Experience supplies us with notions of transcendentals such as goodness. To refer these concepts to God, we first strip them of imperfections associated with their instantiation in creatures. The resultant, abstract concept is univocal to God and creatures. But, before it is attributed to God, it must be joined with the notion of God's infinite being. Scotus states that an infinite being 'exceeds the finite in being beyond any relative measure or proportion that could be assigned' (Scotus 1975: 5.9). Yet this suggests a difference in kind between God and creatures that would vitiate the univocity of religious language. Indeed, Scotus himself seems to have been discontented with his theory of univocity, holding it open to revision should he find a more satisfactory way to protect natural knowledge of God (Marrone 1983; Hall 2007a). Likely as a consequence, Scotus' disciples were (as modern commentators are) divided over whether Scotus intended a weak sense of univocity that preserves divine transcendence at the expense of concepts that signify God's essence (Dumont 1992).

RAYMONDE OF SABUNDE: LETTERS WRITTEN BY THE HAND OF GOD

The *Natural Theology* of Raymonde of Sabunde (d. 1436) was placed on the Index of Prohibited Books prepared by the Council of Trent in 1559. In 1564, the Council restricted the prohibition to the prologue, and the *Theology* is entirely absent from the 1900 Index prepared under the authority of Leo XIII. Given the Council's tasks of determining Church doctrine and initiating reform, the censorship is unsurprising, as the *Theology* by and large dispenses with religious authorities:

> This science teaches every man to know...infallibly, without difficulty and labour every truth that it is necessary to man to know, as of man so too of God...Through this science man knows...whatever is contained in sacred Scripture...Through this science, any person whatsoever knows with ease all the holy doctors...Moreover, this science does not require some other science or any art...And it can be had in less than a month and without labour...This science does not rely on any authority, neither sacred Scripture nor any doctor. On the contrary, this science confirms sacred Scripture for us. [Sabunde 1966: 27*–35*]

Comments such as these, taken from the prologue, are likely what led Maurice DeWulf to accuse Raymonde of embracing a 'theosophy' that seeks to demonstrate all 'the data of Christian revelation' (DeWulf 1909: 172, cf. 271). Though understandable, DeWulf's assessment seems incorrect; for Raymonde elsewhere acknowledges that our knowledge of God is by extrinsic denomination, i.e. from works 'outside' God's essence (Sabunde 1966: 271), and that God's triunity is 'incomprehensible' (Sabunde 1966: 64). Rather than developing a theosophy such as DeWulf detects, Raymonde appears to reach back to the pre-Ockhamist tradition and teach a natural theology that is indebted to Aquinas, Anselm, and the Augustinian notion of the Book of Nature:

> There are two books given to us by God, namely the book of the universe of creatures or the Book of Nature, and the other, sacred Scripture...No creature exists save as a certain letter, written by the hand of God. And out of many creatures, as out of many letters, the first book is composed, which is called the book of creatures...And as letters and words made out of letters carry and include knowledge and diverse significations...so too creatures themselves. Joined and compared to one another, they import and signify diverse significations and thoughts and they contain the science necessary to man. [Sabunde 1966: 35ˣ–36ˣ]

We read the Book of Nature with our senses (Sabunde 1966: 2), refining our understanding through experimentation (Sabunde 1966: 314), by which we discover four orders of creatures:

> (1) all that is, or all that merely is, and does not live, nor sense, nor understand, nor discern nor will freely; (2) what merely lives, but does not sense, understand, etc.; (3) what lives and merely senses, but does not understand, etc.; (4) what lives, senses, understands and wills freely. [Sabunde 1966: 3–4]

Reflection on the lower orders teaches man 'himself, and that which is above him, namely God, his creator' (Sabunde 1966: 7):

> It is impossible that all things measure themselves and give to themselves what they have, and nonetheless they are ordered and measured. Therefore, something external and superior to all these orders, measures, limits and gives to them what they have. [Sabunde 1966: 9]

The Book of Nature and Scripture are both from God and thus will not contradict one another (Sabunde 1966: 37*). Yet, unlike Scripture, the Book of Nature is available to all and cannot be falsified, destroyed, or misinterpreted (Sabunde 1966: 36*). Moreover, knowledge of the Book of Nature 'orders every other [science] to the good end and to the truth useful to man' (Sabunde 1966: 31*). Nonetheless, the unbaptized cannot read all that is in the Book of Nature (Sabunde 1966: 38*) and, as noted, Raymond holds that certain truths surpass reason. Hence there is some need of Scripture.

Anselm's influence is felt in Raymonde's perfect being theology. Humans differ from the lower orders on account of the abilities to learn, desire, and will. These capacities are boundless; thus whatever 'gave to man this power is infinite and without measure' (Sabunde 1966: 82). From this, Raymond derives an 'infallible rule ... that is the root and foundation for proving and conceiving with certainty and effortlessly all things [said] about God' (Sabunde 1966: 82–3); namely: 'God is something than which nothing greater can be thought.' Hence, whatever is 'better, nobler, etc.; man can attribute to God' (Sabunde 1966: 83).

YVES OF PARIS: THE AFTERLIFE
OF MEDIEVAL NATURAL THEOLOGY

Yves of Paris (1588–1678) practiced law and travelled widely before he joined the Capuchin Friars in 1619 at the age of thirty, after the death of his father. Here he rounded out his earlier studies of Marsilio Ficino and Raymon Lull with a synthesis of Aquinas and Bonaventure. Yves was a prolific author, actively engaged in the controversies of his age and he rose through the Capuchin ranks to become first Definitor of his province. The Parisian gazette Le Mercure galante reported Yves' death at the age of ninety as the passing of 'an extraordinary man' (1991: 24). Yet Yves' work soon fell into obscurity, where it remained until its twentieth-century revival by Henri Bremond (1928).

A contemporary of Descartes and Pascal, Yves outlived both. He denied the heliocentric hypothesis and did not believe that a Christian gentleman need study the new science (Fastiggi 1991: 25–6). Rather, he views nature as a theophany, full of beauties that display 'the omnipotence of their lord in the magnificence of their attire' (Yves 1991: 172). Moreover, Yves sought to re-establish the philosophy as handmaiden paradigm, and thus undermine secular rationalism (Yves 1991: 168), and to defend the synthesis of faith and reason:

> Natural reason can be brought into harmony with the divine faith, and ... following St. Thomas, these two lights, which have the eternal truth as their common source, are united and strengthened rather than weakened by their encounter. [Yves 1991: 195]

Martin Luther held that Scripture alone suffices to provide knowledge of God, a sign of this being his insistence on lecturing from a Psalter that was stripped of glosses and commentary (Harrison 2006: 125). Other sixteenth-century developments saw the translation into Latin of Sextus Empiricus' sceptical writings and Pietro Pomponazzi's revival of the Averroist theory that philosophy can contradict Scripture. Seventeenth-century thinkers were therefore amenable to a sceptical, secular morality such as developed amongst the learned libertines 'who doubt the one God' (Yves 1991: 106) and other agnostic thinkers against whom Yves composed his *Natural Theology* (1633–7):

> In order to provide a remedy for these great abuses, I have designed to counter these spirits by a detailed consideration of the marvels of nature. [Yves 1991: 124]

Yves' *Theology* uses traditional arguments from order, contingency, and motion to prove God's existence (Chesneau, 1936: 281). However, Yves devotes special attention to demonstrating that we possess an innate awareness or sentiment of God. Providence 'gives us an awareness of God with an element of necessity' (Yves 1991: 151) and we 'would not be capable of even thinking about God if God Himself had not imprinted the idea in us' (Yves 1991: 139). Hence, this awareness is a necessary condition of natural theology: 'The reasonings of this world can but persuade of a God by means of the natural sentiment already implanted in the soul' (Yves 1928: 380).

Libertines deny this sentiment out of a desire to free themselves of moral obligation:

> [The libertine] raises up clouds to obscure a sun that would expose his deformities; he imposes silence on a voice which accuses him; and he tries to remove himself from a judge who pronounces his condemnation. [Yves 1991: 167]

Nonetheless, the attempt cannot succeed. Yves warns the libertine, 'You will yet see that there is a God; you do not know how to stop this light which you try to dim because it is inside of you, and it operates over your mind...without your consent' (Yves 1991: 149). Since the libertines deny their inner awareness and 'make fun of the authorities', Yves contends with them by means of philosophical arguments, deploying only 'natural reason in the melee', lest his proofs 'expose the Temple to sacrilege'. Yves' *Natural Theology* will then leave 'aside the authorities of the church', attempting, rather, 'to clarify the first truths by reason taken solely from nature...and which can be understood by minds not crippled by passion' (Yves 1991: 106). This is in keeping with Yves' conception of reason as ancillary to theology: 'If man turns his eyes away from this [inner, divine] light...God appoints him with reason just as a magistrate will supply minors with a tutor' (Yves 1991: 168).

Yves supports his claim that we have an inner awareness of God by noting that the rituals of diverse cultures reflect a desire for a higher power: 'It is after this infinite goodness that all the nations of the earth yearn; it is for it that they have their vows and sacrifices' (Yves 1991: 135). Against the Pyrrhonian objection that this awareness is a by-product of convention, Yves points out that conventional belief differs from society to society, while belief in divinity is universal and enduring. Individuals may doubt God's existence, 'but never would we find an entire people living inside this blindness' (Yves 1991: 155). Likewise, rulers do not cultivate this awareness for their own benefit: 'What would be the advantage for them to dissemble a God whose majesty would...obscure the brilliance of the scepter?' (Yves 1991: 160).

Having shown we have an inner awareness of God, Yves argues that 'the awareness which humanity has of God comes from God Himself' (Yves 1991: 137), by means of reasoning nearly identical with that which Descartes offers some four years later in the *Discourse on Method* (published in 1637). Hence, having dismissed the notion that our inner awareness of God comes from opinion, Yves adds that this awareness cannot arise from reflection on one's own nature and thus must proceed from God:

> How could the medium of our soul…have by itself the idea of a God who is an intellectual being, perfectly pure and completely devoid of corporeality?…How could our mind, which has only limited powers, form by itself a concept of infinity if there isn't an infinite being which has communicated this understanding to it? [Yves 1991: 140–1]

Yet where the father of modern philosophy uses God to provide his novel scientific enterprise with a firm and lasting foundation, Yves' *Natural Theology* defends the medieval tradition that studies the design of the natural world to acquire knowledge of God and views philosophy as a handmaiden of theology against a new breed of sceptics who place 'themselves against the truths that nature makes evident' (Yves 1991: 123) and attempt 'to make human reason independent of Heaven and religion' (Yves 1991: 111).

ACKNOWLEDGEMENTS

I would like to thank my readers, James C. Doig and Ronald Jackson.

REFERENCES

Abelard, Peter (1948). *Abelard's Christian Theology*. Translated by J. R. McCallum. Oxford: Blackwell.
—— (1984). 'Peter Abelard's "Solilquium": A Critical Edition'. Edited and translated by Charles Burnett. *Studi Medievali* 25/2: 857–94.
—— (1992). 'Prologue to the "Yes and No"' in *Medieval Literary Theory and Criticism*. Edited by A. J. Minnis and A. B. Scott. Rev. edn. Oxford: Clarendon: pp. 87–100.
—— (2007a). 'Abelard's Confession of Faith' in *Abelard and Heloise: The Letters and Other Writings*. Edited and translated by William Levitan. Indianapolis: Hackett: pp. 260–1.
—— (2007b). 'The Calamities of Peter Abelard' in *Abelard and Heloise: The Letters and Other Writings*. Edited and translated by William Levitan. Indianapolis: Hackett: pp. 1–46.
—— (2007c). 'Seventh Letter' in *Abelard and Heloise: The Letters and Other Writings*. Edited and translated by William Levitan. Indianapolis: Hackett: pp. 170–256.
Anselm (1998a). 'Monologion' in *Anselm of Canterbury: The Major Works*. Edited by Brian Davies and Gil Evans. Translated by Simon Harrison. Oxford: Oxford University Press: pp. 5–81.
—— (1998b). 'On the Incarnation of the Word' in *Anselm of Canterbury: The Major Works*. Edited by Brian Davies and Gil Evans. Translated by Richard Regan. Oxford: Oxford University Press: pp. 233–59.
—— (1998c). 'Proslogion' in *Anselm of Canterbury: The Major Works*. Edited by Brian Davies and Gil Evans. Translated by M. J. Charlesworth. Oxford: Oxford University Press: pp. 82–104.

Aquinas, Thomas (1975). *Summa contra gentiles*. Translated by Anton Pegis. Notre Dame: University of Notre Dame Press.

—— (1987). *Thomas Aquinas: Faith, Reason and Theology: Questions I-IV of his Commentary on the De Trinitate of Boethius*. Translated by Armand Maurer. Toronto: Pontifical Institute of Mediaeval Studies.

—— (2006). *The Treatise on the Divine Nature: Summa theologiae I 1-13*. Translated by Brian Shanley. Introduction by Robert Pasnau. Indianapolis: Hackett.

—— (2007). *Commentary on Aristotle's 'Posterior Analytics'*. Translated by Richard Berquist. Notre Dame: Dumb Ox Books.

Aristotle (1984). 'Posterior Analytics' in *The Complete Works of Aristotle*. Vol. I. Translated by Jonathan Barnes. Princeton: Princeton University Press: pp. 114–66.

Augustine (1948). 'Enchiridion' in *The Basic Writings of Saint Augustine*. Edited by Whitney J. Oates. Translated by J. F. Shaw. New York: Random House: pp. 658–732.

—— (1958). *On Christian Doctrine*. Translated by D. W. Robertson. Indianapolis: Prentice Hall.

—— (1974). 'Sermon, Mai, 126, 6' in *The Essential Augustine*. Edited and translated by Vernon J. Bourke. Indianapolis: Hackett: p. 123.

—— (1982). *The Literal Meaning of Genesis*. Vol. I. Translated by John Hammond Taylor. New York: Newman Press.

—— (1998). *The City of God against the Pagans*. Translated by R. W. Dyson. Cambridge: Cambridge University Press.

Bosley, Richard, and Martin Tweedale, eds. (1997). *Basic Issues in Medieval Philosophy*. Ontario: Broadview Press.

Bradley, Denis J. M. (1981). 'Aristotelian Science and the Science of Thomistic Theology'. *Heythrop Journal* 22: 162–71.

Bremond, Henri (1928). *A Literary History of Religious Thought in France*. Vol. I. Translated by K. L. Montgomery. New York: McMillan.

Chesneau, Charles (1936). 'L'Argument de l'ordre du monde dans la théologie du P. Yves de Paris'. *Études franciscaines* 48: 280–99.

Clairvaux, Bernard (1993a). 'Epistolae no. 188'. Translated by Eileen Sweeney in Sweeney, 'Rewriting the Narrative of Scripture: Twelfth-Century Debates over Reason and Theological Form'. *Medieval Philosophy and Theology* 3: 1–34.

—— (1993b). 'Epistolae no. 193'. Translated by Eileen Sweeney in Sweeney, 'Rewriting the Narrative of Scripture: Twelfth-Century Debates over Reason and Theological Form'. *Medieval Philosophy and Theology* 3: 1–34.

DeWulf, Maurice (1909). *History of Medieval Philosophy*. Translated by P. Coffey. London: Longmans, Green and Co.

Dumont, Stephen (1992). 'Transcendental Being: Scotus and Scotists'. *Topoi* 11/2: 135–48.

Fastiggi, Robert (1991). *The Natural Theology of Yves de Paris*. Atlanta: Scholars Press.

Grant, Edward (1979). 'The Condemnation of 1270 and 1277, God's Absolute Power and Physical Thought in the Late Middle Ages'. *Viator* 10: 211–44.

Hall, Alexander (2007a). 'Confused Univocity?'. *Proceedings of the Society of Medieval Logic and Metaphysics* 7: 18–31. <http://faculty.fordham.edu/klima/SMLM/PSMLM7/PSMLM7.pdf>.

—— (2007b). *Thomas Aquinas and John Duns Scotus: Natural Theology in the High Middle Ages*. London: Continuum.

Harrison, Peter (2006). 'The Bible and the Emergence of Modern Science'. *Science and Christian Belief* 18: 115–32.

Holopainen, Toivo (2007). 'Anselm's Argumentum and the Early Medieval Theory of Argument'. *Vivarium*, 45/1: 1–29.

Lindberg, David (1992). *The Beginnings of Western Science*. Chicago: The University of Chicago Press.

Lombard, Peter (2006). *Sentences*. Translated by Alexis Bugnolo [maintained by the Franciscan Archive] <http://www.franciscan-archive.org/lombardus/opera/ls-prolo.html> accessed 1 May 2010.

Mandonnet, Pierre (1908). *Siger de Brabant et l'Averroisme latin au XIIIme siècle*. 2nd edn. Louvain: Textes inédits.

Marrone, Steven (1983). 'The Notion of Univocity in Duns Scotus's Early Works'. *Franciscan Studies* 43: 347–95.

Ockham, William (1938). '*Centilogium theologicum*' in *Ockham: Studies and Selections*. Translated by Stephen Tournay. La Salle: Open Court.

Paris, Yves de (1928). 'Natural Theology' in Henri Bremond, *A Literary History of Religious Thought in France*. Translated by K. L. Montgomery. New York: McMillan.

—— (1991). 'Natural Theology' in Robert Fastiggi, *The Natural Theology of Yves de Paris*. Translated by Robert Fastiggi. Atlanta: Scholars Press.

Le Mercure galante (1991) [Paris, 1678]. Translated by Robert Fastiggi in *The Natural Theology of Yves de Paris*. Atlanta: Scholars Press.

Sabunde, Raymonde (1966). *Theologia naturalis seu liber creaturarum*. Edited by F. Stegmüller. Translated by Alexander Hall. Stuttgart-Bad Cannstatt: Frommann.

Scotus, Duns. (1950–). *Opera Omnia*. Edited by C. Balić et al. Vatican City: Typis Polyglottis Vaticanis.

—— (1975). *God and Creatures: The Quodlibetal Questions*. Translated by Felix Alluntis and Allan Wolter. Princeton: Princeton University Press.

—— (1987). *Philosophical Writings: A Selection*. Translated by Allan Wolter. Indianapolis: Hackett.

—— (1995). *Duns Scotus: Metaphysician*. Translated by Allan Wolter. West Lafayette: Purdue University Press.

Spinoza, Baruch (1991). *Tractatus theologico-politicus*. Translated by Samuel Shirley. Leiden: Brill.

Suárez, Francisco (1993). '*Disputationes metaphysicae*' in Frederick Copleston, *A History of Philosophy*. Vol. III. Translated by Copleston. New York: Image Books-Doubleday.

Tempier, Stephen, et al. (1973)'Condemnations of 1277' in Arthur Hyman and James Walsh ed., *Philosophy in the Middle Ages* (2nd edn, Indianapolis: Hackett): pp. 582–92.

Torrell, Jean-Pierre (1996–2003). *Saint Thomas Aquinas*. Translated by Robert Royal. 2 vols. Washington: The Catholic University of America Press.

Varro, Marcus Terrentius (1998). 'Antiquities of Human and Divine Things' in Augustine, *The City of God against the Pagans*. Translated by R. W. Dyson. Cambridge: Cambridge University Press.

CHAPTER 5

....

EARLY MODERN NATURAL THEOLOGIES

....

SCOTT MANDELBROTE

THE PHILOSOPHY OF ADAM
....

WRITING in 1669, the physician and controversialist Henry Stubbe (1632–76) took up his cudgels against the nascent Royal Society of London (Stubbe 1671: 26–8). He attacked a line of argument that he found in the apologetic *History of the Royal Society* that Thomas Sprat had published in 1667, but which also characterized the writing of other apologists for novelty in natural philosophy, in particular the Platonist writers, Joseph Glanvill (1636–80) and Henry More (1614–87). Stubbe lit upon Sprat's claim that '[the *Natural and Experimental Philosopher*] will be led to admire the wonderful contrivance of the *Creation*', and his belief that 'this was the first service that *Adam* perform'd to his *Creator*' (Sprat 1667: 349–50). According to Sprat, humanity at the time of its creation, and before the Fall, both gained knowledge of the nature of God and performed an act of worship when studying and ordering the natural world. Similar points had been made by Glanvill, who suggested that Adam had originally had a natural understanding of nature which meant that he had known things which were only now being recovered by natural philosophers, or by More, when he described the special nature of Adam's intellect (Glanvill 1661: 1–9; More 1653b: 40–3). Stubbe, who felt slighted by the Royal Society and was eager to curry favour with institutions that offered alternative visions of natural philosophy (such as the University of Oxford or the London College of Physicians), pointed out that 'No man ever taught, that *Adam*'s fall (which was a breach of his RELIGIOUS DUTY *towards God*) was a deficiency from the study of EXPERIMENTAL PHILOSOPHIE: or that *he* was not ejected from *paradise* for the breach of a *positive command*, but for not minding the *cultivation of the Garden*, and *natural curiosities*.' '[A]s if', he went on:

> NATURAL and *Experimental* PHILOSOPHIE, not *Natural Theology*, had been the *Religion* of *Paradise*: nor doth [Sprat] mention any thing of the obligation *Adam* had

to fulfill the *Moral Law*, or obey the *positive occasional precepts*, or to *believe the incident Revelations* with which his *Creator* might acquaint *him*. [Stubbe 1671: 28]

HISTORIES OF NATURAL THEOLOGY

Stubbe was writing polemic. Nevertheless, his words suggest that understandings of natural theology, as well as those of the meaning and practice of natural philosophy, might be contested in the late seventeenth century. The natural theology of Adam, or of any other human being not yet in possession of Christian revelation, was not necessarily the same as the natural theology of contemporary Platonists or that of contemporary natural philosophers. The uncertainty of this debate raises questions about the constitution of early modern natural theology and complicates understandings of what natural theology was for. This is important because of the existing state of our knowledge of natural theology in this period. Historians have recognized both the pervasiveness and the inclusivity of early modern natural theology (Brooke 1991: 82–225). This was a form of argument that was practised across the confessions that divided Christian Europe after the Reformation, providing something of a common language for Catholics, Lutherans, and members of the Reformed Churches. Despite the role of natural theology in moments of doctrinal controversy over the scope of natural philosophy (most obviously in the early 1630s, during and after the trial of Galileo), historians have also suggested that it granted legitimacy to an emerging scientific culture of 'modernity'. Stephen Gaukroger, for example, has suggested that:

> a good part of the distinctive success at the level of legitimation and consolidation of the scientific enterprise in the early modern West derives not from any separation of religion and natural philosophy, but rather from the fact that natural philosophy could be accommodated to projects in natural theology: what made natural philosophy attractive to so many in the seventeenth and eighteenth centuries were the prospects it offered for the renewal of natural theology. [Gaukroger 2006: 23; cf. McMullin 2005]

Thus natural theology was able to tame and incorporate the increasingly prevalent idiom of a mechanical philosophy from the mid-seventeenth century onwards and to accommodate the increasing mathematization of nature, in part through a willing acceptance of the lawfulness of divine superintendence of the cosmos (Harrison 1995; Hurlbutt 1965). Knowledge of nature and understandings of God were alike beneficiaries of a revived Augustinianism, which promoted a search for certainty in unfamiliar territory. In such an environment, both probabilistic arguments for faith and historical and descriptive accounts of natural evidences carried greater weight (Harrison 2007; cf. Hacking 1975). Comprehension of intentions of the divine author of the two books of nature and scripture was aided by the growing preponderance of the literal sense in the hands of Protestant biblical critics. This paralleled and promoted a culture of fact among interpreters of nature, which reflected a change in understandings of the relationship between words and things (Harrison 1998; Shapiro 2000). Initially successful as a response to classical and Renaissance ideas of scepticism, the evidences for religion which early modern natural theology provided were in turn buffeted by new currents of criticism. In part, this may have been because natural theology presented what Amos Funkenstein has called 'a secular theology', insufficiently attuned both to new forms of piety and to the philosophical challenges of rationalism and materialism (Funkenstein 1986). Peter Harrison argues that:

> the corpuscular philosophy, the idea of laws of nature, and the tendency towards occasionalism in conceptions of causation—developments that can plausibly be associated with theological developments—may be regarded, together with Protestant hermeneutics, as having promoted the desacralization of the world. [Harrison 2008: 359]

Without doubt, there were eighteenth-century critics of the philosophical basis for the argument from design (and other tenets of natural theology), from Hume to Kant (Addinall 1991). Similarly, the weight of contradictory evidence, from geology to biology, available by the mid-nineteenth century generated significant problems for standard attempts to reconcile the literal sense of scripture with the factual understanding of the natural world (Klaver 1997; Thomson 2005).

Classical Writers and Natural Theologians

To focus briefly on the contested nature of natural theologies brings other factors to the fore. The most critical of these, scarcely neglected in the historiography of natural theology, is the continuing significance of a dialogue with classical interpretations of nature and divinity in forming early modern interpretations (cf. Funkenstein 1986; Hooykaas 1972). While the importance for early modern writers of countering ancient forms of atheism has often been recognized, the survival of classical writers as genuine interlocutors in this period does not always receive the attention that it deserves. Classical atomism was Christianized in the mid-seventeenth century by Pierre Gassendi (1592–1655) or Walter Charleton (1620–1707) in order to defend both divine providence and human freedom (Joy 1987: 130–64; Osler 1994: 36–101; Sarasohn 1996: 51–75). The poetry of Lucretius could be used by Edmond Halley (1656–1742) as the model for celebrating the achievement of Isaac Newton (1642–1727) in describing a universe of mathematically lawful physical forces (Albury 1978). Yet Epicureanism might also provide an example for the moral behaviour of deist or libertine writers, for whom Ciceronian scepticism about the nature of the gods underpinned criticisms of both the providential authority of Christian revelation and the limits imposed on human freedom by the political activities of the clergy (Rivers 2000: 28–31, 249–53). At the same time, polite critics of the

Epicurean denial of design in the universe, such as the third Earl of Shaftesbury (1671–1713), defended Ciceronian deportment as the best way to protect manners and religious order (Klein 1994). The same body of classical writing inspired both spiritualist and materialistic interpretations of the mechanical philosophy. It lay behind defences of Christian providence as well as attacks on clerical superstition. Engagement with classical writing on the nature of divine involvement in the physical world was stylistic, not just theoretical. It directed the choice of specific examples of providential design (for example, the suitability of parts of the human body to their supposed purposes), and its influence was not confined therefore to those who might be committed to specific grand theories of nature (Rivers 1993).

Plato, the Fathers, and Non-Christian Religion in Early Modern Natural Theology

The decision of Augustine of Hippo (354–430) in *The City of God* (especially Book 7, chapter 29) to consider the shortcomings of the natural theologies of the schools of ancient philosophy, as summarized in the (now lost) writings of Marcus Terentius Varro (116–27 BCE), underpinned the Christian practice of natural theology during the early modern period. Augustine believed that classical writers had confused worship of the creation with worship of God the creator, which alone was proper for Christians. He recognized, however, that some classical philosophers, in particular Plato and his followers, had acknowledged the existence of a world soul and the presence of living souls in human beings. The fifteenth-century revival of Platonism, of which both Augustine and mainstream medieval natural philosophy had been critical, was important both for the form and the function of much early modern natural theology.

Proponents of Platonism, from Marsilio Ficino (1433–99) or Gianfrancesco Pico della Mirandola (1469–1533) to Ralph Cudworth (1617–88) or Henry More, believed that the essentials of the Christian religion, perhaps including the doctrine of the Trinity, had been communicated to Plato, either through contact with Moses himself in Egypt or through access to what they believed to be proto-Christian scriptures, such as the *Corpus Hermeticum* (Grafton 1991: 162–77; Schmitt 1967: 56–63; Hutton 1992). Throughout the early modern period, an essential claim of natural theology was that it had been the original religion of mankind. This claim was buttressed by beliefs about human rationality, according to which noble and intelligent individuals, abandoned in an environment without human contact, might nevertheless develop an idea of a personal and benevolent deity and his superintendence of a morally coherent universe. Christian natural philosophers were sufficiently committed to this interpretation of human nature that they were happy to find endorsement for it in a range of non-Christian texts, including at least one example from the Islamic tradition. Known to Giovanni Pico della

Mirandola (1463–94) through a Hebrew translation, edited in Arabic and translated into Latin by the younger Edward Pococke (1648–1726) under the direction of his father, the story of Ḥayy ibn-Yaqẓān by Ibn-Tufayl (d. 1185) provided an example of autodidacticism that proved compatible both with Platonic and experimental forms of natural theology (Ben-Zaken 2011). More normal, however, was a stress on the communication (often corrupted over time) of revealed religious principles from Adam to Noah to Moses to Christ, in which humanity's common descent from a single source allowed for the possibility of common belief. This was usually held to be visible in the supposedly universal forms of natural religion or natural law. Often held to be the product of directly transmitted traditions, natural law was also believed by some writers (notably the jurist and Hebraist, John Selden (1584–1654)) to reflect the constant activity of God in moving individual human intellects towards knowledge of the divine (Müller 1998; Tuck 1993; Westfall 1982). The presence of such remnants of common belief both justified attempts to convert pagans (indeed underpinning claims to the humanity of those living in a natural state, such as native Americans) and made it possible to propose accommodation between Christian worship and the practices of other faiths, above all in the Jesuit mission to China (Gliozzi 1977; Pagden 1982; Mungello 1994). In debate with the competing religious traditions of Islam, such as that engaged in by Catholic missionaries in Persia and the Middle East, moreover, easily agreed natural theological points and the claim that knowledge of the natural world gave authority to speak about God provided the basis from which to advance to more contested points of positive truth (Heyberger 1994: 319–26; Hillgarth 1971: 5–27). Access to traditions of natural religion explained the glimmers of truth found even in materialistic classical philosophy, whereas direct knowledge of the Judaeo-Christian tradition made plausible the deeper, spiritual insights that some detected in ancient Platonism (Creech 1683: sig. c1r–v).

Platonist traditions of natural theology received a substantial boost from the progress of humanist scholarship in recovering and editing the texts of the Greek Fathers of the Church. Centres of activity and publication in this regard included late sixteenth-century Augsburg, early seventeenth-century Eton and Oxford, and, pre-eminently, Paris from the late sixteenth to the early eighteenth centuries (Bury and Meunier 1993). The partial rehabilitation, in particular, of the reputation of Origen (c.185–c.254) gave encouragement to Platonic interpretations of the life of the soul, many of them couched in terms of allegorical readings of the evidence of both the Bible and the natural world (Hutton 2006; Lewis 2006; Schär 1979). In the context of the Platonic revival in English natural theology, which had its focus in mid-seventeenth-century Cambridge, it is possible to discern many of the distinctive features of this kind of natural theology. Cudworth, for example, built on the idea of the development of pagan or gentile theologies, derived from contemplation of nature, which he and his contemporaries found set out in the natural legal tradition of Arminian writers such as Hugo Grotius (1583–1645) or Gerardus Joannes Vossius (1577–1649). He sorted through the confusions of classical natural theology, to which Augustine had drawn attention, in order to identify the hidden truth of belief in a Christian deity, knowable through his demonstrable activity in nature and understood in Trinitarian terms by Plato himself (Cudworth 1678: 183–598).

Both Cudworth and Henry More endorsed methods of textual interpretation that they associated with Jewish Kabbalah. More generally, Christian understandings of Kabbalah, especially the *Zohar*, appeared to offer another route to revealing hidden truths in both nature and scripture (Coudert 1999).

They created a textual route that could help to account both for the supposed apostasy of the Jews, who, despite the testimony of natural and revealed religion, rejected Christ, and for the success of Christianity among the gentiles (Mornay 1605: 395–694). The Cambridge Platonists similarly wove together histories of religion and philosophy, openness to novelty in knowledge of nature, and esoteric readings of the Bible that often proved extremely disturbing to mainstream religious orthodoxy, and that had at least something in common with the writings of Lutheran mystical theologians or the contemporary Quakers. Their interest in the collecting of evidence for the activity of spirits and demons in the contemporary world underpinned a broad sense of the importance of the wondrousness of nature and the continuing providential guidance of God (More 1653a; cf. Glanvill 1681). To Enlightenment readers, their writings thus sometimes appeared tainted by incredulity, even if they remained important witnesses to the value of the history of philosophy and the essential truth of natural theology (Hanegraaff 2012: 5–152).

ALLEGORY AND MAKING SENSE OF NATURE

Like most of their Protestant (and, indeed, Catholic) contemporaries, the Cambridge Platonists were committed to the importance of the literal sense of the Bible. Thomas Burnet (?1635–1715) explored the possibilities of the technique of accommodation, advanced by Augustine as a means of reconciling the literal truth of the Bible with the truths of nature (Burnet 1681–9, 1684–90). In common with Cudworth and More, Burnet sought to apply ideas derived from the natural philosophy of René Descartes (1596–1650), whose work was understood in part as renewing the Platonic tradition. Despite this, it is difficult to feel comfortable with attempts to recruit Neoplatonist writers in support of narratives that stress the interconnectedness of the books of scripture and nature and argue that interest in the literal sense underpinned attention to scientific fact. Neoplatonic readings of the Bible went beyond simple figurative and typological interpretations of the text to explore multiple layers of meaning, each with different applications for the believer (for example, More 1653b). As the Devonian Platonist, Richard Burthogge (1638–1705), put it: 'This Theologie indeed is Hieroglyphical and *Figurative*; Nature, an Allegory, God is represented in her and in Providence, as a Cause in its Effects' (Burthogge 1675: 409–10). Platonists drew on models of the interrelatedness of nature, humanity, and God that relied on symbolic methods of interpretation, such as the doctrine of signatures or the idea of the microcosm and the macrocosm.

The importance of these models for fifteenth-, sixteenth- and early seventeenth-century reformers of medicine and philosophy, such as Ramon Sibiuda ([Raymond

Sebonde], d. 1436), Paracelsus (1493–1541), or Robert Fludd (1574–1637), should not obscure their survival in the context of both learned and popular cosmologies into the eighteenth century (Hillgarth 1971: 274–6; Wright 1971: 3–5, 13–14; Curry 1989: 95–117). Platonism (and also Stoicism) encouraged open-mindedness towards allegorical readings of both the Bible and nature (according to which, for example, forms of knowledge, discoveries of peoples, animals, or plants might be illustrated in ways that emphasized moral rather than factual truths), but they were not the only justification for such methods of understanding, which embraced the representations of nature produced by craftsmen as well as the writings of philosophers (Park 2011; Smith 2004: especially 59–93). Although a culture of observation may have displaced an emblematic view of natural history, some of its most painstaking and influential adherents, such as the Dutch entomologist and mystic, Jan Swammerdam (1637–80) or the Swiss physician, geologist, and physico-theologian Johann Jakob Scheuchzer (1672–1733), nevertheless remained able to locate moral as well as physical meaning in the animals and objects that they studied (Jorink 2006: 187–265; Scheuchzer 1723: 45–59; Felfe 2003; Müsch 2000; cf. Ashworth 1990; Harrison 1998: 129–38).

Conscience, Nature, and Scripture

One reason for this was the widespread belief in the importance of faith as a route to understanding. This was a position that might unite Platonists and Augustinians, and, like those two philosophies, it was one that crossed the principal confessional divides of early modern Europe. Although John Locke (1632–1704) at the end of the seventeenth century was willing to limit the evidence of faith to the experience of the divine, most earlier writers (and many of Locke's contemporaries) believed that faith guided reason at some level and that, without it, fallen human beings were bound to err or fall into enthusiasm (Yolton 1956; Spellman 1988; van Leeuwen 1970: 13–48; Heyd 1995). Religious choices were responses to a divine call, rather than being simple acts of human rationality. The books of nature and scripture, according to the English natural theologian and Independent divine, Matthew Barker (1618–98), were written 'to amend the Book of Conscience', which when fully opened would reveal the election or depravity of the individual. Of the two other books, Barker was clear that, in the Bible, 'Conscience hath . . . a clearer account, not only of the Will and Counsels of God, but even of his very Nature and Being.' Natural theology was, by contrast, deficient, since it showed neither how to make reconciliation for sin, nor how to order the worship of God (Barker 1674: 16, 111–12). English divines were unsure how many books God had composed for the benefit of his people (some believed three, some four, some five), but they agreed with Christians everywhere that openness to God through faith provided the best opportunity to understand his works and his will (cf. Byfield 1626: 521–2; Cheynell 1645). As the French natural philosopher and Jansenist, Blaise Pascal (1623–62), put it, in a work whose translation was dedicated to the pre-eminent contemporary

English student of nature, Robert Boyle (1627–91), 'Faith tendeth principally to teach these two things, the Corruption of Nature, and Redemption by Jesus Christ' (Pascal 1688: 44). One confession doubted this consistently. For Socinians, who stressed the historicity of the Bible and the importance of the freedom of the human will, the idea that people might have innate knowledge of God seemed, however, to undermine the rationality of human religion (Mortimer 2010: 13–38). Useful though natural theology was when dealing with pagans, for Christians it often represented an uncertain beginning. One might build theories, such as those of Thomas Burnet, on such foundations, but doctrine needed firmer moral ground.

Jewish Theologies of Nature and their Impact

Such anxieties were not confined to Christian writers: they were shared, for example, by Jewish critics of the spread of Lurianic Kabbalah during the seventeenth century, such as the Venetian rabbi, Leon Modena (1571–1648). Modena's works also proved popular with Christian readers. The return to the works of Maimonides (1135–1204) that he espoused in rejecting the idea of the oral transmission of an otherwise lost esoteric tradition, was one that found favour among Protestants. It especially interested those, such as Vossius, who wanted to discover the historical nature of Jewish and gentile religions (Dweck 2011; Katchen 1984). Maimonidean history, in particular through its openness to ideas of biblical accommodation, also informed much more radical rewritings of the place and authority of God in both scripture and nature. The *Tractatus Theologico-Politicus* (1670) and *Ethics* (1677) of Baruch de Spinoza (1632–77), taken together, provided the most subversive form of natural theology written during the early modern period. Republican in politics, materialist and mechanist in natural philosophy, pantheist in natural theology, sceptical with regard to miracles and biblical authority, and humanist in its interpretation of prophecy, Spinoza's work was the embodiment of what most terrified Christian natural theologians about the classical world (Nadler 2001). At the same time, its endorsement of the corporeality of God and apparent denial of the natural immortality of the soul chimed with the writings of Thomas Hobbes (1588–1679), the most important Christian critic of clerical authority, who had himself been the target of extensive criticism by natural theologians (for example, Ward 1652, also Cudworth 1678, and many others; cf. Mintz 1962; Parkin 2007). In his *Leviathan* (1651), Hobbes had mocked the contradictions of contemporary natural theology, which he characterized as 'so repugnant to naturall Reason, that whosoever thinketh there is any thing to bee understood by it, must needs think it supernaturall' (Hobbes 1991: 463). To Spinoza, natural theological arguments for the necessity of God from the act of creation were 'a reduction, not to the impossible, but to ignorance': they told one nothing either about God or about nature (Spinoza 1955: 78). For many of those who made natural theology an arena of controversy in the eighteenth century, in particular French and English deist writers, Hobbes and Spinoza provided powerful examples to follow (Israel 2001: 563–627).

THE ROLE OF METAPHYSICS

This is, however, to get ahead of the story and it risks losing sight both of mainstream early modern natural theology and of its most significant modifications during the later seventeenth century. For when Hobbes attacked natural theology, the term he used was 'metaphysics', and his target was the Aristotelian philosophy of the universities. As the Independent minister and tutor, Theophilus Gale (1628–79) acknowledged: 'Aristotle's *Metaphysicks* passe in the *Scholes* under the splendid title of *Natural Theologie*' (Gale 1670: 415). The history of metaphysics (defined as 'a Science which enquires of the form and end (as Physicks doth of the efficient and matter) of things', Coles 1677: sig. Aa3v) has been curiously underexplored in accounts of early modern natural theology, even when its importance in late medieval theology has been acknowledged (for example, Gaukroger 2006: 80–6). This is despite the fact that, as Hobbes pointed out, Aristotle's *Metaphysics* continued to play an important role in the scholastic curriculum. Its place in the curriculum had certainly changed, however, in the context of the long-running debate over the teaching of Aristotle, which began in the late thirteenth century. Doubts about the success of the synthesis of Aristotelian philosophy and Christian theology achieved by Thomas Aquinas (1225–74) focussed much debate on metaphysical concerns (such as the limits of the body or location of God with regard to the blood shed by Christ on the cross). Meanwhile, political and ecclesiastical disputes between the various religious orders that were responsible for teaching heightened intellectual differences (Fitzpatrick 2011). At this stage, metaphysics served, as Aristotle himself had intended, as a theoretical science, which dealt with unchanging things that existed separately from matter. As such it was akin to theology, and different from both mathematics and physics (the science of changeable things). Its impact on the teaching of natural philosophy was therefore strictly circumscribed (Grant 1996: 135; Grant 2010: 91–118).

Pietro Pomponazzi (1462–1525), a professor of philosophy at the University of Padua whose background lay in the secular discipline of medicine, intervened in the debate among theologians regarding proofs of the immortality of the soul to deny that it was possible to present such a demonstration in properly Aristotelian terms (Schmitt 1983: 98–103). The responses to his arguments helped to generate realignment in the study and application of Aristotle within the scholastic curriculum. This had the effect both of bringing material from Aristotle's *Physics* much more closely into debate with his *Metaphysics*, and of moving discussion of metaphysical issues away from a process of commentary into the more active sphere of disputation and demonstration. In the hands of the Jesuit Francisco Suárez (1548–1617), therefore, metaphysics came increasingly into contact with natural philosophy, rather than being confined to theology. Suárez taught at universities across the Iberian peninsula as well as in Rome, and his writings were widely read by both Protestants and Catholics (Lohr 1991; Schwartz 2012). Jesuit colleges across Europe, moreover, ensured the spread of his teaching, even when it conflicted with older models of Catholic divinity (Feldhay 1995: 73–198).

PROTESTANTISM AND SCHOLASTICISM

A different reorganization of the curriculum, which nevertheless had the effect of bringing the subject matter and the methods of natural philosophy to bear on questions which had previously fallen in the domain of metaphysical theology (above all, those relating to the nature of the soul), was carried through by Philip Melanchthon (1497–1560) at the University of Wittenberg (Kusukawa 1995). Melanchthon argued that the traditional topics of metaphysics should not be part of the undergraduate arts curriculum. Yet the stress that he placed on the regularity of nature, which directed attention to questions of what God had done, rather than those relating to what He might be, implied a divine element to the study of physics. Elsewhere, Lutheran theologians followed Melanchthon in finding signs of divine providence in the natural world, in ways that both raised the status and value of natural theology and made discoveries about nature (for example, the motion of comets) problematic for Aristotelian physics (Kusukawa 1999; Methuen 1999). Despite the confessional outlook of many writers in this tradition, it would be wrong to see the search for providential signs of divine activity in nature or for the spiritual meaning of plants and animals (whether in the contemporary or the biblical world) as being confined to Lutheran authors. Catholic writers such as Levinus Lemnius (1505–68) or Franciscus Vallesius (1524–92), whose works were often published together, similarly sought out natural evidence of divine providence from the world around them and philological proof of the interrelatedness of divine will and natural facts in biblical texts (Lemnius 1574; Vallesius 1622; Crowther 2008). Reformed authors also included such pious meanings in their encyclopaedic treatments of natural history and divine grace (Blair 2000). They did so within a curriculum in which doctrine was held to derive from the systematic presentation of human knowledge, and in which metaphysics took on the role of first philosophy, the prelude to other forms of knowing. Despite the reservations expressed about metaphysics by Petrus Ramus (1515–72), both Lutheran and Reformed writers of the late sixteenth and early seventeenth centuries, such as Bartholomaeus Keckermann (c.1572–1609), Johann Heinrich Alsted (1588–1638), or Clemens Timpler (1563–1624), came to accept the value of combining theoretical with practical knowledge of God, thus adapting natural philosophy to theological ends in part through awareness of metaphysical concerns regarding divine will, freedom, and consistency. What might be conceivable in terms of metaphysics helped to shape what might be knowable about both God and nature through natural theology (Lohr 1999; Freedman 1999; Friedrich 2004; Hotson 2007; Daston and Stolleis 2008). Thoroughgoing critiques of such positions, for example the efforts of Lambert Daneau (c.1535–c.1590) to establish a Christian physics on revealed truth and to reject pagan natural philosophy, were rare regardless of the theoretical appeal to Protestant theologians of a biblically grounded physics (Daneau 1578).

THE PLACE OF NATURAL THEOLOGY IN NATURAL PHILOSOPHY

Despite the strength of confessional differences, therefore, there was a good deal of agreement about the form and content of natural theology and its place in the under-graduate curriculum of late sixteenth- and early seventeenth-century Europe. This did not imply that 'natural philosophy was about God and his creation', as Andrew Cunningham has argued. Instead it meant that topics that might once have been con-fined to metaphysical theology and that related particularly to the form and intentions of God and human beings were now being taught as part of the propaedeutic to the study of physics (itself a part of natural philosophy) within the arts curriculum (Brockliss 1987: 205–16; Sassen 1941; cf. Cunningham 2000: 266–70; Cunningham and French 1996). This was the setting in which the young Isaac Newton encountered natural theo-logical questions in Cambridge during the 1660s (McGuire and Tamny 1983: 446–53; Ducheyne 2005). It was also the context for revision of the curriculum by writers influ-enced by Epicureanism, Platonism, Stoicism, or other ancient forms of philosophy that provided distorting lenses through which to view forms of study that otherwise remained heavily indebted to Aristotle (Galama 1954: 39–100; Sassen 1962: 16–26). Physics and metaphysics were studied together in the second year of the curriculum set out by the Cambridge tutor, Richard Holdsworth (1590–1649), to be followed in the third year by more detailed study of Aristotle's natural philosophy and in the fourth year by reading that added Seneca and Lucretius to Aristotlean pneumatology and metereology (Cambridge, Emmanuel College, Ms 48). Holdsworth influenced teaching at both St John's College, Cambridge, and Emmanuel College. Students at Emmanuel also encoun-tered a Platonist strain of natural theology, through the teaching of Benjamin Whichcote (1609–83). The shared effects of such influences can be traced in the later writings of Peter Sterry (1613–72), a pupil of Whichcote and a Fellow of Emmanuel when Holdsworth was the College's Master. Sterry later became an Independent minister, and composed his mystical theology for hearers outside the established Church of England and its sem-inaries. Despite his stress on the importance of the light of faith, Sterry held that God's nature was too high for anyone to have immediate natural knowledge of Him, and thus He ought to be approached by degrees through inferior things. This Sterry believed to be the work of natural philosophy, which he divided into five parts, the last of which was natural theology, which 'comprehendeth the knowledge of divine things, of spiritual, that is invisible, and immortal substances...' (Cambridge, Emmanuel College, Ms 291, 16–21; cf. Pinto 1934: 224).

INTELLECTUAL AND SOCIAL CHANGE

This chapter has so far attempted to establish the following essential facts about early modern natural theologies. First, this was a contested arena, in which a number of different standpoints might be justified on the basis of the history of classical or Christian thought. Secondly, those different positions reflected in part disagreements about how one should read the evidence of nature, and what weight one should give to the Bible and to reason as lights to guide one in doing so. On both of these points, mainstream writers clashed with followers of Platonism, as well as with more materialist natural theologies (for example, Parker 1666; Tenison 1670). Thirdly, natural theology had an important and changing role to play in the Aristotelian curriculum that dominated the universities of Western Europe until at least the late seventeenth century. Moreover, its position in that curriculum, although not unaffected by confessional differences, largely transcended the major religious divides created by the Reformation. In part, it did so because people accepted that its role in debate lay primarily in the sphere of discussion with non-Christians, and that questions of the nature and being of God or 'the highest things, as far as they are discernable by the light of Nature', could not normally determine points of doctrinal division within Christianity (Blome 1686: 15).

As the source for this quotation makes clear, natural theology (which the bookseller, Richard Blome (?1635–1705), discussed under the heading, 'Metaphysicks') was, at least by the second half of the seventeenth century, a topic of interest to lay people as well as theologians. In part, that was a reflection on the place that it held in the arts curriculum, which was followed in England and elsewhere during the late sixteenth and early seventeenth centuries by unprecedented numbers of young men, mostly from the gentry, who did not intend to become professional lawyers, doctors, or theologians. This fact also helps to explain the extent to which discussions of natural theology had moved into vernacular languages by the late seventeenth or early eighteenth centuries. This shift, together with the spread of translations, itself aided the dissemination of natural theology as a topic of debate that might engage polite rather than simply learned society. Certainly the fame (or in some cases the notoriety) of a wide variety of lay commentators on theology rested on their contributions to natural theology, whether these were overtly pious (as in the works of Boyle, Scheuchzer, or the Dutch physician, Bernard Nieuwentijt (1654–1718)) or not.

PHYSICO-THEOLOGIANS

That said, some of the most successful of late seventeenth- and early eighteenth-century natural theologies were written by theologians and had their origins in the teaching of the universities. Perhaps the most remarkable of these was John Ray's *Wisdom of God*

(1691), which developed out of lectures that Ray (1627–1705) had delivered while a Fellow of Trinity College, Cambridge, during the 1650s, and which was explicitly structured as an extended commentary on a verse from Psalm 104 (Ray 1691: sig. A6r–v). Other clerical authors, notably Thomas Burnet, were frequently cited by lay readers (as well as by ministers who dissented from the Church of England) because of the skill with which their natural theologies brought landscapes to life as a place of providential action and invested natural phenomena with moral and scriptural significance (Pepys 1926: II, 6; Rastwick 2010: 139–40; Nicolson 1997: 184–270). More generally, the work of Burnet and others helped Protestant readers to disenchant landscapes that had once been populated with reminders of the supernatural powers of saints and demons, and fill them instead with echoes of divine providence (Walsham 2011: 376–94). Moreover, in their hands, providence could threaten as well as reassure (cf. Zuidervaart 1995). Such authors reached a wide audience outside the academy. Burnet's Latin works were republished on the Continent and his writings, as well as those of Ray and other English natural theologians of the late seventeenth or early eighteenth centuries, were often translated, especially into Dutch and German, and attracted comment from Catholic as well as Protestant critics (Keynes 1977: 170–80; Burnet 1695–6; Haller 1940). Commercial success, however, did not always imply that readers shared the pious aims of the authors that they read. Dutch and German Spinozists, for example, were also enthusiastic consumers of works that demonstrated the natural causes behind allegedly providential events (Vermij 1991a).

Revolutions in Knowledge and Natural Philosophy

Ray and others in the mid-seventeenth century were conscious of a rapidly changing environment for natural philosophy, in which developments in metaphysics and natural theology also played a part. In England, explicit criticism came from those who wanted to change the nature of the curriculum as a means to a more thoroughgoing alteration in Church and State. They included Hobbes, and also the chemical philosopher, John Webster (1611–82), who attacked 'Metaphysicks, or Natural Theology, the Vanity, Vselessnesse, and Hurtfulnesse of which we shall shew in some clear arguments' (Webster 1654: 10). In responding to such criticism, the natural theologians of Oxford (notably Seth Ward (1617–89) and John Wilkins (1614–72)) and Cambridge (notably Cudworth and More) made use of two lay writers whose reformulations of natural philosophy also implied revisions of the functions of natural theology. Those authors were Francis Bacon (1561–1626) and René Descartes (1596–1650). Bacon's programme of experimentation provided a model for Wilkins and others at Oxford and lay behind the projects of the early Royal Society, of which Wilkins was secretary (for example, Wilkins 1648; Sprat 1667). An interpretation of Descartes's natural philosophy as being compatible with a true, Platonic metaphysics lay behind the early enthusiasm for his work displayed by More and others (More 1653b; Gabbey 1982).

As early as 1605, Bacon had criticized the confusion of metaphysics (understood as first philosophy) with natural theology, which he defined as 'DIVINE PHILOSOPHIE... that knowledge or Rudiment of knowledge concerning GOD, which may be obtained by the contemplation of his Creatures' (Bacon 1605: fol. 22r–v). Bacon was perhaps the first writer to suggest that the Book of Nature might be subjected to interpretation in a manner analogous to the interpretation of law or that of the Bible (Serjeantson forthcoming). His ideas about cosmology, influenced by Paracelsianism, provided specific if problematic questions for investigation on the part of Wilkins and others interested in determining just how God had created the universe (Rees 1975a, 1975b, 1977). More significantly, the Royal Society appropriated the Baconian idea of experiment as a means of revealing the secrets of nature, and building from them the evidence of the lawful principles by which God governed the world. For Thomas Sprat, with whom this chapter began, experiments were thus a route to contemplation of divine goodness through natural theology. Properly analysed, they provided demonstrations of the activity of God in nature, which might be legitimately compared to the miracles that Christ had performed to make manifest the divine truth of his own teaching, 'which...I would even venture to call *Divine Experiments* of his *Godhead*' (Sprat 1667: 352). Both Wilkins and Boyle wrote works that used the idea of the lawfulness of nature as a means to counter the supposed atheism of classical philosophers and their modern proponents (Wilkins 1678; Boyle 1686). Despite their stress on the regularity of nature, the extrinsic teleology of the writings of Wilkins and Boyle made their arguments quite different from the theological reasoning of older types of natural history, while betraying the influence of Stoicism on both authors (Ogilvie 2005).

Boyle's targets included contemporary Platonists, who appeared at times to reify nature and to make it into a creative principle. He also took aim at Descartes and the notion of extension, which had appeared to provide a means of understanding the relationship between spirit and matter to Henry More and others. Descartes' ideas about substance (in which God was uncreated substance, mind was created and thinking, and matter was created and unthinking) and extension, which gave geometrical form to material bodies, just as thought gave form to the mind, allowed him to create a new account of how natural knowledge might be possible and of what it might look like. The metaphysical physics that resulted rewrote the terminology and tore up much of the understanding of scholastic natural philosophy. It provided a powerful Christian argument against ancient doctrines of atomism. At the same time, it sought to demonstrate how God might rule a geometrically ordered universe through mechanical laws that governed how matter in motion must behave in an act of continuous creation. The natural theological implications of Cartesian physics were immediately apparent to contemporaries, although they differed in the extent to which they found his system conducive to or threatening for faith (Ariew 1999; Garber 1992; Watson 1987). Those differences made French collèges de plein exercice and Dutch schools and universities, in particular, into battlegrounds between proponents and opponents of Descartes. In practice, Cartesian ideas touched almost everyone who wrote or taught about the relationship of

God and nature in the second half of the seventeenth century (Clarke 1989; Sassen 1963: 48–75; Verbeek 1992). While relatively few people endorsed Descartes' ideas whole-heartedly, in the modified form of occasionalism—best exemplified in the writings of Nicolas Malebranche (1638–1715)—they met with broader acceptance (even though Suárez and other Thomists had already attacked ideas of this kind). On this basis, God provided the causation for interactions between otherwise passive bodies of matter, which were the occasion for the projection of divine will into the world.

The Impact of Descartes

Cartesianism promoted controversy in the fields of metaphysics and natural theology. It gave life to materialist criticisms of traditional natural philosophy, as well as encouraging new ways of understanding divine activity in nature. Platonists sometimes joined more orthodox scholastics in rejecting Cartesianism, once they appreciated the materialistic challenge that could be mounted from it. Successful hostility to Cartesianism helped to explain the survival of scholastic metaphysics and pneumatology at institutions like the University of Utrecht, or more generally in the natural theology of adherents of the Further Reformation of Calvinist theology in the Netherlands (Sassen 1961; Goudriaan 1999). This came at a price, however, which was often either the rejection of much of the new learning in natural philosophy that was otherwise transforming institutions of higher education in the late seventeenth and early eighteenth centuries, or the undermining of the role of metaphysics as first philosophy in the curriculum. Similar battles were fought at reformed institutions in France and Geneva, where the introduction of Cartesian physics was carried out without undermining scholastic metaphysics, or in the German-speaking lands (Heyd 1982: 135–44; Neele 2009: 33–4). In Lutheran Germany, by contrast, and notably at Halle, the reaction to Cartesianism helped to promote the hermetic, quasi-mystical and Platonic natural theology of Christian Thomasius (1655–1728), which sought to make sense of the spiritual principles underlying nature (Ahnert 2006: 107–19).

Despite this debate, the principles by which natural theology was carried out had not changed at the end of the seventeenth century. Natural theology could not provide for salvation; it did not represent a sufficient basis for overcoming doctrinal division either among Christians or between Christians and other faiths; and it could not be used to propagate doctrine (Whitby 1705). In the eighteenth century, however, the positive aspects of natural theology as something which led the reader to approach revelation with a suitable sense of awe, or as the basis for a moral philosophy endorsed by the Bible, were increasingly added to its long-term use as an argument to counter paganism and materialism. What drove this process was again controversy, in particular the increasingly loud voices of Spinozists in the Netherlands, and English and French deists, all of whom were themselves users of natural theology. Yet English interest in a revival of natural theology predated these challenges, and gained new vigour in the early 1690s.

This was the period of the publication of Ray's natural theology and the debate over the significance of Burnet's work. It was also the point of introduction of the ideas of Isaac Newton, who first realized that his mathematical proofs of the physical lawfulness of the universe might have natural theological implications at the end of 1691, and who later provided a 'General Scholium' to the second edition of *Philosophiae naturalis principia mathematica* (1713) to make those implications clearer (London, Royal Society, Ms 247, fol. 1v; Newton 1713: 481–4).

THE IMPACT OF NEWTON

Mathematical descriptions of natural laws now underpinned the physico-theology of the argument from design as enunciated by Richard Bentley (1662–1742), Samuel Clarke (1675–1729), or William Derham (1657–1735). Each of these authors was given a platform by the foundation in Robert Boyle's will (28 July 1691) of a series of sermons to be delivered annually in London 'for proving the Christian religion against notorious Infidels, *viz.* Atheists, Theists, Pagans, Jews, and Mahometans, not descending lower to any controversies, that are among Christians themselves' (Birch 1744: 353–4). By no means all of the Boyle lectures consisted of physico-theology, let alone Newtonian physico-theology. Nevertheless, the success of these three writers, together with the increasing role of mathematics in the Cambridge curriculum, helped to ensure the long-term visibility of Newton as a guarantor of the scientific accuracy of natural theology (Gascoigne 1988). The importance of the lawfulness of creation that thus came to dominate English natural theology was disseminated beyond the borders of England by Scottish Newtonians, such as David Gregory (1659–1708) or Archibald Pitcairne (1652–1713), and by those influenced by them, such as Bernard Nieuwentijt (Vermij 1991b). As a result, the place of natural theology in the curriculum again shifted, coming to depend upon the successful teaching of mathematics and natural philosophy, rather than to be taught before or alongside them. At the same time, recent vernacular works of natural theology, including several of those discussed here, began to serve as textbooks in the study of both metaphysics and moral philosophy (Wood 1993: 33–74; Wordsworth 1877: 64–81, 129–32; Sassen 1963: 88–100).

Newtonianism was itself controversial, both within England and overseas. English writers were concerned about Newton's own anti-Trinitarianism. They worried either that his philosophy might be another form of materialism, or that the mathematics on which it was based was irrational and therefore a misleading foundation for truths that were supposed to derive from reason (English 1999; Cantor 1984). In the Netherlands, Newtonianism often found its first footing in the curriculum because of the critical perspective that it provided on Cartesianism and Spinozism, or as the result of the passing of a generation of teachers who had been committed to Cartesianism (Galama 1954: 227–35; Wiesenfeldt 2002: 89–96). Many Lutheran philosophers, by contrast, shared the concerns expressed by Gottfried Wilhelm Leibniz (1646–1716) about the 'General

Scholium', which included fears about the potential materialism of Newton's work (Koyré and Cohen 1961). Nevertheless, eighteenth-century natural theology had the opportunity to base itself on a different kind of lawfulness than that which its precursors had found in nature. At the same time, it was able to advance a far wider range of evidences for divine creation, design, and superintendence than had been available to earlier philosophers. Similarly, it could draw on much wider and more critical accounts of the historical forms of natural religion and of the shared moral world that might cross the divide between the religions of the book (Stroumsa 2010). In contrast, critics of natural theology were no longer so sensitive to its similarities with ancient forms of atheism. Instead, they worried about the extent to which it collapsed religion into an awareness of lawful nature, and, as a result, threatened to make faith too much a matter of fact. Natural theology reached out successfully to an increasingly broad audience. In terms of social status, this stretched from monarchs (for example, the patron of Leibniz and Samuel Clarke, Caroline of Ansbach (1683–1737)) to provincial artisans (such as the Franeker wool carder, Eise Eysinga (1744–1828), who turned his living room into a working model of the lawful universe) (Bertoloni Meli 1999; van Swinden 1851). Practitioners of the design argument could be found, for the first time, on all the inhabited continents of the earth during the eighteenth century, and nature never appeared so wondrous as it did in the discoveries in the South American rainforest or the Pacific Ocean that eighteenth-century naturalists made (Figueira de Faria 2011; Gascoigne 1994: 57–183). Yet the creation of a culture of fact around religion brought with it the danger that other facts might come to make revelation seem less true.

Conclusions

Early modern natural theologies were ubiquitous but limited in their success. Despite playing a changing role in the education of learned readers throughout the period, they remained controversial in most places and at most times. Their place in the curriculum, let alone in wider culture, was often threatened and frequently had to change. They functioned as a means of communication and debate with other cultures, and at the same time exposed scepticism about religion within Christian European culture itself. While confessional divisions did not often scupper arguments in natural theology, competing scientific outlooks threatened the universality of their appeal, especially after the mid-seventeenth century. Yet there remained remarkable resilience in the idea that God and his purposes might be known and understood independently of revelation, and in the theologically subversive claim that they might reach out to all of humanity. Wonder at the bounty or the regularity of nature drew people powerfully to faith more often than materialism or mechanism encouraged them to doubt. Had an eighteenth-century traveller claimed to rediscover paradise, his chances of being believed might have been increased for asserting that its priests indeed practised natural and experimental philosophy (cf. Psalmanaazaar 1704: 290–1).

Acknowledgements

I am grateful to Ian Maclean and Richard Serjeantson for helpful discussions and the provision of relevant materials. Michael Ledger-Lomas and Tabitta van Nouhuys both kindly read drafts of the chapter.

Further Reading

Several works describe clearly the relationship between science and religion in the early modern period. The best of these are Brooke 1991 and the chapters by Henry and Topham in Harrison 2010. Funkenstein 1986 and Harrison 1998 both advance strong claims for particular readings of natural theology. Commentary on their positions as well as much general information about individual natural theologies may be found in van der Meer and Mandelbrote (2008a and 2008b). The history of metaphysics is best approached through the articles of Lohr (1988, 1991, 1999). Gascoigne 1988 provides a good introduction to eighteenth-century material, and relevant examples for this and earlier periods can be found in Kleeberg and Vidal 2007. Daston and Stolleis 2008 provide wide-ranging material about natural law and its implications.

References

Unpublished sources

Cambridge, Emmanuel College, Ms 48: Richard Holdsworth. 'Directions for a Student in the Universitie'. c.1640.
Cambridge, Emmanuel College, Ms 291: Copy of a notebook of Peter Sterry.
London, Royal Society, Ms 247: Papers of David Gregory.

Published sources

Addinall, Peter (1991). *Philosophy and Biblical Interpretation: A Study in Nineteenth-Century Conflict*. Cambridge: Cambridge University Press.
Ahnert, Thomas (2006). *Religion and the Origins of the German Enlightenment*. Rochester, NY: University of Rochester Press.
Albury, W. R. (1978). 'Halley's Ode on the *Principia* of Newton and the Epicurean Revival in England'. *Journal of the History of Ideas* 39: 24–43.
Ariew, Roger (1999). *Descartes and the Last Scholastics*. Ithaca: Cornell University Press.
Ashworth, William B., Jr. (1990). 'Natural History and the Emblematic World View' in *Reappraisals of the Scientific Revolution*. Edited by David C. Lindberg and Robert S. Westman. Cambridge: Cambridge University Press: pp. 303–32.
Bacon, Francis (1605). *The Twoo Bookes…Of the Proficience and Advancement of Learning, Divine and Humane*. London: Henrie Tomes.
Barker, Matthew (1674). *Natural Theology, or, The Knowledge of God, from the Works of Creation*. London: Nathaniel Ranew.
Ben-Zaken, Avner (2011). *Reading 'Ḥayy ibn-Yaqẓān': A Cross-Cultural History of Autodidacticism*. Baltimore: Johns Hopkins University Press.

Bertoloni Meli, D. (1999). 'Caroline, Leibniz and Clarke'. *Journal of the History of Ideas* 60: 469–86.

Birch, Thomas (1744). *The Life of the Honourable Robert Boyle*. London: A. Millar.

Blair, Ann (2000). 'Mosaic Physics and the Search for a Pious Natural Philosophy in the Late Renaissance'. *Isis* 91: 32–58.

Blome, Richard (1686). *The Gentlemans Recreation*. London: Richard Blome.

Boyle, Robert (1686). *A Free Enquiry into the Vulgarly Receiv'd Notion of Nature*. London: John Taylor.

Brockliss, L. W. B. (1987). *French Higher Education in the Seventeenth and Eighteenth Centuries*. Oxford: Oxford University Press.

Brooke, John Hedley (1991). *Science and Religion. Some Historical Perspectives*. Cambridge: Cambridge University Press.

Burnet, Thomas (1681–9). *Telluris theoria sacra*. 2 vols. London: Walter Kettilby.

—— (1684–90). *The Theory of the Earth*. 2 vols. London: Walter Kettilby.

—— (1695–6). *Heilige beshouwinge des aardkloots*. Amsterdam: Daniel van den Dalen.

Burthogge, Richard (1675). *Causa dei, or an Apology for God*. London: Lewis Punchard.

Bury, Emmanuel, and Bernard Meunier, eds. (1993). *Les Pères de l'église au XVIIeme siècle*. Paris: Editions du Cerf.

Byfield, Nicholas (1626). *The Rule of Faith*. London: R. Rounthwaite et al.

Cantor, Geoffrey (1984). 'Berkeley's *The Analyst* Revisited'. *Isis* 75: 668–83.

Cheynell, Francis (1645). *The Man of Honour*. London: Samuel Gellibrand.

Clarke, Desmond M. (1989). *Occult Powers and Hypotheses: Cartesian Natural Philosophy under Louis XIV*. Oxford: Oxford University Press.

Coles, Elisha (1677). *An English Dictionary*. London: Peter Parker.

Coudert, Allison P. (1999). *The Impact of Kabbalah in the Seventeenth Century*. Leiden: Brill.

Creech, Thomas, ed. and trans. (1683). *T. Lucretius Carus. The Epicurean Philosopher, His Six Books 'De Natura Rerum', Done into English Verse*. 2nd edn. Oxford: Anthony Stephens.

Crowther, Kathleen M. (2008). 'Sacred Philosophy, Secular Theology: The Mosaic Physics of Levinus Lemnius (1505-1568) and Francisco Valles (1524-1592)' in *Nature and Scripture in the Abrahamic Religions: Up to 1700*. Vol. II. Edited by Jitse M. van der Meer and Scott Mandelbrote. 2 vols. Leiden: Brill: pp. 397–428.

Cudworth, Ralph (1678). *The True Intellectual System of the Universe*. London: Richard Royston.

Cunningham, Andrew (2000). 'The Identity of Natural Philosophy: A Response to Edward Grant'. *Early Science and Medicine* 5: 259–78.

Cunningham, Andrew and Roger French (1996). *Before Science: The Invention of the Friars' Natural Philosophy*. Aldershot: Scolar Press.

Curry, Patrick (1989). *Prophecy and Power: Astrology in Early Modern England*. Princeton: Princeton University Press.

Daneau, Lambert (1578). *The Wonderfull Woorkmanship of the World*. Translated by T[homas] T[wyne]. London: Andrew Maunsell.

Daston, Lorraine and Michael Stolleis, eds. (2008). *Natural Law and Laws of Nature in Early Modern Europe*. Aldershot: Ashgate.

Ducheyne, Steffen (2005). 'Newton's Training in the Aristotelian Textbook Tradition: From Effects to Causes and Back'. *History of Science* 43: 217–37.

Dweck, Yaacob (2011). *The Scandal of Kabbalah*. Princeton: Princeton University Press.

English, John C. (1999). 'John Hutchinson's Critique of Newtonian Heterodoxy'. *Church History* 68: 581–97.

Feldhay, Rivka (1995). *Galileo and the Church*. Cambridge: Cambridge University Press.

Felfe, Robert (2003). *Naturgeschichte als kunstvolle Synthese. Physikotheologie und Bildpraxis bei Johann Jakob Scheuchzer*. Berlin: Akademie Verlag.

Figueira de Faria, Miguel (2011). 'De Filosofische Reis van Alexandre Rodrigues Ferreira (1783–1792)' in *Terra Brasilis*. Edited by Eddy Stols. Brussels: Ludion: pp. 130–41.

Fitzpatrick, Antonia (2012). 'Mendicant Order Politics and the Status of Christ's Shed Blood'. *Historical Research*, 85–228: 210–22.

Freedman, Joseph S. (1999). *Philosophy and the Arts in Central Europe, 1500–1700*. Aldershot: Variorum.

Friedrich, Markus (2004). *Die Grenzen der Vernunft. Theologie, Philosophie und gelehrte Konflikte am Beispiel des Helmstedter Hofmannsstreits und seiner Wirkungen auf das Luthertum im 1600*. Göttingen: Vandenhoeck und Ruprecht.

Funkenstein, Amos (1986). *Theology and the Scientific Imagination from the Middle Ages to the Seventeenth Century*. Princeton: Princeton University Press.

Gabbey, Alan (1982). 'Philosophia Cartesiana Triumphata: Henry More (1646–1671)' in *Problems of Cartesianism*. Edited by Thomas M. Lennon, John M. Nicholas, and John W. Davis. Kingston and Montreal: McGill-Queen's University Press: pp. 171–250.

Galama, Sybrand Haije Michiel (1954). *Het wijsgerig onverwijs aan de Hogeschool te Franeker (1585–1811)*. Franeker: T. Wever.

Gale, Theophilus (1670). *The Court of the Gentiles. Part II: Of Philosophie*. Oxford: Thomas Gilbert.

Garber, Daniel (1992). *Descartes' Metaphysical Physics*. Chicago: Chicago University Press.

Gascoigne, John (1988). 'From Bentley to the Victorians: The Rise and Fall of British Newtonian Natural Theology'. *Science in Context* 2: 219–56.

——(1994). *Joseph Banks and the English Enlightenment*. Cambridge: Cambridge University Press.

Gaukroger, Stephen (2006). *The Emergence of a Scientific Culture: Science and the Shaping of Modernity, 1210–1685*. Oxford: Oxford University Press.

Glanvill, Joseph (1661). *The Vanity of Dogmatizing*. London: Henry Eversden.

——(1681). *Saducismus Triumphatus: Or, Full and Plain Evidences concerning Witches and Apparitions*. London: J. Collins and S. Lownds.

Gliozzi, Giuliano (1977). *Adamo e il nuovo mondo*. Florence: La Nuova Italia.

Goudriaan, Aza (1999). *Philosophische Gotteserkenntnis bei Suárez und Descartes, im Zusammenhang mit der niederländischen reformierten Theologie und Philosophie des 17. Jahrhunderts*. Leiden: Brill.

Grafton, Anthony (1991). *Defenders of the Text*. Cambridge, MA: Harvard University Press.

Grant, Edward (1996). *The Foundations of Modern Science in the Middle Ages*. Cambridge: Cambridge University Press.

——(2010). *The Nature of Natural Philosophy in the Late Middle Ages*. Washington, DC: Catholic University of America Press.

Hacking, Ian (1975). *The Emergence of Probability*. Cambridge: Cambridge University Press.

Haller, Elisabeth (1940). *Die barocken Stilmerkmale in der englischen lateinischen und deutschen Fassung von Dr Thomas Burnets Theory of the Earth*. Bern: A. Francke.

Hanegraaff, Wouter J. (2012). *Esotericism and the Academy: Rejected Knowledge in Western Culture*. Cambridge: Cambridge University Press.

Harrison, Peter (1995). 'Newtonian Science, Miracles, and the Laws of Nature'. *Journal of the History of Ideas* 56: 531–53.

—— (1998). *The Bible, Protestantism, and the Rise of Natural Science*. Cambridge: Cambridge University Press.

—— (2007). *The Fall of Man and the Foundations of Science*. Cambridge: Cambridge University Press.

—— (2008). 'Hermeneutics and Natural Knowledge in the Reformers' in *Nature and Scripture in the Abrahamic Religions: Up to 1700*. Vol. I. Edited by Jitse M. van der Meer and Scott Mandelbrote. 2 vols. Leiden: Brill: pp. 341–62.

—— (2010). *The Cambridge Companion to Science and Religion*. Cambridge: Cambridge University Press.

Heyberger, Bernard (1994). *Les Chrétiens du Proche-Orient au temps de la Réforme catholique*. Rome: Ecole Française de Rome.

Heyd, Michael (1982). *Between Orthodoxy and Enlightenment: Jean-Robert Chouet and the Introduction of Cartesian Science in the Academy of Geneva*. The Hague: Nijhoff.

—— (1995). *'Be Sober and Reasonable': The Critique of Enthusiasm in the Seventeenth and Eighteenth Centuries*. Leiden: Brill.

Hillgarth, J. N. (1971). *Ramon Lull and Lullism in Fourteenth-Century France*. Oxford: Oxford University Press.

Hobbes, Thomas. (1991). *Leviathan*. Edited by Richard Tuck. Cambridge: Cambridge University Press.

Hooykaas, R. (1972). *Religion and the Rise of Modern Science*. Edinburgh: Edinburgh University Press.

Hotson, Howard (2007). *Commonplace Learning: Ramism and its German Manifestations, 1543–1630*. Oxford: Oxford University Press.

Hurlbutt, Robert H., III (1965). *Hume, Newton and the Design Argument*. Lincoln: University of Nebraska Press.

Hutton, Sarah (1992). 'Edward Stillingfleet, Henry More, and the Decline of *Moses Atticus*: A Note on Seventeenth-Century Anglican Apologetics' in *Philosophy, Science, and Religion in England 1640–1700*. Edited by Richard Kroll, Richard Ashcraft, and Perez Zagorin. Cambridge: Cambridge University Press: pp. 68–84.

—— (2006). 'Iconisms, Enthusiasm and Origen: Henry More Reads the Bible' in *Scripture and Scholarship in Early Modern England*. Edited by Ariel Hessayon and Nicholas Keene. Aldershot: Ashgate: pp. 192–207.

Israel, Jonathan I. (2001). *Radical Enlightenment: Philosophy and the Making of Modernity 1650–1750*. Oxford: Oxford University Press.

Jorink, Eric (2006). *Het Boeck der Natuere. Nederlandse geleerden en de wonderen van Gods schepping, 1575–1715*. Leiden: Primavera.

Joy, Lynn Sumida (1987). *Gassendi the Atomist*. Cambridge: Cambridge University Press.

Katchen, Aaron L. (1984). *Christian Hebraists and Dutch Rabbis*. Cambridge, MA: Harvard University Press.

Keynes, Geoffrey (1977). *John Ray, 1627–1705: A Bibliography, 1660–1970*. Amsterdam: Van Heusden.

Klein, Lawrence E. (1994). *Shaftesbury and the Culture of Politeness*. Cambridge: Cambridge University Press.

Klaver, J. M. I. (1997). *Geology and Religious Sentiment: The Effect of Geological Discoveries on English Society and Literature Between 1829 and 1859*. Leiden: Brill.

Kleeberg, Bernhard and Fernando Vidal, eds. (2007). *Believing Nature, Knowing God*. Special Issue of *Science in Context* 20: 3.

Koyré, Alexandre and I. Bernard Cohen (1961). 'The Case of the Missing *Tanquam*: Leibniz, Newton, & Clarke'. *Isis* 52: 555–66.

Kusukawa, Sachiko (1995). *The Transformation of Natural Philosophy*. Cambridge: Cambridge University Press.

—— (1999). 'Lutheran Uses of Aristotle: A Comparison of Jacob Schegk and Philip Melanchthon' in *Philosophy in the Sixteenth and Seventeenth Centuries*. Edited by Constance Blackwell and Sachiko Kusukawa. Aldershot: Ashgate: pp. 169–88.

Leeuwen, H. G. van (1970). *The Problem of Certainty in English Thought, 1630–1690*. 2nd edn. The Hague: Nijhoff.

Lemnius, Levinus (1574). *De miracvlis occvltis natvrae*. Antwerp: Plantin.

Lewis, Rhodri (2006). 'Of "Origenian Platonisme": Joseph Glanvill on Pre-Existence of Souls'. *Huntington Library Quarterly* 69: 267–300.

Lohr, Charles H. (1988). 'Metaphysics' in *The Cambridge History of Renaissance Philosophy*. Edited by Charles B. Schmitt et al. Cambridge: Cambridge University Press: pp. 201–35.

—— (1991). 'The Sixteenth-Century Transformation of the Aristotelian Division of the Speculative Sciences' in *The Shapes of Knowledge from the Renaissance to the Enlightenment*. Edited by Donald R. Kelley and Richard H. Popkin. Dordrecht: Kluwer: pp. 49–58.

—— (1999). 'Metaphysics and Natural Philosophy as Sciences: The Catholic and the Protestant Views in the Sixteenth and Seventeenth Centuries' in *Philosophy in the Sixteenth and Seventeenth Centuries*. Edited by Constance Blackwell and Sachiko Kusukawa. Aldershot: Ashgate: pp. 280–95.

McGuire, J. E. and Martin Tamny, eds. (1983). *Certain Philosophical Questions: Newton's Trinity Notebook*. Cambridge: Cambridge University Press.

McMullin, Ernan, ed. (2005). *The Church and Galileo*. Notre Dame: University of Notre Dame Press.

Meer, Jitse M. van der and Scott Mandelbrote, eds. (2008a). *Nature and Scripture in the Abrahamic Religions: Up to 1700*. 2 vols. Leiden: Brill.

—— (2008b). *Nature and Scripture in the Abrahamic Religions: 1700-Present*. 2 vols. Leiden: Brill.

Methuen, Charlotte (1999). 'The Teaching of Aristotle in Late Sixteenth-Century Tübingen' in *Philosophy in the Sixteenth and Seventeenth Centuries*. Edited by Constance Blackwell and Sachiko Kusukawa. Aldershot: Ashgate: pp. 189–205.

Mintz, Samuel I. (1962). *The Hunting of Leviathan*. Cambridge: Cambridge University Press.

More, Henry (1653a). *An Antidote against Atheism*. London: Roger Daniel.

—— (1653b). *Conjectura Cabbalistica*. London: James Flesher.

Mornay, Philippe Duplessis (1605). *De Veritate religionis Christianae*. Leiden: Andreas Cloucquius.

Mortimer, Sarah (2010). *Reason and Religion in the English Revolution: The Challenge of Socinianism*. Cambridge: Cambridge University Press.

Müller, Klaus (1998). *Tora für die Völker*. Berlin: Institut Kirche und Judentum.

Mungello, David, ed. (1994). *The Chinese Rites Controversy*. Nettetal: Steyler Verlag.

Müsch, Irmgard (2000). *Geheiligte Naturwissenschaft. Die Kupfer-Bibel des Johann Jakob Scheuchzer*. Göttingen: Vandenhoeck und Ruprecht.

Nadler, Steven (2001). *Spinoza's Heresy*. Oxford: Oxford University Press.

Neele, Adriaan C. (2009). *Petrus van Mastricht (1630-1706). Reformed Orthodoxy: Method and Piety*. Leiden: Brill.

Newton, Isaac (1713). *Philosophiae naturalis principia mathematica.* Edited by Roger Cotes and Richard Bentley. 2nd edn. Cambridge: Cambridge University Press.

Nicolson, Marjorie Hope (1997). *Mountain Gloom and Mountain Glory.* Edited by William Cronon. Seattle: University of Washington Press.

Ogilvie, Brian W. (2005). 'Natural History, Ethics, and Physico-Theology' in *Historia: Empiricism and Erudition in Early Modern Europe.* Edited by Gianna Pomata and Nancy G. Siraisi. Cambridge, MA: MIT Press: pp. 75–103.

Osler, Margaret J. (1994). *Divine Will and the Mechanical Philosophy.* Cambridge: Cambridge University Press.

Pagden, Anthony (1982). *The Fall of Natural Man: The American Indian and the Origins of Comparative Ethnology.* Cambridge: Cambridge University Press.

Park, Katharine (2011). 'Allegories of Knowledge' in *Prints and the Pursuit of Knowledge in Early Modern Europe.* Edited by Susan Dackerman. Cambridge, MA: Harvard Art Museum and Yale University Press: pp. 358–65.

Parker, Samuel (1666). *A Free and Impartial Censure of the Platonick Philosophie.* Oxford: Richard Davis.

Parkin, Jon (2007). *Taming the Leviathan.* Cambridge: Cambridge University Press.

Pascal, Blaise (1688). *Monsieur Pascall's Thoughts, Meditations, and Prayers.* Translated by Joseph Walker. London: Jacob Tonson.

Pepys, Samuel (1926). *Private Correspondence and Miscellaneous Papers.* Edited by J. R. Tanner. 2 vols. London: Bell.

Pinto, Vivian de Sola (1934). *Peter Sterry: Platonist and Puritan.* Cambridge: Cambridge University Press.

Psalmanaazaar, George (1704). *An Historical and Geographical Description of Formosa.* London: Daniel Brown.

Rastwick, John (2010). *The Life of John Rastwick, 1650–1727.* Edited by Andrew Cambers. Cambridge: Cambridge University Press for the Camden Society.

Ray, John (1691). *The Wisdom of God Manifested in the Works of the Creation.* London: Samuel Smith.

Rees, Graham (1975a). 'Francis Bacon's Semi-Paracelsian Cosmology'. *Ambix* 22: 81–101.

—— (1975b). 'Francis Bacon's Semi-Paracelsian Cosmology and the *Great Instauration*'. *Ambix* 22: 161–73.

—— (1977). 'The Fate of Bacon's Cosmology in the 17th Century'. *Ambix* 24: 27–38.

Rivers, Isabel (1993). ' "Galen's Muscles": Wilkins, Hume, and the Educational Use of the Argument from Design'. *Historical Journal* 36: 577–97.

—— (2000). *Reason, Grace, and Sentiment.* Vol. II: *Shaftesbury to Hume.* Cambridge: Cambridge University Press.

Sarasohn, Lisa T. (1996). *Gassendi's Ethics.* Ithaca: Cornell University Press.

Sassen, Ferd. (1941). *Het oudste wijsgeerig onderwijs te Leiden (1575–1619).* Amsterdam: Noord-Hollandsche Uitgevers Maatschappij.

—— (1961). *Johannes Horthemels. De laatste 'Aristotelische' hoogleraar te Utrecht.* Amsterdam: Noord-Hollandsche Uitgevers Maatschappij.

—— (1962). *Het wijsgerig onderwijs aan de Illustre School te Breda (1646–1669).* Amsterdam: Noord-Hollandsche Uitgevers Maatschappij.

—— (1963). *Het wijsgerig onderwijs aan de Illustre School te 's-Hertogenbosch.* Amsterdam: Noord-Hollandsche Uitgevers Maatschappij.

Schär, Max (1979). *Das Nachleben des Origenes im Zeitalter des Humanismus.* Basel: Helbing und Lichtenhahn.

Scheuchzer, Johann Jakob (1723). *Herbarium Diluvianum.* New edn. Leiden: Van der Aa.

Schmitt, Charles B. (1967). *Gianfrancesco Pico della Mirandola (1469–1533) and His Critique of Aristotle.* The Hague: Nijhoff.

—— (1983). *Aristotle and the Renaissance.* Cambridge, MA: Harvard University Press.

Schwartz, Daniel. ed. (2012). *Interpreting Suárez.* Cambridge: Cambridge University Press.

Serjeantson, Richard (forthcoming). 'Francis Bacon and the "Interpretation of Nature".'

Shapiro, Barbara J. (2000). *A Culture of Fact. England, 1550–1720.* Ithaca: Cornell University Press.

Smith, Pamela H. (2004). *The Body of the Artisan: Art and Experience in the Scientific Revolution.* Chicago: Chicago University Press.

Spellman, W. M. (1988). *John Locke and the Problem of Depravity.* Oxford: Oxford University Press.

Spinoza, Baruch de (1955). *On the Improvement of the Understanding: The Ethics. Correspondence.* Edited and translated by R. H. M. Elwes. New York: Dover.

Sprat, Thomas (1667). *The History of the Royal Society of London, for the Improving of Natural Knowledge.* London: John Martyn.

Stroumsa, Guy G. (2010). *A New Science: The Discovery of Religion in the Age of Reason.* Cambridge, MA: Harvard University Press.

Stubbe, Henry (1671). *A Censure upon Certain Passages Contained in the History of the Royall Society.* Oxford: Richard Davis.

Swinden, J. H. van (1851). *Beschrijving van het Rijks-Planetarium te Franeker.* Edited by W. Eekhoff. Schoonhoven: Van Nooten.

Tenison, Thomas (1670). *The Creed of Mr Hobbes.* London: Francis Tyton.

Thomson, Keith (2005). *Before Darwin: Reconciling God and Nature.* New Haven: Yale University Press.

Tuck, Richard (1993). *Philosophy and Government, 1572–1651.* Cambridge: Cambridge University Press.

Vallesius, Franciscus (1622). *De Iis qvae scripta sunt, physice in libris sacris, sive de sacra philosophia.* Lyon: Antonius Soubron.

Verbeek, Theo (1992). *Descartes and the Dutch.* Carbondale: University of Illinois Press.

Vermij, Rienk. 1991a. 'Le Spinozisme en Hollande: le cercle de Tschirnhaus'. *Cahiers Spinoza* 6: 145–68.

—— (1991b). *Secularisering en Natuurwetenschap in de zeventiende en achttiende eeuw: Bernard Nieuwentijt.* Amsterdam: Rodopi.

Walsham, Alexandra (2011). *The Reformation of the Landscape.* Oxford: Oxford University Press.

Ward, Seth (1652). *A Philosophicall Essay.* Oxford: Leonard Lichfield.

Watson, Richard A. (1987). *The Breakdown of Cartesian Metaphysics.* Atlantic Highlands: Humanities Press.

Webster, John (1654). *Academiarum Examen, or The Examination of the Academies.* London: Giles Calvert.

Westfall, Richard S. (1982). 'Isaac Newton's *Theologiae gentilis origines philosophicae*' in *The Secular Mind.* Edited by W. Warren Wagar. New York: Holmes and Meier: pp. 15–34.

Whitby, Daniel (1705). *A Discourse of the Necessity and Usefulness of the Christian Revelation; By Reason of the Corruptions of the Principles of Natural Religion among Jews and Heathens.* London: A. and J. Churchill.

Wiesenfeldt, Gerhard (2002). *Leerer Raum in Minervas Haus. Experimentelle Naturlehre an der Universität Leiden, 1675–1715.* Amsterdam: KNAW.

Wilkins, John (1648). *Mathematicall Magick.* London: Samuel Gellibrand.

—— (1678). *Of the Principles and Duties of Natural Religion.* London: T. Basset et al.

Wood, Paul B. (1993). *The Aberdeen Enlightenment: The Arts Curriculum in the Eighteenth Century.* Aberdeen: Aberdeen University Press.

Wordsworth, Christopher (1877). *Scholae Academicae.* Cambridge: Cambridge University Press.

Wright, Thomas (1971). *An Original Theory of the Universe, 1750.* Edited by Michael A. Hoskin. London: Macdonald.

Yolton, John W. (1956). *John Locke and the Way of Ideas.* Oxford: Oxford University Press.

Zuidervaart, Huib J. (1995). *Speculatie, wetenschap en vernuft.* Leeuwarden: Fryske Akademy.

CHAPTER 6

....

NINETEENTH-CENTURY NATURAL THEOLOGY

....

MATTHEW D. EDDY

PHILOSOPHERS AND THEOLOGIANS

....

DURING the nineteenth century, natural theology was 'natural' because the evidence was taken from direct observation of the natural world (including the human body), or from observations made in the increasingly specialized settings of science. It was 'theological' because such evidence was interpreted in light of the attributes of God laid out in the Bible and in Christian doctrine; however the extent to which the evidence of revelation was augmented or superseded by the facts provided by reason varied from author to author (Powell 1838). In formal educational settings, as well as within the wider world of print culture, several terms were used synonymously with 'natural theology', including, 'design-argument', 'argument for design', 'argument from design', 'the argument from mind', 'doctrine of teleology', and 'doctrine of final causes'. Since these terms were used loosely by some thinkers, and more specifically by others, it is usually a good idea to consider natural theologies in light of the author's education, doctrinal convictions, personal experiences, and style of writing. At the most basic level, primary school students were often instructed to observe the wisdom of God evinced in nature, and university students were taught that there were generally three kinds of natural theological arguments: cosmological, teleological, and moral (Dick 1851; Fleming 1858). These were used across the denominational spectrum and appeared in a variety of genres. For example, after returning from Calcutta, the missionary Joseph Mullens succinctly summed up the three strands of natural theology in *The Religious Aspects of Hindu Philosophy* (Mullens 1860) in the following manner:

> There are three branches of the argument of Natural Theology usually employed by English writers to prove the existence of God. First: the argument from existence and causation. Second: the argument from mind. And thirdly: the argument from design exhibited both in mind and matter.

From a traditional standpoint, cosmological arguments traced the affects of primary and secondary causes—forces, laws, and motion. Teleological arguments addressed final causes as evinced in nature or the body—that is, the final shape or form of objects like hands, leaves, and crystals. Drawing on the long-standing Christian belief that all humans were made in the image of God (*imago dei*), moral arguments focussed on final causes related to the structure of the human mind. Proponents of this viewpoint usually held that the moral capacity of humans pointed to the presence of a divine moral agent.

When it came to structuring design arguments, most authors avoided deductive logic, especially since it was widely associated (rightly or wrongly) with the defunct scholasticism that had been overturned by the scientific revolution. The majority of arguments were a posteriori and inductive. They were seldom presented in a straightforward syllogistic format and they exhibited the usual ambiguities of language that so frequently add colour to arguments of any age. Additionally, design arguments were filled with verbs like 'create', 'make', and 'fashion' that connoted purposeful causation, and authors employed divine names like 'Maker', 'Law Giver' and 'Artificer' that inherently pointed to an intelligent agent. These kinds of volitionally charged words were common in academic discourse, including textbooks that addressed logic, which many styled a science in itself. A good example of this kind of language occurs in the section on scientific reasoning in J. J. Tigert's widely used *Hand-Book of Logic*. Like many Victorian philosophers, he couched laws in the language of agency by asserting that 'Laws of nature are not self-executive any more than natural causes are self-creative' (Tigert 1889: 98). Sir William Hamilton, one of the most influential logicians of the century, followed a similar path in his work, most notably in his translation of Wilhelm Esser's definition of a universal law (natural or mental): 'a law is that which applies to all cases without exception, and from which a deviation is ever, and everywhere, impossible, or at least, *unallowed*' (Hamilton 1866: 25; Day 1865: 17). Tigert was professor of moral philosophy at Vanderbilt University and Hamilton was Edinburgh's professor of logic and metaphysics. Though both professors lived in different countries and came from different educational backgrounds, they are representative of the many instructors who taught logic in religiously supported or administered colleges or universities in the Americas, Europe, and its colonies. Anthropomorphisms abounded in such settings and implicitly functioned as metaphorical and analogical frameworks for design arguments (Wilson 1861; Coppée 1858; Garden 1867). This point is a particularly important one, especially when one considers that twentieth-century commentators on the history of natural theology have sometimes dismissed analogical argumentation as being 'rhetorical'. As stated in Richard Whately's widely read *Elements of Logic*, 'analogy is the resemblance of *ratios* (or relations)' (Whately 1867: 123). This view was shared by many logicians and analogies remained a key part of logic until the late nineteenth century when they were extinguished by the various forms of probability being employed by scientists and government administrators alike.

Natural theology arguments seldom came in neat analytic packages, especially since the traditional division between teleological and cosmological arguments was altered, especially in Britain, by Isaac Newton and his followers. Newtonian natural theology was a diverse intellectual movement, but two recurring tenets retained strength into the twentieth century. The first was that God actively superimposed force upon animate and inanimate matter. The second was the equating of the divine attributes, namely omniscience and omnipresence, to the forces of nature—a move that fused a biblical understanding of God with empirical observation. Much of Newton's natural theology was slowly released to the reading public through the pens of disciples like Richard Bentley and, just as importantly, through posthumous publications that continued to pour off the press well into the nineteenth century. As these appeared in print, they were duly put into the service of design arguments. For example, Thomas Chalmers, Edinburgh's professor of divinity, seized upon the popularity of a recent edition of Newton's letters to Bentley in *On the Power, Wisdom and Goodness of God* (1833). In his comments on natural laws, Chalmers included several quotations from Newton's letters, including the remark that 'the growth of new systems out of old ones, without the mediation of a divine power, seems to be apparently absurd' (Chalmers 1834: 28; Nichols 1822). Such references to Newton were common and the upshot of his theology of nature was that the proofs of design in the heavens, the world, the body, and the mind were undergirded by divinely guided forces.

Such an interlocked view of design influenced intellectual culture throughout the century. William Paley's best-selling *Natural Theology*—see fig. 6.1—suggested that specimens of anatomical and planetary design were caused by divinely appointed forces that guided the growth of bodies and the formation of matter. As noted in the numerous nineteenth-century editions of Dugald Stewart's *Elements of the Philosophy of the Human Mind* (1792–1827), the collocation of primary, secondary, and final causes created a design argument that could be used to embrace just about any kind of regularity that occurred in the natural world. This sentiment continued to be echoed in the philosophically calibrated theology of notable professors like Cambridge's William Whewell, St Andrews' John Tulloch, and Princeton's James McCosh (Whewell 1833, 1845; Tulloch 1855; McCosh 1888). When it came to evolutionary causation, McCosh held that 'It is caused always by divine arrangement, by means of the development of one thing from another, with which it is thereby connected.' Such a view allowed him to conclude that 'evolution does not undermine the argument from Final Cause, but rather strengthens it' (McCosh 1888: 64, 66). However, the chain of events that stretched of a first cause to a final cause could sometimes be long and the precise involvement of a divine power at each stage was interpreted differently. Some marvelled at the number of links in a long causal chain. In the words of Oxford's Baden Powell: 'If the number of links were truly infinite, so much more infinite the skill of its framer' (Powell 1856: 153). Other professors, like Edinburgh's James Buchanan, Bangor's Enoch Pond, and, later in the century, Princeton's Benjamin Breckinridge Warfield, saw the finger of God continually turning the wheels of nature (Buchanan 1857; Pond 1867; Livingstone and Noll 2000).

Within higher education settings, natural theology continued to influence candidates for holy orders, especially in lectures on dogmatics and apologetics. This was reflected in the 1887 edition of the Church of England's *Outlines of Theological Study*, where its section on probable evidence states: 'Paley's *Natural Theology*, edited by Le Gros Clark, and

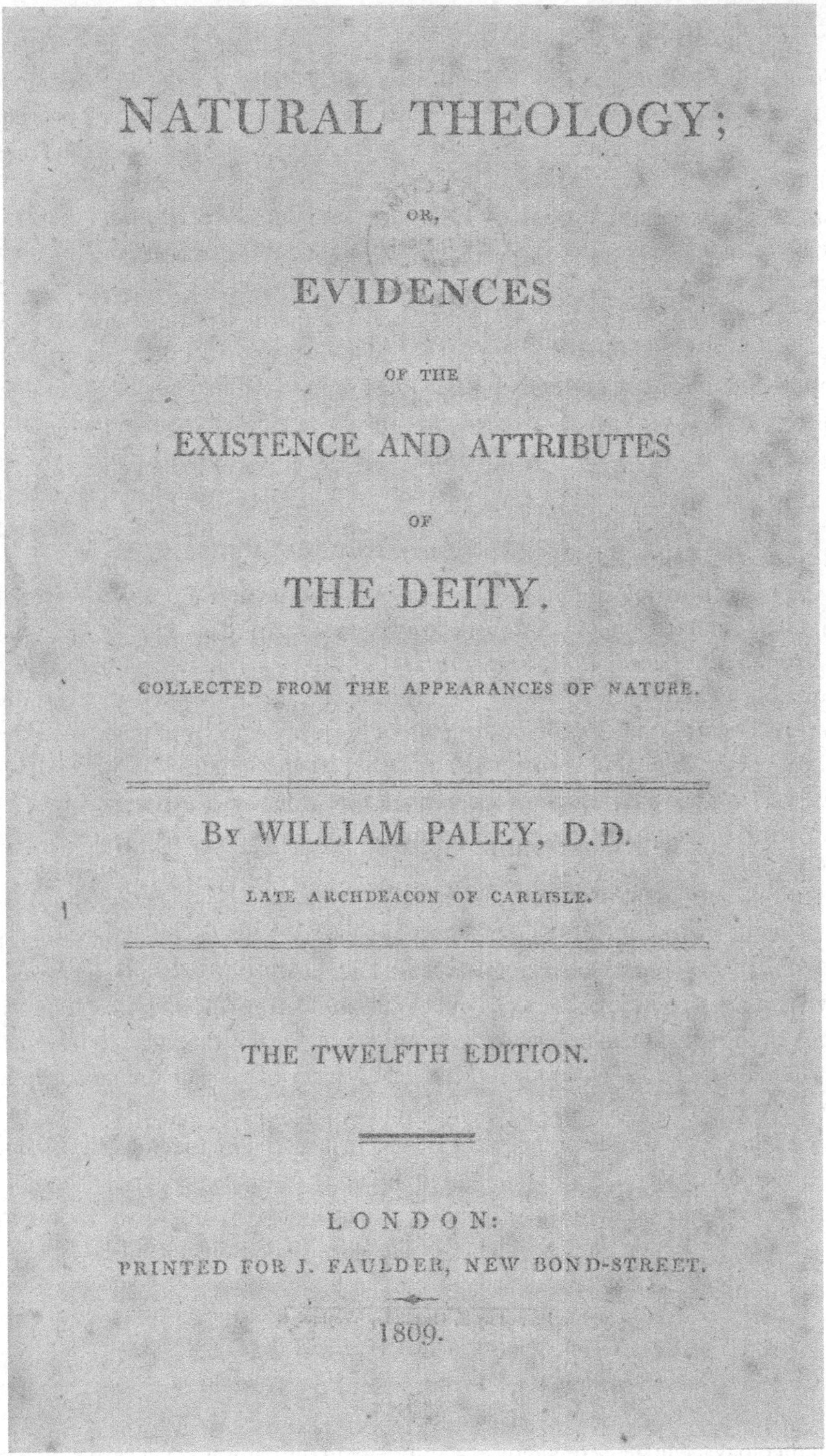

NATURAL THEOLOGY;

OR,

EVIDENCES

OF THE

EXISTENCE AND ATTRIBUTES

OF

THE DEITY.

COLLECTED FROM THE APPEARANCES OF NATURE.

BY WILLIAM PALEY, D.D.

LATE ARCHDEACON OF CARLISLE.

THE TWELFTH EDITION.

LONDON:
PRINTED FOR J. FAULDER, NEW BOND-STREET.

1809.

FIGURE 6.1 Title-page, William Paley, *Natural Theology; or, Evidences of the Existence and Attributes of the Deity* (London: Faulder, 1809).

Bishop Barry's *Natural Theology*, should be studied under this head, together with Pearson and Barrow. Flint's *Theism* and *Antitheistic Theories* will be the best general guides, especially in reference to modern controversies' (Conference upon the Training of Candidates for Holy Orders 1887: 52; see also Le Gros Clark 1875; Barry 1880; Flint 1876, 1879). A chronological perusal of the foregoing books would reveal that, as the nineteenth century moved forward, teleological and cosmological arguments became explicitly, sometimes inseparably, linked to evidence provided by the rapidly expanding disciplinary domains of science. New examples from thermodynamics and ether were embraced, while old stand-bys, like the finger and the eye, were retained. Like arguments that used cutting-edge scientific knowledge to promote the benefits of technological consumerism, the use of new evidence in natural theologies provided more tantalizing examples for thinkers usually predisposed to a foregone conclusion. There were, however, those of faith who became troubled over the infinite regress of material causes and instances of artefactual *naturalia* (Edgerton 2006). Many of these people turned to moral arguments for the existence of God.

An important proponent of the moral argument was Immanuel Kant, whose work had a strong impact on Continental Europe from the 1790s forward, and in the Anglophone world from the 1830s onward. For Kant, the fact that humans were capable of recognizing and pursuing good (over evil) pointed to existence of a 'highest good'—that is, a divine attribute of God. He made this point throughout his many works, but it is voiced clearly in chapter 5 of the *Critique of Practical Reason* (1788). There he states, 'the highest good in the world is only possible insofar as a supreme cause of nature is assumed, which has a causality corresponding to the moral disposition' (cited in Byrne 2007: 85; see also Barth 2001: Chs. 2, 3, and 7). As evinced throughout Kant's earlier work, he was no stranger to teleological or cosmological arguments (Kant 1994). Yet, like many of the scholars who followed in his footsteps, he believed that the inherently moral capacity of the human mind offered the strongest proof of God's existence. This view, however, received criticism from various intellectual corners. For liberally minded philosophers like John Stuart Mill, one of the biggest challenges to the moral argument was theodicy. In his posthumous *Three Essays on Religion* (1874), Mill effectively criticized the divine attribute of goodness, suggesting that it was completely undermined by evil and suffering in the world (Sell 2004). On the other end of the intellectual spectrum, theologically orthodox thinkers like James McCosh continued to maintain that teleological and cosmological arguments were inherently more rational than the intuitive nature of the moral arguments provided by Kantian transcendental philosophy (McCosh 1866: 377–8).

SAVANTS AND SCIENTISTS

Natural theology facilitated a metaphysical mind-set in the natural sciences in which God was treated as the cause of the forces associated with gravity, stratification, electromagnetism, thermodynamics and, sometimes, life itself. For many scientists, finding order in the world through the process of scientific discovery pointed to the presence of the divine orderer of revealed religion. This kind of search was of course influenced by the doctrinal training of a given scientist but, more often than not, it was existential in nature, allowing inquisitive minds to find meaning in the world and motivating them to study the laws and principles of nature. Statements to this effect were made in university courses near the beginning of the century. But after the Napoleonic Wars, science professors started to stress the different, but complementary, kinds of evidence presented in the Book of Nature and the Book of Scripture. In the physical sciences this distinction was frequently made in lectures given in the nascent discipline of geology. Benjamin Silliman, Yale's professor of chemistry and geology, taught his students during the 1820s that 'geological facts are not only consistent with sacred history, but that their tendency is to illustrate and confirm it' (Silliman 1829: 7). Yet, as the century progressed, the increased disciplinary specialization reflected in science curricula taught across the Americas, Europe, and its colonies facilitated the removal of specific references to natural theology, and to the arts and humanities in general. But this silence should not be mistaken as absence. Natural theology was communicated to science students orally in tutorials and during fieldwork. A clearer picture of this more intimate side of science is sometimes available in private notes and letters. When these are consulted, deeply held theologies of nature emerge in the work of leading physical scientists like Michael Faraday, William Crookes, and James Clerk Maxwell. Indeed, James Clerk Maxwell once stated in a letter that:

> I think that each individual man should do all he can to impress his own mind with the extent, the order, and the unity of the universe, and should carry these ideas with him as he reads such passages as the 1st chapter of the Epistle to Colossians (see 'Lightfoot on Colossians,' p. 182), just as enlarged conceptions of the extent and unity of the world of life may be of service to us in reading Psalm viii., Heb. ii. 6, etc. [Campbell and Garnett 1884: 394]

Maxwell, like many scientists of his generation, saw the Bible through the framework of higher criticism, but it was still treated as an indispensible guide to the attributes of God so amply illustrated by the regularities of nature. On the other side of the coin, some scientists of faith were keen to bolster the natural theology taught in divinity schools and seminaries. Such was the case for John Trowbridge, Harvard's assistant professor of physics, when he wrote a letter to *The Popular Science Monthly* in 1875 claiming, 'If the young student of theology has had a rigid scientific training, it will prove of great advantage to him in the future' (Trowbridge 1875: 737).

The natural theology of curricular settings was also presented outside the academy in the ever-growing corpus of journalistic pieces written by scientists. Here Christian teleology abounded. Although some university professorships offered moderate salaries, many scientists pursued their experiments outside their full-time commitments as teachers, lecturers, tutors, curators, shipmen, clergy, and government officials. To make ends meet, or to maintain a more comfortable living, many scientists wrote articles and books for popular consumption, or gave lectures at the many literary and philosophical societies that sprung up throughout the century in Britain, as well as in American venues like Boston's Lowell Institute and New York's Brooklyn Institute. A good early example of this kind of natural theology is the set of eight *Bridgewater Treatises* published during the 1830s. These treatises were written by leading scientists (each of whom was paid a handsome £1,000) and they focussed on specific aspects of nature. Thus, like the natural sciences, natural theologies written by scientists were becoming more specialized. As intimated earlier, physicists continued to walk the meaningful path of Newtonian natural theology, tending to focus on laws and forces. New ideas like entropy and ether theory were also brought under the wing of design and revealed religion. A good example of this practice occurred in 1875 when Balfour Stewart and Peter Guthrie Tait published *The Unseen Universe*. Stewart was professor of natural philosophy at Owens College (Manchester) and Tait occupied the University of Edinburgh's chair of natural philosophy. They used energy physics to argue that 'the visible universe has been developed by an intelligence resident in the unseen'. Here the 'unseen' was the all-pervasive ether that bathed the universe and 'intelligence' was interpreted to be God as described in key passages of the Bible (Stewart and Tait 1880). By 1880 this book had gone through nine editions, therein demonstrating the popularity of the subject matter.

Not to be outdone, chemists also added their voice to the chorus of specialized natural theologies. Their works tended to concentrate on how the elements and chemical reactions facilitated optimum conditions for human life. The physiologist William Prout wrote about these topics in *Chemistry, Meteorology, and the Function of Digestion* (1834) and the tradition continued in the work of Josiah Parsons Cooke, Harvard's professor of chemistry and mineralogy, and George Wilson, Edinburgh's professor of technology and director of the Industrial Museum of Scotland (Cooke 1864; Wilson 1862—see fig. 6.2). Sitting in the conceptual space between the foregoing cosmological to microcosmic theologies of matter was a final subgenre that focussed on geology and which interpreted the Genesis cosmogony in relation to recent geological and palaeontological evidence. William Buckland, Oxford's professor of geology, was one of the leading authors of such geological theology, sometimes called 'scriptural geology', early in the century. His *Reliquiæ Diluvianæ* (1823) and *Geology and Mineralogy Considered with Reference to Natural Theology* (1836) influenced a generation of earth scientists, palaeontologists, and theologians alike. Other notable authors on this topic were the savant Hugh Miller, Princeton's Arnold Guyot, the University of Michigan's Alexander Winchell, and, more implicitly, Harvard's Nathanial Southgate Shaler (Miller 1857; Winchell 1870; Guyot 1884; Shaler 1898; King 1850). Guyot aptly characterized the method of many geological theologians in the 1884 preface of his *Creation, or, the Biblical Cosmogony in the Light of Modern Science*: 'Let us receive from the Bible, on trust, the fundamental truths to which human science cannot attain, and let the results of scientific inquiry serve as a running commentary to help us rightly to understand the comprehensive statements of the Biblical account'. One of the side effects of interpreting the Mosaic record and the stratigraphical record in tandem was that it sometimes motivated geologists of faith to mix revealed religion with palaeontology and human origins—a point well evinced in the fact that all of the foregoing geologists published works on these topics (Miller 1858; Guyot 1849; Winchell 1878; Shaler 1904; see also Livingstone 2008).

RELIGIO CHEMICI.

ESSAYS

By GEORGE WILSON, F.R.S.E.

Late Regius Professor of Technology in the University of Edinburgh.

All things were made by Him ; and without Him was not anything made that was
made. In Him was life ; and the life was the Light of Men.—JOHN i. 3, 4.

London and Cambridge:

MACMILLAN AND CO.

1862.

FIGURE 6.2 Title-page, George Wilson, *Religio Chemici. Essays* (London: MacMillan, 1862).

Throughout the century the proliferation of evolutionary theories based on transmutation and natural selection challenged scientists to rethink the relationship between the life sciences and natural theology, especially as envisioned by Enlightenment empiricism. Even before Darwin's *Origin*, thinkers influenced by transmutationism had turned to versions of Neoplatonism that advocated a divine unity of nature in which natural forces adhered to a purposeful blueprint that had existed since the beginning of time. Within the life sciences, this viewpoint influenced natural theology as interpreted by leading scientists like William Whewell and Georges Cuvier, and by scientifically informed savants like Samuel Taylor Coleridge and Johann Wolfgang von Goethe. It was also promoted after the publication of *Origin* by a number of Darwin's followers, including Louis Agassiz, Harvard's professor of natural history (see Yeo 1979; Nartonis 2005; Hedley Brooke 1991: 246; Nisbet 1972: 6–22). Such appeals to a supreme and transcendental artificer often stemmed from a deep-seated belief in the existential relevance of the revealed truths of the Bible. Sometimes these beliefs functioned as guiding precepts in university lectures. For example, James Bovell, microscopist and dean of the medical faculty at Trinity College, Toronto, drew much of the material in his *Outlines of Natural Theology* (1859) from points that he had made in his physiology course. However, as noted by scientifically informed theologians like Princeton's Charles Hodge, the downward slope between Christian Neoplatonism and pantheism was indeed a slippery one (Hodge 1874: 7–8). This Faustian dilemma between revealed and natural religion often played itself out silently in the careers of scientists of faith, and this explains why there were numerous attempts to 'Christianize' both transmutation and natural selection. James Dwight Dana, Yale's professor of natural history, perhaps epitomized this approach when he interpreted the 'doctrine of evolution' through purposeful natural causes rather than a purposeless natural selection. Many such harmonizations appeared throughout the century, offering respite for those tired of the many debates within the scientific community concerning the applicability and meaning of Darwin's theory (Livingston 1997; Numbers and Stenhouse 1999).

Within the human sciences, anatomists and biochemists fostered natural theologies premised on vitalism—that is, the notion that powers or forces of chemistry and physics were categorically different from those exhibited in a living organism. Vitalists maintained a wide spectrum of teleological positions which ranged from an efficient cause that set the mechanical causes of embryos in motion, to a vital force or power that both guided embryological development and sustained the vital functions of all organisms. With characteristic verve, James Cowles Prichard summed up the latter position in *The Doctrine of the Vital Principle* (1829):

> All these phenomena evidently point to the operation of a much higher power than merely mechanical principles. They are undoubted manifestations of that designing Intellect, whose plans are perspicuously discovered throughout all Nature, but most strikingly in the organising part of it. [Prichard 1829: 138]

Similar positions were promoted by numerous biomedical scientists, but representative proponents with commitments to Christian theology were Johann Friedrich

Blumenbach, Lionel Smith Beale, and Sir Bertram C. A. Windle (Blumenbach 1781; Beale 1871; Windle 1908; see also Driesch 1914; Strick 2000; Ramberg 2000). In a related vein, analogies were frequently drawn between the vital forces that governed the body and volitional forces operating in the brain. Again, this connection sometimes had Neoplatonist undertones. Indeed, Beale, a cellular biologist, concluded that, '[human] *will*, so far from being a result of certain chemical change induced in matter, should rather be regarded as the *power which influences the material particles and causes them to move and take up new positions*' (Beale 1870: 156; see also Bovell 1859: ii). Once such a metaphysical point was established, the conceptual basis of a divine will as an omnipotent and omnipresent mover had been laid. This came full circle back to the analogy between divine and human minds that was characteristic of the moral argument for God's existence. It should come as no surprise, therefore, that vitalism and nascent anthropology were sometimes bedfellows. For example, barring Beale, all of the vitalists mentioned above were also notable anthropologists in their time. For many naturalists and travellers writing on this subject, a number of whom were missionaries or the spouses of colonial administrators, the morality evinced in ancient artefacts or in the minds of 'natives' clearly pointed to the existence of a supreme moral mind (Jasanoff 2005; Gange 2006; Augstein 1999). Such a view was applied not only to the 'savage' minds abroad, but also in the minds of Europeans, which is why moral therapy, a leading psychiatric cure during the century, was predicated upon a natural theology of morality. Everyone, European or not, sane or insane, could be taught to see the truth of revealed religion because of the morality inherent to the human mind.

Priests and Pedagogues

Natural theology is often treated as a kind of argument, but it could also be seen as a type of genre that not only included formal treatises like Paley's, but also textbooks, sermons, and autodidactic literature used by the increasingly lettered populations of the West and its colonies (Numbers 2007; Rose 2001). From a pedagogical perspective, the nineteenth century was a time of great educational reform. As mentioned above, new scientific disciplines were introduced in universities and the divisions between different faculties were widened. Yet there were also tectonic changes in primary and secondary educational settings, especially with the introduction of compulsory education in many European countries and American states. Natural theology was actively present in this 'march of mind', especially since many school teachers were either clerics or educated in religious settings. This produced a strongly moral vision of the human mind and of education in general, a point summed up by John Abercrombie in his popular high-school philosophy textbook, 'Moral impressions and revealed religion: These two sources of knowledge cannot be separated' (Abercrombie 1859: vi; see also Richardson 1994). Here the experiential aspect of design continued to play an important role. Even though natural theological arguments presented in school settings sometimes did not contain direct appeals to revelation, many educators saw the very nature of the genre as being a supplement to attributes of God, presented in the Old and New Testaments, which they already believed. At the very least, in the words of the popular author and Unitarian minister Henry A. Miles, 'The feeling of *wonder*, also, which an acquaintance with the truths of Natural Theology so much inspires, is in the highest degree friendly to intellectual culture' (Miles 1849: 111).

For students in rural settings, design arguments provided a way of making the natural world relevant in a manner that had been practiced since antiquity. For students living in the cramped and smog-filled urban centres of the Industrial Revolution, they provided escape, evoking images of open skies and bucolic bliss. By the 1820s printing had become cheaper, lowering the cost of books, and this laid the foundation for a flow of natural theology class books for young or autodidactic readers to be published throughout the century. Popular examples include the work of Henry Fergus, Thomas Hopkins Gallaudet (see fig. 6.3), Margaret Bryan, and Maria Hack (Fergus 1833, 1838a, 1838b; Gallaudet 1832; see also Gates 1998: 8–44). Narratives of natural theology also filled the pages of evangelical periodicals printed by the Religious Tract Society and the Society for Promoting Christian Knowledge (Fyfe 2004). Authors of such works were often inspired by the style and examples used by Paley. Indeed, many of them summarized his arguments and reproduced the plates made by James Paxton for *Natural Theology's* 1826 edition. This was the case for the third edition of Fergus's *Class Book*, which included additional notes by Charles Henry Alden, the principal of Philadelphia's High School for Young Ladies. The review for his book in *American Annals of Education and Instruction* stated: 'We like the idea of having every body study Natural Theology. For beginners we prefer Gallaudet's little work, *The Class Book of Natural Theology*. For more advanced pupils, in general, we like Paley's admirable work' (Alcott and Woodbridge 1837: 335–6). This pedagogical hierarchy, from simple to advanced books, simply mirrored the progression used to teach curricular subjects to students. For those wishing to ease from Gallaudet to Paley, there were intermediary books like those written by J. W. Baker and James Lawson Drummond (Baker 1817; Drummond 1832).

While instructional texts based explicitly on natural theology enjoyed wide circulation as educational reforms gained strength, in some quarters these gave way to, or sometimes were replaced by, science books for the general reader that were fundamentally committed to promoting a designed world. Like the aforementioned textbooks, many of these works were written by clerics, but also by a rising number of science journalists, many of whom were women. Natural history, anatomy, and cosmology (via laws) continued to provide evidences for design, with examples ranging from those so eloquently collected by Paley, to new items of interest like sunspots or telegraphic wires. New natural laws and theories played a role, but to varying degrees. Within science texts written by Anglican divines, some, like the Reverend John Alexander Johns, ignored Darwin's theories altogether. Darwinian motifs also were indirectly popularized in the science compendia of the Reverends Thomas William Webb and Ebenezer Cobham Brewer, and co-opted by the natural history guides and children's stories of the Reverend Charles Kingsley (Lightman 2007: 39–94; Bottigheimer 1996). Some divines, like the Reverend Henry Baker Tristram, canon of Durham Cathedral, openly shared some of Darwin's views.

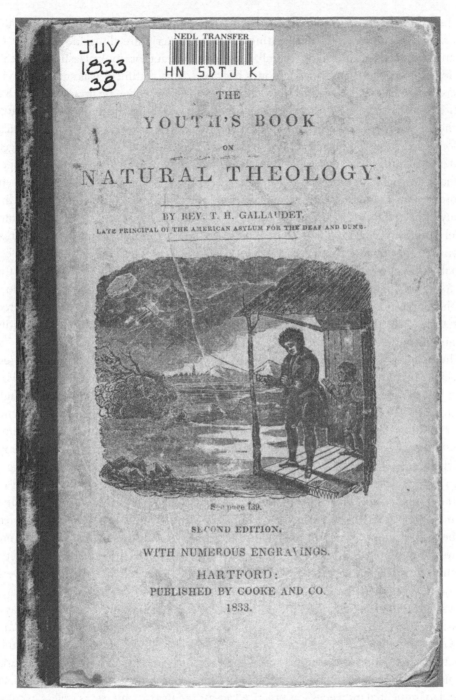

THE

YOUTH'S BOOK

ON

NATURAL THEOLOGY.

BY REV. T. H. GALLAUDET,

LATE PRINCIPAL OF THE AMERICAN ASYLUM FOR THE DEAF AND DUMB.

See page 139.

SECOND EDITION,

WITH NUMEROUS ENGRAVINGS.

HARTFORD:

PUBLISHED BY COOKE AND CO.

1833.

FIGURE 6.3 Title-page, T. B. Gallaudet, *The Youth's Book on Natural Theology* (Hartford, Cooke and Co., 1833).

Books produced by such authors often entertained the public's fascination with the natural history of the Holy Land, setting quotes from Scripture alongside evidences of botanical and zoological design. Overall, popular science authors took pleasure in appealing to evidence of design evinced in one's backyard. This sentiment was summed up in Kingsley's preface of his *Madam How and Lady Why* (1870): 'You begin to find out that truly Divine mystery...by watching the common natural things around you.' Here natural theology was not just a matter of passive pontificating, it was matter of active participation. Mixing teleology with a kind of existential consumerism, authors encouraged readers to acquire picks, spades, shovels, magnifying glasses, microscopes, and telescopes so that they might see microcosms and macrocosms of design for themselves. Indeed, before explaining how to build and manage 'warm pits', 'hot beds', and 'garden frames', the anonymous author of *Every Lady's Guide to Her Own Greenhouse* (A Lady 1851) wrote, 'I feel among my plants as if I were worshiping the Creator through his most lovely works' (1851: 3) In the previous century, this kind of activity was primarily the domain of professionals (like Paley) and wealthy savants who advocated a visual pedagogy that trained the eye to see design in nature. But, as the relative price of books and journals declined during the nineteenth century, this Enlightenment vision of science and piety was transferred directly to Victorian schools, lecture halls, and public libraries used to educate the rapidly expanding middle class.

The pedagogical power of natural theology was recognized by many missionaries, especially because it jointly appealed to the pious contemplation of nature espoused by Evangelicals, and to the analogues between natural and social order championed by High Church devotees. Missionaries taught languages and mathematics with a view to inculcate Christian values and they replicated the school curricula used in their native countries. Students were taught to read vernacular and classical languages in grammar schools and then those with promise progressed to an academy-style setting where lessons were given on specialized topics. A good example of this setup existed in the Church of Scotland mission in Pune (Poonah), India. This city had a large Hindu population and the missionaries taught well over 500 children in their boys' and girls' schools. As noted in the 1842 edition of *The Missionary Register*, males who had mastered English were allowed to move into 'A Class of promising young men, all of the highest ranks of society' (Church Missionary Society 1842: 230). The specialized subjects taught to this group were geometry, algebra, and, notably, natural theology. A similar approach was used in many places, including the mission to the influential Parsi population in Mumbai (Bombay). This community was Zoroastrian and, as noted in 1865 by *The Church Missionary Atlas*, '[Wealthy Indians] are beginning to be quite Europeanized in their social habits, their private morals, and in a great measure, in their religious views, as far as relates to Natural Theology' (Church Missionary Society 1865: 31). The pattern of using education as an inroad to influential indigenes was practiced across the British Empire, as well as in colonies of other European countries. When this did not work, divine design was also promulgated via the translation of adolescent works like Gadaullet's *The Youth's Book on Natural Theology* (1832)—a move that was also made by missionaries operating in Eastern European countries like Greece (Newcomb 1860: 373).

Whether it was through oral or written means, colonial conversions to Christianity motivated many Churches to establish seminaries outside of Europe. Natural theology played a role in the curricula of these institutions as well. For instance, the theological students at the London Mission, Madras, were required to study Paley's *Natural Theology*, as the set text for the Moral Philosophy component (Murdoch 1862: 212). Over the course of the century, natural theology, for better or worse, became a fixture in the intellectual culture of European colonies. Yet, perhaps one of the most interesting outcomes of Western design arguments promoted in the East did not occur amongst Christians. Building on Islam's utilitarian view of technology, Sir Saiyid Ahmad Khan, a British subject from modern-day Pakistan, set out a blueprint of coexistence between Islam and science. In addition to being influenced by Paley's *Natural Theology*, his synthesis utilized the work of the Reverend John Henry Pratt, the polymath Archdeacon of Calcutta (Kahali 1994). Khan was particularly impressed by Pratt's *Scripture and Science Not at Variance* (1859) and it inspired him to argue that Western science was merely a tool that could be used to understand the natural world—a world created by Allah. This move fashioned a conceptual road that allowed Islam to keep in step with modern science and, implicitly, to change the system of education in Muslim countries (Robinson 1993). Today, Khan is often called the founder of Islamic modernism.

CONCLUSION

Most histories of nineteenth-century natural theology tend to give a significant amount of attention to teleological and cosmological arguments. Whilst such studies have yielded a rich intellectual context, they are often presented in analytic terms that implicitly bracket the deep-seated existential and educational worth that Victorians attributed to design arguments. Such a historical gaze does not give adequate attention to the fact that design arguments were increasingly recalibrated to incorporate new scientific evidence. Nor does it give a robust explanation as to why the basic premise of a theistically designed world still enjoyed notable acceptance at the dawn of the twentieth-century amongst scientists and the reading public alike. In short, the *fin-de-siècle* adaptability, or perhaps resilience, of teleological and cosmological arguments challenges the notion that late Victorian natural theology was definitively undermined by the rise of institutions and methods of science. Yet, there is no denying the more subdued presence of natural theology within Western educational settings as the new century moved forward. It is here where this chapter's comments on the moral argument become particularly helpful. Whereas the relevance of Victorian teleological and cosmological arguments were usually framed in relation to an organism's or object's singular place in the world, moral arguments were fundamentally social, extending the meaningfulness of design into larger issues that gripped society as a whole. Given the subtly strong presence of moral arguments within nineteenth-century Europe and its colonies, it would not be going too far to say that one the biggest blows to Victorian natural theology was not necessarily theological liberalism or scientific positivism, rather, it was the moral devastation of the First World War. The psychological impact of this event in other areas of life is well documented and the existential bewilderment that it engendered helps to explain why it was theodicy, not solely logic-chopping, that weakened the cultural appeal of design arguments. It was very difficult for many people to see design in the face of the horrific atrocities that a moral God seemed to be allowing in such a devastating global war. This point had been foreseen by John Stuart Mill, but thanks to the rise in literacy and the rapid development of technologies like the telegraph, photograph, and the steam press, the impact of the war was immediate and visceral. The inexplicable presence of such pervasive evil undermined the ways in which natural knowledge had been aligned with divine attributes like omniscience and omnipresence. These kinds of alignments provided the conceptual foundation of modern natural theology and, without them, proponents of divine design were forced to reconsider their beliefs in relation to the increasingly humanistic morality of the postmodern world.

REFERENCES

'A Lady' (1851). *Every Lady's Guide to Her Own Greenhouse, Hothouse and Conservatory*. London: Orr.

Abercrombie, John (1859). *The Philosophy of Moral Feelings*. Rev. edn. New York: Collins.

Alcott William A. and William C. Woodbridge, eds. (1837). 'Case Book of Natural Theology'. *American Annals of Education and Instruction* 7: 335–6.

Augstein, H. F. (1999). *James Cowles Prichard's Anthropology*. Amsterdam: Rodopi.

Baker, J. W. (1817). *A Grammar of Moral Philosophy and Natural Theology*. New York: Longworth.

Barry, Alfred (1880). *The Manifold Witness for Christ*. London: John Murray.

Barth, Karl (2001). *Protestant Theology in the Nineteenth Century*. London: SCM Press.

Beale, Lionel Smith (1870). *Protoplasm; Or, Life, Matter, and Mind*. 2nd edn. London: Churchill.

—— (1871). *Life Theories: Their Influence upon Religious Thought*. London: Churchill.

Blumenbach, Johann Friedrich (1781). *Über den Bildungstrieb und das Zeugungsgeschäft*. Göttingen: Dieterich.

Bottigheimer, Ruth B. (1996). *The Bible for Children: From the Age of Gutenburg to the Present*. New Haven: Yale University Press.

Bovell, Nathaniel (1859). *Outlines of Natural Theology*. Toronto: Rowsell and Ellis.

Brooke, John Hedley (1991). *Science and Religion*. Cambridge: Cambridge University Press.

Buchanan, James (1857). *Modern Atheism under its Forms of Pantheism, Materialism, Secularism, Development, and Natural Laws*. Boston: Gould and Lincoln.

Byrne, Peter (2007). *Kant on God*. Aldershot: Ashgate.

Campbell, Lewis and William Garnett, eds. (1884). *Life of James Clerk Maxwell, with a Selection from His Writings*. London: Macmillan and Co.

Chalmers Thomas (1834). *On the Power, Wisdom and Goodness of God as Manifested in the Adaptation of External Nature to the Moral and Intellectual Constitution of Man*. Vol. I. London: Pickering.

Church Missionary Society (1842). *The Missionary Register*. London: Watts.

—— (1865). *The Church Missionary Atlas*. 4th edn. London: Seely.

Conference upon the Training of Candidates for Holy Orders (1887). *Outlines of Theological Study*. Cambridge: Deighton, Bell & Co.

Cooke, Josiah P. (1864). *Religion and Chemistry; or Proofs of God's Plan in the Atmosphere and Its Elements*. New York: Scribner.

Coppée, Henry (1858). *Elements of Logic*. Philadelphia: Butler.

Day, Henry N., ed. (1865). *The Logic of Sir William Hamilton: Reduced and Prepared for Use in Colleges and Schools*. Cincinnati: Moore, Wilstach & Baldwin.

Dick, John (1851). *Lectures on Theology*. Vol. I. New York: Carter.

Driesch, Hans (1914). *The History and Theory of Vitalism*. Translated by C. K. Ogden. London: Macmillan.

Drummond, James Lawson (1932). *Letters to a Young Naturalist on the Study of Nature and Natural Theology*. London: Longman.

Edgerton, David (2006). *The Shock of the Old: Technology and Global History since 1900*. Oxford: Oxford University Press.

Fergus, Henry (1833). *The Testimony of Nature and Revelation to the Being, Perfections, and Government of God*. Edinburgh: Oliver & Boyd.

—— (1838a). *Readings in Natural Theology*. London: John W. Parker

—— (1838b). *Class Book of Natural Theology*. Boston: Gould.

Fleming, William (1858). 'Causality' in *The Vocabulary of Philosophy, Mental, Moral and Metaphysical*. London: Griffin.

Flint, Robert (1876). *Theism*. Edinburgh: Blackwood.

—— (1879). *Anti-Theistic Theories*. Edinburgh: Blackwood.

Fyfe, Aileen (2004). *Science and Salvation: Evangelical Popular Science Publishing in Victorian Britain*. Chicago: University of Chicago Press.

Gallaudet, Thomas Hopkins (1832). *The Youth's Book on Natural Theology*. New York: American Tract Society.

Gange, David (2006). 'Religion and Science in Late Nineteenth-Century British Egyptology'. *The Historical Journal* 49: 1083–103.

Garden, Francis (1867). *An Outline of Logic*. London: Rivingtons.

Gates, Barbara T. (1998). *Kindred Nature*. Chicago: University of Chicago Press.

Guyot, Arnold (1849). *The Earth and Man*. Translated by C. C. Felton. Boston: Gould, Kendall, and Lincoln.

—— (1884). *Creation*. New York, Charles Scribner's Sons.

Hamilton, William (1866). *Lectures on Logic*. Vol. I. Edinburgh: Blackwood.

Hodge, Charles (1874). *What is Darwinism?* New York: Scribner, Armstrong, and Company.

Jasanoff, Maya (2005). *The Edge of Empire*. London: Harper Perennial.

Kahali, Manidipa (1994). 'John Henry Pratt, Archdeacon of Calcutta and His Theory of Isostatic Compensation'. *Indian Journal of History of Science* 29: 23–30.

Kant, Immanuel (1994 [1763]). *The One Possible Basis for a Demonstration of the Existence of God*. Translated by Gordon Treash. Lincoln: University of Nebraska Press.

King, David (1850). *The Principles of Geology: Explained, and Viewed in their Relations to Revealed and Natural Religion*. 2nd edn. London: Johnstone and Hunter.

Le Gros Clark, Frederick, ed. (1875). *Paley's Natural Theology Revised to Harmonize with Modern Science*. London: SPCK.

Lightman, Bernard (2007). *Victorian Popularisers of Science*. Chicago: University of Chicago Press.

Livingstone, David N. (1987). *Darwin's Forgotten Defenders*. Vancouver: Regent College

—— (2008). *Adam's Ancestors*. Baltimore: Johns Hopkins University Press.

Livingstone, David N. and Mark A. Noll (2000). 'B. B. Warfield (1851–1921): A Biblical Inerrantist as Evolutionist'. *Isis* 91: 283–304.

McCosh, James (1866). *The Intuitions of the Mind Inductively Investigated*. New York: Carter.

—— (1888). *The Religious Aspect of Evolution*. New York: Putnam.

Miles, Henry A. (1849). 'Lecture IV. On Natural Theology as a Study in Schools' in *The Board of the Censor*. Lectures Delivered before the American Institute of Instruction. Boston: Marsh: pp. 103–18.

Miller, Hugh (1857). *The Testimony of the Rocks*. Edinburgh: Thomas Constables and Co.

—— (1858). *The Cruise of the Betsy*. Constable: Edinburgh.

Mullens, Joseph (1860). *The Religious Aspects of Hindu Philosophy*. London: Smith, Elder & Co.

Murdoch, John, ed. (1862). *Indian Year-Book for 1861*. London: Nisbet.

Nartonis, David K. (2005). 'Louis Agassiz and the Platonist Story of Creation at Harvard, 1795–1846'. *Journal of the History of Ideas* 66: 437–49.

Newcomb, Harvey, ed. (1860). *A Cyclopedia of Missions*. New York: Scribner.

Nichols, John (1822). *Illustrations of the Literary History of the Eighteenth Century*. Vol. IV. London: Nichols.

Nisbet, H. B. (1972). *Goethe and the Scientific Tradition*. London: Institute of Germanic Studies.

Numbers, Ronald L. (2007). *Science and Christianity in Pulpit and Pew*. Oxford: Oxford University Press.

Numbers, Ronald L. and John Stenhouse, eds. (1999). *Disseminating Darwinism: The Role of Place, Race, Religion, and Gender*. Cambridge: Cambridge University Press.

Pond, Enoch (1867). *Lectures on Christian Theology*. Boston, Congregational Board of Education.

Powell, Baden (1838). *The Connexion of Natural and Divine Truth*. London: Parker.

—— (1856). *The Unity of Worlds and of Nature*. London: Longman.

Prichard, James Cowles (1829). *A Review of the Doctrine of a Vital Principle as Manifested by Some Writers on Physiology*. London: Arch.

Ramberg, Peter J. (2000). 'The Death of Vitalism and the Birth of Organic Chmistry: Wöhler's Urea Synthesis and the Disciplinary Identity of Organic Chemistry'. *Ambix* 47: 170–95.

Richardson, Alan (1994). *Literature, Education and Romanticism: Reading as Social Practice 1780–1832*. Cambridge: Cambridge University Press.

Robinson, Francis (1993). 'Technology and Religious Change: Islam and the Impact of Print'. *Modern Asian Studies* 27: 229–51.

Rose, Jonathon (2001). *The Intellectual Life of the British Working Classes*. New Haven: Yale.

Sell, Alan P. F. (2004). *Mill on God: The Pervasiveness and Elusiveness of Mill's Religious Thought*. Aldershot: Ashgate.

Shaler, Nathaniel Southgate (1898). *Outlines of the Earth's History: A Popular Study in Physiography*. London & New York: D. Appleton and Co.

—— (1904). *The Neighbor*. Boston: Houghton, Mifflin, and Co.

Silliman, Benjamin (1829). *Outline of the Course of Geological Lectures Given in Yale College*. New Haven: Howe.

Stewart, B. and P. G. Tait (1880). *The Unseen Universe*. London: Macmillan.

Strick, James E. (2000). *Sparks of Life*. Cambridge: Harvard University Press.

Tigert, J. J. (1889). *Hand-Book of Logic: A Concise Body of Logical Doctrine*. 7th edn. Nashville: Barbee & Smith.

Trowbridge, John (1875). 'Science from the Pulpit'. *The Popular Science Monthly* 6: 734–9.

Tulloch, John (1855). *Theism: The Witness of Reason and Nature to an All-Wise and Beneficent Creator*. Edinburgh: Blackwood.

Whately, Richard (1867). *Elements of Logic*. 9th edn. London: Longmans.

Whewell, William (1833). *Astronomy and General Physics Considered with Reference to Natural Theology*. London: William Pickering.

—— (1845). *Indications of the Creator*. London: Parker.

Wilson, George (1862). *Religio Chemici. Essays*. London: MacMillan.

Wilson, W. D. (1861). *An Elementary Treatise on Logic*. New York: Appleton.

Winchell, Alexander (1870). *Sketches of Creation*. New York: Harper & Brothers.

—— (1878). *Adamites and Preadamites*. Syracuse, NY: J. T. Roberts (republished under the title *Preadamites*).

Windle, Bertram C. A. (1908). *What is Life? A Study of Vitalism and Neo-Vitalism*. London: Sands.

Yeo, Richard (1979). 'William Whewell, Natural Theology and the Philosophy of Science in Mid-nineteenth Century Britain'. *Annals of Science* 36: 493–516.

CHAPTER 7

NATURAL THEOLOGY IN THE TWENTIETH CENTURY

RODNEY D. HOLDER

OVERVIEW

As the twentieth century dawned, with evolutionary biology embraced by mainstream theology and with physics entering a period of revolution, there was the potential for a new creative interaction between science and religion, and, although both extremes were propagated, there was no need for a false choice between a materialist interpretation of science and fundamentalist rejection of science. Most especially, the Gifford Lectures in natural theology in Scottish universities had been inaugurated in 1888 with a munificent bequest by Lord Gifford. Yet, as will transpire, these were mixed blessings, especially for those who were concerned with theological orthodoxy and the centrality of God's revelation in Jesus Christ, a concern that will be reflected in the bulk of this chapter. Lord Gifford stated in his will that the lectures established in his name were for 'Promoting, Advancing, Teaching, and Diffusing the study of Natural Theology' (Jaki 1986: 2). The lecturers could be of any religion or denomination or none and they should 'treat their subject strictly as a natural science, the greatest of all possible sciences, indeed, in one sense the only science, that of Infinite Being, without reference to or reliance upon any supposed special exceptional or so-called miraculous revelation' (73–4). The lecturers should, furthermore, be under no restraint and should be able to discuss 'all questions about man's conceptions of God or the Infinite' including 'whether he can have any such conceptions' (74).

In light of the above it is no surprise that the lectures and lecturers have been so diverse. Thus William James, while attacking materialism, argued for 'pluralism', i.e. the fragmentation of the universe, and acknowledged that his study of 'the varieties of religious experience' could lead merely to polytheism. Many other early lecturers sat light to the orthodoxy of the Church, being sceptical about miracles, or espousing a less than personal God (say as Hegel's 'Absolute Spirit'), or seeing Jesus as just a special human being. Anthropological accounts of the origin of religion, most famously expressed by J. G. Frazer, could also be troubling to traditional Christian belief. Ultimately religion could be explained as evolved from magic, with science now superseding both (Witham 2005: 71). Perhaps, in view of all this, it is no wonder that Karl Barth stormed in to give a lecture series denouncing natural theology altogether! He did that by choosing to speak, conveniently for his purpose, on the Scottish Confession of 1560, rather than the later Westminster Confession of Faith which is more positive for natural theology. Of course, while natural theology may not say much about the particulars of Christian doctrine, it was Barth's concern that so many saw reconciliation with science effectively as the capitulation of theology to science and necessitating abandonment of basic doctrines. On the other hand some Gifford lecturers have espoused a traditional faith and re-presented traditional arguments. This has happened mainly in the post-Second World War period, though there is still no discernible unity or agreement. On the positive and orthodox side would be Austin Farrer, Stanley Jaki, E. L. Mascall, and Richard Swinburne, whose work has become central to the modern discussion. Yet the atheist logical positivist Freddie Ayer is also a contributor, maintaining the extreme diversity of the earlier period.

The mention of Ayer raises the issue of the philosophy of science which has been through a number of significant phases during the twentieth century that have been influential on whether and how religious belief may be justified, and thus on natural theology. The logical positivism of the Vienna Circle, propagated in Britain by Ayer, was wholly negative for religious belief. The verification principle espoused by the logical positivists accorded meaning only to statements about empirically observed facts. Statements about God were deemed not false, but meaningless. Karl Popper, although early associated with the Vienna Circle, argued convincingly that scientific hypotheses, which are of general application, cannot be verified by the observation of particular instances. Instead he proposed the criterion of falsification: though not verifiable, a general law may be falsified by a single counter-example.

Popper also denied that theology or ethics were meaningless, since they were not required to conform to the same norms of rationality as natural science. One problem with Popper's approach is that falsificationism ('critical rationalism') does not seem to capture the way science works in practice. Sometimes a theory is overthrown but in some cases the data are questioned, and in others the theory can be saved by adjusting background assumptions. Imre Lakatos proposed instead a 'methodology of scientific research programmes', which accommodates all these cases by postulating a well-established 'hard core' of theory and a surrounding ensemble of 'auxiliary hypotheses' which are more open to correction (Lakatos 1978). Lakatos sees scientific hypotheses as explanatory. Several philosophers have seen explanation as central and that competing alternative explanations be evaluated by 'inference to the best explanation' (Harman 1965). The inference is made on such criteria as scope, elegance, and simplicity.

All these philosophical approaches have been influential on natural theology, even those which are negative towards it. That may account for a lack of confidence in theological claims or an unwillingness for theology to engage at all in the public square at times when the philosophy of science has been perceived as threatening to religious belief. At any rate, there are positions in the philosophy of religion which deny that theology is explanatory or even that it relates to ontological reality at all. Most notable is 'expressivism', the view that God-talk is really expressive of an attitude to the world rather than referring to God as truly existent. Yet this view would seem to be hard to maintain in the face of what believers themselves generally say and it also has difficulty in explaining loss of faith. Evidence, say the negative evidence of evil and suffering, does seem to count for something after all. A different approach is that of Alvin Plantinga who sees belief in God as 'properly basic', like belief in the truths of logic or the delivery of sense perceptions, and therefore not in need of justification. One problem with this is that I may have a properly basic belief in God but how am I to commend it to others?

Nevertheless, in the latter part of the twentieth century natural theology in the traditional sense of providing arguments for the existence of God has undergone something of a revival, both in the context of the science–religion dialogue and of the philosophy of religion. Notable figures in this revival are the Cambridge 'scientist-theologian' John Polkinghorne and the Oxford philosopher of religion Richard Swinburne. Polkinghorne sees the rational order of the universe, and the openness of the universe to scientific enquiry (its 'comprehensibility' as Einstein put it), as suggestive of a mind behind the universe (Polkinghorne 2006). He further invokes the so-called 'fine tuning' of the cosmos, identified by cosmologists in the late 1970s, as being best explained on a theistic basis. Polkinghorne nevertheless sees natural theology as a limited endeavour, requiring revelation to provide the 'meat on the bone' as it were for an otherwise somewhat emasculated picture of God. Swinburne is rather more robust than Polkinghorne in reviving the classical arguments for God's existence to build up a cumulative case (Swinburne 2004a). He goes beyond his Oxford predecessor Basil Mitchell's approach by applying the analytical framework of Bayesian confirmation theory to evaluate alternative hypotheses. Swinburne sees the epistemic probabilities going into Bayes's theorem as logical and objective, and so the argument, which infers that God's existence is more probable than not, should normatively lead to theistic belief. Swinburne moves to an examination of the specifics of Christian belief through a 'ramified' natural theology (Swinburne 2004b).

There is much to be said pertaining to the success or otherwise of these arguments in their own terms. There are also new challenges to be faced, such as are posed by the 'new atheists', Richard Dawkins and his allies (Dawkins 2006). However, for the bulk of this chapter I shall return to the fundamental theological challenge to the whole enterprise of natural theology posed by Karl Barth. Barth has been highly influential in twentieth-century theology and it would seem that if natural theology is misguided or worse from the point of view of dogmatic theology, as Barth claims, then those who indulge in it are doing a disservice to the Church rather than aiding her cause. In what follows, I re-examine Barth's criticism and look at how a key group of theologians following Barth has reacted to it. These theologians have all engaged with the natural sciences, but all also share similar concerns to Barth in terms of prioritizing revelation and of maintaining or defending an orthodox theology. Nevertheless each provides for some movement away from Barth's ultra-dogmatic position and room for natural theology to re-enter mainstream theological endeavour. I shall show in this chapter how both the theological concerns and opportunities for natural theology of these theologians might be united in the context of the revived natural theology referred to above.

KARL BARTH'S 'NEIN!'

Barth's rejection of natural theology is robust and unequivocal: 'even if we only lend our little finger to natural theology, there necessarily follows the denial of the revelation of God in Jesus Christ' (Barth 1957: 173). His major concern is that we should see God only as he has graciously revealed himself to us, namely in the person of Jesus Christ. Any other approach is to seek to have God on our own, human terms. This was the problem with nineteenth-century liberal Protestantism. It amounts to hubris and for Barth was shown to be bankrupt when his teachers signed a declaration in support of the Kaiser's war aims in the First World War. It arose again in the context of Nazism which Barth saw as offering a new revelation which was leading to 'the transformation of the Christian Church into the temple of the German nature- and history-myth' (173).

Barth's views brought a clash with a number of his contemporaries. These included his teacher Adolf von Harnack. Among other complaints Harnack asserted that theology should be tested at the bar of scientific reason: 'Is there—admitting sloth, short-sightedness, and numerous ills—really any other theology than that which has a firm connection and blood relationship to science?' (von Harnack 1968: 166). Barth's response was typically robust:

> If theology regained the courage to be objective, the courage to become a witness of the *word* of revelation, of judgment, and of the love of *God*, then it could also be that 'science' in general would have to look out for its 'firm connection and blood relationship' to theology, rather than the other way around. [Barth 1968: 170]

Equally sharp was the exchange between Barth and his friend Heinrich Scholz, who provoked Barth's response with an essay entitled, 'How is an evangelical theology possible as science?' (Scholz 1931). Scholz puts forward criteria by which to judge theology as scientific; Barth is equivocal even about the principle of non-contradiction and asserts that it is necessary for theology to transgress all of Scholz's other criteria such as testability and freedom from prejudice (Barth 1936: 8; see also McGrath 2007).

The most famous dispute was that between Barth and his erstwhile colleague and dialectical theologian Emil Brunner, and directly concerned natural theology following publication of the latter's essay *Nature and Grace* (Brunner 1946). In rehabilitating a natural theology Brunner invoked the doctrine of the *imago dei*, asserting that there is a 'point of contact' (*Anknüpfungspunkt*) in human nature for God's self-revelation to latch onto. This point of contact could include an awareness of God in nature, conscience, and knowledge of sin. All this Barth vehemently denied in his reply, simply entitled '*Nein!*' (Barth 1946): God himself creates the point of contact, which does not exist prior to faith in Christ but is realized through faith. Brunner's view implies, for Barth (though not for Brunner), that humans contribute something to their salvation. Barth is keen to repudiate Luther's notion of 'orders of creation', such as the family and the state which were being dangerously appropriated at the time by the Nazified wing of the Church, the so-called 'German Christians'. However, Brunner distinguished marriage and family as orders of creation from the state, which is an order of preservation having to do with sin—an important distinction taken up by Dietrich Bonhoeffer as we shall see.

The essential problem with Barth's approach is that, if there is no natural knowledge of God, theology becomes isolated from other areas of human enquiry. It becomes difficult to commend the Christian faith if it is not to be supported by some kind of scientific rational argument—even with 'scientific' broadly conceived. A notable critic of Barth from this perspective is W. W. Bartley (Bartley 1984). Bartley says that Barth's theology is irrational precisely because it makes itself immune to criticism. It starts from an unfalsifiable premise and argues in a circle and, as we have seen, denies that it should conform to the standards of rationality appropriate to the sciences in general. We shall see that this charge may not have entirely been met by subsequent theology in the Barthian tradition.

DIETRICH BONHOEFFER AND 'POSITIVISM OF REVELATION'

Dietrich Bonhoeffer was heavily influenced by Barth, and was encouraged by Barth in the Church struggle against Nazism. Nevertheless, while showing a Barthian antipathy to natural theology, especially in his earlier writings, Bonhoeffer begins a critique of his mentor and offers significant opportunities for natural theology.

Unlike Barth, Bonhoeffer engages with the natural sciences. This is most evident in his early work *Creation and Fall*, and also in his maturing, though inevitably fragmented, theology in *Letters and Papers from Prison* (Bonhoeffer 1997, 1971). In *Creation and Fall*, an exposition of the early chapters of Genesis, Bonhoeffer certainly expresses an aversion to natural theology. Arguing towards God from the contingency of the creation would 'enthrone reason in the place of God' (Bonhoeffer 1997: 27). On the contrary, we do not believe in God because of the creation but that the world is a creation because the word of God says so and 'we *believe* this word' (41). As for Barth, our belief in the resurrection of Jesus Christ is prior to belief in the creation and in the creation as 'out of nothing'. And when it comes to the Fall, the temptation is for human understanding to trump the word of God, to sit in judgement over it, and to place human understanding above God's command (106–8). But despite these strictures, more positive possibilities for natural theology can be discerned.

In *Creation and Fall* Bonhoeffer substitutes Luther's 'orders of creation' with 'orders of preservation'. These are tasks to be fulfilled rather than orders of being and are temporary; they are God's means of preserving the world from descending into chaos as it awaits God's redemption through Christ (140). In the *Ethics* they undergo a further change, into 'divine mandates', and Bonhoeffer lists labour, marriage, government, and the Church in their number (Bonhoeffer 1964: 207). 'Orders of preservation' or 'mandates' would seem to be closely related to another concept from the *Ethics*, namely 'last and penultimate things'. The ultimate is the word of grace but the penultimate comes before grace. The penultimate embraces a host of activities, such as feeding the hungry and freeing slaves, which are not grace per se but which prepare the way for grace. Very importantly, for Bonhoeffer the penultimate quite simply amounts to the same thing as 'the natural'. Indeed Bonhoeffer goes on to develop what looks very similar to a 'natural law' ethic. He finds after all a place for human reason as 'the organ of knowledge of the natural' and describes human rights and duties which reason should take account of. All this resonates with a traditional view of natural theology, as preceding and preparatory to the gospel. And if, as Bonhoeffer notes, people are better able to receive the gospel if they are well fed (and reason should see the rightness of feeding them), then perhaps they are also better able to receive the gospel if this is added into their pre-existing awareness of deity, however tentative, obtained from nature and reasoned argument. This is not the direction which Bonhoeffer took, but nevertheless it is one opened up to us by his theology (Holder 2008).

In prison for his anti-Nazi activities Bonhoeffer read widely, and in particular he read Carl Friedrich von Weizsäcker's book *The World View of Physics* (von Weizsäcker 1952). From this he gleaned two major points related to science and theology. The first is that God should not be used as a stop-gap (*Lückenbüßer*) when knowledge runs out (Bonhoeffer 1971: 311–12). This 'God of the gaps' idea is routinely invoked nowadays as a complaint against certain theological approaches, such as 'Intelligent Design', which invoke God to explain structures in the natural world which science doesn't currently explain, but has a habit of explaining at a later date. Bonhoeffer's second point is related to this, namely that an infinite universe is self-subsistent, unlike the finite world of the Middle Ages: 'An infinite universe, however it may be conceived, is self-subsisting, *etsi deus non daretur*' (360). Bonhoeffer thinks that science is an autonomous discipline, and that this point is reinforced if the universe is infinite. It is not entirely clear why an infinite universe does not require ultimate explanation in terms of God as necessary being, as a finite universe does. However, Bonhoeffer has been vindicated in the sense that many cosmologists today invoke a multiverse, widely conceived as an ensemble of causally disconnected sub-regions within an overarching infinite space-time, as a way of avoiding the need for God as an explanation of this universe's fine-tuned character (Holder 2004).

Bonhoeffer's comments here again do not get us to natural theology; indeed they seem rather negative once more. It is when he comes to criticize his erstwhile mentor, Karl Barth, that we begin to see a change of direction in *Letters and Papers*. He accuses Barth of offering a 'positivism of revelation'. The most critical passage comes in the letter of 5 May 1944. Here Bonhoeffer endorses Barth's criticism of 'religion' but says that Barth 'put in its place a positivist doctrine of revelation which says, in effect, "Like it or lump it!": virgin birth, Trinity, or anything else; each is an equally significant and necessary part of the whole, which must simply be swallowed as a whole or not at all. That isn't biblical' (Bonhoeffer 1971: 286). Bonhoeffer further argues that there are 'degrees of knowledge and degrees of significance' and that this positivism of revelation sets up 'a law of faith', thereby mutilating what is God's gift. Barth criticized religion but did not offer a 'non-religious' interpretation of theological concepts. His theology ends up being fine for the Church but not for the 'religionless'. Religion becomes a pre-condition to faith just as did circumcision in the New Testament. And the 'liberal question' is answered neither by such 'positivism of revelation' nor by the demythologization programme of Bultmann, which is reductionistic and so still liberal.

For Bonhoeffer, Christ is central and the 'mythology' essential. He also repudiates metaphysics in favour of sharing the sufferings of Christ in the world—and the latter seems to be an important aspect of what he means by being 'non-religious'. Nevertheless he also acknowledges that engagement with the world at the intellectual level is vital: 'We must move out again into the open air of intellectual discussion with the world, and risk saying controversial things, if we are to get down to the serious problems of life' (378). Furthermore, 'Karl Barth and the Confessing Church have encouraged us to entrench ourselves persistently behind the "faith of the church", and evade the honest question as to what we ourselves really believe' (382). It would seem that at the very least, in moving away from the 'revelation positivism' of Barth, Bonhoeffer has re-opened the need for reasoned argument with both the church and the world as to the contents of the faith. And that is encouraging for natural theology (Holder 2009a).

Wolfhart Pannenberg: Theology as Explanatory

Pannenberg has engaged extensively with the natural sciences and his approach to theology can be described as rationally justified in a manner comparable to the sciences. He thus represents a stark contrast to Barth and offers considerable scope for natural theology.

Pannenberg is clear that theology is engaged in the pursuit of truth and must be so in close connection with the sciences (Pannenberg 1994: 59–60):

> Only if we can understand the world as the creation of the biblical God and God himself as its Creator can we raise a truth claim for belief in the sole deity of God.... Theology must make this claim in dialogue with the sciences... A failure to claim that the world that the sciences describe is God's world is a conceptual failure to confess the deity of the God of the Bible.

This passion for truth makes Pannenberg thoroughly opposed to relativism: '*My* truth cannot be mine alone. If I cannot in principle declare it to be truth for all—though perhaps hardly anyone else sees this—then it pitilessly ceases to be truth for me also' (Pannenberg 1991: 51).

Pannenberg first impacted the theological world with his edited volume *Revelation as History* (Pannenberg et al. 1968), and the theme of history remains central to his subsequent theology. God reveals himself in history, most clearly in Jesus Christ (as for Barth), but does so indirectly. Ultimate conclusive universal disclosure will come at the eschaton and retrospectively validate this revelation. In that sense the end of history has been proleptically revealed in the resurrection of Christ. Nevertheless Christian truth claims are based on publicly accessible evidence and what we have *now* in history is enough to go on to command normative assent: 'Nothing must mute the fact that all truth lies right before the eyes, and that its appropriation is a natural consequence of the facts' (136). While Pannenberg has a place for the traditional philosophical arguments for the existence of God, this is relatively minor. However, his use of history is analogous to Swinburne's appropriation of historical evidence for the particulars of the Christian faith in his so-called 'ramified' natural theology.

Pannenberg further developed his philosophy of history, and also began his serious engagement with the natural sciences, in *Theology and the Philosophy of Science* (Pannenberg 1976). Here we also find Pannenberg agreeing with Bonhoeffer's accusation of 'positivism of revelation' against Barth, and with Scholz that an evangelical theology cannot be a science unless it is subjected to formal criteria of scientific validity. If the call of God cannot be tested then, despite Barth's complaint against Schleiermacher that he has reduced theology to the study of religious consciousness, theology becomes precisely that for Barth himself! This point has also been noted by Wentzel van Huyssteen (van Huyssteen 1989: 19). Pannenberg is concerned to establish whether history and metaphysics are sciences. He begins by examining logical positivism and agrees with Popper that this is inadequate because general laws cannot be verified from particular instances. However, Popper's falsificationism is also inadequate to account for history as a science since history concerns unique and unrepeatable events and is united in this with historical sciences such as cosmology and biology.

Very importantly, Pannenberg sees the ability to explain evidence, and to unify and interpret the data, as crucial for both science and history. Moreover, metaphysical assertions also count as scientific because they can be tested for their 'coherence (freedom from contradiction), the efficiency of their interpretative components (the avoidance of unnecessary postulates), and the degree of simplicity and subtlety they achieve in their interpretations of reality' (Pannenberg 1976: 69). Theology is thus included since it accounts for how the all-determining reality of God gives meaning and unity to the whole of reality other than it. Philip Hefner and Nancey Murphy each see Pannenberg proposing theology as a Lakatosian-style scientific research programme (Hefner 1988: 281 ff.; 1997: 109 ff.; Murphy 1990: 174–211; 1997). God the all-determining reality is the hard core of this programme and the auxiliary hypotheses relate to biblical and theological tradition and science as at least open to manifesting the effects of God's all-determining reality.

A difficulty with this approach is that theology, for it to be a progressive research programme, is then required to predict novel facts. Murphy notes that Pannenberg accepted this formulation of his theological programme from her (Murphy 1990: 178). He then suggested certain 'novel facts', namely that anthropology would find a more constructive place for religion and that physics would come up with a field theory which showed the irreversibility of time. These are not predictions in the normal, empirical, scientific sense, and they are also somewhat of a hostage to fortune. Can theology really dictate what physics might discover? Pannenberg's appropriation of field theory is problematic in any case and has been criticized by, for example, Polkinghorne (Polkinghorne 1999). Pannenberg is on safer ground in arguing for the explanatory nature of theology, for example in his statement: 'The fundamental contribution of general statements within general theories is their ability to "explain the evidence at hand"' (Pannenberg 1976: 335). This indeed marks out a commonality between theology and the sciences. Pannenberg states: 'we may speak of a theory as "proved" when it is able to explain the facts at hand' (336). The word 'proved' is of course too strong here, but 'confirmed' in the probabilistic sense of Bayesian confirmation theory would capture the true sense, although any hypothesis should be evaluated alongside its competitors.

Pannenberg disagrees with Barth that there is no knowledge of God prior to God revealing himself to us in Christ. Indeed Pannenberg sees the gospel precisely as filling out, albeit in a dramatic way, what is already known about God (Pannenberg 1991: 75). This would seem to be in accord with scriptural passages such as Romans 1:19–20 and Acts 17:22–31. Natural knowledge of God is clearly limited, and indeed the philosophy of religion also gives only a limited view of God as an impersonal 'Absolute' (Hegel's term), says Pannenberg. The task of Christianity is to supply concrete meaning to this concept and do this in competition with other religions (175–7). When Pannenberg discusses the doctrine of creation, he is clear that creation is the bringing about of a reality distinct from God by the free decision of God (Pannenberg 1994: 9, 20). The creation is therefore contingent. Pannenberg sees human beings as the goal of creation (74). He is impressed by the cosmic fine tunings which were necessary for humans to arise in the cosmos, and which reverse the trend in science since Copernicus to demote humans from the centre.

Pannenberg recognizes contingency in many physical processes, not just those at the quantum level, though contingency is balanced by the regularity of scientific laws. However, the laws themselves are also contingent and only if this is so will the biblical view be confirmed. Again, we see Pannenberg's boldness in the way theology impacts science: a final theory of everything with only one self-consistent set of physical laws all of whose parameters are determined would be incompatible with his view. But it would also run counter to the experimental method, whose development, on one influential reading of history, is owed to theology's insight of the contingency of the universe in the first place. The diametrically opposed taste for multiverses also seems to be leading to necessity, but now in the sense that all possible laws and initial conditions are instantiated in the various universes of an infinite ensemble.

Pannenberg questions Hermann Bondi's assumption of uniformity in time and space (the so-called 'perfect cosmological principle'), which undergirded the 'steady-state theory' of the universe. This violates the second law of thermodynamics which shows an arrow of time, and, furthermore, the 'continuous creation' of the Hoyle-Bondi-Gold theory violates the law of conservation of mass. These and oscillatory theories of the universe have no empirical support. As Pannenberg recognizes, there are ideological interests at stake here, and an eternal and unchanging universe would again contradict the Christian revelation. One imagines him predicting that multiverse theories will ultimately founder for this reason. He is led to pose the counter-question, 'Should a theological interest in the finiteness and irreversible historicity of the world also become involved?' (Pannenberg 1993: 95). Pannenberg is, yet again, rather daring in suggesting that theology should influence the content of scientific theories.

Much of Pannenberg's engagement with the natural sciences could be described as a 'theology of nature' rather than natural theology (cf. the book with this expression in the title). However, his concern for public evidence and espousal of the explanatory nature of theology place him firmly in the camp of those who recognize that there is some knowledge of God available to all simply on the basis of being human. And that is what is meant by natural theology in the traditional sense (Holder 2007).

THOMAS F. TORRANCE: NATURAL THEOLOGY FROM WITHIN

Thomas Torrance was heavily influenced by Barth, yet also engaged seriously with the natural sciences. He also has a place for natural theology, though not as traditionally conceived.

Theology is scientific for Torrance for precisely the same reason it is for Barth, namely that it relates to its object in the way appropriate to it. This is the main point of his book *Theological Science* (Torrance 1969a). As we have seen this is a very different position to that of Pannenberg, who sees theology as making and confirming explanatory hypotheses, and possibly even making novel predictions. For Torrance, 'Christian theology arises out of the actual knowledge of God given in and with concrete happening in space and time' (26). It begins with 'the fact of God's self-revelation'. The problem is, of course, how do we know this is a fact? Torrance, like Barth, presupposes it, and this lays him equally open to W. W. Bartley's charge of irrationality.

Torrance sounds closer to Pannenberg when he says that, since God is creator, theology must engage with the natural sciences (57):

> Thus arising out of the very heart of theology there is an unquenchable interest in the scientific understanding of creaturely being, and for the whole fabric of worldly existence as the medium within which God has placed man and constituted him what he is in relation to Himself.

Like Pannenberg he also sees theology as informing natural science by reminding it of the God-given rational contingency of the world. Thus science should be open to its ground in God's transcendent rationality (Torrance 1998: 84). But that does not lead Torrance to rational argument for God's existence from nature; on the contrary natural theology in that sense is utterly repudiated. As noted by W. Travis McMaken, any natural knowledge of God is firmly denied (McMaken 2010). As for Barth it is Christology, and supremely the cross of Christ, which is central for Torrance. But that means that 'there is no hidden God, no *Deus Absconditus*, no God behind the back of the Lord Jesus, but only the one Lord God who became incarnate in him' (McGrath 1999: 74). Natural theology, which is guilty precisely of proclaiming this 'hidden God', must therefore be excised from theology as a 'sort of foreign body' (Torrance 1969a: 103).

When Torrance does at last find a place for natural theology, it is perhaps not surprising that he completely redefines it. No longer a *praeambulum fidei* or preliminary to the gospel, natural theology is brought within theology proper. To do so, Torrance draws an analogy with what Einstein did in bringing geometry into physics in his profoundly unifying general theory of relativity. Torrance writes (Torrance 1969b: 69–70):

> In physics, this means that geometry cannot be pursued as an axiomatic deductive science detached from actual knowledge of physical processes or be developed as an independent science antecedent to physics, but must be pursued in indissoluble unity with physics.... In theology, this means that natural theology cannot be undertaken apart from actual knowledge of the living God as a prior conceptual system on its own... Rather must it be undertaken in an integrated unity with positive theology in which it plays an indispensable part in our inquiry and understanding of God.

Natural theology is now indispensable because God has revealed himself in time and space, but of course Torrance still has a 'prior conceptual system' of his own, namely the assumed fact of God's self-revelation in Christ. And Torrance's new version of natural theology moves from God to nature and not the other way round.

It would seem, for Torrance as for Barth, that there are no commonly accepted rational grounds for accepting Christian claims. Theology makes itself once again immune to criticism. But despite this, Torrance offers opportunities for the more traditional kind of natural theology which he rejects. We noted above his reference to the rational contingency of the cosmos being rooted in the transcendent rationality of God, and his refusal to base an argument for God's existence on this. However, if God's rationality explains the world's rationality, it follows that the world's rationality is evidence for God being behind it. The contingency of the world, a key theme for Torrance as for Pannenberg, can also be used to provide evidence for God's existence. However, there is some confusion in Torrance's thought about just where contingency lies. Strangely he sees it in Einstein's general relativity which is in fact deterministic, making a similar mistake to Pannenberg regarding the field concept; and he downplays quantum theory which is genuinely indeterministic (Torrance 1998: 14).

Adding further confusion, Torrance says that Einstein gives us 'a finite but unbounded universe with open, dynamic structures grounded in a depth of objectivity and intelligibility which commands and transcends our comprehension' (11). Although a finite and unbounded universe is a possibility in general relativity, it is not demanded by it.

Moreover, a finite universe is technically 'closed' (i.e. of positive spatial curvature) rather than 'open' (of negative curvature). However, what Torrance means by 'open' is that reality is layered with laws at higher levels irreducible to those at lower levels. This makes levels of reality 'open upward but not reducible downward' and not containing within themselves their own sufficient reason (20). As Torrance recognizes, Gödel's incompleteness theorem in mathematics is the ultimate defeater of any reductionist programme in science (1969a: 255).

Despite the confusions in Torrance's presentation, the contingency of the universe, its openness to new, emergent, higher-level structures of reality, and the special initial conditions at the Big Bang to which Torrance also draws attention, can all be very well explained theistically. The universe is neither self-sufficient nor self-explanatory but is grounded in the transcendent rationality of God, as Torrance constantly avers. If the Christian doctrine of creation provides the best explanation, then once again we have a good natural theological argument. Torrance is right to see scientists attempting to move again in the direction of necessity to avoid this conclusion, a point we also noted with reference to Pannenberg (Holder 2009b).

ALISTER McGRATH: SCIENCE
AS *ANCILLA THEOLOGIAE*

Alister McGrath writes on a wide variety of themes but in recent years has turned to the science–religion dialogue and natural theology. In engaging with the natural sciences McGrath has the advantage of an early scientific training, unlike the other theologians we have considered. For McGrath the natural sciences function as an *ancilla theologiae*, much as philosophy has in the past (McGrath 2001: 7, 18–20).

Like Barth and Torrance, whose biography he has written, McGrath sees theology as a science because it adopts methods appropriate to its object. Echoing Polkinghorne's phrase 'epistemology models ontology', McGrath puts it this way: 'ontology determines epistemology' (Polkinghorne 1994: 156; McGrath 2009: 214). In making this claim, McGrath appeals to Roy Bhaskar's concept of 'critical realism'. Indeed this is one of several insights McGrath gleans from secular philosophy. Another insight from Bhaskar's critical realism is the many-layered texture of reality, although this is widely acknowledged by many other authors in the science–religion field, not least Torrance as noted above. McGrath also sees natural theology in Torrance's redefined sense as part of dogmatic theology, and carried out on the basis of a prior commitment to a fully Trinitarian, Chalcedonian Christian orthodoxy (McGrath 2001: 283–6). Natural theology therefore only tells us about a God who is already known. Nature, which for McGrath is a socially constructed notion, and may be interpreted either atheistically or theistically, can then be replaced by 'creation' (McGrath 2005: 53–7). However, this all seems to close down debate on what is under dispute in the modern world, namely whether we can speak of the universe as created by God; indeed whether God exists at all (Peters 2003: 28).

McGrath justifies his position by appeal to Alasdair McIntyre's denial of any universal rationality, but only tradition-based rationalities (McGrath 2002: 64). The Enlightenment project has failed and that licenses theology to advance its own rationality (McGrath 2008: ch. 7). However, although theology is tradition-based it is also tradition-transcendent. That is to say, Christian theology has the capacity to account for other rationalities, including those of other religions (2002: ch. 8). Another insight from secular philosophy is Harman's idea of 'inference to the best explanation'. Hypotheses should be evaluated competitively and the 'best' chosen. McGrath gives criteria such as parsimony, elegance, and explanatory power for this evaluation (2008: 155). The problem is that these seem to be universal rational criteria, which is how they are seen by Swinburne, for example. If Christian theology possesses a tradition-transcendent rationality, and offers the best explanation among competing hypotheses or rationalities, including providing the best account of its competitors, then it seems that universal rationality, which McGrath sought to avoid, is back in (Schwenke 2007). Theological claims ought to be normative for all people; indeed much of what McGrath says, including the dictum 'ontology determines epistemology', sounds as if it should command normative assent. And McGrath's view then becomes indistinguishable from the traditional natural theology which, like Torrance, he rejects.

In demonstrating the explanatory scope of the Christian revelation, McGrath cites much that is common to other authors. There is the fact that science works and the correspondence between the human mind and the rationality of the cosmos including the remarkable and surprising connection between the two through mathematics (McGrath 2006: 59; 2008: 149–50). There are a host of 'fine tunings'. McGrath helpfully cites not just the cosmological fine tunings but much else that needs to be 'just right' for humans to exist in the universe, for example the conditions necessary for life to develop from dead matter, the remarkable chemical properties of water, the dependence of evolution on the properties of key metallic catalysts, and the phenomenon of convergence in evolution (2009: chs. 9–15). He sees all this as consistent with St Augustine's notion of *rationes seminales*, primordial seeds embedded in the initial creation with the potential for the development, under God's guidance, of much greater complexity over time. McGrath notes in several places the Platonic triad of 'truth, beauty, and goodness'. Most of the discussion regarding natural theology relates to the first of these. However, McGrath alerts us to the explanatory power of Christian doctrine in the other two areas as well.

The fundamental ambivalence remains: are all these insights simply confirmatory of beliefs already held or do they constitute arguments meant to command normative assent? That is not to say that they constitute proof; simply that they show with a high degree of plausibility, if not probability (*pace* Swinburne), that Christian claims might be true. Even so, McGrath has drawn our attention to a wider range of explananda than many other authors and, as with Torrance, thereby provides opportunities for natural theology in the traditional sense.

CONCLUDING REMARKS

The twentieth century began on a high note and, through much ambivalence, has ended with natural theology once more a lively topic of investigation. For the theologically orthodox, Karl Barth's challenge was timely, yet his negative critique has been seen to isolate theology from other areas of human enquiry. Bonhoeffer's charge of 'positivism of revelation' was apposite, and Bonhoeffer offered opportunities for intellectual engagement with the world through his notion of the penultimate and in other ways. The most positive of the theologians considered here is Wolfhart Pannenberg who brings scientific rationality to bear directly on theology. Although it is in the realm of history that the truth claims of Christianity will be ultimately validated, theology is explanatory in the realm of nature too. Thomas Torrance and Alister McGrath retreat into making natural theology dependent on prior commitment to a fully orthodox, Trinitarian dogmatic position. However, each offers further opportunities for natural theology as traditionally conceived, by highlighting features of the universe such as its rational contingency which point to the grounding of the universe beyond itself.

Of course this brief survey has been unable to cover all developments in philosophy, theology, and the sciences which are relevant to natural theology. There are other analytic philosophers besides Swinburne who argue for metaphysically realist claims about God. Thus William Lane Craig advances the *kalām* cosmological argument, a deductive, if controversial, argument for God's existence based on the supposed fact that the universe had a beginning in time (Craig 1979). William P. Alston analyses religious experience, though in very different style from William James, and argues for its evidential force in justifying theistic belief (Alston 1991). The rejection of natural theology is also alive not just among Barthians but in the more recent radical orthodoxy school of John Milbank and his colleagues, which is suspicious both of secular reason and of dialogue with other disciplines (Milbank, Pickstock, and Ward 1999). On the other hand there is a flourishing dialogue between science and theology, a significant representative of which, besides Polkinghorne, would be the late Arthur Peacocke. Peacocke sees the existence of a creator as the best explanation of all-that-is, his critique of scientific reductionism and espousal of emergence, especially of persons, being particularly relevant to this (Peacocke 1993). One recent development which may be positive for natural theology is Simon Conway Morris's notion of convergence in biological evolution (referred to by McGrath), which seems to indicate that, were the evolutionary tape to be run again, the result would not be dramatically different and that therefore the emergence of humans is in some sense built in to the way the universe is set up (Conway Morris 2003). On the other hand, new challenges for natural theology are arising from the cognitive psychology of religion and evolutionary psychology.

It would seem that, for the Christian faith to be commended in the modern world, natural theology is vital. It is true that looking at nature alone can only lead to a limited view of God, and that revelation is essential (Barth was right about that). However, revelation itself needs also to be rationally evaluated, which is where Pannenberg helps. The building of a cumulative case for God's existence, using the many insights described here, is justified. But then going on to examine the specific claims of Christianity in a 'ramified natural theology' (as suggested by Swinburne, though his detailed arguments clearly need scrutinizing) would also seem to be vindicated. Natural theology and revealed theology are then hardly to be distinguished at all.

ACKNOWLEDGEMENTS

In the above I have summarized several articles which treat the subject matter much more fully. I am grateful for permission to do so from the following:

Taylor and Francis Ltd (<http:www.tandf.co.uk/journals>, copyright © Center for Theology and the Natural Sciences): Rodney D. Holder (2008). 'Modern Science and the Interpretation of Genesis: Can We Learn from Dietrich Bonhoeffer?'. *Theology and Science* 6/2: 213–31; Rodney D. Holder (2009). 'Thomas Torrance: "Retreat to Commitment" or a New Place for Natural Theology'. *Theology and Science* 7/3: 275–96.

John Wiley and Sons: Rodney D. Holder (2009). 'Science and Religion in the Theology of Dietrich Bonhoeffer'. *Zygon* 44/1: 115–32.

Petr Sláma (ed., Protestant Theological Faculty of Charles University in Prague): Rodney D. Holder (2007). 'Creation and the Sciences in the Theology of Wolfhart Pannenberg'. *Communio Viatorum* XLIX/II: 210–53.

The Gospel Coalition: Rodney D. Holder (2001). 'Karl Barth and the Legitimacy of Natural Theology'. *Themelios* 26: 22–37 (formerly published by the Religious and Theological Studies Fellowship of the Universities and Colleges Christian Fellowship).

REFERENCES

Alston, William P. (1991). *Perceiving God: The Epistemology of Religious Experience*. New York and London: Cornell University Press.

Barth, Karl (1936). *Church Dogmatics*, I.1. Edinburgh: T. & T. Clark.

—— (1946). 'No!' in *Natural Theology*. Translated by Peter Fraenkel. Introduction by John Baillie. London: Geoffrey Bles, The Centenary Press.

—— (1957). *Church Dogmatics*, II.1. Edinburgh: T. & T. Clark.

—— (1968). 'Fifteen Answers to Professor van Harnack' in *The Beginnings of Dialectical Theology*, Vol I. Edited by James M. Robinson. Translated by Keith R. Crim. Richmond, Va: John Knox Press: pp. 167–170.

Bartley, W. W., III (1984). *The Retreat to Commitment*. 2nd edn. La Salle, IL and London: Open Court.

Bonhoeffer, Dietrich (1964 [1949]). *Ethics*. Edited by Eberhard Bethge. Translated by Neville Horton Smith. London: Collins.

—— (1971). *Letters and Papers from Prison*. Edited by Eberhard Bethge. Enlarged edn. London: SCM Press.

—— (1997). *Creation and Fall: A Theological Exposition of Genesis 1–3*. Edited and translated by Martin Rüter and Ilse Tödt. English edition edited by John W. de Gruchy and translated by D. S. Bax. Minneapolis: Fortress Press.

Brunner, Emil (1946). 'Nature and Grace' in *Natural Theology*. Translated by Peter Fraenkel. Introduction by John Baillie. London: Geoffrey Bles: The Centenary Press: pp. 15–64.

Conway Morris, Simon (2003). *Life's Solution: Inevitable Humans in a Lonely Universe*. Cambridge: Cambridge University Press.

Craig, William Lane (1979). *The 'Kalām' Cosmological Argument*. London: Macmillan.

Dawkins, Richard (2006). *The God Delusion*. London: Bantam.

Harman, Gilbert (1965). 'The Inference to the Best Explanation'. *The Philosophical Review* 74/1: 88–95.

Harnack, Adolf von (1968). 'Fifteen Questions to those among the Theologians who are Contemptuous of the Scientific Theology' in *The Beginnings of Dialectical Theology*, Vol I. Edited by James M. Robinson. Translated by Keith R. Crim Richmond, Va: John Knox Press: pp. 165–166.

Hefner, Philip (1988). 'The Role of Science in Pannenberg's Theological Thinking' in *The Theology of Wolfhart Pannenberg: Twelve American Critiques, with an Autobiographical Essay and Response*. Edited by Carl E. Braaten and Philip Clayton. Minneapolis: Augsburg: pp. 266–86.

—— (1997). 'The Role of Science in Pannenberg's Theological Thinking' in *Beginning with the End: God, Science, and Wolfhart Pannenberg*. Edited by Carol Rausch Albright and Joel Haugen. Chicago and La Salle, IL: Open Court: pp. 109 ff.

Holder, Rodney D. (2004). *God, the Multiverse, and Everything: Modern Cosmology and the Argument from Design*. Aldershot, UK, and Burlington, VT: Ashgate.

—— (2007). 'Creation and the Sciences in the Theology of Wolfhart Pannenberg'. *Communio Viatorum* XLIX/II: 210–53.

—— (2008). 'Modern Science and the Interpretation of Genesis: Can We Learn from Dietrich Bonhoeffer?' *Theology and Science* 6/2: 213–31.

—— (2009a). 'Science and Religion in the Theology of Dietrich Bonhoeffer'. *Zygon* 44/1: 115–32.

—— (2009b). 'Thomas Torrance: "Retreat to Commitment" or a New Place for Natural Theology?' *Theology and Science* 7/3: 275–96.

Huyssteen, Wentzel van (1989). *Theology and the Justification of Faith: Constructing Theories in Systematic Theology*. Grand Rapids, MI: Wm B. Eerdmans.

Jaki, S. L. (1986). *Lord Gifford and his Lectures: A Centenary Retrospect*. Edinburgh: Scottish Academic Press; Macon, GA: Mercer University Press.

Lakatos, Imre (1978). *The Methodology of Scientific Research Programmes: Philosophical Papers*. Vol. I. Edited by John Worrall and Gregory Currie. Cambridge: Cambridge University Press.

McGrath, Alister E. (1999). *T. F. Torrance: An Intellectual Biography*. Edinburgh: T & T Clark.

—— (2001). *A Scientific Theology*. Vol. I: *Nature*. Edinburgh: T & T Clark Ltd.

—— (2002). *A Scientific Theology*. Vol. II: *Reality*. Grand Rapids, MI and Cambridge, UK: William B. Eerdmans.

—— (2005). *Dawkins' God: Genes, Memes, and the Meaning of Life*. Oxford: Blackwell.

—— (2006). *The Order of Things*. Oxford: Blackwell.

—— (2007). 'Theologie als Mathesis Universalis? Heinrich Scholz, Karl Barth und der wissenschaftliche Status der christlichen Theologie'. *Theologische Zeitschrift* 63/1: 44–57.

—— (2008). *The Open Secret: A New Vision for Natural Theology*. Oxford: Blackwell.

—— (2009). *A Fine-Tuned Universe: The Quest for God in Science and Theology*. The 2009 Gifford Lectures. Louisville, KY: Westminster John Knox Press.

McMaken, W. Travis (2010). 'The Impossibility of Natural Knowledge of God in T. F. Torrance's Reformulated Natural Theology'. *International Journal of Systematic Theology* 12/3: 319–40.

Milbank, John, Catherine Pickstock, and Graham Ward, eds. (1999). *Radical Orthodoxy. A New Theology*. London and New York: Routledge.

Murphy, Nancey (1990). *Theology in the Age of Scientific Reasoning*. Ithaca, NY and London: Cornell University Press.

Murphy, Nancey (1997). 'A Lakatosian Reconstruction of Pannenberg's Program: Responses to Sponheim, van Huyssteen, and Eaves' in *Beginning with the End: God, Science, and Wolfhart Pannenberg*. Edited by Carol Rausch Albright and Joel Haugen. Chicago and La Salle, IL: Open Court: pp. 409–26.

Pannenberg, Wolfhart (1976 [1973]). *Theology and the Philosophy of Science*. Translated by Francis McDonagh. London: Darton, Longman & Todd.

—— (1991). *Systematic Theology*. Vol. I. Translated by Geoffrey W. Bromiley. Edinburgh: T & T Clark.

—— (1993). *Towards a Theology of Nature: Essays on Science and Faith*. Louisville, KY: Westminster/John Knox Press.

—— (1994). *Systematic Theology*. Vol. II. Translated by Geoffrey W. Bromiley. Edinburgh: T & T Clark.

Pannenberg, Wolfhart et al., eds. (1968 [1961]). *Revelation as History*. Translated by D. Granskou. New York: Macmillan, London: Collier-Macmillan.

Peacocke, Arthur (1993). *Theology for a Scientific Age*. Enlarged edn. London: SCM.

Peters, Ted (2003). *Science, Theology, and Ethics*. Aldershot, UK and Burlington, VT: Ashgate.

Polkinghorne, John (1994). *Science and Christian Belief: Theological Reflections of a Bottom-up Thinker*. London: SPCK.

—— (1999). 'Wolfhart Pannenberg's engagement with the natural sciences'. *Zygon* 34: 151–8.

—— (2006). 'Where is Natural Theology Today?' in *Science and Christian Belief* 18:2, 169–79.

Scholz, Heinrich (1931). 'Wie ist eine evangelische Theologie als Wissenschaft möglich?' *Zwischen den Zeiten* 9/1: 8–35. Repr. in Gerhard Sauter, ed. (1971). *Theologie als Wissenschaft*. Munich: Chr. Kaiser Verlag: 221–64.

Schwenke, Heiner (2007). 'Epistemischer Partikularismus als Weg der Theologie? Warum Alister McGraths <naturwissenschaftliche Theologie> nicht naturwissenschaftlich ist'. *Theologische Zeitschrift* 63/1: 58–78.

Swinburne, Richard (2004a). *The Existence of God*. 2nd edn. Oxford: Oxford University Press.

—— (2004b). 'Natural Theology, its "Dwindling Probabilities" and "Lack of Rapport"'. *Faith and Philosophy* 21/4: 533–46.

Torrance, Thomas F. (1969a). *Theological Science*. Edinburgh: T & T Clark Ltd.

—— (1969b). *Space, Time and Incarnation*. Edinburgh: T & T Clark.

—— (1998 [1981]). *Divine and Contingent Order*. Rev. edn. Edinburgh: T & T Clark.

Weizsäcker, Carl Friedrich von (1952 [1943]). *The World View of Physics*. Translated by Marjorie Grene. London: Routledge.

Witham, Larry (2005). *The Measure of God: Our Century-long Struggle to Reconcile Science and Religion. The Story of the Gifford Lectures*. San Francisco: HarperSanFrancisco.

PART II

THEOLOGICAL PERSPECTIVES ON NATURAL THEOLOGY

CHAPTER 8

JEWISH PERSPECTIVES ON NATURAL THEOLOGY

DANIEL H. FRANK

JEWS are a sceptical lot. They tend to take nothing for granted, and often ask why. On *Pesach* (Passover) one asks why this particular night is different from other nights, i.e. why one eats unleavened bread (*matzah*) on this night, why one eats only bitter herbs on this night, why one dips herbs twice, and finally why one reclines at the Seder meal. In this case the questions resolve themselves by recalling a bit of history, but they serve as a quick reminder that Jews and their particular way of life, Judaism, are grounded in a revelation that demands to be understood, not merely accepted.

There is an ongoing tension in the classical Jewish texts between arrogance and humility, between a strong demand for sensible answers to human problems and a deep sense that such answers or reasons are beyond us to comprehend. The *Book of Job* certainly comes to mind here. Job is beleaguered and the narrative goes back and forth between a stern demand for an accounting of his travails and a resignation that human beings cannot expect to understand the ways of God. All is as it should be, or maybe not.

On both counts, there seems to be no question that Job is beset. His trials are just that; they come upon him from the outside. Job suffers, for whatever reason, through no fault of his own. Indeed, the very opening of the book presents God and Satan planning a test for the most pious and faithful of His servants. And then they get to work.

'Poor Job', we say. Why? It is on account of his unmerited suffering. He did nothing to deserve what he got. Implicit in this thought is the idea that one gets, and ought to get, what one deserves. Maimonides (1138–1204), the greatest of the medieval Jewish philosophers, does not disagree with the implicit idea, but vigorously denies that Job is blameless in his suffering. I shall spend some time on recounting Maimonides' strikingly revisionist reading of Job, for in it we discern I think a good example of the 'naturalizing' of Judaism, a reductive and deflationary analysis that re-envisions grand theological categories that have tended to magnify the gulf between divine and human.

In the Jewish philosophical tradition, such a reductive analysis—a philosophical naturalism that can be traced to Aristotle—is typified by such thinkers as Saadia Gaon

(882–942), the first systematic Jewish philosopher, Maimonides himself, and at the very end of the classical tradition, Spinoza (1632–77). All three thinkers were controversial in their own time, though I suspect for most readers only Spinoza stands out as notorious. But Saadia was as polemical as either of his two successors, and Maimonides had the distinction of having some of his books incinerated in the thirteenth century. Indeed, it is a strange irony that by the time of Spinoza in the seventeenth century, Maimonides, the arch-rationalist, had come to stand for the canonical (conservative) tradition, which had to be overcome in the very name of reason.

Maimonides on Job

As noted, Maimonides denies that Job is blameless in his very own suffering. Whatever can he mean? After all, God and Satan connive, and we read the trial of Job as an exercise in theodicy, divine justice: how are divine knowledge, power, and goodness compatible with evil, misfortune, and blameless suffering, for the latter seem to offend against the former? But Maimonides doesn't read the parable of Job that way; he doesn't emphasize the divine wager, which prefaces the book. For him, as for the young Elihu, Job is not so much about God and divine justice, but rather about Job himself and human finitude, human arrogance and presumption, and the insufficiency of moral virtue to secure happiness and beatitude. To be sure, Maimonides takes himself to be illustrating his own view about divine providence—divine knowledge of human affairs and the salvific consequences resulting from this—by the story of Job. But the role of God in the story, as Maimonides presents it, is quite understated. The real 'culprit' in the tale is he who suffers, Job himself. Indeed, as I shall argue on Maimonides' behalf, it is Job himself who is the (real) cause of his own undoing. His 'innocence', understood aright, is far from exculpatory. Further, as I shall attempt to clarify, Maimonides' discussion of the parable of Job is grounded deeply in Aristotle's own discussion of the nature of moral virtue, but, unlike Aristotle's account, Maimonides emphasizes the relative *in*sufficiency of moral virtue to secure permanent happiness. And though I wouldn't press the point too very hard, I think we might understand Job himself along the lines of Aristotle's *phronimos*, the morally virtuous individual, and Maimonides' exegesis as an implied critique of Aristotle's moral paradigm.

As Maimonides says early in his discussion of Job, 'the most marvellous and extraordinary thing about this story is the fact that knowledge is not attributed in it to Job. He is not said to be a wise or comprehending or an intelligent man. Only moral virtue and righteousness in action are ascribed to him. For if he had been wise, his situation would not have been obscure for him, as will become clear' (1995: 3.22). For Maimonides, Job is good, but not wise. As a result, he suffers. He suffers on account of his innocence, now understood, not as guiltlessness, but rather as a *lack* of wisdom. Precisely what sort of wisdom does Job lack, which renders him vulnerable? On a grand level, he lacks the kind of wisdom vouchsafed someone like the Stoic sage, knowledge of the rational order of the universe, that everything is in its place and as it ought to be. It is presumably the beginning of an insight such as this that God offers Job from the whirlwind (38 ff.). But we don't have to abstract to this rather grand level for present purposes.

More locally, Job is bereft of the wisdom that would clarify and explain his predicament. Job follows common sense in imagining that his material possessions, health, wealth, and family are constitutive of true happiness and that they are a sure sign of his goodness. This latter we might denominate Job's 'Calvinism'. Further, Job imagines that (his) moral virtue guarantees happiness—otherwise why is he so utterly confused and embittered, imagining that 'the righteous man and the wicked are regarded as equal by God?' (Maimonides 1995: 3.23; cf. Job 9:22–3). In following common sense Job shows himself both presumptuous and innocent of any understanding of what brings about true happiness and completely lacking any sense of the real link between righteousness and its (purported) reward. For Maimonides, Job suffers precisely because he has no real understanding of what is truly valuable and because in following common opinion about the presumed link between moral virtue and material well-being he cannot in the least fathom what is happening to him, and why. Of course, these two are connected and an understanding of the former is key to unlocking the latter. But let us take the two separately for the moment.

Let us briefly recall Aristotle and his moral theorizing. In outlining the human good Aristotle canvasses a variety of candidates for what constitutes human well-being. Pleasure, honour and esteem, and wealth are proffered, discussed, and rather quickly dismissed from contention, being either too base, too instrumental, or too dependent on an external source to merit serious consideration. Even moral virtue itself is called into question as being the *summum bonum*, for it is compatible 'with the greatest sufferings and misfortunes; but a man who was living so no one would call happy, unless he were maintaining a thesis at all costs' (Aristotle 2002: 1.5). (Indeed, this latter comment reminds one immediately of Job, morally virtuous, but subject to misfortune.) Nevertheless, for Aristotle, each of the rejected candidates has a role to play in happiness, even though, by itself, none is sufficient to guarantee it. Each is a necessary condition of happiness, so much so that Aristotle can appeal to common sense to establish the point that happiness requires both moral virtue, grounded in effort and practice, as well as 'external' goods such as wealth, good birth, physical beauty, etc., which are to a very considerable degree outside our power to control. Nevertheless, without the latter, human flourishing is impossible of attainment and one is rendered an outcast. Interestingly, the very external goods that Aristotle deems so necessary are precisely those that Socrates—poor, ugly, base-born—lacked, an indication of Aristotle's anti-Socraticism, his anti-anti-conventionalism.

Aristotle's position pushes him to the following dilemma, one between his (and our) deepest intuitions: either happiness is something in our control and not easily snatched from us, in which case external goods and moral luck play no role, or happiness is, at least in part, outside our control, dependent on luck and good fortune.

Aristotle does not resolve the dilemma. Nor I think does he want to, wishing thereby to indicate that happiness and the human condition hover between stability and fragility.

On the one hand, happiness is attainable and sustainable by our own efforts and is consequent upon actions chosen by the agent. On the other hand, as a student of tragedy Aristotle could hardly overlook the extent to which a life can be wrecked through no fault attributable to the agent. King Priam of Troy is his explicit example here (2002: 1.9).

For Aristotle, then, contingency is woven into the fabric of human happiness and the human condition. Indeed, he even suggests that the virtue of the virtuous individual shines forth in adversity, in 'bearing with resignation many great misfortunes' (2002: 1.10). Again, one is reminded of Job and his own misfortunes. But in being so reminded one must signal an important contrast here between Aristotle and Maimonides.

In pointing out the importance of external goods in the achievement of happiness—indeed they play a role in the very development of virtue and the doing of morally virtuous deeds—Aristotle imports contingency into the very notion of happiness, and in so doing shows a deep sensitivity to the fragile and ultimately tragic condition of humankind. Try as we might, misfortune can snatch happiness from us, and moral luck counts for much. But Aristotle's tragic sense is matched by nothing in Maimonides. Maimonides does not view the suffering Job, the righteous and morally virtuous man, as a tragic figure. Instead, he views him as a fool, one who, though morally upright, has no idea of what is truly valuable and who is perplexed and utterly uncomprehending of the meaning (and source) of his misfortune. And for Maimonides, such ignorance is causally linked to suffering itself.

For Maimonides, Job represents common sense in holding material goods to be of value and further in imagining that righteousness and virtue do not go unrewarded and are themselves sufficient for happiness. In holding these beliefs, Job had, according to Maimonides, 'no true knowledge and knew the deity only because of his acceptance of authority, just as the multitude adhering to a law know it' (1995: 3.23). Job is, from Maimonides' standpoint, like those who, at a later stage of the *Guide*, countenance traditional authority, 'but do not engage in speculation concerning the fundamental principles of religion and make no inquiry whatever regarding the rectification of belief' (1995: 3.51; cf. 3.23). Such individuals merit no praise from Maimonides, and Job and his friends are no exception. So long as one follows and lives in accord with traditional authority, the analogue to unreflective common sense, one is at risk. Indeed, the unreflective agent, just by virtue of his intellectual slackness, falls outside the ambit of divine providential concern (1995: 3.17–18), and as a result one's felicity is captive to forces beyond one's control. Note that for Maimonides misfortune is a function of ignorance, perhaps even culpable ignorance, and, contra Aristotle, not an ineliminable part of the world, nor a function of the human condition.

Let me stress this point. For Aristotle, as we have seen, happiness requires external goods and is consequent upon good fortune, with the result that to this degree happiness is beyond our control. The human condition is at root tragic. For Maimonides, true human happiness, the insight into which comes through philosophical speculation, does not require external goods for its fulfillment. Job's suffering depends upon himself, not upon forces outside him. If there is a tragic element inherent in Maimonides' view, it is that not all human beings can be philosophers, and hence must live a life mixed with contingency and suffering. But this latter point is not one that Maimonides' stresses, except when he indexes divine providential concern (salvation) to rational speculation.

For Maimonides, the antidote to human suffering is knowledge, specifically knowledge of God. We need not worry now about precisely what such knowledge amounts to, save to be clear that such knowledge has the effect of putting everything into perspective, clarifying what is truly of value, and what is not. Heretofore, Job took happiness to consist of things such as health, wealth, and offspring—commonly held goods—with the result that when these were taken away suffering ensued. But with God's pronouncements from the whirlwind at the end of the narrative, and Job's (gradual) realization that his prior perplexity and suffering were grounded in a profound ignorance of the nature and (relative) value of things and a naive presumption about reward and desert, Job commences to understand that not even virtue guarantees felicity, only knowledge does. Only knowledge of God can guarantee that one possesses a sense of the relative value of things.

Maimonides is clear that if Job had been wise, 'his situation would not have been obscure to him', and that 'when he knew God with a certain knowledge, he admitted that true happiness, which is knowledge of the deity, is guaranteed to all who know Him and that a human being cannot be troubled in it by any of all the misfortunes in question' (1995: 3.23). Clarity and knowledge bring with them invulnerability to fortune. This is a very strong claim, and I suspect we think it palpably false. But why? Precisely because we have a view of the self that entails that the self is without remainder part of the material world. But Maimonides doesn't hold this view (1995: 3.54). Nor, finally, does Aristotle, with what effect this had upon his appreciation of moral luck we may speculate (2002: 10.7–8). In the final analysis, both link ultimate felicity with an activity akin to divine activity, a theoretical achievement (Aristotle 2002: 10.7–8; Maimonides 1995: 3.54). It is enough for present purposes to underscore that for both thinkers, the true self is the immortal and divine part of 'ourselves', and correlative to this metaphysical claim, we may understand their choice of philosophical understanding as the human good. For Maimonides, this entails that prophecy is the highest good and the prophet, paradigmatically Moses, the human ideal. Divine providential care is a function of intellectual apprehension of the divine. As Maimonides puts it:

> [P]rovidence watches over everyone endowed with intellect proportionately to the measure of his intellect...Providence always watches over an individual endowed with perfect apprehension, whose intellect never ceases from being occupied with God. On the other hand, an individual endowed with perfect apprehension, whose thought sometimes for a certain time is emptied of God, is watched over by providence only during the time when he thinks of God; providence withdraws from him during the time when he is occupied with something else...and becomes in consequence of this a target for every evil that may happen to befall him. [1995: 3.51]

Indeed, with God's appearance to Job from the whirlwind, Job's education commences: 'I had heard of You by the hearing of the ear; but now my eye sees You; wherefore I abhor myself and repent of dust and ashes' (Job 42:5–6). Maimonides understands this latter to mean not merely that Job is humbled by the divine presence and its fulsome iteration of natural events and powers, but also that he comes to abhor what he used to desire, material goods, now evaluated as no more than 'dust and ashes'. Job has begun to see that true human felicity does not consist of material possessions and, with this realization, he begins to distance himself from the material world, the realm of contingency. In this regard, Job will come to understand that even moral virtue, the heretofore presumptive grounds for happiness and well-being, cannot be the final good. We might presume that Job's arguments for this latter conclusion would parallel Aristotle's against the candidacy of moral virtue as the *summum bonum* at the conclusion of the *Nicomachean Ethics*.

Both Aristotle and Maimonides have a keen sense of the precariousness of the human condition. But they draw instructively different conclusions. Aristotle takes the human condition as ineliminably tragic, admitting of no exit from the twists and turns of fortune. Maimonides does not draw this conclusion, because as we see from Job's misfortunes, Job's suffering is his very own doing, a function of his ignorance, his lack of wisdom. For Maimonides, like the anti-Aristotelian Stoics, we are much more in control of our destiny than Aristotle imagined. Though prophecy, the *summum bonum*, is for Maimonides not wholly a natural occurrence, the preliminary steps are very much in our power. For Maimonides, knowledge has the power to vanquish the vicissitudes of fortune.

Let us briefly return to our starting point. We noted that Maimonides, in his own way and illustrated by his revisionist reading of Job, exemplifies a 'naturalizing' tendency in Jewish theological speculation. He is most intent on placing the blame for suffering directly on Job, and with it, the real possibility for a *human* resolution of the problem at hand. Divine grace plays virtually no role in the tale told. To be sure, there is a divine intercession (from the whirlwind), but Maimonides' gloss is to understand this moment as part of Job's ongoing education, a reward for his perseverance and questioning, less as a bolt out of the blue. Here, as elsewhere, Maimonides works hard to explicate Judaism, his religious tradition, as committed to rational reflection and a healthy alliance with science and philosophy. Though we have noted a manifest disagreement between Maimonides and Aristotle on the nature of the human condition, this is in the end less important than a manifest agreement about a (natural) human capacity to achieve well-being. The Maimonidean wise man (a prophet) differs from the Aristotelian *phronimos*, but the emphasis placed upon the role of human agency is clear. Without effort, there is no hope for success.

SAADIA ON TRADITION AND EMPIRICAL STARTING POINTS

Saadia Gaon (882–942) was born in Egypt but spent much of his life in Sura, near Baghdad, as head (*gaon*) of the rabbinic academy. A pugnacious, controversial figure, Saadia may lay claim to be the *fons et origo* of (medieval) Jewish philosophy. The very idea of philosophizing about Judaism, taking the religious tradition itself to be a topic for philosophical reflection, is new with him. Even though Maimonides was a critic of Saadia on certain issues pertaining to the nature of law, he was demonstrably beholden to the latter's general project. That said, Saadia's ultimate purpose in speculating about his own religious tradition was to defend rabbinic Judaism against its detractors, some of whom were to be found even within Judaism itself.

Saadia's defence of Judaism is a species of (Muslim) *kalam*. What is *kalam*? Literally meaning 'speaking, speech, discussion' and often glossed as 'dialectical or speculative theology', *kalam* is in fact a science (*'ilm*) or branch of knowledge that, according to Farabi, a contemporary of Saadia, though like Maimonides at a later date a critic of *kalam*, enables a person to support specific beliefs and actions laid down by the legislators of the religion and to refute all opinions contradicting them. And some three centuries after Farabi, the great philosophical historian ibn Khaldun seconds Farabi by understanding *kalam* as a science that involves rational proofs for defence of the articles of faith and refuting 'innovators' who deviate from the beliefs of early Muslims and Muslim orthodoxy. What is manifest here is the apologetic nature of *kalam*, its use for purposes of defending the faith by philosophical argument. One notes immediately the constructive role of philosophy in *kalam* (Islamic or Jewish). Philosophical speculation is not at odds with orthodox belief but, quite the opposite, its ally. However, it is not a traditional ally but a new-found one, and in Jewish circles the project commences with Saadia.

Saadia has been called 'the revolutionary champion of tradition', and his philosophical magnum opus, *The Book of Doctrines and Beliefs*, written in Arabic and completed in 933, is an outstanding example of Jewish *kalam*, and the greatest work of Jewish philosophy before Maimonides' *Guide* (1190). The 'revolutionary' nature of the book lies in its underlying assumption that Judaism—traditional rabbinic Judaism—is in fact (reducible to) a set of doctrines and thus amenable to systematic theological speculation. It was due to Saadia that a defence of Judaism took the form of a (Mutazilite-inspired) theological discussion of such issues as creation *ex nihilo,* the unity of God, free will, and divine reward and punishment. What a defence of the faith might have been for the religious fundamentalist, a (reactionary) call to cease philosophizing, becomes in Saadia's hands a rich philosophical fare of argument and counter-argument. Saadia's book is a full participant in contemporary intellectual life, while defending traditional Judaism.

The Book of Doctrines and Beliefs was written in Arabic under the title *Kitab al-Amanat wa'l-I'tiqadat* (translated into Hebrew as *Sefer ha-Emunot ve-ha-De'ot* in 1186 by Judah ibn Tibbon). As we begin to trace aspects of 'naturalizing' (empiricist) tendencies in Saadia, we will do well to attend to the very title of the book. *Amanat* (Hebrew *emunot*) are beliefs held 'on the basis of scriptural authority' (alone). Contrarily, *i'tiqadat* (Hebrew *de'ot*) are the very *amanat* subjected to rational reflection and critical scrutiny. Thus, the purpose of Saadia's treatise is to enable the reader to reach a stage where the *amanat* become the (scrutinized) subject of *i'tiqadat*. In the very introduction to the ten chapters, or mini-treatises, that make up *Emunot ve-De'ot*, Saadia indicates the dynamic of the work when he says that 'the believer who blindly relies on tradition will turn into one basing his belief on speculation and understanding'.

Our prior discussion of Maimonides' gloss on Job and his troubles come to mind. In understanding the deepest purpose of Jewish theology to be speculation on the foundations of (traditional) belief, we may readily see the enormous influence that Saadia had on his successors, especially Maimonides. It will be recalled from our prior discussion of Maimonides' gloss on Job that Job, in holding material goods to be of value and further in imagining that righteousness and virtue do not go unrewarded and are themselves sufficient for happiness, has, according to Maimonides, 'no true knowledge and knew the deity only because of his acceptance of authority, just as the multitude adhering to a law know it' (1995: 3.23). Job is precisely like those individuals, described in a famous parable at the end of the *Guide*, who countenance traditional authority 'but do not engage in speculation concerning the fundamental principles of religion and make no inquiry whatever regarding the rectification of belief' (1995: 3.51).

We can range even further properly to contextualize Saadia's (and Maimonides') philosophical project(s). Viewed as the foundational project that it is, one is reminded of Aristotle's general way of proceeding philosophically. Commencing with the status quo, generally the untutored beliefs and customary actions of the neophyte, Aristotle proceeds to transport the 'student' to the point where he begins to understand the grounds for those beliefs and customs. In his own way, Saadia wishes to turn (mere) belief into rationally grounded conviction. So, too, we should understand Maimonides' very own project in the *Guide*. It too is Aristotelian in the way just noted, addressed as it is to a traditional Jew, 'perfect in his religion and character' (1995: Preface), who, on account of having unquestioningly accepted traditional beliefs, has finally become perplexed by the 'externals of the law' (its literal meaning) by 'having studied the sciences of the philosophers'. Traditional, unreflected-upon beliefs square off against natural science and philosophy, with disastrous effect. And so it becomes Maimonides' grand project in the *Guide* to clarify the tradition in such a way that its 'philosophicality' is revealed, and the addressee's perplexities are removed.

Writing at a different time and in a different place, Saadia's audience is manifestly different from Maimonides'. Maimonides writes for an elite, intellectual group, who worries about how dual affiliations to a religious tradition and to contemporary science may both be maintained, without a lessening of commitment to either. This is not Saadia's audience. Writing at a time of major intellectual and social change and growth within Islam itself, of sectarian confrontation with the fundamentalist Karaites in his own community, and finally of interreligious disputation with orthodox Christianity and Gnostic dualists, the Jewish community found itself beset by a bewildering array of rival creeds. The manifest need for a clarification and defence of the faith was apparent, and Saadia writes to this end.

With such a mass of ideas swirling about, it is little wonder that traditional religious beliefs were subjected to scrutiny and attenuated through the sheer welter of new ideas. How ought one to proceed to defend the tradition, given such a situation? Saadia proceeds just as he should, from the ground up. In taking a look at his methodology we can glimpse his empiricism, his naturalizing tendencies to ground belief in reason unaided, and a correction of the senses. In the crucial introduction (prolegomena) to *Emunot* ve-De'ot, Saadia addresses the sources 'why men...become involved in errors' and then proceeds to outline the means whereby this situation can be ameliorated. The sources of error and doubt are for Saadia both intellectual and moral. Uncritically employed, the senses can be unreliable; reason may be derailed if inferential skills are lacking; and overarching all this is the propensity to impatience in inquiry (one is minded of Descartes' plea in the fourth Meditation to bind the will to the understanding, lest it lead the inquirer into irrationality). Error and sceptical doubt arise quite naturally. Rectification of belief follows from treating (correcting and compensating for) the aforementioned sources of error. If sense perceptions are properly interpreted, if inferential skills are appropriately developed, and arguments are carefully analysed, errors will be removed and true belief will take their place. Saadia's common-sensical empiricism is here manifest, something perhaps to be expected given the 'foundational' nature of his project. Not for Saadia is an anti-philosophical (fideist) reaffirmation of the faith an antidote to scepticism. But a surprise lurks.

To the list of the sources of insight and true belief, Saadia adds another, tradition (al-kabar). For Saadia, tradition refers to the Torah in a wide sense, including both Scripture and the oral (rabbinic) tradition. For him, this tradition is a reliable and authentic one, which transmits to humankind the prophetic revelation, the truth (compare Muslim hadith). Why does Saadia add tradition to his list? In countenancing tradition as an (independent) source of truth, he is not defending (the) tradition in an almost question-begging way, but is evidently pointing to some insufficiency or weakness that bedevils the standard empirical sources of knowledge, requiring some kind of supplementation. The latter often mislead, are employed uncritically, and at best provide for some the starting point for an arduous and lengthy journey towards truth. Contrarily, the revealed truth (the tradition), witnessed by many and transmitted by a reliable tradition, is indubitable and immediately worthy of acceptance.

Prima facie this addition of tradition is surprising. We noted above that the problems that beset the various empirical sources of truth do not lead Saadia to any form of fideism, rather the emphasis is placed on a careful and sober correction and strengthening of those very sources. Given this, his appeal to tradition, revealed truth, seems odd. In countenancing the 'necessity' of revelation, and the authentic tradition that transmits it to us, Saadia seems to run the risk of making philosophy and natural scientific speculation irrelevant. Why should one engage in philosophical speculation and scientific inquiry—empirical science—if the truth is *already* at hand? Given that, 'He [the deity] announced them [the doctrines of religion, ie the truths about creation, divine unity and justice, etc] to us by way of prophetic revelation and verified them by proofs and signs of a visible character [miracles], and not by rational arguments', there would appear to be no constructive role left for philosophy and science to play in the acquisition of knowledge. Philosophy and scientific inquiry would appear to be redundant.

But I think that to draw this conclusion is rather too quick, and that Saadia's empiricism remains intact. For him, the manifest weakness of human reason, its propensity to error and confusion, necessitated a divine project of what we might call 'proleptic enlightenment'. Out of benevolence God revealed the truth ('which cannot be assailed by doubts') to everyone through the prophets, lest humankind persist in error and darkness, enjoining at least some to complete the speculative task in the fullness of time. The revelation serves as a beacon as one strives for knowledge and to overcome confusion. In short, tradition serves as an invitation to do philosophy and science. Saadia writes:

> [i]t cannot be thought that the Sages should have wished to prohibit us from rational inquiry, seeing that our Creator has commanded us to engage in such inquiry in addition to accepting the reliable tradition. Thus He said, 'Know you not? Hear you not? Has it not been told you from the beginning? Have you not understood the foundation of the earth?' (Isaiah 40.21)

As Saadia understands the tradition, a *duty* to speculate, to philosophize is embedded in it, even as the truth is presented up front.

The prophetic message, revealed by God, transmitted by the rabbis, and codified by Saadia into doctrinal form, is rather like those answers one finds at the end of a study guide. Upon perusal of the answer (the truth), one works backward, from conclusion to premises, to ascertain how one arrives at the answer. In time, if one figures out the means (the premises) whereby the answer, the conclusion, is attained, one has achieved certain knowledge. I believe that this is precisely Saadia's position. The tradition (the truth) about creation, the nature of God, divine reward and punishment, etc. revealed to the prophets, witnessed by many, transmitted by the rabbis, and (finally) codified by Saadia, provides a starting point, but no more than this, for speculation and interpretation. Without such revelation humankind would have muddled about. But important to note, revelation is not thereby superior to reason, much less an antidote to it. It has a manifest educational and pedagogic function in the ongoing evolution of humanity. Revelation provides a starting point for speculation. It does not trump rational inquiry. In the end, Saadia's magnum opus is nothing other than a philosophical reconstruction in defence of traditional teachings on creation, divine unity, prophecy, human freedom, immortality, resurrection, and reward and punishment. Saadia's empiricism, his naturalizing tendencies, and commitment to scientific inquiry remain intact.

SPINOZA AND THE HISTORICIZING OF SCRIPTURE

In principle, a theological programme such as Saadia's, a defence of traditional religious beliefs (*kalam*), will always have its detractors. Maimonides himself viewed *kalam* with hostility (1995: 1.71), as constricted—not open-ended—and consequently unphilosophical and unscientific because of its very apologetic nature. But Maimonides' verdict is not the final word in the adjudication of the defence of traditional beliefs. In turning now to Spinoza a certain wicked irony emerges, for in Spinoza's view Maimonides' himself stands accused of a manifest disingenuousness in his own philosophical project. According to Spinoza, Maimonides' project, far from being open-ended and 'philosophical', 'assumes that we are permitted to explain and distort the words of Scripture according to our own preconceived opinions, and to reject the literal sense, even when it is perfectly lucid and explicit, and bend it to some other sense'. And Spinoza goes on to describe such a methodology as he believes Maimonides' to be as 'excessively audacious' (2007: 7.115).

In his own way, Spinoza accuses Maimonides, as Maimonides accused Saadia, of a kind of (a priori) question-begging, closed-mindedness on account of his (Maimonides') assumption that Scripture is inerrant, and that it *must* therefore cohere with whatever scientific truths are discovered. 'But of course', says Spinoza, 'this [assumption] is the very thing that should emerge from a critical examination and understanding of Scripture...not assume[d] at the very beginning as a rule of interpretation' (*Treatise*, preface [9]). While Maimonides does not defend traditional views because they are, well, traditional, Spinoza berates him for assuming that Scripture is a repository of all truth, and must be (re)interpreted, if needs be, in such a way that renders it consistent with contemporary science.

Spinoza (1632–77) has always been a liminal case in the history of Jewish philosophy. Expelled from the community into which he was born and raised, Spinoza lived the last half of his short life in close association with the most recent scientific trends in Europe and England. His *Theological-Political Treatise*, published anonymously in 1670, presents a biblical hermeneutics that deflates supernatural pretensions and argues for a demo-cratic and republication form of government that liberates individuals from the tyranny of religious authorities. And Spinoza's philosophical magnum opus, *Ethics*, published posthumously, is prima facie a rigorous deduction, over the span of five books, of a way of life consistent with a metaphysical outlook that is strictly determinist. Spinoza's politi-cal and philosophical concerns seem far removed from particularly Jewish concerns, but for present purposes his explicit critique of Maimonides positions him as part of a tradition committed to deflating the supernatural pretensions of religion. Once again, the irony is that his critique (of Maimonides) is of one who himself is deeply committed to deflating the supernatural pretensions of religion.

In the first six chapters of the *Theological-Political Treatise* Spinoza in rapid succes-sion 'naturalizes' prophecy and the prophets, divine election, the revealed (divine) law including the ceremonial laws, and miracles. His general strategy is to put the story of the Hebrews and the development of their monotheistic culture into historical relief and thereby to understand it and them shorn of any metaphysical or supernatural overlay. Prophecy is a function of an overactive imagination, and has application solely to the moral sphere; divine election refers to material prosperity, not to a special, unique mis-sion for the Hebrew nation, and the only divine laws that Spinoza countenances are the universal moral law and the eternal laws of nature; and finally for Spinoza, miracles are unintelligible and hence impossible. As will immediately be seen, Spinoza's critique leaves the biblical account of a skeptical but finally faithful people at least saved, if not rewarded, by a demanding deity in shambles.

Upon completion of the refutation of revelation, Spinoza's presents in the seventh chapter, 'On the Interpretation of Scripture', a highly influential biblical hermeneutics.

I shall focus on this, as it provides a final instructive instantiation of natural theology in the Jewish tradition, but before turning to Spinoza, a little history of ideas is required.

Spinoza is both a creature of his time as well as a trailblazer in biblical criticism. One of his correspondents and a member of his philosophical inner circle was Ludwig Meyer. Meyer was a radical biblical critic, whose *Philosophia Sacrae Scripturae Interpres* (1666) precipitated considerable debate among both conservative and liberal theologians. Most importantly, it was this very work of Meyer which motivated a response from Spinoza himself, and this response is none other than the *Theological-Political Treatise*, published in 1670. As the very title of his book makes clear, Meyer's radical biblical hermeneutic enthrones philosophy as the criterion by which biblical ideas are to be evaluated and truth is to be revealed. This programme is hardly novel, for, as we have noted, Maimonides and other philosophically minded theologians proposed to reinterpret Scripture when it offended against common sense; nevertheless, such a 'theoretical' project was at odds with the Protestant ways to approach Scripture. Protestant theology emphasized (against Rome) the autonomy of Scripture (*sola Scriptura*)—that Scripture could be approached directly by the lay reader and needed no external source or authority, ecclesiastical or philosophical, to ground, explain, or enforce it. Scripture is a revealed text that stands on its own, and the 'conservative' Protestant response to Meyer is in large measure offered in the name of simple faith, a gross distinction between secular wisdom and revealed truth, and the uniqueness and radical (ahistorical) contingency of Christianity and the Bible. And from the 'liberal' side the Protestant response to Meyer and his philosophical interpretation of Scripture is to insist that the text is not in fact a philosophy text, but rather an historical one that requires the skills of an exegete sensitive to language and contextual nuance to wrest meaning from it. In this debate, liberals can be seen to counter conservatives in the name of history and comparative analysis, while both liberals and conservatives counter Meyer's a priorism, with its dogmatic and potentially authoritarian implications. Nevertheless, disagreements aside, all parties, including Meyer, share the view that the Bible is a repository of divine truth, and that it is the job of the interpreter of the text—philosopher, historian, or simple believer—to reveal the truth in its pristine form.

Enter Spinoza. What distinguishes Spinoza from Meyer and the latter's Protestant critics on the left and the right is his insistence on understanding and interpreting the Bible as (just) a historical text *and* consequently as one without any divine significance and meaning, a wholly human text written by human beings a long time ago. Though beholden to conservatives for the strong dualism between faith and reason (religion and science) and to liberals for invoking history in any viable interpretation of Scripture, Spinoza is finally at odds with all in denying the Bible any authoritative status as a revealed text. Giving a new twist to the Protestant notion of the autonomy of Scripture (*sola Scriptura*), that the text must be understood in its own terms, Spinoza counters Meyer and his evaluation of the Bible against the external canon of philosophical reason, counters conservative theologians and their emphasis on subjective faith and the ahistoricity of the Bible, and finally counters liberal theologians in their misguided attempt to mine an historical text for timeless truths.

What Spinoza offers is a 'natural history of religion'. A famous section of chapter 7 says:

> [T]he method of interpreting Scripture is scarcely different from the method of interpreting nature, and is in fact in complete accord with it. For just as the method of interpreting nature consists essentially in composing a natural history from which we can infer definitions of the things of nature as deriving from assured data; so also for the interpretation of Scripture it is necessary to provide its authentic history, and by drawing logical consequences from that, as from assured data and principles, to infer the intention of the authors of Scripture. [*Treatise* 7.98]

For Spinoza, the analogy between the natural scientist and the (scientific) biblical interpreter is an extremely close one. Just as one comes to understand nature from nature herself (inductively and empirically), so one must come to understand and interpret Scripture from Scripture itself. Scripture stands on its own (*sola Scriptura*), as the conservatives strenuously suggested, but its meaning ('the intention of the authors of Scripture'), *not* to be confused with any sort of extra-historical, timeless truth, is to be inferred by close philological and historical analysis. The Baconian, empiricist methodology should not be missed.

With Spinoza's vigorous critique of Maimonides and (what he takes to be) an indefensible a priorism, we seem to have come full circle. Jewish philosophical theology appears to have become fully naturalized. Truth is revealed through patient scholarly analysis, and does not wait upon divine intervention. Torah, divine revelation, and supernatural miracles give way to physics, and with this substitution modernity commences.

I do not wish to deny the gradual 'disenchantment' of the world with which the modern era is associated. But it is important not to draw such a stark distinction between the modern and the pre-modern periods that we fail to note the naturalizing tendencies in thinkers such as Saadia and Maimonides. We should recall that for both Saadia and Maimonides their respective 'foundational' projects, of turning unreflective beliefs into rationally grounded ones, demand that one engage in science by studying the divine creation. Importantly, this is ordained by the law (Torah) itself. Philosophy and science are religious obligations, we might say. Admittedly this is not and cannot be demanded of all, for only some have the intellectual wherewithal to ground their beliefs in a scientific manner. For the mass of humankind, like Job's comforters and for a while Job himself, platitudes take the place of hard work. But, as Maimonides has shown us in his gloss on the tale of Job, the good life, one grounded in truth and affording the thinker a certain invulnerability, depends upon rising above common sense. Job's perseverance, his questioning of his fate, is ultimately rewarded by a divine intercession; but, for Maimonides, this event, which reveals the order of nature to Job, is important mainly for its strong underscoring of the kind of wisdom that is salvational. Indeed, at the tale's end Job has become wise, and is materially rewarded. He has come to understand that what heretofore he imagined to be of value, and a sign of divine favour, is ephemeral, and a commitment to its value was a recipe for pain and misery. The antidote to this misplaced prioritizing is natural science (and a certain scepticism), and love of God—the *summum bonum*—is a function of coming to understand and appreciate the divine creation. Job is closer to God (*sc.* divine providence spreads over him), precisely because of his moving beyond mere hearsay.

For a theist such as Maimonides, God plays a substantive role in creation and salvation. There is no denying that. But his deflationary accounts of prophecy, miracles, and even creation are an indication of a felt need to confront theological issues in such a way that they interest the intellectual. Maimonides understands his own (rabbinic) tradition as demanding study, not just of religious texts, but of philosophical and scientific ones. And we have seen that Saadia, writing in a time (and place) where fundamentalist literalism was rife in his own community and conformist pressures hovered, proceeded to defend his tradition by understanding it as enjoining rational speculation. Saadia points to the tradition itself as mandating his own philosophical project of transforming simple, unreflective beliefs into rationally grounded ones. Saadia's defence of Judaism is ipso facto a defence of the duty to inquire and to philosophize. Revelation is not so much the inevitable conclusion of his project as its necessary starting point, demanding interpretation and clarification.

Spinoza's atheism, his strong critique of the revealed tradition of Saadia and Maimonides, shares with that very tradition a belief that superstition and idolatry are overcome by natural science. The fact that Saadia and Maimonides are theists, finding a substantive role for divinity, should not hide important common ground, the penchant for natural theologizing that all parties share.

REFERENCES

Aristotle (2002). *Nicomachean Ethics.* Translated by C. Rowe. Oxford: Oxford University Press.
Maimonides (1995). *The Guide of the Perplexed.* Abridged and translated by C. Rabin and D. Frank. Indianapolis: Hackett.
Saadia Gaon (2002). *The Book of Doctrines and Beliefs.* Abridged and translated by A. Altmann and D. Frank. Indianapolis: Hackett.
Spinoza (2007). *Theological-Political Treatise.* Translated by M. Silverthorne and J. Israel. Cambridge: Cambridge University Press.

CHAPTER 9

....

ISLAMIC PERSPECTIVES ON NATURAL THEOLOGY

....

ROBERT G. MORRISON

THE noted philosopher Ibn Rushd (d. 1198) wrote *The Decisive Treatise on the Harmony of Religion and Philosophy* (*Faṣl al-maqāl fī mā bayn al-sharīʿa wa-ʾl-ḥikma min al-ittiṣāl*) in which he argued that the law (*sharīʿa*) enjoined the study of philosophical topics in the ancient tradition (Ibd Rushd 1976: 44–9). Then, Ibn Rushd wrote: 'Now since this religion is true and summons to the study which leads to knowledge of the Truth, we the Muslim community know definitely that demonstrative study does not lead to [conclusions] conflicting with what Scripture has given us; for truth does not oppose truth but accords with it and bears witness to it' (50). This statement meant that human reason, when exercised correctly, might dispense with the need for revelation. Ibn Rushd, despite his contemporary relevance, does not represent a definition of natural theology in Islam for three reasons. First, the Arabic word *ḥikma* included in the title of Ibn Rushd's work means either wisdom or philosophy; *ḥikma* does not mean 'theology', so Ibn Rushd was defending philosophy and not articulating a position within theology. The term *kalām*, denoting the field of thought closest to theology, is better defined as rational speculation about God (Sabra 1994: 5; Dhanani 1996: 157–8). But because the term *kalām* is more wide-ranging than the term 'theology', the problem of translation, and the absence of natural theology as an actors' category are, regarding the question of natural theology in Islam, surmountable. Still, the question of whether the premises of natural theology might conceivably be at odds with the revealed premises of Islamic law had to be addressed. Secondly, Ibn Rushd's equating of reason and revelation depended on the allegorical interpretation of scripture rather than on understanding nature to be another sort of revealed text. Thirdly, Ibn Rushd implied that revelation could be, for some Muslims, superfluous. The second and third reasons will be investigated at the greatest length in this chapter.

VARIETIES OF NATURAL THEOLOGY
AND ISLAM

Whatever the complexities of locating discussions of natural theology in Islamic texts are, Islam has deemed nature relevant to knowing about God. Consider the definition of natural theology implicit in the title of William Paley's 1802 work on natural theology, *Natural Theology: or, Evidences of the existence and attributes of the Deity, collected from the appearances of nature*. This brief definition of natural theology encapsulated in the title certainly calls to mind the *Qur'ān*'s references to nature and creation that stand as a rhetorical argument for God's existence. *Āya* (verse) 50 of *Sūra* (chapter) 20 (*Ṭāhā*) reads: 'Our Lord is He who gave everything its creation.' *Sūra* 7 (*al-A'rāf*): 57 presents God's control over natural processes as evidence of God's ability to resurrect: 'It is He who looses the winds...till, when they are charged with heavy clouds, We drive it to a dead land and therewith send down water, and bring forth therewith all the fruits. Even so (*kadhālika*) we shall bring forth the dead.' The *Qur'ān* is clearly saying that a considered view of nature yields evidence for God's existence and God's attributes of wisdom and power. But the *Qur'ān*'s own claim for the authority of its account of God's existence, unity, and power depends also on the *Qur'ān*'s status as a revealed text, not just on the conclusions of one's intellect.

Islam's position on what could be known only through an examination of nature, without the aid of revelation, is therefore complex and is something that modern Muslim authors are aware has changed over time. In contrast, early Christian texts on natural theology understood the promise of finding God through one's intellect to be in the *New Testament*. In the seventeenth century, Matthew Barker wrote:

> By Natural Theology, that all may understand, I mean that knowledge of God, and our duty to Him, which the Light of Nature may lead Man up to, and which is concreat with his Soul. The Image of God upon Man in his first Creation, confided in Knowledge as well as Holiness and the knowledge Adam had of his Creator, was partly by the Character of his Being engraven upon his Soul, which is by some stiled *verbum* εμφυτον, an implanted Word, and partly by what the large power of his intellectual Faculty might gather from the Works of Creation; by both which he was led to God as his ultimate end. [Barker 1674: B2v]

To this end, at the beginning of Chapter 1 of *Natural Theology*, Barker cited Romans 1:20: 'Ever since the creation of the world his eternal power and divine nature, invisible though they are, have been understood and seen through the things he has made. So they are without excuse.' The chapter of Romans continues: 'And since they did not see fit to acknowledge God, God gave them up to a debased mind and to things that should not be done. They were filled with every kind of wickedness, evil, covetousness, malice. Full of envy, murder, strife, deceit, craftiness, they are gossips.' (Romans 1:28–9)

Barker's definition of natural theology meant that it was possible for humans to have positive knowledge of God, beyond God's existence, without aid of revelation and, moreover, without revealed law. Christianity's particular concern for arguing that revealed law is unnecessary for (and perhaps detrimental to) salvation is understandable as part of Christianity's attempt to legitimate itself and to contrast itself with Judaism. Christian views of natural law resembled those of Aristotle, notably the idea that the source of natural law was the intellect (Griffel 2007:41). But that position on the necessity of revealed law presented a possible contrast with Islam, for the *Qur'ān* made revealed law a key locus for one's relationship with God. The *Qur'ān's* principle of *naskh* (abrogation) meant that the differences between the Hebrew Bible, the *New Testament*, and the *Qur'ān*, all texts due to Allah, mattered.

Since adherence to revealed laws is part of the *Qur'ān's* core message, argument from natural theology has never been necessary to legitimize Islam and, therefore, one might justifiably conclude Islam would be amenable to the kind of natural theology alluded to by the title of William Paley's book but not to that described in the previous quote from Matthew Barker. Yet the *Qur'ān* and *Ḥadīth* speak of *ḥanīf*s, pre-Islamic monotheists who foreshadowed Islam's message and who, apparently, obeyed God's desires without possessing a revealed scripture (see Q6:75–9; Rubin 2001–6). The *Qur'ān* also refers to and appeals to humans' *fiṭra*, humans' instinctive sense that there is one God. Early Islamic literature did cite natural events as heralds of Muḥammad's birth and early Islamic astrology accounted for the cycles of prophets via planetary conjunctions, meaning that while nature might not communicate moral obligations, nature could contain evidence for the authenticity of a prophet (Morrison 2009). The idea that Islam is in accord with one's *fiṭra* resembles the Christian claim that natural law is part of Christian law, and we will find that contemporary Muslim thinkers such as Sayyid Quṭb refer to the *fiṭra* in their own writings (March 2009, 2010a). These references to the *ḥanīf*s and to the *fiṭra* could be understood as part of a discourse of natural law. But *Sharī'a* (in the sense of norms for human behavior), though it agrees with one's *fiṭra*, is not part of one's *fiṭra* (Griffel 2007: 44–5). Thus the initial question, particularly for *Sunnī Ash'arī mutakallimūn* (practitioners of *kalām*) was whether one's *fiṭra*, one's intellect, or nature (when examined through the intellect) could reliably communicate anything found in the *Sharī'a*.

KALĀM AND REVELATION

Kalām texts were the locus for these discussions, the contours of which will lead to an understanding of what reason might be able to discover independent of revelation. *Mutakallimūn* sceptical of the intellect's role upheld a God who could be more than the sum of human reason; *mutakallimūn* who allowed the intellect a role in providing knowledge about God grappled with the question of whether God's actions could be constrained by human reason and if so, how? Because *mutakallimūn* who were opposed to any idea reminiscent of natural law nevertheless had to engage their opponents, who often had different positions on Islamic thought, a variety of ideas appeared in *kalām* texts even when those ideas were not those endorsed by the text's author. The first *falāsifa*, philosophers in the Hellenistic tradition and frequent opponents of the *mutakallimūn*, tried to harmonize Islam with the doctrines of Plato and Aristotle. Fārābī (d. *c.* 950), for instance, held that the *Sharī'a* was, essentially, the truths of *falsafa* in a form that the masses could grasp (al-Fārābī 1991: 79). Though the view of Islam implied by such an argument explains in part why Fārābī's view of the function of *falsafa* did not predominate, the *falāsifa* did consider themselves Muslim and their position on the truth of revelation and of the value of rational investigations resembled the type of natural theology entailed by Christian texts. Ibn Rushd's *Decisive Treatise* was a defence of *falsafa* that rebutted Abū Ḥāmid al-Ghazālī's (d. 1111) criticisms of *falsafa*.

The interactions of *mutakallimūn* with their opponents, a group not limited to the *falāsifa*, began early in the history of Islam. Early *mutakallimūn* took note of what natural philosophers had to say because certain philosophers' ideas competed with Islam. Put differently, *mutakallimūn* had to engage, rather than ignore, the question of whether the intellect was more than just an instrument for defending the supremacy of revelation. Could the intellect, without the aid of revelation, impart divine guidance? One of the projects of certain early *Mu'tazilī mutakallimūn* was to posit a conception of matter (i.e. an alternative physical theory) very different from that of the *falāsifa* (Dhanani 2003: 133). With these *mutakallimūn*, the intellect became more than just a defender of revelation (Sabra 1994: 9). Rather than explain matter in terms of four elements (earth, air, fire, and water) with combinations of different qualities (cold, wetness, heat, and dryness), many *mutakallimūn* proposed that matter was composed of indivisible atoms in which God created various accidents. Time, too, was atomic, and no longer continual. Though this early engagement of *kalām* with physical theory was not explicitly connected to broader religious questions, the *mutakallimūn* must have grasped that there was *something* meaningful about *falsata* (Dhanani 1993: 3–5). By arguing that everything was composed of fundamentally uniform, indivisible atoms, early *mutakallimūn* could conclude that nature was no longer fundamentally differentiated. Thus, drawing independent religious lessons from nature would be more difficult if not impossible. Later, 'Abd al-Jabbār would criticize the *falāsifa* for following Aristotle's opinion that the sun can be neither hot nor cold but was animate; planets were not animate, but 'rocks in the heavens' (Dhanani 2003: 137).

Kalām of the first half of the tenth century remained concerned with other competing views on the composition of matter. Abū Manṣūr al-Māturīdī (d. 944), in his *Kitāb al-Tawḥīd*, critiqued the views of non-Peripatetic thinkers known as the *Dahriyya* (materialists) (al-Māturīdī 1970: 141; Madelung 1998–2004). This was a group that existed during the ninth century CE. Māturīdī's descriptions as historiography should be read critically, but they did depend on an earlier *Mu'tazilī*, Ibn Shabīb. One subset of the *Dahriyya* were the *aṣḥāb al-ṭabā'i'* who alleged that matter was composed of four natures: heat, coldness, wetness, and dryness. These natures existed eternally. The *aṣḥāb al-ṭabā'i'* seemed to think that the natures (*ṭabā'i'*) were analogous to dyes and that the proportions of the natures changed via celestial motions. Māturīdī rebutted them by arguing that dyes did not mix on their own; God mixed the dyes (al-Māturīdī 1970: 141–2). Māturīdī also contended that the natures had to be either accidents or atoms. Māturīdī argued that, since these natures were opposites and since opposites naturally repelled each other, the only way something could exist with its opposite would be due to another agent (al-Māturīdī 1970: 143). Māturīdī's argument led to God's necessary existence but to little else about why God acted and what humans' obligations to God were.

Also of concern to Māturīdī were the astrologers (*al-munajjima*). For them, the stars were connected to the world and controlled it just as the instrument of the weaver controlled the threads (al-Māturīdī 1970: 143). This position was problematic in that it postulated eternal motions of the heavens. Māturīdī wrote, against both the astrologers and *aṣḥāb al-ṭabā'i'*, that there was nothing one might observe that would be evidence either for the natures or the stars' control over terrestrial events. As for the elements, one finds that it is motion that causes heat and that stillness causes cold. Thus, heat and cold are not likely to be the fundamental cause of anything. Likewise, sensory evidence would suggest that it is the scattering (*tafarruq*) and inversion (*taqallub*) of things on earth, with the ensuing release of vapours (*bukhār*) that leads to the motions of the planets, not the reverse (al-Māturīdī 1970: 145). Both the astrologers and *aṣḥāb al-ṭabā'i'* failed to notice that the natural systems that they observed must have been due to a wise creator. Māturīdī's final comment relating astrologers to *aṣḥāb al-ṭabā'i'* reads: 'Then the doctrine of these that the elements (*al-jawāhir*) are created from the original motions of, and likewise is the doctrine of the astrologers, it is known that *jawāhir* exist in every direction through these motions, so it is established that this is null' (al-Māturīdī 1970: 150). I have dwelt on Māturīdī because he was an early *mutakallim* who linked his position on the composition of matter to other qualms *mutakallimūn* might have about astrology. Note that Māturīdī held these positions about God's omnipotent role in the composition of nature without affording humans an opportunity to learn something, via astrological prognostications, about how God operated. Māturīdī did not reject science and the power of the human intellect per se; he held that the astrologers and *aṣḥāb al-ṭabā'i'* had misunderstood God's wisdom and power. The debate between the *mutakallimūn* and their opponents was about the implications of a reasoned study of nature; there was no question that nature was a valid locus of argumentation.

AL-GHAZALI AND THE INCOHERENCE
OF THE PHILOSOPHERS

In the eleventh century, criticisms of *falsafa* were presented systematically by al-Ghazālī (d. 1111) in his *Incoherence of the Philosophers* (*Tahāfut al-falāsifa*). His most notable conclusion from that text was that the statements of the philosophers about the necessity of causes were incorrect. Natural causes were simply a perception based on two events (Ghazālī's example was burning occurring whenever fire and cotton were brought together) being correlated time after time (al-Ghazālī 1997: 166–77). Ghazālī did not have to deny the existence of secondary causes; rather, all that was necessary was to argue that humans would be unable to determine reliably what the secondary causes of a certain phenomenon are. Or, causes and effects could exist; it was just that their connection was not necessary (Griffel 2009: 149). In addition, in the same text, Ghazālī also upheld certain findings of science, such as astronomy's explanation for why eclipses took place (al-Ghazālī 1997: 6). In his *Deliverer from Error*, Ghazālī deemed three doctrines of the philosophers (denial of bodily resurrection, denial of God's knowledge of particulars, and the affirmation of the eternity of the world) objectionable (Watt 1982: 37–8).

Ghazālī's work has been perceived to refute or at least nuance *falsafa*'s claim to authority; but Ghazālī's work eliminated neither the study of philosophy nor a philosophical approach to religious questions, nor, of course, discussions of causality in scientific texts. Rather, by 1200, aspects of science and *falsafa* had entered *kalām* as a means to provide evidence for God's glory and existence and as a way to approach the debate about the reliability and independence of reason as a source of knowledge. Traditions of religious scholarship had developed new hierarchies of disciplines and metaphysics was no longer queen of the sciences. Thus the claims of science and *falsafa* were clearly not perceived to be a threat to religion, as these areas became part of the education of religious scholars and were discussed in *kalām* texts. The study of nature demonstrated God's glory, reinforced perceptions of God's omnipotence and suggested that God's actions, while not subject to human conceptions of justice and reason, could be profitably explored by human reason. As science came to be incorporated into a tradition of religious scholarship, nature became implicitly and explicitly a source of information about God's wisdom and glory. Two critical questions arose. One was the extent to which scientific explanations of nature, with their dependence on secondary causes, affected understandings of God's control of the universe. The second was whether the findings of the intellect were reliable. The two questions were related because the effect of science's explanations upon understandings of God's power in the universe depended on the findings of the intellect being reliable.

AL-NISABURI AND THE REASONED STUDY OF NATURE

Niẓām al-Dīn al-Nīsābūrī (d. *c.* 1330) was a *Shīʿī* religious scholar expert in science whose career grew out of the integration of science into a tradition of religious scholarship that flourished after Ghazālī's career. Nīsābūrī argued not that one could discover the law through reason, but, rather, that the *Sharīʿa* could be rationalized. In his comments on Q1:6 ('Guide us in the Straight Path'), Nīsābūrī made parallels between the *qurʾān*ic concept of the straight path and philosophical ethics. He wrote:

> So there is, in the appetitive faculty, the extreme of excess; it is debauchery. And there is the extreme of negligence; it is deterioration, and both of them are blameworthy.

And the mean, which is using the appetitive faculty in its place and equitably (*'adāla*) and according to the *Sharī'a*, is praiseworthy, and it is abstinence. [quoted in Morrison 2007: 71]

Nīsābūrī's comments on Q48:4 ('that they might add faith to their faith') stated that the righteous would be rewarded and the wrongdoers punished (as alluded to at the beginning of the *sūra*) according to *hikma* (i.e. philosophy, wisdom, or rational knowledge). Throughout his *Qur'ān* commentary, entitled *Gharā'ib al-Qur'ān wa-raghā'ib al-furqān*, Nīsābūrī expressed greater confidence in the reasoned study of nature as a means to understand revelation and God's role in nature than had the earlier philosophically informed *Qur'ān* commentator Fakhr al-Dīn al-Rāzī (d. 1210) from whom Nīsābūrī borrowed a great deal (Morrison 2007: 76).

More interestingly, Nīsābūrī wrote, in a Persian text on astrology, that the *uṣūl* (the hypotheses or principles) that humans used in jurisprudence (*fiqh*) were like those used in astronomy (*hay'at*). Nīsābūrī's statement was more about the parallels between scholarly disciplines than about how revealed truths could be found in nature by the human intellect. But since jurisprudence was a discipline indispensable for humans' grasp of the *Sharī'a*, then the *uṣūl* of jurisprudence must be reliable. The comparison between the *uṣūl* of jurisprudence and those of astronomy meant that astronomy's *uṣūl* must have been reliable too. Nīsābūrī's comments, then, buttressed the value of science as a means of one's appreciation of God's majesty and wisdom in creation. Indeed, the approach of *kalām* itself, as a practical matter, depended on the reliability of the intellect. Nīsābūrī's career reflected a stage in Islamic intellectual history in which the study of *falsafa* had become part of religious education. The reasoned study of nature did not diminish one's understanding of God's omnipotence, but rather enhanced one's appreciation of God's awesome work in creation.

Scholars in the same intellectual tradition as Nīsābūrī used a reasoned study of nature to show how God's wisdom was embedded in the cosmos. Ghazālī had explored whether the principle of theodicy, a version of which Ghazālī accepted, meant that God's actions had to adhere to the dictates of human reason (Ormsby 1984). Ghazālī did not state explicitly that God's actions had to conform to human standards of justice; but God's actions did have to be for the best (*al-aṣlaḥ*) (Morrison 2007: 72–5). Rather, Ghazālī's position that the created world was the best possible world held that 'there is not in possibility anything whatever more excellent, more complete, or more perfect than it is' (quoted in Ormsby 1984: 35). Ghazālī's position contradicted the view of Sayf al-Dīn al-Āmidī that humans could not even tell the difference between the licit and illicit without revelation (Morrison 2005: 28; al-Āmidī 1971: 234). A scientific parallel to Ghazālī's understanding of theodicy exists in the work of Quṭb al-Dīn al-Shīrāzī (d. 1311), Nīsābūrī's astronomy teacher and a religious scholar of note. In an astronomy text, *al-Tuḥfa al-shāhiyya*, Shīrāzī wrote that there could be no unnecessary excess in the heavens (Morrison 2005: 27). Instead, the physical models that astronomers proposed to explain celestial motions had to be founded on an economy of orbs. Nīsābūrī, in his final astronomy text, *Tawḍīḥ al-Tadhkira* (*The Elucidation of the Tadhkira*), contained a lengthy expression of wonder at how two simple hypotheses were sufficient to account for the complexities of the planets' retrograde motions (Morrison 2007: 88). There was no question that the elegance, and thus the perfection, of astronomy's explanations, for certain *mutakallimūn*, could be an argument for God's glory. More subtly, the fifteenth-century scientist and *mutakallim* 'Alī Qushjī (d. 1474) thought 'that the correspondence between our human constructions and external reality is itself a source of wonder' (Ragep 2001: 63). These arguments about how the complexity of creation is evidence for God's glory meant that, in the opinion of some Muslim scholars, the human intellect can tell one something about God.

NATURAL THEOLOGY AND RELIGIOUS OBLIGATIONS

In Iran, in Qom, Islamic astronomy remains a part of religious scholarship in the current millennium. In *Durūs-i hay'at va-dīgar rishtahhā-i riyāḍī*, the author, Ayatollah Ḥasan Ḥasan Zādah Āmulī cited Nīsābūrī's *Gharā'ib al-Qur'ān* when commenting on *Mālik yawm al-dīn*, a phrase from the first *sūra* of the *Qur'ān*, as a source for the definition of a day: 'A day is the period from the rising (*ṭulū'*) of half of the body of the sun to the setting of half of its body, or from the beginning of its rising to its setting or from the rising of the second dawn to its setting and that is revelation (*al-shar'*)' (Āmulī 2007: 1.74). Setting aside momentarily the scientific details of the definition, it is fascinating that a book about science referenced a *Qur'ān* commentary on a matter of science. The author praised Nīsābūrī for providing three definitions of a day, all based on astronomical principles and commented that Nīsābūrī included the definition of the day according to revelation so that people would know the times to perform deeds of worship (*mawāqīt-i a'māl-i 'ibādī*) (Āmulī 2007: 1.74–5). Despite that distinction, Nīsābūrī, in his definition of the day, resorted only to material taken from astronomy texts. Elsewhere, Ḥasan Zādah Āmulī cited *Gharā'ib al-Qur'ān* as an authority for the sphericity of the earth (Āmulī 2007: 1.279). This comment came à propos Q18:86 (*'wajadahā taghrub fī 'ayn ḥami'a'*); the scientifically determined size of the earth, according to Nīsābūrī, meant that a metaphorical interpretation (*ta'wīl*) was necessary. The fluidity of boundaries between religious and scientific disciplines in Ḥasan Zādah Āmulī's vision means, in certain intellectual contexts, that the study of nature is the study of revelation, though not that the Book of Nature is the book of God (i.e. revelation).

Definitions of natural theology in the Christian tradition imply that a reasoned examination of nature can communicate at least some of one's religious obligations. David King's enormous corpus of research has shown that, in Islam, the intellect was important for fulfilling obligations already laid out in the *Sharī'a*. King's prolific research on the application of science to problems posed by religion has shown that scientific methods, in the cases of *qibla* computation and religious timekeeping, could supplant solutions found in the revealed texts (King 1985; 2004–2005). In other cases, scientific evidence could (and can) play a determining role in legal reasoning; for example, an expert knowledge of medicine could be probative. Wael Hallaq has pointed to a passage from Nawawī's *Majmūʿ* in which physicians' findings that wine actually increased thirst were used to overrule Ghazālī and his teacher Juwaynī's view that wine consumption was permitted to quench thirst (Hallaq 2001: 140–1). In Islamic law, which accepts probative arguments, human reason contended with legal texts, particularly *ḥadīth*, reports of Muḥammad's words and deeds. Recent scholarship on *ḥadīth* has found that much *ḥadīth* was viewed to be probable (*ẓannī*) rather than certain (*yaqīn*), but also has reminded us that these same *ẓannī ḥadīth* were taken to be effectively true (Hallaq 1999; Brown 2009). In both cases mentioned above, science served to redefine and interpret, but not alter, obligations (to pray and to pray facing Mecca) found in the *Qurʾān* (Q2:144 for Mecca).

The preceding examples have come closer to showing that the intellect was a tool for determining one's religious obligations than to finding that nature was a separate source of moral authority. After all, from an Islamic point of view, nature contains things such as pork, the consumption of which the *Qurʾān* bans (Emon 2004–5: 361). While nature could help *mutakallimūn* and *fuqahāʾ* (jurists) figure out why things were the way they were, nature lacked the 'moral authority' to tell humans about the way that things should be (Daston and Vidal 2004). To make a comparison with language from the European Middle Ages, the *Sharīʿa* did not describe prohibited actions as 'against nature' (Cadden 2004: 220). There would seem to be no reason for an Islamic text to make such a statement. After all, a central purpose of the *mutakallimūn*'s non-Peripatetic physics was to defend God's total control over nature; another possible motivation was to undercut those who worshipped nature and natural forces. Taken together, these two motivations served to remove or diminish the status of nature as an independent entity. Though the atomist theory of matter came before the critique of independent causality, nature's independent causal efficacy often came to be connected to concerns about detracting from an appreciation of God's omnipotence. Even scholars well-versed in science such as Nīsābūrī talked, in religious texts, about secondary causes, but did so with the recognition that those causes were instruments through which God can enact God's will (a nod to the prerogative of divine omnipotence). Was there any way in which the intellect, unaided by revelation, might determine moral instruction on the basis of an examination of nature?

An important point of contention in the *Muʿtazilī-Ashʿarī* debate in *kalām* in the first few Islamic centuries was whether God's actions were bound by a certain understanding of justice and rationality; the *Muʿtazilīs* took the position that God was so bound (Blankinship 2008: 47–51). The *Ashʿarīs* (and *Māturīdīs*) held, generally, that God's actions could be rationalized but *not* that God was bound by those rationalizations. al-Ashʿarī (d. 935), himself once a *Muʿtazilī*, explained that while God was certainly just, God was not bound by a given human understanding of God's justice (Ibn Fūrak 1987: 139–48).

Specifically, *Ashʿarī kalām* freed God from having to act with the best interests of humans (*ṣalāḥ li-ʾl-ʿabīd*) in mind (al-Ghazālī 1988:115). In his treatise on *Ashʿarī kalām*, *al-Iqtiṣād fī al-i'tiqād*, Ghazālī wrote, against the *Mu'tazilīs*, that while God might have a child die in order to avert future sins and to preserve a place in heaven, God might also allow a sinner to reach maturity, even though having that sinner die as a child might have saved that sinner from Hell (al-Ghazālī 1988: 116). Ibn Fūrak had made a similar point, and had added that were God to choose to terminate the life of a future sinner in order to avert further sin and the resultant punishment, then the state of obedience in which the would-be sinner had died would have been coerced ('alā al-iljā') (Ibn Fūrak 1987: 130). Likewise, it would not be impossible for God to pardon all of the infidels and punish all of the believers. Neither of those explanations from Ghazālī necessitate or even imply that God would act capriciously; rather, simply, the possibility that God might do so could not be excluded. Ghazālī wrote, in the same treatise, *al-Iqtiṣād*, that it is revelation (*al-shar'*), not human reason as the *Mu'tazilīs* contended, that obligates humans (*al-'ibād*) to know God and to thank his kindness (*shukr ni'matih*) (al-Ghazālī 1988: 118). Though Ghazālī did not deny that the intellect could play an important role in helping one follow God's law, Ghazālī pointed out that there were reasons why God might prefer that one use one's intellect for things other than determining one's legal obligations (119). Richard Frank, and, now, Frank Griffel have questioned the extent to which Ghazālī was truly committed to these positions; I have cited these texts simply because they were influential (Frank 1994; Griffel 2009). These positions argue that since the human intellect is incapable of grasping why God might engage in certain actions, humans should not constrain God's actions with human definitions of the reasonable.

Sharī'a and Natural Law

The *Mu'tazilī mutakallimūn*, by valorizing human reason and by constraining God's actions with the principle of justice, advocated a sort of natural law since the *Sharī'a*, in the *Mu'tazilī* understanding, would always mandate that God act according to human conceptions of justice. When the *Mu'tazilī* 'Abd al-Jabbār argued why God does not do morally repugnant (*qabīḥ*) acts, 'Abd al-Jabbār pointed to the wisdom in God's elaborate creation (al-Jabbār 1962: 6.180). For instance, al-Jaṣṣāṣ (d. 981) commented that any act in nature that was not specifically banned was thought to be permitted; then these acts should be evaluated through one's reason (Emon 2004–5: 354–6; al-Jaṣṣāṣ 2000: 1.104). Certain *Ash'arīs* later acknowledged that *Mu'tazilīs* such as Jaṣṣāṣ were not simply legislating through reason. Rather, they had concluded that because God had commanded people to seek benefits (*manāfi'*), anything unmentioned by revelation that reason found to be beneficial might be obligatory or commendable (Emon 2004: 358). For example, Ghazālī allowed reason a role in determining the purposes of the law (*maqāṣid al-Sharī'a*); more generally, as we have seen, human reason and nature played a role in jurists' discretionary decisions, but not in establishing obligations.

Reformers in the nineteenth century would turn to the idea of *maṣlaḥa* (public welfare) as a justification for modernist developments in Islamic law. Muḥammad ʿAbduh expanded *maṣlaḥa* (public welfare) from a principle for interpreting the *Qurʾān* and *ḥadīth* to a way to determine what Islamic law should be (Hourani 1983: 151–2). Although revelation was a source for the moral laws that governed society, books of ethics were another source (137).

Discussions of natural law have proliferated among modern and contemporary Muslim thinkers. Given an increased scientism, questions of natural theology have taken on a greater urgency in that understandings of nature have affected how Muslims define and determine Islamic law in the current Islamic world. Even a few generations earlier, ʿAbduh's follower Rashīd Riḍā (d. 1937) had held that scientific progress meant that classical definitions of the duration of pregnancy were no longer 'a divine prescription (*naṣṣ dīnī*)' (Shaham 2010: 167–8; Coulson 1990: 174–6; Spectorsky 1993: 88). Commenting on Sayyid Quṭb (d. 1965), Frank Griffel has observed that, for Sayyid Quṭb, humans are created with the ability and responsibility to know good from bad. Moreover, '[r]evelation is not necessary to act adequately in response to this responsibility. Revelation does, however, help humans master this task' (Griffel 2009: 51–2). In fact, Sayyid Quṭb's argument for Islam stood on how only the *Sharīʿa* went along in full with God's creation; e.g. God's proclamations about gender differences reflected biological reality (50, 53). Another example would be how the provision for polygamy both recognizes and then controls men's natural instincts. As Griffel observed, Sayyid Quṭb's thought blended philosophical *and* anti-rationalist trends. Thus, it would be imprecise to say that nature was a moral exemplar for Sayyid Quṭb. Instead, Islam was the most natural religion in the same way that Islam did the most to advance social justice (a topic of another of Sayyid Quṭb's books, *Social Justice in Islam*).

Recently, Tariq Ramadan has taken a more radical stance on the value of nature and science as a source for Muslims' knowledge of their ethical obligations; nature and the universe have become sources on a par with revelation (March 2010b: 254). This valorization of the place of nature goes along with Ramadan's shift towards placing applied ethics (and not law) at the focus of Muslims' concerns. Ramadan saw his move as the next step after what he terms the 'Maqāṣid School'. Reminiscent of Nīsābūrī's comment about the parallels between scientific and religious disciplines, Ramadan wrote: 'Both the Universe and the text only reveal their order, structure, and meaning through the complementary mediation of human reason' (259). In fact, Ramadan wrote explicitly that 'The Book of the Universe' was a source of law and ethics. His statements on concrete questions of medical ethics are much more cautious and in line with precedent (263–4). Given this apparent disjuncture between Ramadan's theoretical arguments and their practical applications Andrew March notes that Ramadan's true goal is to argue that Muslims should divorce their consciousness of nature and the universe from *fiqh* (270). In that sense, he is arguing for a conception of natural theology of which earlier scholars such as Nīsābūrī, who related his understanding of nature to *fiqh* by likening the *uṣūl* of astronomy to those of *fiqh*, did not conceive.

NATURAL THEOLOGY, SCIENCE, AND ISLAM

Also relevant to understanding Islamic perspectives on natural theology are reactions to Darwin in the nineteenth and early twentieth-century Near East that engaged the moral implications of the principles of natural selection and the idea of humans' descent from apes. Where Darwin's ideas were rejected, this was due to their implicit materialism and determinism, not simply because they contradicted a literal reading of the *Qur'ān*, though Darwin's ideas could certainly be understood to be in conflict with major themes of the *Qur'ān* (Keddie 1983). For instance, one prominent opponent of Darwin, Jamāl al-Dīn al-Afghānī (d. 1897) was a supporter of science who opposed Darwin's theories due to their potential political implications and due to their origins within a colonial power (Dallal 2010: 166–8). On the other side, the *ṣūfī shaykh* Ḥusayn al-Jisr used Darwin's theories to assert that there was nothing in Islam that opposed science (Elshakry 2007: 212). Even Afghānī's follower, Muḥammad 'Abduh, held that nothing in the *Qur'ān* could contradict what was found in nature (Elshakry 2008: 500–1). In modernity, the locus of the debate shifted from one about the epistemological certainty of science (the dominant concern of pre-modern religious scholars) to the religious implications of science. In the past decade, support of creationism has revived in the Islamic world, though there is nothing exclusively Islamic about what Muslim creationists are saying (Dallal 2010: 168–9).

An interesting contemporary parallel to reactions to Darwinism would be the case of medical ethics, as medicine's abilities are not in doubt but the ethical implications of medicine can be controversial. The concepts of euthanasia and brain death present the possibility that neither God nor, for that matter, other Muslims, will decide one's time of death (Brockopp 2003: 178–9; Krawietz 2003: 194, 202). Birgit Krawietz has found that while the modern conception of brain death has not upended the Islamic understanding of death as the departure of the soul, 'a number of them [Muslim scholars] realize that brain death challenges the death *criteria* of Islamic law, the inappropriateness of which can no longer be overlooked' (Krawietz 2003: 195). Modern Muslims have proposed multiple understandings of brain death, none of which challenge the traditional definition of death as the departure of the soul (207). Thus the traditional sources have retained their position as the final source for what is ethical or unethical, but the need for these new interpretations was posed by scientific developments, a succession of events that would not have been conceivable earlier. Krawietz pointed out that it was the diversity of scientific opinions over the definition of death that was most significant in leading Muslim scholars not to let science define death (202).

Finally, scientific techniques have been applied to contemporary Islamic law. Though Egyptian courts today are not *Sharī'a* courts in the classical sense, these courts are understood to be Islamic (Lombardi 2006). Indeed, in a development from the last decade, Egypt's chief *muftī* wrote, regarding a paternity case, that mandating DNA testing is wholly Islamic. Thus, if adultery were a possibility, DNA testing would implicitly supersede traditional rights to deny paternity through the practice of *li'ān* (Shaham 2010: 178–9). Even in an earlier time, a 1937 text book from al-Azhar University's Faculty of the *Sharī'a* held that blood tests could be probative support for the denial of paternity (180). In modern times, science has certainly affected how Muslims define and apply Islamic law, and the effect of science seems more pronounced than in pre-modern, scientifically-informed *Qur'ān* commentaries such as Rāzī's *Mafātīḥ al-Ghayb* or Nīsābūrī's *Gharā'ib al-Qur'ān*. Arguments for the power of human reason, such as Tariq Ramadan's, seem innovative, but, again, the *Qur'ān's* reference to *ḥanīf*s as well as Ibn Rushd's *Decisive Treatise* suggest a *qur'ān*ic precedent, for people being capable of determining correct religious lessons on the basis of reason alone. Perhaps the increased confidence in reason engendered by modern science's successes has led to positions such as Ramadan's.

REFERENCES

'Abd al-Jabbār, al-Qāḍī Abū al-Ḥasan (1962). *al-Mughnī fī abwāb al-tawḥīd wa-'l-'adl*. Edited by Dr Aḥmad Fu'ād al-Ahwānī. Rev. Ibrāhīm Madkūr. Cairo: Wizārat al-thaqāfa wa-'l-irshād al-qawmī.

al-Āmidī, Sayf al-Dīn (1971). *Ghāyat al-marām fī 'ilm al-kalām*. Edited by Ḥasan Maḥmūd 'Abd al-Laṭīf. Cairo: al-Majlis al-a'lā li-'l-shu'ūn al-islāmiyya.

al-Fārābī(1991). 'The Attainment of Happiness' in *Medieval Political Philosophy*. Edited by Ralph Lerner and Muhsin Mahdi. Translated by Muhsin Mahdi. Ithaca, NY: Cornell University Press: pp. 58–82.

al-Ghazālī (1988). *al-Iqtiṣād fī al-i'tiqād*. Beirut: Dār al-kutub al-'ilmiyya.

—— (1997). *The Incoherence of the Philosophers*. Translated by Michael Marmura. Provo, UT: Brigham Young University Press.

al-Jaṣṣāṣ, Abū Bakr Aḥmad ibn 'Alī (2000). *al-Fuṣūl fī al-uṣūl*. Beirut: Dār al-Kutub al-'Ilmiyya.

al-Māturīdī, Abū Manṣūr (1970). *Kitāb al-Tawḥīd*. Edited by Fatḥ Allāh Khulayf. Beirut: Dār al-mashriq.

Āmulī, Ḥasan Ḥasan Zādah (2007). *Durūs-i hay'at va-dīgar-i rishtahhā-i riyāḍī*. Qom: Markaz-i intishārāt-i daftar-i tablīghāt-i islāmī.

Barker, Matthew (1674). *Natural Theology, or the Knowledge of God, from the Works of Creation; Accommodated and Improved, to the Service of Christianity*. London: Printed for Nathaniel Ranew.

Blankinship, Khalid (2008). 'The Early Creed' in *The Cambridge Companion to Classical Islamic Theology*. Edited by Tim Winter. Cambridge, UK: Cambridge University Press: pp. 33–54.

Brockopp, Jonathan E. (2003). 'The "Good Death" in Islamic Theology and Law' in *Islamic Ethics of Life*. Edited by Jonathan E. Brockopp. Columbia, SC: University of South Carolina Press: pp. 177–93.

Brown, Jonathan A. C. (2009). 'Did the Prophet Say It or Not? The Literal, Historical, and Effective Truth of Ḥadīths in Early Sunnism'. *Journal of the American Oriental Society* CXXIX: 259–85.

Cadden, Joan (2004). 'Trouble in Paradise: The Regime of Nature in Late Medieval Christian Culture' in Daston and Vidal (2004): pp. 207–31.

Coulson, N. J. (1990 [1964]). *A History of Islamic Law*. Edinburgh: Edinburgh University Press.

Dallal, Ahmad (2010). *Islam, Science, and the Challenge of History*. New Haven and London: Yale University Press.

Daston, Lorraine and Fernando Vidal, eds. (2004). *The Moral Authority of Nature*. Chicago and London: University of Chicago Press.

Dhanani, Alnoor (1993). *The Physical Theory of Kalām: Atoms, Space and Void in Basrian Mu'tazilī Cosmology*. Leiden, New York, Köln: Brill.

——(1996). 'Kalām Atoms and Epicurean Minimal Parts' in *Tradition, Transmission, Transformation*. Edited by F. J. Ragep and Sally P. Ragep, with Steven Livesey. Leiden, New York, and Köln: E. J. Brill: pp. 157–72.

——(2003). 'Rocks in the Heavens?!: The Encounter Between 'Abd al-Ğabbār and Ibn Sīnā' in *Before and After Avicenna: Proceedings of the First Conference of the Avicenna Study Group*. Edited by David C. Reisman, with the assistance of Ahmed H. al-Rahim. Leiden: Brill: pp. 127–44.

Elshakry, Marwa (2007). 'The Gospel of Science and American Evangelism in Late Ottoman Beirut'. *Past and Present* 196: 173–214.

——(2008). 'The Exegesis of Science in Twentieth-Century Arabic Interpretations of the Qur'ān' in *Nature and Scripture in the Abrahamic Religions: 1700-Present*. 2 vols. Vol. I. Edited by Jitse M. van der Meer and Scott Mandelbrote. Leiden: Brill: pp. 491–523.

Emon, Anver (2004-5). 'Natural Law and Natural Rights in Islamic Law'. *Journal of Law and Religion* XX: 351–95.

Frank, Richard M. (1994). *al-Ghazālī and the Ash'arite School*. Durham, NC: Duke University Press.

Griffel, Frank (2007). 'The Harmony of Natural Law and Shari'a in Islamist Ideology' in *Shari'a: Islamic Law in the Contemporary Context*. Edited by Abbas Amanat and Frank Griffel. Stanford, CA: Stanford University Press: pp. 38–61.

——(2009). *al-Ghazālī's Philosophical Theology*. Oxford: Oxford University Press.

Ḥallaq, Wael B. (1999). 'The Authenticity of Prophetic Ḥadīth: A Pseudo-Problem'. *Studia Islamica* LXXXIX: 75–90.

——(2001). *Authority, Continuity, and Change in Islamic Law*. Cambridge: Cambridge University Press.

Hourani, Albert (1983 [1962]). *Arabic Thought in the Liberal Age 1798-1939*. Cambridge: Cambridge University Press.

Ibn Fūrak (1987). *Mujarrad Maqālāt al-shaykh Abī al-Ḥasan al-Ash'arī*. Edited by Daniel Gimaret. Beirut: Dār al-Mashriq.

Ibn Rushd (1976). *Averroes on the Harmony of Religion and Philosophy*. Translated by George F. Hourani. London: Luzac & Co.

Keddie, Nikkie (1983). *An Islamic Response to Imperialism*. Berkeley and London: University of California Press.

King, David (1985). 'The Sacred Direction in Islam: A Study of the Interaction of Religion and Science in the Middle Ages'. *Interdisciplinary Science Reviews* X: 315–28.

——(2004-5). *In Synchrony with the Heavens: Studies in Astronomical Timekeeping and Instrumentation in Medieval Islamic Civilization*. 2 vols. Leiden: Brill.

Krawietz, Birgit (2003). 'Brain Death and Islamic Traditions: Shifting Borders of Life' in Brockopp (2003): pp. 194–213.

Lombardi, Clark (2006). *State Law as Islamic Law in Modern Egypt*. Leiden: E. J. Brill.

Madelung, W. (1998-2004). 'al-Māturīdī' in *Encyclopaedia of Islam*. Vol. VI. New edn. Leiden: E. J. Brill: pp. 846–8.

March, Andrew (2009). 'The Uses of Fiṭra (Human Nature) in the Legal and Political Theory of 'Allal al Fasi: Natural Law or "Taking People as They Are"?' Yale Law School, Public Law Working Paper 190.

—— (2010a). 'Taking People as They Are: Islam as a "Realistic Utopia" in the Political Thought of Sayyid Quṭb'. *American Political Science Review* 104/1: 189–207.

—— (2010b). 'The Post-Legal Ethics of Tariq Ramadan: Persuasion and Performance in Radical Reform: Islamic Ethics and Liberation'. *Middle East Law and Governance* 2/2: 253–73.

Morrison, Robert (2005). 'Quṭb al-Dīn al-Shīrāzī's Hypotheses for Celestial Motion'. *Journal for the History of Arabic Science* 13: 21–140.

—— (2007). *Islam and Science: The Intellectual Career of Niẓām al-Dīn al-Nīsābūrī*. London and New York: Routledge.

—— (2009). 'Discussions of Astrology in Early Tafsīr'. *Journal of Qurʾanic Studies* 11: 49–71.

Ormsby, Eric (1984). *Theodicy in Islamic Thought: The Dispute Over al-Ghazālī's 'Best of All Possible Worlds'*. Princeton: Princeton University Press.

Ragep, F. J. (2001). 'Freeing Astronomy from Philosophy: An Aspect of Islamic Influence on Science'. *Osiris* XVI: 49–71.

Rubin, Uri (2001–6). 'Ḥanīf' in *Encyclopaedia of the Qurʾān*. Edited by Jane McAuliffe et al. Leiden: Brill.

Sabra, A. I. (1994). 'Science and Philosophy in Medieval Islamic Theology: The Evidence of the Fourteenth Century' in *Zeitschrift für Geschichte der Arabisch-Islamischen Wissenschaften* IX: 1–42.

Shaham, Ron (2010). *The Expert Witness in Islamic Courts: Medicine and Crafts in the Service of Law*. Chicago and London: The University of Chicago Press.

Spectorsky, Susan (1993). *Chapters on Marriage and Divorce: Responses of Ibn Ḥanbal and Ibn Rāhwayh*. Austin: University of Texas Press.

Watt, W. M. (1982 [1956]). *The Faith and Practice of al-Ghazālī*. Chicago, IL: Kazi Publications.

CHAPTER 10

NATURAL THEOLOGY IN EASTERN RELIGIONS

JESSICA FRAZIER

Discoursers on God say:
"What is the cause? God? Why were we born?
Whereby do we live? And on what are we established?
... Time, or inherent nature, or necessity or chance

Those who have followed after meditation and abstraction
Saw the self-power of god hidden in his own qualities.
He is the one who rules over all these causes,
From 'time' to 'the soul'.

[*Śvetāśvatara Upaniṣad* 1.1–3]

IN Eastern cultures, the familiar arguments of natural theology are revealed through the looking glass of traditions that have very different presuppositions about thought, nature, and God. It is natural that Hindu, Buddhist, Taoist, and Confucian philosophical theologians started with quite different theological sources from those of cultures rooted in Abrahamic theologies and Greek notions of reason. This chapter begins by exploring the possibility of a broader definition of 'natural theology' aiming to encompass the different forms that it takes outside the Abrahamic religions. The chapter will then go on to look at some of the ways in which Eastern natural theologies can offer answers to Western questions, by focussing on Hindu approaches to the causal argument.

The notion of new solutions to old questions is central to this cross-cultural exploration of natural theology. Philosophical problems in religion are largely constituted out of the contradictions between different cosmological, epistemological, and theological assumptions; it follows that a change of assumptions often offers a change of solutions. This happens naturally within the dynamics of any philosophical system, through the innovations of brilliant individuals, or the introduction of new cultural resources. But the *comparative* philosophy of religion also offers new solutions by enabling thinkers to approach the familiar issues through a different filter. Thus cross-cultural natural philosophy demands courage of its practitioners: they must recognize the contingency of beliefs in their own traditions. But the ultimate effect can be both illuminating and refreshing in its reassurance that we are not trapped in an agonistic struggle between reason and hope: the bigger picture often reveals unexpected paths out of the labyrinth.

FORMS OF NATURAL THEOLOGY IN WESTERN AND EASTERN RELIGIONS

What is natural theology? The broadest definition would equate it with 'philosophical theology': the philosophical explanation of theological ideas. A narrower definition might include the holding of those ideas to philosophical standards of coherence. A narrowest definition might take it as the attempt to prove theological ideas based on empirical observation of nature. Each of these definitions would produce a different set of instances in each culture—some philosophical traditions, for instance, prioritize observation as the basis of inquiry, and others prioritize other sources such as intuition; some see ultimate reality as continuous with nature, and others do not; some theologies seek proof, others seek only commensurability and non-contradiction with the laws that we observe in the world. Taking the relationship between our mundane experience and ultimate reality as a central concern of natural theology, in this article we will focus on a middle definition, taking it to be the process of discovering ultimate truths via the capacities (both empirical and logical) of the human mind, as opposed to relying only on revelation.

Such a process has taken a very specific form in European and more lately in Anglo-analytic traditions of philosophy. Yet the very definition of natural theology admits of variables. In order to speak of natural theology across cultures, it may be helpful to define it as an activity that triangulates the relationships between three spheres of reality: humanity with its reflective ability, the natural world which is our immediate object of reflection, and the ill-perceived ultimate reality, which, as we will see, can be defined in a variety of ways. Each of these three levels—humanity, nature, and the level at which a higher 'saving' truth is located—is crucial in determining the character and conclusions of any rational investigation into divinity or ultimate reality. This opens up the possibility of a range of models of natural theology.

As a rule of thumb, in most cultures the form of human reflection that is believed to bring us to knowledge of ultimate reality reflects the nature that is attributed to that reality: some Abrahamic theists tend to see human rational reflection as the best way to arrive at an understanding of a God who is—like humans—the possessor of an intelligence characterized by reflection, planning, will, and action. Other theists who stress the transcendence of God may abjure rational reflection in favour of faith, conceived as an emotion, disposition, or some other attitude that does not require a clearly defined conceptual object for the rational mind.

Early Taoist views conceived of the higher level of reality not as a person, but rather as a pervasive pattern of order. The principles of energy and calm, plenitude and emptiness, and all other semantic relations which give meaning to the phenomenal world, along with the equilibrium which seems to reign between them, are categorized and highlighted in the hexagrammatic archetypes of the *I Ching*. On the basis of such observations, the *Tao Te Ching* propounded the theory of a principle of order called the *Tao*, or 'way of things'. Thus, employing a sort of design argument, these early anonymous Taoist natural philosophers relied on empirical observation and inferential reasoning to prove an ultimate order in reality. But the Taoist culture had no monotheistic scriptural narrative demanding that the discovery of an ultimate order be pressed into the personalist mould of an intelligent design argument—instead it was the order itself, the 'Tao' or 'way' of things, that was deemed ultimate or 'divine'. One consequence of this perspective was that mental *knowledge* of reality was considered less valuable than mental concordance with it. Accordingly, the *Tao Te Ching* advocates an almost ascetic restriction of propositional thought in order to let mental activity settle into its own natural pattern; rather than *showing us* the order of reality, the Tao, the goal was to directly instantiate it.

Hindu Mīmāṃsā thinkers believed that the study of the Sanskrit language in which the Vedic texts are written is the best method for bringing to light the semantically structured 'ultimate reality' that underlies them. By contrast, Hindu Advaitic thinkers such as Śaṃkara held that in its true nature, reality has no defining features to be perceived and possesses no point of continuity whatsoever with the natural order; consequently, while he was eager to explain the philosophical coherence of his doctrines (philosophical theology), he had no choice but to reject the possibility of a natural theology that leads to those doctrines via empirical reasoning, insisting that one can only acquire understanding of the divine through scripture and direct non-propositional experience.

In each of these cases, an appropriate means of knowing is selected according to the nature of what it is that needs to be known. A range of different methods for doing natural theology could be laid out in Table 10.1.

These and other possibilities are realized in the wide range of natural theologies. Many of the strategies that they adopt are quite different from the three or four main arguments that dominated Abrahamic 'proofs' of God. But all these ways of arriving at knowledge of the reality considered highest in that culture share an assumption that the truths of religion are continuous with the truths routinely available to all humans, however limited our mundane experience may seem. In contrast to revealed theology, all of these views see our natural capacity of reflection as a universal ladder that can give each of us access to the highest levels of reality.

Table 10.1 Epistemological foundations for natural theological reasoning

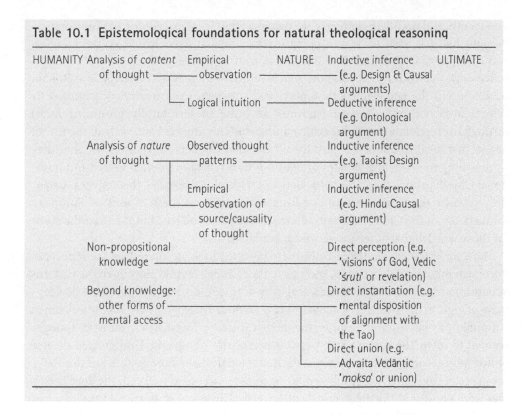

HUMANITY			NATURE		ULTIMATE
Analysis of *content* of thought	Empirical observation			Inductive inference (e.g. Design & Causal arguments)	
	Logical intuition			Deductive inference (e.g. Ontological argument)	
Analysis of *nature* of thought	Observed thought patterns			Inductive inference (e.g. Taoist Design argument)	
	Empirical observation of source/causality of thought			Inductive inference (e.g. Hindu Causal argument)	
Non-propositional knowledge				Direct perception (e.g. 'visions' of God, Vedic '*śruti*' or revelation)	
Beyond knowledge: other forms of mental access				Direct instantiation (e.g. mental disposition of alignment with the Tao)	
				Direct union (e.g. Advaita Vedāntic '*mokṣa*' or union)	

A Short History of Western Interest in Eastern Solutions

As a result of their complex cultural heritage, the Eastern traditions of natural theology have developed as part of the interweaving of many ideas—in India of the monist (Advaitic), dualist (Dvaitic), logical realist (Nyāya), linguistic (Mīmāṃsā), atomist (Vaiśeṣika), gnostic (Sāṃkhya), materialist (Lokāyata), Buddhist, Jain, and other schools, and in China of the Taoist, Confucian, Buddhist, and other religious perspectives. But despite its own mixed heritage, the European tradition by contrast became relatively restricted to a fixed Semitic/Greek set of sources at an early period. Judaism and Islam played the part of a collaborative other, but contact with radically different paradigms of thought was rare. As a result, natural theology as it is known in the West has long sought new solutions while working with the same basic range of philosophical building blocks.

Yet in the modern period, certain Western philosophers saw emerging contact with other cultures as a pool of fresh resources. In particular, some members of the European rationalist movements felt sufficiently liberated from the revelatory authority of the Bible to turn to Asia as an alternative resource of ideas. Throughout the eighteenth, nineteenth, and twentieth centuries, for instance, the German tradition of philosophical thought had felt itself to be struggling towards new answers to old epistemological and metaphysical questions. The introduction of Indian texts seemed to offer a new framework that could go beyond the much-mined resources of the Greek and Roman traditions. In the late eighteenth century a 'Pantheism Controversy' was ignited by Friedrich Jacobi (1743–1819—a vigorous advocate of scripturally grounded faith) through his repudiation of Spinozistic pantheism. This great debate, with all the fear of heresy that it called out of the past, forced German thinkers to consider whether they were willing to follow the dictates of reason if those dictates pointed away from traditional Christian doctrines. This battle between natural and revealed theology was ostensibly won by the Christian traditionalists—there was no mass exodus of European thinkers out of the Church towards alternative religious beliefs. But it sowed the seeds for those who felt that other answers were available.

Thus, for instance, Gottfried Leibniz (1646–1716) took an interest in the reports of European missionaries in China, and saw in the *I Ching*'s cryptic plotting of the patterns of nature, a fundamentally mathematical form of reasoning that prefigured the development of logic in the West. His *Discourse on the Natural Theology of the Chinese* welcomed a number of philosophical improvements that Chinese Taoist and Confucian thought seemed to offer. The voluntaristic personalism of the Abrahamic God created diverse philosophical complications, whereas the impersonal laissez-faire qualities of the Tao— the principle by which nature follows its own order—accorded well with the deist beliefs that were popular at the time. Shortly afterwards, Christian Wolff (1679–1754) claimed that Confucian philosophy had proved humanity's ability to arrive at moral values unaided by revelation.

As the accounts of Jesuit missionaries in China gave way in popularity to the translations of Persian and Indian texts, Hindu and Theravada Buddhist thought came into vogue in Europe. Karl Krause (1781–1832) borrowed Indian ideas in formulating his own panentheist doctrine of God as a non-personal essence (*Wesen*) with which the world must eventually be reunited. Transcendentalists like Ralph Waldo Emerson (1803–82) championed the 'democratic' character of religion based on individual reason rather than revelation, and in his poem 'Brahma', Emerson has the divine reality claim 'They reckon ill who leave me out ... I am the doubter and the doubt ... thou, meek lover of the good! Find me, and turn thy back on heaven' (Lounsbury 1912). Philosophers such as Friedrich Schlegel (1772–1829) were influenced by Indo-Aryan philological theories proposing that ancient Indian Sanskritic civilization was at the root of German culture, and hoped that Indian ideas would heal the philosophically problematic doctrines that had resulted from what was seen as the mythological 'decay' of Christianity. Arthur Schopenhauer (1788–1860) by contrast had little attachment to Christianity and was concerned with the practical aid that Asian philosophy offered. He famously saw in Hindu and particularly in Buddhist disciplines of 'dispassion' a solution (rather than a theodicy) for the problem of suffering.

With increasing global exchange in the twentieth century, students in Eastern and Western cultures began to study each other's philosophical systems and religious beliefs first-hand. Martin Heidegger (1889–1976), who had been so deeply concerned with the 'healing' of what he saw as Western philosophy's misdirection by the Greek heritage, welcomed conversations with Japanese and Chinese thought later in his life. In the other direction, some Asian thinkers, particularly during the colonial periods, drew on European philosophy to elucidate their own theologies. Further east, Japanese philosophers of the Kyoto school used post-Kantian ideas to explain the validity and use-value of Buddhist notions of contradiction, non-determinate truths, and nothingness.

While the German–Asian exchange has been most prolific, a handful of twentieth- and twenty-first-century philosophers in the Anglo-analytic tradition have sought answers in Asia—Jonardon Ganeri tries to illuminate notions of self and subjectivity by reference to Hindu and Buddhist thinkers, and Keith Ward has pointed to the value of Hindu approaches to issues in the philosophy of religion such as the nature of the divine and of the soul. Above all, Asian philosophies have been helpful in exploring the ways in which a weaker commitment to personalism affects the outcome for philosophical problems. For instance, in an article on Chinese philosophical theology John Berthrong uses the Confucian notion of *xian* as a test-case for Tillich's notion of religion as oriented towards a 'supernal reality' rather than a theistic being (Berthrong 2009). However Asian philosophical approaches have rarely been used to augment the classic arguments. In the section that follows we will focus on Hindu approaches to a Western *a posteriori* argument that will be familiar to the average scholar of natural theology—the causal argument.

INDIAN NATURAL THEOLOGY AND THE CAUSAL ARGUMENT

Hinduism, like the classical Greek philosophical tradition, contained early atheistic metaphysical schools such as Mīmāṃsā, Nyāya, Sāṃkhya, and Vaiśeṣika. But unlike its slightly later parallel tradition, Buddhism, most of the Hindu schools agreed that there is *something* eternal lying beyond the finite natural world that is accessible to our routine perceptions. Most also agreed that correct association with it can secure a soteriological transformation in our current human state. In the Vedanta tradition of thought, and those schools which incorporated its ideas, the notion that this eternal counterpoint to the changeful world must be the *source* of the universe—self-existent and characterized by extraordinary ontological powers of 'creation'—arose with all the force of an intuitive leap.

In those schools which considered a cause of the universe to be inductively necessary, it was not the argument against the possibility of an infinite temporal regress of causes that was most convincing. Temporal regress was not seen as hopelessly counterintuitive: indeed, while early cosmogonic narratives in the Ṛg Veda and later the Purāṇas speak about the event of creation, other texts such as the *Bhagavad Gītā* portray it as but one point in a beginningless and potentially unending cycle of creations and dissolution: the linear notion of a start and end point to the universe simply did not seem self-evident, as demonstrated by the belief in an eternal divine being. If God is eternal, why should not the temporal succession of the universe also be eternal? Induction shows us that objects, actions, and events usually begin and end somewhere and so the physical world may raise the question of a beginning, but not time itself. This meant that there could indeed be an infinite regression of past efficient causes. Indeed, a number of schools were quite happy to posit the existence of non-divine substances (such as matter, or mental 'stuff') that had existed eternally: for the medieval theologian Madhva for instance, God's role is as independent (*svatantra*) ontological support for multiple *eternal* realities, not as a temporal creator of them (Sarma, 2003: 52–64).

It is the argument from sufficient reason that generates most Indian approaches. One can reasonably ask of anything we know to exist, 'how did it come to exist?', and inductively it was thought reasonable to ask this of the universe as well. Hindu conceptions of such a cause tended to be very cautious and precise in their reply—they did not automatically assume that such a source has to be a personal, knowing, all-powerful (in the more complex senses of being able to do *any*thing), all-good being. They sought only to derive the idea that there must be something with the characteristics of an ontological foundation: eternal self-existence and the power to somehow give existence to the world that we know.

In one particular tradition, the speculative school of Vedānta arising out of Sanskrit scripture, these ontological qualities alone were enough to establish an enduring conception of the divine as the source and support of the world. The word that is used for God in the Upaniṣads, the earliest texts of the Vedāntic tradition, is *brahman*—literally that which 'bears up' the world. The Indian subcontinent had stood within a vast continuum of polytheistic cultures, not unlike that which generated the earliest stratas of the Hebrew Bible: until this point gods were merely the largest among the beings in the world, and little more proof of their existence was needed than for the human and other creatures which stalked the landscape. But the notion of an entity that stood as the sufficient support for all existence transformed ideas of the divine permanently. On this basis the causal conception of God became particularly widely debated and well-developed (Clooney 2001: 35–58). Indeed, the subsequent 2,500 years of thought allowed a wider variety of formulations of the principles behind the causal argument than are clearly expressed in the mainstream discussions of the Christian tradition. The sources behind these ideas are found in seed in the different analogical models of creation suggested in the proof texts of the tradition.

The Vedāntic texts presented a conception of the divine formulated in contrast to the apparent limitations of the anthropomorphic beings of the earlier polytheistic texts. This contrast is seen in one of the first instances of natural theological reflection, found in the late Vedic/early Vedāntic hymn 10.130, sometimes called the *Nāsadīya Sūkta*— the 'not non-being' verses. This vigorously sceptical cosmogonic poem asks the broad question of the source of the universe, and rejects mythological claims that one of the personal deities could have caused the whole of existence. Regarding the beginning of the universe, it says:

> Then was not non-existent nor existent: there was no realm of air, no sky beyond it. What covered in, and where? And what gave shelter? Was water there, un-knowable depth of water? Then was not existence, nor was there non-existence... Who really knows and who here can say it, whence it was born and whence flows this creation? The Gods are later than this world's production. Who knows then whence it first came into being? [Ṛg Veda 10: 130]

The *Nāsadīya Sūkta* is exceptional as a case of early, almost instinctive scepticism. This cry for an explanation of existence demanded a metaphysics based on a natural theology, and the answer was effectively given by the fragmentary and compendious Vedāntic texts, the Upaniṣads. In the thirteen or so major Upaniṣads, multiple models (often conflated) of the causal relation between the divine and worldly reality are described. Later texts such as the *Bhagavad Gītā*, the *Brahma Sūtras* and also the *Yoga Sūtras*, the *Sāṃkhya-Kārikā* and the philosophical sections of the Sāṃkhya-influenced Purāṇas, all developed the theme further. Eventually professional debaters and scholars who were attached to the schools of Logicians and Empiricists (Nyāya), Atomists (Vaiśeṣika), scriptural philosophers (Vedāntins), Buddhists and Jains, Materialists (Lokāyatas), and others, all became involved in the complex warp and weft of attempts to explain the origin of the universe by recourse to a 'creator'.

One point linked almost all Hindu discussions of divine creation, and axially differentiated them from the Western approach. Hindu thinkers showed a disinclination towards the notion of *creatio ex nihilo*, divine creation of the world from nothing, and more generally the idea that anything can either create, be created from, become, or consign something else to *nothing* (Mohanty 1988: 253). In mainstream Christian theology the idea of God creating the world from nothing is a doctrine assumed necessary to preserve the perfection of God; as Anselm puts it, a material causal relationship to the world 'would mean that the supreme good could be changed and made less good' and as a result Anselm concluded that 'one is just not allowed to say this' (*Monologion* 7). Yet the doctrine of creation from nothing has also caused philosophical difficulties with its counterintuitive claim that something can come from nothing, and its willingness to admit that something other than God exists (i.e. the created world)—an idea that would seem to contradict divine infinity and sovereignty.

This rejection of creation from nothing left a fork between a world-comes-from-God model, and a world-is-eternally-separate-from-God. Thinkers tended simply to choose and stay faithful to one side or the other: Sāṃkhya, Vaiśeṣika, and the Jains agreed that other eternally self-existent things than God can exist. Amongst Vedāntins, the c.tenth-century Sāṃkhya-influenced Vaiṣṇava thinker Yamunācārya, and the thirteenth-century dualist Vedāntin Madhva, for instance, held that God, world, and souls are indeed separately, independently eternally existing entities—although the world is *dependent* on God ontologically. By contrast, Bhāskara, the early mitigated-monist Vedāntin argued that the world is indeed an extension of the divine being, and a number of influential theologians cautiously followed him along this fork.

In either case, *creatio ex nihilo* has little or no place in Indian views of creation, and the analogical reasoning of the early source texts rejected a radical account of creation as 'making to exist'; they inductively reasoned that the fixed economies which we see in the natural world should hold for the divine creation of the world. The result was a nuanced range of 'material-causal' and other accounts, many of which are almost unknown in the Western cosmogonic discussions.

THE PHYSICAL-MATERIAL CAUSE ARGUMENT

Reasoning from the idea that the divine must be the sole eternal foundation of existence, the *Chāndogya Upaniṣad* uses a material causal model to describe the divine creation of the world, portraying the divine as the clay, copper, or iron 'substance' that constitutes all other things (6.1.1). The *Taittirīya Upaniṣad* backs this up with images of the divine having 'flowed' into creation, and in the *Bhagavad Gītā* God (now speaking in an incarnate form explaining His own nature) portrays the divine as the substantial material cause of existence: individual objects emerge from him in the 'morning' of the world and merge back into it in the evening (8.18). Living beings are situated within him (8.22) like a great wind is situated in space (9.6).

In line with this, the early Vedāntic philosophy Bhāskara argued for a mitigated mutability of the divine being through its transformation into the world, holding that all beings are really modifications of the divine. Causes are not thus interactive events in which one thing affects another; they are personal intransitive actions in which God merely undergoes a change. Thus the early 'Viśiṣṭādvaitin' position is that within the divine being, cause and effect are different states of the same divine subject. Rāmānuja, the most famous advocate of this school, echoes this idea by claiming that the divine has both a causal condition (as transcendent creator) and an effect condition (as created world), but remains the same substance throughout (see Rāmānuja's *Śrī Bhāṣya* 1.4.23, translated in Lipner 1986: 84). A few centuries later this was a position defended by Jīva Gosvāmi, a devotional Sāṃkhya-influenced Vedāntin who strongly affirmed that the divine 'is situated everywhere', that the creation in turn is 'always situated in Brahman'. Both Rāmānuja and Jīva, however, would argue that there is an unaffected portion of the divine (See Jīva Gosvāmi's *Catuḥsūtrī Ṭīkā*, translated in Gupta 2007: 176).

The reality is that few upheld a *simple* material causal account of God's creation as it seemed too difficult to maintain the key divine qualities of eternity, immutability, and necessity for the portion of the divine being that remained 'untransformed' in the creative process. And of course it immediately countered the attribute of simplicity—the one-ness of the divine. An eternally subdivided God could not be *akṣara*—undivided and without parts—and just like the Aristotelian scholastic thinkers of Europe, the Hindu theologians saw this as contravening divine sovereignty and inviting a 'decayable' God. To abandon divine one-ness was to return to an era of multiple entities, each sharing a meagre portion of supremacy. As a result qualifying strategies would be necessary to counter this implication. But before going on to look at these approaches, it is important to note that a very different material-causal argument was also used by Hindu philosophical theologians.

THE MENTAL-MATERIAL AND MENTAL-EFFICIENT CAUSE ARGUMENTS

The natural world perceived externally to each inquirer, was not the only field of data which presented itself for fruitful inductive reasoning. Hindu thinkers give systematic empirical consideration to mental phenomena as well as physical ones. This allowed natural theologians to reason causally from mental facts as well as from physical facts (and sometimes in preference to the latter). As Rāmānuja puts it, for all inquiry there is both an external and an internal source of knowledge (see *Vedānta Sūtra Sribhasya* commentary on 3.3). The source of this 'phenomenological' tendency in Indian thinking is not clear—perhaps it was the gnostic trends of the Yogic culture that was so pervasive in Vedic, Tantric, Jain, and Buddhist thought. Whatever the reason, the 'mental-material cause' approach took a strong hold on the theological imagination, and also served to link the tradition of arguments for God to a parallel tradition of arguments for the existence of the soul. The idea of a cause or substrate of physical reality paralleled speculations about the existence of a cause or substrate of mental reality: in many cases these two issues became philosophically interdependent.

The *Kena Upaniṣad* sketches a rough mental-efficient cause argument that would be influential on later reasoning that an underlying source of thought and volition must exist. It asks 'by what' ('*kena*') do thought, breath, will, and action arise, and implies that the answer is a source which itself does not require a source (1.1–8). The *Aitareya Upaniṣad* speaks of brahman as that by which one sees, hears, smells, speaks, perceives, and discerns (31–4), and it summarizes: 'brahman is knowing'. The *Kaṭha Upaniṣad* and, following it, the *Bhagavad Gītā* carry through this idea of brahman as the first cause not only of the existence of sentient beings, but also of their actions, as the inner 'controller' (*Kaṭha Upaniṣad* 5.12), 'that by which one perceives', the 'honey-eating self' (*Bhagavad Gītā* 4.4–5) who enjoys all perceptions but—as it is not itself seen to be created or destroyed—is thought to be 'self-existent' (4.1) and 'without beginning and end' (3.15). The *Brahma Sūtras* try to bring coherence to these ideas, and the notion of the divine as an originary inner compeller recurs in the first section and is repeated in the *Bhagavad Gītā*, in which Arjuna plays the role of a natural theologian, asking 'what is nature? What is mind? What is the field [of experience]? What is *the knower of the field*?' (13.1). The answer is that the divine is the 'knower of the [mental] field', the experiencer who serves as a substrate for the changing and contingent realm of thought.

The above notion of brahman as controller seems to correspond to an *efficient-cause* conception of mental causality. By contrast, the thinker who comes closest to a *material-cause* conception of divine creation is surely the tenth-century Kashmiri theologian, Abhinavagupta. Aiming at a philosophical union of both theistic and radically monistic perspectives, he argued for a form of idealism that resolved a number of ontological difficulties by identifying the world as a movement (*spanda*) of the divine consciousness. Few Western thinkers have followed this path towards a mental-causal argument, but arguably it is to such a category of accounts that the sub-culture of natural theologians which included Spinoza, Leibniz, and Hegel belonged. It is an argument that still 'has legs' in the modern period: John Locke touched on it in claiming that matter could not produce thought, and that thus a first cause is also required to explain the existence of thought, and in the twentieth century Richard Swinburne has made a comparable probabilistic argument, in response to which J. L. Mackie has drawn on Donald Davidson to criticize the analogy between the causal laws governing mental and physical events respectively (Mackie 1982: 119–32). It would seem that the success or failure of this particular argument is linked to questions still hovering around the issue of mind–brain reductionism.

QUALIFIED MATERIAL CAUSALITY
AND ANALYTIC DIVISIONS OF THE DIVINE

Many of those who accepted a material causal account of creation, nevertheless sought to avoid certain implications of a substantial sharing of God's being with the physical world. As a result the medieval and early modern periods in India saw a flourishing of new variations on the old, cruder material images in the classical sources. The new 'qualified' forms of material causality sought to create a bi-level account of the divine, retaining an immutable and unaffected transcendent part and a materially transforming part. But few adopted a simple quantitative division according to which one portion or quantity of God would stay unaffected while another 'becomes' the world. In order to articulate a more convincing division of the divine being—one which could preserve the integrity of the divine being *in its essence rather than just in a part*—a number of theologians established an analytic rather than a quantitative divide, and held that the transformation of the divine into the universe is a change only in the less essential part.

Thus, for instance, Rāmānuja, who is renowned for such strategies, uses the metaphor of a person and his or her body to suggest the divide between a thinking subject and its embodied form. This is not a case of two parts of one thing, identical in nature, yet able to exist independently, but of an aspect (*amśa*) and the possessor of the aspect (*amśin*) (Lipner 1986: 86). The world is a distinct aspect of the divine, one which is able to become multiple, to change and be finite in nature, etc. This Sāṃkhya-Yoga-influenced notion of a being who has a transformable world-body while remaining distinct as a subject, accorded well with the broadly panentheist personalism that was popular in a new genre of theistic religious texts, the Purāṇas.

Here we have a notion of 'partitive' material causality, as Julius Lipner puts it, in which God has explanatory power as both material and efficient cause of the universe, and the absurdity of *creatio ex nihilo* is avoided whilst preserving the transcendental divine attributes. But this idea alone could not safeguard the divine simplicity, for a subject–body division still implies that its possessor has 'parts'. So Rāmānuja develops the idea further; on closer philosophical examination, he claims, the relationship appears like that of an entity to the qualities that inhere in it (*viśeṣya-viśeṣana*). We are merely one of many non-essential characteristics inhering in the divine substance. This strategy was evocative and compelling for many theologians who took Rāmānuja's lead. Jīva Gosvāmī draws on an image from the *Bṛhad Āraṇyaka Upaniṣad*: 'just as the light of a fire situated in one place spreads' in the same way, the creation's existence arises by Bhagavan's (God's) existence (Gupta 2007: 176). Jīva clarifies that he sees the world as an epiphenomenon of God, an accidental non-essential quality, not as an essential one. The Bhedabheda Vedāntic school considered this an unsuccessful strategy however, and as contemporary Western philosophy has seen, the idea of a clear-cut distinction between essential and accidental properties is perennially disputed. Nevertheless this was a clever analytical division of the divine being that sought to preserve an untouched portion away from the ravages of finite and mutable worldly existence.

THE EFFICIENT-CAUSE ARGUMENT AND DIVINE INTELLIGENCE

Alongside this flourishing 'alternative' tradition of material-causal accounts of the divine as an explanation for the universe, many also maintained a notion of divine efficient causality of the kind that is familiar to the West. The relatively theistic *Śvetāśvatara Upaniṣad* affirmed the notion of God as the 'impeller', and 'the one who set in motion the real' (3.12). This was also an important idea for thinkers outside the Vedāntic tradition, for example the Nyāya school of theistic material realists such as Jayanta Bhatta, who argued in a detailed and coherent way that closely parallels Western causal inductions that our experience of temporary objects having an initial cause is so widespread, and the analogy between such objects and the world sufficiently close, that we should indeed assume that the world must have a cause, and one of adequate qualities (power, intelligence, will) to have created such an extraordinary cause. Rāya Narasimha developed these points into an argument for *personal* theism through the idea that causation is an activity that requires an agent (a point argued much later in the West by William Lane Craig).

But the efficient causal arguments were generally seen as weaker than their material or necessary-causal alternatives. Such thinkers saw, as did David Hume in a later era, that such a prime-mover would not necessarily possess all of the characteristics of divinity, and this was particularly clear in uses of the design argument: Vaiśeṣika atomists who saw God as the great assembler of the chaos of eternal parts, essentially favoured a 'design' approach to creation, and Madhva, the arch-dualist of the Vedāntic tradition, and key Nyāya thinkers agreed. But the deity that they thereby sought to prove was only the efficient or even merely instrumental cause, as in the tales of 'creator deities' such as Brahma shaping or assembling separate, prior, eternal, and more fundamental realities (real objects or atoms or even an underlying eternal divine being) that were the material cause, into the world we know. Thus for instance, Madhva had to assume that God, souls, and the world had all existed separately from eternity.

The Necessary-cause and Ontological Arguments

The existence of such deistic lesser-deities suggests that efficient causality need not necessarily be a defining feature of divinity; a model might claim that one or more things exist eternally (as some scientists do about the fabric of the actual universe), and that one could set in motion a chain of events upon another (e.g. a 'creator' deity shapes the world and initiates active force and beings upon it). By contrast, material causality was favoured because it supported the idea of a single eternal pre-existing being, infinite because unlimited by the existence of other entities, sovereign because not dependent on any other entities, from whom all things come and on whom all things depend. There is no being which exists except through God (*Bhagavad Gītā* 10.39), and all beings are in God but he is not in them (7.12, 9.4). God meanwhile is himself undecaying (*avyaya*, 7.13), non-composite (*akṣara*, 8.3), self-existent (*svabhava*, 8.3) and is, intriguingly, both being and non-being (9.19). The *Gītā* even makes a tacit confirmation that it is answering the cosmogonic question posed to the *Nāsadīya Sūkta*: 'the gods cannot comprehend my origin and neither do the receivers of revelation [*ṛṣis*]' (10.2).

This is a divinity conceived as the basis of all existence, answering the question 'why is there anything rather than nothing?' Clearly the Hindus did not agree that the universe is just a 'brute fact', as Bertrand Russell put it. Why? Modern developments in philosophy have taught us to look for the 'historically-determined' values, as Hans-Georg Gadamer calls it, that underpin even a philosopher's rational choice, and Jonardon Ganeri has more recently reminded us to attend to the positional vindicatory genealogy that motivates the strategies of Indian philosophical discourse (Ganeri 2011). Where Christian theologians emphasized the attribute of personality with its capacity to bless and save, classical Hindu Vedāntins emphasized the value of being a *foundation* for other things and possibilities. The impermanence of the world featured prominently as a fault or *doṣa* in the intellectual discourse of the early Vedāntic, Buddhist, and Jain periods, and like medieval thinkers in the West the Hindus craved certainty, reliability, something that would outlast themselves and any possible contingencies. Thus perhaps the postulate of a permanent support for all existence should be seen in the light of an argument from mundane contingency to divine necessity. This is driven home by the Vedāntic notion that the divine lies beyond existence and non-existence, encompassing them both (e.g. *Taittirīya Upaniṣad* 2.6, *Bhagavad Gītā* 9.19). An image from the *Gītā* describes God as the continuous thread that runs through all beings like the string on which beads are strung; one's own life need not be permanent and certain, as long as something of value is.

This is not an argument from formal necessity; few if any Indian thinkers formulated the divine as that which could not intelligibly be denied (one definition of a necessary being in the technical sense of the arguments used in the West). But the tendency to argue for a sole existent entity and to define it primarily in terms of its existence militates in this direction. Kant (who particularly has Leibniz in mind) links the argument for necessary existence to the ontological argument, and in many ways the Vedāntic approach is informally employing a sort of inverted ontological argument: whatever is necessarily existent—i.e. that which is the required premise for any existence—must possess the qualities of eternity, certainty, sovereignty, and self-existence which constitute, in effect, *divinity*.

Indian Natural Theology

Most of the thinkers discussed above were implicit natural theologians: they demanded a cosmological account of the divine. Some were explicit natural theologians: Nyāya realists such as Jayanta Bhatta rejected revelation as evidence, and argued against a variety of sceptical opponents including the Indian equivalents of David Hume, contemporary Buddhist philosophers who were sceptics about the existence of causality itself. But many Hindu thinkers were led by a defence of revealed theology, to reject the determining evidential force of natural theological arguments: Ramanuja, for instance, rejects the idea that causal explanations can prove the existence of a single God, foreshadowing David Hume in arguing that this would not prove a single causal line, but many. As a result, he argues that only reliance on the Upaniṣadic scriptures can show us that it is in fact a single divine being which lies at the origin of the universe (see *Vedāntasūtra Śrībhāṣya* commentary on 2.2).

Thus natural theological accounts of the divine were seen by many as adding a required coherence and explanatory force to beliefs already 'proved' by their presence in scripture. But it is helpful to remember that the adherence to scripture was also a vote in favour of direct empirical perception of the divine reality. Whereas the Western scriptures are either human testimony to natural *events* that inferentially proved God (miracles and the lives of god-inspired individuals), or to *communications* directly from the divine (the words of Jesus in the Gospels, of the Hebrew God, or of Allah in the *Qur'ān*), the Hindu model based on the Veda and carried forward in the Tantras and some

Purāṇas, is of scripture as testimony to direct observation of the divine reality itself. The Vedas are thus said to have been perceived by *rṣis*, and as such even revelation in the Vedic tradition is an expression of faith in the human capacity to arrive at independent knowledge of ultimate realities.

CONCLUSION

These Hindu conceptions of the divine offer us a view of what the options would be if the West had not decided to uphold divine transcendence by means of the doctrine of *creatio ex nihilo*. This doctrine is a curious item in the Western natural theological vocabulary as it is not wholly based on revelation (it has dubious roots in the Bible which speaks ambiguously in Genesis of a formless void with darkness over the deep, and in John of the life which all things had before creation in the 'Word'), and it ill-accords inductively with our experience; as Elizabeth Anscombe points out in support of the causal argument, not only have we never seen something come out of nothing, we cannot even really imagine it. The doctrine is largely there to uphold the Hebrew personalism of the Bible and the Neoplatonic value of the perfection of the divine nature. *Creatio ex nihilo* does not feature in Hindu thinking, perhaps because the Hindu source-scriptures for philosophy, like those of Taoism and unlike the essentially *narrative* source-texts of Judaism, Christianity, and Islam, themselves take the form of early attempts at natural reasoning.

However these observations are not meant to criticize the West's decision to uphold the doctrine of creation from nothing, but rather to show us the way in which a comparative practice of natural theology reminds us of at least two things. First, the Western arguments are composed of both propositions from nature and propositions from the narratives of revealed theology, and a look at reasoning in other theologies often shows us the constitution of the ideas we are debating more clearly, allowing us to assess the coherence and importance of each part independently.

Secondly, in analysing the constitution of the ideas, the comparative perspective also asks us to consider more closely why we have arrived at those ideas, and whether we endorse the values which they are designed to secure. Natural theology is not simply a process of scientific argumentation. Every time a thinker encounters a genuine philosophical choice, his or her underlying motivations surface in the making of that decision. Once any genuine mistakes are remedied the real decisions are about our theological priorities; whether we prefer transcendence and immutability, or accessibility and engagement; simplicity or the complexities of a thinking, willing agent; infinity or perfect goodness; material or efficient, physical or mental, personal or abstract conceptions. It is the underlying value-commitments that are in question every time a thinker—or a culture—faces a philosophical fork: thus in its way, on a global scale natural theology is also a spiritual practice of revealing and recommitting to faith-based belief.

REFERENCES

Berthrong, John (2009). 'Chinese (Confucian) Philosophical Theology' in *The Oxford Handbook of Philosophical Theology*. Edited by Thomas Flint and Michael Rea. Oxford: Oxford University Press.

Clooney, Francis (2001). *Hindu God, Christian God: How Reason Helps Break Down the Boundaries between Religions*. New York, Oxford University Press.

Ganeri, Jonardon (2011). 'Interpreting Indian Rational Traditions'. *Journal of Hindu Studies* 4/1: 12–22.

Gupta, Ravi (2007). *The Caitanya Vaiṣṇava Vedānta of Jīva Gosvāmī*. Abingdon: Routledge.

Lipner, Julius (1986). *The Face of Truth: A Study of Meaning and Metaphysics in the Vedāntic Theology of Rāmānuja*. London: Macmillan Press.

Lounsbury, Thomas R., ed. (1912). *Yale Book of American Verse*. New Haven: Yale University Press.

Mackie, J. L. (1982). *The Miracle of Theism: Arguments for and Against the Existence of God*. Oxford: Oxford University Press.

Mohanty, J. N. (1988). 'A Fragment of the Indian Philosophical Tradition'. *Philosophy East and West* 38(3): 251–60.

Sarma, Deepak (2003). *An Introduction to Madhva Vedānta*. Aldershot: Ashgate.

CHAPTER 11

....

CATHOLIC PERSPECTIVES ON NATURAL THEOLOGY

....

DENIS EDWARDS

THE Catholic tradition has tended to give an important place to reason in the life of faith. Pope John Paul II began his recent encyclical *Fides et Ratio* with the words: 'Faith and reason are like two wings on which the human spirit rises to the contemplation of truth' (John Paul II 1998: 9). The First Vatican Council (1869–70) resisted both rationalism and fideism and insisted that it is possible to know God with certainty from created reality. The Second Vatican Council (1962–5) repeated these positions, but also reflected on the conditions that give rise to atheism and proposed a dialogical stance towards it. The close relationship between faith and reason in Catholic thought, of course, echoes the close relationship that is understood to exist between nature and grace.

In the approach taken here, natural theology is thought of as based, not on 'pure nature', which, after all, does not exist, but on the natural world that is God's creation, in which the Word has become incarnate and the grace-bearing Spirit dwells. I will begin with Michael Buckley's proposal that a particular approach to natural theology has contributed to modern atheism, which I see as setting the scene for renewed natural theology in the Catholic tradition. In the central section, I will explore the approaches of Karl Rahner and Hans Urs von Balthasar, and show how Walter Kasper's natural theology builds creatively on them. In the last section I will consider briefly some developments that raise important questions for natural theology today: first, liberation, feminist, and ecological theologies; secondly, postmodern thought; and, finally, the theology–science dialogue.

MICHAEL BUCKLEY ON THE ORIGINS OF MODERN ATHEISM

Michael J. Buckley's reading of the origin and development of modern atheism has been widely influential among Catholic theologians, and of course, in the wider Christian community. His original work, *At the Origins of Modern Atheism*

(Buckley 1987), focussed on the beginning of this story, and his more recent book, *Denying and Disclosing God: The Ambiguous Progress of Modern Atheism* (Buckley 2004), further extends the analysis. His fundamental argument is that religion betrayed itself in turning to philosophy and science for its own substantiation. Implicitly it was declaring its own lack of warrant for the existence of the God it proclaimed. The last sentence of *At the Origins of Modern Atheism* sums up Buckley's thesis: 'The origin of atheism in the intellectual culture of the West lies thus with the self-alienation of religion itself' (Buckley 1987: 363).

A key moment in this story occurred when the sixteenth century Louvain theologian Leonard Lessius overturned the medieval tradition of using Peter Lombard's *Liber sententianum* as a basic theological text, and replaced it with Thomas Aquinas' *Summa theologiae*. In the process he abstracted Aquinas' philosophical arguments for the existence of God, the *quinque viae*, from their theological context. He brought forth his own parallel arguments based simply on philosophy, arguments that owed more to Cicero than to medieval theology. He saw the existence of God simply as an issue for philosophy. Buckley thinks this fails to grasp the structure of Aquinas' work as a whole. Aquinas' *Summa* stands within Christian faith, as an integrated demonstration of the personal God revealed in God's works, the greatest of which is the Incarnation. Lessius treated it as if it could be broken up into independent units, separating out the content proper to philosophy from revelation. His warrant for God came from the natural world, and was expressed in the language of philosophy. This kind of natural theology is fundamentally independent of Christian revelation.

Marin Marsenne (1588–1648) is a second key theologian in Buckley's analysis. He too was a man of great intellectual ability, closely connected to thinkers like Galileo and Descartes. He wrote in an encyclopedic way, organizing the sciences of his day as he commented on Genesis. Marsenne, like Lessius, attempted to defend Christian faith in an apologetic fashion that built on the new sciences, understood in the light of the mechanics whose origin was in Epicurus. Buckley sees it as deeply and sadly ironic that Lessius and Marsenne, two of the most influential theologians of their time, able not only to incorporate but also to contribute to the new sciences, were unable to respond with the resources of Christian theology: 'The drama that was to become atheistic humanism was opening upon the European stage, and Catholic theologians stood ready to greet it as philosophers' (Buckley 1987: 65). Without the resources of Christology and Pneumatology, Christianity entered into the defence of the Christian God without appealing to anything Christian.

The task of defending God thus fell to the philosophers, and Buckley shows how both Newton and Descartes recognized that the theological office had fallen to them. For Newton's Universal Mechanics, God was needed at the last moment when these mechanics resolved the movement back to a non-mechanical principle, to a dominion that underlay the universe and sustained the coordinates of space and time. For Descartes, God was the necessary condition for his Universal Mathematics. Buckley comments: 'For Descartes, God was a presupposition for physics; for Newton, God was a corollary.

Nothing manifests more the difference between the two philosophies that inaugurated modernity than the location of their natural philosophies' (Buckley 1987: 347). Two influential proponents of Enlightenment atheism, Denis Diderot and Baron Paul d'Holbach, were able to use Newton and Descartes as resources. Both of them accepted the universality of mechanics, but also developed a notion of matter as dynamic, and were then free to abandon Newton's idea that his mechanics lead to a non-mechanical or transcendent source, and to reject Descartes' view that God was a necessary first principle of mechanics. God was no longer necessary, either as an explanation in mechanics or in natural philosophy.

Tracing this process in close detail, Buckley sees religion as abandoning the justification that is intrinsic to its own nature and experience, and seeking its vindication in another discipline, philosophy. It is as though religion had to become philosophy in order to justify its own most critical cognitive claims. The unique character of religious language does not survive this reduction. The self-alienation of religion leads to atheism: 'For if religion itself has no inherent grounds on which to base its assertion, it is only a question of time until its inner emptiness emerges as positive denial' (Buckley 1987: 360). Buckley makes it clear that he accepts that it is appropriate for philosophy to enquire about God, as many great philosophers from Plato to Whitehead have done. His point is about the responsibility of Christian theology for substantiating its own view of God:

> The Christian God cannot have a more fundamental witness than Jesus Christ, even antecedent to the witness of faith; Christian theology cannot abstract from Christology in order to shift the challenge for this foundational warrant onto philosophy. Within the context of a Christology and a Pneumatology of both communal and personal religious experience, one can locate and give its own philosophical integrity to metaphysics, but Christology and Pneumatology are fundamental. [Buckley 1987: 361]

The Christian claim is of a personal God, and both what this God is, and that this God is, have their primordial evidence in Jesus Christ. Buckley makes it clear that he is not attempting a comprehensive account of the rise of modern atheism but simply exploring a pattern that is evident in its rising. He sees this pattern as inevitably recurring whenever a theology, for which God is personal and involved with human subjectivity and history, takes its evidence for this God from what is impersonal and brackets out all reference to religious experience, witness, history, or events. This is closely interconnected with a second problem: 'In religion, God is worshipped as a presence and asserted in a real assent; in mechanics and philosophy, God is inferred as a conclusion from what is more evident' (Buckley 2004: 37). It can be difficult to move from an inferential form of thought to the form of thought involved in assent, above all in a culture where religious assent is dismissed as a 'soft' form of thought. Buckley insists that one cannot bracket out the interpersonal in the quest for God. Religion must be able to appear in all its richness: including its interpersonal, intuitional, emotional, volitional, rational, institutional, traditional, and historical aspects.

KARL RAHNER (1904–84)

Because Rahner's early work, *Spirit in the World,* was philosophical in character, engaging with Aquinas in the light of Kant and Heidegger, some have seen the metaphysics of knowledge that he develops there as *the* foundation for his extraordinarily diverse and rich theological corpus. But with a number of commentators I think this is a mistake that misses what is deepest in Rahner, the fact that his philosophical and theological work springs from his appropriation of the spirituality of Ignatius of Loyola (Egan 1998; Endean 2004). Rahner says of himself that his own theological thinking 'sprang from the practice of the Ignatian Exercises and so in fact was fashioned in the light of reflection on the effective operation of the Spirit' (Rahner 1979: x–xi).

Rahner is not a 'foundationalist' thinker, but one who thinks critically from within the Christian tradition. The content of Ignatius's *Spiritual Exercises* is Jesus Christ the Word made flesh, his birth, life, death, and resurrection. The goal of the *Exercises* is a personal commitment to Jesus in radical discipleship that shapes a retreatant's life. This is transparently a Christ-centred spirituality, but also one that is also fully pneumatological. The *Exercises* assume that God is really encountered in the experience of the Spirit. In one of his late works, Rahner writes as if he were Ignatius speaking today: 'I was convinced that first, tentatively, during my illness in Loyola and then, decisively, during my time as a hermit in Manresa I had a direct encounter with God. This was the experience I longed to communicate to others' (Rahner and Imhof 1979: 11). From this kind of Ignatian mysticism, Rahner draws two themes that shape his theology: that God has given God's self to us in Christ radically, irrevocably, and eternally, and that in our ordinary lives we really do experience God in the Holy Spirit.

Rahner's Ignatian conviction that the self-giving of God can be experienced faced two obstacles. One was the neo scholastic theology which Rahner had been taught, which separated the natural world and the world of grace into a two-tiered reality and insisted that we have access only to the natural world, thus ruling out any genuine experience of God. The other was modern, post-Kantian philosophy which seemed to deny this kind of knowledge of God. Both neo-scholastic theology and the philosophy of modernity seemed to deny the possibility of the experience of God that Rahner took to be at the heart of Ignatian spirituality—and Christian spirituality more generally.

It is in this context and, of course, in the context of Catholic resistance to modernity in general, that Rahner proposed a theological 'turn to the subject'. Rereading Aquinas, in the light of the philosophy of Kant, Hegel, and Heidegger, and following a path opened up by Joseph Maréchal, Rahner offers an analysis of the human person in his or her knowledge and freedom as constituted as 'absolute and limitless transcendentality' (Rahner 1974a: 94). He shows how the experience of transcendence occurs in the encounter between the knowing, free subject and the *other* in the world. In the knowledge of another, and also in our freedom towards the other, two things occur which may or may not be attended to fully: first, we become aware of ourselves in self-distinction from the other; and second, we know this particular and historical other against an 'horizon' that opens our subjectivity out towards the transcending infinite (Rahner 1978: 31–39). There is a boundless expanse to the human mind and heart, and this boundless expanse is always there as the context of ordinary knowledge and love.

Rahner sees this way of approaching the knowledge of God as involving a 'unity' of philosophy and theology (Rahner 1978: 10–11). It is philosophy that can open up the radical question that the human person is to herself, and provide an understanding of the transcendental and historical conditions for revelation. And it is theology, based on God's self-revealing, that offers an answer to the human question. Rahner recognizes that the Christian tradition has acknowledged both 'natural' knowledge of God from the experience of creation and a knowledge of God through revelation. But he proposes a more original unity of the two (Rahner 1978: 55). From revelation we know that God is a God of radical grace, a God who is always present to the human person in self-offering love. This means that there is no such thing as a purely natural knowledge of God, because by God's free gift we live in a world of grace. While philosophical reflection can show that a person is always open to unlimited transcendence in her knowledge and love of another in the world, it cannot tell us about the term of this transcendence. It is revelation that tells us that we are surrounded and held in grace, that the term of our transcendence, the 'whither' of transcendence, is a God of boundless, forgiving love (Rahner 1978: 62).

What of the traditional proofs for the existence of God? Rahner calls these 'signs' that point to God but insists that they do not make God a reality we can grasp. They are necessary and helpful, but are to be seen as a reflective development from the more primordial experience of God as holy mystery. They are not to be presented as if they were demonstrations from outside to a person of something previously unknown. The approach that Rahner advocates is one that shows the hearer that he or she is already involved with the question. Then the 'proofs' are really an explication of something that has already taken place, that in a person's free and spiritual action with regard to others in the world, he or she acts, thinks, loves, and hopes only in a context of a preconceptual transcendental openness to holy mystery. Rahner notes that for different individuals, the subjective intensity of this experience varies in different contexts:

> If, therefore, he is really to understand this reflection on 'proofs' for God's existence, the individual person must reflect precisely upon whatever is the clearest experience for *him*: on the luminous and incomprehensible light of his spirit; on the capacity for absolute questioning ... on annihilating anxiety ... on that joy which surpasses all understanding; on an absolute moral obligation in which a person really goes beyond himself; on the experience of death in which he faces himself in his absolute powerlessness ... Because he experiences himself as finite in his self-questioning, he is not able to identify himself with the ground which discloses itself in this experience as what is innermost and at the same time what is absolutely different. The explicit proofs for God's existence only make thematic this fundamental structure and its term. [Rahner 1978: 69–70]

The various proofs for God's existence simply clarify that one proof that comes from the different points of departure for the transcendental experience of God as holy mystery. In Rahner's view, this is already the revelation of God in the Spirit. This is a universal revelation that is made fully explicit, concrete, historical, and irreversible only in the life, death, and resurrection of Jesus. These constitute the two interrelated aspects of God's self-communication, which Rahner calls transcendental and historical. Transcendental revelation occurs in the historical encounter with our world, and it always needs to find categorical expression in concepts and words, no matter how inadequate these are, and in community life and its institutions (Rahner 1978: 172). The revelation of God in the incarnation, handed on in the Church, in its bible and liturgy, is the 'unsurpassable climax' of categorical revelation. God's very self is expressed and communicated in the historical humanity of Jesus (Rahner 1978: 174).

The human subject, for Rahner, is one who in the encounter with the other in the world, experiences an openness to radical mystery, and looks to history seeking an illumination of this mystery, and finds this graciously given in God's self-bestowal in Christ. Christ is the beginning, the centre, and the final goal of this theology. What happens in Christ constitutes an unthinkable commitment of God to humanity and to this world, the promise and the beginning of the divinization of human beings and with them, in some way, of the whole creation (Rahner 1974b: 129).

Hans Urs von Balthasar (1905–88)

Hans Urs von Balthasar's approach to theology differs from that of Karl Rahner, and he has been critical of Rahner's theology, arguing that it runs the danger of reducing religious truth to anthropology, and eclipsing the drama of divine and human freedom expressed in the Christ-event, particularly in the cross (Balthasar 1987). As I have indicated, I see Rahner's theology not as trapped in anthropology, but as establishing a necessary turn to the subject, within the context of a Christ-centred theology. Balthasar's own contribution is influential today in many circles, including those of postmodern theologies and the 'Radical Orthodoxy' movement. Balthasar's theology, like Rahner's, is deeply grounded in the *Spiritual Exercises* of Ignatius (O'Donnell 1992: 154–9). He believes that good theologies embody spirituality in their inmost being (Balthasar 1983: 44; 1993: 95). In my view, the theologies of Rahner and Balthasar are best seen in non-competitive terms, as major twentieth-century theologies that each have something to offer to the twenty-first century.

Balthasar has developed his theology through a series of fifteen volumes in the shape of a triptych. In the first part he outlines a theological aesthetics, in which the appearance of God in Christ is understood from the perspective of beauty. In the second, he considers God's engagement with us in Christ from the perspective of dramatic theory and explores it in relation to praxis and ethics. In the third part he explores it in terms of its logic, its *logos*. In this theological synthesis, the beautiful (*pulchrum*) is the starting-point and this then unfolds into a drama and a logic, so that the *Gestalt* of revelation may come to be seen in its fullness.

Philosophy finds its place within a theology carried out in the light of faith. Balthasar sees fundamental theology and dogmatic theology as 'in the last analysis, inseparable'. The apologetic task of reason cannot be separated from revelation. The very path towards God's self-revelation 'already stands in the rays of the divine light'. And reason is not simply left behind in dogmatics. Reason is drawn into faith. An adult faith continues to grow as a *fides quaerens intellectum*: 'the facts of revelation are perceived initially in the light of grace, and faith grows in such a way that it allows the self-evidence of these facts—an evidence that itself was "enrapturing" from the outset—to continue to unfold according to its own laws and principles' (Balthasar 1982: 126).

In his theological aesthetics, Balthasar points to the objectivity of the *Gestalt* that is Jesus of Nazareth. He calls this wholeness of the Christ-event its form: 'The beautiful is above all a *form*, and the light does not fall on this form from above and from outside, rather it breaks forth from the form's interior' (Balthasar 1982: 151). It is from this form, the Christ-*Gestalt*, that there comes the light which draws us to itself. This light is 'the ground of the experience of rapture, the experience by which the observer is seized by beauty and drawn into its dazzling radiance' (O'Donnell 1992: 21). The grounds of credibility are found within the Christ-*Gestalt* itself.

It is love that is spoken in Christ, the love of the triune God, a love revealed finally in the paschal mystery, in the vulnerability of the cross. What is revealed is the triune God whose very nature is kenotic love, love that is complete and utter self-giving. In the event of the incarnation, in the life and ministry of Jesus, in the obedience of the cross, in the mystery of Holy Saturday, and in the glory of Easter, the divine word of love is spoken and acted in our world. The death of the innocent one is the word that God speaks, the word that reveals, and the word that challenges us to follow the path of Jesus in our world. Jesus himself is the archetype and the norm of our response to God's self-revealing. To deal fully with the dynamic nature of the Christ-event, and the demand upon us to play our part in response, Balthasar turns to dramatics: 'Aesthetics must surrender itself and go in search of new categories' (Balthasar 1988: 16).

For Balthasar, there is a sign of God imprinted on nature, but this sign comes fully to light only when Christ, the sign of absolute love, appears. Nature is theophanic, but theophanic in the light of Christ:

> If the cosmos as a whole has been created in the image of God that appears—in the First-born of creation, through him, and for him—and if this First-born indwells the world as its Head through the Church, then in the last analysis the world is a 'body' of God, who represents and expresses himself in this body, on the basis of the principle not of pantheistic but hypostatic union. [Balthasar 1982: 679]

To recognize God in the world, we need to see the Form of the world in the love revealed in Christ.

What is needed is a theological aesthetic that recognizes that created beings derive their beauty from their participation in this love which is their transcendent ground.

This aesthetic enables us to be taken by wonder at the theophanic nature of beings in which the light of divine love shines. This involves seeing this specific finite creature of the natural world, being enraptured by it, in all its sensuous beauty, and recognizing it as radically given. It involves being open to this creature before me, that it might appear to me as a true epiphany, that it might give itself, and speak itself.

To find the beautiful in the contingent is also to raise again the fundamental metaphysical question: 'Why is there anything at all and not simply nothing' (Balthasar 1991: 614). Balthasar insists on the importance of Aquinas' conception of the real distinction between essence and existence (*esse*). It is this that underpins the infinite distinction between the absolute uncreated Being of God and created Being and all created entities. Balthasar finds the origin of some of the false paths of modernity in Duns Scotus' rejection of Aquinas when, following an Averroist reading of Aristotle, Scotus took being as a univocal concept that applied to both created and uncreated being (Balthasar 1991: 9–21). This eventually leads to an overestimation of human reason and to all the problems associated with 'ontotheology', where God is seen as one among other beings.

Our existence is a miraculous gift. Existence is a cause of wonder and astonishment, and this wonder is the beginning of all metaphysics. There is a fourfold distinction at the heart of Balthasar's metaphysics. First there is the experience of wonder at the miracle of one's own distinct contingent existence that begins with a child first seeing the love in its mother's eyes. The child begins to awaken to its own 'I' in distinction from its mother, and then from others. Secondly, Balthasar points to the difference between Being and the whole range of existing entities. On the one hand, the abundance of Being surpasses all the existing entities that partake in Being and, on the other, Being does not exist in itself, but only in existing beings. This raises a further question about the relationship between Being and existents: Being might be understood as alien, indifferent, or meaningless and thus lead to nihilism; or Being might be understood in glorious terms as wonderfully excelling all the beauty and order of the world. In the fourth distinction, revelation resolves this ambiguity with the doctrine of creation, where Being is revealed as the pure gift of divine freedom and love (Balthasar 1991: 613–27).

Fergus Kerr comments on this line of thought: 'Perhaps there is more assertion here than supporting argument. For students accustomed to modern Anglo-American styles of metaphysical discourse, much more seems to be claimed that is ever actually demonstrated' (Kerr 2004: 237). But I think that Balthasar recognizes the limits of the philosophical argument, with his indication, in the third distinction, that reason by itself cannot absolutely establish whether Being ends in nothingness or in glory and grace. It is revelation that shows that Being is the sheer gift of God. Balthasar's argument seeks to establish the plausibility of Christian faith not on reason alone, but on reason that finds its completion in God's free self-revelation.

As the incarnation reveals the kenotic character of divine love, so the beauty of creatures, their sheer existence instantiates and reflects this same generosity. Balthasar has said: 'A moment of grace lies in all beauty: it shows itself to me far beyond what I have a right to expect, which is why we feel astonishment and admiration' (Balthasar 2004: 66). This already happens in the simple realization of the givenness of Being in finite entities.

But the grace of Being is elevated to a qualitatively new level, when the Absolute is illuminated and formed in the finite—in Christ: 'What is demanded of us now, as we stand before this pure grace, which no longer reveals beauty but rather glory, is not to admire and be enraptured. Now we must worship' (Balthasar 2004: 67). Balthasar does not attempt an independent metaphysical proof for God, but develops a metaphysics that is incomplete in itself and that is preserved in, but transcended by, a theology done in the light of God's free self-revealing in Christ.

WALTER KASPER (1933–)

In his *The God of Jesus Christ* (1983), Walter Kasper begins from the God-question today, explores the God revealed in Christ, and articulates a relational, fully trinitarian theology of God as a dynamic mystery of love, which he sees as the answer to modern atheism. In the first section, he offers a thorough treatment of natural theology that builds on Rahner and Balthasar, among others. He begins with atheism, and then takes up the experience and language of God and the 'proofs' for the existence of God. He sees natural theology as sustained reflection on the presuppositions of faith (Kasper 1983: 65). This does not mean reducing faith to reason: 'faith can be substantiated only by itself, or more accurately, by its proper object, which is the revelation of God in Jesus Christ. Natural theology cannot substitute for this substantiation or even attempt simply to supplement it' (Kasper 1983: 71). The task of natural theology is to show the internal reasonableness of faith that has its substantiation in itself.

Kasper asks: to what extent is it possible today to speak of experiences of God? He sees experience as involving both subjective and objective dimensions, as emerging in history, always related to language and as stored and communicated through narrative. We experience the finiteness and incompleteness of our experiences, and it is here that we encounter, indirectly, religious experience, as the basic experience present in other experiences: 'In religious experience, there is revealed to us, via other experiences, the ultimate, all-inclusive, sheltering horizon of human experience, namely, the dimension of that mystery out of which all experience emerges and to which all experience points' (Kasper 1983: 85). Kasper recognizes that the experience that arises in 'disclosure' situations can be interpreted today not only theistically but also in atheistic or nihilistic terms. Nevertheless, it poses a fundamental question about the meaning of reality itself.

Kasper sees the language we use for God as an urgent matter for Christian proclamation. He traces the twentieth century discussion of language from logical positivism to Wittgenstein's 'language games' and Heidegger's concept of language as 'the house of being'. With Ricoeur he explores the parabolic and metaphorical nature of language as opening up a new vision of reality. This is how the word 'God' functions. It gives expression to the 'plus' of reality, invites us to see the world as a parable and calls for conversion. The word 'God' opens up a place of freedom and a future. Kasper insists that even when language is not explicitly religious it contains a movement to transcendence: 'Language draws its life from a pre-apprehension of the total meaning of reality and gives expression to this meaning in metaphors and similes' (Kasper 1983: 94). Language reaches its full stature in explicitly religious language. In this light, Kasper proposes a renewal of the doctrine of analogy, where God is understood as perfect and absolute freedom to which our finite freedom reaches forward. In thinking of God within the horizon of freedom, humans look to history to find whether God freely reveals God's self.

Kasper's discussion of experience and language leads to the question of the knowledge of God. Can we know, or even prove God? He sees the word 'proof' as an analogical concept. It suggests a repeatable process of substantiation. But it is used differently by the mathematician, the natural scientist, the lawyer, the historian, the literary researcher, and the medical doctor. The proof of the existence of God reaches beyond the empirical and the merely rational to the infinite and the metaphysical. If one attempted to prove God in the manner of the natural sciences, then one would profoundly fail to know God. Kasper says that 'we should not expect more from the proofs for God's existence than a well-founded invitation to faith' (Kasper 1983: 100). The value of the proofs is as constituting a reasonable appeal to human freedom and offering an account of the intellectual honesty of faith in God. Kasper considers four kinds of arguments: cosmological, anthropological, historical, and ontological.

The point of departure for the cosmological argument is the cosmos itself, its order and beauty, mobility, frailty, and contingency. Kasper sees the heart of this proof, which remains useful today, as the argument from contingency and the question: why is there anything at all instead of nothing? When we take the possibility of non-being as our horizon, we discover the positive character of being. This argument is really 'an explanation of the astonishment felt at the wonder of being' (Kasper 183: 103). In this astonishment, the mind reaches beyond itself, to the groundless ground that is beyond our explanatory thinking. In this situation there is the invitation to a conversion that involves radical trust in this ground. This conversion does not disclose God's being in itself, but enables us to grasp reality as image and likeness of God and thus as meaningful.

The anthropological argument begins with the inner reality of the human spirit. It is an exploration of the openness to the ultimate that occurs in human experience of the world, to what Rahner calls the experience of mystery. Kasper focusses on freedom and finds in every exercise of freedom a hopeful, but unsatisfied pre-apprehension of the complete realization of freedom. This pre-apprehension makes possible and supplies the light and strength for specific free acts. But does absolute freedom exist? Kasper recognizes that many today think we cannot determine that it does. What can be said, he argues, is that if there is to be an absolute fulfillment of meaning for the human person, then this requires absolute freedom as a condition. Furthermore, he says that if God is the perfect freedom that brings our freedom to fulfillment, then God cannot simply be demonstrated to someone from outside. A person must freely open himself or herself up to this absolute freedom, and be open to recognize it, if and when it freely discloses itself in history (Kasper 1983: 105).

Kasper's third argument is from the philosophy of history. In our history we have practical experiences of meaning that keep alive the meaningfulness of history as a whole. It is not possible to prove from reason that there is an unconditioned meaning to history itself, but we do have the basis for an educated hope. Ultimately we live in hope of justice. This is a condition for living as a human being—'As human beings we simply cannot stop hoping that in the end the murderer will not triumph over his innocent victim' (Kasper 1983: 108). If we abandon such hope we abandon ourselves. This hope by which we live can be seen as a pre-apprehension of the Reign of God. Kasper argues that this hope must involve a God who gives life to the dead. The future for which we hope is not simply the continuation of the present but the advent of God as the power of the future. Kasper proposes this not as an absolute proof, but as a justifiable decision about a way of viewing history, which has proved its validity in biblical tradition and in the lives of Christians down to our own day, and which we in turn must verify in our own experience.

These three arguments ask about the ultimate meaning and goal of our cosmological, anthropological, or historical experiences. But modern atheism and nihilism deny that the ultimate ground of our being can be identified as God. Modern philosophy has made it clear that no obvious statements can be made about this ground. This brings out the importance of the ontological argument, associated with Anselm of Canterbury, but rethought by Kasper in agreement with insights of Pannenberg. It begins not from below, but from above 'interpreting reality from the standpoint of the historically transmitted idea of God' (Kasper 1983: 113). The received idea of God thus defines the absolute, and it substantiates itself by the way it functions: 'the reality of the idea of God shows itself capable of opening up reality, making connections visible, facilitating life and encouraging freedom' (Kasper 1983: 113). Kasper sees these arguments as having a cumulative weight. He finds an important place for natural theology within Christian theology, but he believes that both modern philosophy and the ancient Christian commitment to the incomprehensibility of God mean that it is not possible to demonstrate, in any absolute way, the existence of God from the empirical world. It is possible, however, for the believer to bear witness to the existence of God with good arguments.

FURTHER DEVELOPMENTS

There are other developments that might well have been discussed in these pages. The work of Bernard Lonergan, along with Rahner, has opened up a viable way for many Catholic theologians to come to terms with modernity. Important Catholic philosophers have continued to explore natural theology in the tradition of Aquinas. René Latourelle and Rino Finichella have laboured to replace the defensive apologetics that characterized pre-conciliar Catholic theology with a more ecumenical, dialogical, and holistic approach to the plausibility of faith in a renewed fundamental theology (see Latourelle and Finischella 1994). Leaving all this unexplored, I will touch on three further developments: (1) the emergence of liberation theology, feminist theology, and ecological theology; (2) the impact of postmodern philosophy; and (3) the science–theology dialogue.

Gustavo Gutierrez, the founding figure of Latin American liberation theology, defines this kind of theology as 'critical reflection on praxis in the light of the Word of God' (Gutierrez 1988: 11). Where European theology's focus is on the non-believer, liberation theology's focus is on the poor, on those treated as a non-person. Gutierrez sees theology as so inextricably intertwined with social and political processes that there can be no such thing as a 'neutral' theology. The only way that theology can be responsible is to stand at the side of the poor in the midst of their struggles. In a situation of conflict between oppressors and oppressed, theology must be partisan, it must take sides. In this focus on the poor, liberation theology is introducing another dimension to the credibility of faith: God must be shown to be the liberating God of the poor if this God is to be credible in a situation of oppression. In her feminist theology of the triune God, Elizabeth Johnson insists that 'the symbol of God functions' (Johnson 1992: 36). The practice of naming God exclusively in terms of powerful men has pernicious effects: it leads to an understanding of God in literal terms as male and thus reduces God to an idol; it functions to justify patriarchy in Church and society; and it implies that women are less like God than men (Johnson 2007: 97–100). Feminist theology insists again on the classical insight into a God beyond all names, and opens up myriad images and names for God. It asks of any theology of God whether it functions to diminish the full humanity of women or to enable it to flourish. The hermeneutical role of the oppressed that functions in liberation theology and feminist theology has its parallel in ecological theology. A key dimension of ecological thinking and practice is the intrinsic value of non-human creation. Ecological theology challenges all unthinking anthropocentrism and asks about the meaning of our God language for other species and for the whole creation. A natural theology for the twenty-first century will need to show the meaningfulness of talk of God from the perspective of the poor, of women in patriarchal societies, and of Earth and all its creatures.

Postmodern thought opens up a new situation and further questions about our knowledge of God. John Caputo, in an analysis that by his own account is simplistic, suggests that the postmodern can be understood in terms of three background ideas, which he names the 'hermeneutical' turn, the 'linguistic' turn, and the 'revolutionary' turn—this last associated with Thomas Kuhn who showed how science works through changing paradigms (Caputo 2006: 44–9). Caputo sees the postmodern as bringing about a new relationship between faith and reason. In the modern view, reason (science and philosophy) and faith seemed opposed, with reason very much dominant. In the postmodern, a scientific paradigm, for example, is itself a kind of faith, a 'seeing as' in order to discover more. Science and philosophy are seen to involve 'an ongoing faith and trust in its ensemble of assumptions and presuppositions, which function like an anticipatory set of fore-structures that enable us to make our way around—a lab or an archive, a poem or an ancient language, an economic system or a foreign culture' (Caputo 2006: 56). The distinction between philosophy and theology is thus not simply between reason and faith, but between two kinds of faith, two ways of 'seeing as'. In spite of the secularist tendencies of many postmoderns, postmodern thought opens up a new place for theology, explored, for example, in Caputo's own engagement with

Derrida and in Jean-Luc Marion's influential theology of God (Caputo 1997). Marion rejects the metaphysical tradition and, following pseudo-Dionysius, appeals to 'Good beyond being', to the love that gives all, to the gift that is to be received only in love and praise. He sees God as pure giving and the theological task as to 'give pure giving to be thought' (Marion 1991: xxv).

An indispensable aspect of natural theology is the twentieth- and twenty-first-century dialogue between science and theology. The great Catholic pioneer in this was palaeontologist and theologian Teilhard de Chardin who presented a vision that sought to integrate the long sweep of evolutionary history and what he saw as its future promise with the New Testament vision of the cosmic Christ (Teilhard de Chardin 1999). In a very different way and working only as theologian Karl Rahner entered into dialogue with evolutionary thought, particularly in his vision of God's ongoing creative acts as enabling creatures to have the capacity for self-transcendence (Rahner 1966). Contemporary theologians such as John Haught have continued to respond to contemporary science, particularly to Darwinian evolutionary theory, in creative ways (Haught 2000). Jesuit scientists of the Vatican Observatory, such as George Coyne, S.J., and William Stoeger, S.J., have cooperated with Robert John Russell and the Center for Theology and the Natural Sciences at Berkeley to bring scientists, philosophers, and theologians together for a series of research conferences and publications on issues such as divine action, and the suffering that is built into creation. I see this dialogical work as an indispensable contribution to natural theology—a fine example is found in the book of the first major gathering, *Physics, Philosophy and Theology* (Russell, Stoeger, and Coyne 1988). The theologians participating in this dialogue are not attempting to prove the existence of God from gaps in the natural sciences, whether they concern the cosmological anthropic principle, the origins of life, or the so-called 'irreducible complexity' advanced by proponents of 'Intelligent Design'. The focus is on a creative interrelationship with the sciences.

I have proposed that while natural theology has an important role in showing forth the reasonableness of faith in God, the Christian God cannot be defended by reason in an adequate way without taking into account what is truly religious, including the experience of Jesus Christ in our history and the experience of the grace of the Spirit in our lives. Arguments from the natural world have an important place, but need to be treated with care. On the one hand, natural theology must avoid the idolatry of placing God as one being among others, as the highest along a scale of beings, by consistently pointing beyond itself, in language that is self-consciously limited and analogical, to the incomprehensible and the unspeakable. On the other hand, it must humbly recognize that there is no automatic movement from the experience of transcendence to identification of the term of this transcendence with the living God. One can always freely choose to say that the experience of openness to transcendence ends in nothing, and thus embrace bleak nihilism. Christians, with good reason, positively and freely identify the experience of transcendence in terms of the God of Jesus precisely because they are thinking from, and finding meaning, freedom, and hope in the received Gospel of Jesus Christ and in the experience of the Spirit.

REFERENCES

Balthasar, Hans Urs von (1982). *The Glory of the Lord: A Theological Aesthetics*. Vol. I: *Seeing the Form*. Edinburgh: T&T Clark.

—— (1983). *Convergences: To the Source of Christian Mystery*. San Francisco: Ignatius Press.

—— (1987). *Cordula oder der Ernstfall*, 3rd edn. Einsiedeln: Johannes Verlag.

—— (1988). *Theo-Drama: Theological Dramatic Theory*. Vol. I: *Prolegomena*. San Francisco: Ignatius Press.

—— (1991). *The Glory of the Lord: A Theological Aesthetics*. Vol. V: *The Realm of Metaphysics in the Modern Age*. Edinburgh: T&T Clark.

—— (1993). *My Work: In Retrospect*. San Francisco: Ignatius Press.

—— (2004). *Epilogue*. San Francisco: Ignatius Press.

Buckley, Michael J. (1987). *At the Origins of Modern Atheism*. New Haven: Yale University Press.

—— (2004). *Denying and Disclosing God: The Ambiguous Progress of Modern Atheism*. New Haven: Yale University Press.

Caputo, John D. (1997). *The Prayers and Tears of Jacques Derrida*. Bloomington: Indiana University Press.

—— (2006). *Philosophy and Theology*. Nashville: Abingdon Press.

Egan, Harvey D. (1998). *Karl Rahner: The Mystic of Everyday Life*. New York: Crossroad.

Endean, Philip (2004). *Karl Rahner, Spiritual Writings*. Maryknoll, NY: Orbis.

Gutierrez, Gustavo (1973, 1988). *A Theology of Liberation*. Rev. edn with a new introduction. Maryknoll, NY: Orbis Books.

Haught, John F. (2000). *God after Darwin: A Theology of Evolution*. Boulder, CO: Westview Press.

John Paul II (1998). *Fides et Ratio (Faith and Reason)*. Strathfield, NSW: St Paul Publications.

Johnson, Elizabeth A. (1992). *She Who Is: The Mystery of God in Feminist Theological Discourse*. New York: Crossroad.

—— (2007). *Quest for the Living God: Mapping Frontiers in the Theology of God*. New York: Continuum.

Kasper, Walter (1983). *The God of Jesus Christ*. London: SCM Press.

Kerr, Fergus (2004). 'Balthasar and Metaphysics' in *The Cambridge Companion to Hans Urs von Balthasar*. Edited by Edward T. Oakes and David Moss. Cambridge: Cambridge University Press: pp. 224–38.

Latourelle, René and Rino Finischella, eds. (1994). *Dictionary of Fundamental Theology*. Middlegreen, Slough: St Pauls.

Marion, Jean-Luc (1991). *God Without Being*. Chicago: University of Chicago Press.

O'Donnell, John (1992). *Hans Urs von Balthasar*. London: Geoffrey Chapman.

Rahner, Karl (1966). 'Christology within an Evolutionary View of the World' in *Theological Investigations* V. London: Darton, Longman & Todd: pp. 157–92.

—— (1974a). 'Reflections on Methodology in Theology' in *Theological Investigations* XI. New York: Crossroad: pp. 68–114.

—— (1974b). 'Dogmatic Questions on Easter' in *Theological Investigations* IV. London: Darton, Longman & Todd: pp. 121–33.

—— (1978). *Foundations of Christian Faith: An Introduction to the Idea of Christianity*. New York: Crossroad.

—— (1979). 'Foreword' in *Theological Investigations* XVI. New York: Crossroad: pp. vii–xii.

Rahner, Karl and Paul Imhof (1979). *Ignatius of Loyola*. London: Collins.

Russell, Robert John, William R. Stoeger, and George V. Coyne, eds. (1988). *Physics, Philosophy and Theology: A Common Quest for Understanding*. Vatican City State: Vatican Observatory.

Teilhard de Chardin, Pierre (1999). *The Human Phenomenon*. Edited and translated by Sarah Appleton-Weber. Brighton: Sussex Academic Press.

CHAPTER 12

PROTESTANT PERSPECTIVES ON NATURAL THEOLOGY

RUSSELL RE MANNING

THE Protestant tradition seems to be in two minds regarding natural theology. On the one hand, some of the most powerful theological critiques of natural theology have come from the pens of Protestant, in particular, Reformed, theologians. Indeed, for some, Protestantism is, in its very essence, antithetical to natural theology. If natural theology is defined in distinction from 'revealed theology' then it seems only to be expected that the Protestant commitment to *sola scriptura* is incompatible with the endorsement of the possibility of knowledge of God based on the unaided efforts of human reason. At the same time, that other Reformation slogan 'justification by faith alone' seems to sit uneasily with an acceptance of the potential for a natural knowledge of God on the basis of the exercise of our natural cognitive faculties. The stinging condemnations of natural theology from a list of prominent Protestant theologians including Abraham Kuyper, Herman Bavinck, Cornelius van Til, Karl Barth, John Baillie, Alvin Plantinga, and Nicholas Wolterstorff (to name just a few) suffices for most to accept that the Protestant perspective on natural theology is a decidedly negative one. However, on the other hand, many of the most passionate defences and developed examples of natural theology are the works of Protestant authors. Both the so-called 'heyday' of natural theology from the late seventeenth to early nineteenth centuries and the current theological, philosophical, and scientific revivals of natural theology are, unquestionably, dominated by Protestant writers. Indeed, it is tempting to go so far as to claim that whilst Catholic natural theology in the 'traditional' Augustinian/Aquinian mode has been in a protracted slow decline since the eclipse of 'high scholasticism', it was its Protestant counterpart (decisively shaped by 'modern' philosophy and science) that became increasingly dominant.

In this chapter I will explore the apparent contradiction of the simultaneous rejection and endorsement of natural theology within Protestantism by focussing on two distinct, but interrelated perspectives: historical-theological and philosophical. It is beyond the scope of one chapter to trace a comprehensive survey of the divergent Protestant perspectives on natural theology (many of which are, in any case, dealt with in detail in other chapters of this *Handbook*, see especially chapters 5, 6, 7, and 14). Instead, I will focus on two contentious issues as illustrative of the tensions within Protestant perspectives on natural theology. First, I will consider the historical/theological question of the attitude to natural theology amongst the Reformers and the post-Reformation Protestant Orthodoxy. Here I will engage with the established consensus that the increasingly positive evaluation of the possibility and value of natural theology within Protestant Orthodoxy represents a regrettable discontinuity with the 'original' rejection of natural theology by the early Reformers. Secondly, I will explore the place of natural theology within contemporary Protestant philosophical theology, looking in particular at Alvin Plantinga's powerful and influential 'Reformed objection to natural theology'. Here, I will dispute Plantinga's argument that the Reformers' rejection of classical foundationalism in favour of a Reformed epistemology in which belief in God can be properly basic entails a Reformed objection to natural theology. On the contrary, I will suggest the possibility of an alternative Reformed natural theology consistent with the epistemological framework characteristic of Reformed dogmatic theology.

REDISCOVERING THE REFORMATION ENDORSEMENT OF NATURAL THEOLOGY

Overcoming the Barthian 'Nein!'

Karl Barth's blistering condemnation of natural theology, most famously in his 1934 exchange with Emil Brunner and his 1937 Gifford Lectures, has decisively shaped recent evaluations of the place of natural theology in Protestant thought. Whilst the details of the debate are complex (see chapters 7 and 14), Barth is clear about one thing: even if the Reformers 'occasionally made a guarded and conditional use of the possibility of "Natural Theology"' this should not distract from the basic theological conviction of the Reformation, namely 'that the revival of the gospel by Luther and Calvin consisted in their desire to see both the church and human salvation founded on the Word of God *alone*, on God's *revelation in Jesus Christ*, as it is attested in the Scripture, and on faith in that Word' (Barth 1938: 8–9). In Barth's view, the central distinction between the theology of the Reformation and the scholastic Catholicism that it subjected to a thoroughgoing critique was the former's scriptural and Christological exclusivism. For Barth, the Reformers rallied against the isolation of Scripture from revelation and the subjection of a scriptural Christology to a metaphysical account of God's giving of Himself to humanity. By, as he sees it, reuniting the doctrine of creation to the doctrine of God's atoning work in Jesus Christ, Barth affirms that the distinctiveness of Protestant theology lies in its forthright rejection of all natural knowledge of God:

In this sense, as a possibility that is proper to man *qua* creature, the image of God is not just, as it is said, destroyed apart from a few relics; it is totally annihilated. What remains of the image of God even in sinful man is *recta natura*, to which as such a *rectitudo* cannot be ascribed even *potentialiter*. No matter how it may be with his humanity and personality, man has completely lost the capacity for God. Hence we fail to see how there comes into view here any common basis of discussion for philosophical and theological anthropology, any occasion for the common exhibition of at least the possibility of inquiring about God. The image of God in man of which we must speak here and which forms the real point of contact for God's Word is the *rectitudo* that through Christ is raised up from real death and thus restored or created anew, and which is real as man's possibility for the Word of God. The reconciliation of man with God in Christ also includes, or already begins with, the restitution of the lost point of contact. Hence this point of contact is not real outside faith; it is real only in faith. [Barth 1975: 238–9]

By holding together the doctrines of creation and redemption and by sharply opposing natural and revealed knowledge of God, Barth effectively succeeded in placing natural theology off-limits for consideration by serious Protestant theologians for most of the twentieth century. What made Barth's position on this matter so influential is, of course, a complex matter that requires further reflection. Crucial factors no doubt include the dominance of Barthian neo-orthodox theology within Protestantism more generally (itself not unconnected to the real, albeit often exaggerated, decline of alternative 'liberal' strands of Protestant theology), the political context in which Barth's critique of 'natural theology' served simultaneously as a critique of the accommodation of Christianity to National Socialism by the German Christians, and the wider scepticism of metaphysics and the related theological drift towards existentialist voluntarism (Ericksen 1987). Equally important here is the way that Barth's judgement is grounded not only within systematic but also historical theology. At a time of self-proclaimed crisis within German Protestantism, Barth (along with other leading figures of his generation) sought to restate the core doctrine (*Centraldogmen*) of Protestant theology by reinterpreting the Reformers as instituting a radical break from previous Catholic scholasticism; a discontinuity that Barth urged must be repeated to free twentieth-century Protestant theology from so-called *Kulturprotestantismus*' debilitating enthral to contemporary philosophy and science. The solution, which dominated most twentieth-century Protestant historical theology, was to retrieve—and to radicalize—the theological discontinuity of the early Reformers. As Barth put it in his 1934 debate with Brunner, in which both men sought to support their claims with frequent 'proof-texting' references to Calvin (the most iconoclastic of the Reformers):

> If we really wish to maintain the Reformers' position over against that of Roman Catholicism and Neo-Protestantism, we are not in a position today to repeat the statements of Luther and Calvin without at the same time making them more pointed than they themselves did. [Brunner and Barth 1946: 101]

Barth was, of course, not alone in his judgement of the radical core of the early Reformers coupled with their failure, as he puts it, to clarify 'the problem of the *formal* relation between reason and the interpretation of nature and history on the one hand and the absolute claims of revelation on the other' and the subsequent relapse of Protestant Orthodoxy into pre-Reformation metaphysics; his view was echoed by his brother, Peter, in his 1935 corrective to Brunner's 'misunderstanding' of Calvin (a piece that finishes by citing 2 Corinthians 5.7, 'Wir wandeln im Glauben und nicht im Schauen!'), as well as by Paul Althaus's influential 1914 account of the scholasticism of reformed orthodoxy (Barth 1935; Althaus 1914). But it was above all Barth's passionate debate with Brunner that took centre stage, with a twofold result. On the one hand, as James Barr notes:

> Though many people liked Brunner more, for what was thought to be his modera-tion and his good presentation of ideas, it was Barth who seemed to win the day in the end.... The sequel, curiously, was that the issue of natural theology became less of an issue, came to be less talked about. One heard less of it, as if it were no more a question—this although a great many people had not been convinced that Barth's absolute opposition to it was right. Many people doubted it, but did not summon up the force for an outright counterattack against him. [Barr 1993: 13]

On the other hand, which perhaps goes some way to explaining Barr's observation of the curious decline in interest in natural theology precisely as Barth insists upon the centrality of its rejection to Protestant systematic theology, as Stephen Grabill notes, for many twentieth-century theologians, 'the Barth–Brunner debate solidified the trend to enshrine the doctrine of revelation as the centrepiece of Protestant theological systems, and in so doing it assumed the status of a watershed event in the twentieth-century inter-pretation of Calvin's doctrine of the knowledge of God' (Gabrill 2006: 25).

The real result, then, of this bad-tempered exchange was not so much that the sys-tematic theological case was definitively made against the place of natural theology in Protestant thought (it was not), but rather that the actual, historical, endorsement of natural theology by the Reformers was effectively airbrushed out of the picture. Like Jean-Paul Sartre's cigarette on the famous French postage stamp, it was as though it had never really existed in the first place. Recently, however, historians of Protestant theology have begun to contest this Barthian historical orthodoxy and to suggest, first that there is a consistent history within Protestant theology of an endorsement of natural theology (not only of the possibility of natural theology but also of its posi-tive value), and secondly that the crucial issue for the Reformers and their immediate successors was not so much the epistemological question of the sources of knowl-edge of God (nature or revelation) and their interrelations but the theological ques-tion of our responsibility in the light of our natural and supernatural (graced) encounters with God.

Central to this revisionary historical theology is the rejection of the dichotomy, insisted upon by Barth, between 'natural theology' and 'revealed theology'. As Richard Muller insists in his four-volume history of post-Reformation Reformed dogmatics:

> Although a contrast is frequently made, sometimes even in the scholastic systems themselves, between *theologia naturalis* and *theologia revelata* (or *theologia revelata*

sive supernaturalis), it should already be clear that the contrast is imprecise insofar as natural theology is a form of revealed theology. The precise distinction is between *revelatio naturalis* and *revelatio supernaturalis* and the forms of theology resting upon these revelations, *theologia naturalis* and *theologia supernaturalis*, the former being conceived according to the natural powers of acquisition belonging to the mind, the latter according to a graciously infused power bestowed on the mind by God. Natural theology arises out of the order of nature, whereas supernatural theology, transcending the power of nature, belongs to the order of grace—but both arise as revealed knowledge, not as a matter of mere human discovery. [Muller 2003: I. 283]

On the basis of this fundamental rejection of the distinction between natural and revealed theology in favour of the (to Barthian ears unwelcomely paradoxical) contrast between 'natural revelation' and 'supernatural revelation', two crucial points can be stressed about the endorsement of natural theology within post-Reformation Reformed theology.

Calvin's Endorsement of the Possibility of Natural Theology

First, while he acknowledges that Calvin does not use the term *theologia naturalis*, Muller is emphatic that, in common with other early Reformers, Calvin 'does not deny that there is or can be a genuine natural theology based on natural revelation' (Muller 2003: 275). Calvin does not aim to reject the possibility of true knowledge of God from nature, 'rather his intention is to declare that no natural theology contributes to salvation' (Muller 2003: 275). Indeed, on Muller's reading, Calvin endorses the potential for a genuine knowledge of God on the basis of natural revelation (for the regenerate), even as he insists on the insufficiency of natural theology for salvation:

> Calvin, therefore, testifies not only to the existence of natural revelation and to the fact of pagan, idolatrous, natural theology, but to the real possibility of a natural theology of the regenerate. He also appears to have a sense that humanity in general, apart from the issue of sin and regeneration, does have enough logical and rational apparatus to develop some valid teachings concerning God, creation, and providence from examination of the natural order. Yet there is a double problem for natural theology. First, such theology is not saving: it exists as praise rather than as proclamation. Second, it is not dependable in its religious result and contains errors concerning God and his work that can only be corrected through the use of Scripture. [Muller 2003: 276]

Muller directly links what he calls 'the problem of natural theology' to Calvin's understanding of the *imago dei*: 'it is not utterly lost, but it provides no basis for man's movement toward God' (Muller 2003: 276). In essence, this twofold knowledge of God (*duplex cognitio dei*) in Calvin corresponds to a distinction between knowledge of God as creator and knowledge of God as redeemer, with the further distinction spelt out in Book 1 of the *Institutes* between natural knowledge of God:

> available both as a false, pagan theology and as a true, Christian theology clarified by the 'spectacles' of Scripture. God is manifest as Creator both in the workmanship

of the universe and in 'the general teaching of Scripture' but as Redeemer only in Christ. Although Calvin speaks of a twofold knowledge of God, he points to three forms taken by that knowledge—a corrupt, partial, and extrabiblical knowledge of God as Creator, a biblical knowledge of God as Creator, and a knowledge of God in Christ as Redeemer. [Muller 2003: 290)]

'So That They Are Without Excuse': *Sensus Divinitatis* and our Culpable Natural Knowledge of God

An interesting variant of this *duplex cognitio dei* is found in the writings of Calvin's Genevan contemporary Pierre Viret, which leads us to the second point to come out of the revisionary account of the place of natural theology in Reformation thought: culpability for sin. For Viret, knowledge of God comes in two basic varieties. The first, the unfaithful sort, is exemplified by the behaviour of demons, for they acknowledge God but 'fear him as an evil doer fears his judge'. The second, the faithful sort, is seen among true believers who also fear God but 'as a good child fears his father' (Gabrill 2006: 75–6, citing Viret 1548: f. Bi). Without believing through Christ that God is a merciful father and gracious saviour, Viret argues, God can only be known as a 'cruel tyrant' and hence there is little merit in developing philosophical arguments about God on the basis of his 'natural revelation' as any such efforts will unavoidably be warped by our sinful fear of our (justifiable) punishment by the God revealed to us by nature. For Viret, then, in distinction from Calvin and the later Reformed Orthodox, the nature of the true knowledge of God revealed by God 'in this human flesh that he hath put on by his son Jesus Christ, in which he hath declared his goodness, love, mercy, and favor toward man' renders true knowledge of God from nature impossible (Viret 1548: ff. Bi–ii). For Calvin, however, the contrast is not between God as judge and redeemer, but between God as creator and redeemer. Indeed, perhaps ironically, it is Calvin's emphasis on sin—and our culpability for our degeneracy—that leads him to a more positive evaluation of the possibility of natural theology than Viret's, even as he insists that the knowledge of God that it represents is incomplete. Gabrill neatly summarizes this complex understanding of Calvin's nuanced endorsement of natural theology; he writes that 'Calvin holds to the existence of an objectively knowable, and ultimately culpable, knowledge of God that may be perceived by anyone' (Gabrill 2006: 81).

In passages that would not be out of place in Anglican natural theologies of the eighteenth century, Calvin, echoing the natural theologians' favourite Psalm (Psalm 19), writes that:

> There are innumerable evidences both in heaven and on earth that declare his wonderful wisdom; not only those more recondite matters for the closer observation of which astronomy, medicine, and all natural science are intended, but also those that thrust themselves upon the sight of even the most untutored and ignorant persons. [Calvin 1960: 1.5.2]

Similarly, commenting on Acts 17:27 ('that they should seek God'), he writes:

> For God has not given obscure hints of his glory in the handiwork of the world, but has engraved such plain marks everywhere, that they can be known also by touch by the blind. From that we gather that men are not only blind but stupid, when they are helped by such very clear proofs, but derive no benefit from them. [Calvin 1966: 2.119]

Finally, with reference to another favoured source of later Enlightenment natural theologians, Calvin celebrates Galen's account of the 'articulation, symmetry, beauty, and use' of the human body, remarking approvingly that:

> Certain philosophers, accordingly, long ago not ineptly called man a microcosm because he is a rare example of God's power, goodness, and wisdom, and contains within himself enough miracles to occupy our minds, if only were are not irked at paying attention to them. [Calvin 1960: 1.5.2–3]

This unequivocal commitment to the possibility of natural theology is grounded in Calvin's insistence that, even without 'true religion or piety', genuine knowledge of God is possible on the basis of the mutually reinforcing notions of *sensus divinitatis* and *semen religionis*—notions which feature centrally in classical pre-Christian natural theologies (Grislis 1971). In *Institutes* 1.3, for example, Calvin states that 'there is a sense of deity inscribed in the hearts of all' and that all men have been 'imbued with a firm conviction about God, from which the inclination to religion springs as from a seed' which cannot be 'effaced from their minds' (Calvin 1960: 1.3.1–2). Commenting on Romans 1.19–20, Calvin affirms that for Paul:

> God is in himself invisible; but as his majesty shines forth in his works and in his creatures everywhere, men ought in these to acknowledge him, for they clearly set forth their Maker... He does not mention all the particulars which may be thought to belong to God; but he states, that we can arrive at the knowledge of his eternal power and divinity, for he who is the framer of all things, must necessarily be without beginning and from himself. [Calvin 1979: 19/II, 70]

Whilst the final sentence here seems to approach something of a scholastic deduction, Calvin nonetheless holds back from deductive proofs, instead employing discursive and rhetorical arguments that emphasize again and again the primary purpose of the possibility of natural knowledge of God: that we are, in St Paul's term, 'without excuse' for our sin. 'There is', he states, 'within the human mind, and indeed by natural instinct, an awareness of divinity.... To prevent anyone from taking refuge in the pretense of ignorance, God himself has implanted in all men a certain understanding of his divine majesty' (Calvin 1960: 1.3.1). However, 'all degenerate from the true knowledge' of God and 'plunge headlong into ruin' being led inevitably—and yet on reflection obviously wrongly—into the errors of either atheism or idolatry. In both cases, it is as though a negative silhouette of a theology emerges almost in spite of our failures properly to elucidate on the *sensus divinitatis* that is revealed to us in our nature. Neither atheists nor idolaters can in the end deliver on the arguments that they are led to through the misdirected application of reason; their failure fully to efface their true, naturally occurring knowledge of God is, in effect, the demonstration of its truth. As Grislis puts it: 'Such a situation does not, of course, mean that mankind has now so far departed from God as no longer to have any natural knowledge of Him' (Grislis 1971: 25). Nor, of course, does it mean that we are excused for our failure to capitalize on our God-given natural knowledge of God. As Grabill helpfully summarizes it, as a final corrective to the Barthian picture of the Reformer's total rejection of natural theology:

> The main difficulty attending the natural knowledge of God, in Calvin's mind, is not its nonexistence but its lack of clarity. 'It appears that if men were taught only by nature, they would hold to nothing certain or solid or clear-cut, but would be so tied to confused principles as to worship an unknown god.' Contrary to the consensus among Barthians, the key question for Calvin in the debate over the natural knowledge of God pertains to its post-lapsarian status as an ongoing reliable and culpable *knowledge* of God. Calvin does not frame the issue in terms of the *ontology of revelation*—that is, whether all objective traces of the Creator have been removed from the created order—but from the standpoint of the *epistemological consequences of sin*. Calvin argues that God is revealed in nature but that humans misperceive this revelation because of sin, which ultimately leads them to suppress, distort, and abuse the knowledge God has placed at their disposal. [Grabill 2006: 81]

Overcoming the Reformed Objection to Natural Theology

In his seminal paper 'The Reformed Objection to Natural Theology' (1980) (first delivered at a meeting of the American Catholic Philosophical Association!), Alvin Plantinga, the leading theorist and exponent of so-called 'Reformed Epistemology', sets out in no uncertain terms his view of the negative judgement on natural theology within Protestant thought, claiming that 'Reformed or Calvinistic theologians have for the most part taken a dim view of this enterprise' and that 'for the most part the Reformed attitude has ranged from tepid endorsement, through indifference, to suspicion, hostility and outright accusations of blasphemy' (Plantinga 1980: 49). Plantinga's verdict is echoed by Nicholas Wolterstorff in his account of philosophy of religion in the Reformed tradition:

> One of the most salient features of contemporary philosophy of religion in the Reformed tradition of Christianity is its negative attitude toward natural theology— this negative attitude ranging all the way from indifference to hostility. In this regard, the philosophers of the tradition reflect the dominant attitude of the theologians of the tradition, going all the way back to its most influential founder, John Calvin. [Wolterstorff 1999: 165]

Importantly, in their objections to natural theology, Plantinga and Wolterstorff differ significantly from the Barthian rejection of the possibility of natural (non-revealed) knowledge of God. What they are fundamentally opposed to is not so much the possibility of a natural knowledge of God as the legitimacy of natural theology as 'the attempt to prove or demonstrate the existence of God' by rational argument (Plantinga 1980: 49). Consistent with the narrow definition of natural theology within Anglo-American analytical philosophy of religion, Plantinga and Wolterstorff direct their attention to theistic arguments to prove the existence of God that, in William Alston's famous definition, provide 'support for religious beliefs by starting from premises that neither are nor presuppose any religious beliefs' (Alston 1991: 289). These, so Plantinga and Wolterstorff claim, simply have no place in Reformed philosophy of religion for one simple reason: knowledge of God is not the result of a series of logical arguments constituting a justified proof of the existence of God; rather it is, in Plantinga's terminology, 'properly basic' (Plantinga 1980: 53).

The Invention of the Reformed Objection

As already noted, Plantinga and Wolterstorff present this position as being the consensus view within the Reformed tradition, a claim that is roundly disputed by Michael Sudduth in his recent work, *The Reformed Objection to Natural Theology* (2009). Sudduth acknowledges that he borrows his title from Plantinga and yet his dedication of the book to Richard Swinburne—the defender par excellence of arguments to prove the existence of God of recent years—is telling. Sudduth examines the history of accounts of natural theology within the philosophy of religion and concludes that 'the notion that most Reformed thinkers have rejected natural theology runs deeper than the recent ruminations of Plantinga and Wolterstorff, but perhaps not too deeply. There is good reason to suppose that it is the product of twentieth-century thinking' (Sudduth 2009: 43). Central to this 'invention' of the 'Reformed objection' to natural theology, Sudduth claims, are two factors common to much twentieth-century analytical philosophy of religion:

> (a) an overly narrow view of the nature of theistic arguments and (b) an inaccurate view of the function of these arguments within the dogmatic systems of early and high orthodoxy. [Sudduth 2009: 48]

In terms of the first point, Sudduth draws attention to the distinction, common within Reformation accounts of the place of philosophy in theology, between 'natural' and 'philosophical' arguments. By 'natural arguments' is intended 'the simple design argument and the collection of historic-anthropological arguments (for example from universal consent, conscience, and prophecy), typically cast in a rhetorical form and having their historical ancestry in Cicero and Stoic natural theology' (Sudduth 2009: 48). These clearly feature heavily in all writers of the Reformation and are a central component of the Reformers' consistent claims to the naturalness of knowledge of God (through such natural revelation). By contrast 'philosophical arguments' refers to 'arguments from efficient and final causality, Aquinas' arguments from motion and degrees of perfection, and arguments from the contingency and beginning of the universe' (Sudduth 2009: 48).

Aristotelian and scholastic in their provenance and form, these arguments are presented as rational proofs and logical demonstrations and have little place in most Reformation theology (although they are admittedly more prominent in Reformed Orthodoxy), partly no doubt on account of the antipathy towards Catholic high scholasticism but also because of a widespread sense that these arguments add nothing to the natural knowledge of God already derived from the 'natural arguments'. As Muller confirms:

> If, then, the *Institutes* does not contain demonstrations of the existence of God, it certainly contains arguments to the point, several of which relate to the traditional proofs. Both these less logically stated forms of the logical proofs and Calvin's rhetorical and hortatory arguments find, moreover, precise parallels in the Reformed orthodox systems, in which rhetorical arguments stand alongside the logical proofs and in which the logical proofs often take on rhetorical rather than purely demonstrative forms. [Muller 2003: 3, 174]

In effect, then, rather than a rejection of rational arguments for the existence of God, what is found in the Reformers is a broader understanding of the character of such arguments; logical demonstration is not the only (and by no means the most compelling) form of rational argument. By contrast, the dominant tendency within twentieth-century analytical philosophy of religion has been to narrow the scope of rational arguments for the existence of God to those arguments that can accommodate the full rigour of logical analysis; a narrowing that happens to coincide with the traditional approach of Catholic natural theology, albeit with reference to an alternative logical paradigm. In this context, it is perhaps hardly surprising that Plantinga and Wolterstorff are so firm in their rejection of the place of rational argument in Protestant philosophical theology. In this sense Plantinga's dismissive characterization of Protestant philosophical theologians as 'Peeping Thomists' (borrowing the phrase from Ralph McInerny), on account of their inability (or better unwillingness) to embrace Aquinas as 'the natural starting point for Christian philosophical reflection', seems ironically appropriate, given the quasi-scholasticism of much work in the philosophy of religion by Protestant writers (Plantinga 1980: 49). There are, however, signs that the stranglehold of logical analysis on the philosophy of religion is loosening; in particular, recent work on emotions, the imagination, and the spiritual in the philosophy of religion, as well as developments in feminist epistemology and the increasing permeability between the analytical and the continental traditions, indicate that a richer notion of rational argument can have a place within contemporary philosophical natural theology (Wynn 2005; Hedley 2008; Cottingham 2005; Anderson 1998; Trakakis 2007).

With reference to Sudduth's second factor, the 'Reformed objection to natural theology' is clearly influenced by another common misunderstanding characteristic of most twentieth-century philosophy of religion, namely that in order for philosophical arguments to prove the existence of God to be philosophically efficacious they must be capable of 'standing alone' independently of any reference to religious or theological commitments. Whilst the roots of this misapprehension clearly lie in the Cartesian and Wolffian rationalism that inaugurates 'modern' philosophy as an autonomous and foundational discipline, it is all too frequently 'read back' into the history of philosophy—and particularly philosophy of religion—to present the distorting picture of a continuous tradition of natural theology as the attempt to prove the existence of God without any religious or theological presuppositions (a tendency that is clearly visible is almost all twentieth-century introductory textbooks or anthologies of philosophy of religion). Hence, it has been assumed that Reformed natural theology, if it is indeed present in the writings of the Reformers, must take the form of a 'rational, pre-dogmatic foundation for revealed theology' (Sudduth 2009: 49). Given that such an approach is clearly not found in the writers of the Reformation period, but only appears within post-Enlightenment theological systems under the influence of Descartes and Wolff, the obvious conclusion has been reached, namely that there is no natural theology within the 'original' Protestant theologies and hence that there should be no place for natural theology within contemporary Protestant theology. What such an argument overlooks, however, is that early Protestantism consistently understood natural theology as Christian 'dogmatic natural theology' undertaken within the context of the systematic expression of their faith. Sudduth identifies two features of such an approach to natural theology, typical of the Reformers:

> (a) the reversal of the noetic effects of sin through regeneration and sanctification and (b) the influence of Scripture in justifying and reliably guiding the project of developing natural theistic arguments. [Sudduth 2009: 145]

The possibility for natural theology that this dogmatic location entails is centrally important for the Reformers and places their natural theology between the undesirable extremes of a pre-dogmatic justificatory preface to the system of revealed theology on the one hand and a theology of nature based exclusively on scriptural revelation on the other. In Calvin's famous image, Scripture functions as a pair of spectacles, improving upon our dull and confused vision such that the illumination of faith 'does not prevent us from applying our senses to the consideration of heaven and earth, that we may thence seek confirmation in the true knowledge of God' (Calvin 1960: 1.6.1; 1979: 1, 64). Interestingly, as with the broadening of the understanding of rational argument within some recent Protestant philosophy of religion, so there has been a similar move by some recent proponents of natural theology from a Protestant perspective to embrace a 'dogmatic' understanding of natural theology as within yet not wholly subservient to a scripturally founded systematic theology (Torrance 1969; McGrath 2008).

The Reformed Epistemological Objection to Natural Theology

Whatever the background factors influencing Plantinga's formulation of the Reformed objection to natural theology, the two components of his critique are clear: (a) natural theology is unnecessary as we have an immediate knowledge of God and hence we have no need to strive to arrive at knowledge of God through rational argument and (b) natural theology is mistaken as knowledge of God is properly basic and not the result of rational argument. Both these elements are summed up by Plantinga in his claim that Reformed thinkers are 'best understood as rejecting classical foundationalism', defined as the normative epistemological doctrine according to which it is rational to hold certain beliefs to be true immediately (the foundations) and to hold other beliefs to be true mediately by virtue of being based on foundational beliefs (Plantinga 1980: 57). Of course, as Plantinga notes, the formal structure of foundationalism is as old as Western philosophy itself and various criteria for basicality (what makes some beliefs foundational and others not) have been proposed over the years. However, he claims that the consensus of classical foundationalism (defined as 'the disjunction of ancient and medieval with modern foundationalism') is that 'the foundations of a rational noetic structure can at most include propositions that are self-evident or evident to the senses or incorrigible' (Plantinga 1980: 57). By contrast, according to Plantinga, the Reformers were 'prepared to insist that a rational noetic structure can include belief in God as basic' and that 'one who takes belief in God as basic can also *know* that God exists' (Plantinga 1980: 57, 58). In other words, unlike natural theology, as Plantinga understands it, Reformed epistemology has no need to establish and prove the existence of God as according to Reformed epistemology belief in God is immediate and rationally warranted without demonstration (properly basic). But, we may ask, how does the Reformed thinker *know* that her belief in God is properly basic? What are the criteria for proper basicality? In reply, Plantinga sets out the classical foundationalist answer ('For any proposition A and person S, A is properly basic for S if and only if A is incorrigible for S or self-evident to S') and turns the question back onto the classical foundationalist: 'But how does one know a thing like that?' (Plantinga 1980: 59). The answer to this question brings us to the heart of Plantinga's Reformed epistemology and its rejection of natural theology:

> The fact is, I think that neither [the classical foundationalist's criterion] nor any other revealing necessary and sufficient condition for proper basicality follows from obviously self-evident premises by obviously acceptable arguments. And hence the proper way to arrive at such a criterion is, broadly speaking, *inductive*. We must assemble examples of beliefs and conditions such that the former are obviously properly basic in the latter, and examples of beliefs and conditions such that the former are obviously not properly basic in the latter ...
>
> But there is no reason to assume, in advance, that everyone will agree on the examples. The Christian will of course suppose that belief in God is entirely proper and rational; if he doesn't accept this belief on the basis of other propositions, he will conclude that it is basic for him and quite properly so. [Plantinga 1980: 60]

For the Reformed epistemologist, the only 'argument' that is necessary for the Christian to give to justify the proper basicality of her belief in God is the very reason for being a Christian in the first place: the illumination of faith through Scripture. In the course of his paper, Plantinga cites Hermann Bavinck approvingly (twice):

Scripture does not reason in the abstract. It does not make God the conclusion of a syllogism, leaving it to us whether we think the argument holds or not. But it speaks with authority. Both theologically and religiously it proceeds from God as the starting point. [Bavinck 1951: 76]

Notwithstanding the strength of Plantinga's conviction to the contrary, it is, however, by no means clear that the Reformed epistemologists' critique of classical foundationalism in fact entails Plantinga's Reformed objection to natural theology. As has already been noted, there seems to be more to the enterprise of natural theology, especially in the thought of the early Reformers, than simply the application of the 'rules' of classical foundationalism to the question of our knowledge of God. Whilst the Cartesian and Wolffian rationalist natural theologies of the later Protestant scholasticism may fall foul of Plantinga's critique (as might some of the more rationalist forms of contemporary philosophy of religion), this may ironically serve only to strengthen our appreciation of the subtleties of the dominant Protestant perspectives on natural theology, rather than attempting once again to airbrush the enterprise out of existence. Indeed, as Alister McGrath has repeatedly argued (from an explicitly Reformed perspective), in this way 'the Christian tradition repositions the whole enterprise of natural theology, shifting it from an autonomous intellectual exercise outside the community of faith to a discipline that arises and is undertaken within the context of the Christian revelation' (McGrath 2006: 87). Such a project of natural theology, construed, to use Anselm's famous phrase, as *faith seeking understanding*, is surely independent of the normative epistemological view of classical foundationalism; indeed on the contrary, the early (and hence we might say normative) Protestant endorsements of natural theology are at the same time critiques of the dominant (high scholastic) subjugation of scriptural dogmatic theology to natural philosophical arguments. Just as the Reformers should not be thought of as opposing natural theology to revealed theology, neither should their rejection of 'philosophical' arguments for the existence of God (dependent, as all 'philosophical' arguments are, on some form of foundationalism) be mistaken for an objection to all forms of natural theology. Even if, as we may concede to Plantinga, the Reformers can be characterized as opponents of classical foundationalism and hence proponents of a new, Reformed form of epistemology, there is no reason to conclude from this that they were, and that Reformed thinkers should now be, implacable opponents of natural theology. Surely, a Reformed epistemology demands instead a Reformed natural theology; and this is precisely what we find in Calvin's *duplex cognitio dei*. Far from restricting our knowledge of God to an immediate and properly basic belief in the saving authority of Scripture, Calvin not only distinguishes between two aspects of our knowledge of God (*cognitio dei creatoris* and *cognitio dei redemptoris*), but also further distinguishes between knowledge of God the creator 'as belonging to the order of nature and to the general teaching of Scripture' (Gabrill 2006: 83). As such, we might say that Calvin recognizes two forms of natural theology: 'a corrupt, partial, and extrabiblical knowledge of God as creator' and 'a biblical knowledge of God as Creator' (alongside these two, of course, is what we might call the 'un-natural' theology of the scandal of the Christian Gospel, namely the 'knowledge of God in Christ as

Redeemer') (Muller 2003: 290). Crucially, here, both forms of natural theology (the extrabiblical and the biblical) entail the possibility of true knowledge of God—both are based on true natural revelations of God—however, only the scriptural natural theology (and we must not shy away from such apparently paradoxical formulations) does in fact lead us from that true knowledge of God as creator to what Calvin calls 'true religion'. As Grabill summarizes:

> So, far from denying that the pagan philosophers (or even the common folk) have received an elementary and useful knowledge of God as Creator from natural revelation, Calvin showed that because of sin they failed to move from that knowledge to true religion, and thus, in the end, their gifts rendered them yet more inexcusable. Commenting on the phrase in Romans 1.20, 'That they may be without excuse', he writes: 'We must, therefore, make this distinction, that the manifestation of God by which he makes his glory known among his creatures is sufficiently clear as far as its own light is concerned. It is, however, inadequate on account of our blindness. But we are not so blind that we can plead ignorance without being convicted of perversity'.
>
> Accordingly, scriptural revelation was necessary to attain even a true knowledge of God the Creator. [Gabrill 2006: 83, citing Calvin 1979: 31]

And yet, as we have already seen, Calvin insists that the true knowledge of God as creator made available to us through Scripture should not be set against the false knowledge of God as creator, in the sense that both come from God—the corruption of the latter is the result of our degeneracy, not the result of a deficiency in the natural revelation itself. In a similar manner, as Willis affirms, our (culpable) knowledge of God as creator and our (saving) knowledge of God the redeemer (or, in my earlier formulation, 'natural' and 'un-natural' theologies) should not be set against each other:

> The two facets of our knowledge of God are not *creatoris et Christi* but *creatoris et redemptoris*, because for Calvin Christ is not only the redemptive Word of God but also the creative Word of God, just as the Spirit is not only regenerative but also creative. And, equally important, Calvin for the same reasons does not envisage a *cognitio redemptoris* that does not presuppose the *cognitio creatoris*. [Willis 1966: 121]

Clearly, this final point stands as a sharp corrective to the denigration of natural theology and the affirmation of a sharp dichotomy between nature and revelation within the Protestant tradition, characteristic of the Barthian theological consensus. It also stands as a corrective to Plantinga's argument that the Reformers' rejection of the epistemology of classical foundationalism entails their objection to natural theology. Far from it; the Reformers not only endorsed the possibility of natural theology, but also radically transformed it, in accordance with their radically new (Reformed) epistemology, according to which rational argument is repositioned: from a narrowly logical ratiocination independent of any religious concerns (as it was in late medieval scholastic metaphysics and would again become in modern rationalist analysis) to a broader affect-laden discourse situated explicitly within the context of revealed religion. This is certainly not natural theology as the attempt to argue to the existence of God without reliance on religious presuppositions, but it is still natural theology nonetheless.

References

Alston, William P (1991). *Perceiving God: The Epistemology of Religious Experience*. Ithaca, NY: Cornell University Press.

Althaus, Paul (1914). *Die Prinzipien der deutschen reformierten Dogmatik im Zeitalter der aristotelischen Scholastik*. Leipzig: Deichert.

Anderson, Pamela S. (1998). *A Feminist Philosophy of Religion: The Rationality and Myths of Religious Belief*. Oxford: Blackwell.

Barr, James (1993). *Biblical Faith and Natural Theology*. Oxford: Clarendon Press.

Barth, Karl (1938). *The Knowledge of God and the Service of God according to the Teaching of the Reformation, Recalling the Scottish Confession of 1560*. Translated by J. L. M. Haire and Ian Henderson. London: Hodder and Stoughton.

—— (1975). *Church Dogmatics* 1.1, *The Doctrine of the Word of God*. Edited by G. W. Bromiley and T. F. Torrance. Translated by G. W. Bromiley. Edinburgh: T & T Clark.

Barth, Peter (1935). *Das Problem der natürlichen Theologie bei Calvin*. Munich: Chr. Kaiser.

Bavinck, Hermann (1951). *The Doctrine of God*. Translated by William Hendricksen. Grand Rapids: William B. Eerdmans.

Brunner, Emil and Karl Barth (1946). *Natural Theology* ('Nature and Grace' by Brunner and the Reply 'No!' by Barth). Translated by Peter Fraenkel. London: Geoffrey Bles.

Calvin, John (1960). *Institutes of the Christian Religion*. 1559 edn. Edited by John T. McNeill. Translated by Ford Lewis Battles. Philadelphia: Westminster Press.

—— (1966). *Commentary on the Acts of the Apostles*. 2 vols. Edited by David W. Torrance and Thomas F. Torrance. Translated by John W. Fraser. Grand Rapids: William B. Eerdmans.

—— (1979). *Commentary on the Epistle to the Romans* in *Calvin's Commentaries*. 22 vols. Edited and translated by John Owens. Grand Rapids: Baker Book House.

Cottingham, John (2005). *The Spiritual Dimension: Religion, Philosophy and Human Value*. Cambridge: Cambridge University Press.

Ericksen, Robert P. (1987). *Theologians Under Hitler*. New Haven: Yale University Press.

Grabill, Stephen J. (2006). *Rediscovering the Natural Law in Reformed Theological Ethics*. Grand Rapids: William B. Eerdmans.

Grislis, Egil (1971). 'Calvin's Use of Cicero in the *Institutes* 1:1–5: A Case Study in Theological Method'. *Archiv für Reformationsgeschichte* 62: 5–37.

Hedley, Douglas (2008). *Living Forms of the Imagination*. London: Continuum.

McGrath, Alister E. (2006). *The Order of Things: Explorations in Scientific Theology*. Oxford: Blackwell.

—— (2008). *The Open Secret: A New Vision for Natural Theology*. Oxford: Blackwell.

Muller, Richard A. (2003). *Post-Reformation Reformed Dogmatics: The Rise and Development of Reformed Orthodoxy, ca. 1520 to ca. 1725*. 4 vols. Grand Rapids: Baker Academic.

Plantinga, Alvin (1980). 'The Reformed Objection to Natural Theology'. *Proceedings of the American Catholic Philosophical Association* 54: 49–63.

Sudduth, Michael (2009). *The Reformed Objection to Natural Theology*. Farnham: Ashgate.

Torrance, Thomas F. (1969). *Theological Science*. Edinburgh: T & T Clark.

Trakakis, Nick (2007). 'Meta-philosophy of Religion. The Analytical-Continental Divide in Philosophy of Religion' in *Ars Disputandi* 7, <http://www.ArsDisputandi.org>.

Viret, Pierre (1548). *A Very Familiar and Fruitful Exposition of the Twelve Articles of the Christian Faith Contained in the Common Creed, Called the Apostle's Creed*. London: John Day.

Willis, E. David (1966). *Calvin's Catholic Christology: The Function of the So-Called Extra Calvinisticum in Calvin's Theology*. Leiden: E. J. Brill.

Wolterstorff, Nicholas (1999). 'The Reformed Tradition' in *The Blackwell Companion to the Philosophy of Religion*. Edited by Philip L. Quinn and Charles Taliaferro. Oxford: Blackwell: pp. 165–70.

Wynn, Mark (2005). *Emotional Experience and Religious Understanding. Integrating Perception, Conception, and Feeling*. Oxford: Oxford University Press.

CHAPTER 13

NATURAL THEOLOGY AND THE EASTERN ORTHODOX TRADITION

CHRISTOPHER C. KNIGHT

THE theology of the Orthodox Church is based on a self-consciously conservative stress on the writings of the 'Fathers' of the early centuries of the Christian era—especially those of the Greek-speaking east—and on the later Byzantine expansion of this patristic thinking. More recent perspectives do exist, but are accepted only because they are seen as a valid extrapolation from this heritage, and thus as part of the authentic, living tradition of the Church. Since the schism between the Eastern and Western parts of the Christian world, conventionally dated to 1054, Orthodox theology has been influenced by theological developments in the West only for relatively brief periods, and these influences have had little lasting impact. Indeed, even prior to the schism, important aspects of Western theology—such as the Augustinian understanding of original sin—had had little impact in the East.

The term *natural theology* is frequently understood in terms of Western theological developments of the post-schism era, which included both an increasing focus on attempts at logical 'proofs' of God's existence and a growing sense that a firm separation should be made between natural and supernatural revelation. Partly because of this, the term *natural theology* is not often used by Orthodox theologians, since these Western developments are not reflected in their Church's theological thinking. Indeed, the Orthodox tendency to make 'no separation between natural and supernatural revelation' (Staniloae 1994: 1) sits uneasily with much of the scholastic and later Western development of natural theology, which to Orthodox theologians often seem to ignore the action of God in natural revelation, and mistakenly to see the human being as 'the only active agent' in its appropriation (Staniloae 1994: 21). However, as we shall see, the term *natural theology* may—if it is understood more broadly—legitimately be applied to aspects of the Orthodox theological tradition, since some Eastern theologians have certainly made use of the term *natural revelation,* and all of them—following patristic precedent—have accepted that philosophical or scientific insights may contribute to an understanding of the existence or attributes of the divine creator.

The different trajectories taken by natural theology in East and West are understandable in part in terms of the way in which any *natural theology* is linked to the broader notion of *natural religion*. This latter term has itself been understood in many different ways (Pailin 1994), but if we speak of it in the broadest possible way—defining it in terms of the intrinsic human capacity to know something of God independently of God's revelation of himself in historical acts—then it is clear that Orthodox theology has a strong sense of this capacity, but understands it in a different way to that which became common in the West. Crucial to this difference is that the Orthodox notion of original sin is not the Augustinian one that has so strongly influenced Western Christian perspectives. The image of God in humanity is seen, in Orthodox theology, as having been distorted, but not destroyed, through human rebellion against God, so that the created, 'natural' capacity to know God—though partially eclipsed in 'fallen' human nature—has not been obliterated.

In some Western traditions—and especially in late medieval scholasticism—the effects of the fallenness of human nature have been seen as applying less to discursive reason than to other human capacities. The Eastern notion of original sin has, however, meant that Orthodox theology—especially in its development since the fourth century—has tended, if anything, to move in the opposite direction to that taken in the scholastic approach, seeing the unaided human reason as potentially misleading, and focussing, in its natural theology, on other capacities. Thus, for example, Orthodox thinkers, following the example of St John Chrysostom, have sometimes invoked the concept of *natural law* in their thinking about ethics. However, while some have explored parallels between natural and scriptural law in a way that may be compared to aspects of the scholastic development of the Western natural law tradition, the Orthodox approach to natural law has tended, in general, to stress the divinely given nature of conscience rather than the sort of logical reasoning from observations of the world that was characteristic of this scholastic tradition.

One of the reasons for this Orthodox stress on something in human nature deeper than discursive reasoning is that its theology is characteristically an experiential one. Its approach is 'mystical'—not in the sense of being anti-rational, but in the more complex sense in which it is stressed that Christian dogma, often appearing at first as 'an unfathomable mystery', is something that must be approached 'in such a fashion that instead of assimilating the mystery to our mode of understanding, we should, on the contrary, look for a profound change, an inner transformation of the spirit, enabling us to experience it mystically' (Lossky 1957: 8).

THE CLASSICAL PHILOSOPHICAL INHERITANCE

Behind this approach lies the way in which—in the Greek patristic understanding and especially in the later Byzantine appropriation of it—knowledge of God is far more than an understanding based on the discursive reasoning faculty. Such knowledge is, in the

Orthodox understanding, based first and foremost on contemplation (*theoria*), the perception or vision of the highest human faculty, the 'intellect' (*nous*). This intellect is not the same as the discursive reasoning faculty (*dianoia*), which latter is understood as functioning properly in theological analysis only if rooted in the spiritual knowledge (*gnosis*) obtainable through the intellect. According to the Orthodox understanding, the intellect—when purified through ascetic practice—provides not knowledge *about* the creation but rather a *direct* apprehension or spiritual perception of the divine Logos (Word) incarnate in Christ, and of the inner essences or principles (*logoi*) of the components of the cosmos created by that Logos. It is only when the functioning of the reasoning faculty is in accord with this immediate experience that it can function adequately in theological analysis. It is for this reason that, although a general philosophical attempt at proving God's existence is sometimes to be found in patristic works that are held in high regard in the Orthodox world—St John of Damascus's *Exposition of the Orthodox Faith*, for example—a stress on 'proofs' of this kind, based primarily on the discursive reason, is not a major characteristic of Orthodox natural theology.

This does not mean that Orthodox theology does not have a strong sense that a proper reading of the creation points towards the reality and character of its divine creator. Indeed, if anything, the Eastern approach, compared with most Western ones, has a particularly strong emphasis on the way in which the created order is transparent to the glory of God. One aspect of this is exhibited in the way in which many of the Greek fathers see nature as exhibiting a unity with spiritual realities in such a way that these realities can be illuminated by what Gregory of Nyssa speaks of as moving 'anagogically from matters that concern ourselves to…transcendent nature' (*Oratio catechetica magna* 2). This approach is related to the allegorical technique of spiritual exegesis that Origen adopted from Philo, in which every passage in scripture is a mystery that can be unfolded to reveal truths of mystical or moral application. A comparable mode of interpretation may, according to many of the Greek fathers, be applied to the created order.

For example, one of the most common ways of reading nature in this manner is to see rebirth in nature as an 'anagogue' of the resurrection of the body. Another very common use of this kind of understanding focusses on a group of images concerning light and heat, which are held to indicate something of the nature of God. The possibility of this kind of interpretation is seen as far more than what one commentator has called 'mere illustration in which heterogeneous objects are placed side by side for comparison'. Rather, such interpretation is seen as being rooted in 'a principle, part of the structure of nature'. The creation is understood to be such that it is 'possible to argue straight from nature to the spiritual, and then to pass back to nature with new understanding of its significance in this respect' (Wallace-Hadrill 1968: 126).

Wallace-Hadrill goes on to note, however, that the Greek Fathers:

> for all their intense appreciation of nature, for all their interest in the structures of nature and their insistence upon nature as a means by which God reveals his nature, nevertheless hold that God and nature are not identical and that the mind must penetrate nature to find God. The beautiful, the useful, the intellectually fascinating, even the spiritually beneficial—all these characteristics of nature can, if allowed to

become an end in themselves, distract the mind from its proper activity, the knowledge of God. [Wallace-Hadrill 1968: 129]

This knowledge of God is not usually seen as something that can arise straightforwardly from abstract reasoning, but rather is the result of a more complex interplay of human faculties made possible by the purification of the intellect.

This is not to say that the patristic writers see a philosophical and scientific understanding of the world as having no role to play in human spiritual development prior to the full purification of the contemplative faculty. On the contrary, they frequently seem to see this understanding as having a role for all, but one that is focussed at least in part on evoking a movement of the intellect towards God through wonder and awe. For example, the most influential of the Cappadocian Fathers, Basil the Great (d. 379), uses the scientific understanding of his time to try to 'penetrate' the hearers of one of his homilies 'with so much admiration that...the least plant may bring to [them] the clear remembrance of the Creator' (*Hexameron* 5.2). In this respect, he is using the scientific understanding of his time in a way that is reminiscent of that found in some works of Western natural theology of the period of early modern science.

Behind the subtlety of the Eastern patristic attitude towards natural theology, lies a complex attitude towards the philosophy of the classical world, which involves neither uncritical acceptance nor rejection. This complexity may be seen especially in the works of the two other Cappadocian Fathers: Gregory of Nyssa (d. *c*.395) and Gregory of Nazianzus (d. 389), the latter of whom was typical of all three in seeing both 'sight and the law of nature' as giving rise to belief that 'the creative and sustaining cause of all exists' (*Orationes* 28: 6).

In certain respects, what this means is slightly different for each of the Cappadocians. Gregory of Nyssa, for example, can speak explicitly about three legitimate sources of understanding: the thought of 'those who philosophized outside the faith'; the 'inspired writings' of the Old and New Testaments; and what he calls 'the common apprehension' of humanity (*Contra Eunomium* 1: 186). Basil, on the other hand, is less explicit about—and perhaps more ambiguous towards—the role of Greek philosophy, preferring a tri-partite taxonomy involving conceptions that are 'common', those 'that have been gathered...from Holy Scripture', and those which 'we have received from the unwritten tradition of the fathers' (*De Spiritu sancto* 9: 22). As a modern commentator has noted, however, such differences of emphasis are not of major significance compared to what unites the Cappadocians: the implicit natural theology of the Greek philosophical tradition is, for all of them, an authentic source of insight (Pelikan 1993: 24–5).

Jaroslav Pelikan, has produced an insightful account of the Eastern Christian encounter with the classical philosophical tradition of natural theology, making a useful distinction between what he calls 'natural theology as apologetics' and 'natural theology as presupposition' (Pelikan 1993). The former of these categories takes seriously the need to expound what Gregory of Nyssa calls 'the rational basis of our religion' for those who are 'seriously searching for the rational basis of the mystery' (*Oratio Catechetica* 15: 4). The latter relates to the way in which—even when apologetic needs are no longer paramount—theology is still inevitably influenced by what Alfred North Whitehead has called the 'fundamental assumptions' of any particular epoch and culture: those notions which 'adherents of all the various systems within the epoch unconsciously presuppose... [since] no other way of putting things has ever occurred to them' (Whitehead 1948: 49–50). For Pelikan, who quotes this passage as supporting his understanding of the Cappadocians' work, the preconceptions of the classical philosophical tradition are an integral part of the way in which at least some of the assumptions transmitted by the Cappadocians 'as part of their doctrinal patrimony to the inheritors of Nicene orthodoxy... were rooted in natural theology' (Pelikan 1993: 185).

Worship and Eschatology

Pelikan's study ends with two chapters of great importance for understanding the Orthodox use of natural theology, since they not only pick up themes that have been central to that usage up to modern times, but they also illustrate the way in which the Cappadocians' natural theology is not only developed in tandem with theology rooted primarily in revelation in history, but is also, in important respects, moulded by that theology. These chapters are on 'The Worship offered by Rational Creatures' (Pelikan 1993: 296 ff.) and on 'The Life of the Aeon to Come' (Pelikan 1993: 311 ff.).

In the first of these chapters, Pelikan speaks of the way in which it is characteristic of the Cappadocians to see the characteristic natural theology of classical philosophy as being wrong in its perception that the 'worship which we, as rational creatures, should offer' stands in opposition to 'the external sacrifice, the antitype of the great mysteries'. Rather, as Pelikan goes on, Gregory of Nazianzus, in particular, sees this 'rational worship as expressed most fully of all, at any rate here below, in the liturgical mysteries' (Pelikan 1993: 297). These mysteries are seen, at one level, as being beyond analysis in terms of natural theology, and yet at the same time as being capable of illumination through arguments rooted in natural theology. All three Cappadocians, in their exposition of the content of these mysteries, 'seem to have been willing to invoke the vocabulary of Greek science and philosophy' so that in speaking of the effects of baptism, for example, a definition of the duality of human nature is—especially for Gregory of Nazianzus—a presupposition that is 'not only a doctrine of divine revelation but a demonstrable fact available also to human reason' (Pelikan 1993: 299–300).

The Cappadocians' linking of natural theology to a sacramental understanding was to have a strong effect on later Orthodox theology, as also was their linking of it to the second theme to which Pelikan draws our attention: the Christian eschatological vision. In part, this linkage is manifested in their detailed understanding of that vision, so that, for example, they all tend to see the immortality of the soul as common to both natural and revealed theology. Indeed, even though they see the resurrection of the body as principally being a matter of historical revelation, Gregory of Nyssa—in *De hominis opificio* 25–6—claims that it is rendered at least plausible by arguments rooted in natural theology.

More generally, however, it is the particularity of the Christian eschatological understanding that actually moulds the Cappadocians' general understanding of the character and limitations of natural theology. They share Basil's perception that 'the whole of human life is fed not so much on the past as on the future' (*Epistolae* 42:1), and their:

> interpretation of the life of the *aeon* to come was…an epitome of the entire relation between natural and revealed theology…It was by identifying the eschatological goal toward which [the] 'advance to perfection' was moving that the Cappadocians could articulate a universalism that permitted them to comprehend not only Christianity but Classical culture within a single system. [Pelikan 1993: 312]

Thus, for example, Gregory of Nazianzus sees the unity of mankind as manifested by the link between the heavenly Jerusalem of New Testament imagery and the philosophical understanding that is in principle available to all. 'Everyone that is of high mind', he says, 'has one country, the heavenly Jerusalem, in which we store up our citizenship' (*Orationes* 33:12).

Creation and the Limits of Natural Theology

For the Cappadocians there is, however, an essential hiddenness to God's ultimate intentions, and this places an important limit on the scope of any natural theology. For example, the concept of the eschatological divinization (*theosis*) of men and women, which they affirm, is not one that they see as having any relationship with the kind of divinization sometimes spoken of in pagan religion. Indeed, any attempt to link the two is anathema to them, so that, as Pelikan (1993: 318) notes, in this sense their understanding is 'not to be defined as natural theology at all'. Gregory of Nyssa, in particular, speaks about the 'inexpressible knowledge of the divine' (*De vita Mosis* 2) and, for all the Cappadocians, the divine nature, even when 'holding out to humanity the prospect of a future and final participation in itself, retained a transcendence of which it was finally permissible to speak only in *apophatic* language' (Pelikan 1993: 314). Ultimately—as later Orthodox theology was sometimes to insist even more firmly—natural theology can only be valid when integrated into a mystical knowledge of God and of his creation—a knowledge that transcends any cataphatic affirmation.

This characteristic Orthodox focus on the limitations of human language is clearly tied to the perceived need, which we have already noted, for direct, contemplative apprehension of the inner essences or principles—*logoi*—of created things. This focus on inner essences is related to the way in which the Orthodox understanding of the cosmos stresses that the notions of creation and redemption are strongly and intimately linked in terms of the fourth gospel's assertion that the divine Logos both created the world and was incarnate in the person of Jesus of Nazareth. Here, all the nuances of the Greek term *logos* come into play. As a modern commentator has expressed it, to say that the universe is created by the Logos entails, for the Greek speaker, 'that the universe has a meaning, both as a whole and in each of its parts. That "meaning" is *logos*; everything that exists has its own *logos*, and that *logos* is derived from God the *Logos*. To have meaning, *logos*, is to participate in the *Logos* of God.' Behind this, he continues, lurks the Platonic idea that everything that exists does so 'by participating in its form, or idea, which is characterized by its definition; the Greek for definition (in this sense) is, again, *logos*'. As he goes on to note, however, by the time these notions reached their most complex and complete Christian expression—in the work of Maximos the Confessor (d. 662)—the Platonic character of this kind of language had already for centuries been adapted to the requirements of the Christian revelation. Because the world is seen as having been created by God through his Logos, it could no longer be 'regarded as a pale reflection of the eternal reality, as in Plato's world' (Louth 2004: 188).

The early background to this particular way of focussing on the world as God's creation is a complex one, with Irenaeus' battle against Gnosticism and Athanasius' attempts to solve some of the problems of Origenism as significant factors. It is, however, in the work of the Cappadocian Fathers that we see the outline of later Orthodox thinking about the created order most clearly taking shape. As another commentator has remarked, the Cappadocians use the Platonist language of their day in a way that might make 'the modern reader, to whom this language is alien... mistake their Platonic starting point for their conclusion' (Theokritoff 2008: 65). They do, she admits, 'speak in terms of a divide between the intelligible and the sensible, and even of an "affinity" between intelligible creatures and the Godhead' (Theokritoff 2008: 65). However, she insists, 'the main thrust of their thinking is the way in which these inequalities are evened out in the Christian doctrine of creation... It is for the sake of the whole creation that man the microcosm receives the divine inbreathing, so that nothing in creation should be deprived of a share in communion with God' (Theokritoff 2008: 65). This sense of solidarity in createdness has, she goes on to note, 'remained a leitmotif in Eastern Christian theology' (Theokritoff 2008: 65).

Here, it is worthy of notice that this emphasis on the distinction between creator and creature has tended, in Orthodox theology, to be seen as far more important than any other distinction. (It is noteworthy, for example, that John of Damascus's attempt to prove God's existence, which we have noted, was based on this distinction.) In particular, a distinction between what is 'natural' and what is 'supernatural' is far less often stressed in Eastern theology than it is, for example, in Western Christian writings of the late medieval period. This tendency is in part related to the tendency, already noted, to see natural and supernatural revelation as working in tandem and therefore being effectively inseparable. It is also in part related to the fact that, even when the concept of being 'above nature' is used in Orthodox writings, it is understood in terms of a concept of nature that is subtly but vitally different to that which is common in Western Christian thought, so that the term has a rather different technical meaning to that which in the West is associated with the term 'supernatural'. In particular, as Vladimir Lossky has noted, the Eastern tradition 'knows nothing of "pure nature" to which grace is added as a supernatural gift. For it, there is no natural or "normal" state, since grace is implied in the act of creation itself' (Lossky 1957: 101).

This sense of the grace inherent in the created order is not, it should be noted, oblivious to the consequences of the Fall. Indeed, some Eastern patristic writers, as we shall note presently, see the ramifications of the Fall as extending beyond humanity to the entire cosmos. (As Knight (2007: 86–95) has noted, there are interesting implications in this approach for an understanding of divine action and of the problem of natural evil.) Yet, just as the notion of the human Fall does not, for Orthodox theology, imply the obliteration of the image of God in humanity, so also, for this theology, the ramifications of the Fall do not—even for the writers who speak of nature itself as fallen—obliterate the way in which the cosmos is a revelation of the divine.

Panentheism and the Struture of Theophany

This sense of the revelation to be found in the cosmos is particularly stressed in the late fifth- or early sixth-century writings of pseudo-Dionysius the Areopagite, which had major impacts in both parts of the medieval Christian world. These impacts were different, however. While these writings have usually been seen as a vehicle for Neoplatonic influences in the West, they have been seen as representing, in the East, a moderating factor on—or even as a triumph over—such influences. While taking up the Neoplatonist idea of the scale of being, these writings turn it into what has been called 'a structure of *theophany*, revelation of God. Its purpose is to allow each creature to reflect the divine glory in its own unique way.' In this approach, what is envisaged is:

> a structure in which vastly incommensurate elements—angelic, human, animate and inanimate—are all held together and function as a coherent whole, focused on their Creator. And it is a cosmos shot through with the radiance of divinity. God is at once totally other, totally beyond everything that is, and in everything by the ecstatic power inseparable from himself. [Theokritoff 2008: 65–6]

This sense of God being in everything takes up an antinomy that is found at least as early as the work of Athanasius, for whom God has no affinity with the world in his *essence*, but by his *powers* pervades the whole cosmos. This latter concept was developed by later writers in such a way that Orthodox theology has come to stress, not only that God is in everything, but also that everything is in God. This understanding—sometimes known as *panentheism*—is very different from the presumption of the mainstream philosophical theism of the West, in which—as Philip Clayton (2004: 75–84) has noted—an earlier 'substance' metaphysics discouraged it, while later attempts to move away from this metaphysics tended to lead (as in the work of Spinoza) to the kind of pantheism in which the world and God were simply identified with one another.

Orthodox theology has avoided this Western dilemma, not only by eschewing a substance metaphysics, but also in two related and more positive ways. One has been to stress the connection between the divine Logos and the *logoi* of created things, in the way that we have already noted. This is especially the case in the work of Maximos the Confessor (d. 662), according to whom—in the words of a modern commentator— 'Christ, the Creator Logos has implanted in every created thing a characteristic logos, a "thought" or "word" which is God's intention for that thing, its inner essence, that which makes it distinctively itself and at the same time draws it towards the divine realm' (Ware 2004: 160). These *logoi*, he goes on, are described by Maximos:

> in two different ways, sometimes as created and sometimes as uncreated, depending upon the perspective in which they are viewed. They are created inasmuch as they inhere in the created world. But when regarded as God's presence in each thing—as divine 'predetermination' or 'preconception' concerning that thing—they are not created but uncreated. [Ware 2004: 160]

Alongside this model, there exists another, to be found in embryonic form in the writings of Clement of Alexandria and of Basil, and developed most systematically in the much later work of Gregory Palamas (d. 1359). In this approach, what is central is the distinction between God's transcendent essence (*ousia*) and his immanent energies or operations (*energeiai*). This second approach, the same commentator continues, is:

> not contrary to the first but complementary.... In his essence God is infinitely transcendent, utterly beyond all created being, beyond all participation from the human side. But in his energies—which are nothing less than God himself in action—God is inexhaustibly immanent, maintaining all things in being, animating them, making each of them a sacrament of his dynamic presence. [Ware 2004: 160]

This panentheistic view of the relationship between the creation and its divine creator never falls into pantheism because the characteristic Orthodox stress on God's immanence is balanced by an equally strong stress on the utter transcendence of the divine essence, which is seen as unknowable and beyond all creaturely participation.

Over and above the implications of these two complementary models, a third factor discourages any descent from panentheism into pantheism. This is the strong sense of the ramifications of the Fall to be found in Orthodox writings, typically expressed in the patristic era in terms of the biblical notion of the 'garments of skin' given by God to fallen humans (Genesis 3.21). Especially in the work of Gregory of Nyssa, these are seen as referring to 'the entire postlapsarian psychosomatic clothing of the human person' (Nellas 1997: 33). For some writers—as we have already noted in passing—this fallenness of the human being extends to the whole cosmos. The 'natural' world that we experience is, for these writers, both a revelation of God and yet also profoundly 'unnatural', since it reflects the fallenness of humanity rather than the fullness of God's original and eschatological intentions for his creation. Indeed, some Orthodox writers use the term 'natural' only to signify this 'original' or 'eschatological' state, and explicitly criticize the kind of Western natural theology or natural law thinking which uncritically attempts to 'read' God's intentions from the 'unnatural', empirical world of everyday experience (e.g. Sherrard 1976: 25–7).

Even for those writers who stress the 'unnaturalness' of the empirical world, however, the notion that each created thing is a reflection of the divine glory—a sacramental reality at least in potential—is still present. Among modern Orthodox writers, this has been especially the case for Alexander Schmemann and Philip Sherrard, the latter of whom has taken up the notion of the world as sacrament, and related it to the specific sacraments of the church in a way that expands on the general notion of a sacrament as 'a revelation of the genuine nature of creation' (Schmemann 1987: 33–4). Because he stresses the created order's 'estrangement and alienation from its intrinsic nature', Sherrard is able to see in the sacrament something in which 'this divided, estranged and alienated state is transcended' so that the created order's 'essential and intrinsic nature is revealed' (Sherrard 1964: 35). Moreover, he notes, this revelation is by no means limited to those sacraments used within the Church. Everything, he says, 'is capable of serving as the object of the sacrament', and their number cannot be fixed. If we must speak of 'particular' or 'greater' mysteries, this simply means, he says, that we recognize 'a sacred hierarchy of mysteries established in view of the particular conditions of individual existence in the world' (Sherrard 1964: 133–4).

A major achievement of Orthodox theologians of the last century or so has been, in ways like this, to express the traditional cosmic vision of Orthodox theology in a way that has avoided some of the problems of the attempts of the previous century to express this vision (the sophiology of Russian religious philosophy, in particular). As Elizabeth Theokritoff (2003: 221–38) has noted, writers like Vladimir Lossky and George Florovsky have elucidated the Eastern patristic view of creation as a resource for current thinking, while others—Paul Evdokimov, Dumitru Staniloae, John Meyendorff, John Zizioulas, Alexander Schmemann, and Olivier Clement, to name but a few—have more recently expanded this elucidation in terms of an understanding of humanity's place in creation. A strong characteristic of much of this recent work has been the sacramental emphasis we have noted, particularly as linked to the Eucharist. An interesting emphasis here—an expansion of patristic notions rather than simply a restatement of them—has been that human beings are to be understood as the priests of creation, called constantly to give thanks to God for all created things, constantly referring the creation back to its creator and thereby unveiling its eschatological reality.

SCIENCE AND THEOLOGY IN ORTHODOXY

When we look at recent work on the theology of creation, however, what is very noticeable is that—despite general encouragement by influential theologians like Dumitru Staniloae—very few Orthodox theologians have attempted to expand their rich heritage in terms of the insights of modern science, Many of them, of course, have no competence to do this, but this is true also of most members of the Western theological community, among whom a rich 'dialogue between science and theology' has existed for at least half a century. Why, we must ask, has Orthodox theology not, in this period, pursued this dialogue in a similar way? Is it explicable, perhaps, in terms of the way in which Orthodox theology and spirituality have often put more emphasis on knowing the creation through direct contemplative experience than on knowing about it through human reason? Or in terms, perhaps, of the nature of modern Orthodox theology, in which an essential orientation towards 'Tradition' is interpreted, in some circles, as implying a rather narrow conservatism? Or in terms of differences in the apologetic needs associated with the widespread (but questionable) notion that science and theology are in conflict?

Certainly, if the last of these factors is a significant one, this is at least partially understandable in sociological terms. Many Orthodox Christians lived until very recently in situations in which they were inevitably influenced by the need to react against the Marxist-Leninist version of atheism, with its supposed support from the sciences. This has meant that, even after the downfall of that ideology in their countries, many of them have tended, almost instinctively, to see science and atheism as having an intrinsic connection. In addition, at least some influential Orthodox in the West have developed a similar attitude for reasons that are susceptible to comparable sociological analysis. Especially if reacting against the recent 'liberalization' of many of the mainstream Western forms of Christianity, they too may tend to associate science with the ideologies of those they perceive to be the enemies or diluters of faith. It is perhaps difficult to assess how significant these sociological factors are, but it is notable that where neither of them has been a major factor in local Orthodox ecclesial life—in Greece, for example—there often seems to have been a greater openness to scientific insights than there is elsewhere.

It is important to recognize, however, that if suspicion of science among some Orthodox Christians does exist, it should not be equated in its origins or effects with the superficially similar attitude of some of the 'fundamentalist' protestant Christians of the West. While the two groups may sometimes be comparable in sociological terms, their theological views are usually very different. For example, even though a generally conservative approach to Scripture is usual in Orthodox circles, this approach is strongly influenced by the way in which theologians of the patristic period often read the Old Testament Scriptures using an allegorical rather than a literal mode of interpretation, and with due acknowledgement of the science and philosophy of their time. This means, for example, that the creation accounts in Genesis are not seen by most educated Orthodox Christians as expressing literal, 'scientific' truths about the way in which the cosmos came into being. (Indeed, patristic writers such as Augustine and Gregory of Nyssa quite explicitly set aside the literal meaning of these texts.) Given this historical background, it is not science and philosophy as such that are looked at with suspicion by some Orthodox Christians, but only what are perceived by them (rightly or wrongly) to be perverted forms of these disciplines. Neo-Darwinian insights in biology, for example, are still sometimes held to be incompatible with Orthodox faith, though advocates of these insights do seem to be becoming more numerous in the Orthodox community—a trend that has perhaps been encouraged by the observations of some Orthodox theologians that their tradition does not preclude those insights.

One such theologian, for example, has commented that although Maximos the Confessor assumes, with all his contemporaries, that natures are fixed, his thought is still dynamic enough to be implicitly open 'to the idea of evolution...as a way of expressing God's providence' and that his cosmic vision can 'be re-thought in terms of modern science' (Louth 2004: 189). Another, in a similarly helpful way, has commented that, for patristic writers, 'the essence of man is not found in the matter from which he was created but in the archetype on the basis of which he was formed and towards which he tends' (Nellas 1997: 33). It is precisely for this reason, he goes on, that for the Orthodox understanding of creation, 'the theory of evolution does not create a problem... because the archetype is that which organizes, seals and gives shape to matter, and which simultaneously attracts it towards itself' (Nellas 1997: 33).

Despite such assurances, however, there is, as yet, no consensus about how to formulate a contemporary Orthodox response to the sciences in general and to neo-Darwinism in particular. A creative intellectual ferment in this area—characteristic of Western Christianity for several generations—has been effectively absent from Orthodox circles until relatively recently, and this, coupled with the sociological factors already mentioned, means that a wide spectrum of views still exists.

At one end of the spectrum is the essentially anti-scientific attitude expressed by writers such as Seraphim Rose (2000) and Philip Sherrard (1992). The former of these effectively defends a kind of fundamentalism in relation to the patristic literature. The latter—whose concerns about ecology and about the need for the revival of a 'sacred cosmology' are widely shared by his fellow-Orthodox—fails to perceive any validity in the distinctions commonly made between technology and pure science and between science and scientism. For both of them, the natural theology implicit in the Western dialogue between science and theology represents an unacceptable dilution of Christian theology.

At the other end of the spectrum lie writers such as Basarab Nicolescu and Christopher Knight. These, while insisting that Orthodox perspectives have an important role to play in the science–theology dialogue of the future, do not reject the Western dialogue of the last half-century, with its positive attitude to science and its view that science provides genuine insights into major theological themes. Nicolescu—who in his Romanian homeland has led the first major effort to develop a structured and widespread science–theology dialogue in a traditionally Orthodox country—has focussed on essentially philosophical issues, taking bold and controversial strides to formulate a 'transdisciplinary' approach that affects not only the science–religion dialogue but every area of human thought (Nicolescu 1992). Knight, in a rather different way, has focussed on theological issues, arguing that one of the main resources that Orthodoxy can bring to the current dialogue is what he calls the 'teleological-christological' understanding of created things enunciated by Maximos the Confessor. In an updated form that acknowledges current scientific insights, he argues, this traditional Orthodox understanding can provide a new framework—an 'incarnational naturalism'—within which the legitimate questions enunciated by participants in the Western dialogue can be answered more satisfactorily than they have been when examined in a purely Western context (Knight 2007).

Between these extremes of the Orthodox spectrum lie writers who, while not rejecting science, effectively deny the validity of the kind of dialogue between it and theology that has taken place among Western Christians over the last few generations. Of the exponents of this kind of position, Alexei Nesteruk (2008) perhaps presents the most sophisticated argument. While affirming science as a legitimate expression of the human spirit, he tends to by-pass questions about truth in science and theology, and about the consonance or dissonance between them, by interpreting both in terms of the philosophical approach known as phenomenology. Major themes in Orthodox theological thought can, he claims, be incorporated in this approach.

Given this situation, the future of the Orthodox community's development of its distinctive version of natural theology—and of its response to the sciences in particular—is hard to predict. In a tradition with such a rich and nuanced history of natural theology, however, it is surely likely that there will emerge from it an approach that is consonant with earlier perspectives but also sensitive to the new questions and insights that now abound.

References

Clayton, Philip (2004). 'Panentheism in Scientific and Metaphysical Perspective' in *In Whom We Live and Move and Have Our Being: Panentheistic Perspectives on God's Presence in a Scientific World*. Edited by Philip Clayton and Arthur Peacocke. Grand Rapids: Eerdmans: pp. 73–91.

Knight, Christopher C. (2007), *The God of Nature: Incarnation and Contemporary Science*. Minneapolis: Fortress Press.

Lossky, Vladimir (1957). *The Mystical Theology of the Eastern Church*. Cambridge: James Clarke.

Louth, Andrew (2004). 'The Cosmic Vision of St. Maximos the Confessor' in *In Whom We Live and Move and Have Our Being: Panentheistic Reflections on God's Presence in a Scientific Word*. Edited by Philip Clayton and Arthur Peacocke. Grand Rapids: Eerdmans: pp. 184–96.

Nellas, Panayiotis (1997). *Deification in Christ: Perspectives on the Nature of the Human Person*. Crestwood: St.Vladimir's Seminary Press.

Nesteruk, Alexei (2008). *The Universe as Communion: Towards a Neo-Patristic Synthesis of Theology and Science*. London: T and T Clarke.

Nicolescu, Basarab (1992). *Manifesto of Transdisciplinarity*. New York: State University of New York.

Pailin, David (1994). 'The Confused and Confusing Story of Natural Religion'. *Religion* 24/3: 199–212.

Pelikan, Jaroslav (1993). *Christianity and Classical Culture: The Metamorphosis of Natural Theology in the Christian Encounter with Hellenism*. New Haven and London: Yale University Press.

Rose, Seraphim (2000). *Genesis, Creation and Early Man*. Platina: St. Herman of Alaska Brotherhood.

Schmemann, Alexander (1987). *The Eucharist: Sacrament of the Kingdom*. Crestwood: St. Vladimir's Seminary Press.

Sherrard, Philip (1964). 'The Sacrament' in *The Orthodox Ethos: Essays in Honour of the Centenary of the Greek Orthodox Diocese of North and South America*. Vol. I. Edited by A.J. Philippou. Oxford: Holywell Press.

—— (1976). *Christianity and Eros: Essays on the Theme of Sexual Love*. London: SPCK.

—— (1992). *Human Image: World Image: The Death and Resurrection of Sacred Cosmology*. Ipswich: Golgonooza.

Staniloae, Dumitru (1994). *The Experience of God: Orthodox Dogmatic Theology*. Vol. I: *Revelation and Knowledge of the Triune God*. Brookline: Holy Cross Orthodox Press.

Theokritoff, Elizabeth (2003). 'Embodied Word and New Creation: Some Modern Orthodox Insights Concerning the Material World' in *Abba: The Tradition of Orthodoxy in the*

West—*Festschrift for Bihop Kallistos (Ware) of Diokleia*. Edited by John Behr, Andrew Louth and Dimitri Conomos. Crestwood: St.Vladimir's Seminary Press.

Theokritoff, Elizabeth (2008). 'Creator and Creation' in *The Cambridge Companion to Orthodox Christian Theology*. Edited by Mary B. Cunningham and Elizabeth Theokritoff. Cambridge: Cambridge University Press.

Wallace-Hadrill, D. S. (1968). *The Greek Patristic View of Nature*. Manchester: Manchester University Press.

Ware, Kallistos (2004). 'God Immanent Yet Transcendent: The Divine Energies according to Saint Gregory Palamas' in *In Whom We Live and Move and Have Our Being: Panentheistic Reflections on God's Presence in a Scientific World*. Edited by Philip Clayton and Arthur Peacocke. Grand Rapids: Eerdmans: pp.157–68.

Whitehead, A. N. (1948). *Science and the Modern World*. New York: Mentor Books.

CHAPTER 14

···

THEOLOGICAL CRITIQUES OF NATURAL THEOLOGY

···

ANDREW MOORE

INTRODUCTION

THERE is a variety of Christian understandings of natural theology and a corresponding range of theological critiques of it. Many of these are represented in what is often regarded as the *locus classicus* of modern theological disputes about natural theology, the 1934 debate between Karl Barth (1886–1968) and Emil Brunner (1889–1966) published as *Natural Theology: Comprising 'Nature and Grace' by Professor Dr Emil Brunner and the reply 'No!' by Dr Karl Barth* (Barth 1946; Brunner 1946b; henceforward, references to this work by these authors will be by date only.). This chapter locates that debate in the broader context of the mature theological perspectives Barth and Brunner were developing at this time and seeks to highlight aspects of it whose importance have often been overlooked.

Christian arguments about natural theology sometimes resemble re-enactments of historic battles, of interest only to the eccentric minority who like that kind of thing: familiar old positions are painstakingly laid out and well-rehearsed campaigns from the past are repeated, but nothing new or relevant is established (White 2011 is a notable and welcome exception). That was decidedly not the case in the Barth–Brunner debate; each protagonist felt that he was contending for the heart of the Gospel and the *esse* of the Church. So the principal importance of their debate lies less in the range of opinions on natural theology that it represents than in the way that these were generated by the context in which it took place. As we shall see, the debate was precipitated by a major crisis in twentieth-century Church life which provided the dramatic occasion for decisive dogmatic, methodological, and ecclesiological issues to come into sharp focus. The context of the debate was the background against which the content of the gospel was to be discerned afresh, and the topics under dispute were such that it continues to illuminate why natural theology has been a focus of Christian controversy.

A further reason for taking the Barth–Brunner debate as the focus of this chapter is that there are striking parallels between the divergent paths Barth and Brunner took in relation to the questions of judgement and action posed by the puzzles to Christian discernment of their context and the options faced by Christians today. These puzzles and options concern the right understanding of the relationships between social and political context, Christian doctrine, theological method, and Christian witness. To spell out the parallels is beyond the scope of this chapter and, in any case, the demands of Christian obedience are to be met in the present—though this is not to say that instructive generalizations cannot be made from the Barth–Brunner debate and the environment in which it took place. They can; the reasons for adopting, and the reasons for rejecting, natural theology are little different now from then.

The historic re-enactment view supposes, rather crudely, that the differences between those in favour of, and those opposed to, Christians doing natural theology can be summarized in a series of dilemmas: 'nature or grace', 'analogy of being or analogy of faith', 'general or special revelation', 'reason or faith', 'pride and self-assertion or repentance and conversion', 'the idolatrous God of the philosophers or the living God of the Bible', and even 'Roman Catholicism or Protestantism'. (This is to present the contested relations in a Protestant way; for Catholics the issues have more to do with the correct harmonization of nature *and* grace, faith *and* reason, and so on. The dilemmas may be more apparent than real.) Although these topics certainly were in play in the Barth–Brunner debate, one of the most striking things about their disagreement is that, though Barth is rightly regarded as opposing natural theology, Brunner repeatedly draws attention to his agreement with Barth on these dilemmas and to his desire to uphold the latter disjunct in each case (with the exception of the second and, in a qualified sense, the third where Barth emerges as the more ecumenically hospitable of the two). Indeed, as we shall see, Brunner strongly opposes some forms of natural theology, one of which is that nowadays most frequently represented in the literature as the canonical form of natural theology. Clearly, for Barth and Brunner, the question of the propriety of natural theology could not be reduced to a series of straightforward, independently stateable, independently resolvable dilemmas. Despite the way in which the still all-too-common caricatures (and some more sympathetic presentations) of the debate portray the matter, both Barth and Brunner thought that there was more at stake than an understanding of the opposing terms taken apart from wider dogmatic, methodological, and ecclesiological considerations might be supposed to imply. At the heart of the disagreement lay the questions of what theology and the Christian gospel are.

THE BARTH–BRUNNER DEBATE IN CONTEXT

Theological debates are not, and should not be, conducted as though theology can be separated from the Church and its witness. Both Barth and Brunner were acutely aware of this. Their debate took place in Germany in 1934 (Barth composed his reply to

Brunner in September/October) during the rise of Nazism. (For background on the relationship between Barth and Brunner up to this time, see Hart 2004: 19–43.) Hitler's government had come to power in January 1933 with considerable support amongst Protestant Christians. It was hard to escape the question of the relationship between gospel and culture, and between Church and State. Where was God's hand to be found in recent events?

Many Christians saw it in the rise of Hitler and his promise of clear moral leadership. Some regarded him as a German Moses. In June 1933 the German Christian movement had elected as its first bishop a man whom Hitler personally favoured. In the same year, Hitler himself had warned a Protestant Church leader that both Protestants and Catholics 'stood in danger of losing contact with the nation and spoke a language which the nation did not understand; the German Christians wanted to re-establish contact with the nation' (quoted by Wright 1977: 407). In March 1934 the German Christians claimed that 'Christ, as God's helper and saviour, has, through Hitler, become mighty among us ... Hitler (National Socialism) is now the way of the Spirit and Will of God for the Church of Christ amongst the German nation' (quoted by Jüngel 1992: 22). They had adopted the view that belief in Christ was 'racially innate' and, echoing a Lutheran phrase which was to be a focus of Barth's and Brunner's disagreement, declared race, people, and nation to be 'orders of life given and entrusted by God, the care for the preservation of which is for us God's law' (quoted by Wright 1977: 408). Though Hitler's tyranny was only just beginning, both Barth and Brunner recognized it and its threat to the Church.

So the immediate cause of the argument between Barth and Brunner was not natural theology as such; it was how Christians were to discern their vocation in this specific context, to engage it theologically, and to bear faithful witness to the gospel. The atmosphere of moral confusion and the urgency of these far from academic questions helps explain the strong opinions of Barth and Brunner and the force with which they conveyed them.

BRUNNER'S OBJECTIONS TO, AND HIS USE OF, NATURAL THEOLOGY

Brunner opens his contribution to the debate by seeking to establish common ground with his old friend and collaborator. Like Barth, he wished to affirm the traditional principles of Reformed theology: *sola gratia*, salvation uniquely offered through the cross of Christ and justification being by faith alone; and *sola Scriptura*, 'the doctrine that in all questions of the church's proclamation Holy Scripture alone is the ultimate standard' (1946b: 18). He agreed with Barth about the 'orders of creation': Barth had been right to warn against Gogarten's understanding of the doctrine, for this had opened up 'a whole political and cultural programme of a distinctly authoritarian stamp' (1946b: 51; cf. Barth 1938: 21). The German Christians mistakenly (and calamitously) thought they could read how God means things to be from how things are experienced to be—an error they shared with the anti-Christian Hitler (Bucher 2011: 49–57). Against them, Brunner held that 'a false theology derived from nature is also at the present time threatening the church to the point of death' (1946b: 59). Brunner like Barth saw in the government's encroachments upon it a serious threat to the Church's freedom.

And on the issue that now divided them? Brunner declares that '[t]here really can be no difference of opinion between us that a false natural theology did great damage to the Protestantism of the last century—or should we say of the last three centuries?' (1946b: 59). He seems to have had in mind both natural religion and its undergirding in proofs for the existence of God, both of which had undergone a massive revival during early modernity and the Enlightenment in the works of Descartes, Locke, Clarke, and Leibniz, whose cogency had been profoundly questioned by Hume and Kant, and which provide the indispensable background to contemporary natural theology (see 1946b: 17, 34 f.). Brunner summarizes his critique of this natural theology as follows:

> For the Enlightenment the light of reason reaches upwards into the sphere of redemption to the extent of doing away completely with the distinction between the *lumen naturale* and the revelation in Christ. The *lumen naturale* now becomes a revelation, indeed the only one that there really is. Thus the whole of theology becomes *theologia naturalis*, or at least the distinction between the revelation in Christ or in the Scriptures and rational knowledge becomes blurred and uncertain. [1946b: 47]

If the natural theology of the seventeenth and eighteenth centuries strove upwards from humanity to God, in Brunner's view Catholicism makes a similar mistake by promulgating 'religion without a Mediator' (1946a: 38; cf. 1946b: 45–6): it affirms a distinction between special and general revelation that Brunner must deny (at least in the form he is now discussing it; as we shall see, he himself strongly affirms general revelation). 'This graded scheme of a special revelation erected on the basis of general revelation destroys the significance of the fact of Christ' and thereby of *sola gratia* (1946a: 32). To seek a foundation for revealed theology in 'natural' or 'rational' theology in this fashion is to ignore sin and to erect 'a *system* of natural theology, a self-sufficient rational system, detachable from *theologia revelata*' (1946b: 46. Ironically enough, Barth will turn Brunner's criticism against him). Understandably, Brunner felt aggrieved at Barth's reproaches (Barth 1986b: 73, 76–7; cf. Barth 1962b: 341–4) and his repudiation of his position on natural theology. So, given the apparent common ground, what brought Barth to this?

The answer lies in Brunner's *eristic* theology. This form of theological engagement with culture and secularity combined apologetics with polemics with the aim of promoting 'explicit "discussion" between the Christian and non-Christian knowledge of God and of the Good' (Brunner 1937: 61; cf. 1946b: 35, 59). Brunner describes its polemical purpose as ' "laying bare" the true character of existence by destroying the fictions of every *Weltanschauung*. But this "laying bare" cannot be performed except by using what man can of himself know about himself' (Brunner 1932: 529 f. quoted by Barth 1946: 114).

However, eristic theology is not an end in itself. 'What is central is not dogmatics, nor eristics, nor ethics, but solely the proclamation of the Word of God. But', Brunner continues, 'a true understanding of *theologia naturalis* is of decisive importance for all three and also for the manner of proclamation' (1946b: 59; cf. 9). So the apologetic purpose of eristic theology lies in the way in which it serves preaching.

The eristic theology Brunner's natural theology serves does not set out to prove God's existence, though in its engagement with unbelievers, the Church may, Brunner thinks, discuss evidence of God's existence. Brunner's natural theology is not philosophical but theological. It is based upon 'the natural knowledge of God' (1946b: 35; cf. 58) that is available to human beings in virtue of the fact that God has placed his imprint upon nature. 'The creation of the world is...a revelation, a self-communication of God' (1946b: 25). Thus, in addition to the revelation of God in Jesus Christ, Brunner holds that there is also a 'natural revelation': 'The term "nature" can be applied to such permanent capacity for revelation as God has bestowed upon his works, to the traces of his own nature which he has expressed and shown in them' (1946b: 27).

How are fallen, sinful humans able to hear the Word of God when it is proclaimed? Brunner's answer is that it is on account of there being a 'point of contact' between God and humanity. The subjective condition of our capacity for revelation is our having been made in God's image, but this capacity is a passive receptivity; humans have no control over revelation (1946b: 9). Brunner distinguishes between a 'material' *imago* that has lost the capacity for relationship with God on account of sin and a 'formal' *imago* that has not. The latter is the seat of 'the "point of contact": capacity for words and responsibility'. Our 'consciousness of responsibility' is to be understood as 'conscience' (1946b: 56, 25): God has made us capable of hearing him address us personally and morally. This point of contact between God and man is given along with our createdness and cannot be destroyed by the Fall. 'Not even sin has done away with the fact that man is receptive of words, that he and he alone is receptive of the Word of God' (1946b: 31). So human beings have a capacity to receive proclamation by virtue of their being human: 'The Word of God could not reach a man who had lost his consciousness of God entirely' (1946b: 32).

Human responsibility before God comes to light not only in preaching but also through social interactions within the orders of creation. This is a sphere in which God's providential guidance of human affairs and his 'preserving' grace (1946b: 27–31) may be found. The orders of creation are:

> those existing facts of human corporate life which lie at the root of all historical life as unalterable presuppositions, which, although their historical forms may vary, are unalterable in their fundamental structure, and, at the same time, relate and unite men to one another in a definite way. [Brunner 1937: 210]

They are instituted by God as the sphere of human action in which we are to express our obedience to God: they are 'orders in accordance with which we have to act, because in them, even if only in a fragmentary and indirect way, God's will meets us' (Brunner 1937: 291). So, because we are made in God's image and God meets us through his creation, all humans are capable of having some knowledge of God, albeit without knowing that they do.

For Brunner only the Christian enjoys the fullness of knowledge foreshadowed in *theologia naturalis* (1946b: 26) and only in relation to Christ may a person enjoy the blessings of the 'redeeming' grace that is anticipated in God's preserving grace manifest through the orders of creation. Thus, whilst Brunner affirms 'the contrast between the Gospel and the natural knowledge of God' (1946b: 34) he also denies that his argument for natural theology posits a knowledge of God independent of revelation. This means that although eristic 'theological work can indeed be a preparation for the hearing of the Word of God' (1946b: 62, n. 14) by quickening the unbeliever and preparing him or her to hear the Word, it cannot take the place of that Word.

However, Brunner argues, if human language is to be used by God in proclamation, and if human beings have a capacity to hear God's word judging their disobedience and their stricken consciences, then this is dependent on the 'formal' *imago*, on there being some fundamental 'likeness to [God that] is not destroyed even by sin'. This likeness rests 'upon the doctrine that man as we know him, sinful man, is the only legitimate analogy to God, because he is always a rational being, a subject, a person'. Hence Brunner asserts that there is an *analogia entis* and that this is 'the basis of every theology, of Christian theology as much as pagan'. What differentiates Brunner's Protestant use of the analogy of being from Catholic and pagan usages is that 'the determining factor . . . that God is a subject is . . . maintained in theology' (1946b: 55). In his debate with Barth, Brunner offers little more than these few words to guide interpretation of his understanding of the analogy of being; there is no argument for it. The same applies to what it means to say that 'God is a subject'. This seems to underscore a point indicated by the overall tenor and direction of Brunner's contribution to the debate: his attention is focussed on the practical outworkings of doctrine rather than on the underlying and mutually implicated doctrinal and metaphysical issues.

Barth will base his attack on Brunner on his separation of praxis from doctrine and metaphysics. As Catholic theology has long known and as Barth's work tacitly acknowledged, the metaphysical issues cannot be separated from the doctrinal ones. Though they might be addressed in distinctly theological (rather than philosophical) ways, they cannot be avoided. Brunner skirts round the metaphysical issues because he 'thinks as a missionary' (1946b: 11); his priority is engagement with culture and effective preaching. It is not Christian dogma but the demands of the context that required a 'point of contact' and a natural theology on which to base it. As he insists: 'The church's proclamation must be *comprehensible* else it is useless, however true its contents.' The *analogia entis* assures the comprehensibility of proclamation both in so far as it underwrites the fact that, despite sin, human beings are capable of receiving revelation and in so far as it offers an account of language by means of which we can 'choose from amongst human words those that somehow correspond adequately to the divine Word'. Without this 'creaturely relation between the word of man and the Word of God' effective preaching would not be possible. Thus, the human likeness to God that has not been destroyed by sin 'is the *objective possibility* of the revelation of God in his "Word" ' (1946b: 56). Without an *analogia entis* God could not reveal himself.

So strong is Brunner's emphasis on responding to (his perception of) the demands of his situation, and his sense that Barth is evading them, that he launches a thinly veiled personal attack on Barth: 'A pastor might…go to heaven on account of the What [of his preaching] but go to hell on account of the How. To despise the question of How is a sign, not of theological seriousness but of theological intellectualism' (1946b: 56, 58; cf. Barth 1946: 124). Brunner summarizes the purpose of his eristic theology and of the natural theology that underlies it in a passage written in response to Barth's 'No!' which neatly illustrates his response to the How question. 'No missionary has ever preached, or can preach, otherwise than thus: the God whom ye, perverted by your sinful blindness, unknowingly worship as unknown, him do I proclaim to you as he who has "made known the secret of his will" to us in Jesus Christ the Crucified and Risen.' This preaching, based on a general revelation of God in creation and on human culpability in face of its perversion, is productive of repentance, and this 'alone makes possible the preaching of justification. Everything depends on the establishment of this responsibility, which makes man guilty; and the responsibility itself depends on the reality of a general revelation in creation which precedes the revelation of reconciliation in Jesus Christ, and indeed precedes all historical life' (1946b: 11–12). (Against Brunner's reading of St Paul, see Campbell 2009: e.g. 31, 162, 205 ff., 948 n. 13. Against his reading of Acts 17 (alluded to here), see Rowe 2009: 27–41).

Barth's Argument against Brunner's Natural Theology

Barth denies neither the Church's missionary task nor the need for Christians to engage with their cultural and political setting, but since the theologian's vocation is to reflect critically upon the Church's proclamation in the light of the gospel, Barth thinks that his or her primary task is to think theologically (see Barth 1933). Christian doctrine should not be adjusted to the apparent demands of the How of proclamation, for theology consists in obedient thinking in the light of God's mission to humans. Barth's criticisms of Brunner's natural theology should be read in this perspective.

Contrary to the impression given by many interpreters of the Barth–Brunner debate, Barth's objections to Brunner are not principally focussed around Brunner's understanding of the relationship between nature and grace, on general versus special revelation, or on the question of the 'point of contact' (1946: 74 f.). In fact, Barth's objections to natural theology fall only on the periphery of his criticisms of Brunner. 'For', Barth argues, ' "natural theology" does not exist as an entity capable of becoming a separate subject within what I consider to be real theology—not even for the sake of being rejected' (1946: 75). Real theology turns aside from natural theology as one does from an 'abyss'; as with a snake, so with natural theology: 'you hit it and kill it as soon as you see it' (1946: 76). Natural theology is a 'side issue' (1946: 75) for neither it nor its rejection forms part of the creed—which is what claims the attention of real theology.

There is something shocking about Barth's refusal to address directly the question of the propriety of natural theology, not just because of his blunt language but because at first sight his position seems wilfully obtuse. Yet, 'How slow is man, above all when the most important things are at stake!' Some succour is offered to Barth's interpreters by this comment he made about himself in 1939 as he looked back on his own earlier failure to recognize what, in the decade 1928–38, he came to learn was of first importance. The basis for his refusal is arrestingly simple:

> Christian doctrine, if it is to merit the name and if it is to build up the Christian church in the world as she must needs be built up, has to be exclusively and conclusively the doctrine of Jesus Christ—of Jesus Christ as the living Word of God spoken to us men. [Barth 1969: 43]

The reason Barth objects to natural theology is because it would establish some other focus for theology than Jesus Christ and claim a position in our thinking that ought to belong solely to the living Word. The purpose of Christian doctrine is to build up the Church for its witness in the world. The theological vocation is modest; it serves, but is not itself, proclamation.

With this in mind we can make sense of a vital passage in 'No!' which, even though it expresses the essential themes of Barth's critique of natural theology, is often overlooked in discussions of the Barth–Brunner debate.

> By 'natural theology' I mean every (positive *or* negative) *formulation of a system* which claims to be theological, i.e. to interpret divine revelation, whose *subject*, however, differs fundamentally from the revelation in Jesus Christ and whose *method* therefore differs equally from the exposition of Holy Scripture. [1946: 74–5; cf. Brunner 1946b: 46]

Barth finds Brunner to be constructing just such a system and engaging in 'an abstract speculation concerning a something that is not identical with the revelation of God in Jesus Christ' (1946: 75).

Barth's objection to natural theology is rooted in his core convictions about the subject matter of theology and its method, and his definition of it invites us to consider what theology is—which is why his opinions about the analogy of being continue to stimulate valuable theological debate (see White 2011).

Thus, to think that whether or not to engage in natural theology is a question of which horn of the dilemma mentioned in the Introduction is to be taken is to have tacitly assumed an interpretation of divine revelation when it is just that which is in dispute. It is to assume (for example) that the concepts of 'nature' and 'grace', or of what is scriptural, are well-understood and have stable, fixed meanings. But perhaps they are not; perhaps we need instead first to establish a properly theological understanding of them in the context in which they are being used. Much to Barth's annoyance, Brunner seems to have thought that his argument was to be construed in just such a dislocated way (1946b: 20), but Barth objects that this use of *sola gratia* and *sola scriptura* betrays a fundamental misunderstanding. If these foundational principles of Reformed theology are used as independently established, self-standing datum points and interpreted contrastively in relation to external matters (for example, the Church's context) rather than in the context of the scriptural witness to God's revelation in Christ, they fail to do the work for which they were framed as principles. If the doctrines of *sola gratia* and *sola scriptura* are not grounded in, and their implications worked out from, the revelation in Christ—rather than the apparent demands of Christian proclamation—the result is likely to be 'abstract speculation' about, for example, general revelation, points of contact, and orders of creation. (Of course, the possibility must remain that these could be *properly* theological topics but unless they are shown to take Jesus Christ as their subject and to be grounded in the exposition of Scripture, for Barth they will remain abstract speculation.) But just as Barth will not accept speculation that arises from an abstract use of these principles, so neither will he accept the principles unless the theological work that founded them has been done afresh: it could turn out that they themselves are not borne out by Scripture and its witness to Christ. And that is why Barth sees directly combating natural theology as a 'side issue' and a distraction from the proper task of what he considers to be 'real theology': it is to engage in some task other than building up the Church by some method other than 'the doctrine of Jesus Christ—the living Word of God spoken to us men'.

Barth's seemingly narrow understanding of what it is to think theologically generates a correspondingly broad definition of natural theology—broader, for example, than when it is taken to be the project of coming to, or providing support for, knowledge of (the existence of) God and his attributes on the basis of evidence generally available, by unaided reason, and without appeal to revelation or religious authority (see e.g. Kretzmann 1997, 1999; Swinburne 1994, 2004a, 2004b, 2005). Brunner also would reject this conception, but Barth's understanding of natural theology embraces both because, for him, theology should be focussed precisely and exclusively on the actuality and particularity of the Christ-event and on expounding Scripture's witness to it. Barth expresses this powerfully in his 1933 lecture on 'The First Commandment as an Axiom of Theology' (1986b):

> Is it really true that theology hangs by as thin a thread as…the written account about the temporal event of the god who is merciful in Jesus Christ?…[I]s it this and only this god, who is revealed here and in that way, the god to whom theology clings? It is here and here only where theology recognizes its highest value, its source of knowledge, its criterion of certainty, its practical motive…Should God really be delineated by the walls of the church, a book, the events of the years 1 to 30, the revelation and faith of the old and New Israel? Poor theology which has so small a god! Poor theology which has to resemble a pyramid standing on its tip! [Barth 1986b: 72–3]

Barth's position reflects not unthinking subjectivism but is the expression of an epistemological and methodological obedience to God.

To treat natural theology as a theme worthy of separate theological consideration, even if only to reject it, would be to fail to think in the light of the truth in Christ's call—a failure of Christian obedience. 'Real rejection of natural theology can come about only in the fear of God' (1946: 76):

The fight against natural theology, which is unavoidable in view of the first commandment as an axiom of theology, is a fight for right obedience in theology. Right obedience, the good work of theology, must consist in right theological thought and speech. Theology is right and good when it corresponds to the first commandment and does not oppose it. Even theology has good reason to examine 'what is the will of God, what is good and acceptable and perfect' (Roms. 12:2). Such an examination leads us to conclude that theology today...should take its leave of each and every natural theology and dare, in that narrow isolation, to cling solely to the god who has revealed himself in Jesus Christ. Why? Because that and only that has been commanded of it. Because everything else is arbitrariness which does not lead to, but leads away from, that god. [Barth 1986b: 77; cf. 1986a: 56 ff., 58 ff.]

For Barth, obedience to the gospel demanded not eristic theology's polemical-apologetic engagement with culture but a still deeper resolve to attend to 'the good work of theology'. A system of thought drawing on divine revelation but in addition to that also including in its subject matter concerns other than the unique claim of Christ—such as the claims of social, political, and cultural circumstance—might seem fit to meet the demands of the situation, but would in fact imperil theology by setting up a demand in apparent competition with that of God. But the claim of revelation is unique and incommensurable with other claims. To construct such a system would be to engage in 'an abstract speculation concerning something that is not identical with the revelation of God in Jesus Christ' and, owing to the distractions of that speculation, ultimately to compromise theology's exclusive obedience to the revelation of God in Christ. Barth recognized that, in face of the false claims of the Nazis and the German Christians, only taking the first commandment as its axiom could give theology the clarity of purpose its service of the Church's witness required (cf. Jüngel 1992: xxiii).

Barth's refusal of natural theology is therefore not a refusal to read the signs of the times or to engage with culture. But, since Brunner discerns the Church's situation more clearly than the theologians amongst the German Christians (not to mention other theologians such as Karl Adam), so, with stronger reason, as Barth has opposed them he must he also oppose Brunner (1946: 67 ff.). Barth agrees that the Church should pursue those things Brunner thinks the context demands—discussions with unbelievers, teaching the faith to young people, and the practice of dogmatics—but where Brunner puts the latter last in his list of the theologian's priorities, Barth would order them differently. Brunner was allowing the content of the gospel to be distorted by the context in which it was to be expressed (1946: 122); he was not simply failing to address the context in an appropriate way; his ordering of theology's tasks was mistaken *tout court*.

In Barth's view it is Brunner's mistaken sense of the theologian's priorities that had led him in 1929 to write of the first things on his list as representing 'the *other* task of theology' (1946: 123, quoting from the title of Brunner's article in *Zwischen den Zeiten*, 1929, pp. 255 f., Barth's emphasis). But, Barth continues, 'I fail to see how the abstraction which this title expresses is possible in theology' (1946: 123). Brunner mistakenly coordinates the task of theology with the claims of its context. He therefore separates the question of '*what* has to be done?' from '*how* is it to be done' (1946: 122) and treats the latter in abstraction from theology's proper subject matter and method. But '[w]hoever makes such an abstraction will inevitably get into some kind of natural theology' (1946: 123)—'inevitably' because once theology departs from its proper subject matter and method, it is thrown back upon theologically underdetermined creaturely resources. Equally inevitably, Brunner finds the answer to the 'how' in natural theology and, Barth argues, is thereby led away from the sufficiency of Scripture and of grace implicit in the Reformed 'solas'.

In separating the 'how' from the 'what', Brunner forgets that theology has not a double but only a single theme: 'theology and human life in general is concerned with God, his Word, his acts and his rule' (1946: 123). He mistakenly thinks that Mary's question of the angel—'How can this be, since I am a virgin?'—requires to be treated as a separate problem in abstraction from, bracketing out of consideration, the angel's reply. But the what-will-be of the virginal conception finds its 'how' in God's merciful provision. Hence in pondering its own 'how's, the Church need not seek, and should not expect, to 'find help elsewhere than in the revelation of God'. The 'how' of Christian witness is already embraced within theology's single theme, as the prophets and Apostles well knew: 'only God can be called to witness for God', and God has done this in raising Jesus Christ from the dead for our sake (1946: 124).

So even in the crisis that has befallen Germany and the Church in that country, Barth argues that the single task of theology suffices. The Church must continue to speak of God's unconditional demand; of the coming of Christ; of God's victory; of Christian confidence in God, his Word, and the sacraments; of the love of God for his creatures; and of the perseverance he grants. To do otherwise, as Brunner proposes, would be merely to proffer 'useless bridges and crutches' to believers and unbelievers alike (1946: 125). In preaching, rather than correlating the Word of God with the audience's context, the speaker 'should *allow* [his or her] language to be formed and shaped and adapted as much as possible by what the text seems to be saying' (1946: 127). For in fact, Barth writes:

> In my experience the best way of dealing with 'unbelievers' . . . is not to try to bring out their 'capacity for revelation', but to treat them quietly, simply (remembering that Christ has died and risen also for them), as if their rejection of 'Christianity' was not to be taken seriously. It is only then that they can understand you, since they really see that you are standing as an evangelical theologian: on the ground of justification by faith alone. [1946: 127; cf. Barth 1960: 66–70]

Given Barth's fundamental disagreement with Brunner's theology of engagement, it is not surprising that he finds his proposals concerning the point of contact, the orders of creation, and the *imago Dei* and the natural theology which undergirds them to be otiose to the degree of endangering the very principles of *sola Scriptura* and *sola gratia* to which Brunner had appealed. At each point, Barth finds Brunner departing from these principles and abstracting from theology's proper subject matter and method. The result is a 'theology of compromise which has shown itself as the cause of the present unhappy state of the Evangelical Church in Germany'—little wonder the German Christian theologians had applauded Brunner (1946: 72).

In reifying the orders of creation, Brunner goes beyond what Scripture warrants, and his moral epistemology fails to take sin seriously and presumes a knowledge of God's will apart from Scripture and the work of the Holy Spirit (1946: 86 f., cf. 128; 1938: 21 ff.). As Barth saw it, this implies a knowability of, and a requirement of obedience to, God's will in the structures of society, but this was a gift to the German Christians for it permitted an all-too-easy move from an 'is' to an 'ought' readily exploitable by a tyrant. To speak of God's 'preserving grace' being knowable to the non-believer through the orders of creation and thereby mediating God's command would more likely be taken in the Germany of the 1930s to announce 'our condemnation to a kind of antechamber of hell!' (1946: 84; cf. Jüngel 1992: xxiii, 26–9; Barth 1957: 172–8).

Brunner's teaching about the *imago Dei* rests, Barth argues, on an equivocal understanding of the *imago* that results in theological incoherence. Brunner must choose between affirming either that we are fallen, in which case we can contribute nothing to our salvation and *sola gratia* is upheld, or that we are not fallen and can contribute to our salvation, but then *sola gratia* is denied. Either humanity is like a drowning man who cannot swim, or he can put in a few strokes of his own to assist his saviour (1946: 79, 82). The root of this dilemma lies in Brunner's abstracting from revelation. The natural knowledge of God on which Brunner's argument relies is 'a possibility in principle, but not in fact, not a possibility to be realised by us. One might call it an objective possibility, created by God, but not a subjective possibility, open to man. Between what is possible in principle and what is possible in fact there inexorably lies the Fall. Hence this possibility can only be discussed hypothetically: *si integer stetisset* Adam' (1946: 106 quoting Calvin 1960: 40 = I. ii. 1; cf. 1946: 105–9). Brunner cannot simultaneously maintain *sola Scriptura* and affirm both horns of the dilemma. So if he would maintain *sola Scriptura* he must choose: either fallen humans do, or they do not, have a capacity for revelation prior to God's creating it in his work of redemption. Since it is the Holy Spirit who gives humans 'living knowledge of the word of the Cross', Brunner's positing a 'receptivity for words' implies, again, that humans can contribute to their salvation (1946: 79; see also 79–83, 88–94, 116 ff.; O'Donovan 1986).

For Barth, not only is it not possible to affirm a positive natural knowledge of God prior to his revelation in Christ but, granted the regenerating work of the Holy Spirit, it is not necessary to posit or to attempt to establish a point of contact for the Word of God to hook onto as a condition of the possibility of humans being addressed in preaching. Brunner intends his eristic theology to prepare the ground for proclamation by disclosing the plight of humanity separated from God and he seeks to do so by use of human beings' own knowledge of their situation. But again, Brunner needlessly abstracts from revelation. Not only can a point of contact not disclose the human plight, in fact 'the truth, presented in the Scriptures, Creeds and Confessions' does this. Apart from revelation:

> man is of himself unable to find access to the revelation of God. Just because Christ is born, we have to regard the world as lost in the sight of God. The Word of God declares man to be unfree in his relations with God. The fact that we become hearers and doers of the Word of God signifies the realisation of a divine possibility, not of

one that is inherent in our human nature. Freedom to know the true God is a miracle, a freedom of God, not one of our freedoms. Faith in the revelation of God makes this negation inevitable. [1946: 116–17]

So, Brunner's natural theology fails at the point it most needs to succeed: it denies the free grace of God in Jesus Christ and threatens to leave humanity without the hope that comes from the gospel alone. In so far as the human plight is knowable by us it is owing to the work of the Holy Spirit. 'All the comfort, all the power, all the truth of the revelation of God depends on the fact that it is God who is thus revealed to us' (1946: 117). In the end, therefore, Brunner's teaching about a point of contact needlessly abstracts from the third article of the creed: 'The Holy Ghost, who proceeds from the Father and the Son and is therefore revealed and believed to be God, does not stand in need of any point of contact but that which he himself creates' (1946: 121).

By alerting us to the third article of the creed with its confession of the double procession of the Holy Spirit, Barth implies that Brunner is in danger of severing the doctrine of creation from soteriology and even of misconstruing the relations amongst the persons of the Trinity. The epistemological implication of the double procession are important, for if it is true that, as the Pauline author affirms, Jesus Christ is 'the first-born of all creation' (Col. 1:15), and that, following John, the incarnate Word is the one pre-existing 'with God' (Jn. 1:1 ff.), then we ought not abstractly to separate our knowledge of God in creation from our knowledge of God in redemption and sanctification. The perichoresis of the divine persons requires us to think the three, and the works *ad extra* appropriated to them, together and not separately. If we deny the double procession, Barth asks, is it 'not inevitable that the relation of God to man will be understood decisively from the standpoint of Creator and creature, and that it will thus acquire a more or less developed naturalistic and unethical character, so that the Mediator of revelation, the Son or Word, will be set aside as the basis and origin of revelation' (1975: 481)?

What then of Brunner's reliance on the *analogia entis*? Barth's own understanding of the concept is complex and changes over time but the only form in which it is ever acceptable to him is one that is founded on the way that God comes alongside human beings in Christ (see e.g. 1938: 14 f.; 1957: 79–84; 1975: xiii; 1986a: 38 ff.; see also Johnson 2010). Barth is severely critical of Brunner's 'sadly distorted' account of Catholic natural theology for which, in fact, Barth insists 'a true knowledge of God derived from reason and nature is *de facto* never attained without prevenient and preparatory grace... nature presuppose[s] grace' (1946: 95, 96; cf. 95–99, 116; 1962a; 1962b):

> According to the Roman Catholic, reason, if left entirely without grace, is incurably sick and incapable of any serious theological activity. Only when it has been illumined, or at least provisionally shone upon by faith, does reason serve to produce those statements about God, man and the world, which, according to Roman Catholic doctrine, are not only articles of revelation but have to be considered truths of reason. [1946: 96]

The fatal flaw in Brunner's natural theology, illustrated by his misuse of the concept *analogia entis* and his misrepresentation of Catholic teaching, is that he separates revelation and grace. But Barth knows that his own theology faces the same tribunal as Brunner's. So, 'we must learn again to understand revelation as *grace* and grace as *revelation* and therefore turn away from all . . . natural theology by ever making new decisions and being ever controverted anew' (1946: 71).

BARTH AND CONTEMPORARY
NATURAL THEOLOGY

In his 1933 lecture on 'The First Commandment as an Axiom of Theology' (1986b), Barth springs a surprise on those who think his work inhibits discussion of Christian faith with non-believers and practitioners of other academic disciplines. His exposition of the first commandment illustrates a theological use of the concept 'axiom' that is analogous to its use in other axiom-based disciplines such as mathematics and philosophy. Hence, 'the concept "axiom" may serve as a "point of contact" for a discussion about the presupposi-tions of theology' (1986b: 64). Analogous use, not univocal: the content of theology's statements is *sui generis* and incommensurable with those of other disciplines because its source is unique and requires a different method. An understanding of these topics will help us appreciate some wider implications of Barth's critique of natural theology.

Barth regarded his 1931 study of Anselm as his key methodological work (Barth 1960: 11). It is beyond the scope of this chapter even to outline his argument but a very impor-tant aspect of it is his affirmation, common to the great majority of Christian thinkers before modernity, that the order of being precedes the order of knowing. Thus:

> The establishing of knowledge of the object of faith consists in recognition of the basis that is peculiar to the object of faith itself . . . The element of reason in the knowl-edge of the object of faith consists in the recognition of the rationality that is peculiar to the object of faith itself. Ontic rationality precedes noetic. [Barth 1960: 50]

God is knowable to human reason because he precedes human reason; rational thought about God follows after the rationality which God is in himself and in his self-revealing. Since God exists in that fullness of existence which is his alone (necessary existence), creaturely (contingent) existence depends on him for its existence, its continuing exist-ence, and its fulfilment. Creaturely reasoning about God and creation should therefore share this orientation and goal. The consequences of this for the project of natural theol-ogy are important.

First, since 'it is the Existence of God that is the criterion of general [creaturely] exist-ence' (1960: 155), it is an error to think that we can use the latter as a basis of the former. Judgements about God's existence and his perfections are misguided when they are made on the basis of creaturely existence and what we predicate of it: they mistakenly subordinate the order of being to the order of knowing. God's existence and essence are made known in and through his self-revealing to humans; there is no 'independent knowledge alongside that of faith... able to draw from its own sources' (1960: 53). This means that reason turns against its proper orientation in the attempt to argue from crea-ture to creator. A contemporary example of this is the opinion that *creatio ex nihilo* is provable by a version of the cosmological argument based on Big Bang cosmology. Not only does this argument falsely presume that general existence as known to science can be a criterion of God's existence, but it ignores the historical fact that the doctrine of *cre-atio ex nihilo* was a theorem deduced from God's merciful self-revealing in Christ, and that one purpose of the doctrine is to uphold divine aseity. It is unsurprising that the mistake of supposing creaturely existence to be a criterion of God's existence results in the category error of thinking that the doctrine of *creatio ex nihilo* is a quasi-scientific explanation of existence.

Secondly, such is the incomparable fullness of God's existing that creatures can nei-ther ascend to God nor presume to occupy a place of judgement over his (non-)exist-ence. God's gracious self-revelation in Christ both humbles and exalts humans. Hence Barth echoes Anselm: 'No one, nothing else at all confronts me as thou dost—in such a way that this *ascendere* above and *iudicare* on the object is made impossible for me and the only question is of obedience or disobedience' (1960: 156; cf. Anselm 1979: 113, 115 = *Prosl.* I). The early modern historian Peter Harrison has argued that natural theology 'did not exist before the modern period (i.e. the sixteenth and seventeenth centuries)' (Harrison n.d.: 1). This is plausible, especially in the light Michael Buckley's important argument that the origins of modern atheism lie in early modernity (Buckley 1987). But early modernity gave birth to a brave, new child who reached maturity and full flourish-ing in the Enlightenment.

Hitherto, so the story goes, humans had existed under a 'self-incurred tutelage' and lacked the courage to use reason without direction by authority (Kant 1985: 3 = 35). Whilst reason had been an instrument of enquiry, now, with the assistance of Kant (the ground having been partially prepared by John Locke (1975: 688–706 = IV.18–19)), it was determined that reason should ascend to the judicial bench and 'secure its rightful claims... according to its own eternal and unchangeable laws':

> Our age is the genuine age of criticism, to which everything must submit. Religion through its holiness... commonly seek[s] to exempt [itself] from it. But in this way it excite[s] a just suspicion against [itself], and cannot lay claim to that unfeigned respect that reason grants only to that which has been able to withstand its free and public examination. [Kant 1998: 100–1 = A xi - A xii]

Earlier in the eighteenth century David Hume had subjected to devastating criticism arguments for the existence of God that had been put into currency in early modernity. But at the end of that century, Kant's own criticisms of them and his denial of the possi-bility of knowledge of God gave a new lease of life to natural theology. Henceforth, before any theological claim could be entertained, the conditions of its possibility had to be rationally demonstrated. Judicial, neutral reason became the unimpeachable criterion of all proposed truth claims, especially those of religious belief, and thus the argu-ments of natural theology became an apparently essential component of Christianity.

So effective has been the promulgation of this line of thought and so complicit in it have most Christian apologetics been that for many it still has the status of a dogma. But dissenters might think that with the Enlightenment's demand for rational demonstration came, *per impossibile*, a human *ascendere* above, and *iudicare* on, the object of faith: knowledge of God is conformed to the measure of human reason and a new system of thought is born whose subject is an inference, deified, and whose method is human ingenuity.

Karl Barth's critique of natural theology challenges the Enlightenment's then-novel conception of reason's judicial authority. For him, theology is one form of the Church's obedient, rational response to God's address to humans; it is faith seeking understanding. And, since the sole measure of its truth is the divine λογοσ incarnate, it is before him alone that it will give account. So, in theology's attending to the 'question as to the correctness of [the Church's] utterance it does not measure by an alien standard but by its own source and object' (Barth 1975: 4; cf. 12). This side of eternity, theology's question about the truth of its discourse can never finally be settled, and certainly not by the 'alien standard' of judicial reason as the Enlightenment tradition has insisted. 'God's revelation is…for man a court from which there can be no possible appeal to a higher court' (Barth 1975: 305). But sanctified instrumental reason is a gift from God by which faith is granted to understand its source and object and to test its speech—as Barth has been doing in his reply to Brunner. As his Anselm book shows, Barth is misrepresented if he is thought to be advocating or warranting any departure from the instrumental use of reason in obedient 'recognition of the rationality that is peculiar to the object of faith itself' (Barth 1960: 50).

Just as Anselm in his use of reason was not a disciple *manqué* of Kant but one who knew divine truth to be the measure of theological statements, so Barth in his criticisms of the Enlightenment and the natural theology it generated is not an irrationalist: for him the divine rationality, revealed to and received by faith, is the source and goal of faithful human reasoning. Reason is the God-given instrument by which faith seeks understanding: sanctified human rationality participates in the divine rationality. Without it, to understand and, in the Anselmian sense, to prove the Church's faith is an impossibility. To the extent that natural theology defers to the pretensions of judicial rationality ('sanctified judicial rationality' is an oxymoron), it will not be capable of rising to either of these tasks, still less to establishing the existence of the God whose λογοσ sanctified instrumental rationality seeks to follow. To the extent that natural theology demonstrates the virtues of sanctified instrumental rationality, it will have lost its reason to exist.

REFERENCES

Anselm of Canterbury (1979). *Proslogion with a Reply on Behalf of the Fool by Gaunilo* and *The Author's Reply to Gaunilo*. Translated by M. J. Charlesworth. Notre Dame: University of Notre Dame Press.

Barth, Karl (1933). *Theological Existence Today!: A Plea for Theological Freedom.* Translated by R Birch Hoyle. London: Hodder and Stoughton.

—— (1938 [1929]). *The Holy Ghost and the Christian Life.* Translated by R. Birch Hoyle. London: Frederick Muller.

—— (1946 [1934]). 'No!' in *Natural Theology: Comprising "Nature and Grace" by Professor Dr Emil Brunner and the Reply "No!" by Dr Karl Barth.* Translated by Peter Frankel. Introduction by John Baillie. London: Geoffrey Bles: pp. 65–128.

—— (1957 [1940]). *Church Dogmatics, II/1: The Doctrine of God.* Edinburgh: T&T Clark.

—— (1960 [1931]) *Anselm: 'Fides Quaerens Intellectum', Anselm's Proof of the Existence of God in the Context of his Theological Scheme.* Translated by Ian W. Robertson. London: SCM.

—— (1962a [1928]) 'Roman Catholicism: A Question to the Protestant Church' in *Theology and Church: Shorter Writings 1920–1928.* Translated by Louise Pettibone Smith. London: SCM: pp. 307–34.

—— (1962b [1926]). 'Church and Culture' in *Theology and Church: Shorter Writings 1920–1928.* Translated by Louise Pettibone Smith. London: SCM: pp. 334–54.

—— (1969). *Karl Barth, 1886-1968: How I Changed my Mind.* Edinburgh: The St Andrew Press.

—— (1975 [1932]) *Church Dogmatics, I/1: The Doctrine of the Word of God.* Edinburgh: T&T Clark.

—— (1986a [1929]). 'Fate and Idea in Theology' in *The Way of Theology in Karl Barth: Essays and Comments.* Edited by H. Martin Rumscheidt. Allison Park, Pennsylvania: pp. 25–61.

—— (1986b [1933]). 'The First Commandment as an Axiom of Theology' in *The Way of Theology in Karl Barth: Essays and Comments.* Edited by H. Martin Rumscheidt. Allison Park, Pennsylvania: pp. 63–78.

Brunner, Emil (1932). 'Die Frage nach dem "Anknüpfungspunkt" als Problem der Theologie'. *Zwischen den Zeiten* 10: 505 ff.

—— (1937 [1932]) *The Divine Imperative.* Translated by Olive Wyon. London: Lutterworth Press.

—— (1946a [1932]). *The Mediator: A Study of the Central Doctrine of the Christian Faith.* Translated by Olive Wyon. London: Lutterworth Press.

—— (1946b [1934]). 'Nature and Grace' in *Natural Theology: Comprising "Nature and Grace" by Professor Dr Emil Brunner and the Reply "No!" by Dr Karl Barth.* Translated by Peter Frankel. Introduction by John Baillie. London: Geoffrey Bles: pp. 15–64.

Bucher, Rainer (2011). *Hitler's Theology: A Study in Political Religion.* Translated by Rebecca Pohl. London: Continuum.

Buckley, Michael S. J. (1987). *At the Origins of Modern Atheism.* New Haven: Yale University Press.

Calvin, John (1960). *Institutes of the Christian Religion 1.* Edited by John T. McNeill. Translated by Ford Lewis Battles. Philadelphia: The Westminster Press.

Campbell, Douglas A. (2009). *The Deliverance of God: An Apocalyptic Rereading of Justification in Paul.* Grand Rapids, Michigan: Eerdmans.

Harrison, Peter (n.d.). 'Reading the Book of Nature in the Early Modern Period'. Unpublished MS.

Hart, John W. (2004). 'The Barth-Brunner Correspondence' in *For the Sake of the World: Karl Barth and the Future of Ecclesial Theology.* Edited by George Hunsinger. Grand Rapids: Eerdmans: pp. 19–43.

Johnson, Keith L. (2010). *Karl Barth and the Analogia Entis.* London: T & T Clark.

Jüngel, Eberhard (1992). *Christ, Justice and Peace: Towards a Theology of the State in Dialogue with the Barmen Declaration.* Translated by D. Bruce Hamill and Alan J. Torrance. Edinburgh: T&T Clark.

Kant, Immanuel (1985). 'What is Enlightenment?' in *On History*. Translated by Lewis White Beck et al. New York: Macmillan: pp. 3–10.

—— (1998). *Critique of Pure Reason*. Translated by Paul Guyer and Allen W. Wood. Cambridge: Cambridge University Press.

Kretzmann, Norman (1997). *The Metaphysics of Theism: Aquinas's Natural Theology in 'Summa contra gentiles' I*. Oxford: Clarendon Press.

—— (1999). *The Metaphysics of Creation: Aquinas's Natural Theology in 'Summa contra gentiles' II*. Oxford: Clarendon Press.

Locke, John (1975). *An Essay Concerning Human Understanding*. Edited by Peter Nidditch. Oxford: Clarendon Press.

O'Donovan, Joan F. (1986). 'Man in the Image of God: The Disagreement between Barth and Brunner Reconsidered'. *Scottish Journal of Theology* 39/4: 433–59.

Rowe, C. Kavin (2009). *World Upside Down: Reading Acts in the Graeco-Roman World*. New York: Oxford University Press.

Swinburne, Richard (1994). *The Christian God*. Oxford: Oxford University Press.

—— (2004a). *The Existence of God*. Oxford: Oxford University Press.

—— (2004b). 'Natural Theology, its "Dwindling Probabilities" and "Lack of Rapport". *Faith and Philosophy* 21/4: 533–46.

—— (2005). *Faith and Reason*. Oxford: Oxford University Press.

White, Thomas Joseph, O.P., ed. (2011) *The Analogy of Being: Invention of the Antichrist or Wisdom of God?* Grand Rapids: Eerdmans.

Wright, Jonathan (1977). 'The German Protestant Church and the Nazi Party in the Period of the Seizure of Power 1932-3' in *Renaissance and Renewal in Christian History*. Edited by Derek Baker. Oxford: Oxford University Press.

PART III

PHILOSOPHICAL PERSPECTIVES ON NATURAL THEOLOGY

....

CHAPTER 15

PERSPECTIVES ON NATURAL THEOLOGY FROM ANALYTIC PHILOSOPHY

....

KEITH M. PARSONS

THE DEFINITION OF NATURAL THEOLOGY IN ANALYTICAL PHILOSOPHY

....

NATURAL theology is the endeavour to support the truth or rationality of theism using only the resources of natural human reason. Natural theology, as opposed to revealed theology, may not appeal to any premise that presupposes the authenticity of a particular alleged revelation or the supposed authority of any scripture. Only premises certifiable by the application of the usual tools, standards, and methods of intellectual inquiry are permissible. Such premises may be taken as simply obvious, as Aquinas seemed to regard the premises of his *quinque viae*, or they may be rather recondite, involving theorems of modal logic or the data of biochemistry. The point is that the arguments of natural theologians may not beg the question in favour of theism. Notable historical examples of natural theology have been Anselm's ontological argument, Aquinas' *quinque viae*, Paley's 'watchmaker' argument, and Leibniz's cosmological argument from the principle of sufficient reason.

Analytic philosophy is a genre or style of philosophy, typically practiced among philosophers in English-speaking countries (though with notable exponents from Scandinavia, Germany, and elsewhere), that advocates rigorous forms of logical or conceptual analysis as the central method of philosophy. Analytic philosophers are the intellectual progeny of major philosophers of the nineteenth and twentieth centuries such as Gottlob Frege, Bertrand Russell, G. E. Moore, Ludwig Wittgenstein, and Rudolf Carnap. These philosophers, though differing over many points, generally repudiated the traditional philosophical quest for speculative or metaphysical truth and focussed on elucidating the deep logical structures which, they held, lurk beneath the 'surface grammar' of many of our propositions. By such a process they thought that it would be possible to solve, or dissolve, many long-standing philosophical conundrums, which were consequences of the bewitchment of our intellects by language.

The usually cited paradigm of philosophy in the analytic mode is Russell's theory of descriptions, which employed first-order predicate logic to clarify denoting expressions so that they no longer seemed to commit us to a questionable ontology. Though we may point to such paradigmatic instances, no comprehensive definition of 'analytic philosophy' seems possible. At most, the different types of analytic philosophy exhibit an overlapping set of family resemblances with respect to content, aim, and technique. Perhaps all we can comfortably say is that analytical philosophers are a loose aggregation, chiefly connected by a shared commitment to the rigorous examination of philosophical problems in the light of tools and methods drawn from formal logic, set theory, and the natural sciences.

From the Rejection of Natural Theology in Analytical Philosophy to the Rise of Analytical Theism

With analytic philosophy thus broadly characterized, what can we say about the attitude of analytic philosophers towards natural theology? At one time it would have been safe to say that the attitude was generally hostile or even dismissive. When analytic philosophy was largely dominated by logical positivism, with its employment of the verifiability criterion of meaning, the tendency was to regard theological claims as literally meaningless (see e.g. A. J. Ayer's positivist manifesto *Language, Truth, and Logic*). The claims of natural theology, such as 'an omniscient, omnipotent, creator of the universe exists', would have been taken as pseudo-propositions—that is, as utterances that fail to express any meaningful claim at all.

Perhaps the most famous instance of an a priori rejection of theological claims by an analytic philosopher is found in Antony Flew's essay, 'Theology and Falsification' (Flew 1955: 96–9). Flew argued that theological assertions, unlike empirical claims, are incapable of falsification. A scientific claim, such as the double-helix structure of DNA, is potentially falsifiable (though not actually falsified) by many kinds of scientific tests or data. Theological assertions, says Flew, are not similarly falsifiable by contrary data or counterexample. Consider 'God loves you and has a wonderful plan for your life'. Flew contends that such assertions, as intended by those who assert them, do not admit of falsification, not even in principle. For instance, the fact that God's 'wonderful plan' for some people seems to be that as infants they are burned to death in house fires is not taken as contradicting theological asseverations about the love of God. Flew concludes that theological assertions, though they bear a superficial resemblance to factual propositions, should not be taken as factual propositions at all since they do not meet a condition regarded as necessary for all such claims, viz. that they be in principle falsifiable. Questions of evidence for theological claims do not arise at all if theology does not even succeed in making factual claims.

With the demise of the verifiability criterion, and the repudiation by most philosophers of allied efforts, such as Flew's, to impose a linguistic veto on theological claims, natural theology once again became a topic of possible philosophical interest. A new generation of analytic philosophers of religion arose in the 1960s and 1970s including, most notably, Alvin Plantinga and Richard Swinburne. Plantinga's *The Nature of Necessity* (1974) and Swinburne's *The Existence of God* (1979) were, rightly, seen as setting a new and much higher standard of rigour and sophistication in the treatment of traditional issues in the philosophy of religion. These works employed such powerful, but abstruse, tools as modal logic, possible worlds semantics, and Bayesian confirmation theory to elucidate and reformulate a number of theistic arguments and to provide potent rejoinders to atheistic arguments. In fact, Plantinga and Swinburne spearheaded a remarkable burgeoning of what we might call analytic theism, the articulation and defence of theism using the tools and techniques of analytic philosophy.

Other notable analytic theists have included (in no particular order) William Lane Craig, J. P. Moreland, Douglas Geivett, Paul Copan, William Alston, John Hick, Nicholas Wolterstorff, Robert Merrihew Adams, Marilyn McCord Adams, George Schlesinger, Robin Collins, Robert C. Koons, William Hasker, Stephen T. Davis, Victor Reppert, George Mavrodes, Philip L. Quinn, and Keith Yandell. Naturally, this burst of activity by theistic philosophers has elicited responses from nontheist analytic philosophers, including (again in no particular order) Antony Flew, Wallace Matson, Kai Nielsen, Richard Gale, Adolf Grunbaum, William L. Rowe, Michael Martin, J. L. Mackie, Daniel Dennett, Evan Fales, Michael Tooley, Quentin Smith, Jordan Howard Sobel, Robin Le Poidevin, Theodore Drange, Walter Sinnott-Armstrong, Nicholas Everitt, J. L. Schellenberg, and Graham Oppy.

The above lists, though very far from comprehensive, indicate that the analytic philosophy of religion has been an extremely active area of philosophical inquiry for the last forty years. One remarkable aspect of the new analytic theism has been its theological conservatism. The analytic theists generally have no truck with any sort of secularized or demythologized religion, but make an unabashed and vigorous defence of traditional creeds. One consequence of this conservative approach has been a renewal of interest in the arguments of natural theology, which, though part of the stock-in-trade of theologians of earlier centuries, had largely been abandoned by the most eminent theologians of the twentieth century.

The Fine-tuning Argument

Clearly, in a short examination such as this, even the most superficial survey of the work of recent analytic philosophers of religion on the arguments of natural theology would be impossible. Obviously, this chapter can be no kind of overview or conspectus, but only a way of communicating the flavour of the debates and style of some of the salient practitioners of the analytic philosophy of religion. Hence, I will focus on just one of the most prominent arguments debated in recent discussions of natural theology, the so-called fine-tuning argument (FTA). The FTA is a sophisticated version of the traditional argument from design, one that appeals to the apparent 'fine tuning' of the fundamental constants of nature, such as the gravitational constant, such that even a minute variation in these values would not have permitted the development in our universe of complex forms of life or, *a fortiori*, intelligent and sentient creatures.

Focussing on just one argument will allow a much more in-depth examination of the nature of recent debates on natural theology by analytic philosophers and permit a richer appreciation of the logical rigour and sophistication of these arguments. I will first present the statement of the argument by two of its defenders, William Lane Craig and Robin Collins, and then look at criticisms by such philosophers as Robin Le Poidevin and Graham Oppy. Following this expository section, I conclude by asking whether the recent debates among analytic philosophers of religion have really advanced the case for natural theology. That is, does the undoubted success of analytic theists in making the arguments of natural theology more logically rigorous and scientifically informed really make those arguments more cogent, or only make it plainer why the project of natural theology must fail?

Fine Tuning: The Theistic Statement

Craig offers a succinct formulation of the FTA:

1. The fine-tuning of the universe is due to physical necessity, or to chance, or to design.
2. It is not due to physical necessity or chance.
3. Therefore it is due to design. [Craig 2007:79]

He explains the fine-tuning concept as follows:

> The physical laws of nature, when given mathematical expression, contain various constants, such as the gravitational constant, whose values are independent of the laws themselves; moreover, there are certain arbitrary quantities that are simply put in as boundary conditions on which the laws operate, for example, the initial low entropy condition of the universe. By 'fine tuning' one means that the actual values assumed by the constant and quantities in question are such that small deviations from those values would render the universe life-prohibiting, or, alternatively, that the range of life-permitting values is exquisitely narrow in comparison to the range of assumable values. [Craig 2007: 80]

Put simply, a universe capable of supporting any conceivable form of complex life will be possible only within a very narrow range of values of the fundamental physical constants. Had, for instance, the strength of the gravitational constant been only *very* slightly less or greater, then no galaxies, stars, or planets could have formed, and there would have been no environment in the least suitable for the evolution of complex life. Further, so far as we know, the gravitational and other such constants could have had any of an enormous range of possible values, only a tiny fraction of which would permit conditions necessary for the development of complex life. We may therefore envision a vast ensemble of possible universes, representing all possible combinations of values for the basic physical constants. Only a very, very tiny minority of these possible universes would be life-friendly; the overwhelmingly vast majority would prohibit the development of complex life. Craig illustrates this point as follows:

> Take a sheet of paper and place on it a red dot. That dot represents our universe. Now slightly alter one or more of the finely-tuned constants and physical quantities... As a result we have a description of another universe, which we may represent as a new dot in proximity of the first. If that new set of constants and quantities describes a life-permitting universe, make it a red dot; if it describes a universe that is life-prohibiting, make it a blue dot. Now repeat the procedure arbitrarily many times until the sheet is filled with dots. What one winds up with is a sea of blue with only a few pinpoints of red. [Craig 2003: 164–5]

It certainly seems, then, that it is extremely implausible that it could be a matter of sheer chance that out of that vast assemblage of possible universes our universe would just happen to be one of the very, very few with life-permitting values. In public lectures Craig has further illustrated this vast improbability by comparing it to firing a randomly aimed rifle shot into the Grand Canyon and having it kill a particular cockroach crawling on the canyon wall. Craig therefore thinks that we can rule out that the fine tuning of our universe is due to chance.

Perhaps, though, there is a way that the values of the physical constants in our universe could be due to chance. Perhaps, as a number of cosmologists now posit, there is not one universe, but a vast ensemble of universes. Perhaps the big bang was not a unique event, but has occurred many, many times generating endless numbers of universes. If the values of physical constants are randomly distributed among these various universes, then, by sheer chance, some tiny subset of those universes would have life-friendly values. Unsurprisingly, we find ourselves in one of those few life-friendly universes, not because we were providentially placed here, but because complex life such as humans could only develop in such a universe.

This is the multiple-worlds hypothesis (MWH), and Craig considers and rejects it. When compared to the design hypothesis—that is, that the fine tuning of our universe is due to providential design—Craig thinks that the MWH has four disadvantages:

1. *The design hypothesis is simpler.* According to Occam's Razor, we should not multiply causes beyond what is necessary to explain the effect. But it is simpler to postulate one cosmic designer than to postulate the infinitely bloated and contrived ontology of the MWH...
2. *There is no known way of generating a world ensemble...*
3. *There is no evidence for the existence of a world ensemble apart from the fine-tuning itself.* But the fine tuning is equally the evidence of a cosmic designer.

4. *MWH faces a severe challenge from evolutionary theory.* According to the prevailing theory of biological evolution, intelligent life such as ourselves, if it evolves at all, will do so as late in the lifetime of a star as possible… Hence, if our universe is but one member of a world ensemble, then it is overwhelmingly more probable that we should be viewing a very old sun than a relatively young one. [Craig 2007: 81–2]

Craig therefore rejects the possibility that the values of the physical constants could be due to chance.

Often, though, in the history of science, when the values of certain parameters have appeared arbitrary or random, further inquiry has shown that those values are in fact physically necessary—that is, determined by natural law. For instance, Johannes Kepler discovered three laws of planetary motion. The third law states that for each planet of the solar system the square of its period of revolution about the sun divided by the cube of its mean distance from the sun equals a constant. For Kepler, this law was an empirical discovery; no one knew why that relation *had* to hold until Newton demonstrated that Kepler's three laws are a consequence of the more basic laws of motion and gravitation propounded by Newton. Craig therefore must consider the possibility that a more basic law, a Theory of Everything (TOE) could entail the basic physical constants, thereby making their values determinate and a matter of physical necessity rather than chance.

Craig rejects this possibility also. His argument is that any such TOE will itself require fine tuning:

For example, in the most promising candidate of a TOE to date, super-string theory or M-theory, the physical universe must be 11-dimensional, but why the universe should possess just that number of dimensions is not addressed by the theory. M-theory simply substitutes geometrical fine-tuning for fine-tuning of forces… Furthermore, it seems likely that any attempt to reduce fine-tuning significantly will itself turn out to involve fine-tuning. This has certainly been the pattern in the past. In the light of the specificity and number of instances of fine-tuning, it is unlikely to disappear with the further advance of physical theory. [Craig 2007: 81]

If, therefore, the fine tuning of the universe cannot be due to chance or physical necessity, then the second premise of Craig's version of the FTA is supported. If, as the first premise of his argument states, the only options are that fine tuning is due to chance, physical necessity, or design, then design is left as the only option.

Robin Collins also addresses the MWH and his critique is similar to Craig's (Collins 2003: 130–4). Since space here is limited, we will focus on his defence of the FTA against what Collins calls 'the atheistic single universe hypothesis': 'According to the atheistic single-universe hypothesis, there is only one universe, and it is ultimately an inexplicable, "brute" fact that the universe exists and is fine-tuned' (Collins 2003: 123). Collins states his version of the FTA against the atheist single universe hypothesis (ASUH) as follows:

Premise 1. The existence of the fine-tuning is not improbable under theism.

Premise 2. The existence of the fine-tuning is very improbable under the atheistic single universe hypothesis.

Conclusion: From premises (1) and (2) and the prime principle of confirmation, it follows that the fine tuning argument provides strong evidence to favor the design hypothesis over the atheistic single universe hypothesis (Collins 2003: 125).

The 'prime principle of confirmation (PPC)' is defined by Collins:

> *Simply put, the principle says that whenever we are considering two competing hypotheses, an observation counts as evidence in favor of the hypothesis under which the observation has the highest probability (or is the least improbable).* (Or, put slightly differently, the principle says that whenever we are considering two competing hypotheses, H1 and H2, an observation, O, counts as evidence in favor of H1 over H2 if O is more probable under H1 than it is under H2.) Moreover, the degree to which the evidence counts in favor of one hypothesis over another is proportional to the degree to which the observation is more probable under the one hypothesis than the other. [Collins 2003: 123–4; emphasis in original]

Collins regards his first premise as relatively uncontroversial. Surely, it seems, a perfectly good God would want intelligent, conscious beings to exist, and so would create a world friendly to the development of such life. Collins thinks that most criticisms will be directed at the second premise. For instance, atheists could argue that since there is only one universe, the idea that the fundamental constants of nature are improbable is meaningless. In this case the PPC could not be applied to favour theism over the ASUH, since, on this latter hypothesis, there is no probability, high or low, that the universe is fine tuned, and so the fact of fine tuning cannot be more probable given theism than given the ASUH.

I have argued in favour of the ASUH:

> The assignment of meaningful probabilities upon the hypothesis of atheism is...difficult. If atheism is correct, if the universe and its laws are all that is or ever has been, how can it be said that the universe, with all of its 'finely tuned' features, is in any relevant sense probable or improbable? *Ex hypothesi* there are no antecedent conditions that could determine such a probability. Hence, if the universe is the ultimate brute fact, it is neither likely nor unlikely, probable or improbable; it simply *is*...If we were in a position to witness the birth of many worlds—some designed, some undesigned—then we might be in a position to say of any particular world that it had such-and-such a probability of existing undesigned. But we simply are not in such a position. We have absolutely no empirical basis for assigning probabilities to ultimate facts. [Parsons 1990: 182]

So, if there is no meaningful sense in which the 'finely tuned' features of the universe are either probable or improbable given the ASUH, then those features cannot confirm theism over atheism.

Collins replies that the sense of probability relevant to the FTA is *epistemic probability*, which he characterizes as follows:

Roughly, the epistemic probability of a proposition can be thought of as the degree of confidence or belief we rationally should have in the proposition. Further, the conditional epistemic probability of a proposition R on another proposition S—written as P(R/S)—can be defined as the degree to which the proposition S *of itself* should rationally lead us to expect that R is true. Under the epistemic conception of probability, therefore, the statement that *the fine tuning of the cosmos is very improbable under the* [ASUH] is to be understood as making a statement about the degree to which the [ASUH] would or should, *of itself*, lead us to expect cosmic fine-tuning. [Collins 2007: 355; emphasis in original]

In other words, the relevant question is this: given *only* the information contained within the ASUH—that only one universe exists as an ultimate brute fact—and no other information at all (such as the fact that we *are* alive, and so the universe must be life-friendly), to what degree should we rationally expect the basic constants of the universe to be finely tuned?

Collins answers that the rational expectation of fine tuning given only the ASUH is much lower than it would be given theism. He imagines a disembodied being who is highly intelligent and thoroughly familiar with the laws of physics as known today, but who does not know whether the actual values of the physical constants are such as to allow complex embodied life (CEL). Collins says that such a being would have a much greater rational expectation that those constants would fall within the range permitting CEL given theism than given the ASUH:

it is not difficult to see that the conditional epistemic probability of a constant of physics having a CEL-permitting value under the [ASUH] will be much smaller than under theism. The reason is simple when we think about our imaginary disembodied being. If such a being were a theist, it would have some reason to believe that the values of constants would fall into the CEL-permitting region...On the other hand, if the being were a subscriber to the [ASUH], it would have no reason to think the value would be in the CEL-permitting region instead of any other part of the 'theoretically possible' region *R*. Thus, the being has more reason to believe the constants would fall into the CEL-permitting region under theism than the [ASUH], or put differently, the existence of a CEL-permitting universe is more surprising under the [ASUH] than theism. [Collins 2007: 356]

In short, the finely-tuned features of the universe are more probable (rationally expected) given theism than given the ASUH, so, the PPC tells us that the existence of those features counts much more strongly in favour of the hypothesis of theism than the ASUH.

FINE TUNING: THE ATHEIST CRITIQUE

I turn now to the critique of the FTA by analytic atheists. Collins's chief disagreement with the proponents of the ASUH will be over whether we can have rational expectations about ultimate metaphysical posits. The ASUH posits the primordial condition of the universe, encompassing the universe's initial state and its physical laws, as ultimate brute facts. To posit something as an ultimate brute fact is to say, *inter alia*, that it is not caused by, derived from, reducible to, composed of, conditioned by, an epiphenomenon of, or supervenient upon anything else. In other words, an ultimate brute fact is a sheer given: a basic or primordial reality that is not in any sense dependent upon or explicable in terms of any antecedent or more fundamental reality.

In our ordinary assessments of epistemic probability, we base our expectations on a body of empirical or theoretical information that we take as background knowledge. For instance, we expect a tossed coin to turn up heads about fifty per cent of the time given that it is a fair coin. We think that there is a 40 per cent chance of rain tomorrow given a body of meteorological knowledge. Ultimately, we base our rational expectations about physical phenomena upon our knowledge of the laws of physics. But against what background are we supposed to judge, as Collins would have us do, that the laws of physics *themselves* are highly unexpected? As Robin Le Poidevin pointedly asks, against what possible background could we judge, say, that it was extremely improbable that the charge on the electron would be 1.602×10^{-19} coulomb (Le Poidevin 1996: 49–50)? The laws of physics cannot constitute the background since they will either be irrelevant to the charge on the proton or will entail precisely the charge it has.

As defenders of the ASUH see it, rational expectations must have a rational basis— that is, some information of a theoretical or empirical nature to provide grounds for the expectation. Yet, when we are talking about ultimate posits, then, *ex hypothesi*, all such information has been withheld. We are asked to make a probability assessment that is purely unconditioned and a priori. In that case, as the proponent of the ASUH sees it, the only *rational* expectation of the values of the constants is that they will be whatever we find them to be. In other words, the only universe we have a right to expect is the one we actually have.

Collins, however, does think that there can be a rational basis for an expectation of the values of the constants given ASUH. He appeals to the *principle of indifference*, which he characterizes as follows:

> Applied to the case at hand, the principle of indifference could be roughly stated as follows: *when we have no reason to prefer any one value of a parameter over other* [sic], *we should assign equal probabilities to equal ranges of the parameter given that the parameter in question directly corresponds to some physical magnitude.* [Collins 2003: 129; emphasis in original]

He next shows how this principle would apply in forming our rational expectation about the value of the gravitational constant:

> Specifically, if the 'theoretically possible' range (that is, the range allowed by the relevant background theories) of such a parameter is R and the life-permitting range is r, then the probability is r/R. Suppose, for instance, that the "theoretically possible" range, *R*, of values for the strength of gravity is zero to the strength of the strong nuclear force between those protons—that is, 0 to $10^{40}G_0$, where G_0 represents the current value for the strength of gravity. As we saw above, the life-permitting range

for the strength of gravity is at most to $10^9 G_0$... Thus, assuming the strength of the forces constitute a real physical magnitude, the principle of indifference would state that the equal ranges of this force should be given equal probabilities, and hence the probability of it the [sic] strength of gravity falling into the life-permitting region would be at most $r/R = 10^9/10^{40} = 1/10^{31}$. [Collins 2003: 129]

It appears, then, that if we accept the principle of indifference, and given only the ASUH, our rational expectation that the values of the gravitational constant would fall within the CEL-permitting region would be only about one in 10^{31}, a very small expectation indeed.

Many objections could be raised against Collins's invocation of the principle of indifference. For one thing, it is hard to see what Collins means by the 'theoretically possible' range R of the constant values. What are the relevant background theories when we are talking about possible worlds and ultimate metaphysical posits? Why wouldn't the 'theoretically possible' values be from zero to infinity? If, on the other hand, Collins wants to define a finite upper limit, R, then, as Graham Oppy notes, it is hard to see what, other than axe-grinding, would determine the choice of R:

> If, on the other hand, we suppose, for example, that the various force strengths can fall anywhere in the interval [0, R] where R is an upper limit to the possible force strengths to which it is legitimate to appeal for the purposes of the 'cosmic fine-tuning' argument for design, then we face the apparently intractable problem of justifying the choice of R. Are we to suppose that there is some value R, such that it is *impossible* for the force strengths to exceed that value? (What reason is there to suppose that there is any such value?) If not, what grounds could we possibly have for ignoring all of the possible worlds in which the value of the force strength is greater than R when we compute the probability that the value of a given parameter falls within the life-permitting range? After all, if a proponent of the 'cosmic fine-tuning' argument is free to choose a value of R that suits the purposes of proponents of the argument, why shouldn't an opponent of the 'cosmic fine-tuning' argument be free to insist on a value of R that suits the purposes of opponents of the argument? [Oppy 2006: 206; emphasis in original]

Unquestionably, there are contexts where, when properly restricted, the principle of indifference is useful in solving certain problems and performing certain calculations of probability (see e.g. Applebaum, 1996: 52–3). The crucial question is not whether that principle is ever useful, but whether it can do the metaphysical heavy lifting that Collins wants it to do. Clearly, it is quite a leap to think that a principle useful in certain rather modest and restricted contexts can justify rational expectations about which ranges of possible worlds are likely to actualized.

Can we have rational expectations about ultimate metaphysical posits? It may help to note that the defenders of the ASUH have one thing in common with theists—each group posits something as a brute, inexplicable, metaphysical ultimate. For ASUH supporters, it is the primordial state and laws of the universe; for theists it is God. John Hick states this point clearly:

> It is true that no naturalistic theory can account for the *existence* of the universe, or for its having the basic character that it has; this simply has to be accepted as the ultimate inexplicable fact. But religion also has its ultimate inexplicable fact in the form of God or a non-personal Absolute. And the skeptical mind prefers to rest in the mystery of the visible world without going beyond it to a further invisible mystery. [Hick 2004: 111]

Further, it seems that in either the naturalistic or the theistic case we can imagine possible worlds in which things are different. We can imagine possible worlds in which the values of the fundamental physical constants are other than they are in the actual world. Likewise, we seem to be able to imagine possible worlds in which something other than the theistic God would be the ultimate, uncaused, brute supernatural reality. Indeed, it seems that there could have been (i.e. there seem to be possible worlds in which) one or more of an indefinitely numerous set of supernatural entities could be the ultimate existent(s) instead of the theistic God. Maybe, for instance, there could have been Platonic ideas, or a Neoplatonic One, or a non-personal Absolute, or a being that preferred to be alone, or, tragically, a lonely god who yearns for companionship, but does not have the power to create.

If it *is* possible to have rational expectations about which of a range of possible worlds is likely to be actualized, where do we stop? If someone insists that we are very, very lucky—impossibly lucky—to have a universe as 'life friendly' as the one we inhabit, and therefore there must have been a supernatural fine-tuner to set things up, don't we have to ask why that same reasoning should not apply to putative supernatural beings? Why is it, that of all the ultimate, uncaused supernatural beings that might have existed, we were so impossibly lucky as to get one that was a personal being who, amazingly, just happened to want creatures like us and also had the power to do the fine tuning? Instead of solving the fine-tuning problem, doesn't the hypothesis of theism merely set it back a step? Instead of a finely tuned universe we seem to need a finely tuned God. If the former is wildly unlikely, then why not the latter? If the universe is rationally unexpected, then why not God?

Theistic philosophers have historically recognized the force of such queries and have attempted to obviate them by countering that the theistic God is in some sense uniquely ultimate so that his existence is not a metaphysical mystery in the sense that any other postulated ultimate would be. Some have postulated that God is logically necessary or is the only being that is its own sufficient reason. Some, like Richard Swinburne (1979) argue that the hypothesis that posits God as the ultimate inexplicable existent is a simpler hypothesis than any other, and therefore more a priori likely. Each such suggestion has very serious problems that we do not have space to pursue here (but see Mackie 1982; Parsons 1989; Oppy 2006).

Oppy offers further critiques of the FTA (Oppy 2006: 202–28). He distinguishes a number of versions of the argument and Collins's version is what Oppy calls a 'likelihood' argument (Oppy 2006: 203). That is, by his invocation of the prime principle of confirmation, Collins argues that the evidence of fine tuning confirms theism over the ASUH because the fine tuning evidence is much more likely given theism than given the

ASUH. Yet in determining the acceptability of hypotheses, likelihoods are only part of the story. It might well be that hypothesis H_1 is far more probable given evidence e_1 than hypothesis H_2, but we still regard H_2 as far more probable than H_1. Why? Because probabilities must be decided with respect to the *total* evidence, and, while H_1 may be more expected given e_1 than is H_2, we might have other pieces of evidence, e_2, e_3, e_4, ... e_n, that collectively strongly favour H_2 over H_1.

The upshot is that a likelihood argument, at most, can only achieve limited results—showing how probable a hypothesis is given *some* of the evidence. Oppy doubts that the FTA can achieve even such a modest success. He asks us to consider the kind of designer that is postulated by the FTA:

> Given only the hypothesis that there is an intelligent designer of the universe—and given no further assumptions about the *preferences* of that designer—it is not clear to me that there is very much that one can conclude about the kind of universe that the designer is likely to produce. [Oppy 2006: 207]

Those who invoke intelligent designers are often quite coy about the specific nature of the putative designer. Given only that the universe had *some* sort of intelligent designer, and given that we do not know what the aims or abilities of such a designer might have been, we cannot conclude that the finely tuned features of the universe are very much expected given the hypothesis of such a generic designer. On the other hand, if, like Collins, we specifically invoke the *theistic* God (the God worshipped by Christians, Muslims, and Jews), then we have to face some difficult questions about evidence that appears to disconfirm that hypothesis. For instance, some atheists have argued that God's existence is very unlikely given the abundance of apparently superfluous evil in the universe (Parsons 1989). Others have argued that God's existence is highly improbable given the persistence of unbelief or considering the 'hiddenness' of God (Drange 1998; Schellenberg 1993). Indeed, sceptics have made many claims which, if true, could be adduced as evidence against the God hypothesis: that intelligence and consciousness seem to be functions of neurological machinery; that all alleged holy scriptures contain absurdities, contradictions, and morally opprobrious teachings; and that biology and social construction seem sufficient to account for the existence of theistic belief. The upshot is that God's existence might be far more probable than naturalism given only the fine-tuning evidence, but less probable overall, i.e. given all the evidence we have.

What about Craig's argument that the finely tuned features of the universe are not due to necessity or chance, and therefore must be the product of design? This argument can work only if we have a reliable means of eliminating the possibility that the values of the constants were due to chance. In general, how do we tell whether some state of affairs is due to chance or design? William Dembski proposes a procedure that he calls an 'explanatory filter' for determining whether something is due to Regularity (e.g. a law of nature), Chance, or Design (Dembski 1998). Craig specifically connects his version of the FTA to Dembski's 'filter' (Craig 2003). However, Oppy carefully examines Dembski's 'filter' and shows that it suffers from extensive vagueness and ambiguity (Oppy 2006: 211–13). He concludes:

In sum, it seems to me that there are many good reasons to deny that Dembski's 'explanatory filter' provides an infallible template for inferences to design. Apart from the various points of detail that have been mentioned above... the most important problem to note is that there is no reason at all to suppose that one can rule out all of the hypotheses that belong to Regularity or Chance without ever pausing to compare them with the hypotheses belonging to Design. Before we begin, we know that, for any observation E, we can frame design hypotheses that have greater *likelihood* than any chance hypotheses, given this observation or evidence. But it may nonetheless be the case that, on this observation or evidence, there is no design hypothesis that has greater *probability* than any of a number of chance hypotheses. [Oppy 2006: 213]

Oppy has put his finger on a crucial feature of design hypotheses: it is easy—far too easy, sceptics think—to tailor a design hypothesis to fit any set of data so that such data will be highly likely given that hypothesis. From the hypothesis that an all-powerful being wants x, we are 100 per cent sure to get x. Given that God wanted turtles, we were sure to get turtles. By contrast, evolution by natural selection cannot guarantee turtles; far from it. Indeed, many evolutionists say that the chance that evolution would have generated any particular kind of creature is very small. Start the world over again and run evolutionary history over again, and the chances are very small that we would get turtles—or you and me (see Gould 1989). So is special creation (which is a kind of design hypothesis) a more reasonable explanation for the existence of turtles than evolution? Not if you think that special creation is strongly disconfirmed vis-à-vis evolution by the total evidence and background knowledge, i.e. by everything else we know. And so, it seems, with all design hypotheses. Critics like Oppy may concede that certain phenomena are more likely given design, but hold that the proponents of design theories have not shown that their hypotheses are overall more probable than competing hypotheses that appeal to law or chance.

Conclusion: Old Wine in New Wineskins

We have looked at some length at a very revealing case study—arguments by analytic philosophers over the FTA, a new version of an ancient sort of argument. The claim that the natural world bears evidence of design goes back at least to Plato. It has always been a salient claim of natural theologians. Now analytic theists have produced the FTA, a very sophisticated argument that draws upon high-powered philosophical tools of great subtlety and rigour. Therefore, one goal of analytic theists, to produce arguments that are clear, precise, scientifically informed, and logically stringent, has been successfully achieved. These arguments are impressive pieces of philosophy, and their proponents are clearly outstanding philosophers.

Yet, have the analytic theists attained their deeper goal, to make the arguments of natural theology more cogent, persuasive, and impervious to sceptical attack? Has putting the old wine of natural theology into the new wineskins of analytic philosophy really strengthened the theist's case? Here the verdict is much less clear. The sceptics appear just as capable of deploying sophisticated, scientifically informed, and logically rigorous counter-arguments. In the end, analytic philosophy, for all of its vaunted rigour and logical stringency, may have succeeded only in making it clearer just where theists and atheists diverge.

They diverge where they always have. The core of their disagreement does not lie in the details of probability calculations or the subtleties of modal logic. It lies in a fundamental difference between two types of human being and two ways of experiencing the world. One sort of person says with St Augustine, 'Our hearts are restless until they rest in thee, O Lord.' For such persons, the order, beauty, and contingency of the natural world cry out for explanation in terms of the choices and acts of a personal being. The other sort of person says with the physicist Laplace, when Napoleon asked him where God entered his theory, 'Sire, I have no need of that hypothesis.' Perhaps more insight into the unbeliever's view lies in the saying attributed to the Russian physicist Yakov Zel'dovich: 'The atheist pays God the compliment of saying that the universe is so perfect that it does not need a creator.'

The conclusion of our case study seems to be that natural theology, if construed as a project intended to persuade (or at least intimidate) unbelievers by the sheer force of evidence and logic, has failed and will continue to fail. Whatever accounts for the fundamental divide between believers and unbelievers, it does not appear to be that one side is reasonable and the other not. Both sides are capable of deploying arguments of great rigour and sophistication. Each can cite evidence that seems to tilt the argument in its favour. Yet logic did not cause this divergence between human beings, and, even when wielded by analytic philosophers, is far too weak a tool to bridge this divide. Perhaps it is wisest to follow John Hick in his masterful *An Interpretation of Religion* (2004) and concede that both theism and naturalism are rational options, and that there are no logical or evidential resources whereby one can compel the submission of the other.

However, natural theology need not be viewed as a sort of logical bludgeon. Perhaps a less aggressive natural theology could have the aim merely of defending theistic belief from the attacks of unbelievers, like those issuing from the group of truculent 'new atheists'. Perhaps natural theology could function mainly to provide rational support for those who already believe. There is no reason why such a 'kinder and gentler' natural theology cannot flourish for the foreseeable future.

REFERENCES

Applebaum, D. (1996). *Probability and Information: An Integrated Approach*. Cambridge: Cambridge University Press.

Collins, R. (2003). 'God, Design, and Fine-Tuning' in *God Matters: Readings in the Philosophy of Religion*. Edited by R. Martin and C. Bernard. New York: Longman.

—— (2007). 'The Teleological Argument' in *The Routledge Companion to the Philosophy of Religion*. Edited by C. Meister and P. Copan. London: Routledge.

Craig, W. L. (2003). 'A Reply to Objections' in *Does God Exist: The Craig–Flew Debate*. Edited by S. W. Wallace. Burlington, VT: Ashgate.

—— (2007). 'Theistic Critiques of Atheism' in *The Cambridge Companion to Atheism*. Edited by M. Martin. Cambridge: Cambridge University Press.

Dembski, W. (1998). *The Design Inference: Eliminating Chance through Small Probabilities*. Cambridge: Cambridge University Press.

Drange, T. M. (1998). *Evil and Nonbelief: Two Arguments against the Existence of God*. Amherst, NY: Prometheus Books.

Flew, A. (1955). 'Theology and Falsification' in *New Essays in Philosophical Theology*. Edited by A. Flew and A. MacIntyre. New York: Macmillan.

Gould, S. J. (1989). *Wonderful Life: The Burgess Shale and the Nature of History*. New York: Norton.

Hick, J. (2004). *An Interpretation of Religion: Human Responses to the Transcendent*. 2nd edn. New Haven: Yale University Press.

Le Poidevin, R. (1996). *Arguing for Atheism: An Introduction to the Philosophy of Religion*. London: Routledge.

Mackie, J. L. (1982). *The Miracle of Theism: Arguments for and Against the Existence of God*. Oxford: Clarendon Press.

Oppy, G. (2006). *Arguing about Gods*. Cambridge: Cambridge University Press.

Parsons, K. M. (1989). *God and the Burden of Proof: Plantinga, Swinburne, and the Analytic Defense of Theism*. Buffalo: Prometheus Books.

—— (1990). 'Is there a Case for Christian Theism? in J. P. Moreland and K. Nielsen, *Does God Exist?* Nashville: Thomas Nelson.

Plantinga, A. (1974). *The Nature of Necessity*. Oxford: Clarendon Press.

Schellenberg, J. L. (1993). *Divine Hiddenness and Human Reason*. Ithaca, NY: Cornell University Press.

Swinburne, R. (1979). *The Existence of God*. Oxford: Clarendon Press.

CHAPTER 16

A PERSPECTIVE ON NATURAL THEOLOGY FROM CONTINENTAL PHILOSOPHY

RUSSELL RE MANNING

CONTINENTAL philosophy is perhaps best defined as a style of philosophical thought associated with developments in modern, that is to say post-Kantian, philosophy that emphasize the interpretation of experience over against the analysis of language, characteristic of so-called analytical philosophy. Whilst rooted in the various nineteenth-century reactions to the Kantian restriction of philosophy to *critique*, the continental tradition as such is generally identified with those twentieth-century philosophical developments that do not form part of the analytical school's distinctive embrace of the linguistic turn and consequent limitation of the philosophical task to logical and conceptual analysis. Predominantly German, French, and American, continental philosophy is standardly agreed to include such broad philosophical movements as phenomenology, existentialism, hermeneutics, critical theory, post-structuralism, postmodernism, and, the newest arrival, so-called 'speculative realism'.

THE TURN TO RELIGION AND THE AVOIDANCE OF NATURAL THEOLOGY IN CONTINENTAL PHILOSOPHY

One helpful way of characterizing continental philosophy is to describe it as a tradition of thought responding to the Kantian prioritizing of the transcendental subject as an autonomous self-positing agent (Goodchild 2002). In contrast to Kant's naive confidence in the capacity of the transcendental subject to reason free from imposed conditions, on the basis of pure, natural, human *ratio*, limited only by itself, the central thinkers of the continental tradition insist upon the external limitations upon thought. Thus, unlike the analytical tradition, continental thinkers prioritize *synthesis* over *analysis*, and seek to avoid the arrogation of a particular set of philosophical assumptions to an alleged universality. Already with Hegel, self-consciousness was located within the temporal flow of history, inseparably bound up with—and unavoidably determined by—its historicalness. In the lines of thought that trace through continental post-Kantian developments, a series of similar locations are identified and foregrounded, including nature, language, tradition, culture, and gender. More recently, religion itself has been added to this list. Thus, 'continental philosophy of religion'—unlike its analytical counterpart—is predominantly interested in what Goodchild identifies as 'the "outer" components of religion—its traditions, worship, liturgy, narratives, and practices' (Goodchild 2002: 15). One of the results of this is that whereas analytical philosophy of religion has been (and remains) predominantly concerned with topics within traditional natural theology (most centrally, of course, the question of the capacity of the unaided human mind to find out truths about God), continental philosophy of religion is occupied with the particularities of religion itself, thus presenting something of a block to any interest in natural theology within continental philosophy.

A further barrier to an engagement with natural theology from the perspective of continental philosophy is to be found in the particular style of thinking that the tradition adopts. Whereas the analytical tradition primarily apes the methods, concerns, and specialisms of the natural sciences, the continental strand tends to a closer engagement with the arts and humanities, to the extent that it is often difficult to characterize many writings in continental philosophy as specifically philosophical, as opposed to literary; a tendency that routinely provokes accusations of a lack of rigour and clarity from the analytics (Trakakis 2007). More particularly, in spite of many recent efforts to develop so-called 'continental philosophy of religion', the departmentalized disciplinary segmentation so beloved of analytics is very hard to impose upon continental philosophy. Hence, it can be difficult to separate out those elements of continental philosophy that engage issues in natural theology from those elements that engage political and aesthetic concerns. This is not necessarily because continentals are any more systematic than their analytical colleagues; more often it is grounded in the characteristic indirection of continental philosophy that precisely aims to undermine the straight linear pretensions of the modern Kantian project of pure reason.

Nonetheless, notwithstanding these justified cautions, it is clear that continental thought is vitally marked by an engagement with issues that are essential to natural theology, albeit more ambiguously than its analytical counterpart. The pervasiveness of theological concerns within continental philosophy both justifies and complicates an account of the perspectives on natural theology from the continental tradition. On the one hand, the central features of natural theology, as normally conceived, seem to be strikingly absent from the writings of continental philosophers. There is, for instance, very little in the way of consideration of the canonical arguments for the existence of God, nor is there much sustained engagement with claims for or against the ability of the natural sciences to disclose the divine. Indeed, if anything, the continental philosophers seem to share with their continental theological colleagues an insistence upon an either/or assessment of the relation between philosophy and theology: either a secular philosophy concerned with the interpretation of human experience or a positive theology occupied with the specifics (or *positum*) of a particular religious tradition. Just as Karl Barth's 'Nein!' set the scene for the relative neglect of natural theology amongst continental theologians, so too Martin Heidegger's call for the separation of phenomenology from theology it seems has set the agenda of the continental philosophers' reluctance to engage, explicitly at least, in philosophical natural theology. Perhaps the most striking example of this philosophical *laïcité* is the recent anxiety over the so-called 'religious turn' within French phenomenology, in particular in the form of the avowedly theological phenomenology of Jean-Luc Marion. However, as so often with continental philosophy, all is not as it seems on the surface. Notwithstanding the 'official' separation of philosophy and theology, continental thinkers are deeply concerned with and engaged in fundamental issues in natural theology. The preoccupations of continental philosophy are those of natural theology: questions of order, intelligibility, and dependence; of sovereignty, ultimacy, and unconditionality; of alterity and moral imperative; of anxiety and hope; and of the paradoxes and ambiguities of a rational mysteriousness at the centre of human life and experience. True, the continental tradition has no place for the highly technical arguments of analytical perfect-being natural theology, but its leading figures—from Husserl and Heidegger, Jaspers and Sartre, Arendt and Adorno, Gadamer and Habermas, Foucault and Derrida, Ricoeur and Levinas, Deleuze and Badiou, Kristeva and Irigaray, Nancy and Marion, Caputo and Taylor, through to Meillassoux and Žižek—have all contributed to the development of a distinctive and provocative perspective on natural theology.

In what follows, I am not, however, primarily interested in what these philosophers themselves have to say about natural theology—they say very little explicitly on the subject but are far more interested in religion. Instead I will set out a distinctive perspective on natural theology that is informed by a more synthetic account of the general tendencies of continental philosophy. I will take my lead from a perhaps unexpected source to consider a continental perspective on natural theology via what the American sociologist Peter Berger calls 'signals of transcendence'. Whilst not presented explicitly as a work in natural theology, in his suggestive 1969 book *A Rumour of Angels* Berger identifies five aspects of human experience that move, as he puts it, 'inductive faith' to make statements about God. Berger's list, which he acknowledges is personal and open to further supplementation, names the following five natural phenomena as open to pointing beyond themselves to a suggestion of transcendence: order, play, hope, damnation, and humour. For Berger, attention to these signals of transcendence, understood as 'prototypical human gestures' proper to 'ordinary everyday awareness' (Berger 1969: 70) enables the rediscovery of the supernatural as a possibility for theological thought capable of 'overcoming the triviality' (119) of a situation marked by a divisive either/or of the secular vs the religious. In this chapter, I aim to follow Berger and to present an account of an alternative perspective on natural theology from continental philosophy as a discourse for those, in George Steiner's terms 'who lack or reject any formal creed' (Steiner 1989: 218).

NATURAL THEOLOGY AND PISTIC THEOLOGY

The first essential move in this discussion of natural theology from the perspective of continental philosophy is definitively to reject the definition of natural theology that has become normative within analytical philosophy with its determinative contrast between natural and revealed. To define natural theology with William Lane Craig and J. P. Moreland as 'that branch of theology that seeks to provide warrant for God's existence apart from the resources of authoritative propositional revelation' (Craig and Moreland 2009: ix) is immediately to adopt and endorse a perspective that is radically alien to continental philosophy. Far from drawing a confident distinction between autonomous human reason (the domain of natural theology) and heteronomously imposed revelation, the continental tradition instead emphasizes the porousness of this central binary opposition, the acceptance of which has been so characteristic of the progress of religion in modernity. In their admittedly very different ways, continental philosophers from Hegel to Derrida (with Nietzsche, Husserl, and Heidegger as crucial intermediaries) have affirmed the unavoidable interdependence of the natural and the revealed. Radicalizing the Kantian insight into the *aporia* of the rationalist/empiricist either/or, Husserl's phenomenological procedure of *epoche*, for example, far from the ideal of scientific detachment so beloved of the analytics, brings the interpenetration of nature and revelation to the very centre of the philosophical enterprise itself. To characterize phenomenology as a 'response to the given' that remains open to all intuitions is to mark a move beyond the static polarity of nature and revelation as two alternative sources of order and is to affirm instead the radical indeterminacy of subjective experience—of the subject as neither a fully self-determined agency nor a merely passive recipient. In short, from a continental perspective the lazy contrast between natural and revealed theology simply cannot stand.

In the place of the failed opposition between natural and revealed theology, by taking a perspective on natural theology from continental philosophy an alternative contrast presents itself; namely between natural and faithful, or *pistic*, theologies. The guiding thought here is that what natural theology lacks is not so much revelation but faith. From a continental perspective, then, natural theology is not so much a human theology (of the 'bottom-up' kind so derided by its Barthian critics), but a faithless theology. It is, to put it another way, the theology of disappointment; the theology that has thrown off all religious (and secular) certainties in disgust. For such a natural theology, recalling the earliest explorations in natural theology in ancient Greece, God has become 'a problem for thought' (Jaeger 1947: 4). It is important to stress that by setting up natural theology against pistic theology, I do not intend simply to reiterate the Kantian dichotomy between faith and reason of the Preface to the *Critique of Practical Reason*. Just as much as I wish to reject the analytical philosophical definition of natural theology as the attempt to prove the existence of God through the application of human reason alone, so too am I keen to avoid simply reframing natural theology as the sceptical naturalization of religion that generates the contemporary disciplines of the allegedly value-free scientific study of religion. Here the centrality of the important distinction between natural theology and natural religion becomes crucial. To talk of natural religion is to attempt to discern within the various positive religious traditions beliefs and practices that are universal, and hence natural. In effect, it is a reductionist and fundamentalist enterprise of excavating the 'essence of religion' from the surface detritus of human history and culture. Natural religion is thus ahistorical and acultural and aims at nothing other than the subjugation of unnatural religious traditions to its timeless abstractions (an ambition that still haunts even the most rigorously postmodern forms of comparative religious studies).

Understanding Seeking Faith

To talk instead of natural theology over against pistic theology is, to repeat, not to insist upon an 'Athens-and-Jerusalem' opposition between faith and reason, but is rather to reject another standardized definition of natural theology, namely that of the Anselmian position of '*fides quaerens intellectum*'. On this Anselmian view the false antipathy between nature and revelation is resisted in favour of a synthetic approach in which 'blind faith' is illuminated by the divinely inspired work of natural human reason. Of course, we must be careful to resist the distinctly un-Anselmian interpretations of his motto in much contemporary analytical natural theology by recognizing that Anselm hardly aims for clarity but rather a mystical vision of God. As he celebrates in his distinctly Platonic contemplative prayer:

> How far you are from me who have come so close to you.
> How remote you are from my sight,
> While I am thus present in your sight.
> Everywhere you are entirely present,
> And I cannot see you.
> In you I move and have my being,
> And I cannot come to you.
> You are within me and around me,
> And I have no experience of you. [*Proslogion* 540–8]

What is clear, however, is that Anselm's contemplative exercise in the *Proslogion* is as far from natural theology as is Karl Barth's *Church Dogmatics*. God's withdrawl to 'that light inaccessible' (*Proslogion* 524) of his majesty may be difficult for Anselm to understand, but it can hardly be thought of as a discovery of his natural theologizing. Instead, this approach is decisively marked by the incorporation of reason into faith. Anselm is explicit here—there is no way for him to come to God, indeed he cannot even have an experience of God. Instead, as a truly pistic theologian, it is by faith, not sight, that he proceeds.

To present natural theology as the theology of the faithless is, then, clearly to locate it otherwise than the Anselmian conception of faith seeking understanding. Indeed, there is a temptation to reverse the formula: natural theology as 'understanding seeking faith'. Such a reversal is almost right: it certainly captures the dynamism of such an interpretation of natural theology and yet it is far from clear that the direction of movement in such a natural theology is always or indeed primarily towards faith. Far from an enterprise that aims at the overcoming of doubt in the achievement of religious certainty, natural theology considered from the perspective of continental philosophy instead seems to be far more content to remain 'en route', always on the way but never arriving at its conclusion. Of course, as the example of Anselm makes clear, natural theology is hardly alone in its sense of its own incompleteness, but whereas pistic theology's caution stems from a conviction of the incomprehensible excess of the divine to finite fallen human minds, the natural theological iconoclasm against fulfilment is grounded in its radical reluctance wholly to accept any conception of ultimacy as final. It is this commitment-phobia that is most strikingly definitive of natural theology viewed from the perspective of continental philosophy, and we might venture, it is precisely this that makes the enterprise so alluring.

Importantly, of course, such *agnosia* applies equally to both religious and secular forms of faith and differs markedly from both genuine philosophical scepticism and the superficial agnosticism of indecision. Natural theology, as presented here, does not attempt to defeat faith any more than it seeks to bolster it. Natural theology is rather an 'unfaithing' theology; a theology that enacts a gesture of refusal against faith by taking nothing for granted, including the autonomous authority of reason itself. This *anomic* theology is at once then a theology of betrayal that perpetually thwarts its own ambitions and a theology of hope akin to a therapeutic turning towards the future from out of the disenchantment of the past.

Such a perspective on natural theology identifies it as primarily concerned with wagers on transcendence that embrace the uncertain mix of a faithlessness that refuses both the grounded security of acceptance and the ungrounded commitment of a pledged troth. Distanced from a faith in both the self-sufficiency of reason and the Kierkegaardian leap of absurdity, such a stance is constitutionally suspicious and distrustful of all forms of foundational theology, viewing the theological enterprise instead as a radically uncertain and yet unavoidable venture. It is this that Paul Tillich describes as 'absolute faith': the courage to be as rooted in the God above God, a state that Tillich describes as:

> On the boundary of man's possibilities. It *is* this boundary. Therefore, it is both the courage of despair and the courage in and above every courage. It is not a place where one can live; it is without the safety of words and concepts, it is without a name, a church, a cult, a theology. But it is moving in the depth of all of them.
> [Tillich 1952: 188–9]

In sum, if pistic theology can be defined as characterized by faith understood as a 'response to the call of an infinite demand' (Critchley 2012)—be that the revelation of an un-pre-thinkable God or the un-get-roundable requirements of reason—then natural theology can by contrast be defined as characterized by faithlessness understood as an invitation to respond to an infinite opportunity to venture beyond the given towards an unencompassable ultimacy.

HEIDEGGER'S REFUSAL OF A NATURAL THEOLOGICAL VOICE

It is no accident that the period of crisis following Germany's catastrophic defeat in the First World War continues to play such a central role in both continental philosophy and theology and it is to this period that we must look to locate the origins of the continental philosophical refusal of natural theology and its definitive embrace of theological pisticism. Theological analysis of the drawn-out crisis of the Weimar Republic and its collapse into the barbarism of the Third Reich has rightly emphasized Karl Barth's violent rejection of the legitimacy of any form of natural theology. However, less remarked upon is its philosophical parallel in Heidegger's 1927–8 lecture 'Phenomenology and Theology' (Caputo 2002).

Heidegger does not address the question of natural theology explicitly; his concern is to delineate respectively: (i) the positive character of theology; (ii) the scientific character of theology; and (iii) the relation of philosophy, as a positive science, to philosophy. Heidegger's discussion of theology (his 'final adieu' in Caputo's terms) is dominated by the notion of faith, which he specifies in its 'proper existentiell meaning' as rebirth, that is as:

> the mode of existence that specifies a factical Dasein's Christianness as a particular form of destiny. Faith is the believing-understanding mode of existing in the history revealed, i.e., occurring, with the Crucified. [53]

Theology, accordingly, is the positive science of faith, that is to say that theology is the historical, systematic, and practical cultivation of this 'believing-understanding mode of existing', or faithfulness (54–7). Whilst Heidegger denies that 'faithless science' can prove or disprove faith—nontheological science simply 'shatters against' faith—he nonetheless insists on the role of philosophy in discerning the pre-Christian fundamental ontology of Dasein. Here, for example, he claims that whilst 'sin' is 'manifest only in faith', 'guilt' is 'an original ontological determination of the existence of Dasein' (58). Thus Heidegger asserts the prior purity of a faithless philosophy; echoing Nietzsche's horror at the pollution of philosophy by 'the theologians' blood', he declares that 'faith, as a specific possibility of existence, is in its innermost core the mortal enemy of the *form of existence* that is an essential part of *philosophy*' (60).

The result is clear: the strict separation of Jerusalem from Athens, the faithful theology from the faithless philosophy, that makes sense of the simultaneous philosophical discomfort at the thought of a 'turn to religion' and fascination with its own religious other. But what of the possibility of a faithless theology? For all the apparently critical heretical approaches to religion in recent continental philosophy—for example Jean-Luc Nancy's attempts at the 'deconstruction of Christianity' and François Laruelle's 'non-Christianity' (Nancy 2008; Laruelle 2010)—a genuinely faithless theological alternative remains remarkably under-explored.

Political Theology

A good illustration of what such a natural theology conceived from the perspective of continental philosophy might look like in practice can be given by exploring the relation of such a natural theology to recent developments in one of the most hotly contested areas of contemporary continental philosophical engagements with religion, namely political theology. One of the more notable features of recent continental philosophical writings about religion has been the renewed interest in what Simon Critchley calls the 'triangulation' of religion, politics, and violence. From Agamben to Žižek (including Derrida and Habermas), continental philosophers are acutely engaged with a new situation for thinking, characterized primarily no longer by the theoretical ontological concerns about the occlusion of Being within a metaphysics of ontotheology, but rather with the practical political concerns about the possibility of living in a 'time of terror' (Borradori 2003). In response to the events of 9/11 and the subsequent 'war on terror', continental philosophers have turned their attention to religion and to the failures of the liberal project of secularization that promised to put an end to the history of violence in the triumph of democratic capitalism.

Unsurprisingly, continental philosophers have generally responded to the challenges of thinking in a situation marked by the resurgence of 'religiously justified violence [as] the means to a political end' (Critchley 2012: 8) by refusing the liberal modern either/or of secularism or theism, turning instead to explore the murky interrelations between the political and the theological, including igniting a striking revival of interest in Carl Schmitt's 1922 *Political Theology*, with its (in)famous thesis on sovereignty as enabled by and dependent upon the suspension of (natural) law in the decision for a state of exception. Whilst the political lessons that recent continental philosophers draw from Schmitt's analysis are widely divergent, they are united by a common acceptance of the underlying theo-logic of Schmitt's theory, namely that true/effective power relies upon an unnatural breakthrough of an external heteronomy. As such, political theology stands in antithesis to natural theology: political theology reveals the fideistic voluntarism of the various competing and fundamentally ungroundable 'decisions-for' that characterize the political economy. Once again it is faith that lies at the heart of the continental philosophical engagement with religion, such that the possibility of a natural theology is overlooked or dismissively identified with the pretentions of a discredited liberalism.

In contrast to the pistic political theologies of recent continental philosophies, a faithless natural theology would emphasize images of transparency and continuity, in which the weakness of non-coercive non-manipulative communication (Habermas) provides an antidote to the excess of faith that provokes and sustains violent sovereignty and the equally violent reactions to it. To a certain extent there are clear continuities here with the post-secular critiques of the failed modern secularization project, but with the radicalized insistence that the secular itself undergo a process of secularization, in which the liberal faith in the secular is disenchanted. From the perspective of natural theology, the post-secular that emerges is thus far from the triumph of a religious alterative, but a genuinely post-pistic situation in which the political possibilities of natural theology become apparent. By obviating the exceptionalist prerequisites for political authority, such a natural theology offers an alternative vision of a theonomous consensus, transparent to the ultimate reality that truly, albeit abysmally, grounds finite human sovereignty.

Natural Theology and the Miracle of the Ethical

Moving from the political to the ethical, a similar perspective can be opened up on natural theology as heir to the Platonic defence of theonomous morality. In the face of the collapse of the Kantian ethics of universal autonomous submission to the moral law (Arendt 1963) and the lingering distaste for the calculative (shop keepers') utilitarianism that dominates the analytical tradition, continental philosophers have turned once again to religio-theological sources of ethics. One influential option has been Heidegger's effective refusal of an ethical role for philosophy, endorsing a Kierkegaardian suspension of the ethical in favour of the religious: after all, only a God can save us now. However, even those within continental philosophy who have been most concerned to articulate—and enact—a post-Kantian philosophical morality have inextricably been drawn to the idea of faith. For Levinas, for example, the unconditional demand of the face of the other provokes, by means of a minor 'miracle', the 'overthrowing of the natural order':

> Ethics is ... *against nature* because it forbids the murderousness of my natural will to put my own existence first ... [T]he face ... calls for an ethical conversion or reversal of my nature. [Levinas 1984: 60–1]

As Badiou exposes, Levinas's ethics thus depends on an 'ideal of holiness contrary to the laws of being' (Levinas 1998: 114) that in effect equates to a voluntarily accepted 'law of founding alterity' (Badiou 1993: 20). In keeping with the voluntaristic tendency of continental philosophy's wider investment in pistic theology, the result here is that Levinas's ethics depends on an arbitrary 'decision-for' that makes him unequivocally a citizen of Jerusalem and not Athens:

> In truth, there is no philosophy of Levinas. It is no longer even a philosophy 'servant' to theology: it is a philosophy (in the Greek sense of the word) *annulled* by theology,

which moreover is not a theo-logy (a nomination still too Greek, and which supposes an approach to the divine by way of the identity and predicates of God), but, precisely, an ethics... Taken out of its Greek usage (where ethics is clearly subordinated to the theoretical), and taken in general, Levinas's ethics is a category of pious discourse. [Badiou 1993: 22–3]

Similarly the notion of faith is determinative for Deleuze's ethical invocation of a Spinozan-Leibnizian ethics of the immanence of life. In effect calling for an inverted anti-natural theology, Deleuze insists on the need for faith to restore 'our belief in the world' against what he diagnoses as an intolerable loss of faith. He writes:

Whether we are Christians or atheists, in our universal schizophrenia, we need reasons to believe in this world. It is a whole transformation of belief. It was already a good turning-point in philosophy, from Pascal to Nietzsche: to replace the model of knowledge with belief. But belief replaces knowledge only when it becomes belief in this world, as it is. [Deleuze 1989: 172]

Two things stand out in this quotation that set a perspective on natural theology into sharp relief. First, Deleuze's reference to Pascal and Nietzsche (he might equally have referred to Kierkegaard and Heidegger) places his ethics squarely within the voluntarist horn of the Euthyphro dilemma, in which the moral force of a conviction is wholly determined by the power of the free agency of the individual, a position fundamentally at odds with a natural theology that seeks to discern a *telos* or lure within the 'order of things' capable of motivating human behaviour without the need for an arbitrary decision-for. Secondly, the reductionist naturalism of Deleuze's belief in this world 'as it is' starkly opposes the very basis of natural theology. Of course, Deleuze is a long way from scientific naturalists, such as Dawkins and Dennett, but it is unsurprising that his immanentism leads to a pious naturalism in complete contradistinction from the heretical naturalism of a natural theology that rejects both the neo-Darwinian faith in blind evolution and the religious credence in the possibility of divine intervention (dismissively characterized by Robert Boyle as God's 'after-games'). For the natural theologian it is precisely the insufficiency of the world 'as it is' that the turn to nature and life demonstrates and that in turn enables an ethical orientation towards others without the submission to an autocratic Other, be that God or Nature. It is in this sense, paradoxically, that such a natural theology is both without nature and without God (Albertson and King 2009; Meillassoux 2008).

Natural Theology without Religion and after God

In what remains of this chapter, I want to turn to a perspective on natural theology informed by the work of two influential American continental philosopher/theologians, John D. Caputo and Mark C. Taylor. The thought of both Caputo and Taylor has been decisively formed by continental philosophy, notably Derrida's postmodern deconstructionism, but both perhaps have enough of a lingering influence of the Anglo-American analytical style of philosophy of religion that their 'continental philosophies of religion' are more concerned to advance theoretical reflection on the existence and nature of God (albeit in very non-traditional ways) than the general engagement within continental philosophy of religion with the external phenomena of religion. As such, both are less quick to give up the ambition of classical natural theology towards a metaphysics of ultimacy, even whilst they firmly reject pre-Heideggerian metaphysics and celebrate its 'end'. Caputo, for instance, insists that 'we on the continental side of [the] divine have sworn off' traditional philosophy of religion and instead have 'taken our stand with the equally traditional objection to the ontotheological tradition, voiced in a prophetic counter-tradition that stretches from Paul to Pascal to Luther, and from Kierkegaard to the present, with honorary headquarters in a Jerusalem that is constitutionally wary of visitors from Athens' (Caputo 2002: 2). However, whilst there can be no doubting the sincerity of Caputo's foreswearing of analytical natural theology and his desire to ensure a decent burial for the 'God of the philosophers', his constructive work 'after the death of God' can legitimately be characterized as a continental natural 'theology of the event' that 'keeps its ear close to the heart of the pulse or pulsations of the divine in things' (Caputo and Vattimo 2009: 49).

Like Taylor, who notes in his 2007 *After God* that he has 'never left the study of religion behind but ha[s] always attempted to expand its scope and significance' (xiv) Caputo is most passionately opposed to the 'great monsters' and 'large overarching theories that would catch [events] in their sweep, organize them, make them march in step to some metaphysical tune or other, right or left, theistic or atheistic, idealist or materialist, realist or anti-realist' (2009: 48–9). For Taylor:

> The most pressing dangers we face result from the conflict of competing absolutisms that divide the world between oppositions that can never be mediated... In a world where to be is to be connected, absolutism must give way to relationalism, in which everything is codependent and coevolves. After God, the divine is not elsewhere but is the emergent creativity that figures, disfigures and refigures the infinite fabric of life. [Taylor 2007: xvii–xviii]

Neither Caputo nor Taylor explicitly invoke natural theology as descriptive of their enterprises; indeed both are pretty scathing about what they take natural theology to be in its traditional forms. However, in their quests for the interstitial thinking of the divine after God and of religion without religion both are clearly closer to the antipistic kind of natural theological thinking that is emerging in this chapter. Both invoke images of the 'desert' of theology, loosed from the certainties and particularities of faith, and the riskiness of the forever erring attempt to venture after the God who comes after. This is Caputo's *amor venturi* (51) and Taylor's 'unfigurable edge' (347) in which both theism and atheism, transcendence and immanence, naturalism and supranaturalism meet in the paradoxical and rationally mystical concept of 'natural theology'.

THE MYSTICAL ANARCHISM
OF NATURAL THEOLOGY

Importantly, such a natural theology is not simply a responsive accommodating correlationist theology that allows a particular philosophical authority to take up a normative status for theology. Applying an updated version of Michael Buckley's thesis about early modern natural theology, Graham Ward berates Taylor (amongst others) for simply allowing postmodernism to become 'the anti-metaphysical philosophy theology can found itself upon' (Ward 1997: xlii); in effect identifying theirs as simply the latest iteration of the God of the philosophers. Whilst such a charge can indeed be levelled at contemporary analytical philosophical natural theology and recent liberal natural theologies of scientifically mediated religious experience, the accusation seems misplaced when directed at a continental philosophical natural theology that is definitively marked by a denial of faith and an absence of religious experience. Indeed, rather than equating such an approach with the God of the philosophers, a better parallel would seem to be with the mystical theologies of detachment (*Abschiedenheit*) and withdrawl. As Denys Turner emphasizes, such rational mysticism is the polar opposite of experientialist models of religious thought (Turner 1998). The mystic, like the continental natural theologian, precisely does not have a religious experience and leaves behind 'representational' responses to a divine presence in his (or frequently her) ambition of achieving a union with the God who is 'nothing'. Such mysticism, what Critchley identifies as 'mystical anarchism', depends precisely on the distancing characteristic of a natural theology that iconoclastically rejects all images of God, instead striving to see through the transparency of the natural to its forever inaccessible divine ground. Thus this 'ground of being' mystical natural theology stands sharply opposed to the kind of 'phenomenology of revelation' that characterizes Jean-Luc Marion's influential attempts to think, philosophically, of the gift as *es gibt*. In contrast to Marion's accounts of the iconicity of the divine that saturates phenomena with the fullness of God's presence without ever descending into idolatry, a continental natural theology turns to the absence of God, to sites of dereliction and emptiness. It is this excess of absence, figured and disfigured through autodestructive non-images of byss and abyss that recall Boehme and Schelling and that connect natural theology to rational mysticism. At the same time, the natural theological *Bilderverbot* most emphatically necessitates an embrace of the imagination as the privileged faculty of natural theological sense (Hedley 2008). If the pistic theologian sees by faith and not by sight, then the natural theologian's vision is by the imagination; that synthetic faculty (*Einbildunskraft*) of the natural and the theological able to 'bod[y] forth/the forms of things unknown' (*A Midsummer Night's Dream* V.i.14–15). Reading the Book of Nature, such an approach favours allegory and the 'noble lies' of philosophical myth-making, playfully surpassing absolutist attempts at finality or closure through the richness of allusion and a hermeneutics of openness. Yet, as Douglas Hedley notes, the issue is not primarily epistemological, but metaphysical (23). Imaginative natural theology—rooted in Platonic-Romantic metaphysics—is the antithesis to the anti-Platonic, anti-Romantic, and above all anti-metaphysical mainstream of continental philosophy. Yet, as it were, against the grain of continental philosophy's simultaneous allergy to and fascination with faith, such a natural theology emerges as an alternative minority report.

Restlessly utopian, passionately uncommitted, and deliberately ambivalent, this natural theology stands opposed to fideism and pisticism in all their forms—religious and secular. Post-metaphysical, this natural theology responds to the foundational critique of ontotheology not by a non- or a-metaphysical withdrawl from speculative phil-theo-logy but by a retrieval off a participatory metaphysics that denies the either/or formulations of sacred/secular in an a/theological, a/theistic, supra/naturalism. Responding to an invitation, a suggestion, a rumour of angels, such an approach is an unconverted venture, a wager on transcendence in the midst of a tragically antagonistic battle of competing faiths. This, then, is the natural theology opened up from the perspective of continental philosophy, for those faithless enough to risk it.

REFERENCES

Albertson, David and Cabell King, eds. (2009). *Without Nature: A New Condition for Theology*. New York: Fordham University Press.

Anselm (1973). *The Prayers and Meditations of Saint Anselm with the Proslogion*. Harmondsworth: Penguin.

Arendt, Hannah (1963). *Eichmann in Jerusalem. A Report on the Banality of Evil*. New York: Viking Press.

Badiou, Alain (1993). *L'Éthique: essai sur la conscience du mal*. Paris: Hatier.

Berger, Peter L. (1969). *A Rumour of Angels: Modern Society and the Rediscovery of the Supernatural*. Harmondsworth: Penguin.

Borradori, Giovanna, ed. (2003). *Philosophy in a Time of Terror: Dialogues with Jürgen Habermas and Jacques Derrida*. Chicago: University of Chicago Press.

Caputo, John D., ed. (2002). *The Religious*. Oxford: Blackwell.

Caputo, John D. and Gianni Vattimo (2009). *After the Death of God*. New York: Columbia University Press.

Craig, William Lane and J. P. Moreland, eds. (2009). *The Blackwell Companion to Natural Theology*. Oxford: Blackwell.

Critchley, Simon (2012). *The Faith of the Faithless: Experiments in Political Theology*. New York: Verso.

Deleuze, Gilles (1989). *Cinema 2: The Time-Image*. Translated by Hugh Tomlinson and Robert Galeta. Minneapolis: University of Minnesota Press.

Goodchild, Philip, ed. (2002). *Rethinking Philosophy of Religion: Approaches from Continental Philosophy*. New York: Fordham University Press.

Hedley, Douglas (2008). *Living Forms of the Imagination*. London: T & T Clark.

Jaeger, Werner (1947). *The Theology of the Early Greek Philosophers*. The 1936 Gifford Lectures. Oxford: Clarendon.

Laruelle, François (2010). *Future Christ: A Lesson in Heresy*. Translated by Anthony Paul Smith. New York: Continuum.

Levinas, Emmanuel (1984). 'Ethics of the Infinite' in *Dialogues with Contemporary Continental Thinkers*. Edited by Richard Kearney. Manchester: Manchester University Press.

—— (1998). *Entre Nous: Thinking of the Other*. Translated by M. B. Smith and B. Harshav. New York: Columbia University Press.

Meillassoux, Quentin (2008). *After Finitude: An Essay on the Necessity of Contingency*. London: Continuum.

Nancy, Jean-Luc (2008). *Dis-Enclosure: The Deconstruction of Christianity*. Translated by Bettina Bergo, Gabriel Malenfant, and Michael B. Smith. New York: Fordham University Press.

Steiner, George (1989). *Real Presences: Is There Anything in What We Say?* Chicago: University of Chicago Press.

Taylor, Mark C. (2007). *After God*. Chicago: University of Chicago Press.

Tillich, Paul (1952). *The Courage to Be*. New Haven: Yale University Press.

Trakakis, Nick (2007). 'Meta-Philosophy of Religion: The Analytical–Continental Divide in the Philosophy of Religion'. *Ars Disputandi* 7: 1–47.

Turner, Denys (1998). *The Darkness of God: Negativity in Christian Mysticism*. Cambridge: Cambridge University Press.

Ward, Graham, ed. (1997). *The Postmodern God*. Oxford: Blackwell.

CHAPTER 17

PROCESS THOUGHT AND NATURAL THEOLOGY

DAVID RAY GRIFFIN

ALTHOUGH it also has a wider meaning, 'process thought' now refers primarily to the mode of thinking rooted in the philosophies of Alfred North Whitehead (1861–1947) and Charles Hartshorne (1897–2000).

Natural theology was central to the work of both. Whitehead's major work, *Process and Reality*, was an expansion of drafts he had delivered as Gifford Lectures, which were established to advance 'the study of Natural Theology', in which the lecturers would treat this subject 'as a strictly natural science,... without reference to or reliance upon any supposed... miraculous revelation' (Gifford 1885). One of Hartshorne's books is entitled *A Natural Theology for Our Time* (Hartshorne 1967), and most of his other books are also essays in natural theology.

To say that natural (or philosophical) theology is practised without appeal to 'any supposed... miraculous revelation' means that it is based solely on experience and reason, so that the criteria for evaluating it are those for judging any philosophical position: self-consistency and adequacy to the generally available relevant evidence.

This does not mean, however, that the resulting position should pretend to be the product of reasoning that is 'natural' in the sense of being neutral in relation to the various historical traditions. It is now widely accepted that there is no such thing. Our thinking inevitably reflects intuitions shaped by the particular traditions in which we find ourselves. John B. Cobb Jr, pointing out that his use of Whitehead to construct a natural theology, like Whitehead's philosophy itself, was shaped by a 'Christian vision of reality', entitled his resulting book *A Christian Natural Theology* (Cobb 1965: 259–70). But the criteria for evaluation are still strictly philosophical.

Natural theology, in any case, can be understood in a narrow and a broad sense. In the narrow sense, it consists of arguments for the existence of God. In a broader sense, any philosophical cosmology providing a framework for speaking of a divine reality can be called a natural theology. Whitehead and Hartshorne each provided natural theologies in both senses of the term.

While drawing heavily on Whitehead and Hartshorne, especially the former, I will summarize my own process natural theology as articulated elsewhere (Griffin 2001). I begin, however, with a discussion of the decline of natural theology's reputation in modern times.

Supernaturalism, Scientific Naturalism, and the Decline of Natural Theology

In the past two centuries, natural theology fell into disrepute in scientific, philosophical, and even theological circles, primarily for two reasons. On the one hand, natural theology had become associated with a very problematic type of theism. On the other hand, science had become associated with a cosmology that allows neither for a divine being nor for religious and ethical experiences. I will discuss these two factors in order.

Supernaturalistic Theism

Although there are many types of theism, the most important distinction is that between naturalistic and supernaturalistic types.

According to *supernaturalistic* theism, there is a divine being that can occasionally interrupt the world's most fundamental causal processes. Contemporary evangelical theologian Millard Erickson, for example, affirms 'a definite supernaturalism—God resides outside the world and intervenes periodically within the natural processes through miracles' (1985: 304).

Because 'God' had been conceived as such a being by the major theologians of Judaism, Christianity, and Islam throughout most of their histories, theism of this type can also be called *traditional* theism.

The crucial divine attribute for traditional theism, which made it supernaturalistic, was *omnipotence*: God was said to be all-powerful in the sense of having the power to bring about, unilaterally, anything that was logically possible. Although God could not bring about a world with round squares, because 'round square' does not name a logically possible entity, God *could* have unilaterally prevented all of the things, such as wars, holocausts, and diseases, that people have regarded as great evils.

The idea of God as supremely powerful and even capable of performing miracles was contained in the Bible, but the doctrine of divine omnipotence, according to which nothing in the world can offer resistance to divine power, was not developed until the end of the second century AD, at which time the Church began accepting the idea of creation *ex nihilo*, with *nihil* understood as absolute nothingness. Christian and Jewish theologians had previously held, with Plato and the Hebrew scriptures, that our world was created out of chaos, which meant that there was something in the nature of things that could resist the divine will (Levenson 1988: 4–5, 121–3; May 1994: xi–xiii, 7–27, 61, 74, 122, 144).

The precipitating cause of the new doctrine was the gnostic dualism of Marcion, who said that our world is inherently evil because formed out of evil matter. In an overreaction, theologians such as Hippolytus, Tertullian, and Irenaeus declared that God created the world out of absolutely nothing, thereby rejecting not only Marcion's view but also the position of Platonic Christian theologians, such as Hermogenes, according to whom God created our world out of matter that was 'without qualities', hence neutral between good and evil (May 1994: xiii, 40–43, 144–6, 151).

The way in which this new doctrine implied the absolute omnipotence of God can be illustrated by Erickson, who wrote:

> God did not work with something which was in existence. He brought into existence the very raw material which he employed. If this were not the case, God would . . . have been limited by having to work with the intrinsic characteristics of the raw material which he employed. . . . God needs no materials. Therefore, his purposes . . . will not be frustrated by any inherent qualities of material with which he must work. [Erickson 1985, 374–5]

This doctrine created two problems.

The Problem of Evil

Hermogenes warned that the idea of *creatio ex nihilo* would make it impossible to explain the origin of evil consistently with the perfect goodness of God (May 1994: 140–6). Although his warning was ignored, his prescience was borne out by the history of theodicy, which shows that this view of the God–world relation did indeed create an insoluble problem of evil (Griffin 1976: chs. 6–15).

Prior to the Enlightenment, to be sure, the question of how evil could exist was generally seen as merely a 'mystery'. But since the Enlightenment, the contradiction between the world's evil and God's alleged power and goodness has been seen as a problem of such seriousness that theism, given its widespread equation with *traditional* theism, has come to be widely regarded as indefensible.

For example, philosopher John Mackie, who taught at Oxford, entitled his book on God's existence *The Miracle of Theism*. Echoing Hume's ironic remark that no reasonable person could believe the Christian religion without a miracle, Mackie's title expressed his conviction that theism's 'continuing hold on the minds of many reasonable people is surprising enough to count as a miracle' (1982: 12). His argument, however, dealt only with *traditional* theism, according to which God is 'able to do everything (i.e. omnipotent)' (1982: 1). The existence of such a being, Mackie concluded, is rendered improbable by the problem of evil. But people who believe in a deity that is, 'though powerful, not quite omnipotent', Mackie acknowledged, 'will not be embarrassed by this difficulty' (151). Mackie, however, ignored the importance of this caveat, presenting his book as an argument against theism as such, not merely one type.

Similarly, American philosopher Michael Martin wrote a book entitled *Atheism: A Philosophical Justification*, which was intended 'to provide good reasons for being an atheist' (Martin 1992: 24). Atheism is generally understood to be the rejection of any form of theistic belief whatsoever, but Martin argued only against 'an all-good, all-powerful, and all-knowing being' (30). The book provided a philosophical justification, therefore, only for 'atheism in the sense of disbelief in a being who is omniscient, omnipotent, morally perfect, and completely free' (315). Like Mackie, Martin illustrated the way in which theism is commonly rejected because of its widespread identification with the problem-of-evil-afflicted *traditional* theism.

This is the case whether one is referring to the *classical* version of traditional theism, held by Augustine, Aquinas, Luther, and Calvin, which portrayed God as not only having the power to determine all events but actually *doing* so, or the *free-will* version of traditional theism, which portrays God as permitting human beings to exercise genuine freedom—a view that requires time to be real for God. The incoherencies in classical theism, which have been pointed out vigorously (Martin and Monnier 2003), are significantly overcome by the free-will version of traditional theism. But critics have nonetheless concluded—rightly in my view (Griffin 1976, 1991, 2000b)—that the problem of evil undermines the free will as well as the classical version of traditional theism, and this conclusion, when combined with the equation of theism with the traditional type, led to a widespread consensus that natural theology, with its arguments for theism, must be an intellectually bogus enterprise.

The Conflict with Science

Equally problematic, at least in science-based circles, is the fact that theism of this type contradicts the scientific community's most fundamental philosophical presupposition, naturalism, understood in a minimal sense to mean simply that the world involves an unbreakable web of causes and effects.

According to this minimal naturalism—which can be called *generic* naturalism, because it is common to the various types of naturalism—miracles, understood as supernatural interruptions of the world's most fundamental causal processes, cannot occur.

Having started moving towards this naturalistic position in the late seventeenth century, the scientific community—by which I mean science-based philosophers as well as practicing scientists—had fully embraced it by the middle of the nineteenth. Philosopher and biblical critic David Friedrich Strauss, reflecting German currents of thought, declared in his 1835 *Life of Jesus* that the biblical miracles must be interpreted as myths, because modern thought presupposes that 'all things are linked together by a chain of causes and effects, which suffer no interruption' (Brooke 1991: 270). In England, Charles Darwin, rejecting the view that the origin of the human mind could be explained only by a supernatural intervention, said: 'I would give nothing for the theory of Natural selection, if it requires miraculous additions at any one stage of descent' (Darwin 1896: II, 6–7).

Traditional theism, however, says that such interruptions of the world's normal patterns can occur. Erickson, having said that the world was created *ex nihilo*, adds:

> Nature…is under God's control; and while it ordinarily functions in uniform and predictable ways in obedience to the laws he has structured into it, he can and does also act within it in ways which contravene these normal patterns (miracles). [Erickson 1985: 54]

Contemporary British philosopher Richard Swinburne agrees, saying:

> [God] can bring about...any event he chooses...God is not limited by the laws of nature; he makes them and can change or suspend them...God is *omnipotent*: he can do anything. [Swinburne 1996: 7]

Many science-based writers, accepting the equation of theism with theism of this traditional type, hold that scientists must affirm a materialistic world-view that rules theism out. For example, American biologist Richard Lewontin, while admitting the 'patent absurdity' of many explanations based on atheistic materialism, wrote that scientists must hold fast to it anyway: They 'cannot allow a Divine Foot in the door', because '[t]o appeal to an omnipotent deity is to allow that at any moment the regularities of nature may be ruptured, that miracles may happen' (1997: 31). Lewontin illustrates the fact that as long as ideological leaders of the scientific community equate theism with belief in the omnipotent, miracle-working deity affirmed by Erickson and Swinburne, they will be hostile to it.

Scientific Naturalism as Naturalismsam

The other major reason for the widespread rejection of natural theology is the association of science with a version of naturalism that rules out any form of theism whatsoever.

The *generic* naturalism discussed thus far, according to which there can be no interruptions of the world's normal causal laws, simply rules out the supernaturalistic type of theism. Using 'ns' to stand for 'non-supernaturalist', we can call this doctrine naturalismns. In accepting naturalismns, however, the scientific community—for reasons I have explained elsewhere (Griffin 2000a: chs. 2, 5)—embodied it in a form of naturalism that affirms a materialistic view of the world's constituents, along with a sensationist doctrine of human perception, which together imply an atheistic view of the universe. This sensationist-atheist-materialist naturalism can be abbreviated naturalismsam. I will explain how its materialism leads to atheism, then do the same for its sensationism.

Materialism

Naturalismsam is materialistic in a twofold sense. It holds, first, that what we call the physical world is made up of bits of matter that are completely devoid of experience. Whitehead dubbed this the concept of 'vacuous actuality', meaning something that is fully actual and yet 'void of subjective experience' (1978: 167). This view won out in the seventeenth century over competing views for reasons that I have discussed elsewhere (Griffin 2000a: ch. 5).

At first, this materialistic view of nature's ultimate units was combined, most famously by René Descartes, with a dualistic view of human beings, according to which we consisted of two ontologically different types of substances: a material body and an immaterial mind or soul. But this position created a problem: if the brain is composed of insentient bits of matter, which like billiard balls interact by pushing each other around, and the mind is a feeling, perceiving, thinking entity, which can neither push nor be pushed, how can mind and brain interact?

This was no problem for Descartes himself, who simply said that God, being omnipotent, caused them to interact (Baker and Morris 1996: 153–70). Although other philosophers developed somewhat different views (saying perhaps that God made them merely *appear* to interact), it was widely agreed that the coordination between conscious experiences and bodily movements could be explained only by divine omnipotence. 'For thinkers of that age', William James quipped, '"God" was the great solvent of all absurdities' (James 1911: 195).

As the Enlightenment proceeded, however, philosophers and scientists turned increasingly away from this solution and thereby away from dualism. Many philosophers accepted some form of idealism, according to which what we call 'matter' is not ultimately real, but the scientific community turned towards a full-fledged materialism, according to which what we call the 'mind' is not a distinct actuality: it is either identical with the brain or, at most, an epiphenomenal by-product of its activity. In either case, the 'mind' is not an entity with any causal powers of its own—either to act or to perceive.

How Materialism Leads to Atheism

By virtue of being materialist in this second sense, naturalismsam leads to atheism, for three reasons.

First, theism has used the mind–body relation as an analogy for the God–world relation, saying that God acts on the world in somewhat the same way that the mind acts on its body (Swinburne 1986: 51; Moreland and Craig 2003: 507–11). Given materialism's denial that the mind is a distinct actuality, an extrapolation to the universe from the mind–body relation suggests atheism.

Secondly, a materialist view of the world implies that there is no 'place' for God. Arguing that science entails naturalism defined as the 'thesis that *all* facts are facts of nature', Princeton philosopher Gilbert Harman wrote: 'Our scientific conception of the world has no place for gods' (1977: 17; 1989: 381). According to biologist Richard Dawkins, a 'philosophical naturalist' is 'somebody who believes there is nothing beyond the natural, physical world' (2006: 14).

The third way that materialism leads to atheism is by entailing a sensationist doctrine of perception.

How Sensationism Leads to Atheism

If the 'mind' is not a distinct actuality with its own power, then information can come to the mind only by means of the brain and hence via the body's physical senses. Philosopher Willard Quine, for example, said that 'whatever evidence there is for science is sensory evidence', because 'our data regarding the world reach us only through sensory stimulation' (Quine 1969: 75; 1984: 364). Spelling out one implication of this sensationist view, Quine said: 'there is no extrasensory perception' (1981: 1–2). Whereas this term usually refers to telepathy, Quine's doctrine also ruled out any other type of nonsensory perception.

In line with the empiricist conviction that we should not affirm the existence of unperceivable entities, Quine declared that nothing is to be allowed into our ontology that cannot pass the 'tribunal of sense experience' (Quine 1953: 41). Combining this dictum with the fact that we have no sensory perception of values, he declared that moral judgements can be neither true nor false (Quine 1986: 663–5).

Several other philosophers have stressed that the sensationist doctrine of perception rules out knowledge of moral values. Mackie, articulating an epistemological 'argument from queerness', said: '[I]f we were aware of [objective moral values], it would have to be by some special faculty of moral perception or intuition, utterly different from our ordinary ways of knowing everything else [i.e.] sensory perception or introspection', and this would be too queer to be credible (Mackie 1977: 38–9). Gilbert Harman said that one has no way of perceiving 'the actual rightness or wrongness of a given situation', because there is no way it 'can have any effect on your perceptual apparatus' (1977: 9).

Authentic religious experience—at least *theistic* religious experience, understood as the direct perception of a divine actuality (Smart 1970: 12–14; Kwan 2009)—is also ruled out by this doctrine. To affirm a 'feeling of the immediate presence of the Supreme Being', said Immanuel Kant, would be a 'fanatical religious illusion', because it would affirm 'a receptivity for an intuition for which there is no sensory provision in man's nature' (1960: 163). Philosopher J. J. C. Smart wrote:

> It would seem that if mystical experiences are not mere aberrations of feelings…
> explicable in naturalistic terms, then they must be in some way miraculous.… Physics
> and physiology enable us to explain…how we can get in touch with rabbits or even
> with electrons. 'Getting in touch' involves responses to physical stimuli, and it is
> clear that no naturalistic account could be given of mystical cognition of the super-
> natural. [1996: 222–3]

In *Explaining and Interpreting Religion*, Robert Segal says that social scientists rightly assume that 'believers never encounter God' (1992: 71).

Implications for Natural Theology

Although natural theologies commonly include arguments for the existence of God from moral and religious experience (Swinburne 1979: chs. 9 and 13; Craig and Moreland 2009: chs. 7 and 9), thinkers who presuppose the sensationist doctrine of perception will not be persuaded, no matter how sophisticated the arguments, because they will assume that the reported experiences, no matter how impressive, could not have really resulted from non-sensory perceptions of a divine actuality.

Supernaturalists can, of course, explain the occurrence of moral and religious experiences to their own satisfaction by simply claiming that God, being omnipotent, can create such experiences (Swinburne 1979: chs. 9 and 13; Linville 2009: 416–17; Kwan 2009: 518). But such explanations do not provide 'arguments for the existence of God' to people who do not already presuppose the reality of such a deity. Natural theologians need to show the inadequacy of the sensationist doctrine of perception.

That is so, at least, if natural theologians should, as I hold, try to provide a world-view that can be accepted by the scientific community, for which naturalismns is not negotiable. This is the task undertaken by process natural theology.

PROCESS NATURAL THEOLOGY IN THE BROAD SENSE: NATURALISMPPP

Although Whitehead did not employ the term 'naturalism', his affirmation of naturalismns was made clear in his first metaphysical book. It belongs to 'the full scientific mentality', he wrote, to assume 'that all things great and small are conceivable as exemplifications of general principles which reign throughout the natural order', so that 'every detailed occurrence can be correlated with its antecedents in a perfectly definite manner, exemplifying general principles' (1967a: 5, 12).

However, while affirming naturalism in that minimal sense, Whitehead's entire philosophy was presented as an alternative to naturalismsam, which he called 'scientific materialism' (1967a, 17). His alternative can be called naturalismppp, meaning a prehensive-panexperientialist-panentheist version of naturalism. In this alternative, naturalismsam's sensationist doctrine of perception is replaced by a prehensive doctrine of perception, according to which sense-perception is derivative from a non-sensory mode of perception called 'prehension'. Atheism is replaced by panentheism, according to which the world exists within God. And materialism is replaced by panexperientialism, according to which the world is made up of experiencing, partially self-determining events.

Although Whitehead presented this form of naturalism as a way of fusing religion and science 'into one rational scheme of thought', he offered it in the first place in the interest of *science itself* (1967a: 66–7, 83–4; 1978: 9–10, 82, 93–5). The scientific community will surely not move away from its long-standing commitment to naturalismsam unless it becomes aware of its inadequacy as an interpretative framework for science and also of the existence of a superior version of naturalism. I will now briefly indicate how several problems inherent in naturalismsam are overcome by the respective doctrines of naturalismppp.

Materialism's Mind–Body Problems

Panexperientialism rejects the view that the ultimate units of our world are 'vacuous actualities', completely devoid of experience. It thereby avoids several dimensions of the mind–body problem that materialists have found insoluble. I will mention four:

How Could Experience Have Emerged?

One problem has been that of how things with experience could have emerged out of things wholly devoid of experience. Using *pour soi* for that which, having experience, is something 'for itself', and *en soi* for that which, having no experience, is merely something 'in itself', philosopher Thomas Nagel wrote: 'One cannot derive a *pour soi* from an *en soi*.... This gap is logically unbridgeable' (Nagel 1979: 189). Materialist philosopher Colin McGinn, agreeing that we have no understanding of how 'the aggregation of millions of individually insentient neurons [constituting the brain] generate subjective awareness', says at this point 'scientific naturalism runs out of steam', because '[i]t would take a supernatural magician to extract consciousness from matter' (McGinn 1991: 45). Refusing to resort to supernaturalism, McGinn has called the problem insoluble in principle (viii, 1).

How is Freedom Possible?

Philosopher John Searle, believing science to teach that the world 'consists entirely of mindless, meaningless, physical particles', concluded that it 'allows no place for freedom of the will' (1984: 13, 92). Nevertheless, he pointed out, nothing can 'ever convince us that our behavior is unfree', because 'we can't act otherwise than on the assumption of freedom' (97–8). Due to Searle's acceptance of materialism, he found himself committed to both 'freedom and determinism' but 'unable to reconcile the two' (86).

How Is Downward Causation Possible?

We all presuppose in practice that our thoughts, especially our decisions, exert 'downward causation' on our bodies: we know that we walk to a fountain *because* we want a drink. Materialism, however, implies that the behaviour of the human brain, like that of all complex entities, is completely determined by the causal interactions of its most elementary particles, so that all vertical causation goes *upward*. In an early essay on this problem, philosopher Jaegwon Kim pointed out that a position's affirmation of epiphenomenalism, according to which 'our reasons and desires have no causal efficacy at all in influencing our bodily actions', constitutes a *reductio ad absurdum* of that position. Several years later, having realized that the materialism he affirmed could not avoid epiphenomenalism, Kim declared it to be 'up against a dead end' (Kim 1993: 105, 367).

How Is Rational Activity Possible?

Closely related is the problem of how people can engage in rational activity, which is action guided by norms, such as the principles of logic (Kim 1993: 215). According to materialism, the mind is the brain, the activities of which are determined by the causal interactions of its subatomic particles. Asking 'how a physical organism can be subject to the norms of rationality', McGinn admitted that materialism can provide no answer (1991: 23n), thereby illustrating Harvard philosopher Hilary Putnam's charge that most science-based philosophies are self-refuting, because they 'leave no room for a rational activity of philosophy' (Putnam 1983: 191).

Panexperientialism's Avoidance of Materialism's Mind–Body Problems

The first of these problems, involving emergence, does not arise for panexperientialism, because it regards experience as primordial, not as something that emerged in the evolutionary process. There has, to be sure, been real emergence: *conscious* experience arose out of non-conscious feeling, after which *self*-consciousness arose. But panexperientialism does not have the insoluble problem of how experience arose out of things that, being wholly devoid of experience, were absolutely different in kind. Panexperientialism can, therefore, account for the rise of human beings within a fully naturalistic framework, whereas materialists, as McGinn admitted, and dualists, as Swinburne emphasized (1979: 172–3; 1986: 198–9), can do so only through appeal to supernatural intervention.

Panexperientialists can explain the other three features of our experience—freedom, downward causation, and rational activity—the same way dualists do: by distinguishing between the brain, as an organism consisting of billions of low-grade entities, and the mind, as a unitary actuality having power to exercise both self-determination and causal influence on other things. But panexperientialism, saying that the mind is not ontologically different in kind from the brain's neurons, can explain brain–mind interaction in fully naturalistic terms.

Sensationism's Knowledge Problems

Several more problems for science and science-based philosophy are created by naturalismsam's sensationist doctrine of perception. These problems arise because these enterprises claim to be empirical, which means that their fundamental notions must be based on experience, and yet the sensationist version of empiricism does not provide an experiential basis for a number of notions presupposed by the scientific enterprise. I will mention three.

How Can We Have Knowledge of Mathematical Objects?

Mathematics deals with entities that are invariably regarded by mathematicians as real (Hersh 1999, 7; Maddy 1990: 2–3; Moschovakis 1980: 605). And yet these entities are non-physical, which by definition means they cannot be perceived by our physical senses. As Putnam put it: 'We cannot envisage *any* kind of neural process that could even correspond to the "perception of a mathematical object"' (Putnam 1994: 503). Although some philosophers and mathematicians resort to desperate measures—such as denying the existence of numbers (Field 1980; Hellman 1989) or claiming that they are perceivable by the senses because they are embedded in the physical world (Maddy 1990: 44, 59, 178)—most philosophers evidently exemplify the kind of arbitrariness exhibited by Quine, who employed his 'tribunal of sense experience' to deny the existence of moral values (Quine 1986: 663–5) but then allowed 'the abstract objects of mathematics' into his otherwise materialistic world-view (Quine 1995: 14).

Knowledge of the External World

'The belief in an external world independent of the perceiving subject', declared Einstein, 'is the basis of all natural science' (Einstein 1931: 66). According to Hume's widely accepted analysis, however, sensory perception provides knowledge only of sense data, such as shapes and colours, not of an actual world. While a few philosophers have sought consistency by saying that science merely describes sensory phenomena, the dominant position has been to affirm, inconsistently, both sensationism and the independent reality of the physical world. Quine, having said that 'our statements about the external world face the tribunal of sense experience', agreed with Hume that sense perception gives us no knowledge of physical objects, putting them in the same boat with Homer's gods. Quine, nevertheless, 'believe[d] in physical objects and not in Homer's gods' (1953: 41, 44).

Knowledge of Causation and Induction

As Hume also showed, sensory perception provides no basis for affirming causation in the sense of the real influence of one thing on another. Sensory perception therefore provides no basis for affirming a necessary connection between 'cause' and 'effect', hence no basis for scientific induction. Pointing out the seriousness of this problem, philosopher of science Hans Reichenbach said it suggests science to be 'nothing but a ridiculous self-delusion' (1938: 346).

How Prehensive Perception Solves Sensationism's Knowledge Problems

Whereas sensory perception as analyzed by Hume, which Whitehead called 'perception in the mode of presentational immediacy', gives us only sense data, our full-fledged sensory perception, which is a mixed mode of perception termed 'symbolic reference', includes a more fundamental, non-sensory mode of perception, which he called 'perception in the mode of causal efficacy' (1978: 120–1, 180), or 'physical prehension' (33, 64). In this mode, we directly grasp (prehend) the causal influence of other actual things upon us. This non-sensory mode of perception explains why we never in practice doubt, as Hume acknowledged, the external world or causation as real influence.

Whitehead's prehensive doctrine of perception also explains how we can have theistic religious experience, in the sense of a conscious experience of God as Holy. While only occasionally resulting in such an experience, this direct prehension of God, which is a dimension of every moment of experience, also explains—as pointed out below—how we can perceive non-physical entities, such as numbers, norms, and values.

This prehensive doctrine of perception thereby allowed Whitehead to break with the tradition of modern cosmological construction, in so far as it had been based exclusively on the physical sciences, by basing his own naturalistic cosmology on evidence from aesthetic, ethical, and religious experience as well as the sciences (1967a: vii). The resulting cosmology, which amounted to a natural theology, was theistic.

As the term 'process theism' suggests, time is real for God. However, thanks to the 'dipolar theism' developed by Hartshorne, which is based on a distinction between the abstract essence and the concrete actuality of God, the traditional attributes of timelessness, immutability, and impassibility can apply to God without contradiction. The reality of time for God also provides the basis for another dipolarity, emphasized by Whitehead, between God as influencing the world and God as being influenced by it in return. Although Whitehead's own version of dipolar theism was incoherent, I have shown how his and Hartshorne's respective emphases can be combined into a doubly dipolar theism (Griffin 2001: ch. 4).

For our present purposes, the central feature of process theism is its repudiation of the supernaturalistic idea of God, which Whitehead called the 'theory of a wholly transcendent God creating out of nothing an accidental universe' (1978: 95). In rejecting a 'wholly transcendent God', Whitehead meant a deity that exists independently not simply of our *present* universe (which he affirmed) but of any universe of finite existents whatsoever. By 'an accidental universe' he meant one that is *wholly* contingent.

In Whitehead's view, God necessarily exists in relation to a world of finite existents—not our particular world, but some world or other—and our particular universe, which he calls 'our cosmic epoch' (1978: 288), embodies some principles that are *metaphysical*, meaning that they would necessarily be exemplified in *any* world God might create.

The most basic principle is that every individual existent embodies creativity, which gives that existent the twofold power of self-determination and causal influence on other existents. It is for this reason that God cannot interrupt our world's most basic causal laws. Whereas traditional theism saw the God–world relation as wholly contingent, because rooted in the divine will, Whitehead said 'the relationships of God to the World ... lie beyond the accidents of will', being instead 'founded upon the necessities of the nature of God and the nature of the World' (1967b: 168).

The necessary relation between God and the world can be expressed with the label 'panentheism', which means that the totality of finite things exists within God. The metaphysical principles, which God cannot violate, do not confront God as something alien, because God is 'their chief exemplification' (1978: 343). In Hartshorne's language, the metaphysical categories exist in God 'as fixed characteristics of an individual life' (Hartshorne 1961: 171). Just as a divine decision could not violate the divine nature as love, neither could a divine action violate the world's most basic causal principles, as they equally belong to the divine nature. Whitehead expressed his resulting view of divine causation by endorsing Plato's view that 'the divine element in the world is to be conceived as a persuasive agency and not as a coercive agency' (Whitehead 1967b: 166).

Although panentheism and pantheism both hold that the world exists necessarily, they are different in two crucial ways. For panentheism, finite individuals have their own power to act, which they can use to act contrary to the divine persuasion, so the evil in the world does not imply evil in the divine nature. Also, God is not simply the world as the totality of finite individuals. Whitehead reportedly expressed this view thus:

> [I]n respect to the world, God is everywhere. Yet he is a distinct entity.... This is the basis of the distinction between finite and infinite. God and the world have the same locus. [Johnson 1960: 372]

In Hartshorne's language, God is not the universe but 'the soul of the universe' (Hartshorne 1991: 649). As all-inclusive soul of the universe, God both feels the world—suffering with its sufferings and rejoicing with its joys—and acts back upon the world, analogously to the way in which the human soul receives feelings from, and acts back upon, its brain.

PROCESS NATURAL THEOLOGY IN THE NARROW SENSE

The traditional arguments for God provided a cumulative case against an atheistic view of the universe. These arguments failed only in so far as they were presented on behalf of traditional theism, because their cumulative case *for* theism was cancelled out by the cumulative case *against* it (see Davis 1989: 140–2). Process theology makes its main contribution to natural theology in the narrow sense, accordingly, by simply providing a conception of God that is not incoherent, not vitiated by the problem of evil, and not in tension with the scientific world's assumption of naturalismns. The probability of this conception's truth is supported, therefore, by the fact that, while not being contradicted by the traditional anti-theistic arguments, it is supported by the traditional theistic arguments (reformulated, of course, in terms of Whitehead's panexperientialism and prehensive doctrine of perception), plus a few novel ones. I will mention eight Whiteheadian arguments.

The Metaphysical Argument

Consistently with his doctrine of creation out of chaos, Whitehead distinguished between 'laws of nature' specific to our cosmic epoch, on the one hand, and underlying metaphysical principles, which would be exemplified in any cosmic epoch, on the other. Because these metaphysical principles exist necessarily, the question of their origin does not arise. But there is still a question to be answered in light of what Whitehead calls the 'ontological principle', which says: 'Everything must be somewhere; and here "somewhere" means "some actual entity"' (1978: 46). Also termed the 'Aristotelian principle' (40), it simply reaffirms Aristotle's insight that anything that is not itself a substance—not an *actual* entity—can exist only in such an entity.

Accordingly, the existence of metaphysical principles, which are necessarily exemplified at all times and places, can be understood only by positing *an omnipresent, everlasting individual to whose abstract essence the metaphysical principles belong, and who shares these principles with the world by being prehended by all finite actual entities*. The 'ideal realization of potentialities in a primordial actual entity', Whitehead wrote, 'constitutes the metaphysical stability whereby the actual process exemplifies general principles of metaphysics' (40).

The Cosmological Argument

The same reasoning applies to what Whitehead called 'those matter-of-fact determinations—such as the three dimensions of space, and the four dimensions of the spatio-temporal continuum—which are inherent in the actual course of events, but which present themselves as arbitrary in respect to a more abstract possibility' (1967a 161).

Process philosophy's cosmological argument says: *The present universality of finite existents embodying contingent principles, commonly called 'laws of nature', implies the existence of a primordial actuality that, besides having unfathomable wisdom, can make temporal, contingent decisions, then make the content of these decisions effective throughout the realm of finite actuality, so as to create and sustain our universe.* In Whitehead's words: '"God" is that actuality in the world, in virtue of which there is physical "law"' (1978: 283).

The Teleological Argument

Pointing out that 'the doctrine of the survival of the fittest' does not explain evolution's 'upward trend' and, in particular, 'how complex organisms with... deficient survival power ever evolved', Whitehead referred to 'a three-fold urge: (i) to live, (ii) to live well, (iii) to live better' (1968b: 7, 24, 5, 8). This upward trend, which is evident not only in animal evolution but also in 'the purely physical cosmos', requires positing, Whitehead argued, the existence of a 'counter-agency', meaning an agency countering the entropic running down of the universe (25–7). Whitehead thereby pointed to what he elsewhere called the 'primordial nature of God' and the 'Eros of the Universe' (1978: 32–3; 1967b: 11)

The Argument from Novelty

Evolutionary progress involves the realization of novel forms, which had not previously been realized in our world. God is needed, Whitehead said, to answer the question, 'where does novelty come from?' (Johnson 1960: 367). Asking how 'unrealized abstract form [can] be relevant', Whitehead wrote:

> 'Relevance' must express some real fact of togetherness among forms. The ontological principle can be expressed as: All real togetherness is togetherness in the formal constitution of an actuality.... Thus 'proximate relevance' means 'relevance as in the primordial mind of God.' [1978: 32, 46]

Apart from the influence of God, he added, 'there could be nothing new in the world' (1978: 247).

The Argument from Ideals

Having in an early book stated that we have 'a direct intuition of a righteousness in the nature of things' (Whitehead 1996: 63), Whitehead later explicated the argument implicit in that intuition thus:

> There are experiences of ideals—of ideals entertained, of ideals aimed at, of ideals achieved, of ideals defaced. This is the experience of the deity of the universe....

Human experience explicitly relates itself to an external standard. The universe is thus understood as including a source of ideals. The effective aspect of this source is deity as immanent in the present experience. [1968b: 103]

The Argument from Mathematical Knowledge

Mathematicians clearly have knowledge of a realm of abstract entities that exists independently of them. On the basis of naturalismsam, however, mathematicians can explain neither where such entities exist nor, even if they could somehow—as Plato evidently held—exist on their own, how these entities could influence our minds. As Penelope Maddy put it:

[H]ow can entities that don't even inhabit the physical universe take part in any causal interaction whatsoever? Surely to be abstract is to be causally inert. Thus if Platonism is true, we can have no mathematical knowledge. [Maddy 1990: 37]

Agreeing, Whitehead wrote: 'According to the ontological principle, there is nothing which floats into the world from nowhere' (1978: 244). This is because the ontological (Aristotelian) principle says: 'apart from things that are actual, there is nothing—nothing either in fact or in efficacy' (40). The 'mathematical Platonic forms' can influence our minds, the erstwhile senior author of *Principia Mathematica* held, because they exist in 'a basic Psyche whose active grasp of ideas conditions impartially the whole process of the Universe', thereby providing 'the agency whereby ideas obtain efficiency' (1978: 291; 1967b: 147).

The Argument from Truth

Nietzsche famously argued that, if there is no God, there is no truth, only a multiplicity of partial perspectives. Whitehead agreed, saying that 'there can be no determinate truth, correlating impartially the partial experiences of many actual entities, apart from one actual entity to which it can be referred' (1978: 13). Unlike Nietzsche, however, Whitehead knew that it is self-refuting to deny that truth exists, which means that there must be an all-inclusive perspective. 'The truth itself', he wrote, 'is nothing else than how the composite natures of the organic actualities of the world obtain adequate representation in the divine nature' (1978: 12).

The Argument from Importance

Calling importance one of our 'ultimate notions', which cannot be eradicated, Whitehead asked, rhetorically: 'Does not "importance for the finite" involve the notion of "importance for the infinite"?' (1968b: 86–7). British Philosopher Bernard Williams, in spite of his atheism, implicitly gave a positive answer. In addition to the merely *relative* idea of importance, according to which something is found important by a particular person or group, Williams pointed out, 'we have another notion, of something's being, simply, important (important *überhaupt*, ... important *period*)'. Asking what this might mean, Williams indicated that he was certain of only one thing: 'It does not mean that it is important for the universe', because 'in that sense, nothing is important'. Having excluded that answer, however, he had to admit that he could not explain why we have this notion (Williams 1985: 182). Whitehead's explanation was that we have a vague awareness that 'the immediate facts of present action pass into permanent significance for the Universe' (Whitehead 1947: 94)—which he otherwise called the 'consequent nature of God' (345–51).

CONCLUSION

Richard Swinburne, arguing that the evidence for traditional theism outbalances the evidence against it, deemed the existence of God 'significantly more probable than not' (Swinburne 1996: 138–9). John Hick, presupposing the same type of theism but finding the evidence for and against it to be roughly equal, concluded that God's existence is *not* 'in any objective sense more probable than not' (Hick 1989: 211). Critics such as John Mackie and Michael Martin, finding the evidence against this type of theism to be far stronger than that for it, say that God's non-existence is overwhelmingly more probable than not. Be that as it may, Whiteheadian-Hartshornean process philosophy, which portrays a panentheistic conception of deity as an integral part of a naturalistic world-view having a panexperientialist ontology and non-sensationist theory of perception, and which also shows this naturalism$_{ppp}$ to be more adequate than naturalism$_{sam}$ as a framework for interpreting science, has provided a theistic view of the universe that is overwhelmingly more probable than an atheistic view.

REFERENCES

Baker, Gordon, and Katherine J. Morris (1996). *Descartes' Dualism*. London and New York: Routledge.

Brooke, John Hedley (1991). *Science and Religion: Some Historical Perspectives*. Cambridge: Cambridge University Press.

Cobb, John B., Jr (1965). *A Christian Natural Theology: Based on the Thought of Alfred North Whitehead*. Philadelphia: Westminster Press.

Craig, William Lane and J. P. Moreland, eds. (2009). *The Blackwell Companion to Natural Theology*. Oxford: Wiley-Blackwell.

Darwin, Charles (1896). *The Life and Letters of Charles Darwin*. Edited by Francis Darwin. 2 vols. New York: D. Appleton.

Davis, Caroline Franks (1989). *The Evidential Force of Religious Experience*. Oxford: Clarendon Press.

Dawkins, Richard (2006). *The God Delusion*. Boston: Houghton Mifflin Harcourt.

Einstein, Albert (1931). 'Maxwell's Influence on the Development of the Conception of Physical Reality' in *James Clerk Maxwell: A Commemorative Volume*. Edited by J. J. Thomson et al. Cambridge: Cambridge University Press: pp. 66–83.

Erickson, Millard J. (1985). *Christian Theology*. Grand Rapids, MI: Baker Book House.

Field, Hartry (1980). *Science without Numbers*. Princeton: Princeton University Press.

Gifford, Lord Adam (1885). 'Lord Adam Gifford's Will.' The Gifford Lectures, <http://www.giffordlectures.org/will.asp>.

Griffin, David Ray (1976). *God, Power, and Evil: A Process Theodicy*. Philadelphia: Westminster Press.

—— (1991). *Evil Revisited: Responses and Reconsiderations*. Albany: State University of New York Press.

—— (2000a). *Religion and Scientific Naturalism: Overcoming the Conflicts*. Albany: State University of New York Press.

—— (2000b). 'Process Theology and the Christian Good News: A Response to Classical Free Will Theism' (1–38) and 'In Response to William Hasker' (246–62) in *Searching for an Adequate God: A Dialogue between Process and Free Will Theists*. Edited by John B. Cobb, Jr, and Clark H. Pinnock. Grand Rapids, MI: Eerdmans.

—— (2001). *Reenchantment without Supernaturalism: A Process Philosophy of Religion*. Ithaca, NY: Cornell University Press.

Harman, Gilbert (1977). *The Nature of Morality: An Introduction to Ethics*. New York: Oxford University Press.

—— (1989). 'Is There a Single True Morality?' in *Relativism: Interpretation and Confrontation*. Edited by Michael Krausz. Notre Dame: University of Notre Dame Press: pp. 363–86.

Hartshorne, Charles (1961). 'Whitehead, the Anglo-American Philosopher-Scientist.' *Proceedings of the American Catholic Philosophical Association*. Washington, DC: Catholic University of America: pp. 163–71.

—— (1967). *A Natural Theology for Our Time*. LaSalle, IL: Open Court.

—— (1991). 'A Reply to My Critics' in *The Philosophy of Charles Hartshorne*. Edited by Lewis Edwin Hahn. The Library of Living Philosophers. Vol. XX. LaSalle, IL: Open Court: pp. 569–731.

Hellman, G. (1989). *Mathematics without Numbers*. Oxford: Oxford University Press.

Hersh, Reuben (1999). *What is Mathematics, Really?* New York: Oxford University Press.

Hick, John (1989). *An Interpretation of Religion: Human Responses to the Transcendent*. London: Macmillan.

James, William (1911). *Some Problems of Philosophy*. London: Longmans, Green, and Co.

Johnson, A. H. (1960). 'Whitehead as Teacher and Philosopher.' *Philosophy and Phenomenological Research* 29: 351–76.

Kant, Immanuel (1960). *Religion within the Limits of Reason Alone*. Translated by Theodore M. Greene and Hoyt H. Hudson. New York: Harper & Row.

Kim, Jaegwon (1993). *Supervenience and Mind: Selected Philosophical Essays*. Cambridge: Cambridge University Press.

Kwan, Kai-Man (2009). 'The Argument from Religious Experience' in *The Blackwell Companion to Natural Theology*. Edited by William Lane Craig and J. P. Moreland. Oxford: Wiley-Blackwell: 498–552.

Levenson, Jon D. (1988). *Creation and the Persistence of Evil: The Jewish Drama of Divine Omnipotence*. San Francisco: Harper & Row.

Lewontin, Richard (1997). 'Billions and Billions of Demons.' *New York Review of Books* 9 January: 28–32.

Linville, Mark D. (2009). 'The Moral Argument' in *The Blackwell Companion to Natural Theology*. Edited by William Lane Craig and J. P. Moreland. Oxford: Wiley-Blackwell: pp. 498–552.

Mackie, John L. (1982). *The Miracle of Theism. Arguments for and against the Existence of God.* Oxford: Clarendon.

Maddy, Penelope (1990). *Realism in Mathematics.* Oxford: Clarendon Press.

Martin, Michael (1992). *Atheism: A Philosophical Justification.* Philadelphia: Temple University Press.

—— and Ricki Monnier, eds. (2003). *The Impossibility of God.* Amherst, NY: Prometheus Books.

May, Gerhard (1994). *Creatio Ex Nihilo: The Doctrine of 'Creation out of Nothing' in Early Christian Thought.* Translated by A. S. Worrall. Edinburgh: T. & T. Clark.

McGinn, Colin (1991). *The Problem of Consciousness: Essays Toward a Resolution.* Oxford: Basil Blackwell.

Moreland, J. P. and William Lane Craig (2003). *Philosophical Foundations for a Christian Worldview.* Downers Grove, IL: Intervarsity Press.

Moschovakis, Y. N. (1980). *Descriptive Set Theory.* Amsterdam: North Holland.

Nagel, Thomas (1979). *Mortal Questions.* London: Cambridge University Press.

Putnam, Hilary (1983). *Realism and Reason.* New York: Cambridge University Press, 1983.

—— (1994). *Words and Life.* Edited by James Conant. Cambridge: Harvard University Press.

Quine, Willard van (1953). *From A Logical Point of View.* Cambridge: Harvard University Press.

—— (1969). *Ontological Relativity and Other Essays.* New York: Columbia University Press.

—— (1986). 'Replies' in *The Philosophy of W. V. Quine.* Edited by Lewis Edwin Hahn and Paul Arthur Schilpp. Library of Living Philosophers. Vol. XVIII, LaSalle, IL: Open Court: pp. 663–5.

—— (1995). *From Stimulus to Science.* Cambridge: Harvard University Press.

Reichenbach, Hans (1938). *Experience and Prediction.* Chicago: University of Chicago Press.

Searle, John R. (1984). *Minds, Brains, and Science: The 1984 Reith Lectures.* London: British Broadcasting Corporation.

—— (1992). *The Rediscovery of the Mind.* Cambridge, MA: MIT Press.

Segal, Robert A. (1992). *Explaining and Interpreting Religion: Essays on the Issue.* New York: Peter Lang.

Smart, J. J. C. (1996). 'Religion and Science' in *Philosophy of Religion: A Global Approach.* Edited by Stephen H. Phillips. Fort Worth: Harcourt Brace: pp. 217–24. Reprinted from *Encyclopedia of Philosophy.* Vol. VII. Edited by Paul Edwards. New York: Macmillan Press, 1967.

Smart, Ninian (1970). *The Philosophy of Religion.* New York: Random House.

Swinburne, Richard (1979). *The Existence of God.* Oxford: Clarendon.

—— (1986). *The Evolution of the Soul.* Oxford: Clarendon.

—— (1996). *Is There a God?* Oxford: Oxford University Press.

Whitehead, Alfred North (1947). *Essays in Science and Philosophy.* New York: Philosophical Library.

—— (1967a [1925]). *Science and the Modern World.* New York: Free Press.

—— (1967b [1933]). *Adventures of Ideas.* New York: Free Press.

Whitehead, Alfred North (1968a [1929]). *The Function of Reason*. Boston: Beacon Press.

—— (1968b [1938]). *Modes of Thought*. New York: Free Press.

—— (1978 [1929]). *Process and Reality: An Essay in Cosmology*. Corrected edition edited by David Ray Griffin and Donald W. Sherburne. New York: Free Press.

—— (1996 [1926]). *Religion in the Making*. Reprint, with an introduction by Judith A. Jones: New York: Fordham University Press.

Williams, Bernard (1985). *Ethics and the Limits of Philosophy*. Cambridge: Harvard University Press.

....

CHAPTER 18

THE DESIGN ARGUMENT AND NATURAL THEOLOGY

....

NEIL A. MANSON

INTRODUCTION

....

IN the broadest sense, natural theology is the effort to gain knowledge of God from non-revealed sources—that is, from sources other than scripture and religious experience. Natural theology in this sense encompasses an array of activities ranging from attempts to understand the divine attributes (omnipotence, omniscience, moral perfection, and so on) to establishing the existence of the soul. The essays in this volume attest to the vibrancy of natural theology understood in this sense. But there is also a much narrower sense of natural theology: the construction of arguments for the existence of God from empirical evidence. Although this narrower sense technically includes the argument for God's existence from the very existence of a contingent reality—'the Cosmological Argument'—it is most strongly associated with the argument for God's existence from something much more specific: the appearance that the natural world, in whole or in part, has been constructed for a purpose. Philosophers call this 'the Teleological Argument', from the Greek word '*telos*', meaning 'goal' or 'end'. It is more commonly called 'the Design Argument'.

The Design Argument touches on an enormous variety of issues in science, logic, metaphysics, epistemology, and value theory. Furthermore, there is not one version of it, but many. These versions can be distinguished according to two factors: the sorts of scientific evidence to which they appeal and the logical nature of the sorts of inferences being made. Perhaps a dozen distinct fields of inquiry have at one time or another provided fodder for some version of the Design Argument. Additionally, a host of different argument forms have been employed (Manson 2003: 5–8; Oppy 2006: 202–16). Yet three versions stand out in particular.

The most influential version historically is that of William Paley (2006 [1802]), who appealed to functional biological parts (eyes, wings, and so on) whose structures seemed explicable only in terms of a supernatural designer. The version currently generating the most heat is 'Intelligent Design Theory'. Like Paley's argument, this version appeals to functional biological parts, but this time at the cellular level (Behe 1996). The claim is that some of these parts exhibit a feature—'irreducible complexity'—that cannot be explained by some combination of law and chance (i.e. by Darwinian natural selection), leaving design as the only remaining explanation. Finally there is 'the Fine-tuning Argument' (Manson 2009a). According to it, the very laws of physics and constants of nature themselves involve numerical values such that, had they been the slightest bit different, life of any sort would not have been possible in the universe (Barrow and Tipler 1986; Leslie 1989; Collins 2003; Holder 2004). If there is no God to design the universe, we must believe something incredibly improbable happened, whereas if God does exist, we have an explanation of fine-tuning.

Instead of addressing the *philosophical* and *scientific* particularities of each version, this chapter addresses a generic *theological* question confounding the Design Argument. Why would God design or create anything at all, much less a world like this one? Let us call this question 'Why design?' (WD). Oddly, neither opponents nor proponents of the Design Argument have given WD much attention (Manson 2009b). Yet answering WD is obviously crucial if the Design Argument is to succeed. If there is no reason to think God would design or create anything at all, then *a fortiori* there is no reason to think God would fine-tune the universe for life, make irreducibly complex cellular structures, fashion animals with eyes and wings, or bring about any of the other features of the world that supposedly have such a slim chance of being exhibited in a reality lacking God. As we will see, answering WD entangles proponents of the Design Argument in age-old debates about divine freedom, divine moral perfection, and divine rationality. Despite the pretensions of some of its proponents, the Design Argument is not and never has been 'strictly scientific'. Natural theology in the narrow sense demands natural theology in the broad sense.

FRAMING THE ISSUE: POSSIBLE CREATIONS VS. POSSIBLE WORLDS

At the outset, a clarification of WD is in order. Typically it is framed as the question of what God would 'actualize' and why. The picture here is of God contemplating all the possibilities, then picking one for realization ('actualization' in the jargon of analytic philosophy) according to some rationally defensible selection principle. On this picture possibilities are thought of as abstract entities on the 'actualist' model of Alvin Plantinga (1974) rather than as concrete entities on the 'modal realist' model of David Lewis (1986). The point of clarification concerns whether actualization-by-God is to be conceived as the actualization of a *possible creation* or the actualization of a *possible world*.

A possible creation is simply a proper part of a possible world—the part consisting of all and only the objects such that, were they actual, they would be contingent and non-abstract. On the actualist model of possible worlds, abstract objects—objects such as numbers, propositions, properties and other items that seem to be outside of space and time—are necessary and indestructible. As such, they are not subject to being created. Furthermore, though God is not an abstract object, His existence is logically prior to His actualizing anything and He exists independently of any other thing. Thus God, too, is not properly conceived as a part of a possible creation. A possible world, on the other hand, comprises abstract objects as well as 'concrete' (that is, non-abstract) objects, necessarily existing or independently existing objects as well as contingent objects. Possible worlds are maximal states of affairs, including necessary states of affairs as well as contingent ones (Plantinga 1974: 44–5). Thus possible worlds are the sorts of things that might include God, whereas possible creations are not (Plantinga 1974: 196–221).

Since a possible creation is merely a part of a possible world, it seems there could be a possible world without a created part. Two such possible worlds suggest themselves immediately. First is a possible world containing abstract objects and no other things. For reasons beyond the scope of this chapter, metaphysicians have typically held there can be only one such world. Metaphysicians who ask why there is something rather than nothing are asking why it is not the case that this world is actual. Second is the possible world containing abstract objects, God, and nothing else. Call this world 'God Alone' (GA). Thus the philosopher or theologian who asks why God would create anything at all is asking why it is not the case that GA is actual.

If actualization-by-God is conceived as the actualization of a possible *creation*, then, in asking what world God would actualize, the question does not arise of why GA is not actual. On this way of looking at actualization-by-God, God must actualize *some* possible creation, with the only issue being which one He picks. Now this way of conceiving actualization-by-God raises significant theological questions. One is why God would actualize a possible creation with any evil in it. This is the famous 'Problem of Evil'. Another is how God could be both free and morally unsurpassable if, no matter what possible creation He actualizes, there is always another possible creation that is even better (Rowe 2004). Nonetheless, this way of conceiving actualization-by-God cloaks a question, WD, that comes to the fore if actualization-by-God is conceived as the actualization of a possible *world*, since on that conception, God's actualizing GA by not actualizing any possible creation at all is explicitly allowed as possible. This is a strong reason for conceiving of actualization-by-God as the actualization of a possible world rather than of a possible creation: doing so highlights a question of obvious interest. Another reason is simply that talk of actualizing creations is not standard within analytic philosophy whereas talk of actualizing possible worlds is (Swinburne 2003: 121, n. 8).

WD thus breaks into two parts. First, why would God actualize some possible world other than GA? In other words, why would God not content Himself with a reality the concrete part of which was just Himself? Secondly, if God would actualize some possible world other than GA, what kind of world would that be? Adopting the terminology of Norman Kretzmann, we can refer to these two questions respectively as 'the general problem of creation' (Kretzmann 1991a) and 'the particular problem of creation' (Kretzmann 1991b). The focus of the remainder of this chapter is the general problem of creation. Before exploring the general problem of creation, however, we must be aware of some constraints imposed by the concept of the most perfect being.

CONSTRAINTS FROM TRADITIONAL THEOLOGY

'Perfect being theology' (PBT) is the result of constructing a theology on the assumption that God is absolutely perfect—absolutely lacking in any deficiency. How, if at all, does PBT constrain any answer to WD?

Two constraints seem obvious. First, it cannot be that God actualizes some world other than GA out of need; otherwise God's absolute self-sufficiency would be threatened. This point is accepted by theologians as far back as Augustine (Teske 1988: 248–9). Spinoza, controversially, generalized this latter point to argue that it is incoherent to think an absolutely perfect being would have desires, goals, or purposes, since he analysed desires, goals and purposes in terms of the fulfillment of needs. He claimed that 'if God acts with an end in view, he must necessarily be seeking something that he lacks' (Spinoza 1982 [1677]: 59). From Spinoza's perspective, any allegedly perfect being that acts to fulfill a desire, goal, or purpose would be incomplete and hence imperfect.

Secondly, it cannot be that God actualizes some world other than GA contrary to reason or for no reason at all, because that would contradict God's perfect rationality. It might be objected here that what is or is not reasonable is itself determined by the will of God. More modestly, it might be objected that the rationalist, Leibnizian conception of the divine will should not be built into PBT; it should not be presumed that there is a sufficient reason for everything God does. Instead, goes the objection, PBT should be open to a conception of the divine will according to which God could act for no reason whatsoever, so long as God does not act *contrary* to reason (Mawson 2005: 149). Without dismissing this proposal, we may just note here that it marks a significant departure from traditional PBT. The goal of this chapter is to show that it is very difficult *for the traditional theist* to answer WD. Non-traditional theists (e.g. process theologians) may have resources to answer WD that traditional theists do not, but non-traditional theists are not our concern. For the remainder of the chapter we will thus presume that PBT forbids answers to WD whereby God creates for no reason.

A third constraint is more controversial than the first two: that PBT forbids answers to WD whereby God creates of necessity. The thought here is that any such answer would conflict with the idea that God is perfectly free. However, whether divine freedom should be conceived in the libertarian sense rather than the compatibilist sense is a matter of dispute. The libertarian says that if S did X freely, then it was possible that S did otherwise than X. The compatibilist says possibly S did X freely even though S could not have done otherwise than X if S's doing X was what S wanted, desired, or decided. Great minds can be found on either side of the libertarianism/compatibilism issue, with some (e.g. Augustine and Aquinas) vacillating (Kretzmann 1991a: 209–23; Teske 1988; Kretzmann 1999: 101–41; Mann 1991). The vexing question for the compatibilist about divine freedom is why compatibilism should not likewise apply to *human* freedom (O'Connor 2008: 121). That question is vexing because there being no answer to it threatens one very popular solution to the problem of evil—namely, that the possibility of evil is a precondition for the possession by humans of genuine freedom. At this point we can simply note that there are differing opinions on this issue—some think PBT requires a libertarian conception of divine freedom, others think PBT allows that God's actions are both necessitated and free—and that this difference will be relevant when it comes to assessing answers to WD.

Theologian Karl Barth acknowledges precisely these three constraints from PBT at the start of a passage in which he claims to answer WD:

> Creation is the freely willed and executed positing of a reality distinct from God. The question thus arises: What was and is the will of God in doing this? We may reply that He does not will to be alone in His glory; that He desires something else beside Him. But this answer cannot mean that God either willed and did it for no purpose, or that He did so to satisfy a need. Nor does it mean that He did not will to be and remain alone because He could not do so. [Barth 1961: 149–50]

These concessions seem to leave Barth with little room to manoeuvre. How then, does he answer WD?

THE OCCURRENTIST FALLACY

For Barth, the answer lies in the notion of divine love:

> If, then, this positing is not an accident, if it corresponds to no divine necessity and does not in any sense signify a limitation of His own glory, there remains only the recollection that God is the One who is free in His love. In this case we can understand the positing of this reality—which otherwise is incomprehensible—only as the work of His love. He wills and posits the creature neither out of caprice nor necessity, but because He has loved it from eternity, because He wills to demonstrate His love for it, and because He wills, not to limit His glory by its existence and being, but to reveal and manifest it in His own co-existence with it. [Barth 1961: 150]

So, for Barth, God created the world because He loved it. But this answer is befuddling. Doesn't the world have to exist first for it to be loved? If so, how can love explain why the world exists in the first place?

Included within PBT is the idea that God is perfectly loving. Being perfectly loving, God will, of course, love any being that is an appropriate object of love (a human, say, rather than an electron). But that in no way explains why there exist objects of God's love. Barth's statement that God creates because 'He has loved it [creation] from eternity [and] wills to demonstrate His love for it' cannot mean that the creation exists independently of God. Otherwise its existence would run counter to the traditional doctrine of creation *ex nihilo*, another core element of PBT.

So Barth still has not given us an answer to WD. Yes, God is perfectly loving, but why should that lead us to expect God to create objects of His love?

The property of being perfectly loving was just presented as a dispositional property—a property that need not be manifested to be possessed. A dispositional analysis of being perfectly loving might go something like this: S is perfectly loving if, and only if, if X is an appropriate object of love, then S loves X unconditionally. Perhaps Barth thinks being perfectly loving requires more than just the disposition to love unconditionally those things that are appropriate objects of love. Perhaps he thinks that, for a subject S to be perfectly loving, there must be an actual occurrence of unconditional love—there must exist at least one object (other than S) of S's unconditional love. Philosopher Leon Pearl maintains precisely this. He reminds us that Aristotle claimed 'a poor person cannot be charitable. True, if the person was rich, he would be charitable; but not being rich he is in no position to exercise acts of charity; and is, therefore, not charitable' (Pearl 1994: 333).

Yet this position seems mistaken. The case Pearl gives of charity is not analogous to the case of love. To be analogous, the issue would have to be, not whether a person could be charitable while having no riches to give, but whether a person could be charitable while having no one to whom riches could be given. If being charitable requires that there be someone to whom riches could be given, however, then being charitable is no longer an intrinsic property of a person. On that view, a person would cease to be charitable if everyone around her suddenly became wealthy or suddenly died. Intuitively, however, properties such as being charitable, being just, being loving, and so on *are* intrinsic properties—if not in the human case, then certainly in the divine case (according to PBT). That means they must be dispositional properties rather than properties that must be manifested to be possessed. (Call these latter 'occurrent properties' to distinguish them from dispositional ones.) If we think the divine virtues are dispositional rather than occurrent properties, then Pearl's argument falls flat—as does Barth's, for the same reason.

A second criticism of Barth's suggestion is that, since the act of creation necessarily precedes any act of justice or of love (because such acts require that the appropriate objects exist), the act of creating such objects does not qualify as an act of justice or of love. Tim Mawson points this out when he says of created things that 'their not existing prior to His creating them means that they themselves could hardly be said to have previous requirements met by their being created' (Mawson 2005: 149). Aquinas made the same point (Kretzmann 1999: 130–1).

A third problem with Barth's suggestion is that occurrentist accounts of the divine virtues impinge on divine freedom by making God create of necessity, by making God create as a result of God's very nature as loving, benevolent, and just. Aquinas rejected the occurrentist account of justice for precisely this reason. As was noted earlier, there is a disagreement as to whether PBT forbids saying God necessarily creates. Indeed, according to Kretzmann (1997: 223), Aquinas himself was of two minds on this issue. While Aquinas 'explicitly endorses' the libertarian explanation of creation, 'his conceptions of God, goodness, creation, and choice entail a necessitarian explanation to which he was clearly drawn and which gets expressed, perhaps inadvertently, even in the context of a thoroughgoing presentation of his official libertarian line'. Given this controversy, I will merely note here that those with a libertarian conception of divine freedom have additional reason to reject the occurrentist account of the divine virtues, and hence to reject any answer to WD of the sort Barth gives.

It is worth noting that the sort of answer Barth gave has considerable precedent. Both Plato and Augustine suggested that the motive for creation was the lack in God of the vice of envy. Kretzmann calls attention to this passage from Plato's *Timaeus*:

> Let us now give *the reason why* the maker made becoming, and the universe. He was *good*, and in him that is good no envy ever arises regarding anything. Being devoid of envy, he wanted everything to be *like himself*, as far as possible… God desired that everything should be *good* and nothing evil, as far as possible… For him who is most good *it neither was nor is permissible* to do anything other than what is most beautiful. [Plato 1902: 29E–30B; cited in Kretzmann 1991a: 213–14]

Roland Teske cites several passages in which Augustine makes a similar suggestion. The following one is representative:

> But if he could not make good things, there would be no power; if, however, he could and did not, there would be great enviousness (*invidentia*). Hence, because he is almighty and good, he made all things very good. [Augustine: 4.16.27 (PL 34.307; CSEL 28.1, p. 113, lines 10–13), cited in Teske 1988: 249]

As with being loving, however, it seems the property of being envious is a dispositional one. A crude dispositional analysis of envy might go something like this: S1 is envious if, and only if, if there is another subject S2 such that (i) S2 possesses something S1 regards as good and (ii) S1 knows that (i), then S1 bears ill will towards S2. This analysis suggests that lacking envy is also a disposition. Let us help Plato and Augustine along here and suppose that they intend to speak, not of the absence of a vice, but the presence of a virtue: good will. Hence S1 is perfectly good-willed if, and only if, for any other subject S2, if (i) S2 possesses something S1 regards as good and (ii) S1 knows that (i), then S1 bears good will towards S2.

Given this (admittedly crude) analysis of what it is to be perfectly good-willed, can being perfectly good-willed explain why God created? No more so than being perfectly loving can. In all cases, the possession of the dispositional property is consistent with the non-existence of anything that might make the disposition manifest. We get no explanation of why there must exist objects of the disposition by being told God possesses the disposition. Since in this section we have seen that the mistake of thinking otherwise is made often enough, let us create a label for the mistake. Call it 'the occurrentist fallacy'.

THE DIONYSIAN ANSWER: THE GOOD AS ESSENTIALLY DIFFUSIVE

If *all* of the divine attributes are dispositional properties rather than occurrent ones, then it looks as though we simply cannot answer WD by reference to the divine attributes—at least, not without committing the occurrentist fallacy. According to Kretzmann, however, Aquinas held that at least one of the divine attributes should *not* be understood as a mere disposition. That attribute is goodness (Kretzmann 1991a: 215–23; 1997: 220–5; 1999: 120–36). According to Kretzmann (1999: 134), Aquinas endorsed the Dionysian Principle that 'goodness is by its very nature diffusive of itself and (thereby) of being'. Kretzmann (1991a: 217) himself agrees with this principle, saying it 'expresses an important truth about goodness, most obviously about the goodness of agents'. Kretzmann admits that there are coherent dispositional accounts for *some* of the divine attributes (e.g. omniscience), but denies that goodness can be merely dispositional. 'There is no obvious inconsistency in the notion of knowledge that is unexpressed, never shared by the agent who possesses it even if he is omnipotent', he says (1991a: 217), 'but there is inconsistency in the notion of goodness that is unmanifested, never shared, even though united with omnipotence'.

The Dionysian Principle is a beautiful thought, but we get no argument from Aquinas or Kretzmann that it is true. Perhaps it is simply a fundamental aesthetic/moral intuition for which no argument can be given. Appealing to the Dionysian Principle, however, seems to violate the third constraint imposed by PBT—the constraint that any answer to WD cannot entail that God creates necessarily. If God is essentially good, and the good is essentially creative, then God is essentially creative. It is part of God's very nature to be creative, so that God could not refrain from creating a contingent reality and still be God. Kretzmann documents how Aquinas struggled with this implication of his solution. According to Kretzmann (1991a: 215), there are both 'libertarian and necessitarian strains in Aquinas' that Aquinas never reconciled. 'I see no way of avoiding the inconsistency (or, at least, ambivalence) in Aquinas's account as it stands', he adds, tracing the ambivalence back to a fundamental conflict in Greek thought about God between 'Platonist self-diffusiveness and Aristotelian self-sufficiency' (Kretzmann 1991a: 222).

Kretzmann does think there is a way to tie together the competing strains, to reconcile the libertarian and necessitarian conceptions of creation:

> what I think Aquinas *should* say about God's need to create something [is] that goodness does require things other than itself as a manifestation of itself, that God therefore necessarily though willingly wills the being of something other than himself, and that the free choice involved in creation is confined to the selection of which possibilities to actualize for the purpose of manifestation. [Kretzmann 1991a: 223]

Kretzmann is not the only one who finds this compromise plausible. Timothy O'Connor judges:

> there is a strong case to be made that a perfect being would create something or other, though it is open to Him to create any of a number of contingent orders…Perhaps it is inevitable, then, that a perfect God would create. [O'Connor 2008: 112–13]

In response, let me spell out an unwelcome consequence of the Dionysian answer from the perspective of the libertarian about divine freedom. According to the Dionysian Principle, it is metaphysically impossible that God sits on His hands. Doing nothing is not an option for Him. He is not free to actualize GA, according to Kretzmann, despite the seeming possibility that He does so. This is in tension with the idea that we should be grateful to God for not having actualized GA—that is, for having created something other than Himself. Creation can no longer be seen as a gift or an act of grace if the act of creating is necessitated (Rowe 2004: 2).

The restriction on God seems to run further. Suppose, as is highly plausible, that there is no upper bound to the amount of goodness that could be created (this is the presupposition of Rowe's objection to the idea that God is both free and yet morally unsurpassable). Then no creation of finite value is compatible with the Dionysian Principle unless we arbitrarily limit the scope of that principle. Say, for example, that God diffuses His goodness to produce a creation possessing N units of value, even though it is possible for there to be a creation of N + M units of value. Suppose further that the explanation of God's creating just N units of value is that, although His goodness necessarily diffuses itself, it only does so to a limited extent—just enough to produce N units of value but not enough to produce N + M units of value. This would be an arbitrary, brute fact about divine goodness—a very puzzling fact. What force or factor would be confining the divine goodness to just N units of value? Nothing outside of God could restrain His goodness, and it seems nothing internal to God would do so. So if the Dionysian Principle is correct, not only is God not free to actualize GA, He is not free to actualize any possible world with a created component of finite value, on pain of acting arbitrarily. Some recent philosophers enamoured of the Dionysian Principle (Leslie 2001; O'Connor 2008) have embraced this consequence, proposing that God creates an 'infinitely membered super-universe, whose members are ordered by value without upper bound' (O'Connor 2008: 118–19). Yet this consequence is unorthodox, to say the least. In short, serious limitations on God's choice of what world to actualize seem to follow from the Dionysian Principle.

Perhaps some easily accept these consequences, declaring that we have reconciled ourselves to the counterintuitive consequences of other 'limitations of perfection'. I suspect the case of Aquinas is more representative of the actual situation. His appeal to the Dionysian Principle results in an account of creation marked by 'inconsistency or ambivalence' (Kretzmann 1991a: 223). This suggests adherents of PBT seeking an answer to WD should at least be cautious in their appeals to the Dionysian Principle. Not even Aquinas could figure out how to reconcile it with PBT.

MIGHT GA BE LESS THAN THE BEST OF ALL POSSIBLE WORLDS?

Earlier, three constraints PBT imposes on any answer to WD were proposed. Is there a fourth constraint—namely, that PBT forbids answers to WD whereby GA is something less than 'the best of all possible worlds' (BPW)? The idea that GA is BPW seems to follow directly from the idea that God is the best of all possible beings. Kretzmann states that 'the existence of an absolutely perfect being and nothing else at all seems unquestionably the best of all possible worlds' (Kretzmann 1997: 221)—a claim which leads him to ask 'what could motivate God to choose to create anything at all?'

Whether PBT imposes a fourth constraint on any answer to WD will depend on our metric for value and on whether we equate maximal possession of a value with possession of that value to an infinite degree. If there is only one fundamental kind of value— and so only one dimension along which to measure value—and if PBT entails that God possesses that value to an infinite degree, then it seems to follow directly that, of all the possible worlds, GA rates the highest. Given that God has infinite value, and given that there is only one kind of value, God will have that value to an infinite degree. Say, for example, that the only kind of value is happiness. In that case, PBT entails that God has happiness to an infinite degree, so that no possible individual or sum of individuals— including sums with God as a part—surpasses God in happiness. Timothy Chappell (1993) uses precisely these assumptions to prove that God is not a consequentialist— a maximizer of value—for if He were, then He would actualize GA, which He obviously did not. Robert Nozick made a similar point (1989: 225). Of course, there may be more than one ultimate kind of value. Indeed, some forms of ultimate value might even conflict with one another. But if there is only one ultimate value, then GA must be rated BPW on the metric for that value. As Kretzmann just pointed out, this seems to leave us with no way to answer WD.

As William Mann interprets medieval theologian Vital du Four, a startling consequence emerges from the idea that there is only one kind of value and God possesses it to an infinite degree: all possible worlds that God might actualize are of equal value.

> 'Every creature has an accidental relation to the goodness of God, because nothing is added to his goodness from them, just as a point adds nothing to a line.'... One can interpret du Four's remark in such a way that it allows that some creatures have intrinsic value, even that some creatures are intrinsically more valuable than others, but simply denies that the existence of any of them can add to God's goodness. This interpretation would stress that God's goodness is perfect and infinite, thus that the addition of any amount of created goodness cannot increase his goodness. In fact, one can maintain further that the addition of any amount of created goodness cannot increase the aggregate amount of goodness in existence, since God's goodness alone provides an infinite amount of goodness in existence. [Mann 1991: 253–4, citing du Four 1891: 307]

Here du Four seems to have in mind the paradoxical question beloved of beginning maths students: 'What is infinity plus one?' For du Four, the answer is 'infinity'. If an infinite number of marbles is in existence, adding one does not increase the number of marbles, nor does taking one away (nor, for that matter, does adding another infinity of marbles, assuming that both infinities are of the same cardinality). Here du Four conceives of God's creating as adding a finite quantity to an infinite one. Thus the 'goodness rating' of any possible world with God in it is going to be the same: infinity. So on du Four's view, GA is tied for the title of BPW with every other possible world God might actualize—simply by virtue of the fact that all of those worlds include God. No world surpasses GA in goodness, but countless worlds equal GA in goodness.

If we adopt the picture of perfect goodness of du Four, the presumed constraint that God must actualize BPW turns out to be no constraint at all. If every possible world with God in it is equal in its value, then we cannot answer WD in terms of God's wanting to actualize as good a possible world as He can, because God's wanting to do so in no way favours actualization of some world other than GA. The world containing God, abstract objects, and cosmic dust is just as valuable as our world. So is the world containing God, abstract objects and five times as much cosmic dust. So is the world containing God, abstract objects, and one very grumpy cat. And so on. None of these worlds stand above GA in value, and so there is no reason to actualize one of them over GA. Thus to actualize one of them over GA would be for God to act without reason; according to the second constraint of PBT on any answer to WD, God cannot so act.

There are two points to jump off here. First, one might maintain that, while God possesses the maximum value any individual can have, it does not follow that God possesses infinite value. The idea here is that there is an intrinsic maximum to the value that can be possessed by any individual. But this idea is hard to square with the assumption that there is only one fundamental kind of value. If there was more than one kind of value, then we could imagine a function such that maximizing the *combined* value of the several values is inconsistent with maximizing any particular one of the several values. But how can there be an upper limit on the value of an individual being if there is only one kind of fundamental value? What could be imposing the upper limit? There seems to be no way to answer this question. If there is only one kind of value, it seems God having maximal value entails God having infinite value.

This suggests a second option. One might reject the idea that there is only one kind of fundamental value. Nothing about PBT commits us to this idea. The alternative idea, proposed by Mann (1991: 268–76) among others, is that there are plural, incommensurable values—fundamental values with no deeper measure of value against which they might be compared. What might these values be? O'Connor (2008: 117–18) proposes three different measures of the value of a possible creation: the *intensive* value of the parts of a creation (so that a Rembrandt painting rates higher than a tube of toothpaste); the *extensive* or *aggregate* value of the whole creation (so that a world with a thousand happy people rates higher than one with just five); and the *organic* value of the creation (the value attaching to the relational structure of the world).

The idea that intensive and extensive/aggregate value are fundamental yet incommensurable values should be familiar to observers of the debates amongst hedonistic utilitarians. Which is better, the hedonistic utilitarians ask themselves: a world with a small number of extremely happy people or an enormous number of marginally happy people? Which is more important: average utility or total utility? Hedonistic utilitarians have tied themselves in knots over this question, which suggests both to ideal utilitarians and to other outside observers that average utility and total utility are incommensurable values. In a similar vein, O'Connor is suggesting that intensive value, extensive value, and organic value are incommensurable. They are all fundamental values, but since they are fundamental there is no deeper measure of value against which we can compare them.

Schemes of incommensurable values other than O'Connor's can no doubt be proposed. The issue here is whether or not it is possible that these values are capable of all being maximized within a single individual. If one holds that they not only can be, but that they are, in fact, all maximized in God, then appealing to incommensurable values does nothing to solve the problem at hand. If God maximizes every incommensurable value, then GA rates the highest on every measure of value. For every fundamental measure of value there is a BPW with respect to that value, but in each case the BPW is the same: GA. But if GA is BPW on all measures of value, we still have no reason to expect God to actualize any world but GA. Surprisingly, O'Connor himself suggests that, while it may be that no possible creation has maximal value along all three dimensions, GA does, saying that 'the limit case, if attainable at all, could be reflected only by that which is perfect goodness itself—God Himself' (O'Connor 2008: 118). Mann makes a similar suggestion, saying that BPW might 'be so full of so many goods that it is a candidate—in fact, a winner—in every cluster of worlds of incommensurable goods' (Mann 1991: 272).

What if there are incommensurable values that are not all capable of being maximized within a single possible individual? For example, suppose that happiness and organic unity are incommensurable yet fundamental values, and suppose that no individual can have both maximum happiness and maximum organic unity. On this picture, GA is BPW with respect to a limited set of values but GA is not BPW with respect to all values, just because there is no possible world containing only one individual that is BPW with respect to all values.

This alone will not yield an answer to WD, for it would only establish that GA is not BPW with respect to all values, not that some world other than GA is BPW. Suppose, however, that there is a meta-value with respect to possible worlds and that God seeks to maximize the meta-value. The greater the variety of fundamental, incommensurable values displayed in a world, the better a world is with respect to the meta-value. On this view, actualizing GA does not maximize the meta-value. If actualizing some world other than GA does maximize the meta-value—or even if doing so only, in some sense, makes there be 'more' of the meta-value than there would be if God actualized GA—then we will have a general answer to WD.

For this proposal to make sense there must be values displayed maximally in worlds other than GA that are not displayed maximally in GA and that are incommensurable with the values displayed maximally in GA. Plausibly there are many such values (e.g. diversity, harmony, novelty). But if those values are incommensurable with the values displayed in GA (e.g. simplicity) then an unacceptable result follows. Suppose the created part (CP) of a world displays to the maximal degree a value V_1 that cannot be displayed to the maximal degree in GA, which instead displays to a maximal degree a different value V_2. Let us now switch from rating possible worlds to rating concrete beings. If we treat CP as a concrete being—the mereological sum of all of the created beings in that world—then it seems right to say CP displays V_1 to the maximal degree. So which is better—God or CP? On this line of thinking, there can only be a qualified answer to this question. God is better than CP with respect to V_2, while CP is better than

God with respect to V_i. It is not true that God is better than CP *tout court*. So if one says GA is not BPW because there are incommensurable values and no one being is capable of displaying all of those values to the maximal degree, one must deny that God is without qualification the greatest possible being, since CP is also a possible being and it is just as great with respect to the values it displays as God is with respect to the values He displays. Theists confront a powerful dilemma here: deny that God is the greatest possible being *tout court* or admit that GA is BPW. For the reasons already given in this chapter, grabbing the second horn is admitting that there is no good answer to WD.

CONSEQUENCES FOR THE DESIGN ARGUMENT

Unlike its cousin the Cosmological Argument, the Design Argument does not present its premises as *logically guaranteeing* that God exists, but only as giving *strong inductive support* for the claim that God exists. According to it, phenomena improbable or inexplicable on the hypothesis that there is no God are probable or explicable on the hypothesis that God exists: 'Of course God would make a universe that is hospitable to life in which there are magnificent creatures with marvellous features like eyes and wings.' That is what the proponent of the Design Argument needs us to believe. I hope to have shown in this chapter, however, that it is really quite a puzzle for traditional theists why God would design or create anything at all if, as natural theologians ask us to pretend, reason and observation alone are sufficient to support the premises of the Design Argument. Just considering the bare concept of God, and setting aside alleged revelation, there seems to be no obvious reason why God would create a universe and design some or all of its parts.

The difficulty can be presented in the form of a series of questions that can be asked of anyone who advances the Design Argument.

1. 'Are you saying God made the world because He needed something?'
2. 'Are you saying God made the world contrary to reason, or for no reason at all?'
3. 'Are you saying it is necessary that God made the world? Are you saying that God is not free not to make a world like ours?'
4. 'Are you saying God could not have some of His essential properties unless He made the world?'
5. 'Are you saying that a world consisting of God alone is less than the best of all possible worlds? Are you saying that reality is somehow inadequate unless it contains something more than God?'

It seems as though traditional theists are pushed to answer 'no' to every one of these questions. That list of 'no' answers makes it hard for them to then go on and advance the Design Argument. At the very least these deliberations show that one must do considerable work in natural theology in the broad sense before one can proceed to doing natural theology in the narrow sense.

References

Augustine (1887 and 1894). *De Genesi ad litteram* (*The Literal Commentary on Genesis*) in *Patrologia Latina* (PL). Vol. XXXIV. Edited by Jacques-Paul Migne. Paris: Garnier and in *Corpus Scriptorum Ecclesiasticorum Latinorum* (CSEL). Vol. XXVIII.1: *Sancti Aureli Augustini opera*. Edited by Joseph Zycha. Vienna: Tempsky.

Barrow, John D. and Frank J. Tipler (1986). *The Anthropic Cosmological Principle*. Oxford: Oxford University Press.

Barth, Karl (1961). *Church Dogmatics: A Selection*. Translated and edited by G. W. Bromiley. New York: Harper and Row.

Behe, Michael (1996) *Darwin's Black Box: The Biochemical Challenge to Evolution*. New York: Simon & Schuster.

Chappell, Timothy (1993). 'Why God is Not a Consequentialist'. *Religious Studies* 29: 239–43.

Collins, Robin (2003). 'Evidence for Fine-tuning' in *God and Design: The Teleological Argument and Modern Science*. Edited by Neil A. Manson. London: Routledge: pp. 178–99.

Four, Vital du (1891). *De Rerum Principio*, in *Joannis Duns Scoti Opera Omnia*. Vol. IV. Paris: Vives.

Holder, Rodney (2004). *God, the Multiverse, and Everything: Modern Cosmology and the Argument from Design*. Hampshire: Ashgate.

Kretzmann, Norman (1991a). 'A General Problem of Creation: Why Would God Create Anything at All?' in Scott MacDonald, ed., *Being and Goodness: The Concept of the Good in Metaphysics and Philosophical Theology*. Edited by Scott MacDonald. Ithaca, New York: Cornell University Press: pp. 208–28.

—— (1991b). 'A Particular Problem of Creation: Why Would God Create This World?' in *Being and Goodness: The Concept of the Good in Metaphysics and Philosophical Theology*. Edited by Scott MacDonald. Ithaca, New York: Cornell University Press: pp. 229–49.

—— (1997). *The Metaphysics of Theism: Aquinas's Natural Theology in Summa Contra Gentiles I*. Oxford: Clarendon Press.

—— (1999). *The Metaphysics of Creation: Aquinas's Natural Theology in Summa Contra Gentiles II*. Oxford: Clarendon Press.

Leslie, John (1989). *Universes*. London: Routledge.

—— (2001). *Infinite Minds: A Philosophical Cosmology*. Oxford: Clarendon Press.

Lewis, David (1986). *On the Plurality of Worlds*. Oxford: Blackwell.

Mann, William E. (1991). 'The Best of All Possible Worlds' in *Being and Goodness: The Concept of the Good in Metaphysics and Philosophical Theology*. Edited by Scott MacDonald. Ithaca, NY: Cornell University Press: pp. 250–77.

Manson, Neil A., ed. (2003). *God and Design: The Teleological Argument and Modern Science*. London: Routledge.

—— (2009a). 'The Fine-Tuning Argument'. *Philosophy Compass* 4/1: 271–86.

—— (2009b). 'The "Why Design?" Question' in *New Waves in Philosophy of Religion*. Edited by Yujin Nagasawa and Erik Wielenberg. New York: Palgrave-MacMillan.

Mawson, Timothy J. (2005). *Belief in God: An Introduction to the Philosophy of Religion*. Oxford: Clarendon Press.

Nozick, Robert (1989). *The Examined Life*. New York: Simon & Schuster.

O'Connor, Timothy (2008). *Theism and Ultimate Explanation*. Oxford: Blackwell.

Oppy, Graham (2006). *Arguing About Gods*. Cambridge: Cambridge University Press.

Paley, William (2006 [1802]). *Natural Theology*. Oxford: Oxford University Press.

Pearl, Leon (1994). 'God Had to Create the World'. *Religious Studies* 30: 331–3.

Plantinga, Alvin (1974). *The Nature of Necessity.* Oxford: Oxford University Press.

Plato (1902). *Timaeus.* Edited by J. Burnet. Oxford Classical Texts, Oxford: Clarendon Press.

Rowe, William (2004). *Can God Be Free?* Oxford: Oxford University Press.

Spinoza, Baruch (1982 [1677]). *The Ethics and Selected Letters.* Edited by Seymour Feldman and translated by Samuel Shirley. Indianapolis: Hackett.

Swinburne, Richard (2003). 'The Argument to God from Fine-tuning Reassessed' in *God and Design: The Teleological Argument and Modern Science.* Edited by Neil A. Manson. London: Routledge: pp. 105–23.

Teske, Roland J. (S.J.) (1988). 'The Motive for Creation According to St. Augustine'. *The Modern Schoolman* LXV (May):, 245–53.

CHAPTER 19

....

MORALITY AND NATURAL THEOLOGY

....

WILLIAM SCHWEIKER

INTRODUCTION

NATURAL theology has been conceived in a variety of ways, and, additionally, taken vastly different expressions. Usually contrasted with 'revealed theology', and so discourse about God grounded in an authoritative revelation within a specific religious community, natural theology is, most simply put, the attempt to demonstrate the existence of 'God' and divine purpose(s) through the observation of nature, experience, or the working of human reason. There have been attempts, especially in the seventeenth and eighteenth centuries, to establish a 'natural religion' which could secure wide public assent and thus elide the conflict between reason and revelation (however conceived). Often associated with 'deism', the argument was that an order to reality can be discerned which bespeaks the existence of a creator and orderer, but this God is not the God of the Bible and accounts of divine action and miracles. Deism usually entailed three fundamental ideas: the existence of God, immortality of the soul, and reward for virtue and punishment for vice. There were also arguments for natural theology made by Christian divines who marvelled at nature and human beings. These arguments were meant to answer various criticisms of natural and revealed religion made by Enlightenment thinkers like David Hume, Denis Diderot, Voltaire, and others. Analogous ideas of 'natural religion' and ongoing revisions of the agenda of natural theology continue in debates nowadays about the 'God-gene' or 'Intelligent Design'. The criticism of natural theology also continues among major twentieth-century Christian theologians, like Karl Barth and others, as well as forms of philosophy which focus on language-use rather than speculative questions, and likewise attacks on 'theism' among some scientists. So, the enterprise of natural theology reaches back to the dawn of Western thought and into current debates among philosophers and theologians as well as in popular culture.

The purpose of this chapter is to explore one approach to natural theology in the ancient no less than the modern and contemporary world, namely natural theology undertaken with respect to morality. In many cultures and societies there has been, at least intuitively, some connection between what is believed to be sacred and divine and the highest ideals of the good, justice, and the right. Moral beliefs and values are often sensed to have ultimate importance, as somehow holy, and thus the examination of those beliefs, values, and sensibilities would be a proper starting point for natural theology. The inverse is also true: reflection on and the experience of evil and viciousness has provoked many to explore the negation of the holy and divine, namely the demonic, in order to avert moral scepticism and despair that evil might prevail. Granting the wide range of issues that could be considered in exploring the connection between God and morality, we begin by clarifying what is meant by approaching natural theology through ethics. That discussion will be followed by outlining a typology of key positions. The article concludes with prospects for future thought.

NATURAL THEOLOGY AND
THE MEANING OF MORALITY

The possibility of developing a natural theology through morality depends on how morality is conceived. There have been some dominant ethical approaches to understanding 'morality', at least in the West. Ethics, in this context, should be distinguished from morality. 'Morality' is a set of beliefs, values, and practices which actually guide the conduct of some individual or community. Different communities and societies can have, and do have, different moralities, that is, different beliefs and practices about what is deemed good and praiseworthy in human conduct. Ethics, conversely, is critical reflection on and the normative definition of the meaning, source, and validity of 'morality' for the sake of orienting rightly human conduct as well as individual and social flourishing. Ethics arises whenever the dominant 'morality' is questioned or found lacking in orientation for individual and social life. An ethics, then, might validate and clarify, or invalidate and replace, the 'morality' of some community or individual. So, the question of the relation between morality and natural theology is, on this account, a question within ethics, or, same thing said, moral philosophy.

The question of the relation between God and morality arose at the dawn of Western ethical thought in Greek philosophy and also the social consciousness of the Hebrew prophets and sages. In each case, there was a challenge to inherited religious convictions and also the reconstruction of beliefs and practices in ways ethically required. Often called the 'Euthyphro problem', after the Platonic dialogue by that name (Plato 2003), Socrates posed a question to the young man Euthyphro about whether something is good and pious because the gods command it, or, conversely, if the gods command something because it is, independent of the commandment, good and pious.

If some action or attitude is good and pious solely because it is a matter of divine command, then, two logically different conclusions could obtain. First, it would appear that whatever the gods command (say, ritual sacrifice or war no less than justice and truth-telling) is in fact good and pious. That is, there are no grounds to contest the goodness of a divine command because all that is meant by 'goodness' is what is commanded. To violate a divine command would be to do wrong, be immoral, no matter how much that command might seem to contradict moral sensibilities. This possibility is underscored in the dialogue. Euthyphro meets Socrates outside the court. He is taking his father to trial for the unintentional death of a slave, and thus, in Socrates' mind, violates familial obligations. Euthyphro insists that the gods commanded him to do so. A divine command shows that morality is non-natural.

However, the idea that whatever a god commands is good can thus violate basic intuitions about what actions are good and pious, like one's obligation to a father, as well as standard ideas of 'god' and what a god would command. One can always reasonably ask: is a command of god ethically good? In that case a second conclusion about the 'Euthphro problem' is possible. It is obvious, Socrates holds, that morality is not dependent on the gods or divine commands. Religious ideas, if they are to be morally valid, must be redeemed through ethical reflection. With that conclusion a second one seems obvious. Many hold that every form of divine command ethics disallows natural theology, and, conversely, the enterprise of natural theology must, by definition, follow Socrates and find independent rational, social, or metaphysical grounds of morality devoid of religious content or import. In that case, ethics nullifies the enterprise of natural theology in relation to the moral life. The extent to which this second conclusion about the absolute separation of morality and religion can be sustained will be examined below. Some forms of theistic ethics circumvent the 'Euthyphro problem'.

Even before the Socratic enlightenment, ancient religious prophets and sages reached analogous insights. The Hebrew Prophets like Jeremiah or Micah insisted that the true worship of God must include a commitment to justice, and Abraham, the great patriarch, demanded that God abide by the dictates of justice (Genesis 18:22–33). In the New Testament this line of thought continues into Jesus' ministry and his insistence that the Sabbath was made for man and not man for the Sabbath and also that he desired mercy and not sacrifices (Matthew 9:10–13). Further, because of the covenant between God and Noah, the so-called Noahide covenant, rabbis held that every human being has some basic sense of morality. This rudimentary natural moral knowledge is supplemented by the giving of the Law, the so-called Ten Commandments, to Moses at Sinai (Exodus 20:1–26). In a similar way, the Qur'ān and the teachings of Islam advance the idea that human beings, as the vice-regents of God on earth, have an inborn knowledge of justice. On these various accounts and despite obvious differences, morality does indicate something about the divine, and thus seems to open the possibility of natural theology, even while it is also rooted in God's covenant with humanity (Noah), Abraham, or Prophets like Muḥammad and Moses, and thus is not only a matter of natural theology. These traditions stand in contrast to those which are non-theistic and yet endorse strong moral codes and values, like forms of Buddhism, or in which the 'gods' no less than human beings engage in moral wrong-doing, like Greek religion. Thus, two socio-cultural resources, the Greco-Roman and the Hebraic, Islamic, and Christian traditions, are the deep background for the question of the relation between morality and natural theology, at least for the West. This is the case because these resources have funded widely held conceptions of 'morality' and 'God'.

However, despite this shared, if complex, socio-cultural background, approaches to natural theology in relation to morality have profoundly differed. Consider several accounts in the history of thought. As noted, one option in Western thought and religion is that morality is a system of commands and duties given to or imposed on moral agents by a god. In this case, morality, as argued in forms of divine command ethics, would seem to depend on 'revelation'. There can be no moral approach to natural theology since, per definition, morality is not a 'natural' phenomenon. In some forms of Islam and Christianity, for instance, philosophical reflection, especially in ethics, must be denied in light of the revelation of the *Qur'ān* and authoritative legal interpretations. As shown below, the religious negation of natural theology is true only of some forms of 'divine command ethics' and not every form of theistic ethics. Secondly, morality has also been understood to be the set of norms and values to guide human action that arises within the historical legacy of some community and reaches no deeper than evolving social convention. On this account, there is nothing in 'morality' which could facilitate reflection on or arguments about the divine. Morality is only a human 'natural' phenomenon and, as such, cannot disclose or indicate anything about divine reality (if such a reality exists). Between the extremes of these two positions, there is, thirdly, the argument, made by Christian theologians like St Thomas Aquinas and others, that while God is the highest good and the source of (moral and non-moral) goodness, there are parts of morality that are 'natural' to human beings—that is, precepts of action, virtues, and the aims or ends of temporal action—while there are others that depend on divine grace and revelation. An ethical approach to natural theology is thereby possible and valid, but it must be supplemented by appeals to revelation and divine grace because morality is both natural and revealed. An analogous approach is seen among certain postmodern thinkers, like Emmanuel Levinas, who argue that 'God' is a trace within the ethical encounter among human beings. Morality is the condition for the possibility of speaking about God, but the discourse about God drawn from specific religious traditions is not reducible to the ethical relations among human beings.

These positions do not exhaust the historic options in approaching natural theology from within ethics. Thus, fourthly, there are thinkers who argue that while morality is grounded in human reason, sentiment (say, sympathy), or social convention, religion provides sanctions and motivations for following the dictates of morality. Ethics contributes to natural theology at the level of moral motivation, or, more technically, moral psychology. Some who adopt this strategy, like Immanuel Kant and in a different way David Hume, are keen to show the ways in which religious motivations rooted in fear or hope of (natural or supernatural) reward are in fact immoral (Kant 1960, 1993; Hume 1980). Given this, one must either purge the moral life of every non-moral motive (Hume and Kant) or clarify the rational conditions under which it is ethically permissible to conceive of God in relation to human hope (Kant but not Hume). Only in the latter case, can one rightly conceive of something like ethical theism as a kind of natural theology (see below). Fifthly, there are those thinkers, ancient and modern, who understand and define morality in terms of human aspirations to flourishing or happiness and well-being. Again, there are differences. Modern critics of religion, Friedrich Nietzsche no less than Sigmund Freud, insist that morality is merely an ideology of power or repressed human needs and desires and therefore cannot be a valid resource for reflection on God or, for that matter, human beings (Nietzsche 1994; Freud 1961). Conversely, there are ancient thinkers, like Plato and St Augustine, as well as modern and contemporary thinkers who understand God as the highest good and proper object of human desire. The examination of human desire, as explored later, is one way to approach natural theology. Finally, there are positions, like the ancient Stoics and modern thinkers such as Baruch Spinoza, for whom the metaphysical primitive—i.e. the most basic constituent of reality as such—is God, or the divine Logos, and this means that morality and natural theology are convertible (Spinoza 1992). This line of theistic ethics is why Spinoza entitled his major work *Ethics* even as his basic claim is that God alone is substance and every other thing, including human beings, are modes of substance.

We develop in more detail below a typology of options in thought. Here it is important to note that natural theology approached through morality entails the prior question about the nature and source of morality itself. This presents a problem: without some shared conception of 'morality' how can one enumerate, let alone examine and assess, approaches to natural theology from the perspective of ethics? Perhaps the various options enumerated and others as well are so radically different that it is fallacious to conceive of the general idea of morality let alone natural theology? In order to answer this problem, one can draw a distinction (but not a separation) between *formal dimensions* of morality—that is, those elements which any set of beliefs or practices must have to be counted as moral—and the *content* which a specific ethics and morality gives to those formal features. The formal dimensions provide the means for comparing approaches to ethics and natural theology; the differences in content make comparison interesting, important, and (hopefully) useful for natural theology and ethics.

Drawing widely from the history of thought and culture, it can be argued that 'morality' has five formal dimensions the content of which demarcate different moralities (Schweiker 1985, 2005): (1) morality entails a set of norms and values that are obligatory or praiseworthy and thus ought to guide human individual and social conduct; (2) morality entails procedures of practical reason in order to enable persons to answer questions about what one can and ought to do and thereby to reach morally right decisions and form good character; (3) in so far as choices and decisions always take place at some time and in some place, a moral outlook will entail means to interpret situations of moral perplexity and choice; (4) morality presupposes that there are agents (human and perhaps divine) who make choices and decisions, exercise powers of action, and influence or shape reality and their own lives, and, accordingly, a morality will provide an account of what it means to be an agent—individually and socially—and the capacities that entails; (5) a morality claims to be the true or the right framework for the orientation of human actions and relations—even if it might be judged not to be so from some other moral and/or ethical perspective—and thus another dimension is how to show the validity of a morality. In so far as ethics is critical reflection on the morality of a specific community or tradition that seeks to clarify its meaning and determine its truth, ethics will also have these five formal dimensions. Moralities differ, and so too forms of ethics, in terms of the specific *content* given these formal dimensions. For instance, Kantian ethics centred on universalizable duties and rational maxims of action differs from Platonic ethics which seeks the perfection of the human soul in relation to the Good. Each of those positions differs from a Jewish morality that centres on covenant fidelity between Israel and God or a Christian outlook developed around the life and teaching of Jesus Christ. The differences among moralities and forms of ethics remain even though each morality and kind of ethics shares formal dimensions.

Ethical Approaches to Natural Theology

Having isolated the conditions needed to survey options in the history of thought and likewise noting some options, we consider next in more detail some types of natural theology developed within ethics. Granting limitations of space, the typology is developed mainly, but not exclusively, with respect to the grounds and content of norms and values and also with respect to the question of the meaning of moral agency. As will be seen, these dimensions provide the salient points of comparison and also pose the related question of the validity of an ethical position and natural theology. However, several options in the history of ethics noted above do not require further consideration. Strident forms of divine-command ethics disallow the project of natural theology because morality is defined purely in terms of discrete and specific divine commands unrelated to thoughts or intuitions about what is morally good and right. We also need not consider those positions that insist morality is purely a social convention with no implications for thinking about the nature of reality or the divine. Finally, there are a host of positions which argue that morality and religion are rooted in the will-to-power (Nietzsche), a form of psychological repression (Freud), or which seek to show the morally dangerous impact of religion on human sentiments (Hume). They too, albeit in different ways, deny the possibility of natural theology. Accordingly, the typology constructed ranges from positions, on the one extreme, which focus on the convertibility of morality and theism ('theistic ethics') to those, on the other extreme, which see morality as the condition for the possibility of valid claims about God ('ethical theism'). Between these extremes will be positions designated 'aspirational' and 'mediating'.

THEISTIC ETHICS

One of oldest forms of natural theology from the vantage point of ethics are versions of what can best be labelled 'theistic ethics'. God is the supreme reality in relation to which everything else exists, and, further, the divine mind or will is the moral order of the universe to which human conduct can and ought to conform. One might speak here of a divine command, but the content of that command is reality as such and with it a moral order. The capacity of human beings as moral agents to live according to the divine order is rooted in reason or will. For example, ancient Stoic thinkers, like Epictetus, taught that one ought to 'live according to nature' which meant to orient life with respect to reason, the divine spark in the human mind, and in terms of the duties of one's station in life assigned by God. The divine Logos orients reality and the morally good life is to fulfil one's obligations fittingly in conformity to those divine laws. The aim of the moral life is self-sufficiency and this requires distinguishing between what is within human control and what is not, and cultivating an attitude of *apathia* with respect to forces beyond the agent's control, like (say) the fate of one's children. Self-sufficency as the human good is a form of tranquility found in fulfilling one's duty and cultivating apathy towards what is beyond one's control. Out of this Stoic outlook developed 'natural law ethics' (see below), and also a claim important for natural theology, namely that reflection on the laws of moral reason and the ordering of the universe provide evidence of the divine. Morality is theistic even if it is not dependent on discrete divine commands. In fact, God is not conceived as a commander in the way (say) the Bible or the *Qur'ān* speak of God, but, rather, the rational orderer of reality. In this way, the Stoic conception of theistic ethics differed from other ancient philosophical positions which either denied the moral relevance of the gods (Epicureanism) or conceived of the divine as the ultimate object of human aspiration and thinking, say with Plato and Aristotle (see below).

In the modern West a different version of theistic ethics is found, as noted above, in the thought of Spinoza. 'God' is substance while every other thing, including human beings, is a mode of substance, a mode of God. Reflection on the norms and values of human conduct, or ethics, must then be theistic and the aim of the moral life is to increase one's power of being, one's *conatus* as he called it. God is not an 'agent' or personal being but defined as the most knowable self-subsisting thing (substance). In so far as humans do not understand this fact about God, their lives will be misguided and lived in bondage to false ideas and desires. Ethics explores the divine reality and dispels illusions in a way that enables human agents to escape their bondage and thus to attain happiness, the increase of the power of being. It is axiomatic for Spinoza that God and Good are metaphysically one and reflection on morality is necessarily a type of natural theology that begins and ends with rational reflection on the nature of reality.

The fate of theistic ethics of the type seen in the Stoics and Spinoza has been intrinsically linked to the criticisms of metaphysics in much current thought. In so far as this approach to natural theology requires a necessary and undistorted connection or continuum between moral reason and the ultimate nature of reality (God), then the denial of that connection, which first began with Immanuel Kant and has continued in various forms into current philosophy and theology, means the end of this type of natural theology. There have been attempts to rejuvenate theistic metaphysics by so-called process philosophy associated with Alfred North Whitehead, Charles Hartshorne, and most recently in ethics by Franklin I. Gamwell in his work *The Divine Good* (Gamwell 1990). Further, some Christian theologians, like James M. Gustafson and Sallie MacFague, have, in different ways, sought to clarify the relation between God and nature with import for ethics. Gustafson speaks of a natural piety or sense of the divine. Nevertheless, the contemporary post-metaphysical and non-theistic tenor of current moral philosophy has seriously curtailed this type of approach to natural theology. An approach to natural theology from the perspective of 'theistic ethics' faces the challenge of rehabilitating metaphysical speculation in some form and arguing for a natural sense of God.

ETHICAL THEISM

The opposite approach to natural theology from that of metaphysical theistic ethics was most decisively formulated by Immanuel Kant in his critical philosophy. Kant's task was to chart the nature, law-giving capacity, and also limits of human reason and in doing so challenge traditional metaphysics, like the Stoics and Spinoza, which exceed the limits of reason. Additionally, Kant argued that ostensive appeals to revelation exceed human rational capacities and thus cannot claim the status of knowledge. He was mindful, of course, that the human mind can think what it cannot properly know. The grave error is to confuse mental fictions (including religious beliefs) with objects of knowledge. That is, we can think the idea of God but we cannot, according to Kant, know that God is or what God is. Interestingly, the distinction between knowing and thinking allowed Kant within his moral philosophy to clarify the rational warrant for postulating the idea of God and thereby developing another type of natural theology within ethics. He called it 'ethical theism'. In many respects, Kant's position provides a different backing for the three main ideas of deism.

Kant's argument, in brief, is that human reason legislates the supreme principle of morality, the categorical imperative or the moral law, as a maxim for action, and, further, this principle is formulated in terms of universalizability, respect for persons, and a kingdom of ends as an ideal to regulate social conduct. The fact that we can rationally legislate the moral law as a maxim of action, and so what we ought to do, means, further, that we must be able so to act—that is, we must be free. Obligation without capacity is meaningless: we are warranted in postulating the reality of freedom in so far as reason legislates the moral law. To act in accordance with the categorical imperative is to act morally no matter what one's specific pursuit, and, accordingly, to manifest the good will as that which alone is truly good. Further, it is, Kant argues, rational to conceive of the highest good as the perfect coincidence of virtue and happiness. Yet while reason legislates the moral law and we can conceive of the idea of the highest good, it is obvious that human beings, due to inclinations and desires for happiness, often act on non-moral or immoral maxims, namely maxims that cannot meet the test of the categorical imperative. In so far as the purpose of the moral life, according to Kant, is to be worthy of happiness, then, by the logic of moral reason, no finite agent qua finite could ever attain happiness. At the core of the moral life is an insufferable antinomy or conflict, namely, the idea of the highest good colliding with the finite limitation of human agents.

In order to preserve morality from the acids of scepticism and despair, we are rationally justified to postulate, and thus to think but not to know, two other ideas besides the postulate of freedom. One idea is immortality and thus an infinite time to make ourselves worthy to be happy by following the moral law. The other idea is 'God' as the omniscient judge who can perfectly reward virtue with happiness. The postulates of immortality and God are dependent on the more basic idea of freedom. They are limit-concepts we are allowed to think in order to address the conflict between the desire for happiness and the demands of duty. 'Natural theology' is redeemed through ethics but at the cost of understanding God as a postulate of pure practical reason rather than as an object of moral knowledge.

Kant's argument has had profound impact in theology and philosophy. Christian theologians responded to or adopted his argument; philosophers, beginning with the German idealists, sought to challenge his limitation of reason; and still others have flatly rejected his moral and religious thought. The Kantian form of 'ethical theism' has been widely rejected by many. These thinkers argue that the demands of morality can and must be formulated without reference to any comprehensive doctrine (religious or metaphysical), as John Rawls puts it, or in a strictly post-metaphysical way, as Jürgen Habermas does in his discourse ethics. While influenced by Kant, these thinkers reject the need for any postulate of God to sustain the moral life. Some other thinkers, like Ronald Green, have amended the Kantian project by arguing that in addition to ethical reason there is 'religious reason'. That form of reason is meant to answer the antinomy of moral reason but it does so with appeal to specific religious traditions. Relatedly John Hare, in *The Moral Gap*, argues that Kant's argument must be supplemented with appeals to God's grace to motivate moral action (Hare 1996). In a word, the question facing ethical theism as a form of natural theology is the extent to which theological claims are actually needed within a rational conception of morality.

ASPIRATION AND ETHICS

While theistic ethics and ethical theism represent virtually opposite positions in natural theology from an ethical perspective, they do share a focus on rationality as the crucial link between the moral agent and the divine that warrants theological claims. Granted that 'reason' is conceived differently in these forms of natural theology, nevertheless each is a form of ethical rationalism. Spinoza spoke of the 'intellectual love of God' whereas Kant thought theological reflection was a luxury of reason that could be enjoyed only in the face of the antinomy of practical reason or the fact of human evil. Other forms of natural theology from the perspective of ethics focus on the place of love and desire in human action and agency. They seek to show that there are degrees of perfection and love, the apex of which is the divine. These arguments begin with the observation that things matter to us, and that what matters (what is loved and valued) directs conduct. In this respect, they bear some resemblance to 'ethical theism' since the idea of God is ethically reconstructed not in terms of duties (e.g. Kant), but love of and desire for the Good.

The oldest philosophical argument rooted in human aspiration or love is found in Plato's dialogues despite Socrates' criticism of Euthyphro's appeals to divine command-ments. For Plato, the Good is the Form of other Forms of knowing and being. The Good is the ultimate object of human desire. In the *Symposium*, and elsewhere, Plato shows through a dialogue between Socrates and others that there are degrees of love with respect to different objects (Plato 1993). At a crucial point in the dialogue, Socrates explains he was taught by Diotima that one must move, in progressive steps of abstrac-tion, from love of bodies, through love of beautiful things, to love of beauty qua beauty to, finally, the Good. This conception of the Good is the ethical reconstruction of 'God'. That is to say, whatever one might mean by the idea of God the only conception which can stand philosophical scrutiny is one that coheres with the form of the Good. As Iris Murdoch, a twentieth-century Platonist, once put it, 'Good is what the old (idea) of God symbolized' (Murdoch 1970: 55). God is not, as in many religions, an agent analogous to a human agent. God is not the rational ordering of the universe, as Stoics held. God is not a postulate of pure practical reason. Rather, the Good or God is the perfect and unchanging object of rightly directed human love, an object which elevates the human soul beyond itself and the sensible world to union with what is enduring. This entails the ethical reconstruction of customary morality as well as traditional religion. One can ask, as Plato does in the *Republic*, what a proper conception of the Good means for other moral ideas, like justice. And, further, he could argue in the *Timeaus* that one can estab-lish the existence of God in order to explain the orderly movement of the cosmos. All things desire the Good or are moved by attraction to the Good and thus the divine.

The Platonic form of natural theology via an ethics of the Good has had a profound and enduring impact on Western thinking and theistic forms of religion. Aristotle, while differing from Plato in many ways, nevertheless ends his *Nicomachean Ethics* with an account of God as the unmoved mover which is the cause by attraction of all movement, including human action. While friendship is the greatest human social good, contem-plation of God is the highest good reserved for select human beings. Likewise, the idea of the unmoved mover, God who causes the movement of the cosmos through attrac-tion, is developed in his *Metaphysics*. For Plato and Aristotle, then, the perfection of thought is found in the unity of God and Good. Likewise, Christian theologians, Jewish sages, and Islamic philosophers have in various ways charted the ascent of the soul towards mystical union with God and what that means for the moral life. Often these arguments exceed the boundaries of natural theology since they rely on the discourse and ascetic practices of a specific community in order to trace the journey of the soul.

While Platonic forms of natural theology have enjoyed revivals throughout Western thought, especially in the Italian Renaissance and some current forms of phenomenology, the main challenges have focussed on ideas about the human good. Some thinkers, like Martha Nussbaum, argue that Platonic thought wrongly directs one beyond finite goods of natural human life to some supposedly supernatural good and thereby mutilates human flourishing. In order to counter this possibility, and thus to negate the move to natural theology, one must focus on human fragility and the fulfilment of human capabilities. Conversely, Robert Merrihew Adams, in his volume, *Finite and Infinite Goods*, argues that the supreme Good is God and the love of God is fundamental to the moral life (Adams 2002). Drawing on the resources of the Christian tradition, his argument is meant to establish a theistic framework for ethics rooted in the equation of God and Good. Finally, Murdoch, sought, as noted, to retrieve Plato's argument about the good and degrees of perfection supplementing it with a more complex psychology indebted to Freud while also insisting that the idea of God is implausible. In this way, she agrees with Adams against Nussbaum about the priority of a supreme Good and yet denies his equation of God and Good. Clearly, the legacy of a natural theology focussed on human desire remains in dispute around what defines the distinctly human good.

Mediating Theology

The final type of position to be noted is, for lack of a better term, a mediating one which relates and yet distinguishes the domain of what is natural in morality from claims about its supernatural or revealed end. It interrelates rational arguments like theistic ethics but also the aspiration to natural and supernatural ends.

Importantly, mediating positions can be found among both Protestant and Catholic Christian thinkers. It is also found in a different way among Jewish philosophers, like Moses Maimonides, and some Muslim philosophers (Maimonides 1983). Maimonides, for instance, grants natural moral knowledge open to human beings in the Noahide convenant, but then insists that the revelation of the Law, or Torah, is crucial for the highest form of human life. Among Protestants, personal and social life is lived out in specific orders or spheres created by God and human beings in order to sustain life and to restrain conflict and wickedness. In these orders, human reason is a sufficient guide for the moral life. However, religious concerns hamper the enterprise of natural theology. First, Protestants are wary of speculative reason because it might conceive of a God on its terms rather than the God revealed in scripture, a concern that continued in different form in Kant's limitation of reason (see above), but also has analogies in Islamic criticisms of philosophy. And, secondly, Protestants want to insist that virtuous conduct in the civil order might give rise to some form of human righteousness, but that is not sufficient for salvation. Classical Protestants, like Martin Luther and John Calvin, mediated between natural morality and revealed Christian morality, but in ways that challenged the possibility and worth of natural theology. Things were somewhat different among Catholic thinkers. Emblematically found in the thought of the great medieval theologian St Thomas Aquinas, the position is indebted to Stoic theistic ethics, natural law, Aristotelian virtue ethics, and the theology of grace and love found in St Augustine (Aquinas 1981).

Aquinas provides arguments for the existence of God, or at least a framework for understanding discourse about God, in the first part of his *Summa Theologiae*. Rejecting the ontological, or a priori, argument for God, Aquinas begins with experience and develops five proofs, including one from degrees of perfection. It is only in the second part of the *Summa*, dedicated to human action and so morality, that anything like a natural theology from the perspective of ethics is advanced. The divine mind has promulgated an ordering or law for beings to move to their specific ends. In human beings, this takes the form of 'natural law'—that is, the participation of the human mind in the divine Logos. The laws of human action, the most basic precept of which is to 'seek good and avoid evil', are specific to human beings; they are laws of reason and yet find their source in the divine mind. Aquinas also argues that action in accordance with reason is virtue and good conduct rightly shapes intellectual and moral virtues, meaning by 'moral virtues' those excellencies of character with respect to human appetites and desires. In this way, reflection on human reason, the ordering of reality, and also the formation of virtue can be seen as a form of natural theology unfolded within ethical inquiry. As noted, an analogous argument, although one that rejects natural law in the technical sense, is found in the writings of Maimonides.

However, Aquinas, as a Christian theologian, seeks to show how divine grace does not destroy but in fact perfects nature. Not only is there the eternal law which is the divine mind and natural law, or human reason, but also the laws of the civil order and, importantly, 'divine law', the revealed commands of God given in Scripture. Furthermore, human beings are directed to two related but distinct ends: the natural end of individual and social flourishing and also a supernatural end of communion with God, the *beatific vision*. Due to human finitude and sin, divine grace is needed to perfect and elevate human beings to their supernatural end and grace is received through the sacraments of the Church which enable meritorious good deeds. For Thomas there is no conflict between reason and revelation since each is grounded in God's being. Yet that aspect of morality which can fund natural theology is delimited and superseded by revealed knowledge and divine grace. In this way, Aquinas fashioned a grand synthesis of reason and revelation and therefore the connection between natural theology and revealed theology within the domain of morality. In this he joined other medieval thinkers—Maimonides, Averroes, and others—who related reason and revelation within their specific traditions.

The enterprise of relating and yet distinguishing natural and supernatural ends remains pressing within Catholic moral thought. Some twentieth-century Catholic moral theologians, like Bernard Haring, Josef Fuchs, and others, argued that human beings have a fundamental option for divine grace and thus the moral life is concerned with the totality of a person's life, whether Christian or not. These positions were criticised by Pope John Paul II due to his concern for religious authority in the moral life. The attempt to develop a natural theology from within Catholic ethics seems then at an impasse. The twentieth-century Protestant theologian Paul Tillich sought to show how a theonomous ethics, as he called it, was consistent with general ethical reflection and thereby correlated the two. Yet Tillich rejected the idea of natural theology and never probed its possible revision with respect to ethics. In a similar way, the legacy of natural theology has waned among many Jewish and Muslim thinkers. There is suspicion of attempts to unify reason and revelation and thus a turn to reflection on the distinctive discourses and practices of religious communities.

PROSPECTS FOR FURTHER THOUGHT

Having outlined a typology of positions in the history of Western ethics that have funded the work of natural theology, noting challenges and revisions to them, the question arises about the prospects for further thought. To be sure, possibilities have already been noted about thinkers who continue to work within the 'types' noted. And precisely because ideas about God and morality are engrained in Western thought and society, one can expect the various types of ethics and their approaches to natural theology to continue. However, another possibility is also open. It is one that seeks to articulate the importance of the questions of natural theology while also engaging the distinctive resources of particular religions. This possibility rejects a cardinal assumption of much natural theology, namely that there is something called 'reason' unshaped or untainted by historical traditions and, conjointly, that something called 'revelation' is self-interpreting. Once we grant the historical character of human understanding and that every form of discourse, including ostensive divine revelations, demand interpretation, a new trajectory of thought is possible. One might call this type of mediating position a 'hermeneutical' approach to natural theology.

The enterprise of natural theology in relation to morality seemingly arises because of two impulses within human experience: a sense that beliefs about what is good and just have some depth and even sanctity to them, and, further, that human beings seek meaningful and intelligible reasons for action. While ideas about the just and right, for instance, might be the products of social convention, their sense and gravity seem to indicate a breadth or depth of experience not limited to social forces. In this respect religious beliefs and practices are important within ethics. One needs to relate a sense of ultimate concern, a religious sensibility, to the moral life in order to avoid reducing morality to mere utility or failing to grasp the texture of moral experience. Surely what is meant by the term 'God' is then the ultimate object of thought and desire; the labour of natural theology within ethics aims, on this account, to use religious ideas in order to articulate, but not ground, the reach of moral experience. By the same token, moral experience seems to demand publicity and intelligibility—that is, the ability to articulate experience and provide cogent and accessible reasons for beliefs about the proper conduct of life. In this respect, natural theology can serve in the ethical reconstruction of religious beliefs and practice, an agenda, as noted above, already seen within the religions themselves. Surely part of the global challenge to ethics is a thinning of moral experience within advanced consumer-driven societies and also the immoral and too-often violent expression of religious belief. A hermeneutic approach to natural theology within ethics addresses these challenges.

The suggestion, then, is that the enterprise of natural theology within ethics not be conceived as the agenda of 'proving' the existence of God, but, rather, as mutually critical interpretations of forms of discourse and reflection that aim at articulating the depth but also the intelligibility and publicity of moral and religious convictions. The emphasis on 'theology' within ethics seeks to clarify the sanctity and depth of what is good and right; the emphasis on ethics within theology tests religious practices by reasonable and shared standards. This agenda is more humble than either theistic ethics or ethical theism, as explored above, even if it, like them, gives an account of moral understanding. The agenda arises out of the texture of moral experience and the intuition that religious and moral ideas are not foreign to human existence even while specific communities develop distinctive beliefs and practices. The question is what those distinctive features of a community provide for reflection on the shared global moral situation.

If it is correct that religious and moral beliefs seem endemic to the human condition and also that human beings require intelligible and public reasons to orient their lives, then the enterprise of natural theology within ethics seems inevitable. Exploring various 'types' of positions which have pursued such reflection has been the aim of this chapter. Our inquiry, we can now conclude, is that natural theology from within ethics remains salient and pressing for the global situation.

REFERENCES

Adams, Robert Merrihew (2002). *Finite and Infinite Goods: A Framework for Ethics*. New York: Oxford University Press.

Aquinas, Thomas (1981). *Summa Theologica*. Translated by Fathers of the English Dominican Province. Notre Dame, IN: Christian Classics.

Freud, Sigmund (1961). *Civilization and Its Discontents*. Translated by James Strachey. New York: W. W. Norton.

Gamwell, Franklin I. (1990). *The Divine Good: Modern Moral Theory and the Necessity of God*. San Francisco: Harper San Francisco.

Hare, John E. (1996). *The Moral Gap: Kantian Ethics, Human Limits, and God's Assistance*. Oxford: Clarendon Press.

Hume, David (1980). *Dialogues Concerning Natural Religion*. Edited by Richard H. Popkin. Indianapolis: Hackett Publishing Company.

Kant, Immanuel (1960). *Religion within the Limits of Reason Alone*. Translated by Theodore M. Greene and Hoyt H. Hudson. New York: Harper Torchbooks.

—— (1993). *Critique of Practical Reason*. Translated by Lewis White Beck. Upper Saddle River, NJ: Prentice Hall.

Maimonides (1983). *The Ethical Writings of Maimonides*. Edited by Raymond L. Weiss with Charles E. Butterworth. New York: Dover Publications.

Murdoch, Iris (1970). *Sovereignty of Good*. London: Routledge & Kegan Paul.

Nietzsche, Friedrich (1994). *On the Genealogy of Morals*. Translated by C. Diethe. Cambridge: Cambridge University Press.

Plato (1993). *Symposium and Phaedrus*. Edited by Candace Ward. New York: Dover Publications.

—— (2003). *Euthyphro*, in *The Last Days of Socrates*. Translated by Hugh Tredennick and Harold Tarrant. London: Penguin Books.

Schweiker, William (1985). *Responsibility and Christian Ethics*. Cambridge: Cambridge University Press.

——, ed. (2005). *The Blackwell Companion to Religious Ethics*. Oxford: Blackwell.

Spinoza, Baruch (1992). *The Ethics*. Edited by Seymour Feldman. Translated by Samuel Shirley. Indianapolis: Hackett Publishing Company.

CHAPTER 20

RELIGIOUS EXPERIENCE AND NATURAL THEOLOGY

MARK WYNN

RELIGIOUS EXPERIENCE AND THE GROUNDS FOR RELIGIOUS BELIEF

NATURAL theology is commonly associated with various strategies of argument, most obviously the ontological, cosmological, and design arguments; and we might suppose that the data of religious experience are properly of interest for natural theology because they can contribute to the premises of some such argument. We might wonder, for example, whether religious experience, of a certain type and distribution, is more likely on the hypothesis of design than on rival hypotheses. However, in the recent literature, religious apologists have generally taken a different tack, by arguing that the data of religious experience provide non-inferential grounds for religious belief. This approach rests in varying degrees on the thought that religious experience is like sensory experience to the extent that its deliverances are to be treated as prima facie trustworthy. If there is a role for argument on this approach, it will be in responding to objections which maintain that there is reason to doubt the apparent findings of a given religious experience or experience type, either because we have reason for supposing that these deliverances are false, or because we have reason to think that the conditions of the experience, or the subject of the experience, are in some respect unreliable.

A clearly formulated example of this general strategy is Richard Swinburne's defence of the 'argument' from religious experience. He comments that: 'it is a principle of rationality that (in the absence of special considerations), if it seems (epistemically) to a subject that x is present (and has some characteristic), then probably x is present (and has that characteristic)' (Swinburne 2004: 303). The 'principle of credulity' as Swinburne formulates it here does not distinguish between conventional sensory experience and religious experience; so he is proposing that the onus of proof rests upon the person who doubts the veracity of an experience whether or not that experience has a religious content. There is, then, no requirement upon the believer to produce an argument in support of the claim that a given religious experience is to be treated as veridical, except in so far as she has been given reason to think otherwise.

It is significant that Swinburne appeals to religious experience only in the closing stages of his book. At this point, he takes himself to have established, by means of conventional natural theological kinds of argument, including versions of the design and cosmological arguments, that the theistic hypothesis is roughly speaking 'as probable as not' (341). The role of religious experience, or more specifically theistic experience, is to build on this natural theological case, by licensing the further conclusion that theism is overall probable. And in turn, the role of natural theological argument, of the conventional variety, is to establish that religious experience can properly play this role, because it is subject to the principle of credulity. Swinburne notes various cases in which the principle of credulity ceases to apply. Suppose for example that I have very good reason to suppose that x does not exist. In that case, even if it seems to me that x is present, I will not be entitled to conclude, simply on the strength of the appearances, that most probably it is present (311–12). Swinburne thinks that his approach is not vulnerable to an objection of this kind, because he takes himself to have shown in earlier parts of the book that the theistic hypothesis has a reasonable, mid-range probability. So natural theological argument of the conventional variety helps to show that the data of theistic experience fall under the principle of credulity, and supposing that they do, we may then conclude that the existence of God is overall probable.

William Alston's defence of religious experience is rather differently formulated, but develops a similar train of thought. Alston begins not so much with the thought that there are different kinds of experience (sensory, religious, introspective, memory, and so on), all of which are properly subject to the principle of credulity, but rather with the idea that there are various socially constituted belief-forming practices, including sensory doxastic practice (SP) and 'mystical' doxastic practice (MP), all of which can properly be treated as prima facie trustworthy. Again this prima facie case can be overturned in particular instances, as when the outputs of one practice come into conflict with those of another, 'more firmly established' practice (Alston 1991: 171). Just as Swinburne thinks that we have no choice but to adopt the principle of credulity, because if we do not start from the presumption that experience is trustworthy, then we will forfeit all possibility of constructing a substantive picture of the world, so Alston thinks that it is practically rational for the participant in a practice to adopt an initial stance of credulity towards the practice, when 'it is firmly rooted in its devotees from early in life, interconnected with other practices in a form of life, and socially established'—because giving up such a practice would be a costly process, and should therefore only be attempted if there are weighty considerations in its support (Swinburne 2004: 306; Alston 1991: 169).

Alston maintains that objections to the trustworthiness of religious experience are typically committed to 'epistemic imperialism' or 'double standards'—that is, either they take the standards which are appropriate to some other kind of practice (usually, SP) and suppose that MP needs to adhere to these same standards, despite the difference in the character of its purported object, or else they find fault with MP for reasons which are in fact equally applicable to SP (Alston 1991: 249–50). An example of the first failing would be the insistence that MP is defective because it fails to generate ready predictions concerning the conditions under which God will appear (whereas SP does generate detailed predictions concerning the conditions under which a given type of sensory object will appear). But this objection fails to reckon with the fact that God is said to be a transcendent personal intelligence, and in that case, it is not to be expected that God can be reliably brought to appear simply by manipulation of relevant bits of the material world (49). So this objection involves an unwarranted extension of the rules which rightly apply within SP. An example of 'double standards' would be the complaint that there is no non-circular justification of MP—that is, there is no way of stepping outside the practice to check that its apparent findings match reality. After all, the same can be said, Alston notes, for SP, since while we can check some findings of SP against other findings, we cannot check SP as a whole for reliability, because we have no SP-independent mode of access to the material world, which would allow us to correlate the deliverances of SP with some judgement concerning the nature of the world which is not itself reliant on SP (106–7). Yet, radical sceptics aside, no one takes this as a sufficient reason for giving up on SP. So Alston's approach is not straightforwardly an argument from analogy: he acknowledges that there are important differences between MP and SP (to suppose otherwise would be to fall into 'epistemic imperialism'), but at the same time, his case does rest upon the thought that in one fundamental respect sensory and religious experience are alike, because in each case our experience is embedded within a well established doxastic practice, which we have reason to treat as prima facie trustworthy.

Critics of the arguments which Swinburne, Alston, Jerome Gellman, Keith Yandell, and others have deployed in support of religious experience typically cite some feature of religious experience which sets it apart from sensory experience and which yields a reason for taking a sceptical attitude towards it, while continuing to suppose that in general the apparent findings of sense experience are prima facie worthy of belief (Gellman 1997, 2001; Yandell 1993). Candidates include: many people appear not to have religious experience of any kind; the content of religious experience seems to be culturally relative to a significant degree; religious experiences cannot be checked in the same way as sensory experiences; religious experiences can easily be explained without assigning their purported object any causal role in the production of the experience. These differences could be taken to show that religious experiences do not fall under the principle of credulity, or some other rubric which would allow them to count as prima facie trustworthy, or to show that there is typically good reason to suppose that any prima facie justification which they enjoy can be overturned.

Evan Fales, Anthony O'Hear, and others have pressed the objection that religious experiences are not appropriately checkable (Fales 2004; O'Hear 1984; Gale 1991: Ch. 5). This objection appears to challenge Swinburne's principle of credulity, and Alston's claim that the deliverances of well-established doxastic practices can be treated as prima facie trustworthy, by suggesting that the onus of proof rests to some extent on the person who wishes to trust the apparent findings of an experience. This proposal may appear to lead fairly quickly in the direction of radical scepticism—after all, we commonly form beliefs about the sensory world without recourse to any process of checking, and it is hard to see how we could in general proceed otherwise. Fales responds to this consideration by noting that in ordinary perceptual experience there is in fact a good deal of implicit checking: 'We can look and just "see" that the refrigerator in the kitchen is white, in part because we have acquired an understanding of what refrigerators are and what they look like, readily expect such items to appear in kitchens, and know that white things look a certain way under the apparent conditions of illumination' (Fales 2004: 151). So this particular perceptual judgement has the backing of a prior process of checking (of colours against illumination conditions, and so on).

An Alstonian would no doubt raise two contrary considerations. If a doxastic practice is socially established, and has persisted over some time, then its deliverances will presumably have been subject to a degree of cross-checking of broadly the kind that Fales has identified here: like any other properly constituted doxastic practice, MP has an 'overrider system', which allows outputs of the practice to be sifted and tested, as when they are examined in terms of their 'fruits', such as their capacity to contribute towards the believer's 'sanctification' (Alston 1991: 170, 251). Secondly, even if it is true that everyday perceptual experience is more fully informed by prior checking than is religious experience, it will not follow that we ought not to trust the apparent findings of religious experience, because given the difference in the purported object of these two practices, we should not expect checking to be as significant a feature of MP as it is of SP, since we should not expect to be able to control the 'stimulus conditions' for experience of God so readily (49). It is worth noting that even if we agree with Alston's defence of the practical rationality of MP in the face of such disanalogies, we need not infer that there is just as much reason to trust MP as to trust SP. We might suppose, for example, that SP enjoys a larger measure of self-support because in the case of SP it is relatively easy to engage in cross-checking of the kind that Fales considers so important, and that this is an additional reason for treating SP as reliable. In this way, we can give some weight to the considerations which Fales advances, without taking them to overturn our right to take the findings of MP as prima facie trustworthy.

The sceptical case against religious experience can also be developed by appeal to the apparent variability of such experience across faith traditions. Is it not the case that the phenomenological content of religious experience, and what its subjects take it to reveal about religious reality, is to a large extent relative to cultural context? And does this not suggest that even if such experiences are in general prima facie trustworthy, they are not going to issue in any secure account of, for example, the existence and nature of God, because any experience purporting to yield an understanding of these matters will need to be weighed against others of apparently contrary import? Various other objections might be based on this same consideration. For example, if religious experience lacks the uniformity across time and space that is characteristic of sensory experience, should we not conclude that such experiences owe their character to the subject of the experience, rather than to some mind-independent reality whose nature they track across cultural contexts? More exactly, if religious experience is so highly sensitive to social conditions, should we not take it to be simply a product of those conditions?

One might respond to these objections by trying to isolate a phenomenological or doctrinal core which is common to at least a large swathe of religious experience. We could then argue that, so far as this core is concerned, the experiences embedded in different traditions do not after all have any tendency to cancel one another out. For example, as Nelson Pike has noted, there seems to be a degree of consensus among Christian mystics on the phenomenology of their experience, and a common language, of 'spiritual sensations', which enables them to document what it is like to have such experiences (Pike 1992; Turner 1995). Or again, it might be argued that mystical experiences across traditions have much the same phenomenological content, and that differences in the reporting of such experiences are attributable to differences in interpretation or differences in vocabulary for communicating that content (Stace 1961; Katz 1978). Or again, it could be said that providing that we specify their content fairly abstractly, then religious experiences are largely in agreement across traditions, since in general they give the appearance of being directed at a reality which is of supreme value and beyond space and time (Davis 1989).

Alston responds to the challenge of diversity rather differently, by appealing to the distinction between inter- and intra-practice kinds of dispute (Alston 1991: 271). In Alston's terms, the dispute between two equally successful weather forecasting systems will count as a case of intra-practice disagreement, since here there is a consensus on what would it would take for one system to demonstrate its superiority over the other (namely, a better record in predicting the weather). So the systems in this example have failed to achieve a desideratum which is evidently in principle attainable and, in Alston's view, this gives us reason to doubt each of them. By contrast, the dispute between different religious traditions is better regarded, he thinks, as an example of inter-practice disagreement, since in this case there is no shared account of what would count as success. In this kind of dispute, says Alston, the failure of a given system to establish its superiority over others by reference to some common criterion of success is not to be reckoned as a defect in that system, because we lack any clear conception of what it would be for this alleged deficiency to be made good. Allowing for all of this, it seems to be a consequence of this view that the adherents of the different faiths are equally entitled to persist in their tradition-relative doxastic practices, assuming that these practices are properly constituted. And for some this will be enough to leave the basic drift of the challenge from diversity intact: while I may be entitled to persist in my faith-relative doxastic practice, I know that others are equally entitled to persist in theirs, and in that case how much reliance can I place on the outputs of my own practice when they come into conflict with those of another practice? If this deadlock is to be broken, we may need to have recourse to one of the more traditional strategies of natural theological argument.

John Hick has developed a particularly radical response to the challenge of religious diversity. He allows that the relativity of religious experience to cultural context suggests that its content is to be explained very largely in socio-cultural terms. Hick puts this point by saying that one and the same ultimate reality, what he calls the 'Real in itself', is differently manifest in different traditions, depending upon the religious categories which are operative in those traditions. These categories function then as a kind of lens through which the believer views sacred reality, so that it appears in Trinitarian form to those who are wearing Trinitarian 'spectacles', and so on for other traditions. On this account, it is not that the members of different traditions are having much the same experience from a phenomenological point of view, but describing that experience differently, using the categories of their own tradition; rather, those categories inform the experience, so that the phenomenological content of religious experience varies with tradition (Forgie 1984; Zangwill 2004). It is natural to move from this idea, Hick notes, to the idea that we have no experiential access to the Real in itself, and then to the idea that none of our substantive concepts fits the Real in itself, with the consequence that it cannot be said to be one or many, good or evil, purposive or non-purposive (Hick 1989: Ch. 14).

From Hick's perspective, this approach has the merit of supporting a pluralistic conception of the relationship between the major faiths: all are equally successful in experiential terms, in so far as the Real is genuinely manifest in each of them, and all (we could say, though Hick does not put the point quite in these terms) are equally unsuccessful in descriptive terms, since none of the faiths' doctrinal categories will apply to the Real in itself. The immediate focus of devotion in the Abrahamic religions and equally in the Eastern faiths is therefore a divine 'phenomenon' or appearance, rather than ultimate sacred reality as it is in itself. Hick's approach is a very striking example of an experience-focussed form of natural theology, since he discounts the claims of the various traditions to have received any 'special' revelation, and he doubts whether natural theology in its traditional argumentative forms provides a good reason for favouring any particular substantive account of the nature of the Sacred.

To sustain this case, Hick appeals to the principle of credulity: we are entitled to take the deliverances of religious experience as prima facie trustworthy, and accordingly we are entitled to suppose that this experience has as its source a transcendent sacred reality. (Hick's intention is simply to advance a 'hypothesis', so he is not suggesting that these considerations oblige any reasonable person who is acquainted with the relevant facts to suppose that there is such a reality.) However, it seems to follow from this account that the believer's cultural context, or the conceptual scheme with which they operate, provides a full explanation of the content of religious experience. Some commentators have supposed that this combination of ideas is rather unstable: if the nature of the supposed transcendent source of religious experience sets no constraint on the content of religious experience, then would it not be simpler to suppose that culture sufficiently explains not only the content but also the very occurrence of such experience? Peter Byrne, for example, has argued that pluralism needs to postulate at least some minimal convergence in the content of religious experience across traditions, in order to ground the idea that this experience is in cognitive contact with a mind-independent reality, rather than consisting simply of a culturally mediated projection of some sort (Byrne 1995: Ch. 2; Stoeber 1992).

Alvin Plantinga has proposed a rather different response to the reductionist challenge to religious experience. He considers the force of Freudian and Marxist proposals that religious experience and belief derive from processes which are aimed at something other than truth—such as consolation in the face of a hostile world (Plantinga 2000: Ch. 5). These critiques of religious experience, broadly conceived, will be plausible enough, Plantinga suggests, if we start from a naturalistic conception of reality. But if, on the other hand, theism is true, then it is to be expected that God will have conferred upon human beings belief-forming faculties which can be relied upon to generate true beliefs about God and God's purposes, since such beliefs are required for an explicit relationship with God. So on Plantinga's view, the critiques of Marx and Freud, and other naturalistic critiques of religious experience, are persuasive only on condition that naturalism is true; and they provide, therefore, no reason for favouring a naturalistic reading of religious experience in the first place. Perhaps Plantinga is right to say that the plausibility of Freudian and Marxist critiques of religion will depend upon prior metaphysical commitments. But this approach will hold little consolation, presumably, for the person who is wondering whether religious experience provides grounds for supposing that theism is true. For on Plantinga's view, the theistic construal of such experiences is like the naturalistic construal in this respect: in each case, the construal will be cogent only if we have already agreed to the relevant (theistic or naturalistic) world view. To this extent, this stance seems to place religious experience beyond the realm of natural theology as traditionally conceived.

It will be apparent from this brief survey that the recent philosophical literature on religious experience has generally been concerned with experiences which seem to the subject to be focally of God or of some other supernatural 'thing'. This focus perhaps reflects the apologetic concerns of much of this literature, and its interest in the question of how religious experience may in certain respects prove to be like sensory experience. If this is the strategy of argument that we wish to employ, then there may be some pressure to consider God as a particular item of experience, in rather the way that material things are particular items of experience, albeit that God is of course non-material. For instance, Richard Swinburne delimits the range of phenomena which he wishes to consider by observing that: 'For our present purposes it will be useful to define [a "religious experience"] as an experience that seems (epistemically) to the subject to be an experience of God (either of his just being there, or of his saying or bringing about something) or of some other supernatural thing' (Swinburne 2004: 295). The apologetic focus of this literature may also be apparent in its interest in non-sensory forms of religious experience, since such experiences may seem to be particularly resistant to naturalistic explanation. Alston, for example, concentrates upon 'experiences in which the subject takes him/herself to be directly aware of God, with particular emphasis on that subclass in which experience is non-sensory' (Alston 1991: 67).

But of course there are many other kinds of religious experience, in addition to those which appear to involve some non-materially mediated intuition of God considered as a particular item of experience. I shall argue now that these other experiences should also be of some interest for natural theology.

The Bodily, Materially Mediated
Character of Some Forms
of Religious Experience

While many religious experiences may seem to be targeted directly at God, there are of course many others which have as their focus some material context, and the religious meaning borne by that context. The phenomenological literature on the nature of 'sacred space' provides one helpful starting point for a consideration of experiences of this kind. This literature unites around the idea that there are, broadly speaking, three ways in which places can acquire special religious significance (Barrie 1996; Jones 2000; Wynn 2009; Brown 2004). First of all, unsurprisingly, places can acquire such significance because of their histories, whether directly, by virtue of the fact that certain events once took place there, or indirectly, as when for example the relics of a saint come to be stored at a place, so that the relic is the bearer of religious significance in the first instance, and the place then shares in that significance at one remove, as the site where the relic is lodged in the present. We can speak of religious 'experience' in this connection in so far as the history of a place, or of the objects which are stored there, requires of the believer a certain kind of affective and also practical response when they are located there. It is perhaps tempting to say that this is not really a case of religious 'experience' in the conventional sense, but is more a question of someone having certain feelings as a consequence of having rehearsed various thoughts with a religious content. But that can't be a full account of the matter, if we allow that it is particularly fitting that these thoughts should be rehearsed here, and therefore particularly fitting that these feelings should be experienced here, in recognition of what happened at this place. On this view, the storied significance of the place is in a sense encountered, rather than just thought about, because that significance makes an affective as well as practical claim on the believer when they stand in the relevant spatial relationship to the place.

Secondly, a place may acquire special religious significance because of its sensory appearance in the present. Sacred sites commonly pose a challenge of some sort for the body, by virtue of being located in inaccessible places, or being surrounded by a threshold wall, or by threatening to overwhelm or expose the physical vulnerability of the believer on account of their scale or their dim lighting, to mention just a few examples. As Thomas Barrie comments: 'The path [to the sacred site] is rarely easy but is experienced as a trial, either physically or psychologically' (Barrie 1996: 59). It is natural to suppose that these physical challenges are designed to induce the right kind of mental attunement in the believer, broadly speaking one of reverential seriousness, so that they are predisposed to apprehend the meaning of the shrine aright. So such places are not available for casual inspection, but require of the believer a degree of seriousness of purpose, and a setting aside of conventional sources of security and self-worth. Clearly, this account is different from the first: a replica of a sacred site could serve as well as the original on this second account of the significance of sacred sites, but the same cannot be said on the first account, since any such replica will lack the storied significance of the original.

Finally, it is commonly supposed that sacred sites can owe their significance to their capacity to serve as an *imago mundi* or *axis mundi*, so that they stand as a microcosm for the nature of things more broadly, or in some way bear a representative meaning. This third account can easily be combined with the other two, since it may be that a place holds this sort of significance because of its sensory appearance or because of what once happened there.

From the standpoint of traditional natural theology, these observations may seem to be more of anthropological than philosophical interest. But in fact they are of some importance for a natural theological conception of religious experience, I am going to suggest. First of all, the phenomenological literature suggests that sites with these characteristics are a recurrent feature of traditional religious cultures. To this extent, we seem to be dealing with a mode of religious experience which constitutes to some extent a human universal, and which is to that extent a fitting topic for natural theological investigation. Next, this literature is concerned with a materially mediated kind of religious experience: it is by setting themselves in an appropriate physical relationship to a given place that the believer is able to access a sacred meaning. This is another important datum for natural theological reflection: if we are interested in human beings' 'natural' capacities for religious sense-making, then we need to take stock of the fact that religious experiences often have some material context as their focus, rather than taking the form of some non-sensory, non-materially mediated encounter with God which simply by-passes the material order.

Next, it is reasonable to suppose that the Sacred in each of these cases is presented to the believer not so much as an individual item of experience, but rather as the meaning which attaches to a particular material context. Gerardus van der Leeuw has commented that: 'The religious significance of things . . . is that on which no wider nor deeper meaning can follow. It is the meaning of the whole' (Leeuw 1938: 680). And a person can apprehend an encompassing, religious meaning of this kind, we might suppose, in the act of apprehending the meaning of a particular site, when this site bears a microcosmic significance. This finding is again of some interest for a natural theological account of religious experience: such experience, we could say, is not always, perhaps is not even usually, experience of a particular item, or of some 'supernatural object', but is rather a way of cognizing the meaning which attaches to a localized material context, and of cognizing thereby the meaning which attaches to a more broadly defined cosmological or metaphysical context. It is, we could say, a matter of learning how to assign an appropriate significance to individual things in their material context, rather than a matter of coming to apprehend a further and rather special individual thing. In a rather similar vein, Rowan Williams has written that talk of God 'is structurally more like talking about some "grid" for the understanding of particular objects than talking about particular objects in themselves' (Williams 1984: 15).

There is one further, very striking feature of these accounts, and especially of the second account: religious experience requires the believer to undergo, or in part perhaps it just consists in, an appropriate set of bodily affective responses. In other words, such experience depends upon adopting the right mode of engagement with the site, and is not available to someone who simply observes it neutrally. This is a further respect in which the literature on sacred space departs from the mainstream philosophical literature on religious experience. Notwithstanding its interest in the case of non-sensory experience, the philosophical literature does of course acknowledge that some reports of religious experience imply that God can be recognized or indirectly perceived in the data of sense experience. Swinburne cites as an analogy 'the way in which someone may see a vapour trail in the sky as the trail of an aeroplane' (Swinburne 2004: 299; Alston 1991: 21). Here God is non-inferentially recognized in God's effects. However, this example obscures the fact that God is not standardly available simply as an object of observation, in rather the way that tables and trees or vapour trails are. If the literature on sacred sites is a reliable guide, we should suppose that the recognition of sacred meanings depends upon striking the right affective-practical stance, rather than simply upon 'looking' (Scheler 1960: 266).

So a natural theological account of religious experience which is informed by these examples may well wish to say that religious experience, of these kinds, invites a certain conception of God, namely, as an overarching meaning, rather than as a supernatural 'object', and also a correlative epistemology, one which gives due acknowledgement to the sense-making capacities of the human body and of affective responses in particular. It might be objected that this account is concerned with circumstances which, whatever their importance in the religious history of human beings, are no longer of much interest, since 'modern', urbanized human beings evidently have little to do with sacred sites of the traditional kind. In fact, the picture we have been sketching can easily be generalized so that it applies equally to other kinds of experience, and not simply to experience of officially sanctioned 'sacred sites' of the traditional type. For example, most people find that there are certain places where they feel most themselves, or to which they will go if they wish to refresh their sense of the larger direction of their life. The places of childhood, for instance, often carry this sort of significance. Given the third of our accounts of the sacred site, we may say that places such as these can mediate a religious significance: they may not be sacred sites in the traditional sense, but such places store up the wider meaning of things for a person, and so carry a microcosmic significance for them. Once again, it may be because of its history (its association with childhood, for example) or because of its particular sensory qualities that a place is able to assume this sort of significance. Moving further still from the 'sacred site' model, we may add that microcosmic experience need not be tied to particular places, but may be a feature of circumstances which are defined, for example, more in social than simply in physical terms.

So this account of religious meaning can easily be extended to the context of modern, urban existence. And in this way, it can evade the charge of being theologically partisan. After all, many Christians, especially those of a Protestant persuasion, have felt, to say the least, a degree of reserve about the idea of 'sacred places', and many associate this idea with 'pagan' customs, see for instance Harold Turner's distinction between the *domus dei* and *domus ecclesiae* conceptions of church architecture (Turner 1979; White 1995). But if the account we have been considering admits of this broader application, then it need not imply that sacred sites of the traditional sort are especially well suited to serve as the bearers of religious meaning, and to this extent it need not be aligned with, say, a broadly Catholic rather than broadly Protestant religious sensibility.

The literature on sacred sites evidently suggests that the affective phenomenology of religious experiences is in some way integral to their significance. I want to think a little more closely now about how a natural theological appreciation of the epistemology of religious experience might give due recognition to the contribution of emotional feelings. On one account which was much favoured by philosophers in the latter half of the twentieth century, the emotions are to be understood as compound states, comprising a thought component and a feeling component, where the second derives from the first. Hence embarrassment, for example, is to be understood as the state of mind which consists of the thought that I have done something (or someone suitably related to me has done something) which may lower my standing in the eyes of others, together with a feeling of negative hedonic tone which is engendered by this thought. On this account, emotion types are to be differentiated by reference to their thought component, or by reference to the affective response which is engendered by a given thought (as when we distinguish pity and *schadenfreude*, for example) (Budd 1985: Ch. 1). This approach recognizes the emotions' contribution to our intellectual life: they are not to be considered as mere stomach churnings or twinges for example, since they have intellectual content. But on this view, this content resides in the thought component of the emotion, and its feeling component is represented as a kind of thought-induced sensation, which is in itself thought-less. Some more recent accounts of emotional feelings have, by contrast, sought to give them an intellectual significance in their own right (Blum 1994; Goldie 2000). These accounts fit very neatly with the kind of epistemology of the body that is implied in the second of our conceptions of the sacred site. Let's consider just one example of this further approach.

Suppose that I am fearful of a large dog that is fast approaching me. Following the thought-plus-feeling account, we might suppose that my fear consists in the thought that this dog is approaching plus a sensation of discomfort which is induced by that thought. But, more naturally, we might say that my fear does not involve so much an affect-free registering of the scene, which then engenders a felt response; rather, my experience is structured pervasively in normative and affective terms. Thus the dog will assume a degree of salience in my perceptual field while various other things, such as the colour of the linoleum floor on which I am standing, are consigned to the periphery of my awareness; and at the same time I am likely to register in feeling the tensing of my body, as it makes ready to deal with the practical demands of this particular situation. So here we have a unified state of mind which consists in a certain feeling and a correlative mode of salient perception and practical disposition of the body. In such a case, the feeling of fear is, we could say, of itself world-directed, in so far as it participates in the practical reckoning with the world that is implied in the body's stance, and in this particular organization of the perceptual field. At no point need there by any conscious rehearsing of thoughts along the lines of 'the dog is fast approaching, if it sinks its jaws into me I will experience a degree of discomfort' and so on; nor need there be a neutral perception of the dog's advance which is then classified as a bad development once it engenders a feeling of negative hedonic tone. Instead, the feeling of fear, along with a correlative organization of the perceptual field and expressive posture, is the primary mode of my recognition that I am in danger and need to take self-protective action (Pickard 2003; Solomon 2003).

This account of the role of emotional and bodily response in constituting certain evaluative insights is directly consonant with the second of our accounts of the sacred place. It is by virtue of eliciting a certain kind of bodily response that the sacred site, on this second model, succeeds in disclosing its significance, and this disclosure involves not so much the recognition of an additional item of experience, but rather an appreciation of how to view the various items of experience with appropriate salience, so that the 'meaning' or import of a set of circumstances is properly cognized.

An epistemology of religious experience of this kind clearly has a rather different character from those which have provided the focus of the recent literature in philosophy of religion, since it is concerned with the question of how to make sense of a material context, and with the role of emotional feelings in this regard. William Alston writes:

> One nagging worry is the possibility that the phenomenal content of mystical perception wholly consists of affective qualities, various ways the subject is feeling in reaction to what the subject takes to be the presence of God.... Our inability to specify any other sorts of non-sensory phenomenal qualities leads naturally to the suspicion that the experience is confined to affective reactions to a believed presence, leaving room for no experiential presentation of God or any other objective reality. [Alston 1991, 49–50]

This concern obviously trades on the thought-plus-feeling picture of the emotions: given that account, it is natural to suppose that an episode of feeling is a response to some thought rather than contributing more integrally to our reckoning with the nature of things. By contrast, Rudolf Otto's account of religious experience suggests that, in some cases anyway, such experiences involve not so much a discursive thought, with some state of feeling tacked on, but a non-conceptually articulated, affectively toned encounter, where emotional feeling is the primary mode of our recognition of the presence of a 'mysterious' other (Otto 1959: 40; Newman 1979: 108; Proudfoot 1985; Wainwright 1995; Wynn 2005).

We have been considering some of the ways in which experience of a material context can be religiously important. I want to close by noting very briefly one further way in which world-directed experience may serve to mediate a religious understanding. As we have seen from our discussion of Hick, philosophers of religion have been interested in the contribution of religious categories to the appearance of a putative transcendent object. It is reasonable to suppose that these categories can also penetrate the everyday appearances of the material world, and we might add that in this way a religious world-view can give us access to a distinctive life-world. A similar idea is evident in William James's observation that 'a not infrequent consequence of the change operated in the subject [following conversion] is a transfiguration of the face of nature in his eyes. A new heaven seems to shine upon a new earth' (James 1902: 151; Kohák 1984). In a comparable vein, Roger Scruton has noted various ways in which religious thoughts may inhabit the appearances of buildings—as when the thought of the Gothic church as an image of the heavenly Jerusalem enters into the appearance of such churches, so that this thought is rendered in the appearance, rather than just being evidenced by it (Scruton 1979: 74–5). Similarly, others have supposed that the thought of the world as designed can be regis-tered in perception, rather than being affirmed simply on the basis of inference (Ratzsch 2003). Generalizing from these examples, we might suppose that religious thoughts can be cast in sensory form, and that this possibility marks a further way in which everyday perceptual experience can count as a variety of religious experience.

We might wonder whether the capacity of religious thoughts to transfigure the sen-sory appearances of things can be relevant to an assessment of their truth. Clearly con-verts have sometimes taken the new vividness of their experience of the world following conversion as an index of the truth of their religious convictions. Here we return to the question of the evidential significance of religious experience. On this issue, as on a number of others that we have touched upon, the construction of a natural theological appreciation of the data of religious experience is evidently very much a work in progress.

REFERENCES

Alston, William P. (1991). *Perceiving God: The Epistemology of Religious Experience*. Ithaca, NY: Cornell University Press.

Barrie, Thomas (1996). *Sacred Place: Myth, Ritual, and Meaning in Architecture*. Boston, MA: Shambhala.

Blum, Lawrence (1994). *Moral Perception and Particularity*. Cambridge: Cambridge University Press.

Brown, David (2004). *God and Enchantment of Place: Reclaiming Human Experience*. Oxford: Oxford University Press.

Budd, Malcolm (1985). *Music and the Emotions: The Philosophical Theories*. London: Routledge & Kegan Paul.

Byrne, Peter (1995). *Prolegomena to Religious Pluralism: Reference and Realism in Religion*. Basingstoke: Macmillan.

Davis, Caroline Franks (1989). *The Evidential Force of Religious Experience*. Oxford: Clarendon Press.

Fales, Evan (2004). 'Do Mystics See God?' in *Contemporary Debates in Philosophy of Religion*. Edited by Michael Peterson and Raymond van Arragon. Oxford: Blackwell.

Forgie, William (1984). 'Theistic Experience and the Doctrine of Unanimity'. *International Journal for Philosophy of Religion* 15: 13–30.

Gale, Richard M. (1991). *On the Nature and Existence of God*. Cambridge: Cambridge University Press.

Gellman, Jerome I. (1997). *Experience of God and the Rationality of Theistic Belief*. Ithaca, NY: Cornell University Press.

—— (2001). *Mystical Experience of God: A Philosophical Inquiry*. Aldershot: Ashgate.

Goldie, Peter (2000). *The Emotions: A Philosophical Exploration*. Oxford: Oxford University Press.

Hick, John (1989). *An Interpretation of Religion: Human Responses to the Transcendent*. Basingstoke: Macmillan.

James, William (1902). *The Varieties of Religious Experience: A Study in Human Nature*, London: Longmans, Green, & Co.

Jones, Lindsay (2000). *The Hemeneutics of Sacred Architecture: Experience, Interpretation, Comparison*. Vol. II: *Hermeneutical Calisthenics: A Morphology of Ritual-Architectural Priorities*. Cambridge, MA: Harvard University Press.

Katz, Stephen (1978). 'Language, Epistemology and Mysticism' in *Mysticism and Philosophical Analysis*. Edited by S. Katz. London: Sheldon Press: pp. 22–74.

Kohák, Erazim (1984). *The Embers and the Stars: A Philosophical Inquiry into the Moral Sense of Nature*. Chicago: Chicago University Press.

Leeuw, Gerardus van der (1938). *Religion in Essence and Manifestation: A Study in Phenomenology*. Translated from German by J. E. Turner. London: George Allen & Unwin.

Newman, John Henry (1979). *An Essay in Aid of a Grammar of Assent*. Notre Dame, IN: University of Notre Dame Press.

O'Hear, Anthony (1984). *Experience, Explanation and Faith: An Introduction to the Philosophy of Religion*. London: Routledge & Kegan Paul.

Otto, Rudolf (1959). *The Idea of the Holy: An Inquiry into the Rational Factor in the Idea of the Divine and Its Relation to the Rational*. Translated from German by J. W. Harvey. Harmondsworth: Penguin Books.

Pickard, Hanna (2003). 'Emotions and the Problem of Other Minds' in *Philosophy and the Emotions*. Edited by A. Hatzimoysis. Cambridge: Cambridge University Press.

Pike, Nelson (1992). *Mystic Union: An Essay in the Phenomenology of Mysticism*. Ithaca, NY: Cornell University Press.

Plantinga, Alvin (2000). *Warranted Christian Belief*. New York: Oxford University Press.

Proudfoot, Wayne (1985). *Religious Experience*. Berkeley, CA: University of California Press.

Ratzsch, Del (2003). 'Perceiving Design' in *God and Design: The Teleological Argument and Modern Science*. Edited by Neil A. Manson. London: Routledge.

Scheler, Max (1960). *On The Eternal in Man*. Translated from German by Bernard Noble. London: SCM Press.

Scruton, Roger (1979). *The Aesthetics of Architecture*. Princeton, NJ: Princeton University Press.

Solomon, Robert (2003). 'Emotions, Thoughts and Feelings: What is a "Cognitive Theory" of the Emotions and Does It Neglect Affectivity?' in *Philosophy and the Emotions*. Edited by A. Hatzimoysis. Cambridge: Cambridge University Press.

Stace, W. T. (1961). *Mysticism and Philosophy*. London: Macmillan.

Stoeber, Michael (1992). 'Constructivist Epistemologies of Mysticism: A Critique and Revision'. *Religious Studies* 28: 107–16.

Swinburne, Richard (2004). *The Existence of God*. Oxford: Oxford University Press.

Turner, Denys (1995). *The Darkness of God: Negativity in Christian Mysticism*. Cambridge: Cambridge University Press.

Turner, Harold (1979). *From Temple to Meeting House: The Phenomenology and Theology of Places of Worship*. The Hague: Mouton Publishers.

Wainwright, William (1995). *Reason and the Heart: A Prolegomenon to a Critique of Passional Reason*. Ithaca, NY: Cornell University Press.

White, Susan (1995). 'The Theology of Sacred Space' in *The Sense of the Sacramental: Movement and Measure in Art, Music, Place and Time*. Edited by D. Brown and A. Loades. London: SPCK.

Williams, Rowan (1984). ' "Religious Realism": On Not Quite Agreeing with Don Cupitt'. *Modern Theology* 1: 3–24.

Wynn, Mark R. (2005). *Emotional Experience and Religious Understanding: Integrating Perception, Conception and Feeling*. Cambridge: Cambridge University Press.

—— (2009). *Faith and Place: An Essay in Embodied Religious Epistemology*. Oxford: Oxford University Press.

Yandell, Keith (1993). *The Epistemology of Religious Experience*. Cambridge: Cambridge University Press.

Zangwill, Nick (2004). 'The Myth of Religious Experience'. *Religious Studies* 40: 1–22.

CHAPTER 21

POSTMODERNISM AND NATURAL THEOLOGY

CLAYTON CROCKETT

POSTMODERNISM AND THE IMPOSSIBILITY OF NATURAL THEOLOGY

POSTMODERNISM is a complex and often ill-defined term, but it generally indicates a distance taken from modernism or modernity. One way to think about postmodernism is as a periodization, an epoch that succeeds the modern era. Another way to view it is more theoretical or methodological, that postmodernism offers ideas that call the modern into question. I adhere more to the latter, methodological understanding, because I think that postmodernism asks important questions about the nature and stakes of modernity. Postmodernism is not anti-modernism, however, and it does not simply dismiss or oppose modernity.

Natural theology can be seen as a European Enlightenment notion that develops the idea that human reason in its universal capacity can know the divine, or at least the regular laws by which divinity operates. Natural theology, or natural religion, names a predominately modern discourse that attempts to read divinity from the natural world. As a modern Enlightenment discursive practice, this conjunction of nature and divinity is rendered deeply problematic and seen as naive from the standpoint of postmodern philosophy. Postmodernism focusses on language and human culture, and views with suspicion any claims about nature, essence, or given reality. In many ways, postmodernism and natural theology is the story of a disjunctive if not hostile relationship, although this very conclusion is actually more complicated than it initially appears. Just as the relationship between postmodernism and religion or theology was originally seen as hostile and incompatible but has become more and more evident in the late twentieth and early twenty-first century, the connection between postmodernism and nature, and therefore natural theology, may in fact be more compatible than appearances suggest.

Postmodernism emerges as a term closely related to modernism, in literature, history, painting and architecture. According to Perry Anderson, the first use of the term 'postmodernism' occurs in Spanish in the 1930s by Federico de Onís, who 'used it to describe a conservative reflux within modernism itself' (Anderson 1998: 4). Postmodernism later becomes an American interpretative category, and debates swirled and continue to swirl around whether it is actually a conservative or progressive term. For many English-speaking intellectuals, postmodernism is the label that stuck to French post-structuralism as it emerged on the American scene in the 1960s. French existentialism, associated with the work of Jean-Paul Sartre and Albert Camus, remained influential in American intellectual contexts throughout the 1950s, and the structuralist philosophies that emerged in France in the work of Maurice Merleau-Ponty, Claude Lévi-Strauss, and Jacques Lacan did not reach the shores of the United States until the 1960s, when it was already giving way to post-structuralism in the work of Gilles Deleuze, Michel Foucault, and Jacques Derrida. The watershed conference on 'The Language of Criticism and the Sciences of Man' was held at Johns Hopkins University in 1966, and featured Roland Barthes, Jacques Lacan, and Jacques Derrida, among others.

For many English readers of French philosophy, the differences between structuralism and post-structuralism were somewhat blurry. Postmodernism became a catch-all term to indicate and describe French post-existentialist philosophy, even though most of the French philosophers themselves did not use the word. Finally, in a report on knowledge to the government of Quebec in 1979, the French philosopher Jean-François Lyotard spelled out *The Postmodern Condition*. Lyotard defines the word postmodern 'as incredulity toward meta-narratives' (Lyotard 1984: xxiv). We cannot avoid competing narratives, but the postmodern condition names a situation in which we have become suspicious of the two overarching meta-narratives of modernity: the liberal-progressive narrative of gradual reform, and the revolutionary Marxist narrative of an antagonistic clash between good (proletarian class struggle) and evil (bourgeois capitalism) that will lead to the end of history and a communist Utopia. Lyotard claims not only that these two meta-narratives cease to function as meta-narratives, but our reason itself is so conflicted that we cannot agree upon any other meta-narrative to replace them: 'consensus has become an outmoded and suspect value' (Lyotard 1984: 66). Our situation is marked by irreducible dissensus.

In the wake of Lyotard's work, postmodernism becomes a name that expands to include and incorporate various strands of post-structuralism, deconstruction, and avant-garde radical theory. Jean Baudrillard's theory of simulacra helps consolidate an understanding of postmodernism in which humans are utterly cut off from the real, including natural reality. Baudrillard claims that postmodernism is a situation marked by hyper-reality, where images and signs only refer to other signs, and the play of signs is ungrounded by any reality. Instead of a Platonic conception where the original Form exists and is then copied by the thing, there are no originals and no copies, only simulacra. Simulation, according to Baudrillard, 'stems from the utopia of the principle of equivalence, from the radical negation of the sign as value, from the sign as reversion and death sentence of every reality' (Baudrillard 1994: 6). For Baudrillard, there is no objectivity, no objective meaning or value, and no possibility of recapturing the lost real. All we can do is unreservedly throw ourselves into the play of simulacra. God, religion, reality, the universe, and nature itself are merely signs and simulacra, caught up in a play of non-referential simulation.

If postmodernism means what is implied in Baudrillard's extreme conclusion, then there is no possibility of any natural theology. But since postmodernism is also applied to distinct aspects of post-structuralism and deconstruction, there is room to delimit this conclusion about the impossibility of any relation between postmodernism and natural theology. On the one hand, postmodernism is deeply informed by twentieth-century philosophy's strong focus on language, and the thesis that language constructs or shapes reality. In his book *The Philosophical Discourse of Modernity* (1987), Jürgen Habermas says that Western philosophy largely follows a development from philosophies of being to philosophies of consciousness to philosophies of language. Whether the linguistic turn is associated with Nietzsche or with Frege, most forms of twentieth-century philosophy have taken up language as a fundamental object and theme. Language constructs a social world and shapes our perception and our identity, and to ignore this is naive. On the other hand, there is in French structuralism and post-structuralism an attention to science and scientific developments that is often lost in the translation into English.

In the United States, the post-Second World War intellectual situation is characterized by a bifurcation between science and philosophy, or the sciences and the humanities. The most popular and influential book about science among non-scientists is Thomas Kuhn's *The Structure of Scientific Revolutions*, first published in 1962. Kuhn articulates a model of paradigm shift, where the practices of normal science give way to revolutionary science under specific conditions of accumulating anomalies. Kuhn's work, taken up by non-scientists, alienated many intellectuals from what seemed like positivist and empirical practices of normal science blithely being done by obtuse scientists, while these non-scientist intellectuals understood and applied Kuhn's work more in social and cultural terms, absent his scientific contexts. For social, political, and technological reasons, the practice of science receded further and further from the theoretical understanding of science, philosophy, culture, and meaning. Post-structuralist and postmodern notions of the construction of knowledge and reality were read in these terms, even though in France the distance between serious science and serious philosophy was not nearly so great as in the United States (and arguably the United Kingdom). This distance between science and philosophy is so great that when the ground-breaking book by Ilya Prigogine and Isabelle Stengers was translated into English in 1984, the French title *Le Nouvelle alliance*, that is, the new alliance between humanity and nature (the humanities and the natural sciences), had to be downplayed into a subtitle, and the book retitled *Order Out of Chaos: Man's New Dialogue with Nature*. For English readers, a new alliance made no sense.

Neo-orthodoxy and Correlationalism: The Context of Postmodern Theology's Suspicion of Natural Theology

Postmodernism fits neatly into the cultural and intellectual situation of the latter part of the twentieth century where language constructs reality and nature in subjective and even voluntaristic terms. Theology is no exception generally, but for the striking attempt of John Cobb to elaborate *A Christian Natural Theology* using the metaphysics of Alfred North Whitehead. In the 1960s, theologians engaged with and appropriated new manifestations of secularization, and called into question even God's meaning and existence. These radical Death of God theologies were never very popular beyond the academy, but they contributed to the formation of a postmodern theology in the 1980s, which I will discuss below.

The overwhelming influence on theology in the second half of the century remained Karl Barth, and most radical and postmodern theologies followed Barth's strong rejection of natural theology, even if they broke with his neo-orthodoxy. Barth inaugurated twentieth-century theology with his famous commentary on Paul's Letter to the Romans, and he maintained an admirable and uncompromising rejection of human attempts to access, manipulate, and speak for God. From his *Römerbrief* to his multivolume *Church Dogmatics*, Barth attacked all human efforts to grasp the divine, and he contrasted the biblical Word with modern religious humanism. Christ is God's revelation to humanity, but we can only appropriate it by grace, not by our own will or reason, which are corrupted by sin. When his colleague, Emil Brunner, tried to find a sophisticated way to talk about a relationship between nature and grace, Barth's famous reply thundered forth: *Nein!* There could be no point of contact between natural reason and the natural world with God's grace as manifested in Jesus Christ. Barth's absolute opposition to natural theology continued to reverberate throughout the rest of the century, even among theologians who rejected Barthianism.

Theological efforts to delimit Barth took the form of correlationism: there must be some form of correlation between God and the world, between human and divine reason, and between the Bible or Christ and contemporary culture. Paul Tillich is the most famous Protestant representative of correlationism, but his efforts were effective and influential more in terms of cultural correlation than natural correlation, despite his language of being. Tillich offered resources for a theology of culture, and later theologians who took contemporary culture seriously viewed any straightforward language of being or ontology with suspicion.

In twentieth-century Roman Catholic theology, despite intriguing engagements with contemporary science and cosmology in the work of Georges Lemaître (who coined the term 'Big Bang') and Teilhard de Chardin (who took evolution seriously and spiritualized it), most serious work involves engaging, updating, critiquing, and applying

Thomism to contemporary thought and culture. Here Karl Rahner's attempt to modernize Aquinas in *Spirit in the World* and his *Theological Investigations* can be seen as a sort of correlationism, where the Thomistic *analogia entis* (analogy of being) provides the name for an act of understanding and being that possesses important theological implications. Since Thomas Aquinas is the privileged theologian of the Church, and his definition of God is in terms of a pure act, *actus purus*, contemporary action can be redescribed in spiritual terms, following the work of Maurice Blondel and the link between Aquinas and Kant established by Joseph Marechal. There is a correlation between the medieval and the modern tradition, and there is a correlation between thinking and being in terms of action, and this constitutes a liberal Catholic tradition that culminates in Vatican II. Hans Urs von Balthasar, however, follows Barth in rejecting this correlationism (even though he critiques him) and elaborates a Catholic neo-orthodoxy. Balthasar assumes the stance of the tradition against the modern world, and he elaborates a theological aesthetics and then a theological dramatics along broadly postmodern lines.

'How to Avoid Natural Theology': Postmodern Theology and the Turn from Nature

Contemporary theology overall is most engaged with language and culture, and nature is either implicitly or explicitly subordinated to issues of theological language or attempts to shape or change contemporary culture. A heuristic classificatory schema can envision four broad types of contemporary theology. The first type is fundamentalistic, rejecting all modernism and clinging to biblical inerrancy. The second type is neo-orthodox in a broad sense, which involves upholding the truth of the tradition, the Bible, and the Church but recasting those truths in more contemporary forms. The third type is correlationist, which means that it attempts to mediate between traditional truths and contemporary culture. Finally, the fourth type is liberationist, which struggles for human and social emancipation in political terms, associating divinity with social justice. Again, each of these types is centrally concerned with either conserving or updating theological language, and with changing, restoring, rejecting, or improving contemporary culture. Nature is marginal to most forms of theological discourse, with two notable exceptions: first, process theology, as already mentioned; and, secondly, efforts to justify and prove the existence of God in modern rational and analytic terms.

Postmodernism and postmodern theology is distinct in its methodology and aims from process theology, although there are points of intersection and overlap. Postmodernism and postmodern theology are very suspicious of modernist attempts to prove the existence of God in the form of analytic truth claims, however, including efforts to justify or reconcile God with the world in terms of theodicy. All of these efforts, that make up a large portion of analytic philosophy of religion, appear incredible from the standpoint of postmodernism. Postmodern theology consists of a radicalization of traditional theological concepts based on an understanding of 'the Death of God'.

The Death of God theology emerged in the 1960s in the United States and United Kingdom. This Death of God theology can be seen as a radicalized Tillichianism that takes theology further into culture than Tillich's correlational method did. Theologians like Gabriel Vahanian, Thomas J. J. Altizer, William Hamilton, Richard Rubenstein, and John A. T. Robinson argue that traditional concepts of God are irrelevant to contemporary culture, and they break with Barthian neo-orthodoxy. At the same time, however, these Death of God theologians, with their emphasis upon culture, philosophy, and theological language, maintain Barth's suspicion of the viability of any natural theology. The Death of God theology takes many forms, but none of them seriously engages with nature or natural theology.

In the 1980s, a postmodern theology developed that combined insights drawn from Death of God theology with readings of French deconstruction and post-structuralism. Postmodern theologians such as Mark C. Taylor, Carl Raschke, Don Cupitt, Charles Winquist, and Edith Wyschogrod argue that theology is best understood as a discursive social practice. As Raschke puts it in his contribution to a collection of essays on *Deconstruction and Theology*, 'deconstruction is in the final analysis the death of God put into writing' (Raschke 1982: 3). These postmodern theologians attend to and follow the overwhelming focus on language and culture, and emphasize questions of aesthetics, ethics, and epistemology as applied to theological language and contemporary culture.

In the 1990s, following Derrida's more explicit attention to religious and political themes, a Continental philosophy of religion took shape around more phenomenological and hermeneutical methods. This Continental philosophy of religion kept its distance from theology per se, but it showed how French post-structuralism and post-modernism, far from jettisoning religious ideas, was making religion more crucial for a post-modern context. In addition to Derrida, French philosophers like Emmanuel Levinas, Paul Ricoeur, and Jean-Luc Marion were important sources. In the English-speaking world, John D. Caputo, Merold Westphal, Richard Kearney, and Kevin Hart were the central figures in this conversation. Caputo hosted four influential conferences on Religion and Postmodernism at Villanova University in the late 1990s and early 2000s, the first three featuring Derrida. Continental philosophy of religion privileges phenomenological interpretation of texts, cultures, and images, and remains suspicious of any direct or unmediated appeal to nature or natural religion.

In an essay on 'How to Avoid Speaking of God: The Violence of Natural Theology', Caputo argues that natural theology is necessarily violent, but that we cannot avoid this violence if we want to speak of God (Caputo 1992). Natural theology does violence to the reality of God by trying to express it in determinate language, and it commits violence against human beings by claiming to speak in a privileged and possessive way about the nature of God in a way that perpetuates violence on other people. Caputo does not reject natural theology completely, and he criticizes Jean-Luc Marion's effort to separate

God from Being. For postmodern philosophy of religion, language is a kind of ontology. We cannot fully separate language from being, but we should recognize that 'the unmediated is never delivered without massive mediation' (Caputo 1992: 130). In this essay from the 1990s, Caputo affirms the necessity of speaking about God, but still keeps his distance from theology. In his later book *The Weakness of God*, published in 2006, Caputo affirms what he is doing as a kind of weak theology, or a theology of the event. Weakness is here opposed to strong, determinate, and apologetic theologies, which know what they mean when they speak about God. For Caputo, the event means that something is happening in the name of God that we can invoke but cannot completely know or describe (or enforce).

For postmodernism, language is a kind of ontology, or possesses its own being and materiality, even if the ontological aspects of language are usually more implicit. Around the turn of the century, we can see a return to more explicit ontological themes in Continental philosophy. Sometimes this appeal to ontology takes the form of a rejection of postmodernism, as seen in the work of Alain Badiou and Slavoj Žižek. Badiou and Žižek criticize the excesses of postmodernism, including the postmodern obsession with otherness in multicultural terms, and the over-emphasis on language to the exclusion of non-linguistic reality. This return of ontology raises anew questions of nature and the natural world, although not in the conventional terms of natural theology. At the same time, Continental philosophers like Žižek and Badiou maintain and sustain an interest in religion and politics, even though they are both self-professed atheists. This engagement with issues of ontology, politics, and religion provides resources for rethinking questions of natural theology, even if such discussions do not take place in conventional terms.

According to Badiou, in his magnum opus *Being and Event*, mathematics in the form of set-theory provides a fundamental ontology that characterizes being as being (Badiou 2006). Badiou argues that mathematical set-theory indicates an irreducible multiplicity, rather than an overarching One, and unity or oneness emerges as a subtraction from this original multiplicity. He claims that the decision for multiplicity and against the One is a rejection of theism and a liberation of atheism, because Western logic is constrained to think God as One. In his book on *Badiou and Theology*, however, Frederiek Depoortere defends a more traditionalist understanding of God in terms of set-theory by appealing to Georg Cantor and not disqualifying paradoxical sets which include themselves as members (Depoortere 2009). For Žižek, ontology takes the form of a fundamental disjunction, or parallax, where it is not simply that our ideas about reality do not line up with natural reality, but in fact reality itself is disjoined or incommensurable with itself. Rather than a traditional split between thinking and being, Žižek argues that thinking mirrors an originary split within nature. In his book, *The Parallax View*, Žižek discusses contemporary neurology and other cognitive sciences, and claims that:

> the only way effectively to account for the status of (self-)consciousness is to assert the ontological incompleteness of 'reality' itself: there is 'reality' only insofar as there is an ontological gap, a crack, in its very heart, that is to say, a traumatic excess, a foreign body which cannot be integrated into it. [Žižek 2006: 242]

Žižek calls himself a Christian atheist, because he claims that the crucifixion of Jesus demonstrates this ontological gap, which is a gap within nature, humanity, and the divine at once.

Towards a Postmodern Natural Theology

In a narrow sense we could say that this return of and to ontology represents a move beyond postmodernism, in so far as postmodernism indicates a specific discourse prevalent during the late twentieth-century dealing with language, politics, and culture. The predominant mood of this specific postmodernist discourse is critique, or a hyper-suspicion of meta-narratives, overarching truth claims, or naive appeals to nature or the 'way things are'. In an essay, 'Mood Swings', Katherine Hayles and Todd Gannon claim that this narrow form of postmodernism died in the mid-1990s. They trace a 'mood shift' towards 'complex connections with the emergence of network culture and what Manuel Castells has called "informationalism"' (Hayles and Gannon 2007: 102). But we could also view postmodernism more broadly and think about this renewed interest in nature and ontology in more complex terms, where there is a shift in tone but not in substance. Finally, we could see tools for the elaboration of a complex natural theology, a postmodern natural theology that is very different from traditional modern forms of natural theology.

Complexity theory arises out of chaos theory and to a certain extent information theory. Structuralism and post-structuralism are both informed by information theory, and in some ways postmodernism can be identified with a kind of chaos theory. The problem, however, is that information theory, chaos theory, and complexity theory all work across the boundary that divides the natural from the cultural world, whereas postmodern theory in most of its guises has largely confined itself to cultural, social, and linguistic phenomena. Postmodernism in the English-speaking world has forgotten or neglected the fact that the deconstruction of the opposition nature/culture, as performed by Derrida in *Of Grammatology*, does not mean that culture simply swallows up nature (Derrida 1976). Postmodern theory has been over-determined by Richard Rorty's influential book, *Philosophy and the Mirror of Nature*, where Rorty claims that linguistic metaphors go 'all the way down,' and never get to the natural world they attempt to mirror (Rorty 1979). At the same time, most Anglo-American philosophy, including Rorty's, appeals to a kind of minimalist naturalism that is often obscured when it bumps up against postmodernism.

This is a complex discussion, but I am arguing that complexity theory 'better' instantiates some of the most important post-structuralist insights than many of the postmodern appropriations of post-structuralism. In a narrow sense, we need to get beyond the limits of a postmodernism obsessed with language and culture to the exclusion of nature, which is partly the consequence of its American reception and engagement by philosophers, social scientists, and literary theorists who have applied post-structuralism to the contemporary American academy, with its strong methodological divide between the humanities and the natural sciences. In a broad sense, postmodern and post-structuralist insights and ideas are still vitally relevant to reconceptualizing nature in various ways, including theological ones. Here both complexity theories and postmodern ideas deform traditional notions of theology, so that a postmodern natural theology would not be a traditional or neo-orthodox form of theology, but a more radical and open form of theological questioning and understanding.

According to the theoretical physicist Murray Gell-Mann:

> [a] complex adaptive system acquires information about its environment and its own interaction with that environment, identifying regularities in that information, condensing those regularities into a kind of 'schema' or model, and acting in the real world on the basis of that schema. [Gell-Mann 1994: 17]

What is interesting about a complex adaptive system is that it cuts across the organic/inorganic distinction, because non-living systems can be complexly adaptive too. Complex adaptation works by means of nonlinear processes, including recursive feedback loops. These feedback loops are extremely complex, and they cannot be modelled in conventional linear terms. Complex adaptive systems can appear chaotic in so far as they are not linear, but chaos theory is less about literal disorder than sensitive dependence on initial conditions, where small changes can be magnified to create large-scale effects. At the same time, these systems can also display a surprising amount of resiliency, or resistance to external changes.

Complex adaptive systems take place along an edge where technology and science intersect and interact. The philosopher of science Katherine Hayles claims that the complex self-organizing processes that constitute contemporary science and network culture challenge conventional understandings of the human being, and lead towards a 'post-humanism' (Hayles 1999). The post-human is characterized by an interface where robotic technologies, biological processes, and cultural understandings all interact. The post-human is a kind of cyborg, as Donna Haraway explains in her 'Cyborg Manifesto'. According to Haraway, 'a cyborg is a cybernetic organism, a hybrid of machine and organism, a creature of social reality as well as a creature of fiction' (Haraway 1991: 149). Cyborgs transgress boundaries: boundaries between humans and animals, organisms and machines, and finally between physical and non-physical reality. The theological significance of cyborgs and post-humanism resides not in their objective status, but in the internal processes that constitute them in their becoming. This is a kind of postmodern spirit in the world that does not provide evidence of any transcendent God, but embodies traces of divinity immanent to the process of self-organization.

We live in a network culture, one that does not simply subsume nature, but expresses it in a distinct and complex way. The postmodern theologian Mark C. Taylor has been one of the theorists most engaged in discussions of complexity from a broadly religious perspective. Taylor argues that we are living in *The Moment of Complexity*, which marks a historical and technological transition from a modernist world based upon grids to a network culture that works by means of webs (Taylor 2001). According to Taylor, complexity is the emergence of life or self-organization at the edge of chaos. Complexity lies between order and chaos. Taylor draws on the work of the theoretical biologist Stuart Kauffman, who suggests that 'genomic systems lie in the ordered regime near the phase transition to chaos' (Kauffman 1995: 25). Genomic systems and networks both exist and thrive near the edge of chaos, in a constant state of tension that sustains organization but does not simply dissolve into disorder. In a later book, *After God*, Taylor claims that the Infinite itself is fractal—'the Infinite is an emergent self-organizing network of networks that extends from the natural and social to the technological and cultural dimensions of life' (Taylor 2007: 346). The Infinite is not somewhere else beyond the finite, but it is the rhythm of the finite as well as the matrix in which all relation and intermediation occurs.

Taylor draws on contemporary complexity theory to reconceptualize religion and develop a postmodern theology of culture that avoids binary oppositions. Taylor criticizes the obsession with negative critique that marks deconstruction, and moves towards a post-post-structuralism that offers a more complex model or structure than that presupposed by earlier structuralism. Complexity theory and complex adaptive systems allows us to reframe traditional debates, including discussions about chance and design that inform natural theological questions about God. In terms of modern natural theology, either the world is the effect of random chance, or it is the product of intelligent design. For the most part, the attempt to locate and affirm design in nature has been de-legitimated, first by the philosophical criticisms of David Hume in his *Dialogues Concerning Natural Religion* and then the extraordinary success of Darwinian natural selection. Most constructive projects of natural theology have overlooked or ignored Hume's devastating critiques, and have had to take defensive and reactionary positions against the methods or implications of Darwinism. Complexity theory, however, avoids the clumsy arguments for intelligent design and the absolutization of chance in some forms of neo-Darwinism. Complexity is emergent rather than designed, and it involves randomness but not complete and incredible chance due to the predictable effects of recursivity upon systems.

Although it is not solely a natural theology, an understanding of life as an emergent self-organizing process on the edge of chaos as theorized by Kauffman and others offers new ways of thinking about religion and science and what Taylor calls the Infinite (as opposed to God). In terms of cosmology and particle physics, contemporary science provides powerful sources of awe and wonder, although again, its conclusions caution against too-quick an assimilation to more traditionalist categories of religious reflection. Even if Einstein was wrong about some of the implications of quantum physics, his relativity theory shifts and distorts our conventional perspectives about space and time. Furthermore, Einstein himself cultivated and defended a 'cosmic religious feeling' that indicates a sense of awe and wonder when confronted with the complexity of the universe. Many scientists in the twentieth century have followed Einstein in expressing a form of religious feeling in light of the surprising and elusive nature of the cosmos.

Two of the most important problems in contemporary cosmology and particle physics involve first the discovery of the acceleration of the expansion of the universe in 1998, which gives rise to speculation about dark energy, and secondly, the experimental impasse reached in particle physics due to its inability to get down to the Planck scale. Dark energy provides a force to explain the observed acceleration of the universe, and it sometimes consists of the introduction of a cosmological constant, introduced by Einstein in order to stabilize the universe and then abandoned as an absurdity. This new cosmological constant provides a force that is driving the universe apart more and more quickly, and eventually, in the absence of a counter-force, would lead to what cosmologists call a 'big rip' that will tear everything, including atoms, apart. The discovery of dark energy, as well as observations and theories about black holes, has generated much speculation about the nature and functioning of the universe. One idea, offered by theoretical physicist Lee Smolin in *The Life of the Cosmos*, is that the formation of a black hole constitutes a new universe in another dimension (Smolin 1997). Another possibility, which challenges the conventional Big-Bang model of the origin of the universe, is the idea of an ek-pyrotic universe, offered by Paul Steinhardt and Neil Turok (2007). Ek-pyrosis is a cyclic view of the universe, where what we call the Big Bang is actually the crashing together of two brane-worlds that then spread apart an infinitesimal and unmeasurable distance before coming together again about a trillion years later. As Steinhardt and Turok acknowledge, their proposal of a cyclic or ek-pyrotic universe has more in common with ancient Greek and Hindu cosmology than with Christian or Jewish monotheism. In any case, the Big Bang, even though it remains the dominant hypothesis, is by no means settled, and this unsettlement can itself be a stimulus to theological reflection about the nature of the universe, even it if exceeds the limits of Christian theology.

String theory is an extraordinary mathematical and physical theory that claims that the fundamental things in the world are tiny one-dimensional strings. Unfortunately, scientists cannot come anywhere near the scale needed to detect these strings, but the theory is promising precisely because it can (theoretically) unify gravity and quantum physics, the twin legacies of the twentieth century. In 1995 Edward Witten demonstrated that at low energies, a ten-dimensional superstring theory can be compatible with an eleven-dimensional supergravity (Randall 2005: 313). The possibility of unifying quantum physics with gravity is incredibly exciting for physicists, but the problem is that we are unable to experimentally confirm or disconfirm this or any version of string (or superstring) theory. At the same time, alternative efforts exist to formulate a theory of quantum gravity, based on the work of Smolin, Carlo Rovelli, Abhay Ashtekar, and others (Callendar and Huggett 2001). The basic problem is not only our inability to measure such miniscule phenomena as the graviton, but also that the very structure of space-time seems to break down at the Planck scale unit of measurement.

So space and time seem to be themselves emergent, entangled phenomena, and we are forced to speculate, philosophize, and even theologize in the absence of experimental data. One of the main hopes for experimental confirmation or disconfirmation of contemporary particle physics is the Large Hadron Collider, the most powerful supercollider ever built. Based at CERN in Switzerland and France, the LHC became operational in the autumn of 2008 but then almost immediately broke down and had to be repaired. As of this writing, the LHC is working but results are not yet in. The most important task of the LHC is to test for the Higgs particle, which has been dubbed the 'God particle' because if it exists it gives mass to the other particles that make up the standard model of contemporary particle physics. If the Higgs particle is detected, then physicists will feel very confident about the standard model. But if the Higgs is not found at the energies available for the LHC, then serious questions will be raised about the entire model, which includes quarks, leptons, and gluons. Finally, there is some possibility that the LHC might be able to detect indirect evidence for the existence of higher dimensions. String theory posits at least ten dimensions. We experience four—three spatial dimensions plus time—so the other six must somehow be hidden or rolled up in such small ways that we cannot currently detect them. In her book *Warped Passages: Unraveling the Mysteries of the Universe's Hidden Dimensions*, Lisa Randall claims that the LHC *might* detect Kaluza-Klein particles, which are three-dimensional partners of higher-dimensional ones (Randall 2005: 457).

Whatever the results from the Large Hadron Collider, contemporary physics and cosmology have opened up new venues for theoretical reflection, even as complexity provides a better methodology by which to think across disciplinary and natural boundaries. Postmodernism offers ways to think about language, culture, and ideas in complex and unorthodox ways. Although in Anglo-American contexts postmodernism has been largely shorn of connections to nature and to scientific and technological processes, many of these ideas and connections are being made or remade, along what Hayles calls the cusp of meaning. Postmodern religion concerns culture and politics, language and identity, and it coincides with an incredible resurgence of religion in contemporary life, largely but not exclusively in traditionalist and fundamentalist forms. At the same time, a few brave postmodern theologians and theorists have taken up issues and questions concerning nature, the nature of reality, and the universe, as well as the nature of emergent self-organization.

CONCLUSION: A POSTMODERN NATURAL THEOLOGY OF BECOMING

By way of conclusion, I want to briefly consider how Deleuze articulates processes of physical and metaphysical becoming, and show how these reflections on intensity and energy matter for postmodern theology in the work of Catherine Keller. In his book *Difference and Repetition*, Deleuze develops a metaphysical model of repetition based on difference, where repetition is repetition of difference rather than identity (Deleuze 1994). Deleuze avoids and opposes the stereotypical postmodern emphasis on language; he is primarily interested in being or becoming. Becoming is becoming different and it is based on difference. *Difference and Repetition* is an extremely dense book, but it offers a kind of postmodern ontology that has not been fully appreciated or comprehended. According to Deleuze, repetition of difference is possible by means of intensities. Intensity is what drives repetition. Intensity is a kind of energy that differentiates individuals, both human and non-human beings, and it lies underneath extensive qualities.

The energy that constitutes becoming is a kind of spiritual energy. Deleuze contrasts spiritual repetition of difference with bare material repetition of the same. Energy is generally seen in dualistic terms, either as immaterial spirit or material physical stuff. The convertibility of matter and energy formulated by Einstein, combined with the insights of quantum physics and later developments of chaos theory and complexity theory, suggest that energy is a strange and vital phenomenon. Energy transformation, or intensity, makes up what Deleuze calls 'a life', which is not simply an organic phenomenon, but closer to what we understand by complex self-organized systems. Our contemporary material civilization over the last three centuries is based on the exploitation of stored solar energy in the form of fossil fuels, which are not renewable on the time scales of human civilization. Deleuze's post-structuralist philosophy offers a new way to think about energy and becoming, which is a spiritual intensity that takes place upon a plane of immanence rather than on another, higher plane of transcendence.

For the postmodern and process theologian Catherine Keller, Deleuze's thought, when combined with that of Alfred North Whitehead, Jacques Derrida, and others, and applied to an interpretation of Genesis 1:1, contributes to a theology of becoming. In the Genesis account, the creation of heaven and earth occurs at a time when darkness is on 'the face of the deep', which gives the title of Keller's book (2003). The Hebrew word for deep is *tehom*, and Keller elaborates a tehomic theology that deconstructs traditional conceptions of *creatio ex nihilo*, or creation out of an absolute nothing. For Keller, creation is *creatio ex profundis*, or creation out of a profound deep. *Tehom* names 'the depth of God', which is 'the topos of creation', where the world surges in its virtuality, in the *complicatio*, or 'folding together', the 'matrix of all relations' (Keller 2003: 227). The deep is the creative edge of chaos where becoming takes place, and she uses a term that Deleuze borrows from James Joyce, *chaosmos*, to name this productive chaos. The depth, which is a spiritual depth, provides the energy that drives becoming or repetition, and this becoming is always new because it is a repetition of difference. Depth is not a stored resource somewhere else in another dimension, but a part of the process of energy transformation, self-organization, and life. Complex self-organization along the edge of chaos works with a kind of spirituality, a dynamic rather than a static divine intensity that participates in the world rather than stands apart from it in impassive aseity. In her book *The Face of the Deep*, drawing on resources of process theology, Catherine Keller has written perhaps the most compelling account of a postmodern natural theology.

REFERENCES

Anderson, Perry (1998). *The Origins of Postmodernity*. London: Verso.
Badiou, Alain (2006). *Being and Event*. Translated by Ray Brassier. London: Continuum.

Baudrillard, Jean (1994). *Simulacra and Simulation*. Translated by Sheila Faria Glaser. Ann Arbor: University of Michigan Press.

Callender, Craig and Nick Huggett, eds. (2001). *Physics Meets Philosophy at the Planck Scale: Contemporary Theories in Quantum Gravity*. Cambridge: Cambridge University Press.

Caputo, John D. (1992). 'How to Avoid Speaking of God: The Violence of Natural Theology' in *Prospects for Natural Theology*. Edited by Eugene Long. Washington, DC: The Catholic University of America Press: pp. 128–50.

—— (2006). *The Weakness of God: A Theology of the Event*. Bloomington: Indiana University Press.

Deleuze, Gilles (1994). *Difference and Repetition*. Translated by Paul Patton. New York: Columbia University Press.

Depoortere, Frederiek (2009). *Badiou and Theology*. London: Continuum.

Derrida, Jacques (1976). *Of Grammatology*. Translated by Gayatri Chakravorty Spivak. Baltimore: Johns Hopkins Press.

Gell-Mann, Murray (1994). *The Quark and the Jaguar: Adventures in the Simple and the Complex*. New York: Henry Holt.

Habermas, Jürgen (1987). *The Philosophical Discourse of Modernity*. Translated by Frederick J. Lawrence. Cambridge, MA: The MIT Press.

Haraway, Donna (1991). 'A Cyborg Manifesto: Science, Technology, and Socialist-Feminism in the Late Twentieth Century' in *Simians, Cyborgs and Women: The Reinvention of Nature*. New York: Routledge: pp. 149–81.

Hayles, N. Katherine (1999). *How We Became Post-Human: Virtual Bodies in Cybernetics, Literature and Informatics*. Chicago: University of Chicago Press.

Hayles, N. Katherine and Todd Gannon (2007). 'Mood Swings: The Aesthetics of Ambient Experience' in *The Mourning After: Attending the Wake of Postmodernism*. Edited by Neil Brooks and Josh Toth. Amsterdam: Rodopi: pp. 99–142.

Kauffman, Stuart (1995). *At Home in the Universe: The Search for the Laws of Self-Organization and Complexity*. Oxford: Oxford University Press.

Keller, Catherine (2003). *The Face of the Deep: A Theology of Becoming*. London: Routledge.

Lyotard, Jean-François (1984). *The Postmodern Condition: A Report on Knowledge*. Minneapolis: University of Minnesota Press.

Prigogine, Ilya and Isabelle Stengers (1984). *Order Out of Chaos: Man's New Dialogue with Nature*. New York: Bantam Books.

Randall, Lisa (2005). *Warped Passages: Unraveling the Mysteries of the Universe*. New York: HarperCollins.

Raschke, Carl (1982). 'The Deconstruction of God' in *Deconstruction and Theology*. Edited by Thomas J. J. Altizer et al. New York: Crossroad.

Rorty, Richard (1979). *Philosophy and the Mirror of Nature*. Princeton: Princeton University Press.

Smolin, Lee (1997). *The Life of the Cosmos*. Oxford: Oxford University Press.

Steinhardt, Paul J. and Neil Turok (2007). *Endless Universe: Beyond the Big Bang—Rewriting Cosmic History*. New York: Broadway Books.

Taylor, Mark C. (2001). *The Moment of Complexity: Emerging Network Culture*. Chicago: University of Chicago Press.

—— (2007). *After God*. Chicago: University of Chicago Press.

Žižek, Slavoj. (2006). *The Parallax View*. Cambridge, MA: The MIT Press.

CHAPTER 22

....

FEMINIST PERSPECTIVES ON NATURAL THEOLOGY

PAMELA SUE ANDERSON

'NATURAL THEOLOGY' AND PHILOSOPHICAL OPENNESS

....

PHILOSOPHICAL theologians from Thomas Aquinas to Richard Swinburne (2005: 106–21) and Linda Zagzebski (2007: 13–14) would agree that natural theology has its roots in the Christian intellectual tradition, as well as in ancient Greek and scholastic philosophies. In contemporary theological circles at least, 'natural theology' tends to designate an analytic philosophical as opposed to a theological field of knowledge; this is the case in so far as the theologian requires divine revelation, before acquiring any natural knowledge of, or a relationship to, God. Consistent with the sense of natural theology as a form of philosophy and, specifically, as an analytic tradition of philosophy of religion, the philosophical preoccupation of natural theologians has been the arguments from evident features of the natural world to the existence and nature of God (Zimmerman 2007: 1–13; Wolterstorff 2009: 155–70). Other contemporary philosophers would contend that Immanuel Kant discredited this preoccupation of natural theology in the late eighteenth-century (see Anderson and Bell 2010: 40–9).

Another sense of 'natural theology' emerged and persists despite, or possibly because of, Kant's criticisms of the ontological proof on which the other proofs for the existence of the theistic God depend. In this second and much broader sense of natural theology, the contemporary philosopher thinks critically about human beings as they live and interact within a natural world. Consistent with the growth of knowledge in a whole range of modern intellectual fields, including philosophy, psychology, literature, history, and social and physical sciences, a new form of natural theology is created by both philosophers and those philosophical theologians who explore underdeveloped human capacities to think about the nature of our lives, the world, and our relations to other beings who are like and unlike us. For instance, this would include at least some, if not all, of the contributing philosophers in *Philosophers without Gods* (see Antony 2007: x–xiii). Instead of requiring belief in the theistic God, these philosophers and/or natural theologians argue for a more broadly construed theology, or rational religion of life, of living beings and nature itself. A natural theologian of life asks questions about the nature of particular living beings, subjects, and objects; about general terms and concepts which every human being applies to nature, to other beings, to the self, and to some sense of 'the divine'. Questions are also asked about living beings and their relations to inanimate things.

Feminist perspectives on natural theology should cover both the narrow and the broad construals of the field. But very different things would have to be said by feminist philosophers about the philosophical issues in the traditionally narrow sense of natural theology from those things said of the broader sense. It is interesting, for example, to speculate about how many of those philosophers whose writings are examples of analytical natural theology imagine that their rigour and precision on the arguments concerning God manage to avoid completely questions of gender. Feminist theologians would and have challenged the claim that 'rigour' requires complete gender-blindness (e.g. Coakley 2009: 280–312). The result will surely be a critical dismissal of the ambitions and methods of narrowly construed natural theology on the basis of feminist concerns, and a reciprocal rejection of feminist perspectives within this theology. However, it may be more philosophically interesting for feminist critics to turn to the broader approach to natural theology, to render an openness to the whole range of philosophical (and theological) questions of God and gender issues. As such, it is the goal of this chapter to suggest a reflective critical openness to feminist perspectives on natural theology.

This philosophical openness to thinking about nature, about our human relationships, capacities, concepts, and conceptual scheme would enable a constructive feminist perspective on natural theology. To locate this perspective, it is necessary to explore both implicit and explicit responses to natural theology by a few representative women from the present and the previous centuries in western philosophy.

THE SECOND SEX AND NATURAL THEOLOGY

In 1949, Simone de Beauvoir published *Le Deuxieme Sexe*. In the past sixty plus years, *The Second Sex* has persisted as a classic text of philosophy, while still posing a feminist challenge to the Western tradition of natural theology. Beauvoir's challenge is to the ways in which men have created their world and, in the process, produced an unwitting 'theology' of male subjects. Consider her feminist perspective on the singular situation of a female author:

> It would never occur to a man to write a book on the singular situation of males in humanity. If I want to define myself, I first have to say, 'I am a woman': all other

assertions will arise from this basic truth. A man never begins by positing himself as an individual of a certain sex: that he is a man is obvious. [Beauvoir 2009: 5]

To support these facts about men and women as truths of the world, Beauvoir turns to the philosophers and theologians in the history of Western thought. She begins *The Second Sex* with an epigraph from Pythagoras: 'There is a good principle which created order, light, and man, and an evil principle which created chaos, darkness and woman.' In the course of her book, Beauvoir refers to a significant number of the men in philosophy, literature, and theology whose sexist views reinforce her critique of the 'truths' about woman. To quote her text again at some length:

> Woman has ovaries and a uterus; such are the particular conditions that lock her in her subjectivity; some even say she thinks with her hormones. Man vainly forgets that his anatomy also includes hormones and testicles. He grasps his body as a direct and normal link with the world that he believes he apprehends in all objectivity whereas he considers woman's body an obstacle, a prison, burdened by everything that particularises it. 'The female is a female by virtue of a certain *lack* of qualities', Aristotle said. 'We should regard women's nature as suffering from natural defectiveness.' And St Thomas in his turn decreed that woman was an 'incomplete man', an 'incidental' being. This is what the Genesis story symbolises, where Eve appears as if drawn from Adam's 'supernumerary' bone, in Bossuet's words. Humanity is male, and man defines woman, not in herself, but in relation to himself; she is not considered an autonomous being... she is nothing other than what man decides; she is thus called 'the sex', meaning that the male sees her essentially as a sexed being; for him she is sex, so she is it in the absolute. She determines and differentiates herself in relation to man, and he does not in relation to her; she is the inessential in front of the essential. He is the Subject, he is the Absolute. She is the Other. [Beauvoir 2009: 5–6]

Ironically, feminist philosophers continue both to be shaped by and to criticize Beauvoir's account of woman as the Other (Anderson 2009a: 27–8, 37–50; 2010: 175–80). Beauvoir's exposure of this myth of the Other catapulted a generation of women into resisting the complicity which characterized, in Beauvoir's terms, 'the situation' of woman (cf. Le Doeuff 2010: 90–105). A woman's situation is her embodied existence, and in 1949 Beauvoir demonstrates that female embodied existence had been devalued by centuries of natural theologians who had exalted themselves to the position of male supremacy. From a Beauvoirian feminist perspective, this exaltation is nothing else than man's attempt to be God (Beauvoir 1976: 14–16); or, in contemporary terms, male deification is a simulacra (Rea 2009: 23). Following Beauvoir, but more explicitly in the context of natural theology, Mary Daly argued, twenty years later, against the philosophical theologian's God: 'if God is male, then male is God' (Daly 1986: 19). Daly's argument may be incomplete; but it sets the male-human God in the context of Christian myth. She anticipates the decisive role that 'myth' plays in feminist perspectives on natural theology. Continuing on and beyond this path of Christian mythology, Daly would eventually identify herself as 'a post-Christian feminist'.

MYTH, ABSOLUTE TRUTH,
AND MALE SUPREMACY

It is crucial to understand myth's role in a feminist demythologization of the sexism in natural theology. This feminist demythologization aims to extract the myth about women and men from the Thomist tradition of natural theology as seen by Beauvoir and her feminist successors. Beauvoir captures the general structure of myth, in shaping virile figures, 'sex', and the flesh as follows:

> Any myth implies a Subject who projects its hopes and fears of a transcendent heaven. Not positing themselves as Subject, women have not created the virile myth that would reflect their projects; they have neither religion nor poetry that belongs to them alone: they still dream through men's dreams. They worship the gods made by males. And males have shaped the great virile figures for their own exaltation... Undoubtedly there are stylised images of man as he is in his relations with woman: father, seducer, husband, the jealous one, the good son, the bad son; but men are the ones who have established them, and they have not attained the dignity of myth; they are barely more than clichés while woman is exclusively defined in her relation to man.... The representation of the world as the world itself is the work of men; they describe it from a point of view that is their own and which they confound with the absolute truth. [Beauvoir 2009: 166]

What could seem more theological than 'the absolute truth'? Well, Beauvoir's demythologization reveals the self-deception of this theological work: men have represented the world from *a* point of view, while claiming it to be 'universal' and 'neutral'. From Beauvoir's feminist perspective, man thinks he is God in assuming the universal point of view; but at the heart of her feminist legacy is recognition of man's self-projection onto a male God.

As another pivotal woman in philosophy and a feminist in the generation after Beauvoir, Michèle Le Doeuff gives further recognition of the pervasiveness of the virile myth in philosophy generally and in other intellectual fields, too. With Le Doeuff, we find that the at-one-time unwitting misogyny of natural theology persists today as a conscious form of sexism. This persistence is, according to Le Doeuff and other twenty-first century feminists, no longer acceptable. Instead it is irresponsible. And Le Doeuff's rationally and ethically articulated feminist objection to the pervasiveness of male supremacy in every intellectual field unwittingly unites her with feminist theologians in being labelled and alienated as a 'heretic'. In other words, confronted by a feminist critique of virility, philosophers—like theologians—will suddenly become defensive of a strongly held 'religion' of male supremacy. As Le Doeuff explains:

> [When] I have disagreed with the notion of male supremacy, perhaps the major myth all intellectual fields still tend to share... I am doing my job as a philosopher, that's all, and *if* I am therefore seen as a heretic, it simply comes to prove that there is something most unphilosophical in our philosophical world as it is.

Philosophy, although it is philosophy, may function as a form of religion.
[Le Doeuff 2010: 108–9]

It is imperative that Le Doeuff's point is clearly understood. She is not simply making an assertion about the un-philosophical nature of sexist thinking in philosophy. She is admitting an affinity with women who assert their views about a sexist bias—whether we call this male supremacy or virility—in the conceptions which gain an often unwitting status as absolute truths. The objects of Le Doeuff's feminist critiques are precisely the sexist truths of an all too commonly shared myth. In turn, these 'truths' can be wrongly reinforced by arguments from evident features of the natural world to the existence and nature of this most supreme (male) God. Again, the myth which projects the ideal characteristics of the male Subject onto God becomes most problematic when men and women accept the superiority of fathers and sons as a natural feature of human life.

FEMINIST PERSPECTIVES ON SEXUAL DIFFERENCE

Feminist perspectives on the maleness of God, including whether a feminist can call God 'Father' continue to diverge greatly (Soskice 2007: 66–83; Beattie 2006: 60–4, 234–45). In the 1960s Mary Daly's claim that we must go 'beyond God the Father' became a rallying call for women in and outside of Christian theology. Daly's aim is to tackle the misconception that the male being is God, or that man is closer to God than woman, and so her access to the divine was only through man. As seen above, Daly also exhibits an affinity to Beauvoir; Daly's insistence is explicit on the self-deception of the woman who accepts a situation as 'the second sex'. Daly exposes the theological ramifications for women who accept that, like Eve, she brings evil into the world in seducing man and stimulating his concupiscence.

Admittedly, these basic points from Daly's feminist natural theology, premised on the Beauvoirian idea of female becoming and not being, will sound overly stereotypical (to today's theologians) as harmful generalizations about femininity, masculinity, God as Father, Man as Adam, and God as Son and as the Second Adam. Yet the clarity of Daly's earliest, however stereotypical, account of the misogyny in natural theology is what made and still makes her early views most influential—and, of course, heretical! Daly's ideas became far more radical in her later years when she separated from men and from 'the Church'. Nevertheless, Daly's groundbreaking and creative texts explicitly challenge natural theology from the standpoint of a woman (the young Daly herself) who has been an insider to the field of philosophical theology. As both a trained theologian and a philosopher, she knows how to expose the crucial core beliefs of natural theology as it had been developed up until Beauvoir's *The Second Sex*. Daly and Beauvoir each helped to expose what lay beneath the tip of an iceberg: that is, the patriarchal structure which had shaped the virile myth in natural theology. This patriarchal myth, in turn, determined the profound theological meaning given to a woman's love relations to herself, to man, and to God. Due to this patriarchal determination of meaning, these love relations remain strongly resistant to change. The unwitting resistance to seeing the damage done to women in the name of 'love' persists in serious cases of sexual and emotional abuse.

The stranglehold of sexist norms in natural theology over women, especially when it comes to love or sexual union (with 'the divine'), has to be one of the most formidable obstacles for feminists. Oppressive patriarchal forms of 'natural' theology would determine the love between a woman and her children, herself, and everyone else in damaging ways. The implications are huge. A novel feminist perspective appears in Luce Irigaray's writings which are far more critical of Beauvoir than any of those named so far. Irigaray dismisses Beauvoir's feminism for ignoring the issue of sexual difference. Instead Irigaray's psycholinguistic description of the oppressive nature of patriarchal forms of love dramatically portrays a woman's place within patriarchal theology in a story of 'living death'. In her mimetic appropriation of the ancient story of Antigone, Irigaray illustrates how a woman's love, in this case a sister's love for her brother in the place of her own dead mother, results in Antigone as a symbol of familial (or possibly incestuous) love being buried alive (cf. Anderson 1998: 194–200). For Irigaray, it is not enough to expose the myth of the Other in an attempt to achieve Beauvoir's aim of equal standing for women and men.

For example, Irigaray's post-Lacanian reading of Hegel's master and slave relation is strikingly different from Beauvoir's existential reading of a struggle between the master and the slave. In Beauvoir, there is no invisible unconscious space of female *jouissance* whereas Irigaray's play with Hegel's Antigone disruptively mimes the female role. This disruptive mimesis unearths the female language, constituting an invisible substructure, on which the social-symbolic structure (or 'male economy') of relations between men rests. In brief, Irigaray assumes and uncovers an invisible linguistic order of women. Once uncovered this order becomes (according to Irigaray) a language for women and for her becoming divine. All of this, Irigaray insists, depends on 'an ethics of sexual difference' (1993b: 126–9). The ethical imperative is to become divine as male or as female. There is not only one subject who is male, but there are two subjects; and each of the two types of subject needs a God in his or her own image to define two gendered subjects and their love relations.

Perhaps the most often quoted assertion from Irigaray in the field of natural theology is: 'The only diabolical thing about women is their lack of a God' (Irigaray 1993a: 64). Her claim about women lacking a God in her own image is contentious because it exposes male supremacy, while still insisting the problem is a woman's lack of a direct relation to a God of her own gender. This insistence assumes that the divine functions as a projection of human gender onto an ideal which needs to become both the ground and the ideal for gendered subjects; for both women and men to become subjects, two genders are necessary; this gives sexual difference.

However, with Irigaray, we discover a feminist perspective on natural theology which oscillates between highly conservative sexual roles and seemingly radical ideas for gendered subjects. But what makes this ethics feminist? ... that Irigaray claims there are two genders? How does the argument for an ethics of sexual difference avoid reinforcing exclusive theological norms of heterosexuality? Irigaray argues that to become a subject each gender requires a divine in its own gender; since men have a male God they are subjects who become divine; but since women lack a God in their own gender, they must uncover their own sexual morphology in a language, on the stage of a 'female imaginary', which enables them to become subjects and so divine women. Ultimately, divine women are both the presupposition and the goal of Irigaray's feminist form of natural theology. Be it conservative or radical, Irigaray's ethics obligates us to uphold a woman's sexual difference from man.

A Conservative or Radical Feminist (Natural) Theology

We have arrived at a highly contentious and ambiguous feminist perspective on natural theology for both women and men. Ironically in recent years, male theologians are often more attracted to Irigaray's account of sexual difference for natural theology than women in philosophy are to 'difference feminism'. Significant difficulties exist for interpreting Irigaray's provocative contributions to natural theology. Her writings contain endless suggestive remarks about nature, gender, life, love, and divine beings, or to be more precise, 'on becoming divine'. In 'Divine Women', 'An Ethics of Sexual Difference', and numerous other essays such as 'The Universal as Mediation', Irigaray can be read as filling out a natural theology of sexual difference, including the 'elemental passions' from ancient Greek philosophy: that is, fire, air, water, and earth (Irigaray 1993a: 57). Irigaray's textual 'flings with' a range of Western (male) philosophers are intoxicating and seductive; her fluid, poetic, and suggestive style of writing, for example about Heidegger on air and Nietzsche on water, become part of her plundering of ancient myths and Western philosophies for what they can suggest about the stuff making up nature and human nature. This emotionally fluid metaphysical material gives passionate life to abstract doctrines of orthodox Christianity, especially the Christian God's incarnation in a God-man by way of a Virgin mother. But this goes beyond natural theology.

Feminist philosophers inevitably struggle to assess fairly Irigaray's provocative texts, which can be appropriated in strongly divergent ways. Her seductive and obscure poetic style of self-expression draws the (woman) reader into her intense, playful miming of male language, while remaining unclear how beautiful imagery and fluid movements safely connect women to nature—not to mention to politics and concrete gender issues. Irigaray's account of gender and human nature should be of interest to the natural theologian as much as to any feminist metaphysician. She plays, for example, with Hegel's masculine and feminine, finite and infinite. Her aim seems to be to find 'the place' where 'the spirit' might enter human nature; this would be the site for the transformation of an 'economy of sameness', or the one (male), to an economy of sexual difference, or 'being two' in love. To capture a sense of Irigaray's fluid language, here is a brief passage from 'The Universal as Mediation':

> Yet sex does not obey the logic of contradiction. It bends and folds to accommodate that logic but it does not conform. Forced to follow that logic, it is drawn into a mimetic game that moves faraway from life. The woman who acts the man (or the woman...), the man who acts the woman (or the man...), the wife who acts the mother, the man who acts the father, are not spiritualizing their nature.
>
> The process whereby gender might become perfect is lacking...in ourselves. If gender were to develop individually, collectively, historically, it could mark *the place where spirit entered human nature*, the point in time when the infinite passes into the finite, given that each individual of a gender is finite and potentially infinite in his or her relation to gender. [Irigaray 1993a: 139]

At this point, both the non-feminist and the feminist philosophers might worry about treating these thoughts on gender as either metaphysics or natural theology. If we arrive at a place where we not only ignore the logic of contradiction but search for a process to locate what is missing in human nature—that is, 'spirit'—then we don't seem to have anything either concrete or formal with which to philosophize. Perhaps the theologian who needs no arguments from natural theology because her or his work is, instead, grounded in divine revelation finds Irigaray's language resonates with Christian doctrines. Yet this would generate a problematic feminist perspective on natural theology; an Irigarayan conservative theology offers no bridge from divine men and women back to nature, or from revelation to reason.

Questions of Transcendence for the Feminist Philosopher

Patrice Haynes contributes two insightful essays in which she struggles to make sense of what precisely Irigaray has to offer feminist philosophers of religion. In 'Transcendence, Materialism and the Re-enchantment of Nature: Toward a Theological Materialism', Haynes contributes to debates about Irigaray's view of God, transcendence, and material nature (2009). Here another Irigarayan feminist perspective on natural theology begins to emerge. Haynes focusses on the question of God's nature as transcendent and non-sensible, discovering that Irigaray aims to reconceive the divine in terms of a 'vertical' and 'horizontal' transcendence which, at least initially, appears to reconcile human and divine natures in a manner which would be compatible with a woman's 'sexuate' nature as sensible and a man's 'sexuate' nature as transcendent (Haynes 2009: 57, 72; cf. Anderson 2009a: 30–1). In this way, the twofold nature of transcendence in Irigaray's account of a divine for women and for men preserves sexual difference; the divine is, then, two: sensible and transcendent being or immanence and transcendence.

Haynes also considers the significance of the 'sensible transcendental' (Irigaray 1993b: 129) for feminists who reject the traditional theistic God as personal but without a body, eternal, omniscient, omnipotent, impassible, and omni-benevolent. From an Irigarayan feminist perspective, the traditional (Thomist) theistic God is an ideal for a male gender, associated with positive, transcendent atttributes. The problem is that women have commitments associating them with another, sensible ideal; crudely speaking, it is argued that women are necessarily involved in the sensible world, in giving birth, loving, caring, being 'the sex' and flesh for man. To quote Haynes:

> For many feminists, a theoretical commitment to transcendence is politically irresponsible because it is held that this ultimately refuses to address the realities of material immanence: the social and historical conditions of women and men's lives. Supposedly, transcendence calls for a path out of this world and its material complexities, instead of aiming to effect concrete, social transformation that would promote just relations between human beings and the wider environment
>
> In feminist theology and feminist philosophy of religion,...the argument runs, God's relation to the world serves as the model for the dualistic and hierarchical ordering of reality: God-world, spirit-matter, transcendence-immanence, male-female. [Haynes 2009: 56]

But again, the philosopher might expect an argument for the existence of God before any arguments about how terms and concepts are gendered; or, how 'theoretical commitment' can be 'politically irresponsible'—as suggested (above)—in feminist philosophy of religion. Here we might recall Beauvoir's point that the theistic God being male and personal is a projection of the Subject's self-deceptive exaltation. Similarly, Haynes concludes that 'God's transcendence, then, may turn out to be the grand expression of the male ego, a projection that allows man to assuage his fear of finitude and embodiment' (Haynes 2009: 57).

Yet the topic of projection is not merely a psychological matter, but a question of realism. Is God's omnipotence, omniscience, omni-benevolence, and other omni-attributes made up by man to satisfy his own desires, or is the traditional theistic God a real person without a body (Zagzebski 2007)? Feminist philosophers of religion are thus forced to ask questions at the very heart of natural theology. In 'The Problem of Transcendence in Irigaray's Philosophy of Sexual Difference' (2010), Haynes continues to raise pressing questions about natural theology and Irigaray's feminist perspective on sexuate nature. Haynes sets out to expose serious problems for any philosopher—let alone a natural theologian—in Irigaray's conception of a sensible transcendental. This is especially problematic, thinks Haynes, if Irigaray's conception depends upon a Feuerbachian idea of man's projection onto God. Haynes reads Irigaray's conception of transcendence critically as follows:

> Irigaray's re-conception of transcendence unintentionally creates, among other problems, a gulf between male and female such that the two are unable to move towards the mutual recognition necessary for love and social transformation...her picture of transcendence retains a quite traditional emphasis on distance and inaccessibility, but this time figured between the two of sexual difference rather than humanity and a supernatural God. [Haynes 2010: 281; cf. Anderson 2009a: 39–44]

Clearly, although Irigaray does not seem to offer an adequate account of transcendence-in-immanence which might be coherent and liveable for both (feminist) women and men, her feminist perspective makes an original contribution to debates on topics in contemporary natural theology. Haynes herself makes an additional tantalizing suggestion about bringing into Irigaray's account a '*Naturphilosophie* where nature as a whole seeks its divine realization' (Haynes 2010: 294; cf. Stone 2006: 193–215).

What seems exactly right about Haynes's critical interest in the contribution of Irigaray's writings on divine women and sexual difference to feminist philosophy of religion, or what we might call another novel feminist perspective on natural theology, is the drive to keep alive the struggle to unearth the biases against women in theology. The danger in this struggle for sexual difference is revisions in theology which insist upon a woman's different way of thinking, while allowing patriarchy to continue to think in its male ways. In Irigaray's case, this female insistence and male allowance in the context of natural theology would seem to reinforce the old theological divisions between male and female subjects, visible and invisible, divine men and divine women. For a particularly salient example in this context, Irigaray is happy to mime the story of the Virgin Mary for the sake of women's integrity; but much ink has been spilt on the dangers of a feminist perspective that reinstates the symbolic order of orthodox Catholicism for women (Irigaray 1993a: 57–72; cf Beattie 2006: 236–8, 256–70).

In response, a totally different, more sobering statement of a feminist perspective is helpful. Let us think philosophically about Mary Midgley's unequivocal assertion concerning feminism and the day when feminism might no longer be necessary. Midgley's philosophical reflection on feminism recalls the virile myth with which this chapter began. But in Midgley's terms, the situation, however complex, is clear and so is the still long awaited outcome:

> 'feminism' is not the name of some new doctrine, imported into controversies arbitrarily and for no good reason. That name stands for the steady, systematic correction of an ancient and very damaging bias. [Virilism] has always reigned unnoticed. Correcting it is not a single, simple move. It demands different emphasis in different places because the bias has worked unevenly. Like other corrections, feminism might hope in the end to become unnecessary and so to put itself out of business. [Midgley 1997: 58–9]

An Analytic Feminist Perspective on Religious Epistemology

Life and thinking remain the focus of much philosophy today, and, perhaps, especially feminist perspectives on philosophy of religion and on metaphysics (Anderson 2009b: 119–29; Haslanger 2000: 107–26). A philosophical focus on the rationality, rigour, clarity, and precision of religious or metaphysical thinking necessarily involves disagreements, critical analyses, and reformulations of un-philosophical thoughts. Similarly, a philosophical focus on religious life involves critical analyses of diverging views of the origin and nature of living beings, of temporal life, and of natality and mortality. A philosophical hierarchy which privileges certain male subjects over women and other men, but also scientists over artists, poets, and non-analytical philosophers, risks sustaining boundaries that exclude women thinkers. The risk here is also the exclusion of men and women who think philosophically about issues relevant to natural theology, while not reducing their thoughts about God and human life to abstract conceptual analysis. The prejudice of some analytical (male) theologians against the messiness and complexities of real living excludes the philosophical concerns of male and female feminists as sexually and materially specific human beings. To recall Midgley's wisdom, 'virilism' is 'an ancient and very damaging bias' precisely because it 'always reigned unnoticed' (Midgley 1997: 39). This bias is not obvious to (most) analytic philosophers or analytic theologians.

Yet feminist philosophers have produced critiques of analytic natural theology. These are critiques of (i) the biased construction of core concepts, (ii) the un-philosophical nature of sexist reasoning, and (iii) the oppressive effects of patriarchal norms. As implied in early sections of this chapter, some of the crucially relevant concepts which have come under feminist criticism include nature, life (including 'life after death'), thinking, and autonomy but also the God–man relationship. The theistic arguments which have been criticized include arguments for the existence and knowledge of the theistic God, the gender-neutral arguments concerning 'man's place in nature', the free-will defence of God's goodness, the universal nature of reason, the generic nature of persons. The material and social conditions of philosophical thought have been exposed for their exclusion of women from traditional Western philosophy; this includes the disinheritance of those women in the history of natural theology who contributed ideas of their own. Let us consider one final feminist perspective which is squarely within contemporary natural theology.

In 'Dark Contemplation and Epistemic Transformation', Sarah Coakley gives her careful attention to gender in the philosophical theologian's discussions of 'rationality' and its 'epistemic rootedness in circles of trust and mutuality' (2009: 284–306). Coakley turns to the analytic philosophers of religion who, she finds, have unwittingly taken part in 'the feminization of religious rationality' (284, n. 11). At least part of Coakley's feminist argument is that the enormous amount of creative energy directed to religious epistemology (as a vital area for contemporary natural theologians) has to do with the attempts to bring the 'femininity' stereotypically associated with the private realm (that is, trust, affectivity, subjectivity, and affectivity) into the public realm. In brief, Coakley speculates that the public recognition of the epistemic significance of maternal trust and intimacy should have a justificatory effect upon public discussions of the epistemic trust and intimacy with the divine. In this way, feminine—if not, 'feminist'—epistemology can have an enabling effect.

One immediate philosophical problem with Coakley's argument about the feminization of religious rationality is precisely its stereotypical nature, as she herself admits. How does dealing with stereotypes of femininity help either the feminist or the justificatory cause? It seems a huge twofold assumption that: (i) the rich contemporary studies of the rationality of religious belief have something to do with what is stereotypically associated with mothers (presumably, of theistic philosophers); (ii) the association of trust in religious rationality and its epistemic authority is due to a growing public awareness of the significant epistemic role of maternal experiences, especially those when children learn to trust others. Moreover, even if this twofold assumption is accepted there is no reason—or at least none given by Coakley—why we should see this connection between early learning and religious rationality as in any sense feminist. Again, we face a question of how conservative a feminist perspective can be and still remain 'feminist'.

A feminist philosopher could object to Coakley's gendering of religious epistemology because conservative assumptions tie trust to the mother-infant relation. If feminism is to be attributed to the childhood habituation that creates trust, it must have a critical distance from any stereotypical role for woman. At a minimum, feminist philosophers have a political commitment to step back from the biases—in this case about maternal trust—of one's own class, race, religion, sexual orientation. One is not a feminist because of being born a woman; epistemic trust does not just happen because one is and has a mother. The aim of feminist epistemology is not the same as growing up and learning to trust others, or recognizing who is or isn't an epistemic authority. In fact, the aims of feminism and learning to trust might be the reverse. Feminist philosophers are by definition keenly and rightly suspicious of hidden biases, violence, and other pernicious dangers which characterize women's lives in sexist and misogynist societies. In this context, it is crucial to note that women are not all alike as mothers. Moreover, a feminist perspective on natural theology would be suspicious of the forms of rationality and the conceptions of God which characterize women (including mothers) as socially inferior, politically untrustworthy, or spiritually defiled. Each of these social and sexual markings would feed into forms of epistemic injustice (Fricker 2002: 90; 2003: 154–73; Anderson 2004: 90–102).

For example, if a devotedly religious mother of many children is given an epistemic privilege due to her years of experience in being trusted by her own infants, would a devout woman who has never had any children be less trustworthy, especially when it comes to religious matters? In fact, Coakley finds Teresa of Avila the perfect example of a woman who should be trusted on matters of prayer and knowledge of God because of habitual practices of contemplation; but Teresa has had no experience of being a mother. Her political isolation as a mystic hardly recommends itself for developing those rational principles of credulity and testimony which, Coakley insists, come from the upbringing of children in familial circles of trust and mutuality, as well as from a social context of justice and peace.

To make this critical point clear, let us consider two more passages. The first comes from Coakley's introduction to Swinburne's rational principles of credulity and of testimony:

> So here the credulity and testimony principles are not something we wheel on when desperate to give veracity to internal, 'subjective', perceptions that otherwise look epistemically fishy. No, they are principles of *all* rationality, reminding us of our

epistemic rootedness in circles of trust and mutuality. Implicitly...they remind us of the special power of the maternal, which...either inculcates an attitude of trust and security, or of fear and distrust...then epistemology has everything to do with families and upbringing. [Coakley 2009: 292]

To repeat, Coakley places the source of our epistemic trust, as evident in these principles of rationality, primarily in the mother who the infant trusts, and by extension in ideal familial and social contexts. But then, she analyses how the natural theologian's examples are taken from female mystical experiences of a union (in divine love). Coakley concludes that female mystical experience, in supporting the rationality of theistic belief, becomes 'a form of personal empowerment and epistemic expansion (in God)...[which] has the capacity to transcend certain [dualisms] in which woman has always tended to be awarded the "inferior" role' (Coakley 2009: 312). Yet to reach this conclusion Coakley must establish a further connection between rationality and epistemic trust; the trust of an intimacy with and a safety in God must be connected to an original maternal intimacy forming trust:

> The most significant feature of [Teresa's] spiritual maturation was her body's habituation to a (now non-sporadic) state of union. Whereas previously...passing experiences of union would leave her physically prostrate, now—in the close description of that state in *The Interior Castle*, 7—that union has become permanent, and her body is no longer afflicted by it. Rather, her embodied selfhood now exists in a curious tension between complete union and safety-in-God at one level, and yet an equal sensibility of continuing trials, disturbances, and bodily fatigue at another. [Coakley 2009: 298]

The problem is not simply that the child with a mother who cannot be trusted would have no basis for trust in God, but that the mystic's relation to the harsh reality of human life would work against empowerment and expansion in God. Can Coakley render the mystic's experience compatible with the uncertainties of maternal love and of everyday life?

For an indirect response to Coakley's 'feminist' arguments, let us reflect on a non-feminist and non-theological, intellectual Jewish woman's philosophical insight. Hannah Arendt, whose thinking is profoundly shaped by the Holocaust in twentieth-century Europe, offers radical political knowledge of the human condition. For this reason feminist philosophers have increasingly turned to her deep and original insight, specifically, on 'living in a web of human relationships' which are marked by 'that miracle that saves the world...from its normal, "natural" ruin...ultimately the fact of natality' (Arendt 1998: 247; Anderson 2009b: 119–29). For our feminist challenge to Coakley, Arendt makes a subtle and highly significant point about practices of contemplation, or 'the *vita contemplative* over all kinds of human activities'. Arendt's point can be redirected to Coakley's argument for contemplation. Here is Arendt's critique of privileging a medieval form of Christian contemplation and her image for a philosophy of active life:

> The reason why Christianity, its insistence on the sacredness of life and on the duty to stay alive notwithstanding, never developed a positive labour philosophy lies in the unquestioned priority given to the *vita contemplativa*...[Here Arendt refers to

and quotes Aquinas, *Summa theologica* ii. 2. 182. 1, 2], and whatever the merits of an active life might be, those of a life devoted to contemplation are 'more effective and more powerful'. This conviction, it is true, can hardly be found in the preachings of Jesus of Nazareth, and it is certainly due to the influence of Greek philosophy. . . . [Instead] what matters today is not the immortality of life, but that life is the highest good. . . . Only when the *vita activa* had lost is point of reference in the *vita contemplativa* could it become active life in the full sense of the word; and only because this active life remained bound to life as its only point of reference could life as such, the labouring metabolism of man with nature, become active and unfold its entire fertility. [Arendt 1998: 318–20]

What better conception—to replace the traditionally conceived God of Christian theism—for a feminist perspective on natural theology than 'an active life' which will 'unfold its entire fertility'? Feminist perspectives on natural theology might not be able to do better than to seek a conception of life, of nature, and of a thoughtful love of an Arendtian active life as a shared vision for women and men today.

CONCLUSION

In this chapter, a range of feminist perspectives on core topics in natural theology has been sketched. However, this sketch could not be definitive because the terms of the title could not be fixed. 'Natural theology' has traditionally been defined in a fairly narrow manner which, as seen above, is no longer viable generally, though it is still relevant. Coakley helps a feminist philosopher to engage critically with the narrow conservatism of the field. Ongoing contemporary changes in how philosophers think about nature and how (analytic) theology is written have begun to break the theological field open to new possibilities, as well as new perspectives on old philosophical debates. 'Feminist perspectives' cannot be neatly lined up, or easily able to peer into the traditionally exclusive field of natural theology. Instead the ultimate goal here is to encourage more open, philosophical reflection on the various feminist perspectives introduced. Readers are welcome to disagree with the lines drawn in the spirit of critical openness into new possibilities for feminist perspectives on natural theology.

REFERENCES

Anderson, P. S. (1998). *A Feminist Philosophy of Religion: The Rationality and Myths of Religious Belief.* Oxford: Blackwell.

——(2004) 'An Epistemological-Ethical Approach' in *Feminist Philosophy of Religion. Critical Readings.* Edited by Pamela Sue Anderson and Beverley Clack. London: Routledge: pp. 90–102.

——(2009a). 'Transcendence and Feminist Philosophy: On Avoiding Apotheosis' in *Women and the Divine: Touching Transcendence.* Edited by Gillian Howie and J'annine Jobling. New York: Palgrave Macmillan: pp. 27–54.

Anderson, P. S. (2009b). 'A Thoughtful Love of Life: A Spiritual Turn in Philosophy of Religion'. *Svensk Teologisk Kvartalshkrift* Arg 85: 119–29.

—— (2010). 'The Lived Body, Gender and Confidence' in *New Topics in Feminist Philosophy of Religion: Contestations and Transcendence Incarnate*. Edited by P. S. Anderson. Dordrecht, London and New York: Springer: pp. 163–80.

—— and J. Bell (2010). *Kant and Theology*. London: Continuum.

Antony, L. M., ed. (2007). *Philosophers Without Gods: Meditations on Atheism and the Secular Life*. Oxford: Oxford University Press.

Arendt, H. (1998). *The Human Condition*. 2nd edn. With an Introduction by Margaret Canovan. Chicago: University of Chicago Press.

Beattie, T. (2006). *New Catholic Feminism. Theology and Theory*. London: Routledge.

Beauvoir, S. de (1976). *The Ethics of Ambiguity*. Translated by Bernard Frechtman. New York: Citadel Press, Kensington Publishing.

—— (2009). *The Second Sex*. Unabridged translation by Constance Borde and Sheila Malovaney-Chevallier. London: Jonathan Cape.

Coakley, S. (2009). 'Dark Contemplation and Epistemic Transformation: The Analytic Theologian Re-Meets Teresa of Avila' in *Analytic Theology: New Essays in the philosophy of theology*. Edited by O. D. Crisp and M. C. Rea. Oxford: Oxford University Press: pp. 280–312.

Daly, M. (1986 [1973]). *Beyond God the Father: Towards a Philosophy of Women's Liberation*. 2nd edn. London: The Women's Press Ltd.

Fricker, M. (2002). 'Power, Knowledge and Injustice' in *New British Philosophy: The Interviewers*. Edited by J. Baggini and J. Stangroom. London: Routledge.

—— (2003). 'Epistemic Justice and a Role for Virtue in the Politics of Knowing'. *Metaphilosophy* 34/102 (January): 154–73.

Haslanger, S. (2000). 'Feminism in Metaphysics: Negotiating the Natural' in *The Cambridge Companion to Feminism in Philosophy*. Edited by M. Fricker and J. Hornsby. Cambridge: Cambridge University Press: pp. 107–26.

Haynes, P. (2009). 'Transcendence, Materialism and the Re-enchantment of Nature: Toward a Theological Materialism' in *Women and the Divine: Touching Transcendence*. Edited by G. Howie and J. Jobling. New York: Palgrave Macmillan: pp. 55–78.

—— (2010). 'The Problem of Transcendence in Irigaray's Philosophy of Sexual Difference' in *New Topics in Feminist Philosophy of Religion: Contestations and Transcendence Incarnate*. Edited by P. S. Anderson. Dordrecht, New York and London: Springer: pp. 279–96.

Irigaray, Luce (1985). *Speculum of the Other Woman*. Translated by G. C. Gill. Ithaca, NY: Cornell University Press.

—— (1993a). *Genealogies and Sexes*. Translated by G. C. Gill. New York: Columbia University Press.

—— (1993b). *An Ethics of Sexual Difference*. Translated C. Burke and G. C. Gill. Ithaca, NY: Cornell University Press.

Le Doeuff, M. (2010). 'Beauvoir the Mythoclast' and 'Panel Discussion with Michele Le Doeuff'. *Paragraph* (March): 90–124.

Midgley, M. (1997). 'The Soul's Successors: Philosophy and the 'Body' in *Religion and the Body*. Edited by S. Coakley. Cambridge: Cambridge University Press: pp. 53–68.

Rea, M. (2009). 'Introduction' in *Analytic Theology: New Essays in the Philosophy of Theology*. Edited by O. D. Crisp and M. C. Rea. Oxford: Oxford University Press: pp. 1–30.

Soskice, J. M. (2007). *The Kindness of God: Metaphor, Gender and Religious Language*. Oxford: Oxford University Press.

Stone, A. (2006). *Luce Irigaray and the Philosophy of Sexual Difference*. Cambridge: Cambridge University Press.

Swinburne, R. (2005). *Faith and Reason*. 2nd edn. Oxford: Clarendon Press.

Wolterstorff, N. (2009). 'How Philosophical Theology Became Possible with the Analytic Tradition of Philosophy' in *Analytic Theology: New Essays in the philosophy of theology*. Edited by O. D. Crisp and M. C. Rea. Oxford: Oxford University Press: pp. 155–68.

Zagzebski, L. T. (2007). *Philosophy of Religion: An Historical Introduction*. Oxford: Blackwell Publishing.

Zimmerman, D. (2007). 'Three Introductory Questions' in *Persons, Human and Divine*. Edited by D. Zimmerman. Oxford: Oxford University Press: pp. 1–32.

CHAPTER 23

COMPARATIVE NATURAL THEOLOGY

WESLEY J. WILDMAN

INTRODUCTION

TRADITIONAL natural theology (as defined here) aims at direct entailment from the world to God. More precisely, it attempts to infer a partial metaphysics of ultimacy from a partial ontology of nature. Detractors of natural theology assert that no rational knowledge of ultimacy is possible based on any amount of analysis of the natural world. The position defended here is intermediate between these extremes: conceptual traction between the ontology of nature and ultimacy metaphysics is neither entirely absent nor strong enough to support direct inference in the manner of traditional natural theology. Rather, this conceptual traction is such as to have the limited effect of shifting the relative plausibility of ultimacy views in various respects. Indeed, this conceptual traction may render a single ultimacy view simultaneously relatively more plausible than a competitor in one respect of comparison and relatively less plausible than the same competitor in a different respect of comparison. Nevertheless, conceptual traction exists to a degree sufficient to advance inquiries in natural theology, when they are properly framed.

If correct, this position implies that traditional natural theology is impossible, that outright scepticism towards natural theology is needlessly defeatist, and that a different approach to navigating the conceptual and logical linkages between the ontology of nature and the metaphysics of ultimacy is required. This different approach would have to aim not at watertight proof but at evaluating large-scale systems of ideas for their plausibility in relation to every relevant consideration, and thus would necessarily be comparative in character. This is the basis for thinking of the required new approach as comparative natural theology. In addition to being properly fitted to the evidential and logical situation of natural theology, comparative natural theology has the great virtue of overcoming a lamentable pattern of parochialism in traditional natural theology, a pattern that becomes painfully obvious as soon as the religious philosopher or philosophical theologian reaches beyond a single tradition to consider related styles of argument in other traditions.

In addition to the terms 'traditional natural theology' and 'comparative natural theology', already defined above with precision sufficient for present purposes, we require several other definitions.

Ontology of Nature

For the purposes of this chapter, 'ontology of nature' could equally well be called 'philosophical cosmology'; in both cases the point is to establish basic philosophical categories for understanding nature and its operations. The former phrase is preferred here to avoid confusing 'philosophical cosmology' with 'scientific cosmology' or 'physical cosmology', which are scientific ventures. Note that treating philosophical interpretations of nature as the starting point for inference frames natural theology as an act of interpretation and thereby rejects the possibility that inference can ever be simply 'from nature', without the aid (and the complications) of philosophical interpretation. Most scientific theorizing about nature, *as science*, is too constrained to be the basis for inference relevant to natural theology; philosophical mediation is necessary for inquiry at the junction of nature and ultimacy metaphysics to be theologically significant.

Ultimacy

The term 'ultimacy' is here preferred to 'ultimate reality' or 'God' in deference to the results of the Comparative Religious Ideas Project (see Neville 2001). That project sought to identify through a rigorous process of comparison and analysis which categories work best to describe what is important about the ideas of world religious traditions, minimizing distortion and arbitrariness. One of the conclusions of the project is that the term 'ultimate realities', while more generous and more useful than both the singular term 'ultimate reality' and the much-used term 'God', is nevertheless biased against religious traditions that focus on the discovery and living out of ultimate ways or paths and on freeing people from an unhealthy obsession with ultimate realities. A vaguer category encompassing both 'ultimate realities' and 'ultimate paths' is preferable—thus 'ultimacy'. The interest here is in metaphysical theories of ultimacy, of course, and this leans heavily towards 'ultimate realities', yet the term 'ultimacy' is a helpful reminder of the complex diversity of religious thought.

Natural Theology

For the purposes of this chapter, natural theology (whether traditional or comparative in character) is the rational attempt to derive information about ultimacy (God, in some traditions) from philosophical interpretations of nature. Two comments pertaining to the scope of natural theology are in order. First, some definitions of natural theology contrast it with revealed theology. This works in theological traditions for which informative revelation is conceivable and the distinction between revelation and natural processes is plausible. Some theological traditions reject one of these conditions. Indeed, a number of theological outlooks (including 'ground of being' theology within theistic traditions) reject both, and this fact calls into question the advisability of defining natural theology by means of a contrast with revealed theology. Fortunately, neither condition is required to make sense of comparative natural theology. Secondly, some have included in the domain of natural theology rational arguments for the existence of God that make no explicit reference to nature, such as the ontological arguments of Anselm and Leibniz and others. The basis for this appears to be that such arguments make use of the power of 'natural reason' unaided by revelation, a usage indebted to the understanding (just discussed) of natural theology contrasted to revealed theology. For the purposes of this chapter, the 'natural' in 'natural theology' refers to the natural world and 'natural reason' is synonymous with 'reason'. It follows that ontological arguments are mostly insignificant for natural theology, though neither because such arguments are impossible nor because reason is in any sense not a part of nature, but just because they lie outside the scope of reflection on the natural world. Of course, in a minor way ontological arguments remain significant for natural theology as phenomena of nature that need to be explained, like political economies and the laws of cricket. As a logical argument, however, it belongs not to natural theology but to metaphysics.

CHALLENGES FACING NATURAL THEOLOGY

Natural theology faces serious challenges. Each of the four discussed in what follows clarifies why comparative natural theology is a better path than traditional natural theology. These challenges do not disappear in the move from traditional to comparative natural theology but they do become optimally tractable within a comparative natural theology approach.

First, an ontology of nature is a complex intellectual creation, synthesizing a great deal of scientific theorizing about nature and crystallizing principles by which to make sense of such rational structures of nature as exist. This is made difficult by the sheer enormity of the task but also by the fact that the natural sciences constitute a kind of uneven and sometimes ad hoc patchwork of theories about nature rather than a seamless garment of rational comprehensiveness. Realizing this makes the proofs of traditional natural theology seem oversimplified, if not naive. For example, the sciences employ several apparently incompatible concepts of causation, and philosophy of science has struggled more or less in vain to clarify the concept. Cosmological proofs that rely on unanalysed concepts of causation, as many do, appear to be building a house on a foundation of sand. Because of its orientation to weighing the plausibility of large-scale systems of ideas, comparative natural theology is better able to manage the vagaries surrounding ontology of nature.

Secondly, there are always questions about the completeness of the set of ultimacy hypotheses that might have a claim in any natural theology argument. While we can run a natural theology argument through its paces and notice how some ultimacy theories fare better than others in the process, we are never certain that another ultimacy theory not currently in the mix of competing hypotheses may fare better still. For example, Anselm in his *Monologion* makes a good-faith effort to register different possible explanations for ontological dependence, dividing the question as follows (see Anselm 1998): (1) something comes from nothing; (2) all things come from one another in a closed system of interdependence; (3) all things come from something else in one of two ways: (3a) either they derive from multiple things that are individually self-subsisting, or (3b) they derive from one thing. It is striking to see that Anselm effortlessly captures (1) varieties of nihilism, (2) the Buddhist doctrine of dependent co-arising (*pratītya-samutpāda*), and (3a) the ontological pluralism widespread in Chinese philosophy. Equally, it is unsurprising that he could not give the alternatives to his theistic preference (3b) their argumentative due, as he was doubtless unfamiliar with any philosopher or philosophical literature that defends them. Shockingly, though we are not so hobbled in knowledge as Anselm was, the history of traditional natural theology right up to the present day has blatantly disregarded the full range of alternative explanations of ontological dependence, rarely even bothering to mention the range of possibilities as Anselm did. Fortunately, identifying and managing competing conceptual frameworks is the lifeblood of comparative natural theology.

Thirdly, comparative weighing of the plausibility of large-scale conceptual frameworks is relatively new as an explicit form of inquiry, though it has ancient antecedents in all literate cultures. Traditional natural theology had tended to ignore the challenge of large-scale world-view evaluation, in the sense of performing it surreptitiously and often unconsciously through deploying hidden and unanalysed premises. But evaluating large-scale conceptual frameworks is always difficult, including for comparative natural theology. In particular, the comparative criteria by which we discriminate superior from inferior metaphysical proposals about ultimacy are under-explored. For example, exactly how important are the criteria that 'an adequate ultimacy metaphysics should solve the problem of the one and the many' (creation *ex nihilo* traditions prize this criterion), and 'an adequate ultimacy metaphysics should uphold the co-primordiality of principles of law and operations of chance in nature' (dualist Manichaeism and Zoroastrianism prize this criterion)? Is one of them more important than the other? Can they be rendered compatible? Thus, we must allow that a given argument in natural theology could become more (or less) persuasive with time as comparative metaphysics gradually stabilizes and comparative criteria are better understood. This possibility is unwelcome in traditional natural theology but quite at home within comparative natural theology.

Fourthly, and perhaps most importantly, ultimacy may be such that there just is not one superior metaphysical theory of it. This prima facie likelihood barely registers within traditional natural theology, where it bluntly interferes with the aspiration to construct rational proofs. By contrast, comparative natural theology comfortably recognizes that ultimacy may be replete with category-defying cognitive richness that forces perspectival scattering of metaphysical theories. Surely it makes sense that some aspects of ultimacy should surpass human rational capacities altogether.

These difficulties do not constitute a knock-down argument against the possibility of natural theology, and not even traditional natural theology. They do define the senses in which natural theology is difficult and indicate the reasons why comparative natural theology is better placed than traditional natural theology to manage the actual evidential and inferential structure of the conceptual relations between nature and ultimacy. Most profoundly, they suggest that traditional natural theology is in fact an intellectually short-circuited and over-ambitious simplification of comparative natural theology, and that only the latter is properly scaled to the actual challenges facing this type of inquiry.

The Prospects of Natural Theology

The challenges just sketched suggest that the prospects for natural theology cannot be definitively evaluated in the abstract, notwithstanding numerous attempts to do so. Rather, whether natural theology is possible has to be established or refuted through attempts to do it. The chances of success turn decisively on how effectively philosophical interpretations of nature constrain theories of ultimacy. This takes us to the deepest and most perplexing question surrounding natural theology: can nature tell us anything about ultimacy?

This is an ancient question, shared across cultures, and handled differently but in structurally similar ways in West Asian, South Asian, and East Asian philosophical traditions. More often than not, the answer has been a qualified yes: the world around us does tell us something about ultimacy, but not as much as we might want to know. For example, the cosmological arguments of medieval Judaism, Christianity, and Islam concurred that there must be an ultimate reality that gives rise to the proximate reality we know, but we cannot infer much about its character—certainly not as much as the sacred texts of these theistic religions affirm. Similarly, many traditions of South Asian philosophy found it necessary to include authority as a valid form of inference (*pramāña*) because observation and logic alone could not yield the Vedic portrayal of ultimacy. Chinese traditions perhaps have been the most optimistic about reading the character of ultimacy from the way reality shows up for us in natural processes, but the plural and vague visions of ultimacy that typically result confirm the difficulty of the task.

Within this mixed evaluation of the inferential journey from nature to ultimacy there are specialized subplots, some highly sceptical and others extremely optimistic. On the sceptical side, Buddhist philosophy relies heavily on the possibility of inference from human experience to religious insight, but the fruit of this inference in some of the most rigorously philosophical forms of Buddhism (such as the Mādhyamaka School of Mahāyāna Buddhist philosophy) is primarily a spiritually liberating path and only secondarily and vaguely a metaphysical portrayal of ultimacy. According to this way of thinking, reality as we conventionally experience it is deeply misleading. Careful inference from the suffering and contradictions of experience frees us from its delusions, including the twin delusions that there is an ultimate reality lying behind it all, and that we need to explain conventional reality with reference to some ontologically more basic theory of ultimate reality.

Theistic traditions have produced another form of scepticism in the form of exclusive reliance on God's self-revelation conjoined with the denial that we can infer anything about God from created reality. The utter transcendence of God motivates this scepticism (in twentieth-century Swiss Christian theologian Karl Barth's rejection of natural theology, for example), but the counterintuitive result is that there are no natural or scientific constraints whatsoever on revealed traditions' claims about God. Could the loving God Barth believed in really create a world that was utterly misleading as a source of knowledge of God's character?

The extremely optimistic side is rare by comparison. Some thinkers have claimed that the pattern of inference from apparent design in cosmology and biology to a designer can produce detailed knowledge of the character and purposes of ultimacy (which may be distinct from the designer) as well as knowledge of the designer's existence and relation to the world. These natural theology enthusiasts sometimes even reject revealed theology altogether as too burdened with myth to make a useful contribution to knowledge of ultimacy. Twentieth-century American philosopher Charles Hartshorne is an example of one type; early nineteenth-century German philosopher Georg W. F. Hegel is an example of another; and Enlightenment deism, a movement that continues down to the present in transformed ways and under different names, yet another.

In our time, the well-populated middle ground is the domain of discussion among most who are interested in science–religion relations. Most accept that nature constrains what we can say about ultimacy. They do this while admitting that nature does not permit clear lines of entailment from science to detailed knowledge of ultimacy, while tolerating a persistent lack of clarity about what precisely are these constraints. Within these boundaries several debated questions mark out the interior territory, and I note two here.

First, are the constraints from science on hypotheses about ultimacy strict enough to allow direct entailment relations from science to God? Controversial intelligent-design theorists such as American biochemist Michael Behe and American mathematician-philosopher William Dembski say yes, though they admit (consistently with the medieval design arguments) that the entailment does not yield much more than the sheer existence of a designer—and technically speaking, the designer may be clever aliens rather than any deity (see Behe 1996; Behe, Dembski, and Meyer 2000; Dembski 1998, 2002). Atheists say yes, too, and it is the non-existence of a divine being that science supposedly entails (among the new atheists, see Dawkins 2006; Harris 2006; Hitchens 2007). Numerous contemporary sceptical authors from American astronomer Carl

Sagan to Skeptics Society founder Michael Shermer stop just short of evidence-based atheism when they say that science is steadily removing any need we once might have had to postulate God (see Sagan 1996; Shermer 2002). Most in the science–religion dialogue suspect that science is too vague to determine a single view of ultimacy and that the best we can aim for is consonance relations between scientific and traditional religion-based theological understandings of the world (see the survey of types of logical connection between science and religion in Murphy 1996, which thematizes the contrast between holistic justification versus stronger entailment relations between science and theology). Some, such as American metaphysician Robert Neville, deliberately aim for metaphysical formulations of ultimacy that are perfectly neutral with regard to scientific theories (see Neville 1968). He reasons that if there were any inferential traction between the cosmological pictures of science and the metaphysical pictures of ultimacy, then the latter would be too coarsely formulated, too much in thrall to the actual cosmology of our universe, and insufficiently attuned to the ontological conditions for any possible cosmological environment. Overall, it appears that the question of whether scientific constraints on hypotheses about ultimacy are strict enough to support direct entailment relations may be too deeply conflicted to answer.

Secondly, and now more modestly, can science help us choose among competing views of ultimacy, even if it does not select out a uniquely adequate view? This question is under-explored because most people involved in science–religion discussions have not engaged religions beyond their own, or conflicting views within their own religion, well enough to make serious comparative analysis feasible. It is an emerging issue, however, and thinking about it carefully leads to a clarified understanding of what has really been going on in traditional natural theology all along, but hidden in unanalysed premises, as we shall see below.

The Logic of Natural Theology

Comparative natural theology seeks to compare numerous compelling accounts of ultimacy in as many different respects as are relevant, thereby assembling the raw materials for inference-to-best-explanation arguments on behalf of particular theories of ultimacy. Judgements of plausibility and theoretical superiority are central in the final stages of this process, and the best comparative natural theology makes completely clear the criteria that function in those judgements. Schematizing the logic of comparative natural theology in a preliminary way can help to crystallize how it differs from traditional natural theology.

An ontology of nature, O, is enormously complex, logically. At the simplest and most idealized level, O is a finite conjunction of (say, n) propositions, $O_1 \wedge O_2 \wedge O_3 \wedge \ldots \wedge O_n$, each establishing philosophically basic concepts for making sense of natural objects and processes. But the complexity arises when we allow for the facts that: (1) these propositions collectively may not be mutually consistent; (2) the conjunction in any given formulation does not exhaust everything relevant to an ontology of nature; (3) the collection of propositions is a snapshot of a dynamic process whereby the ontology constantly adjusts to the growing insights of those who articulate it and to changes in scientific theories; (4) some of the propositions are more robust than others because they are most closely tied to well-attested scientific theories; and (5) scientific theories themselves are snapshots of dynamic research programmes with complex internal structures and relations to data. This realistic picture of the internal structure of an ontology of nature is utterly neglected in traditional natural theology.

Working from the most superficial characterization of an ontology of nature as a finite conjunction of *consistent* propositions, traditional natural theology tries to establish entailment from propositions in O to propositions about ultimacy, say:

U_1 = 'A First Cause exists and we call it God.'
U_2 = 'An Intelligent Designer exists and we call it God.'

That is, traditional natural theology seeks arguments that, say, $O_3 \rightarrow U_1$ (O_3 might describe the close causal nexus of nature) or $O_{14} \rightarrow U_2$ (O_{14} might describe instances of specified complexity). Because of the hidden but false assumption of the static perfection and internal consistency of O, this amounts to $O \rightarrow U_1$ and $O \rightarrow U_2$. Moreover, despite the fact that the history of theology displays real problems establishing the consistency of all propositions about ultimacy that are pronounced therein, traditional natural theology typically stipulates the desired consistency, which results in the appealing but manifestly oversimplified conclusion that $O \rightarrow U$. Voila! God exists and we even know something about the divine nature, all on the basis of analysing implications of our observations about nature. No wonder there has been so much hostility towards traditional natural theology.

Comparative natural theology is painfully sensitive to all of the fallacies in the argumentative procedure of traditional natural theology. Satisfactorily correcting these fallacies probably requires a fully developed theory of inquiry, but there is no space for that here (see Wildman 2010). The following schematization, however, does give an indication of some of the logical steps involved. At root, this schematization turns on the fact that implications run more soundly from ultimacy theories to ontologies of nature, than in the other direction.

Suppose we have three hypotheses about ultimacy, UH_1, UH_2, and UH_3 (these might be, for example, 'Ultimacy is a personal supernatural being with intentions, plans, and powers to act'; 'Reality is self-caused and ontologically ungrounded'; and 'Ultimacy is Being itself and necessarily surpasses human cognitive grasp'). These examples illustrate how complex an ultimacy hypothesis can be but, for the sake of exposition, let us neglect such details and concentrate on the relation of these ultimacy hypotheses to the ontological theory of nature, O, which is supposed to help us decide among these ultimacy hypotheses. Specifically, and remembering the complexity and possible internal inconsistency of O, suppose that:

$UH_1 \rightarrow \{O_1, O_6, O_8, O_{11}\}$
$UH_2 \rightarrow \{O_1, O_5, O_6\}$
$UH_3 \rightarrow \{O_1, O_2, O_4, O_{14}\}$.

It follows from this that the ontological proposition O_1 is of little use in detecting superiority of one ultimacy hypothesis over the other two, because all three entail it. Other ontological propositions would be more useful but comparative criteria (CC) are required to realize this potential. Consider the following examples:

CC$_1$: 'O_6 is especially important.'
CC$_2$: 'O_8 is especially important.'

In practice, comparative criteria are often much more complex than this, involving several features of an ontology simultaneously, with intricate interpretative dimensions. But even in these simplified cases, we can conclude that:

CC$_1$ ('O_6 is important')$\rightarrow$UH$_1$ and UH$_2$ are superior to UH$_3$.
CC$_2$ ('O_8 is important')$\rightarrow$UH$_1$ is superior to UH$_2$ and UH$_3$.

Subsequent debates over the relative weighting of comparative criteria CC$_1$ and CC$_2$ determine which of UH$_1$, UH$_2$, and UH$_3$ is finally the best explanation of the ontology of nature, O, given the available information. In this instance, UH$_3$ is not faring well and UH$_1$ is looking good. Of course, a final (though always provisional!) decision between UH$_1$, UH$_2$, and UH$_3$ would depend on how all relevant comparative criteria, including CC$_1$ and CC$_2$, are weighted.

Quite commonly, operative comparative criteria support one ultimacy hypothesis in one respect while supporting another in another respect, forcing the careful analysis of comparative criteria and leaving open the possibility that reasonable defences of alternative ultimacy views may coexist without resolving into a single superior viewpoint. At this point, the philosopher is forced to conclude that inquiry lacks sufficient resources, or that sufficient resources exist but the sociality of inquiry is not organized to capitalize on them. Or perhaps sufficient resources exist and the social organization of inquiry is optimal but the conceptual richness of ultimacy supports and demands multiple metaphysical perspectives; in that case, a non-decisive conclusion might be deemed informative in a way that does better justice to ultimacy than isolating a single best ultimacy metaphysics ever could.

The confidence with which we draw a final (again, always provisional) conclusion from an inference-to-best-explanation style of argument of this sort depends upon how sure we are that: (1) we have all of the relevant ultimacy hypotheses in play; (2) we have recognized all of the relevant comparative criteria; (3) we have properly accommodated our reasoning to the complexity of the ontology of nature and of the scientific theories on which it depends; and (4) we are realistic about the perplexities and peculiarities plaguing all arguments concerning ultimacy.

Traditional natural theology flagrantly violates all of these criteria for soundness of reasoning: (1) it usually ignores alternative ultimacy hypotheses; (2) it neglects making explicit comparative criteria, allowing them to function silently, unanalysed, and unchallenged; (3) it oversimplifies both ontological premises and the scientific theories that inform them; and (4) it often treats ultimacy arguments as strictly analogous to arguments in other domains, failing to register the potentially rationality defeating nature of inquiry into ultimacy.

The transparency of criteria for metaphysical superiority (corresponding to comparative criteria) in comparative natural theology is a huge advance on the covert operation of such criteria in traditional natural theology. Transparency also stimulates superior conversation across different views because clearly stated criteria can benefit from criticism in a way that covert criteria cannot. It is an open question whether an extended period of comparative metaphysics of this sort would induce greater agreement among those who initially value criteria for metaphysical adequacy differently. But there is no question that it would promote greater mutual understanding as well as more meaningful and satisfying debate.

INFERENCE TO BEST EXPLANATION REVISITED

This logical analysis of inference-to-best-explanation argumentation in comparative natural theology stands in tension with existing analyses within so-called confirmation theory, which rely on Bayesian probability. The standard Bayesian account of inference to best explanation depends on evaluating the probability of propositions given certain conditioning factors. The relevant formalism is as follows: let $P(A|BC)$ stand for the probability of proposition A given propositions B and C. Suppose that H is a hypothesis intended to explain evidence E in the context of background facts F. How 'good' is H as a hypothesis? To begin with, neglecting the evidence E, hypothesis H might be absurd relative to background facts F, so we need to keep an eye on the *prior probability of H*, which is $P(H|F)$. Prior probability is high when hypothesis H is simple or elegant or possesses other desirable intrinsic features, and also when H fits closely with background facts F. Next, we also need a way to measure the *explanatory power of H*, which is $P(H|EF)$. Explanatory power is high when hypothesis H has high predictive power—that is, $P(E|HF)$ is high, meaning that evidence E is likely on the assumption of the hypothesis H and given background facts F. Explanatory power is high also when evidence E has low prior probability—that is, $P(E|F)$ is low, meaning that evidence E is unlikely to occur just given background facts F and disregarding hypothesis H. Finally, in cases where two hypotheses, H_1 and H_2, have equal explanatory power, namely $P(H_1|EF) = P(H_2|EF)$, the hypothesis with the higher prior probability wins—that is, H_1 wins when $P(H_1|F)>P(H_2|F)$.

Bayesian accounts typically neglect the role of comparative adjudication or rest content with simple pair-wise comparison of competing hypotheses. They also assume the meaningfulness of the 'prior probability' of any hypothesis, which is its likelihood of being true given background information but disregarding the specific evidence pertaining to the situation in which the question about the hypothesis actually arises. This involves using unanalysed concepts of simplicity, elegance, fit with existing knowledge, and other factors involved in judging prior probability. In the case of metaphysical hypotheses, and indeed hypotheses of most kinds, prior probability is a grossly abstracted concept. Even in the classic examples of hypothetical explanations of a crime scene, the idea of prior probability of an hypothesis seems no more than a hand-waving gesture towards actual probability calculations, and thus probability talk functions more as a guiding analogy to keep one's head clear, or an after-the-fact rationalization of vastly complex intuitive judgements.

Many philosophers remain deeply dissatisfied with the Bayesian account of inference to best explanation (see Earman 1992). But this has not prevented some philosophical theologians from making hearty use of this Bayesian way of formalizing inference to best explanation in their arguments for the existence of God. For example, Richard Swinburne makes extensive use of confirmation theory (see the presentation of confirmation theory in Swinburne 1973 and the application of it to the existence of God in Swinburne 1979). Swinburne limits himself to judgements of 'more likely' and 'most likely' rather than attempting to assign numbers for probabilities, which is prudent. But he does not investigate the virtues of alternative hypotheses despite pointing out that it is important to allow for this (1979: 19), which is a serious error. He also does not address in any sustained way the difficulties facing attempts to determine the prior probability of a metaphysical hypothesis about ultimate reality. More pertinently, the philosophy of science has demonstrated that the logic of confirmation is formidably complex in actual practice, certainly not reducible to the terms of Bayesian probability, and possibly not even fully rational at key decision points. This reflects the debate between Imre Lakatos and Paul Feyerabend over the impossibility of stipulating fully rational criteria for deciding to abandon apparently degenerating research programs (see Motterlini 1999; the key background works are Lakatos 1978; Lakatos and Musgrave 1970; and Feyerabend 1993). This leaves these theological adventures in confirmation theory looking both innocent and unhelpfully abstract.

Recent philosophical attempts to refine (or to produce) understanding of judgements of similarity and difference, of consonance and dissonance, of elegance and coherence, have turned especially on the integration of cognitive science and philosophy. Cognitive modelling has proved to be an important tool here: such valuational judgements occur in prodigiously complex brains that may have special ways of detecting overall resonance between two sets of biologically coded information. Connectionist models of brain processes are especially useful here because they can represent hypotheses being compared as distributed activation patterns of nodes in a connectionist machine, which allows consonance and dissonance to be represented as pattern similarity and overlap. This in turn makes judgements of similarity akin to pattern recognition skills (see Churchland 1989; Thagard 1988).

These consonance-detection methods may be irreducible to simple probability calculations or even logical arguments. Yet they may still be logically pertinent if these biologically based mechanisms for assessing resonance produce useful results not merely accidentally but on the basis of neural functions refined through evolutionary pressures to be truth-conducive as well as fitness-promoting (a complex issue in its own right; see Plantinga 1991; Wildman 2009). We might abstract from such processes a Bayesian framework for understanding them but, inevitably, such abstractions will not prove very illuminating.

Human beings may have natural consonance-detection abilities, but we are also vulnerable to serious errors of judgement. Our pattern-recognition skills appear to be over-productive of hypotheses to explain the puzzles we come across. This is useful when we are searching for explanations, and thus highly relevant to evolutionary survival, which probably explains how we got this way. But it can also dangerously mislead us into trusting 'feelings' of similarity where in fact this leads to mistakes—sometimes deadly ones. There are many compendiums of errors due to biological limitations on human rationality, including examples of the ways that unscrupulous people exploit such vulnerabilities for their own profit and amusement (see Gilovich 1993; Piatelli-Palmarini 1996; Plous 1993; Randi 1982; Sagan 1996; Shermer 1997). In the context of comparative metaphysics and religion, especially, this propensity to trust feelings of consonance must be handled with extreme care. It takes decades of training both to help people make use of their abilities for inquiry and to train them to overcome their liabilities as inquirers. Even with such protracted training, experts still make errors of reasoning, particularly around questions of similarity and dissimilarity. Such errors in comparative religion have been traced with impressive precision (for example, see Smith 1982). The result is that a new collaborative approach has seemed necessary if we are to compare religious ideas with any degree of confidence (this was the aim of the Comparative Religious Ideas Project; see Neville 2001).

In light of these complexities, and without even touching on the peculiarities of ultimacy metaphysics, it appears that a Bayesian analysis of inference to best explanation is deficient, and perhaps best understood as an abstraction from a more complex process of inquiry. The alternative analysis I have proposed stresses awareness of many relevant hypotheses, transparency of the comparative criteria that guide judgements of similarity and difference, dynamic complexity of both ontologies of nature and ultimacy theories, and the futility of stipulating a reliable recipe for directing the artful process of evaluating competing conceptual systems. This approach still does not come to terms with the way we make judgements of similarity and difference, of simplicity and fit. But it has been made responsive to the problem by building in the kind of transparency and flexibility that facilitates correction of judgements in an ongoing process of adjustment and improvement.

Conclusion

Natural theology has always depended on a complex kind of comparative argumentation whose logical structure is presented above. Traditional natural theology aims at direct inference from nature to ultimacy only by mistake—a mistake of oversimplification that takes the form of unanalysed and hidden presuppositions. Natural theology properly described—which is to say comparative natural theology—involves surfacing criteria for judgement that operate silently beneath the misleading surface of traditional natural theology. Comparative natural theology also involves acknowledging that many aspects of the judgements involved—especially those of consonance and dissonance, similarity and difference—are aesthetically complex, entangled in philosophical tastes and formative influences, and resistant to complete clarification.

It is important in concluding to recognize that natural theology is only one aspect of theological reflection. Theology takes shape in traditions, with support from religious or secular scholarly institutions. When theology attempts to address metaphysical questions—a move whose current unpopularity may be a seasonal phenomenon—it is no less dependent on such traditions and institutions for the reception and carrying forward of its plausibility conditions and canons of rationality. The results of comparative natural theology can play an important role in structuring and adjusting these plausibility conditions and canons of rationality, thereby helping to guide metaphysical reflection on theological topics. Yet it remains possible to defend within a robust social context and lively intellectual tradition almost any metaphysical theory of ultimacy, more or less indefinitely. Such is the wealth of considerations that are relevant to judging the adequacy of any ultimacy metaphysics.

Metaphysics is not completely arbitrary, nor solely a matter of taste and tradition; natural theology has always held that this pessimistic view is mistaken. But we also need to resist the fantasy that ultimacy metaphysics is exhaustively rational in the sense that every question can be decided. Correspondingly, we should thoughtfully embrace the inchoate forces that dispose us to prefer one hypothesis over another, one aesthetic sensibility to another, one way of balancing criteria rather than another—embrace them, that is, in order to control their power and learn to allow for them.

This non-decisive rational landscape appears to be a fact of life for inquiries into ultimacy of all kinds, including those arising within natural theology. *Philosophical theologians can manage this complex situation to an optimal degree by employing the tools of comparative natural theology.* This requires engagement with the sciences of nature and the philosophy of science—an unappetizing prospect for many and certainly not an easy task. Once properly informed, however, philosophical theologians can build ingenious theories around ultimacy hypotheses that artfully balance criteria in a way that honours the struggles and strange currents of their own lives and the traditions that form them. It is a partly rational process, conditioned by unfathomable drives and intriguing instincts and untraceable influences. Yet the process of inquiry does not fall into the irrational chaos of sheer relativism because the process can be made responsive to the network of conceptual and logical linkages that stretches like an intricate web between our ideas of the natural world and our ideas of ultimacy. Traditions and personal predispositions continue to find voice within the inquiries of natural theology and yet the rational constraints on argumentation are genuine and productive.

It would be easier to embrace personal involvement in metaphysical theory building if the Kantian and logical-positivist detractors, the Heideggerian anti-onto-theological and postmodern anti-logocentric accusers of metaphysics were known to be at least partly mistaken, and if rational constraints deriving from nature were known to make a constructive difference in ultimacy queries. After all, no philosophical theologian wants to be the poster child for deluded metaphysical speculation. The scope of this chapter has not permitted consideration of such arguments (see Wildman 2010).

Nevertheless, once the meaningfulness of the network of conceptual and logical linkages between nature and ultimacy is granted—granted to any degree whatsoever—then comparative natural theology offers the ideal response to the questionable rational status of traditional natural theology. By eschewing rational overreaching, by cautiously accepting the complexities of multidisciplinary comparative inquiry, and by acknowledging the misleading consequences of hidden premises in traditional natural theology, comparative natural theology actually produces credible results that simultaneously overcome cultural parochialism and meaningfully constrain ultimacy metaphysics. Modest achievements build confidence precisely because they do not overreach and do not underestimate difficulties. Comparative natural theology creates confidence to venture speculative arguments about ultimacy and nurtures willingness to accept our emotional and spiritual entanglement in metaphysical theory building. This is not the grand achievement of now discredited traditional natural theology, to be sure, but that may prove to be a great advantage.

REFERENCES

Anselm (1998). *Monologion*. In *Anselm of Canterbury: The Major Works*. Edited by Brian Davies and G. R. Evans. Oxford and New York: Oxford University Press.

Behe, Michael J. (1996). *Darwin's Black Box: The Biochemical Challenge to Evolution*. New York: Free Press.

Behe, Michael J., William A. Dembski, and Stephen C. Meyer (2000). *Science and Evidence for Design in the Universe: Papers Presented as a Conference Sponsored by the Wethersfield Institute, New York City, September 25, 1999*. San Francisco: Ignatius Press.

Churchland, Paul (1989). *A Neurocomputational Perspective*. Cambridge, MA: MIT Press.

Dawkins, Richard (2006). *The God Delusion*. London, UK: Houghton Mifflin.

Dembski, William A. (1998). *The Design Inference: Eliminating Chance through Small Probabilities*. Cambridge and New York: Cambridge University Press.

—— (2002). *No Free Lunch: Why Specified Complexity Cannot be Purchased without Intelligence*. Lanham, MD: Rowman & Littlefield.

Earman, John (1992). *Bayes or Bust? A Critical Examination of Bayesian Confirmation Theory*. Cambridge, MA and London: MIT Press.

Feyerabend, Paul (1993). *Against Method*. 3rd edn. London and New York: Verso.

Gilovich, Thomas (1993). *How We Know What Isn't So: The Fallibility of Reason in Everyday Life*. Boston: Free Press.

Harris, Sam (2006). *Letters to a Christian Nation*. New York, NY: Knopf.

Hitchens, Christopher (2007). *God Is Not Great: How Religion Poisons Everything*. New York, NY: Twelve Books.

Lakatos, Imre (1978). *The Methodology of Scientific Research Programs*. Edited by John Worrall and Gregory Currie. Cambridge and New York: Cambridge University Press.

Lakatos, Imre and Alan Musgrave, eds. (1970). *Criticism and the Growth of Knowledge*. Cambridge and New York: Cambridge University Press.

Motterlini, Matteo, ed. (1999). *For and Against Method: Including Lakatos' Lectures on Scientific Method and the Lakatos–Feyerabend Correspondence*. Chicago: Chicago University Press.

Murphy, Nancey (1996). 'Postmodern Apologetics, or Why Theologians Must Pay Attention to Science' in *Religion and Science: History, Method, Dialogue*. Edited by W. Mark Richardson and Wesley J. Wildman. New York and London: Routledge: pp. 105–20.

Neville, Robert Cummings (1968). *God the Creator: On the Transcendence and Presence of God*. Chicago, IL: Chicago University Press.

—— ed. (2001). *The Comparative Religious Ideas Project*. Vol. I: *The Human Condition*. Vol. II: *Ultimate Realities*. Vol. III: *Religious Truth*. Albany, NY: State University of New York Press.

Piatelli-Palmarini, Massimo (1996). *Inevitable Illusions: How Mistakes of Reason Rule Our Minds*. John Wiley and Sons.

Plantinga, Alvin (1991). 'An Evolutionary Argument against Naturalism'. *Logos* 12.

Plous, Scott (1993). *The Psychology of Judgment and Decision Making*. New York: McGraw-Hill.

Randi, James (1982). *Flim Flam: Psychics, ESP, Unicorns and other Delusions*. Amherst, NY: Prometheus Books.

Sagan, Carl (1996). *The Demon-Haunted World: Science as a Candle in the Dark*. New York: Random House.

Shermer, Michael (1997). *Why People Believe Weird Things: Pseudoscience, Superstition, and Other Confusions of Our Time*. New York: Henry Holt.

—— (2002). *Why People Believe Weird Things: Pseudoscience, Superstition, and Other Confusions of Our Time*. 2nd edn. New York: Henry Holt and Company, Owl Books.

Smith, Jonathan Z. (1982). 'In Comparison a Magic Dwells' in *Imagining Religion: From Babylon to Jonestown*. Chicago: Chicago University Press.

Swinburne, Richard (1973). *An Introduction to Confirmation Theory*. London: Methuen & Co.

—— (1979). *The Existence of God*. Oxford: Clarendon Press, 1979.

Thagard, Paul (1988). *Conceptual Revolutions*. Princeton: Princeton University Press.

Wildman, Wesley J. (2009). *Science and Religious Anthropology: A Spiritually Evocative Naturalist Interpretation of Human Life*. Farnham, UK: Ashgate Publishing.

—— (2010). *Religious Philosophy as Multidisciplinary Comparative Inquiry: Envisioning a Future for the Philosophy of Religion*. Albany: State University of New York Press.

CHAPTER 24

PHILOSOPHICAL CRITIQUE OF NATURAL THEOLOGY

CHARLES TALIAFERRO

THERE are at least two kinds of philosophical critiques of natural theology: what may be called external and internal critiques. External critiques take aim at the whole project, objecting to the metaphysics, epistemology, or theory of values that make natural theology possible at all. Among external critiques, *Kant's Critique of Pure Reason* seeks to undermine all metaphysics, as do contemporary forms of non-realism. Internal critiques allow that natural theology can (in principle) succeed but none of its arguments are cogent or meet high philosophical standards. Let us consider the external critique first.

THE EXTERNAL CHALLENGE

Kantian and other assaults on metaphysics have been formidable and, if successful, would render natural theology null and void. Interpretative debates continue to plague a facile summary of Kant on metaphysics, but philosophers agree that Kant held that human cognition is limited to the phenomenal realm of appearance and cannot penetrate the noumenal world of things in themselves. Kant writes:

> All our intuition is nothing but the representation of appearance; that the things that we intuit are not in themselves what we intuit them to be, nor are their relations so constituted in themselves as they appear to us; and that if we remove our own subject or even only the subjective constitution of the senses in general, then all the constitution, all relations of objects in space and time, indeed space and time themselves would disappear, and as appearances they cannot exist in themselves, but only in us. What may be the case with objects in themselves and abstracted from all this receptivity of our sensibility remains entirely unknown to us. We are acquainted with nothing except our way of perceiving them, which is peculiar to us, and which

therefore does not necessarily pertain to every being, though to be sure it pertains to every human being. [Kant 1998: A42]

Some philosophers today, for reasons other than Kant, take umbrage over ontology. Perhaps the most dramatic recent condemnation of ontology may be found in Hilary Putnam's *Ethics without Ontology*. Putnam compliments ontology but along the way he describes it as a 'stinking corpse'. I cite this partly to document not just the intellectual rejection of ontology, but to convey a current distaste for the enterprise.

> I promised an obituary on ontology, but to extend those remarks would not be so much an obituary as flogging a dead horse. Instead I shall just say this (since it *is* customary to say at least one good word about the dead): even if ontology has become a sinking corpse, in Plato and Aristotle it represented the vehicle for conveying many genuine philosophical insights. The insights still preoccupy all of us in philosophy who have any historical sense at all. But the vehicle has long since outlived its usefulness. (Putnam 2004: 85)

Despite the condemnation of metaphysics and ontology by such prestigious philosophers, metaphysics has proved to be resilient and is currently enjoying a renaissance (see Arrum Stroll's 'Metaphysics Revivified' (2009)). The Kantian project seems to suffer multiple problems. For example, despite Kant's relegating causation to only the phenomenal world, he (inconsistently) held that the phenomenal world was caused by the noumenal world. On this view, causation and its related concepts (space and time) are not restricted to the phenomenal world. For another example, Kant sought to ground necessary truths in terms of the structure of human cognition, but why should necessary human structures be any less mysterious than believing in necessarily existing abstract objects (as in Plato, Leibniz, Frege, Chisholm)? Moreover, extensive critical realist accounts of perception challenge Kant's scepticism. Granted, human perception should not be presumed to be infallible, but perception can be a source of knowledge— e.g. I can be sure that my copy of Kant's first Critique is on my desk right now (see Alston 2001 for a further defence of metaphysical realism).

Putnam's attack on realism is grounded on his view that our access to the way things are is always mediated by conceptual schemes. Putnam claims that 'access to the world is *through* our discourse and the role that the discourse plays in our lives; we compare our discourse with the world as it is presented to us or constructed for us by discourse itself, mainly in the process new worlds out of old ones' (Putnam 1990: 121). Putnam seems to hold that metaphysical realism is undermined because we can never achieve a God's eye point of view or make the assumption that a God's eye point of view is even possible. We cannot escape 'our own skins' (Putnam 1990: 125). Putnam believes that we can and should recognize the truth of multiple, mutually exclusive views of reality. 'Objects are theory-dependent in the sense that theories with incompatible ontologies can both be right' (Putnam 1990: 40). From this vantage point, natural theology is unpromising, to say the least.

Like Roger Trigg, I am not persuaded by Putnam and other anti-realists. One of the problems with most attacks on realism is that virtually all the attacks seem to presuppose some metaphysic or ontology. Putnam, for example, seems to recognize the fact that there are conceptual frameworks, theories, and discourse. This is *an ontological claim* and for his position to be coherent, it must be the case that to deny the existence of such things is mistaken (Loux 1998). Putnam also seems to be led to a deeply implausible position in claiming that incompatible ontologies can both be right if that means both can be true (try to imagine that both atheism and theism are true), albeit incompatible ontologies might have equally good reasons behind them. Furthermore, Putnam seems simply wrong that we cannot escape our own skins through empathetic imagination and the affective identification with others. The case for racial justice has been built, historically, on persons coming to see the world from the point of view of persons of different ethnicity—including imagining one having skin that is quite different (see Taliaferro 2005 for a further defence of this counter-move). Trigg rightly contends that Putnam seems to give us a misleading picture of our options: either we must claim to know everything from every point of view or we must abandon realism:

> We should not be forced into a choice between reasoning about everything and reasoning about nothing. Just because we cannot possess omniscience, does that mean that the only alternative is to be content with the prejudices of our time and place? The function of metaphysics is surely to warn us of the dangers of such parochialism. Where we are is not necessarily where we ought to be. We can reason about our circumstances and our position in them, even if we can never leave them completely. [Trigg 1993: 121]

I suggest that external philosophical critiques of natural theology have been less than successful. What about internal critiques?

INTERNAL CRITIQUES

Let's consider four sets of objections that may be labelled 'The Incoherence of Theism', 'The Poverty of Theism', 'Humean Uniqueness', and 'Kantian Disappointment'.

The Incoherence of Theism

Natural theology has historically involved arguments for non-theistic concepts of God, though in Western philosophy theism has been the preferred model of God and thus the view of God most attacked by critics of natural theology. One of the most serious charges against theistic natural theology is that theism is itself incoherent.

Some philosophers have argued that the very idea of an incorporeal or non-physical subject or agent is incoherent. It has been argued, for example, that the concept of an agent is necessarily the concept of an embodied, physical being and that the concept of a person is necessarily the concept of a being with spatial boundaries. John Hick has argued that, in so far as God is a person (or, for a Trinitarian, three persons), God would have to be bounded but this is impossible because God is infinite (Hick 2010).

388   CHARLES TALIAFERRO

Both lines of reasoning are open to serious doubt. Materialism faces multiple problems, especially when it comes to offering a physical reduction or elimination of consciousness. Non-physicalist accounts of human nature have been growing of late (see Baker and Goetz, forthcoming) and make it increasingly difficult to argue that materialism is necessarily true. As for persons and bodies, theists may rightly (in my view) insist that their concept of God does envision God as a person or person-like but it is not thereby anthropomorphic or a matter of supposing that God would have to have physical boundaries. In theism, God is omnipresent but this is not at all like God being some diffuse material thing—a kind of gas or field (see Taliaferro 1994).

Some philosophers have contended that theism is incoherent on the grounds that it posits God as a necessarily existing reality and, they reason, all of reality is contingent. Hume articulated such an objection:

> It is pretended, that the Deity is a necessarily existent Being and this necessity of his existence is attempted to be explained by asserting, that, if we knew his whole essence or nature, we should perceive it to be as impossible for him not to exist as for twice two not to be four. But it is evident, that this can never happen, while our faculties remain the same as at present: It will still be possible for us, at any time, to conceive the nonexistence of what we formerly conceived to exist; nor can the mind ever lie under a necessity of supposing any object to remain always in being; in the same manner as we lie under a necessity of always conceiving twice two to be four. The words, therefore, *necessary existence* have no meaning; or which is the same thing, none that is consistent. [Hume 1991: 149]

And the idea that God might be self-created seems not to be an option. Dennett observes:

> If God created and designed all these wonderful things, who created God? Supergod? And who created Supergod? Superdupergod? Or did God create himself? Was it hard work? Did it take time? Don't ask! Well then, we may ask instead whether this bland embrace is any improvement over just denying the principle that intelligence (or design) must spring from intelligence. [Dennett 2009: 619]

In reply, many philosophers today believe that there are necessarily existing abstract objects (properties, propositions, states of affairs). If this position is plausible (and I believe that it is) the blanket assertion that all of reality must be contingent seems less than compelling. Those denying the status of necessity are also in the seemingly embarrassing position of holding that it is necessarily the case that there are no necessary realities (Koons 1997). There is no need to think of God as self-created, as Dennett seems to suppose. Dennett's barb about self-creation is amusing but fails to reveal any awareness of the theistic conviction that God exists *a se*, and not through any external power or by God (absurdly) bringing about God's own existence (see Nagel 2010 and his critique of Dawkins for making an assumption like Dennett's).

Some philosophers claim to find incoherence among the divine attributes, but establishing incoherence is an uphill battle given the elasticity of theism. Theism is elastic in so far as it is compatible with multiple accounts of the divine attributes. For example, if it were ever demonstrated that there cannot be an atemporal, eternal being, theists can adopt the view that God is in time but everlasting (without temporal origin or end). If we have good reason for believing that omniscience is incompatible with future free action, theists can hold that omniscience only obtains over possible knowledge (this view is often called 'open theism').

The Poverty of Theism

Some philosophers have argued that theistic explanations are not authentic or intelligible. Jan Narveson claims:

> It ought to be regarded as a major embarrassment to natural theology that the very idea of something like a universe's being 'created' by some minded being is sufficiently mind-boggling that any attempt to provide a detailed account of how it might be done is bound to look silly, or mythical, or a vaguely anthropomorphized version of some familiar physical process. Creation stories abound in human societies, as we know. Accounts ascribe the creation to various mythical beings, chief gods among a sizeable polytheistic committee, giant tortoises, super-mom hens, and, one is tempted to say, God-knows-what. The Judeo-Christian account does no better, and perhaps does a bit worse, in proposing a 'six-day' process of creation. [Narveson 2003: 93–4]

Narveson holds that theism is defective because it is unable to explain how it is that divine agency functions:

> It is plainly no surprise that details about just *how* all this was supposed to have happened [God creating the cosmos] are totally lacking when they are not, as I say, silly or simply poetic. For the fundamental idea is that some infinitely powerful mind simply willed it to be thus, and as they say, Lo!, it was so! If we aren't ready to accept that as an explanatory description—as we should not be, since it plainly doesn't *explain* anything, as distinct from merely asserting that it was in fact done— then where do we go from there? On all accounts, we at this point meet up with mystery. 'How are we supposed to know the ways of the infinite and almighty God?' it is asked—as if that put-down made a decent substitute for an answer. But of course it doesn't. If we are serious about 'natural theology,' then we ought to be ready to supply content in our explication of theological hypotheses. Such explications carry the brunt of explanation. Why does water boil when heated? The scientific story supplies an analysis of matter in its liquid state, the effects of atmospheric pressure and heat, and so on until we see, in impressive detail, just how the thing works. An explanation's right to be called 'scientific' is, indeed, in considerable part earned precisely by its ability to provide such detail. [Narveson 2003: 94]

Narveson concludes that theism is to be rejected due to its profoundly unscientific or anti-scientific philosophy.

Narveson wants theists to have detailed accounts of how divine purposes or God's will accounts for things. His demands, however, seem to be at odds with our recognition of the concept of basic actions. If there are genuine intentional explanations of events, there must be what some philosophers call *basic actions*. These are acts one does for reasons, but one does them directly and without the mediation of other acts. You might do one thing (get your friend's attention) by doing another (calling out to her), but some acts are not mediated. Your calling out to your friend because you want to meet her may require a host of factors to come into play in a full explanation (factors including social expectations, language use, personality type, texting, etc.). But some acts will not be further accountable by other acts. When you called, you did not do so by willing that certain neurons fire or that your nervous system react in some way; you simply did the act. When Narveson complains that theistic explanation lacks certain mechanisms and causal elements his complaint cuts against intentional explanations in ordinary human (and other animal) activities. In everyday, bona fide explanations of human agency, there are basic acts that are not further reducible into 'impressive detail'. It should also be noted that if there must always be an answer to 'how things work' in physical causation, there can be *no basic physical causes*. This seems counter to many views of causation in the physical world and threatens an infinite regress. If divine intentions are basic, so are some human intentions even though the latter are exercised by beings with animal bodies. This implies that Narveson is not successful in ruling out the possibility of theistic accounts. Let us linger on this point a bit more.

Imagine Narveson adopts Daniel Dennett's strategy and insists that any mental explanations have to (ultimately) give way to explanations that involve only clearly non-mental causes. This would, however, have the impact of undermining our reasoning. If reasoning takes place, the embracing of conclusions takes place in virtue of grasping certain reasons. But in non-mental causation there is no reasoning because there are no beliefs, no understanding, no intentions. The difficulty of collapsing or reducing mental, intentional explanations is stated clearly by John Searle:

> So far no attempt at naturalizing content [meaningful beliefs and reasons] has produced an explanation (analysis, reduction) of intentional content that is even remotely plausible. A symptom that something is radically wrong with the project is that intentional notions are inherently normative. They set standards of truth, rationality, consistency etc., and there is no way that these standards can be intrinsic to a system consisting entirely of *brute, blind, nonintentional causal relations*. There is no mean [middle] component to billiard ball causation. Darwinian biological attempts at naturalizing content try to avoid this problem by appealing to what they suppose is the inherently teleological [i.e. purposeful], normative character of biological evolution. But this is a very deep mistake. There is nothing normative or teleological about Darwinian evolution. Indeed, Darwin's major contribution was precisely to remove purpose and teleology from evolution, and substitute for it purely natural forms of selection. [Searle 1992: 50–1]

It will not do to dismiss Searle's point by appealing to the way computers calculate or reason, for they either simply are behaving in accord with programs made by humans or it is unreasonable to believe computers actually have any beliefs or reasons at all. Computers are pure syntactic mechanisms with no intrinsic intentionality.

One more modest point may be added in a reply to Narveson. Scriptural reference to God creating through speech (God said 'Let there be light') may be seen as representing creation as a supremely intentional, purposive act. Among the ancients and many modern thinkers, language-usage is considered the high-water mark of intelligence. By describing God as creating through speech, the key thesis is that creation occurs through purposive agency and goodness ('And God saw that it was good') rather than some thesis about the causal power of divine auditions. (For a further response to Narveson, see Goetz and Taliaferro 2008).

Humean Uniqueness

Hume developed many arguments in response to natural theology. Perhaps one of the most important is the thesis that arguments about whether there is a creator involves a problem of uniqueness. If there were multiple universes that we could compare, we might be able to make reliable inferences as to whether our universe is created, but the universe is absolutely unique. Richard Swinburne articulates the objection and then offers a reply:

> From time to time various writers have told us that we cannot reach any conclusions about the origin or development of the universe, since it is (whether by logic or just in fact) a unique object, the only one of its kind, and rational inquiry can reach conclusions about objects which belong to kinds, e.g. it can reach a conclusion about what will happen to this bit of iron, because there are other bits of iron, the behaviour of which can be studied. This objection of course has the surprising, and to most of these writers unwelcome, consequence, that physical cosmology cannot reach justified conclusions about such matters as the size, age, rate of expansion, and density of the universe as a whole (because it is a unique object); and also that physical anthropology cannot reach conclusion about the origin and development of the human race (because, as far as our knowledge goes, it is the only one of its kind). The implausibility of these consequences leads us to doubt the original objection, which is indeed totally misguided. [Swinburne 2004: 134]

I believe the uniqueness objection would also curtail reasoning about matters that are quite immediate and ordinary. Philosophers have different and sometimes quite well reasoned views about whether some non-human animals are conscious. It seems that we can form some reasonable views on animal minds based on behaviour, anatomy, evolutionary theory, and an inference to the best explanation even if, from a human point of view, animal minds are unique. Putting aside the possibility of reincarnation across species, no humans will become non-human animals and we will never be able to directly know the level or kind of consciousness that non-human animals enjoy or endure (for a famous defence of this position, see Thomas Nagel's 'What Is it Like to Be a Bat?' and Taliaferro and Evans 2011: Ch. 4).

Kantian Disappointment

Both Hume and Kant complain that a plausible natural theology is deficient in so far as it would not justify the awesome attributes of the God of classical Christian theism. Here is Kant's famous qualification about a successful teleological theistic 'proof':

> The proof could at most establish a highest architect of the world, who would always be limited by the suitability of the material on which he works, but not a creator of the world, to whose idea everything is subject, which is far from sufficient for the great aim that one has in view, namely that of proving an all-sufficient original being. If we wanted to prove the contingency of matter itself, then we would have to take refuge in a transcendental argument, which, however, is exactly what was supposed to be avoided here. [Kant 1998: A627]

If one is not a Christian theist, this objection will not be telling. But does this objection give pause to Christian theists?

This is far from obvious. If the teleological argument would generate what Kant thinks it would, this result would suffice to cause many naturalists to undergo a severe philosophical heart attack. But more importantly, any evidence for theism in general will increase the plausibility of Christian theism (just as any evidence that there was life on, say, Mars, would increase, however slightly, the case for there having been intelligent life on Mars). Also, Christian philosophers have developed cumulative arguments for their position (Swinburne 2004) as well as introduced other strategies (arguments from religious experience, reformed epistemology) that would enable the acceptance of revelation claims in the absence of natural theology. The finding of natural theology that there may be some transcendent, teleological force would not give one the God of the New Testament, but perhaps it does not have to. Even so, one should bear in mind that for a non-Christian or a Christian prepared to treat the New Testament in highly restricted ways (e.g. treating the God of Jesus in the biblical narratives as largely metaphors), the Kantian disappointment objection will not be weighty.

The Current State of Play
for Natural Theology

With the revival of philosophical theism and metaphysics since the demise of positivism in the 1960s, we now seem to be working at a time when natural theology can once again be taken seriously as an important, constructive enterprise. John Searle's comment on systematic philosophy may be applied to natural theology:

> What does philosophy look like in a post-epestemic, post-skeptical era? It seems to me that it is now possible to do systematic theoretical philosophy in a way that was generally regarded as out of the question half a century ago. [Searle 2003: 3]

The prominent analytic philosopher Dean Zimmerman recently published a kind of 'all clear' announcement to theologians, alerting them that the current intellectual climate is far more theologian-friendly. His report from the front lines of cutting edge analytic philosophy is worth citing as further testimony that the philosophical critique of theology (including natural theology) is at bay:

> Many theologians and Christian philosophers who belong to groups that rejected analytic philosophy early in the last century assume that the analytic river is still patrolled by theologian-eating sharks; that the only kind of philosophical theology capable of surviving here is a meagre and reductionistic 'analysis of religious language'. But the analytic stream was only toxic for theologians (and metaphysicians and ethicists and...) for at most a third of its hundred-year history. [Zimmerman and van Inwagen 2007: 7]

While there are still hostile forces around (as there are facing virtually every substantial philosophical position), the water seems far safer than several decades ago.

REFERENCES

Alston, W. (2001). *A Sensible Metaphysical Realism*. Milwaukee: Marquette University Press.

Dennett, Daniel C. (2007). 'Atheism and Evolution' in *The Cambridge Companion to Atheism*. Cambridge: Cambridge University Press.

Goetz, S. and C. Taliaferro (2008). *Naturalism*. Grand Rapids: Eerdmanns.

Hick, J. (2010). 'God and Christianity According to Swinburne'. *European Journal for Philosophy of Religion* 2/1: 25–37.

Hume, D. (1991). *Dialogues Concerning Natural Religion*. Edited by S. Tweyman. London: Routledge.

Kant, I. (1998). *Critique of Pure Reason*. Edited by Paul Guyer. Cambridge: Cambridge University Press.

Koons, Robert C. (1997). 'A New Look at the Cosmological Argument' in *American Philosophical Quarterly* 34: 171–92.

Loux, M. (1998). *Metaphysics*. London: Routledge.

Nagel, T. (2010). *Secular Philosophy and the Religious Temperament*. Oxford: Oxford University Press.

Narveson, J. (2003). 'God by Design?' in *God and Design*. Edited by in N. Manson. London: Routledge.

Putnam, H. (1990). *Realism with a Human Face*. Cambridge: Harvard University Press.

—— (2004). *Ethics without Ontology*. Cambridge, MA: Harvard University Press.

Searle, J. (1992). *The Rediscovery of the Mind*. Cambridge: Cambridge University Press.

—— (2003). 'Philosophy in a New Century'. *Journal of Philosophical Research* 28. APA Centennial Supplement: 3–22.

Stroll, A. (2009). 'Metaphysics Revivified' in *The Routledge Companion to Metaphysics*. Edited by R. Le Poldevin. London: Routledge.

Swinburne, R. (2004). *The Existence of God*. 2nd edn. Oxford: Clarendon Press.

Taliaferro, C. (1994). *Consciousness and the Mind of God*. Cambridge: Cambridge University Press.

Taliaferro, C. (2005). 'A God's Eye View' in *Faith and Analysis*. Edited by Harris, H. A. and C. I. Insole. United Kingdom: Ashgate.

Taliaferro, C. and J. Evans (2011). *The Image in Mind*. London: Continuum.

Trigg, R. (1993). *Rationality and Science*. Oxford: Blackwell.

Zimmerman, Dean and Peter van Inwagen (2007). *Persons: Human and Divine*. Oxford: Oxford University Press.

PART IV

··

SCIENTIFIC
PERSPECTIVES ON
NATURAL THEOLOGY

··

CHAPTER 25

NATURAL THEOLOGY: THE BIOLOGICAL SCIENCES

MICHAEL RUSE

THE biological sciences have always been highly pertinent to issues in natural theology. I shall show this by considering in turn three major, and still very much alive, topics: the argument from design, the problem of evil, and the place of humans in the cosmic scheme of things.

DESIGN: THE EARLY YEARS

Socrates is generally given credit for the first exposition of the argument from design, that argument for the existence of God (no implications yet that this is the Christian God) from the design-like nature of the world. It is given by Plato in the *Phaedo*, the dialogue that purports to report on Socrates' last day on earth:

> I had formerly thought that it was clear to everyone that he grew through eating and drinking; that when, through food, new flesh and bones came into being to supplement the old, and thus in the same way each kind of thing was supplemented by new substances proper to it, only then did the mass which was small become large, and in the same way the small man big. [Plato *Phaedo* 96d, cited in Cooper 1997: 83–4]

Socrates then says that he realizes that this explanation is incomplete. There is a sense of purpose about things that cannot be explained just in this way. Flesh and bones have an organization, they exist for ends, to do things, and this cannot just be chance. Somehow we must account for the design-like nature of the world. And so we get to God:

> the ordering Mind ordered everything and placed each thing severally as it was best that it should be; so that if anyone wanted to discover the cause of anything, how it came into being or perished or existed, he simply needed to discover what kind of existence was *best* for it, or what it was best that it should do or have done to it. [Plato *Phaedo* 97b–c]

Later, in the *Timaeus*, Plato elaborated on this God, the 'Demiurge'. Notably, Plato's Demiurge is described as working on already existing matter and that it applied (and could be inferred) throughout the universe: physical things as well as organisms were fully part of the story.

Aristotle did not believe in Plato's God (Sedley 2008). For him, the deities were Unmoved Movers, with little interest in the world as they contemplated their own perfection. However, Aristotle was not only a philosopher; he had been a practicing biologist. Like Plato, he saw things in the world as being end-directed—to use a word from the eighteenth century, as being 'teleological'—and although his thinking like Plato's applied to all physical things, it was he who first made clear that the real action is in the biological world. 'What are the forces by which the hand or the body was fashioned into its shape?' Aristotle noted that a woodcarver (speaking of a model) could well say that it was made as it is by tools like an axe or an auger. Like Plato, however, the philosopher noted that simply referring to the tools and their effects is not enough. One must bring in ends. The woodcarver 'must state the reasons why he struck his blow in such a way as to effect this, and for the sake of what he did so; namely, that the piece of wood should develop eventually into this or that shape'. Likewise against the physiologists:

> the true method is to state what the characters are that distinguish the animal – to explain what it is and what are its qualities – and to deal after the same fashion with its several parts; in fact, to proceed in exactly the same way as we should do, were we dealing with the form of a couch. [Aristotle *On the Parts of Animals* 641a 7–17, in Barnes 1984: 997]

If there is no designing God, no demiurge, then clearly the analogy with the woodcarver can only go so far. There can be no argument from design because there is no designer. What is crucial is the end-directedness, the teleology, or what Aristotle called 'final cause'. This is not cause in the sense of efficient cause—the woodcarver fashioning the wood in various ways—so there is no question of causes somehow in the future affecting the present or past. Rather it is cause in the sense of understanding the present—the activities of the woodcarver—in terms of the future, the finished carving. But if there is no demiurge, then how do things come about? What is it that makes for the hand and the eye and makes them non-random and organized and end-directed? Plato's is an external teleology, with a designer. Aristotle's is an internal teleology with some kind of vital force making everything tick. This force is not necessarily conscious but it is alive in some sense, or at least it infuses that which is alive.

Fast forward now 2,000 years to the Scientific Revolution. The one thing that the scientists and philosophers wanted to do was to kick Aristotelian final causes out of physics (Dijksterhuis 1961). Francis Bacon likened them to Vestal Virgins, decorative but sterile! Using an argument as much theological as philosophical or scientific, René Descartes warned that:

> When dealing with natural things, we will, then, never derive any explanations from the purposes which God or nature may have had in view when creating them <and we shall entirely banish from our philosophy the search for final causes>. For we

should not be so arrogant as to suppose that we can share in God's plans. [Descartes 1985: 202; arrow brackets, < >, denote an addition approved by Descartes in the French translation from the original Latin]

Stick rather to efficient causes:

starting from the divine attributes which by God's will we have some knowledge of, we shall see, with the aid of our God-given natural light, what conclusions should be drawn concerning those effects which are apparent to our senses. [Descartes 1985: 202]

Yet while this may all have been very well in physics, in biology things were not quite so simple. Organisms really did seem to have been designed, to exhibit final causes. The coming of the microscope reinforced this feeling because the very small was, if anything, even more remarkable than the living world we can see with our unaided eyes. The physicist/philosopher Robert Boyle endorsed strongly the expulsion of final cause from the physical sciences—a favourite point of illustration was a magnificent clock in Strasburg built late in the sixteenth century, something that simply worked away according to fixed unbroken laws. The physical universe is just like this—a mechanism without (visible) point or purpose. But when it comes to the biological sciences, things are different. Descartes (and his followers, the Cartesians) in particular were criticized and the human eye was taken as a clear example of something that demands final-cause thinking:

For there are some things in nature so curiously contrived, and so exquisitely fitted for certain operations and uses, that it seems little less than blindness in him, that acknowledges, with the Cartesians, a most wise Author of things, not to conclude, that, though they may have been designed for other (and perhaps higher) uses, yet they were designed for this use. As he, that sees the admirable fabric of the coats, humours, and muscles of the eyes, and how excellently all the parts are adapted to the making up of an organ of vision, can scarce forbear to believe, that the Author of nature intended it should serve the animal to which it belongs, to see with. [Boyle 1688: 397–8]

Boyle argued that supposing that 'a man's eyes were made by chance, argues, that they need have no relation to a designing agent; and the use, that a man makes of them, may be either casual too, or at least may be an effect of his knowledge, not of nature's'. This attitude takes us away from the urge to dissect and to understand—how the eye 'is as exquisitely fitted to be an organ of sight, as the best artificer in the world could have framed a little engine, purposely and mainly designed for the use of seeing'—and also it takes us away from the designing intelligence behind it (Boyle 1688: 397–8).

Note that Boyle did not see this position of his as something threatening expulsion of final cause from physics but as complementing it. The clock analogy was turned around now to make this very point. 'I never saw any inanimate production of nature, or, as they speak, of chance, whose contrivance was comparable to that of the meanest limb of the despicablest animal: and there is incomparably more art expressed in the structure of a dog's foot, than in the famous clock at *Strassburg*' (Boyle 1688: 404). Significantly, Boyle distinguished between acknowledging the use of final causes qua science, and the inference qua theology from final causes to a designing god. First:

> In the bodies of animals it is oftentimes allowable for a naturalist, from the manifest and apposite uses of the parts, to collect some of the particular ends, to which nature destinated them. And in some cases we may, from the known natures, as well as from the structure, of the parts, ground probable conjectures (both affirmative and negative) about the particular offices of the parts. [Boyle 1688: 424]

Then, the science finished, one can switch to theology: 'It is rational, from the manifest fitness of some things to cosmical or animal ends or uses, to infer, that they were framed or ordained in reference thereunto by an intelligent and designing agent' (Boyle 1688: 428). By now, obviously, people like Boyle were identifying the designer with the Christian God, and if challenged would have argued that the goodness or worth of the design points to the goodness or worth of the designer. Obviously there was no proof of all of God's supposed attributes, or creation from nothing, so the argument from design would obviously be thought a part of a range of arguments that collectively do what is needed. Presumably the causal argument can deal with the creation-from-nothing issue.

DESIGN: DAVID HUME AND THE RESPONSES

Boyle was writing towards the end of the seventeenth century. A hundred years later, the Scottish philosopher David Hume drove a horse and cart through all of this kind of reasoning. In his justly celebrated *Dialogues Concerning Natural Religion* (1779), he attacked the argument from design from just about every angle and then some. The argument proves that there were many previous botched worlds, that there will be future worlds better than ours, that there was a squad of designers, that the designer was horrible rather than good, and on and on. Yet, for all this, right at the end of the dialogues, the character who is presumed to speak for the author, admits that there might be something to the argument after all! The nature of organisms surely cannot be by chance, by blind law. If the proposition before us is that '*the cause or causes of order in the universe probably bear some remote analogy to human intelligence*', then 'what can the most inquisitive, contemplative, and religious man do more than give a plain, philosophical assent to the proposition, as often as it occurs; and believe that the arguments, on which it is established, exceed the objections, which lie against it?' (Hume 1947: 203–4; his italics)

The other great eighteenth-century philosopher, Immanuel Kant, picked right up on this, discussing teleology at length in the (second half of his) *Third Critique*, the *Critique of Judgement* (1790). He wanted to keep God out of the picture and had no place for the argument from design:

> if we supplement natural science by introducing the conception of God into its context for the purpose of rendering the finality of nature explicable, and if, having done so, we turn round and use this finality for the purpose of proving that there is

a God, then both natural science and theology are deprived of all intrinsic substantiality. [Kant 1928: 31]

Kant was unbending on this: 'this deceptive crossing and recrossing from one side to the
other involves both in uncertainty, because their boundaries are thus allowed to overlap'
(Kant 1928: 31). But Kant recognized that we simply cannot do without final-cause thinking.
Heuristically, in biology teleology is absolutely essential. Using his characterization of final
cause as a situation where everything is both means and end—the flower causes the fertilization, we understand the flower in terms of the fertilization—we find that we need the maxim:
'*an organized natural product is one in which every part is reciprocally both end and means*'.
  We simply cannot do biology without assuming final cause:

> It is common knowledge that scientists who dissect plants and animals, seeking to
> investigate their structure and to see into the reasons why and the end for which
> they are provided with such and such parts, why the parts have such and such a
> position and interconnexion, and why the internal form is precisely what it is, adopt
> the above maxim as absolutely necessary. [Kant 1928: 25]

Scientists cannot do biology in any other way. Teleological thinking is not a luxury; it is a
necessity. Life scientists:

> say that nothing in such forms of life is in vain, and they put the maxim on the same
> footing of validity as the fundamental principle of all natural science, that nothing
> happens by chance. They are, in fact, quite as unable to free themselves from this
> teleological principle as from that of general physical science. For just as the
> abandonment of the latter would leave them without any experience at all, so the
> abandonment of the former would leave them with no clue to assist their observa-
> tion of a type of natural things that have once come to be thought under the concep-
> tion of physical ends. [Kant 1928: 25]

If we think of this as the Aristotelian side to Kant's thinking, we should note also that
there was a Platonic side. This is less with respect to teleology and more with the essence
of Platonic metaphysics, the theory of Forms, those ideal patterns on which the physical
things of this world are supposedly fashioned. Kant drew attention to the fact—a point
actually that the biologist Aristotle had well appreciated—that organisms of different
species nevertheless show similar patterns of structure. The arm of human, the leg of
horse, the flipper of seal, the wing of bird, is the classic example of such isomorphism.
The English anatomist Richard Owen in the 1840s called them 'homologies', although
today this term is reserved for similarity from common descent, as opposed to other
similarities or 'analogies', for instance just of function, like the wing of bird and the wing
of insect. Kant agreed that these similarities suggest a shared evolutionary origin. But
then he pulled back. Kant could not see how blind, undirected law could lead to the
intricate features that organisms have for their welfare. He thought that final cause pre-
cluded undirected development (Ruse 2006a).
  After Kant, in the realm of science and into the nineteenth century, there were those
biologists who agreed with him completely about final cause. Best known and most
influential was the French anatomist Georges Cuvier. Like Kant (there was probably a

direct influence because Cuvier was educated in Germany) he argued that organisms show final causes or what Cuvier called 'conditions of existence':

> Natural history nevertheless has a rational principle that is exclusive to it and which it employs with great advantage on many occasions; it is the *conditions of existence* or, popularly, *final causes*. As nothing may exist which does not include the conditions which made its existence possible, the different parts of each creature must be coordinated in such a way as to make possible the whole organism, not only in itself but in its relationship to those which surround it, and the analysis of these conditions often leads to general laws as well founded as those of calculation or experiment. [Cuvier 1817: 1, 6, cited in Coleman 1964: 42]

Cuvier also agreed with Kant that final cause precludes evolutionary change. However, particularly in Germany, there were those who took up the other side of Kant's thinking, the Platonic suggestions about isomorphism (Richards 2003). These Romantic thinkers—generally known as *Naturphilosophen*, and ranging from philosophers like Friedrich Schelling to anatomists like Lorenz Oken—stressed the connections between organisms rather than their end-directed nature. Not surprisingly, they were much more given to developmental thinking. Some, like the philosopher Hegel, thought that any development was more idealistic than real, but others became in modern terms full-blown evolutionists. It is thought that by the end of his long life the poet Goethe switched from opposition to evolution to acceptance. (As opposed to the teleological Cuvierian 'Conditions of Existence', the connections between different species were generally known as 'Unity of Type.')

None of this is theological. Although Cuvier was a sincere Protestant, he would never have introduced theology into his science. In Britain, however, for all of the arguments of Hume (and Kant for that matter) the traditional Platonic argument from design went on happily. The classic exposition was given at the beginning of the nineteenth century by Archdeacon William Paley (1802). Likening the eye to a telescope, Paley argued that just as telescopes have telescope designers and makers, so the eye must have a designer and maker—the Christian God. Paley was not alone. By the 1830s, the telling of the argument was becoming voluminous and frenetic. Thanks to the bequest of an Earl of Bridgewater, eight separate works on the topic were published and distributed widely (Gillespie 1950). Although the intent was theological, proving and glorifying the Christian God, the more sophisticated writers did not miss the opportunity to use their conclusion to follow Cuvier (a great British favourite) to put in the teleological boot to arguments about evolution. One should remember also that the authors of the 'Bridgewater Treatises' were also using the opportunity to show to their fellow—and often dubious fellow—Christians, that far from science leading to disbelief, properly understood it could burnish the Glory of the Lord.

As we approach the fateful year of 1859, the year when Charles Darwin published his *On the Origin of Species*, three points are worth making. First, why was it that Paley and company could keep promoting the traditional argument from design in the face of the withering criticisms of David Hume? The answer surely lies in the fact that people were not really thinking of the argument as a traditional analogy—the eye-designer to the telescope-designer, as the eye to the telescope. Rather, they had in mind more what is today generally called 'an argument to the best explanation' (Lipton 1991). As Sherlock Holmes pointed out, when you have eliminated the impossible whatever remain however improbable, must be the truth. You have got to have some kind of explanation. Intricate design-like patterns don't just happen according to blind law. Murphy's Law holds: if it can go wrong, it will go wrong. (Or the alternative: the bread always falls jammy side down.) In fact, they would have agreed with Hume himself. Whatever the problems, in the absence of an alternative, you really have to go with a designer of some sort.

Secondly, the emphasis really was on the biological world. People were at one with Boyle on this. It does not mean that there was no interest in the non-biological. The philosopher and historian of science William Whewell drew astronomy and general physics as his lot for the *Bridgewater Treatises* (1833). But although he laboured manfully, he had to admit that his task would have been easier had he drawn biology—a topic to which he devoted much attention when later he wrote his major works on the history and philosophy of science (Whewell 1837, 1840). What we do find is a variant of the design argument where it is the mere fact of order, of law-bound regularity rather than chaos, that is taken as evidence of God's existence. This obviously could be used in the biological world also, specifically to bring isomorphisms into the design fold.

This brings us to the third point. In the decades leading up to the *Origin*, increasingly within and without biology people started to realize how very non-end-directed were many features of the world. Thanks to Owen particularly, homologies (as we may now call them) were recognized as much more than unimportant side-phenomena but a very significant fact of the organic world and an absolutely crucial tool in working out relationships (real or ideal) between organisms. Then Whewell (1853) of all people started to worry about the universe and its vast emptiness. What could God have been thinking of when He created the world? Most obviously, as homes for other beings (a belief known as the 'plurality of worlds'); but Whewell thought this against the Christian premise that humans are special. So, although he certainly never gave up on the argument from design based on organic final cause (sometimes known as the 'utilitarian' argument from design), increasingly he found himself pushing other versions of the design argument and agreeing that final cause is not all.

THE ORIGIN OF SPECIES

Although this is not our direct concern, the troubles of someone like Whewell strongly confirm a major point about scientific revolutions, one much emphasized by Thomas Kuhn (1962). Change comes as much because the older position was breaking down as because the newer position is all perfect. Having said this, and focussing first on the scientific side to the argument, there is no question but that Darwin's theory of evolution through natural selection, presented in the *Origin of Species*, changed forever our thinking about final cause (Ruse 1999). Two important points stand out. First, Darwin absolutely and completely was committed to final cause in biology. He thought that organic contrivances or adaptations—the hand and the eye, the bark and the leaves—are the fundamental feature of life. Indeed, paradoxically, by the time the *Origin* was published, Darwin was almost out of step on this. He did his creative thinking in the 1830s, when Cuvier and final cause rode high (reinforced ten years before at Cambridge with a heavy diet of William Paley). Hence, although Darwin was very much aware of homology and had used it extensively in a long study of barnacles in the late 1840s and early 1850s, it was never at the forefront in this thinking.

Secondly, Darwin offered a natural, law-bound explanation of final cause. He showed that you do not need either a direct creative designer (Plato) or an internal special life force (Aristotle). Starting with the insights of Thomas Robert Malthus, Darwin argued first to a ubiquitous struggle for existence and, more importantly, reproduction. Then, drawing on the variation we find in all natural populations, he argued that on average the winners in the struggle (the fit) will be different from the losers (the unfit) and that over time this natural form of selection will lead to change. As importantly, he argued that it is the differences in variation that make the difference in success. One will not only get change but change in the direction of adaptive advantage. We have design-like features, but in our science there is no need to invoke a designer. Indeed, Darwin got very cross with those (like his great American supporter, the Harvard botanist Asa Gray) who supposed a designer helped, specifically in making specially directed variations.

Picking up on a point raised just above, the conviction about the importance of final cause and the causal explanation of natural selection was not done through a denial that there are aspects of the organic world that do not show direct function. Darwin was fully aware that the vagaries of history and much more can make for a failure in design. And on the question of homology, Unity of Type, far from belittling or ignoring it, he argued that its explanation was one of the triumphs of his theory. Unity of Type falls right out of the Conditions of Existence!

> It is generally acknowledged that all organic beings have been formed on two great laws—Unity of Type, and the Conditions of Existence. By unity of type is meant that fundamental agreement in structure, which we see in organic beings of the same class, and which is quite independent of their habits of life. On my theory, unity of type is explained by unity of descent. The expression of conditions of existence, so often insisted on by the illustrious Cuvier, is fully embraced by the principle of natural selection. For natural selection acts by either now adapting the varying parts of each being to its organic and inorganic conditions of life; or by having adapted them during long-past periods of time: the adaptations being aided in some cases by use and disuse, being slightly affected by the direct action of the external conditions of life, and being in all cases subjected to the several laws of growth. Hence, in fact, the law of the Conditions of Existence is the higher law; as it includes, through the inheritance of former adaptations, that of Unity of Type. [Darwin 1859: 206]

Turn now to the theological side to things. While he was writing the *Origin*, Darwin was committed to a designer God. He made this very clear in a letter, written in 1860, to Asa Gray. However, given that he wanted no part of God in science, this God had to be one who designed and directed from a distance:

I see no necessity in the belief that the eye was expressly designed. On the other hand I cannot anyhow be contented to view this wonderful universe & especially the nature of man, & to conclude that everything is the result of brute force. I am inclined to look at everything as resulting from designed laws, with the details, whether good or bad, left to the working out of what we may call chance. [Darwin 1993: VIII, 224]

Some years later, like so many of his fellow Victorians, Darwin slid into a form of agnosticism (never atheism) although apparently every now and then he would have flashes of belief.

AFTER DARWIN

There are two major truths here. First, from now on the design argument (certainly the utilitarian form based on biology) had lost its bite. Given natural selection, God was no longer the inevitable conclusion of an argument to the best explanation. One could simply explain the eye and the hand as the consequence of the workings of blind, natural laws. No intelligence needed. In the words of Richard Dawkins:

An atheist before Darwin could have said, following Hume: 'I have no explanation for complex biological design. All I know is that God isn't a good explanation, so we must wait and hope that somebody comes up with a better one.' I can't help feeling that such a position, though logically sound, would have left one feeling pretty unsatisfied, and that although atheism might have been *logically* tenable before Darwin, Darwin made it possible to be an intellectually fulfilled atheist. [Dawkins 1986: 5]

Final cause has been preserved, but there is need neither of a creator God or a vital force.

Secondly, nothing here says that one *has* to be an atheist. You can go on believing in a designer. It is rather that you are not proving the designer's existence. I will deal in a moment whether Darwinian biology says one must be an atheist, but that is not the point here. Showing that design comes through law does not at all, as Darwin says explicitly, show that there is no designer. It is just that the designer must work at a distance. I should say that there were many who found this theologically rather comforting. As the American preacher Henry Ward Beecher (1885) was to say: 'design by wholesale is grander than design by retail' (113). A favourite British reflection was that the Brits had shown how to do things with machines rather than by hand. This was what the Industrial Revolution was all about. Hence, God (who is undoubtedly British) was that much greater if he worked by law rather than by miracle, machine over hands. The cranky social commentator and inventor Charles Babbage (1838) devoted much effort to showing how his machines (he built a proto-computer) could do the most wonderful things purely by working through their motions, that is by law.

Two final points and then we can turn to our next topic. First, one should recognize that the moves being made in and about biology did not occur in isolation. For other reasons, people were already starting to question the argument from design. In Protestant theology, in particular, there were those—Kierkegaard notably—who were condemning the whole natural theological enterprise. He felt, and of course this was something picked up strongly in the twentieth century by Karl Barth, that trying to get at God through reason diminishes faith. The whole point about faith is that it is a leap into the absurd—one has to make an existential commitment, and knowing that there is firm ground on the other side rather defeats the whole purpose of things. John Henry Newman, who started as an Anglican and then moved across to the Church of Rome, also was one who was very uncomfortable about the design argument in particular. In 1870 (twenty-five years after he converted), in correspondence about his seminal philosophical work, *A Grammar of Assent*, Newman wrote:

> I have not insisted on the argument from *design*, because I am writing for the 19th century, by which, as represented by its philosophers, design is not admitted as proved. And to tell the truth, though I should not wish to preach on the subject, for 40 years I have been unable to see the logical force of the argument myself. I believe in design because I believe in God; not in a God because I see design. [Newman 1973: 97]

He continued: 'Design teaches me power, skill and goodness—not sanctity, not mercy, not a future judgement, which three are of the essence of religion.'

Secondly, whatever the doubts and criticisms, this is not to say that the argument died on the spot. Apart from those who like Henry Ward Beecher who were in the business of modifying the argument, there were those who kept going on very old-fashioned paths. Newman may have worried about the design argument, but the Church which he joined continued (and still continues) to endorse it. Among Protestants we find that there were those who wanted no truck with Darwinian refutations or modifications. The then-doyen of theologians, Charles Hodge (1874) was firm on this. 'What is Darwinism?' he asked rhetorically in the title of one of his books. Back came the resounding cry: 'It is Atheism!' The argument had a long shelf life in Britain too. I write with some personal experience as one who was educated in a state school in that country in the 1940s, a time when religious instruction was compulsory. More recently, as is well known, a group of American evangelicals has taken up the argument with some enthusiasm, arguing that Darwin was wrong. There are aspects of the organic world, like the bacterial flagellum and the blood clotting cascade, that are 'irreducibly complex', and hence cannot be explained by natural law, specifically not by Darwinian selection. They therefore appeal to an Intelligent Designer, and although publicly they are careful not to say more about this designer lest they be caught pushing religion—something that cannot be taught in US state-supported schools—privately they are firm that this designer is to be identified with the Christian God; indeed the Logos at the beginning of the Gospel of John, in the words of the mathematician-philosopher William Dembski (Forrest and Gross 2004).

There is little need to linger here over the scientific pretensions of Intelligent Design Theory (IDT). It has been shown that all of the supposed examples of irreducible design give way quickly to completely natural explanations (Pennock 1998; Miller 1999). Moreover, as we shall see shortly, there are some horrendous theological problems over-shadowing it. Nor, since this is beyond our scope, need we linger over those physicists who—like Jesus raising Lazarus from the dead—now argue that the world's physical constants demand reference to a designer (Barrow and Tipler 1986). Others can discuss the 'anthropic principle'. The physicists may be confident, but the biologists with reason are sceptical.

The Problem of Evil

Thus far, at most, it has been shown that Darwinian evolutionary biology destroys the compelling nature of the argument from design (utilitarian version based on organisms). This is no small thing, but it does not actually deny the existence of the Christian God. For that conclusion, more is needed; namely, the belief of many Darwinians, starting with Darwin himself, that more may be on offer. And obviously in respects this is a belief that is hard to gainsay. If your God is one who created in six days, 6,000 years ago, then clearly His existence is in conflict with modern science—not just biology, but physics, geology, and much else. But it should be stated clearly that this God is an invention of an idiosyncratic form of American evangelical Christianity from the nineteenth century—much of it in fact the brainchild of the Seventh-day Adventists. It is not the God of traditional Christianity, the God of Augustine and Aquinas, of Luther and Calvin. It is true that they all held beliefs about the world that we would now reject as untrue, but within their methodology were the tools to work with and accept modern science. So I shall say nothing more here on that topic, and turn to issues where traditional Christianity might be thought to have conflicts. And most important here is the problem of evil.

The canonical text is an earlier part of the already-quoted letter to Asa Gray:

> With respect to the theological view of the question; this is always painful to me.—
> I am bewildered.—I had no intention to write atheistically. But I own that I cannot
> see, as plainly as others do, & as I sh^d wish to do, evidence of design & beneficence
> on all sides of us. There seems to me too much misery in the world. I cannot per-
> suade myself that a beneficent & omnipotent God would have designedly created
> the Ichneumonidæ with the express intention of their feeding within the living bod-
> ies of caterpillars, or that a cat should play with mice. Not believing this, I see no
> necessity in the belief that the eye was expressly designed. [Darwin 1993: VIII, 224]

Expectedly, Richard Dawkins has picked this up, arguing that the essence of Darwinism is a cruel struggle for existence and there is no reason for or expectation of seeing the living world as the product of a good God. Using the notion of 'reverse engineering' for the process of picking backwards to try to work out something's purpose, and of a 'utility function' for the end purpose being intended, Dawkins draws attention to the cheetah/antelope interaction, and asks: 'What was God's utility function?' Cheetahs seem wonderfully designed to kill antelopes. 'The teeth, claws, eyes, nose, leg muscles, backbone and brain of a cheetah are all precisely what we should expect if God's purpose in designing cheetahs was to maximize deaths among antelopes.' But conversely, 'we find equally impressive evidence of design for precisely the opposite end: the survival of antelopes and starvation among cheetahs.' It is almost as though we had two gods, making the different animals, and then competing. If there is only one god who made the two animals, then what on earth is going on? What kind of god is this? 'Is He a sadist who enjoys spectator blood sports? Is He trying to avoid overpopulation in the mammals of Africa? Is He maneuvering to maximize David Attenborough's television ratings?' The whole thing is ludicrous (Dawkins 1995: 105). Truly, concludes Dawkins, there are no ultimate purposes to life, no deep religious meanings. 'The universe we observe has precisely the properties we should expect if there is, at bottom, no design, no purpose, no evil and no good, nothing but blind, pitiless indifference' (Dawkins 1995: 133).

Recently the philosopher Philip Kitcher has dwelt on the suffering brought on by the struggle for existence, the prelude to natural selection. He writes:

> [George John] Romanes and [William] James, like the evangelical Christians who rally behind intelligent design today, appreciate that Darwinism is subversive. They recognize that the Darwinian picture of life is at odds with a particular kind of religion, Providentialist religion, as I shall call it. A large number of Christians, not merely those who maintain that virtually all of the Bible must be read literally, are providentialists. For they believe that the universe has been created by a Being who has a great design, a Being who cares for his creatures, who observes the fall of every sparrow and who is especially concerned with humanity. Yet the story of a wise and loving Creator, who has planned life on earth, letting it unfold over four billion years by the processes envisaged in evolutionary theory, is hard to sustain when you think about the details. [Kitcher 2007: 122–3]

He writes of having believed that Darwinism was reconcilable with Christianity, and—with the fervour of a repenting sinner at an evangelical revivalist meeting—insists that he alone should be held responsible for 'the earlier errors that I recant here' (180).

There are two questions here. First, can anything speak successfully to the problem of evil? Secondly, does biology—Darwinian evolutionary biology specifically—make the problem of evil insoluble? In other words, if you do have a solution to the problem of evil, does Darwinism then destroy this? Speaking for myself, I am not sure that one can solve the problem of evil. I am with the character in *The Brothers Karamazov* who simply says that salvation is not worth the suffering of one small child. For me, Anne Frank's death in Bergen-Belsen was the end of matters. However, this is not really our prime question here. It is the second question that really counts. Does Darwinism specifically make a solution impossible? It certainly exacerbates the problem. Dawkins is right. There is non-stop suffering involved in the evolutionary process. But does it actually on its own destroy any defence? This is another matter and I am not at all sure that this is indeed the case. In fact, I would even go so far as to say that biology helps the defender rather than hinders. To see this, let us start with the fact that most of the critics seem curiously loathe to mention, namely that Christians do have standard responses. I am not now referring to recent trendy—at least in circles seduced by the process philosophy of Alfred North Whitehead—suggestions that God has voluntarily given up some of his powers ('kenosis') and that hence He cannot prevent evil even He wished to. That seems to me to be a deeply heretical reading of the God of Christianity. I am talking now of standard responses within a genuine Christian framework. The usual move is to divide the problem into two: human-caused evil (Auschwitz) and natural-caused evil (Haiti). Free will is the answer to the first; natural law and possibilities is the answer to the second. We take them in turn.

HUMAN EVIL

Following Augustine, Christians argue that human-caused evil comes about through the deliberate choices and actions of humans, their free will, but that God saw it was better that humans have free will despite the consequent evil than that they be determined machines even though no evil follows. Now you might want to say straight off that since Darwinism implies that things follow or are ruled by unbroken law, and that this applies to human beings, then the free-will defence fails. Free will demands that one can stand outside law, and so there is an end to things. But obviously matters are not quite this simple. No one wants to say that humans are entirely outside law. Otherwise why bother with education? Teaching children is predicated on the belief that there are certain laws or rules of learning and that following these is what education is all about. More than this, following David Hume (2000), many think that the whole point of freedom is precisely that we do follow law rather than stand outside it! The crucial distinction is not between freedom and law but freedom and licence. A man who kills his wife because he dislikes her is free. A man who kills his wife because he has been hypnotized is not free. Indeed, suppose someone does something absolutely crazy and then claims that they did it because the laws of nature broke down. We could hardly condemn them as free against being responsible for their actions. They are crazy and perhaps sick but not evil.

But does not Darwinism particularly cut down on free will? When the area of Darwinism dealing with social behaviour (sociobiology) was developed in the 1970s, a common cry from those opposed to its application to humankind was that it implied 'genetic determinism' (Lewontin 1991). Apparently we humans are like marionettes on strings controlled by the DNA. In fact, this is simply not true. As no less a person than Daniel Dennett (1984)—one of the leading new atheists and someone who hates all religion—has pointed out, this simply is a travesty of the Darwinian's thinking on human nature. Ants are genetically determined. They are, to use a metaphor, entirely controlled by the tiny computers that they have for brains. They do not think. They just obey orders. And this is just fine for ants, but it would not be just fine for humans. The reason is simple. Ants have gone the route of many offspring with little care or concern for individual well being. The great thing about being genetically determined is that you do not have to waste effort on education and so forth. The really bad thing about genetic determination is that if something goes wrong, you do not have the ability to put things right. Dennett gives a lovely example. He tells of a wasp which brings food to its nest to provision its young:

> The wasp's routine is to bring the paralyzed cricket to the burrow, leave it on the threshold, go inside to see that all is well, emerge, and then drag the cricket in. If the cricket is moved a few inches away while the wasp is inside making the her preliminary inspection, the wasp, on emerging from the burrow, will bring the cricket back to the threshold, but not inside, and will then repeat the preparatory procedure of entering the burrow to see that everything is all right. [Dennett 1984: 11]

This can go on and on indefinitely: 'The wasp never thinks of pulling the cricket straight in. On one occasion this procedure was repeated forty times, always with the same result.' This is the problem. A thousand ants are out foraging and its starts to rain. A thousand ants are lost because the chemical (pheromone) trails that lead them home are washed away.

Fortunately in the case of the ants it does not matter much. There are hundreds of thousands more where the vanished ants came from. In the case of humans, it would matter very much. We have gone the route of few children who demand much care. We cannot afford to lose even two or three every time it starts to rain. Technically, biologists say that humans are practising K selection whereas the ants are practicing r selection. Of course, everyone thinks that there has been a feedback process in evolution. As we got better at raising children, we could have fewer and having fewer put more selective pressure on being better able to raise children. So how have we set about raising children in the face of adversities like rainstorms and predators and fellow humans? Here is where our brains are important. In Richard Dawkins's (1986) phrase, we have big onboard computers and when we come to challenges we can reason how to overcome them. This does not mean that we move from beneath the net of law, but that we have a dimension of freedom that the ants do not have. To continue with Dennett's examples, we are like the Mars Rover. When it came to a rock, it did not stop, but had the computer-driven ability to reason how to get around the rock. Or to use an example of my own, ants are like cheap rockets that are aimed at the target but if it moves simply miss because they cannot change direction. Humans are like expensive rockets that have homing devices to track a moving target. Both rockets do what they do because of unbroken law, but the expensive rockets—a.k.a. humans—have a dimension of freedom that the non-expensive rockets—a.k.a. ants—do not have. In other words, I suggest that far from Darwinian theory blowing holes in the free-will defence, if anything it comes to its aid.

NATURAL EVIL

Turn now to natural evil—earthquakes, hurricanes, as well as diseases like cancer and tuberculosis. Following Leibniz, the standard reply is that God cannot do the impossible. If the world is ruled by law, then compromises have to be made. Gravity can kill but without gravity we could not function. A hot stove can burn and cause pain, but without the pain we would not be aware of the dangers from burning. An earthquake destroys and causes terrible suffering, but without plate tectonics the world would be a different and much poorer place. A malfunctioning cell causes cancer but without cells we could not live and breathe. Admittedly this argument is open to parody as Voltaire showed in his *Candide*—the best of all things in the best of all possible worlds—but taken seriously, and assuming that God has found the best compromises, it is a good way to explain natural evil.

Once again the new atheists help to make this position more plausible! This time it is Richard Dawkins to the defence. He argues that we could not have a functioning organic world without adaptation—design-like features—and the only way in which you can get such features is through natural selection. The Intelligent Design Theorists' supposition of guided mutations or variations is just not science. Lamarckism, the inheritance of acquired characteristics, is false. Macro-mutations or large variations leading to instant new features simply do not create design-like effects. The second law of thermodynamics kicks in here—things run down and not up and creatively. Chance leads to mistakes not triumphs of design. This really only leaves selection:

> My general point is that there is one limiting constraint upon all speculations about life in the universe. If a life-form displays adaptive complexity, it must possess an evolutionary mechanism capable of generating adaptive complexity. However diverse evolutionary mechanisms may be, if there is no other generalization that can be made about life all around the Universe, I am betting it will always be recognizable as Darwinian life. The Darwinian Law...may be as universal as the great laws of physics. [Dawkins 1983: 423]

Of course all of this rather presupposes that God had to—or decided to—create by law rather than miracle. We have already seen a British argument to this effect, supposing that God is the supreme industrialist and hence prefers machines to hand work. But going back to more traditional sources, there is much in Saint Augustine to suggest that creation was by law—apart from the fact that Augustine thought that miracles are law-governed events about the causes of which we are now ignorant. If God stands outside time, then for him the thought of creation, the act of creation, and the product of creation are as one. Augustine's God has no need of miracles doing things all at once or over six days. Augustine himself spoke of God planting seeds that then develop. I do not mean to suggest that Augustine was an evolutionist or even (like, say, Empedocles) a proto-evolutionist. Rather that there are theological resources in his work that make an evolutionary approach very natural and comfortable.

Finally, swinging back for a moment to the Intelligent Design Theorists, note that their scientific problems are equalled only by their theological problems. If God is designing and creating on an ongoing basis, then since he apparently is prepared to get involved to make the complex but presumably very good (this surely applies to blood clotting), why then was he not prepared to get involved to clean up the simple but very bad? Many horrendous genetic diseases involve only one or two molecules out of place. Surely a good, all-powerful God would have done something about this? Note that this argument is not to say that God never intervenes in the course of nature, perhaps even breaking or going against the laws. Many Christians of course prefer to think of the miracles as more metaphorical—the feeding of the 5,000 was truly an out-pouring of warmth and affection and sharing of food—but for those who demand that they be literal—the Archbishop of Canterbury apparently would give up and become a Quaker if he found that the tomb was not empty on the third day—you simply invoke the distinction between the order of nature and the order of grace. You simply say that God the creator intervened. Science cannot go there. But notice that the intervention is not to prop up or to complete the creation—the intervention has to be something involved in our salvation history. What is going on has nothing whatsoever to do with the realm of science.

HUMAN UNIQUENESS

We come to the final question. It is surely a non-negotiable demand of the Christian that humans had to occur. We might have had green skin. We might have had twelve fingers. I am not really sure about this but it might even be that we did not have to have the two sexes. But we had to exist. There had to be a race of beings that could sense and reason, find out about the world, and interact in a moral fashion. If we don't have these features, then we are simply not made in the image of God. But Darwinian evolutionary theory is a non-directional process (Ruse 2006b). Natural selection is relativistic. There is no absolute better or worse. Given heavy predation, against a black background it might be better to be black and against a white background it might be better to be white. And after this the mutations, the raw building blocks of evolution, are undirected. They are not uncaused. But they do not occur according to need. If you need a white-causing mutation, you are just as likely to get a green or a red one. No promises at all. The appear-ance of humans was at best a lucky chance.

As Stephen Jay Gould used to say, punning on the asteroid that hit the earth, wiping out the dinosaurs:

> Since dinosaurs were not moving toward markedly larger brains, and since such a prospect may lie outside the capabilities of reptilian design..., we must assume that consciousness would not have evolved on our planet if a cosmic catastrophe had not claimed the dinosaurs as victims. In an entirely literal sense, we owe our existence, as large and reasoning mammals, to our lucky stars. [Gould 1989: 318]

He also said that beliefs in biological progress, a line leading from blobs up to humans, are chimerical. He spoke of the idea as 'a noxious, culturally embedded, untestable, non-operational, intractable idea that must be replaced if we wish to understand the patterns of history' (Gould 1988).

How are you to reconcile the Christian demand with the nature of Darwinian evolutionary biology? One starting point might be to note that not everyone agreed with Gould about progress. Many evolutionists, at least as eminent as he, think that there is progress (Ruse 1996). Darwin was one. Today's most eminent evolutionist, the Harvard-based ant specialist and sociobiologist, Edward O. Wilson is another. He writes:

> The overall average across the history of life has moved from the simple and few to the more complex and numerous. During the past billion years, animals as a whole evolved upward in body size, feeding and defensive techniques, brain and behavioral complexity, social organization, and precision of environmental control—in each case farther from the nonliving state than their simpler antecedents did. [Wilson 1992: 187]

Again, Richard Dawkins of all people is a great help here. He is an ardent biological progressionist.

> Notwithstanding Gould's just skepticism over the tendency to label each era by its newest arrivals, there really is a good possibility that major innovations in embryological technique open up new vistas of evolutionary possibility and that these constitute genuinely progressive improvements... The origin of the chromosome, of the bounded cell, of organized meiosis, diploidy and sex, of the eucaryotic cell, of multicellularity, of gastrulation, of molluscan torsion, of segmentation—each of these may have constituted a watershed event in the history of life. Not just in the normal Darwinian sense of assisting individuals to survive and reproduce, but watershed in the sense of boosting evolution itself in ways that seem entitled to the label progressive. It may well be that after, say, the invention of multicellularity, or the invention of metamerism, evolution was never the same again. In this sense, there may be a one-way ratchet of progressive innovation in evolution. [Dawkins 1997: 1019–20]

But how then do you get progress in the face of Darwinism? How do you get progress because of Darwinism? Exploring a line of thinking that goes back to Darwin himself, Dawkins argues that different lines of organisms compete against each other and thus improve their adaptations. There are what we today would call 'arms races'. The prey gets faster and so the predator gets faster. The shell gets thicker and so the boring apparatus gets sharper and stronger. This leads to a kind of relative progress. Taking a leaf from real life arms races, Dawkins argues that the way that such races go is towards more and more electronic equipment, particularly computers. Humans in the organic world have the biggest on-board computers. Hence you can say that we have won. 'The fact that humans have an EQ [encephalization quotient] of 7 and hippos an EQ of 0.3 may not literally mean that humans are 23 times as clever as hippos!' But, Dawkins concludes, it does tell us 'something' (Dawkins 1986: 189).

A somewhat different approach has been taken by the Cambridge paleontologist Simon Conway-Morris (2003)—a person who, unlike Dawkins, is a committed Christian. He argues that not every organic form is possible and those that do exist are constrained by the necessity of finding suitable ecological niches in which they can survive and reproduce. However, he thinks also that selection is always pushing forms to find new available niches and, given the ferocity of the struggle for existence, sooner or later, if such spaces exist, they will be occupied—probably sooner rather than later, and probably many times. Conway-Morris draws attention to the way in which life's history shows an incredible number of instances of convergence—instances where the same adaptive morphological space has been occupied again and again. The most dramatic perhaps is that of sabre-toothed, tiger-like organisms, where the North American placental mammals (real cats) were matched item for item by South American marsupials (thylacosmilids). Clearly there existed a niche for organisms that were predators, with cat-like abilities and shearing/stabbing-like weapons, and natural selection found more than one way to enter it. Indeed, it has been suggested, long before the mammals, the dinosaurs might also have found this niche.

Conway-Morris's claim is that this sort of thing happens repeatedly, showing that the historical course of nature is not random but strongly selection-constrained along certain pathways and to certain destinations. From this, Conway-Morris concludes that movement up the order of nature, the tree of life, is bound to happen, and eventually some kind of intelligent being (what has been termed a 'humanoid') is bound to emerge. We know from our own existence that a kind of cultural adaptive niche exists—a niche where intelligence and social abilities are the defining features. More than this, we know that this niche is one to which other organisms have (with greater or lesser success) aspired. We know of the kinds of features (like eyes and ears and other sensory mechanisms) that have been used by organisms to enter new niches; we know that brains have increased as selection presses organisms to ever new and empty niches; and we know that, with this improved hardware, have come better patterns of behaviour and so forth (more sophisticated software). Could this not all add up to something?

> If brains can get big independently and provide a neural machine capable of handling a highly complex environment, then perhaps there are other parallels, other convergences that drive some groups towards complexity. Could the story of sensory perception be one clue that, given time, evolution will inevitably lead not only to the emergence of such properties as intelligence, but also to other complexities, such as, say, agriculture and culture, that we tend to regard as the prerogative of the human? We may be unique, but paradoxically those properties that define our uniqueness can still be inherent in the evolutionary process. In other words, if we humans had not evolved then something more-or-less identical would have emerged sooner or later. [Conway-Morris 2003: 196]

I hardly need say that neither of these suggestions gives you a cast-iron guarantee of progress up to humans. There is nothing inherently biologically desirable about large brains. Apart from anything else, they need to be fuelled by huge amounts of protein. In other words, in the wild that means meat—and that means the skills and the time to hunt or forage and much more, probably involving social skills also. Try tracking and killing an elephant on your own. If there is lots of cheap fodder around like grass, you might be better off going vegetarian and spending your time grazing and munching. In the immortal words of the paleontologist, the late Jack Sepkoski: 'I see intelligence as just one of a variety of adaptations among tetrapods for survival. Running fast in a herd while being as dumb as shit, I think, is a very good adaptation for survival' (Ruse 1996: 486). Conway-Morris's suggestion is also problematic. Apart from anything else, niches don't just sit around waiting to be discovered. If anything, they are created by organisms as much as found. Many insects live exclusively in the higher branches of trees in the Brazilian rain forests, but without the trees the niches would hardly exist. Beavers in a way, building damns and bottling up rivers, create their own niches. In any case, can one guarantee that organisms will always find their ways into available niches? Many a slip between cup and lip. The Christian says that humans must happen and there is not quite the guarantee here that one needs.

Another option is to take the job away from science and to hand it over to God. This is the gambit played by physicist-theologian Robert John Russell (2008). He wants to put God's direction in down at the quantum level. Apparently all we can see are the averages, but God can decide just when and where the right mutations will occur and as a result the appearance of humans is no chance. In a way, of course, this is a version of Intelligent Design Theory, and as such open to the same problems. If God is involved in doing the good, why does He not prevent the bad while he is at it? He might put the genetic counsellors out of business, but that is a small price to pay for the elimination of so much genetically caused human suffering. I suppose that if Russell insists on his position, there is nothing absolute one can say in refutation. He has hidden his God down at a level where we cannot go. But like IDT, his is ultimately a 'god of the gaps' explanation. We cannot find an answer ourselves, and we suppose therefore that the answer relates directly to God. Theologically there is something a little smelly about this. As Dietrich Bonhöffer said: 'We are to find God in what we know, not in what we don't know.' What we do know is that Darwinian evolution is non-directed, and this kind of evolution is directed.

MANY UNIVERSES?

Let me try an alternative suggestion. We have a theological problem here and so my inclination is to seek a theological solution. Science-based solutions are too open to refutation if and when the science changes. Darwin gives a clue about how to proceed. Somehow complexity just emerges because in a way you are always going to be building on what you have already:

> The enormous number of animals in the world depends on their varied structure & complexity.—hence as the forms became complicated, they opened

fresh means of adding to their complexity.—but yet there is no *necessary* tendency in the simple animals to become complicated although all perhaps will have done so from the new relations caused by the advancing complexity of others.—It may be said, why should there not be at any time as many spe- cies tending to dis-development (some probably always have done so, as the simplest fish), my answer is because, if we begin with the simplest forms & suppose them to have changed, their very changes tend to give rise to others. [Darwin 1987: E 95–7]

Darwin certainly thought of the complexity as ultimately adaptive. Immediately after the just-quoted passage, he added: 'it is quite clear that a large part of the com- plexity of structure is adaptation'. Interestingly, although no progressionist, Gould (1996) conceded that over time we expect to see a rise in organic complexity and all that that entails. This is simply the nature of random change. You cannot get more simple than simple, but you can get more complex. The drunkard walking along a sidewalk with a wall on one side and a gutter on the other is never going to walk through the wall but eventually he will fall into the gutter. So it is with evolution. There is no progress in nature, but there is direction. Will this direction eventually end up with humans or human-like beings? Although Gould was not optimistic about this one-off world of ours, he rather thought that if you extend your gaze out to the rest of the universe and to the many life-forms that surely exist out there, one might reasonably expect to find the evolution of intelligent beings of some sort (Dick 1996).

I am still not sure that this is enough. If you have only a finite number of chances, then there is surely no guarantee that humans will arrive. But suppose you draw on the fact that God is outside time and space and if He wants to create an infinite number of uni- verses that is His choice. You might think this awfully wasteful but as Whewell realized you have a lot of apparent waste in this universe already. Humans did evolve by natural selection so they could evolve by natural selection—whether through the growth of complexity or aided by arms races and niche selection or whatever. All God had to do was to set things in motion and at some point we would appear—and since 1,000 years are as a day in the sight of the Lord, He was not hanging around waiting year after year for this to happen.

Note that this 'multiverses' solution is not appealing to physics but simply to God's supposed attributes. It is theological not scientific. You might say that if God knew that one of the attempts was going to produce humans, He did not really have to bother to do the others. I fear that this move takes you back to guided evolution antithetical to the directionless nature of Darwinian change. If we are bound to appear, there is direction. This rather supposes that although God knows that we will appear, He cannot tell in which universe we will appear. Is that not a constraint on omniscience? Perhaps not, any more than God not knowing how to make 2 + 2 = 5 is a constraint on omniscience. Note that this is not downgrading God to the level of the process philosophers. There is no question of God giving up powers. It is more a question of what powers one has with omniscience.

Conclusion

For all that many people think that natural theology has been refuted by science and rejected by Christianity, it is obviously still a subject of considerable intellectual interest. No doubt more could have been said, but let me simply draw the conclusion of the above discussion. In the light of modern biology, specifically modern Darwinian evolutionary theory, there is little support for definitive proofs of the nature and existence of the Christian God. However, notwithstanding arguments to the contrary, there is nothing in modern Darwinian evolutionary theory that makes impossible a belief in a traditional form of Christianity.

REFERENCES

Babbage, C. (1967 [1838]). *The Ninth Bridgewater Treatise. A Fragment*. 2nd edn. London: John Murray.

Barnes, J., ed. (1984). *The Complete Works of Aristotle*. Princeton: Princeton University Press.

Barrow, J. D. and F. J. Tipler (1986). *The Anthropic Cosmological Principle*. Oxford: Clarendon Press.

Beecher, H. W. (1885). *Evolution and Religion*. New York: Fords, Howard, and Hulbert.

Boyle, R. (1966 [1688]). *A Disquisition about the Final Causes of Natural Things. The Works of Robert Boyle*. Vol. V. Edited by T. Birch. Hildesheim: Georg Olms: pp. 392–444

Coleman, W. (1964). *Georges Cuvier Zoologist: A Study in the History of Evolution Theory*. Cambridge, MA: Harvard University Press.

Conway-Morris, S. (2003). *Life's Solution: Inevitable Humans in a Lonely Universe*. Cambridge: Cambridge University Press.

Cooper, J. M., ed. (1997). *Plato: Complete Works*. Indianapolis: Hackett.

Cuvier, Georges (1817). *Le Règne animal distrubé d'après son organisation*. Paris: A. Belin.

Darwin, C. (1859). *On the Origin of Species by Means of Natural Selection, or the Preservation of Favoured Races in the Struggle for Life*. London: John Murray.

—— (1987). *Charles Darwin's Notebooks, 1836–1844*. Edited by P. H. Barrett et al. Ithaca, NY: Cornell University Press.

—— (1993) *The Correspondence of Charles Darwin*, vol. VIII: *1860*. Edited by Frederick Burkhardt et al. Cambridge: Cambridge University Press.

Dawkins, R. (1983). 'Universal Darwinism' in *Evolution from Molecules to Men*. Edited by D. S. Bendall. Cambridge: Cambridge University Press: pp. 403–25.

—— (1986). *The Blind Watchmaker*. Harlow: Longman.

—— (1995). *A River Out of Eden*. New York, NY: Basic Books.

—— (1997). 'Human Chauvinism: Review of Full House by Stephen Jay Gould'. *Evolution* 51/3: 1015–20.

Dennett, D. C. (1984). *Elbow Room: The Varieties of Free Will Worth Wanting*. Cambridge, MA: M.I.T. Press.

Descartes, R. (1985). *The Philosophical Writings*. Vol. I. Translated by J. Cottingham, R. Stoothoff, and D. Murdoch. Cambridge: Cambridge University Press.

Dick, S. J. (1996). *The Biological Universe: The Twentieth-century Extraterrrestrial Life Debate and the Limits of Science*. Cambridge: Cambridge University Press.

Dijksterhuis, E. J. (1961). *The Mechanization of the World Picture*. Oxford: Oxford University Press.

Forrest, B., and P. R. Gross. (2004). *Creationism's Trojan Horse: The Wedge of Intelligent Design*. Oxford: Oxford University Press.

Gillespie, C. C. (1950). *Genesis and Geology*. Cambridge, MA: Harvard University Press.

Gould, S. J. (1988). 'On Replacing the Idea of Progress with an Operational Notion of Directionality' in *Evolutionary Progress*. Edited by M H Nitecki. Chicago: The University of Chicago Press: pp. 319–38.

—— (1989). *Wonderful Life: The Burgess Shale and the Nature of History*. New York, NY: W. W. Norton Co.

—— (1996). *Full House: The Spread of Excellence from Plato to Darwin*. New York, NY: Paragon.

Hodge, C. (1874). *What is Darwinism?* New York: Scribner's.

Hume, D. (1947 [1779]). *Dialogues Concerning Natural Religion*. Edited by N. K. Smith. Indianapolis, IN: Bobbs-Merrill Co.

—— (2000 [1739–40]). *A Treatise of Human Nature*. Edited by David Fate Norton and Mary J. Norton. Oxford: Oxford University Press.

Kant, I. (1928 [1790]). *The Critique of Teleological Judgement*. Translated by J. C. Meredith. Oxford: Oxford University Press.

Kitcher, P. (2007). *Living with Darwin: Evolution, Design, and the Future of Faith*. New York: Oxford University Press.

Kuhn, T. (1962). *The Structure of Scientific Revolutions*. Chicago: University of Chicago Press.

Lewontin, R. C. (1991). *Biology as Ideology: The Doctrine of DNA*. Toronto: Anansi.

Lipton, P. (1991). *Inference to the Best Explanation*. London: Routledge.

Miller, K. (1999). *Finding Darwin's God*. New York: Harper and Row.

Newman, J. H. (1973). *The Letters and Diaries of John Henry Newman*. Vol. XXV. Edited by C. S. Dessain and T. Gornall. Oxford: Clarendon Press.

Paley, W. (1819 [1802]). *Natural Theology (Collected Works: IV)*. London: Rivington.

Pennock, R. (1998). *Tower of Babel: Scientific Evidence and the New Creationism*. Cambridge, MA: M.I.T. Press.

Richards, R. J. (2003). *The Romantic Conception of Life: Science and Philosophy in the Age of Goethe*. Chicago: University of Chicago Press.

Ruse, M. (1996). *Monad to Man: The Concept of Progress in Evolutionary Biology*. Cambridge, MA: Harvard University Press.

—— (1999). *The Darwinian Revolution: Science Red in Tooth and Claw*. 2nd edn. Chicago: University of Chicago Press.

—— (2006a). 'Kant and Evolution' in *Theories of Generation*. Edited by J. Smith. Cambridge: University of Cambridge Press: pp. 402–15.

—— (2006b). *Darwinism and its Discontents*. Cambridge: Cambridge University Press.

Russell, R. J. (2008). *Cosmology: From Alpha to Omega—The Creative Mutual Interaction of Theology and Science*. Minneapolis: Fortress Press.

Sedley, D. (2008). *Creationism and its Critics in Antiquity*. Berkelely: University of California Press.

Whewell, W. (1833). *Astronomy and General Physics (Bridgewater Treatise, 3)*. London: W. Pickering.

—— (1837). *The History of the Inductive Sciences*. London: Parker.

—— (1840). *The Philosophy of the Inductive Sciences*. London: Parker.

—— (2001 [1853]). *Of the Plurality of Worlds. A Facsimile of the First Edition of 1853: Plus Previously Unpublished Material Excised by the Author Just Before the Book Went to Press; and Whewell's Dialogue Rebutting His Critics, Reprinted from the Second Edition*. Edited and introduction by Michael Ruse. Chicago: University of Chicago Press.

Wilson, Edward O. (1992). *The Diversity of Life*. Cambridge, MA: Harvard University Press.

CHAPTER 26

THE PHYSICAL SCIENCES AND NATURAL THEOLOGY

PAUL EWART

NATURAL theology gathers from the world evidence for the existence of God and clues to his nature. In so doing it responds to a seemingly instinctive response that ascribes the beauty, power, and majesty of the universe to the work of a creator God. We sense that beyond the natural world lies a being that is not only responsible for its existence but gives it meaning and purpose. The physical sciences, on the other hand, examine the world to find explanations in terms of causes and effects. The motives and methods behind each form of enquiry may be different but they can, nonetheless, enlighten each other. Physical science, for example, gives an explanation of how the universe evolved over vast expanses of space and time that may be set beside the theological accounts of Creation such as those given in Genesis. Apart from their impact on biblical interpretation such scientific accounts may seem to raise fundamental questions about God's existence, his nature, and his interaction with the world. Some of these issues are of a highly technical nature and are beyond the scope of this chapter. So, in what follows, I will consider a few key examples that illustrate the impact of physical science on natural theology. The sciences of the very large, cosmology, and of the very small, quantum physics, reveal a deep order in nature that suggests the universe is the product of 'Mind', a supreme designing intellect, with the implication that it exists for a purpose. As well as order, however, chaos and randomness seem somehow 'built-in' to the fabric of reality. At many levels the operation of nature seems to be a matter of chance which suggests we live in an 'accidental universe' with no ultimate cause or purpose. The challenge then for natural theology is to speak meaningfully of what lies beyond nature by giving a coherent account that does justice to all the evidence. This will involve examining the methods of science, its dependence on reductionism, and how interpretation of theory relates to the nature of reality. The 'instinctive response' of awe and wonder at the glories of the universe is echoed in the psalmist's affirmation that 'the heavens declare the glory of God, and the firmament showeth his handiwork' (Psalm 19). So we are encouraged by both the Bible and our curiosity to look beyond nature to find deeper understanding.

THE COSMOLOGICAL ARGUMENT

The existence of the universe is perhaps the most obvious clue to the existence of God. It is argued that only God, who does not require explanation, can provide the ultimate answer to the question 'Why is there something rather than nothing?' This 'cosmological argument' has a history going back to Plato and Aristotle but was revived by Leibniz in his essay, *On the Ultimate Origin of Things* (Ariew and Garber 1989). Aquinas incorporated the idea in his thesis that all motion derives from a 'prime mover' which he identified as God. Muslim philosophers such as Avicenna had earlier placed the argument in the context of creation in time—a form of the argument known today as the 'kalam cosmological argument'. Basically the argument terminates what would otherwise be an infinite regress by finding the ultimate cause of all existing, and contingent, things in an *un*caused or necessary being. The kalam version is based on the logical requirement for a finite history for the universe. If the universe had no beginning, so the argument goes, time would stretch backwards from any point, such as the present, for an infinite span into the past. Since it is impossible to traverse an infinite time span it is impossible for anything, including the universe, to arrive at the present. A universe without a beginning is therefore a contradiction. Notwithstanding this philosophical conundrum, some atheistic thinkers such as Fred Hoyle and Hermann Bondi openly admitted their preference for a universe that had always existed since this avoids the question of a creation. They advanced a theory of 'continuous creation' whereby matter was continually being formed to fill the expanding void of the universe. Some forms of the cosmological argument are consistent with a universe without a beginning. The strongest form of the argument, however, demands a start of the causal sequence of events in time implying a universe with a finite lifetime.

Modern cosmology supports the idea of a finite lifetime of the universe. The 'standard model' describes its beginning approximately 13.5 billion years ago in an explosion from a 'point-like' singularity with enormous energy, an event dubbed pejoratively by Hoyle as the 'Big Bang'. Evidence for such a primeval fireball is provided by the physical sciences on theoretical and observational grounds but it also clearly resonates with theological accounts of creation. The Russian theorist Alexander Friedman found solutions of Einstein's equations of General Relativity that indicated an expanding or contracting universe and the Belgian priest, Georges Lemaitre, produced solutions consistent with an initial expansion from a microscopic source. These mathematical arguments are supported by astronomical observations including the measurement of receding galaxies by Edwin Hubble and, more recently, detection of the cosmic microwave background. The former indicates the expansion of space and the latter—'the smoking gun'—is the present-day remnant of the radiation emitted by the hot early universe in the aftermath of the initial explosion.

At first sight the physics of the 'Big Bang' theory confirms the biblical teaching that 'In the beginning God created...' (Genesis 1:1). It needs to be remembered, however, that the

Bible is making a metaphysical and theological statement about origins and is not concerned with mechanisms. Nonetheless the theological and philosophical implications of modern cosmology continue to be the subject of intense debate. The causal chain running backwards in time (and space) takes us to the limit of both our science and our reasoning capacity. According to the theory, not only matter and energy were created in the Big Bang, but also time and space as an integrated four-dimensional space-time continuum. Thus the questions 'What was happening before the Big Bang?' or 'What is the universe expanding into?' are rendered meaningless. This idea accords with Augustine's affirmation, many centuries before Einstein and Lemaitre, that time itself was created by God who is timeless or eternal. Cosmology gives some explanation for the evolution of stars, galaxies, and large scale structure of the universe but questions remain about the nature of the reality in which our universe is embedded. Physical science takes us to the limit of the knowable from one side; theology and metaphysics approach this frontier from another direction. Natural theology affirms that these views of the borderlands are complementary.

The implications of cosmological theories for natural theology can, however, be double-edged. Newtonian physics described the universe as a clockwork mechanism operating under fixed laws of nature. God was initially ascribed the role of designer and maker of the laws, but in due course he was deemed, most famously by Laplace, to be an unnecessary hypothesis. In one sense the Big Bang explosion offers natural theology no more valuable a gift than the idea of a cosmic watchmaker who wound up the mechanism: God's role in this case is reduced to 'lighting the blue touch-paper'. More recently, speculative theories have emerged that deprive God of even this limited role. These theories explain the Big Bang as a random 'quantum fluctuation' out of 'nothing'. On this basis Stephen Hawking argues that there is then no need of a creator (Hawking and Mlodinow 2010). Hawking is, however, wrong to conclude that God is redundant. First, the 'nothing' from which quantum fluctuations arise is not 'nothing' in the absolute or philosophical sense but refers to a 'zero energy state' of a system obeying well-defined quantum mechanical and gravitational laws. The ultimate origin of these laws and the system in which they operate remains unexplained. Secondly, God is not a hypothesis that can be dispensed with when a satisfactory naturalistic explanation is found. God is the reason why all naturalistic explanations work and why anything exists to be explained. Hawking has made the common 'category mistake' of using physics to answer a metaphysical question. Physical scientists and natural theologians must both be careful not to confuse physics with metaphysics or to present a theological statement as if it was a scientific finding.

If misplaced theological conclusions are sometimes attached to the universe's beginning the same is true in relation to its end. The ultimate fate of the universe depends on whether its present expansion rate is constant, accelerating, or decelerating. A decelerating universe will eventually stop expanding and then contract under the pull of gravity—like a stone falling back to ground after being thrown up into the air. The end will be a 'Big Crunch' as all matter and energy disappear into a singularity where time and space vanish. Recent astronomical measurements seem to indicate that the expansion is accelerating. Whether the expansion is constant or accelerating the fate of the universe is the same—it will be determined by the second law of thermodynamics. This all pervasive law tells us that the entropy, or degree of disorder, always increases in a closed system. Since the universe is the ultimate 'closed system' then all matter will eventually decay into a cold featureless void—the 'heat death' of the universe. The prospects for life in either scenario, Big Crunch or Heat Death, are similarly bleak, leading some commentators to conclude that life is insignificant and pointless.

From a theological perspective such a conclusion is unwarranted. It is interesting to note that, following a brief inflationary phase, the universe has expanded at a rate that has been close to constant for almost all of its lifetime. This rate also has been just right to allow life to develop. Even if the final state of the universe turns out to be lifeless, the fact that this rate has been 'just right' is one of many coincidences that suggest life is in fact highly significant. In any case, the 'point' of life need not be identified with the final state of matter as presently constituted—the possibility of a renewal of matter cannot be discounted. New states of matter with remarkable properties have been one of the surprising discoveries of quantum physics—a topic to which I will return later. Christian eschatology specifically speaks of a 'new heaven and a new earth' and of bodies in the after-life as being qualitatively different from present bodies as a flower differs from its seed (1 Corinthians 15). The eye-witness accounts of Jesus' resurrected body suggest it had physical properties different from those of his pre-crucifixion body. Finally, the purpose of the universe may be as incubator of a new kind of life—a life intended for a new type of world. If that is true, like the baking of a cake from certain ingredients and using a finite cooking time, the ultimate fate of the oven is less important than the quality of the cake. Since time and space are created features of the present universe of matter and energy it may be that the 'point' is discernable only from an eternal, i.e. timeless, viewpoint. Apart from such theological perspectives, the existence of life in the universe turns out to have significance for cosmology and its relationship with natural theology.

'FINE TUNING' AND THE ANTHROPIC PRINCIPLE

The existence of a universe hospitable to life seems to have depended upon a remarkable series of coincidences (Rees 1999; Davies 2007). It appears that the constants of nature, the strength of fundamental forces etc., seem extraordinarily finely tuned to allow human life to exist. For example, if gravity had been only slightly weaker than its present value then no galaxies or stars would have formed. In this starless scenario the universe would be an uninteresting expanse of hydrogen and helium. Life could not have evolved since all the heavier elements necessary for life are formed in the interior of stars. On the other hand, had gravity been only slightly stronger, the universe would have collapsed on itself long ago with insufficient time for the evolution of stars, galaxies, and life. The generation of elements critical for life—carbon and oxygen in particular—relies on a particularly striking 'coincidence' discovered by Fred Hoyle. Carbon is formed by the simultaneous collision of three helium nuclei, a process so improbable that it would never occur at a sufficient rate to explain the present abundance of carbon in the universe. Hoyle predicted that the probability must have been enhanced by a nuclear resonance—a feature of the energy states of nuclei determined by the strength of the nuclear and electromagnetic forces. This resonance was subsequently found to be almost exactly where it was predicted to be. The coincidence is so remarkable that even the atheist Hoyle was moved to comment that it looked as if a super-intellect had been 'monkeying' with the physics (Hoyle 1983)! According to the theoretical physicist Freeman Dyson (1923–) the fact that so many other coincidences were also necessary for life implies that 'the universe knew we were coming' (quoted in Barrow and Tipler 1986). The combination of 'coincidences' and the 'fine tuning' has been given the status of a principle—the 'Anthropic Principle' (Barrow and Tipler 1986). In its strongest form the principle states that the universe must have the properties it does so that conscious rational beings *will exist* to observe it. This is an expression in terms of purpose—teleology—and so goes beyond the usual naturalistic explanation. The second, and weaker, form of the principle states that the fine-tuning of the universe simply created the conditions in which observers like us *could exist*. Even in this weak form the principle seems to point beyond the merely physical content of the world.

The critical factor for interpreting the 'evidence' of fine-tuning is the inconceivably small probability of all the coincidences arising purely by chance. It is often not appreciated exactly how remarkable are the numbers involved. For example, the expansion or contraction of the universe is controlled by the cosmological constant, Λ. If the strength of the gravitational force or the weak nuclear force differed from its actual value by one part in 10^{40} the consequent change in Λ would result either in expansion with such force that galaxies would never form, or a catastrophic collapse under gravity that again would prevent the evolution of stars and life. (The number 10^{40} is 10 multiplied by itself 40 times, i.e. a 1 followed by forty zeroes.) An even more spectacular number concerns the degree of order required in the initial state of the universe immediately after the Big Bang. As noted above, the degree of disorder, or entropy, always increases and so to have a universe with its present degree of order required an amazingly low entropy at the beginning. Roger Penrose has calculated that the precision needed in this initial state to achieve something like our present, life-friendly, universe is one part in $10^{10^{123}}$. This number is unimaginably large—it has vastly more zeroes than there are protons and neutrons in the entire universe (Penrose 1989)! It strains credulity therefore that this precision was the result of pure chance.

When multiple and *independently* improbable events occur the probability of them all happening purely by chance tends to zero and the case for an underlying cause becomes correspondingly stronger. Such an underlying cause could be a single unifying principle that would determine the values of constants of nature, strength of forces etc. This has been the motivation for the search for a grand unified theory, or a 'theory of everything', that would explain all the 'miraculous' coincidences. By reducing everything to a single, simple basis this would be the ultimate triumph of reductionism. As will be discussed later it would therefore also be affected by the limitations of this method. It would also not answer the fundamental metaphysical question—what is the ultimate source of the order, and the unimaginable precision, described by such a theory?

An alternative method to account for the cosmic coincidences invokes an ensemble of universes, a 'multiverse', in which each has a different set of values for the constants of nature etc. The fact that we observe fine-tuning is 'explained' by our being in the one universe, out of a practically infinite number, where this set of values just happens to occur. The multiverse arises in some speculative 'String Theories' that are also designed to unify the forces of nature into a single grand unified scheme. Such theories are beyond experimental validation, or falsification, and so, by Popper's definition that a scientific theory should be falsifiable, may be 'unscientific'. There are also serious philosophical and technical objections to the multiverse idea. For example, if the different universes are unconnected in any way then it cannot be assumed that the laws of physics in our universe apply to others or to the multiverse as a whole. If, on the other hand, the many universes are causally connected then we simply have a larger universe defined as all that exists. In this case it turns out that some of the initial-state problems, such as the entropy problem identified by Penrose, reoccur in a more acute form (Spitzer 2010). So, although the multiverse may be logically possible, it is not necessarily plausible and simply pushes the question of ultimate origin to an even more remote location. In any case the multiverse would then become the object of God's creation act.

The 'fine-tuning' argument and anthropic principle are clearly consistent with theism but are inconclusive in an absolute sense. It is worth remembering that no scientific theory can be absolutely conclusive since theories are always underdetermined by experiment. The argument that the 'coincidences' are unlikely to have arisen by chance alone is, however, persuasive—the odds against a purely chance 'explanation' are truly staggering. The multiverse idea addresses the improbability of the 'pure chance' explanation by replacing it with a different improbability—the existence of a very large number of undetectable universes. The multiverse thus introduces a multitude of extra factors and so, in a sense, maximally violates Occam's principle which demands that the number of explanatory factors should be the minimum necessary. The theistic idea of origins, however, converges to a single ultimate cause which is both simple and elegant.

THE QUANTUM WORLD

Explanations in cosmology for the vast structures of stars and galaxies introduced new concepts, including the creation of space and time, and hence a time 'zero' before which there was no time and a universe expanding, but not into any 'external' void. The nature of reality beyond the observable universe revealed by such concepts challenges our capacity to understand. Nonetheless the orderly behaviour of stars and planets are described by 'laws of nature' relating cause and effect. At the other end of the length scale, however, in the world of atom-sized particles, explanations require a theory that is even more counterintuitive—quantum theory. The classical world-view supposes all events to be linked in an unbroken chain of cause and effect. Change occurs in a continuous stream that seamlessly joins one event or observation to another. There is a world 'out there' that maintains an objective existence independently of us and our observations. In the quantum world, however, these familiar ideas of causality, continuity, and objective reality are called into question. The implications of quantum theory for natural theology are now beginning to be explored.

At the heart of quantum theory lie two important principles that govern our interaction with the world at the atomic scale. First, the principle of complementarity, articulated by Neils Bohr, proposes a 'wave–particle duality' for both light and atomic particles. For example, an atom (or a part of one, such as an electron or proton) will be discerned as either particle-like or wave-like depending on the way it is observed. Secondly, Heisenberg's 'Uncertainty Principle' fundamentally limits the precision of our knowing certain combinations of properties e.g. position and momentum. The more precisely we know one property the less precise becomes our knowledge of the other. Both of these principles involve the observer in a fundamental way. This differs markedly from the familiar world described by classical physics where objects are assumed to have a precise position and motion whether or not anyone is looking.

According to the commonly accepted 'Copenhagen' interpretation of quantum theory, knowledge of 'reality' is limited to mathematical manipulation of symbols and the calculation of *probabilities*, defined by a 'wave function'. The act of measurement results in the 'collapse' of the wave function *randomly* into one of a set of allowed values. Thus nature allows us to know only the probability of finding a particle 'here rather than there' with 'this rather than that motion'. Between any observations at two different positions we can have no definite knowledge of any continuous path between them. The unsettling feature of this interpretation is that it denies any reality to physical parameters until they are observed. Thus the uncertainty in knowing whether an entity is a wave or a particle, or in determining simultaneously its position and momentum, is not due to our ineptitude in measuring these things but is inherent in the nature of reality at the quantum level. The uncertainty is ontological not epistemological. The ontological randomness in the outcome of measurements breaks the chain of continuity and causality and seriously undermines determinism. It was this probabilistic aspect of quantum mechanics that so disturbed Einstein leading him to declare that, 'God does not play dice.'

Quantum theory introduces an inherent randomness but also other bizarre phenomena that further offend our common sense. Wave–particle complementarity leads to particles that seem to be in two places at once. Using their wave-like properties, atoms that normally bounce off each other can be induced to travel, ghost-like, through each other as if the other wasn't there. Clouds containing millions of atoms can be 'organized' using laser light into a new form of matter with 'miraculous' properties such as flowing without friction or slowing light to the speed of a cyclist! But what relevance has all this to natural theology?

One potentially helpful answer to this question is that the mysterious quantum nature of matter forces us to accept paradoxes as an inherent feature of reality. This may help us, by analogy, to accept that paradoxes in theology are not necessarily fatal to its intellectual coherence. Such paradoxes reflect a perspective of reality that is no less valid than physical interpretations of a quantum mystery. Wave–particle duality allows one entity to be two mutually exclusive things at the same time. A similar complementarity could help in thinking about the Trinity. In facing up to the mysterious behaviour in the quantum world physical science has had to accept the way things are and find ways of calculating the consequences of this new non-classical reality. In a similar way theology has had to find ways of expressing spiritual realities as they have been experienced. This similarity reveals what Polkinghorne calls an 'unexpected kinship' between science and theology in the search for truth (Polkinghorne 2007).

A second possible implication of quantum theory for natural theology concerns the problem of divine action. The breakdown of the causal nexus that occurs at the quantum level has led some to speculate that this gives God an opportunity to exercise his influence on the world. The essence of this idea is that since events in the macroscopic world are tightly controlled by a rigid determinism, the inherent 'indeterminism' perceived in quantum mechanics would allow God to act without violating his own 'laws of nature'. Any event is thought to be reducible ultimately to events on the quantum scale and so God can act in a 'bottom up' manner whilst maintaining the regularity of nature on the large scale. The basic idea was expressed by a physicist, William Pollard (Pollard 1958) but has been elaborated and refined by a number of theologians. This is a serious attempt to explore the interface between the scientific and theological perspectives of reality since Christianity certainly affirms that God acts in the real world. The attempt, however, to locate divine action at the quantum level, whilst not excluding his acting at other levels, is plagued with technical difficulties (Saunders 2000). A major problem arises from a failure to appreciate that quantum mechanics is actually rigidly deterministic in the calculation of observable properties. The randomness associated with individual quantum 'events' is soon lost in the statistical certainties of the behaviour of large-scale objects. I would argue also that it is by no means necessary to admit that bottom-up causality is the only possible means of acting on the world either by God or humans for that matter. We take it for granted that our actions may originate in thoughts that are freely willed at a higher level than sub-atomic quantum processes. Since we are a long way from understanding how mind affects body, it seems premature to speculate on exactly *how* God, a Spirit, acts in the physical world.

Other interpretations of quantum theory have been proposed that have different philosophical implications than the standard 'Copenhagen' version. The 'Many Worlds' view put forward by Hugh Everrit III suggests that every measurement is associated with a branching of the universe into a set of 'parallel universes' characterized by having one of the allowed values of the observable. There must therefore exist an almost infinite number of these parallel but undetectable universes and the one we inhabit is a matter of pure chance. An alternative proposed by David Bohm, based on an earlier idea of Louis de Broglie, supposes a deep, underlying order—a wholeness—that is somehow folded, or crumpled up inside reality so that it is only our encounters with it at the quantum level that are random. These alternative interpretations provide the same probabilistic mathe-matical predictions of the standard quantum theory but both are totally deterministic.

Quantum theory introduces the problem of randomness or chance in a particularly acute form since, on at least the standard interpretation, it is ontological and not merely epistemological. The existence of any disorder in the universe could undermine the argu-ment from the orderliness of nature to an origin in the ordered mind of God. Furthermore, the breaking of causal chains by chance events is threatening to determinism and to the power of God to control every detail of creation. Whether the world is fully deterministic or not has serious implications for natural theology. Classical theology has accommo-dated a very deterministic view of God's relations with the world but the role of chance is currently being re-evaluated, partly as a consequence of quantum ideas.

DETERMINISM, ORDER, AND DISORDER

Classical mechanics assumes a rigorous determinism 'all the way down'. This need not imply that everything is predictable. The recent development of chaos theory shows how various systems display unpredictable behaviour since small uncertainties in initial con-ditions may lead to highly divergent outcomes. Although unpredictable, the behaviour is still thoroughly deterministic (Gleick 1987). A further source of uncertainty may be the impossibility of calculating the result of a highly complex process. Chance therefore simply represents our inability to predict outcomes owing to ignorance of causes, insuf-ficient precision of our knowledge of initial conditions, or to overwhelming complexity. The 'chance' involved here is *epistemological*. Classical Theism has also tended to take this view of chance, since an omniscient, sovereign God must be in total control of every event, from large-scale 'accidents' to the decay of every radioactive nucleus. However, if quantum mechanical behaviour, e.g. radioactive decay, is genuinely non-causal and non-deterministic, the unpredictability of events at the sub-atomic level represents pure or *ontological* chance. It is then possible that not even God can predict the microscopic disorder that can arise by chance. For some this represents a threat to the omniscience and omnipotence of God. For some others chance undermines the very existence of God, at least of the God of Classical Theism. I would argue for a third way in which chance is a divinely designed and purposeful feature of nature. In this view natural events may even be unpredictable to God but this does not necessarily deny omniscience if this is understood as knowledge of all that, in principle, can be known. Neither does it deny omnipotence, but rather enhances it, since God has power to deal with whatever chance outcomes occur and to bring about his purpose.

The role of chance in biological evolution has been used by atheistic writers such as Jacques Monod to counter the argument from design (Monod 1971). On the other hand, chance has been accommodated in a theistic evolutionary view by Arthur Peacocke as an integral part of the creator's *modus operandi* (Peacocke 1986). David Bartholomew has presented a wider-ranging study of chance, including its effects in the physical sciences and shown that disorder on one level can lead to order on another (Bartholomew 2008). Recent research has also shown many examples of 'spontaneous' generation of order from disorder by self-organizing systems or randomized systems far from equilibrium. Chance is therefore seen to play a constructive role in creation and can be incorporated into providential acts of God. The process of creation itself requires a certain degree of chaos to allow the full exploration of the possibilities inherent in the properties of matter and living organisms. Yet, as John Polkinghorne has observed, a balance must be struck; too little chaos and nothing gets created, too much and nothing survives.

It seems to me that the combination of order and disorder in nature reflects the character of the creator. Allowing a degree of indeterminacy provides an openness to the future and creates the possibility of meaningful relationship between creature and creator. Einstein rejected quantum indeterminacy and held firmly to a fundamental determinism, an outlook that influenced his concept of God. In his view, everything, including every act of evil, is deterministic and therefore ultimately the responsibility of the creator of the universe. For this reason he concluded that the idea of a personal God was inconsistent since he would be passing judgement on himself. The causal chain and fundamental order of the universe is, in this way, relevant to theodicy and the nature of God. The corollary of Einstein's view would be that indeterminacy could at least open the possibility of a personal God without the moral stain of evil on his character. The conflict between chance and the sovereignty of God may be resolved to some degree if chance is necessary in a world ordered by laws of nature where humans have genuinely free will (Ewart 2008). Assuming such freedom of will, it would be possible, in principle, for us to force God, by the consistency of his nature, to *react* in a predictable way. A God so forced into action has lost his sovereignty. A built-in randomness, however, could break the deterministic chain linking any action of man to a predictable act of God. The omnipotence and sovereignty of God could then be seen as his infinite ability to respond, *in a way that he chooses*, to any event, a free-willed act or even a random physical process, in an appropriate way to effect his will. Thus chance, even ontological chance, does not undermine the concept of a sovereign and personal God. Einstein's instinct to link the source of order in Nature to the moral order is, however, surely correct. The same association is made in Psalm 19 which moves from acknowledgment of God as creator to consideration of moral law.

Full-blown determinism 'all the way down' is certainly fatal to the idea of human free will. It also fits comfortably with some theological views of predestination. The 'fixity' of the future is settled by a scheme whereby God micromanages every detail in an unfolding pre-ordained plan. Free will is also ruled out by the 'Block Universe', based on an interpretation of the special theory of relativity where all events in space-time are accessible 'simultaneously' to a timeless God. On the other hand, if chance is allowed a genuine role, God can retain his sovereignty by his infinite capacity to respond to whatever happens. The outcomes of chance processes are always in any case limited by the laws of physics. Thus the inclusion of a certain degree of indeterminacy at various levels creates an open future of possibilities. This kind of universe allows human free will and freedom for God to interact responsively and to have the ultimate say in how things turn out. This view is consistent more with the ideas of 'Open Theism' than those of Classical Theism (Sanders 1998). Natural theology, in this view, can accommodate both the order and the disorder in the universe as evidence of God's provision of a stable framework for existence that is also sufficiently indeterminate to allow human free will. The order remains evidence of the divine mind and the disorder the clue to his personal nature—a nature that desires a dynamic and open relationship with his creatures.

LAWS OF NATURE, REDUCTIONISM, AND RATIONALITY

The argument that the perceived order in the universe implies the existence of God rests on the link between laws of nature and the need for a 'Law Giver'. However, the validity of the 'Laws of Nature' concept has recently been questioned. Most working scientists recognize the limits imposed by imprecision and inaccuracies in measurement but take a 'critical realist' view that the 'laws' bear some approximate ontological relationship to reality. Reductionism seeks to establish causal links all the way down to some foundational level—usually lying in the domain of physics—and it is this causal chain that underpins the laws. It is often necessary to contrive some abstraction by eliminating unpredictable or complicating factors and so the 'laws' are *ceteris paribus* and apply strictly only within certain specified limits. Therefore, it is argued, since the real world is so complicated by random factors, in the strictest sense there are no 'Laws of Nature' and hence no need for a 'Law Giver'.

Against this it should be recognized that the universe displays a remarkable degree of uniformity—the nature of elementary particles and the forces between them are demonstrably the same on earth and in the farthest reaches of the universe. The laws that govern their behaviour on cosmological and quantum mechanical scales are the same everywhere. Local variations, however, do arise, often by chance—spatial irregularities and random fluctuations—but these too obey laws, albeit of a statistical character. As we have already noted, chance can reasonably be seen as part of the creative plan. In any case, the theist is not committed to one particular and absolutist interpretation of the laws of nature. It is sufficient for theism that there is enough regularity and lawfulness to permit God's purpose to be fulfilled. Purpose, however, cannot be discerned by the methods of physical science but must be sought in the realm of metaphysics.

A more conventional attack upon theism is based on the apparent ability of science, and physical science in particular, to deliver provable certainty in contrast to unprovable faith statements of religion. That science has been so successful is due in part to its methodology and to the self-imposed limits of its enquiry. By reducing a problem to simpler constituent parts and excluding complicating factors, rigorous solutions are obtained. This reductionism gives a beguiling appearance of certainty and completeness in the conclusions. An implicit assumption is often made that more complicated problems, i.e.

problems in the 'real' world, would yield to such an approach given sufficient time and attention to detail. It is then further assumed that once such a naturalistic explanation has been given, there is nothing more to say, because a reductionist explanation includes all relevant causes and effects. The philosophical materialist is then led to conclude that even thoughts can be reduced to 'nothing but' the physics of atoms in our brains. All non-material entities, including spiritual 'realities', are 'explained away' as mere epiphenomena of purely physical processes. In other words the only things that really exist are material things.

There are several logical flaws in this argument. First, '*methodological* naturalism' has been confused with '*ontological* naturalism'. The method deliberately selects only naturalistic explanatory factors so any conclusion that only naturalistic factors exist is implicit in the premise. Elizabeth Anscombe puts it as follows: 'This often happens in philosophy; it is argued that "all we find" is such-and-such, and it turns out that the arguer has excluded from his idea of "finding" the sort of thing he says we don't find' (Anscombe 1981).

Secondly, it is self-defeating. Since the argument itself must have been derived by thought and, if thought itself is nothing more than 'motions of atoms in our brains', its logic rests on a non-rational basis. Reductionism therefore cannot deliver a complete 'theory of everything'. Even in terms of physical science such a theory would not actually explain everything since many phenomena emerge only at higher levels of complexity and require different forms of explanation (Anderson 1972). Superconductivity, for example, is explained only in terms of the quantum mechanical cooperative behaviour that is not inherent in an individual electron. In one sense emergent phenomena, typically found in complex, biological organisms, can provide a kind of 'top down' causality, but the causal connections involve a 'bottom-up' connectedness that is still essential for the operation. Emergence should not be thought of as admitting some kind of mysterious unphysical causation. It is simply a concept that supplies a different framework for explanation that cannot be provided by reductionism.

The essential problem for atheism's attack on natural theology based on reductionism, or naturalism per se, is that it simultaneously questions the validity of our rationality. If our ability to reason is doubted, it cannot be validated by reason alone. This problem prompted Aristotle to note an ancient proverb to the effect that if someone chokes on water what can be used to wash it down? For the theist, rationality may be seen as an emergent property; it requires a degree of complexity in the brain, but a complete validation cannot be provided solely in the physical realm. It is as though our rationality allows us to make statements that are true but not provable. This understanding of the limitations of reason has a formal analogue in Gödel's incompleteness theorem. The truth of some statements cannot be proved from within a closed system but requires a perspective from a 'higher' level. Blaise Pascal wrestled with the paradox that only reason could persuade reason of its inadequacy and that 'Reason's last step is the recognition that there are an infinite number of things which are beyond it' (Pascal 1996).

REFLECTIONS

Natural theology is therefore both encouraged and challenged by the findings of the physical sciences. The scientific method is committed to finding naturalistic explanations, yet the vision that it gives suggests there is more to it than meets this particular eye: the universe seems to be permeated with signs of 'mind'. That the universe is deeply ordered, with fundamental parameters so finely tuned to allow our existence, suggests there is a reason why we are here. At first sight the disorder in the world undermines the inference from order to a rational, order-imposing, and purposeful creator. Yet chance too can be consistent with purpose since it can play a positive and creative role. The balance of order and disorder suggests a world designed to have a reliable structure but free from a rigid determinism. These 'signs' of mind behind or beyond the natural world are consistent with the creator being a personal God rather than some impersonal force or logical principle.

The mysterious quantum world has shown us that new ways of thinking are required to deal with material 'reality'. We have to come to terms with irreducible uncertainty and also to accept mutually exclusive ways of representing sub-atomic matter. The Principle of Complementarity, that accommodates wave–particle duality, prepares our minds for metaphysical paradoxes of spiritual 'reality'.

Quantum theory has also revealed new forms of matter with 'miraculous' properties. These properties are not evidence of supernatural intervention in the normal running of the universe but manifestations of a deeper rationality that lay undiscovered by classical physics. Could it be that all miracles are similarly rational—displaying obedience to laws of nature known only God? This reasoning is not to dismiss miracles as having merely naturalistic explanations or to deny that God can intervene in his world. Rather it affirms that God is a God of reason who does not use magic or act capriciously. The physical sciences have taught us not to limit what may be possible to what we know at present. One can speculate that the possibility of new states of matter—made out of the old stuff—has eschatological implications. If the ultimate fate of the universe is to involve a new heaven and a new earth, we can expect a transformation of existing matter as St Paul describes in his letter to the Corinthians (1 Corinthians 15:35–53).

Einstein commented that 'the eternal mystery of the world is its comprehensibility' (Einstein 1995). The Christian theist explains this 'mystery' by God's gift of rationality that allows us, to some extent, to think his thoughts after him. The physical sciences present an ambiguous picture. We find no overwhelming proof of God or of his nature. It remains possible, given sufficient faith, to dismiss the deep order and remarkable fine tuning in the universe as cosmic coincidences. Einstein also spoke of coincidence as God's way of remaining anonymous but he rejected the idea of a personal God. The reason for God to choose such anonymity may, however, lie in the personal nature of his character. It would be consistent with a personal God, intent on having a relationship of love and trust, that he would not overwhelm us with 'proof'. Most of the founders of quantum theory were moved to a quasi-religious sense of wonder in contemplating the nature of reality. They were, however, adamant that the theory neither confirmed nor denied spiritual things, yet they felt that the evidence pointed beyond physics to a deeper reality. Wolfgang Pauli is reported to have asked Heisenberg if he believed in a personal God (Heisenberg 1971). Heisenberg rephrased the question by asking 'Can you ... reach the central order of things or events, whose existence seems beyond doubt, as directly as you can reach the soul of another human being?' and answered 'Yes'. If 'the central order of things' is the rational principle underlying all things—the Logos, which the New Testament identifies with Christ, the second person of the Trinity (John 1:1–3)—then the Christian would agree. So the physical sciences provide evidence that is consistent with the affirmations of natural theology—the existence and personal nature of God—but to reach Him, as to another soul, requires a step beyond.

References

Anderson P. W. (1972). 'More is Different'. *Science* 177/4047: 393–6.

Anscombe, G. E. M. (1981). 'Causality and Determination'. Inaugural lecture, Cambridge University in *Metaphysics and the philosophy of mind: Collected Philosophical Papers*. Vol. II. Basil Blackwell: Oxford: p. 137.

Barrow, John D. and Frank J. Tipler (1986). *The Anthropic Cosmological Principle*. Oxford: Oxford University Press.

Bartholomew, David (2008). *God, Chance and Purpose: Can God Have it Both Ways?* Cambridge: Cambridge University Press.

Davies, Paul (2007). *The Goldilocks Enigma*. Harmondsworth: Penguin.

Einstein, A. (1995). *Out of My Later Years*. New York, Carol Publishing Group.

Ewart, Paul (2008). 'The Necessity of Chance: Randomness, Purpose, and the Sovereignty of God'. *Science and Christian Belief* 21/2: 111–31.

Gleick, James (1987). *Chaos: Making a New Science*. Harmondsworth: Penguin.

Hawking, S. and L. Mlodinow (2010). *The Grand Design*. New York, Bantam Books.

Heisenberg, W. (1971). *Physics and Beyond: Encounters and Conversations*. Translated by A. J. Pomerans. New York, Harper & Row Publishers Inc.

Hoyle, Fred (1983). *The Intelligent Universe*. London, Michael Joseph.

Leibniz G. W. (1989). 'On the Ultimate Origin of Things' in *Philosophical Essays*. Translated by R. Ariew and D. Garber. Indianapolis: Hackett Publishing Company Inc.

Monod, Jacques (1971). *Chance and Necessity: An Essay on the Natural Philosophy of Modern Biology*. Translated by Austryn Wainhouse. New York: Vintage.

Pascal, B. (1996). *Pensées, 188*. Translated by A. J. Krailsheimer. London: Penguin Books.

Peacocke, Arthur (1986). *God and the New Biology*. London: Dent.

Penrose, Roger (1989). *The Emperor's New Mind*. Oxford: Oxford University Press.

Polkinghorne, John (2007). *Quantum Physics and Theology: An Unexpected Kinship*. London: SPCK.

Pollard, William G. (1958). *Chance and Providence: God's Action in a World Governed by Scientific Law*. London, Faber & Faber.

Rees, Martin (1999). *Just Six Numbers*. London: Weidenfeld and Nicolson.

Sanders, John (1998). *The God Who Risks: A Theology of Providence*. Downers Grove, IL: InterVarsity Press.

Saunders, N. T. (2000). 'Does God Cheat at Dice? Divine Action and Quantum Possibilities'. *Zygon* 35/3: 517–44.

Spitzer, Robert J. (2010). *New Proofs for the Existence of God*. Grand Rapids and Cambridge: Wm B. Eerdmans Publishing Co.

....

CHAPTER 27

CHEMICAL SCIENCES AND NATURAL THEOLOGY

....

DAVID KNIGHT

CHEMISTRY never was a contemplative science. Like surgery, it has always had a strong aspect of a craft. Expertise cannot be gained from books alone, but must be learned by experience on the job. Managing furnaces, Bunsen burners, sand baths, and water baths; blowing and manipulating glass which must be neither too thick (or it will crack) nor too thin (or it will break); sucking up fluids in pipettes and managing them in burettes; blowing out while breathing in with a blowpipe; educating the nose, the tongue, and the eye to distinguish smells (often horrible), tastes (ditto), and colours, and the hands to manipulate weights, gases, retorts and condensers, charcoal blocks, filter papers, hot test tubes, and spatulas, must all be learned (Faraday 1829). Chemists have to think with their fingers, distinguishing the unctuous and the gritty, tweaking their apparatus, drawing out and twisting hot glass. Out walking, or from a book in an armchair, it is easier to admire the starry heavens, the flowers and the butterflies, and be moved to think of their creator than it would be in the laboratory, with its evocative stinks, its necessary manual skills, and its dangers for the uninitiated. Chemistry is hard work as well as hard thinking.

Again, while chemistry is like all sciences concerned with understanding the world, it is also deeply involved with changing and improving it. The world is not a Garden of Eden: we are liable to all sorts of diseases; agriculture is beset with weeds and pests; useful metals like iron and aluminium are hard to extract; dyes, paints, ceramics, yarns, and plastics make life easier and more fun but are hard to make. Chemistry, informal or scientific, has proved its worth in bettering life: but this has not been achieved through contemplation. As Humphry Davy (1788–1829) declared in a Presidential address to the Royal Society in 1822:

> The more we study nature, the more we obtain proofs of divine power and beneficence; but the laws of nature and the principles of science were to be discovered by labour and industry, and have not been revealed to man; who, with respect to philosophy [science], has been left to exert these god-like faculties, by which reason ultimately approaches, in its results, to inspiration. [Davy 1839–40: VII, 41–2]

Chemistry is a science for a fallen world. In the nineteenth century, with its promise of fertilizers, alloys, dyes, and explosives, process- and quality-control, disinfectants, and preservatives, it was popular and admired. It was notably publicized in the widely read writings of Justus Liebig (1803–73) (Liebig 1851). It looked then like the solution to problems of dirt, pests, pollution, and adulteration: but in the culture of suspicion of the later twentieth century 'chemicals' became a dirty word, and 'chemistry' was associated with pollution. Things can be said on both sides; but in reality chemists will be necessary to clean up the world, and everything, whatever its immediate origin, is a chemical. Chemistry has become everybody's service science, ubiquitous if unpopular: chemists invented the graduate student, the laboratory, and experimental science, and have always been practical, with an eye on usefulness. 'Chemical philosophy' was a term used by some prominent chemists of the early nineteenth century to describe their activity as parallel to the much-esteemed 'natural philosophy' of Newtonian physicists: but that disguised the hands-on nature of their science. Chemistry, like farming, did not lend itself to passive adoration of the wisdom and benevolence of God: some ingenuity was required to turn the arduous process of discovery, interpretation, and application into worship.

Chemistry thus went more readily with a theology of nature, enriching the faith of those who already believed in God, than with attempted proofs of His existence, wisdom, and benevolence (Brooke and Cantor 1998: 314–41). It promised a route to riches, and to ameliorating the fallen human condition, by increasing crops, decreasing labour, and through pharmacy improving health and prolonging life. It also promised a deeper understanding of those sciences that lent themselves more readily to advocates of natural theology: astronomy and natural history. Auguste Comte (1798–1857), that great despiser of theology and metaphysics, famously declared that we can never know the chemistry of the stars; but within a generation, chemists armed with spectroscopes were doing just that. Nevertheless, he perceived chemistry as a fundamental science, a bridge linking astronomy to biology through method if not speculative understanding of animal, vegetable, or stellar processes (Comte 1853: I, 138, 298–9; II, 539–43). The nineteenth century was the age of the expert; and in bridging these gulfs in scientific knowledge, chemistry was divided into three great branches: inorganic, organic, and physical. They became further divided into specialisms; and chemists within industry formed societies for the exchange of information and for professional qualification and recognition. By the twentieth century, chemistry had become a congeries of chemical sciences.

BEGINNINGS

Chemistry is very old. The making of ceramics and glass, the refining of gold and silver, the extraction of bronze and iron, the preparation of dyes for the human body and for textiles, all go back into the remote past. By the beginning of the Christian era, in both

China and the Mediterranean, this artisanal knowledge was leading to what we call
'alchemy'. Alchemists were optimists, seeing potential gold within imperfect and
perishable things: in searching for the 'philosophers' stone' or 'elixir' that would
transform base metals into gold, or indefinitely prolong human life, they aspired also to
make themselves better, transforming their own base metal into noble and beautiful
gold. This is the metaphor in George Herbert's poem, 'The Elixer', in which the 'tincture'
was 'for Thy [God's] sake':

> This is the famous stone
> That turneth all to gold;
> For that which God doth touch and own
> Cannot for less be told. [Herbert 1967, 88–9]

From legendary founders such as Hermes Trismegistos and Maria the Jewess,
alchemy was enthusiastically picked up by Renaissance magi, in a 'chemical philosophy' in which God created the world in a dynamical, continuing chemical
process (Debus 2006). All was working towards perfection, so that base metals
within the earth were slowly turning to gold. The adept might accelerate the process, and make gold or even life (a golem or homunculus) provided that he was in a
good moral state: the story of Faust showed what happened if he wasn't. Alchemists'
experiments yielded chemical knowledge as well as practical expertise, notably in
distillation and in the handling of crucibles and furnaces: but they did not succeed
in their main aim, and notoriously there were many charlatans gulling their
clients.

Traditionally, alchemists had been chiefly concerned with the mineral realm, the
extraction and transmutation of metals. The science took a new turn with
Paracelsus (1493–1541), whose real name was Theophrastus Bombastus von
Hohenheim; an unorthodox physician who coined the term 'alkahest' for the philosophers' stone, and who prescribed powerful metallic remedies in place of herbal
concoctions. His disciples spread his practices around Europe, particularly in combating syphilis; and gradually these desperate remedies for desperate diseases
became acceptable to the medical establishment. An eminent disciple, Johannes
Baptista van Helmont (1579–1644) of Brussels, was also a mystic, under grave suspicion from the Roman Catholic authorities. He dedicated his posthumously published *Ortus Medicinae* (1648) to God; pondering the nature of matter, he was
unhappy both with the Aristotelian four elements (earth, air, fire, and water) and
Paracelsus' 'sulphur', 'salt', and 'mercury'. He investigated the growth of trees
(apparently from water alone), and coined the term 'gas' for the various effluviae of
his experiments. Paracelsus, van Helmont, and subsequent disciples brought about
a close alliance of chemistry with medicine (Debus 2001): henceforward, formal
courses in chemistry would, until the middle of the nineteenth century, be taught
mostly in medical schools. This (al)chemical philosophy played an important part
in the 'Scientific Revolution', usually too closely associated by historians with
astronomy and mechanics.

'CHYMISTRY'

In this seventeenth-century Revolution, chemistry occupied a prominent place in the newly founded scientific societies and academies in Italy, France, and Britain: but because it was a rather different science from ours, scholars nowadays often prefer the contemporary spelling 'chymistry' for it. In Britain the most prominent chymist, a leading figure in the Royal Society, internationally respected, and an eminent natural theologian, was Robert Boyle (1627–91), younger son of the (parvenu) Earl of Cork, a deeply religious grandee who could devote himself to the life of a virtuoso in science and natural theology. His life and writings have been in recent years hugely elucidated by the work of Michael Hunter and his associates (Hunter 2003, 2009). Where alchemists had been secretive, veiling their arcana in mysterious verses or pictures, and teaching disciples on a one-to-one basis, Boyle believed that science was public knowledge: he reported everything, as far as possible in the plain language of artisans that the Royal Society expected of its Fellows. He was also, like Descartes, a devotee of mechanical explanations. For him, matter was composed of 'corpuscles', created by God and all of the same basic stuff, which in stable arrangements formed the primary mixts, iron, tin, gold, sulphur, and other substances that resisted chemical analysis, and which in their turn would combine to form compound bodies.

Boyle was famous for his piety, which included firm rejection of the Platonic idea that a demiurge, Nature, came between God and creation. No deist, but seeing the world as a great machine under God's immediate superintendence, he praised design and contrivance wherever he found it; and in his will endowed what became an important series of annual lecture courses in London, demonstrating the goodness and wisdom of God. He ensured that while science might in Restoration London be mocked as a hobby for absent-minded dilettantes, it was generally perceived and popularized by the more serious-minded as a way of understanding God through his works, rather than as atheistic. This kind of natural theology became a feature especially of Britain in the eighteenth and early nineteenth centuries; reading the Book of Nature in concert with the Bible (confident that in the long run at least they would cohere) was a proper activity for gentlemen and their ladies, and the underlying teleology gave the science a framework. Chymistry was the science to which Boyle was particularly devoted, and experiment rather than mathematics the key to knowledge: he was probably the first person to publish uncooked experimental data, and he also wrote refreshingly about the value of experiments that did not go as expected. But his 'corpuscular philosophy' could not explain any chemical process in detail: it was a programme.

Boyle saw no contradiction here with alchemy, and in this he was joined by Isaac Newton (1642–1727). Newtonian scholars have demonstrated how much time Newton spent in alchemical reading and experiment in his laboratory, and in theology: but because he was not a Trinitarian, he kept his heretical religious ideas to himself and published only hints. For him, as he sought prosaically to decode the recipes, alchemy was the sphere of short-range forces, discussed in the famous 'Queries' appended to his *Opticks* (Newton 1952: 394):

> There are therefore Agents in Nature able to make the Particles of Bodies stick together by very strong Attractions. And it is the business of experimental Philosophy to find them out.

This dynamical approach, based on forces rather than what Newton perceived as the hard, indestructible particles of what in a letter to the first 'Boyle lecturer' he called 'inanimate brute Matter' (Newton 1958: 302), greatly appealed to Joseph Priestley (1733–1804), a Unitarian minister and the leading British practitioner of what we can now call 'chemistry' in the late eighteenth century.

THE CHEMICAL REVOLUTION

In the preface to his *History and Present State of Electricity*, Priestley contrasted mechanics, concerned with the 'sensible properties of bodies', with electricity, chemistry, and optics, that promised 'an inlet into their internal structure':

> New worlds may open to our view, and the glory of the great Sir Isaac Newton himself…be eclipsed, by a new set of philosophers, in quite a new field of speculation. [Priestley 1966: xv]

Priestley found his metier in chemistry with the isolation and identification of gases, making chemistry the sphere of all three phases, gaseous, liquid, and solid. His vision of chemistry as awaiting its Newton, who would transform it into a fundamental and dynamic science, dealing with forces rather than just brute matter; his attractive style, welcoming all to join in the excitement of discovery; and the potential of spectacular chemical experiments done in conjunction with lectures all made chemistry an important part of the Romantic science of what has been called the Age of Wonder, the decades either side of 1800. Chemists pondered the 'elective affinities' that (unlike universal gravitation, but like marriage) bound unlike substances together; and Johann Goethe (1749–1832) wrote a novel, *Elective Affinities*, brilliantly exploring this idea and its materialistic implications as the relationships of four people learning about chemical reactions collapse disastrously in a double decomposition, $AB + CD = AD + CB$ (Goethe 1971).

The eighteenth century culminated in revolutions: during 1789 George Washington was inaugurated as first President of the USA; in France the Bastille was stormed and the States General convened; and also in Paris Antoine Lavoisier (1743–94) published his *Elements of Chemistry*, intended to bring about an intellectual revolution. He used that word, which was just ceasing to refer to cycles of history and mean a decisive change. Using Priestley's discoveries, notably of the component of air that supported burning and breathing that Lavoisier named 'oxygen', he reinterpreted combustion and acidity, promulgated a new language which is still essentially in use, and replaced the old elements or principles with a list of 'simple substances' that could not be further analysed. He sought for chemistry the rigour he perceived in algebra, and deplored as 'metaphysical' any speculation about atoms. In 1794 he fell a victim (as an indecently rich tax-collector) to the political revolution he had at first welcomed, but by then his powerful position in the Academy of Sciences in the world's centre of excellence in science had ensured that his new vision would prevail. Like other sciences in France, this chemistry was cut off not only from metaphysics, but also from religion: in Comte's terminology it was 'positive' knowledge. This smacked of a dangerous materialism and atheism, notably in Britain where some delighted in, but many were much alarmed by, events in revolutionary France. In England, although he rejected Lavoisier's chemical reforms, the religious and political radical Priestley was stigmatized by the conservative Edmund Burke, using chemical metaphors, as playing with gunpowder and releasing wild gas. In 1791 his house in Birmingham was sacked by a mob shouting 'Church and King'. He fled to London, but found himself cold-shouldered and in 1794 set sail for the USA, dying there in exile.

By then in Britain, at war with Revolutionary and Napoleonic France for a generation, it was important to demonstrate that the pursuit of chemistry was fully compatible with being a God-fearing and patriotic subject of King George III. The Quaker John Dalton (1766–1844) re-jigged the corpuscular philosophy of his hero Newton, imagining irreducibly distinct atoms for each of Lavoisier's 'simple substances' (our elements). His work impinged little upon religion and politics; but Davy in London became a scientific star as the apostle of applied science, looking forward to a world in which chemistry would have transformed life. His wealthy hearers were reassured that inequality was an essential part of this vision, for capital investment was required; and its success would bring general prosperity, and abate revolutionary sentiments. Davy in 1806–7 realized Priestley's dynamic vision when he demonstrated that chemical affinity was electrical, using a great battery in a dramatic experiment melting and then decomposing potash. Sparks flew around the laboratory, but he succeeded in isolating the extraordinary metals potassium (which he compared to the alkahest) and sodium; and his lectures and researches stimulated Mary Shelley (1797–1851) to write *Frankenstein* (Shelley 1999), depicting the chemist in a darker role, as sorcerer's apprentice.

At the end of his life, Davy wrote a strange series of dialogues, *Consolations in Travel*, intended as a kind of testament (Davy 1839–40: IX). It is the apologia of a chemist and romantic genius, who aspired to be a sage, and has a visionary and unorthodox religious strain; Davy had earlier written a poem about his faith:

> Oh, most magnificent and noble nature!
> Have I not worshipped thee with such a love
> As never mortal man before displayed?
> Adored thee in thy majesty of visible creation,
> And searched into thy hidden and mysterious ways
> As Poet, as Philosopher, as Sage? [cited in Knight 1998: 9]

Orthodox critics of natural theology have been aware that it is as easy to stray into such pantheism as into deism. Davy could not accept the materialism, real or methodological, that he and contemporaries saw in the writings of French-influenced physiologists. Just as matter cannot be destroyed, so the human mind can never die; and in *Consolations* Davy declared his belief in the immortality of the soul, with reincarnation on other planets in a gradual ascent towards more and more spiritual and intellectual being. That means progress, for Davy in Stoic mode identified rationality with goodness. Meanwhile on Earth, the chemist is a hero, facing danger in the laboratory for the good of his fellow-humans, bringing enlightenment and ameliorating the curses of pain and hard labour, in a progressive world dominated by cyclic chemical processes of growth and decay. Davy, following time spent in Ireland, Italy, Austria, and what is now Slovenia, was unusually sympathetic to the Roman Catholic Church, and rejoiced when Catholics in Britain were emancipated in 1829, just before his death. A religious tone, rather liberal and vague, pervades his book; but he was sceptical of attempts to prove God's existence through science and logic.

Priestley (whose atoms were dynamical, point centres of force) had been a Christian materialist, an unusual and unpopular combination, denying the existence of the soul, seeing matter as active and looking forward to the miraculous Resurrection of the Body at the Day of Judgement. Davy in contrast saw immortal souls imprisoned in an otherwise-inert bodily machine that sooner or later wore out, and moving on to new worlds in the heavens. His brother John, editing his *Works*, added a fragment of manuscript dialogue from among Davy's papers to *Consolations* that he thought Davy meant to put there, advocating atoms like Priestley's: but that context seems very unlikely. Michael Faraday (1791–1867), on the other hand, did publish such a 'speculation' after Davy's death, and went on to develop it into his field theory of electromagnetism (Faraday 1844: 284–93): but though he saw the laboratory as a place of worship, he was careful to keep his literalist Sandemanian faith distinct from his science. Unlike those on astronomy or natural history, most chemistry books of the nineteenth century also contained few references to theology of nature.

There were exceptions. One was the very successful *Chemical Catechism* by the Unitarian manufacturer Samuel Parkes (1761–1825), in which the utility of chemistry was vigorously promoted. The frontispiece in some editions was a curiosity, etched on glass using fluoric acid; the idea of the book was that on first reading, the student just went through the questions and answers (modelled on church catechisms), and subsequently read the notes in smaller type that amplify (and dwarf) the text. Some are encomia on the wisdom and benevolence of God, often in the form of quotations in verse or prose, but Parkes himself wrote about cyclic processes, especially that involving water, as:

> Continual circulations whereby all matter is made to subserve various purposes, which have been devised by the Creator for the promotion of his beneficent purposes. [Parkes 1808: 44]

Elsewhere (450) he wrote about the chemistry of life:

All organized beings, whether vegetable or animal, possess the materials of which they are composed only for a limited time: life itself is a boon which is only *lent,* to serve the purposes of infinite beneficence.

At the back of the book, there are further notes, bringing it up to date; and 255 experiments, some suggested by Davy and involving the newly discovered metal potassium. The book also contains (393) a product placement, recommending Parkes's own Haggerstone Chemical Works for the supply of dyes; and boasts a delightful illustrated title-page where, in what was then a new and hi-tech process, coal gas was being generated and chandeliers lit, all rather dangerously near draped curtains. And the main text ends with a quotation from Paley.

A generation on, the Presbyterian James Johnston (1796–1855) published at the end of his life a popular work, *The Chemistry of Common Life.* It became widely known and admired, both in English and in translation. The chapters cover topics like 'The Water we drink', 'The Bread we eat', 'The Liquors we ferment', and 'The Narcotics we indulge in'. It is pervaded with a theology of nature, though Johnston was very conscious of the insufficiency of natural theology without revelation, which told us more of God's purposes and character than could ever be inferred from chemical (or other scientific) discoveries. His conclusion was at once both effusive and sobering:

The Deity willed that this corner of His vast work should be the theatre of new displays of wisdom, of consummate contrivance, of a wonderful fitting-in of means to the accomplishment of beneficent ends, and at last the seat of an intellectual being, with capacity to study and comprehend and admire His works—to praise, and love, and serve Him. [Johnston 1855: II, 448]

But all this could be stopped by God at any time—and the crowning lesson from science must be the insignificance of human beings in the great scheme of things.

CHEMICAL NATURAL THEOLOGIES

Although it was often thus no more than incidental, by the time Davy died there were a few works starting to come out that were explicitly concerned with chemistry and natural theology. When the Earl of Bridgewater bequeathed £8,000 to the Royal Society to commission works on science as demonstrating the goodness and wisdom of God, the physician and chemist William Prout (1785–1850) took on the last one, a rag-bag of chemistry, meteorology, and the function of digestion (Topham 1998; Prout 1834). This final volume in the series of eight in itself would indicate that chemistry was seen as much less apt than astronomy, geology, or the human hand, each of which got a whole book. Prout, the Royal Society's Copley Medallist of 1827, was well-known for his identification of hydrochloric acid in the stomach juices; and is remembered in the history of chemistry for his hypothesis of 1815, at first anonymous but then acknowledged, that the chemical elements were polymers of hydrogen. This idea (in effect making hydrogen

Boyle's fundamental 'corpuscle') required the atomic weights of the elements, relative to hydrogen, to be whole numbers; and at first analyses by Thomas Thomson and his students in Glasgow seemed to confirm this. But subsequent work showed that they diverged, often not much but sometimes considerably, from integers (Brock 1992: 160–2). Nevertheless, various elements, potassium and sodium for example, were extremely similar to each other; and they also behaved very like the ammonium radical, NH4, known to be compound: it was not implausible that Dalton's many different kinds of atoms were stable configurations of one, or very few, ultimate particles. Prout's Hypothesis, though experimentally falsified, therefore survived to tantalize chemists with a vision of a simpler world—notably Josiah Cooke (1827–94), founder of the chemistry department at Harvard University.

Prout was an admirer of William Paley, whose *Natural Theology* he often quoted or summarized in his own work; and he remarked that:

> The argument from design, assures [man] that, insignificant as he is, while he investigates and approves of the order and harmony around him, he is exerting faculties truly godlike. [Prout 1834: 7]

Our reason differed from God's only in not being infinite. Chemistry, a science founded 'solely on experience', was in Prout's opinion particularly apt for demonstrating design more subtle than mechanical contrivances. Having created the chemist's atoms, polarized 'molecules' that are clearly 'manufactured articles', God had gone on to make a 'harmonious, connected series' of compounds that fuel a cumulative argument for His wisdom and benevolence. Thus water, liquid at just the right range of temperatures for conditions on Earth, illustrates the fine adjustments that prove design, which is even more evident in the complex chemical processes that go on in living 'organised beings'. The way in which the properties of compounds are so different from those of their components is a source of wonder and fascination in what Prout clearly found a delightful science (19, 31, 165, 180, 184). The Bridgewater Treatises were a surprising success from the publishing point of view, and several went through a number of editions; but Prout's was never one of the popular ones.

In 1844 George Fownes (1815–49) published his essay, focussed entirely upon chemistry, which had won the prize of a hundred guineas established at the Royal Institution by Hannah Acton (Fownes 1844). He referred to the small number and useful distribution of elementary substances that constituted all the variety that we see in the world, and to the laws of chemical composition, as pointing to a wise lawgiver. Then the contiguity, for example, of iron ore and vast forests in otherwise-barren parts of Sweden were indicators of a divine plan. The labour required to extract useful materials was not a curse, but a blessing: it went with health and happiness, whereas idleness was the real curse for humanity. Fownes was well-aware of the new developments in chemistry, and his book has 'flow charts' indicating the course of reactions, diagrams indicating the play of affinities, tables, symbols for the elements, and even equations. More important than these then-hypothetical constructions was the dramatic rise of organic chemistry, particularly associated with Liebig and his new methods of analysis. That was Fownes's field of interest and research. Animals and plants had been found to consist almost entirely of carbon, hydrogen, oxygen, and nitrogen, in great series of compounds where they were differently arranged: sometimes indeed the same elements in exactly the same proportions constituted two or more different substances, in the phenomenon of isomerism. At last animal and vegetable chemistry was being understood.

Thus the body was a low-temperature furnace, in which carbon and nitrogen were gently combusted: chemical reactions could evidently go on under very different circumstances, and at different speeds. Chemical equilibria, reversible reactions, and cyclic processes, were hugely important in the processes of nature, and chemists who were beginning to understand them could not but reflect that:

> It is difficult to avoid the conclusion, that these exquisitely beautiful laws and relations have been framed and adjusted to each other by an intelligent mind. [Fownes 1844: 184]

They indicated enlightened, active benevolence. Natural theology was thus for Fownes the ultimate object of science; and chemistry an excellent subject for such religious meditation.

Fownes's textbook published the following year established itself as a classic, in print in revised editions for over forty years; but in that year he was struck down by lung disease, and died in 1849. Similarly, Prout by the time he wrote his *Bridgewater Treatise* was suffering from severe deafness which seriously impaired his social and scientific life. Nevertheless, there seems to be some truth in the idea that dilating upon the wisdom and goodness of God is easiest for those like Paley generally in good health and comfortable circumstances: and Prout and Fownes also did well financially out of it, as some crabby critics noted. There is a facile aspect to what they wrote, as George Wilson (1818–59) pointed out in his writings, interesting and profound reflections upon God and chemistry by a lifelong invalid, who had in 1843 suffered the amputation of his left foot without anaesthetics (for which he subsequently became a fervent advocate). Wilson was in 1855 appointed the first Professor of Technology in the University of Edinburgh, and spent much time explaining what that meant; and he was also director of the museum, which in due course became the Royal Museum of Scotland and preserves elements of his vision. In 1858 he was urged to apply for the better-endowed chair of chemistry, but his failing health made that impossible. After his death his sister Jessie wrote his biography, including his poems and his horrifying subjective account of his amputation; and also edited articles and papers into a volume to which she gave the title *Religio Chemici*. He had intended if spared to write a book with that title, on the model of Sir Thomas Browne's *Religio Medici* (1642–3); what we have instead is a stimulating collection of essays, including brief and perceptive biographies of Boyle, Dalton, and William Hyde Wollaston as well as the religious reflections that would presumably have filled the projected volume. He delighted in the history of science, and had written a full-scale biography of the reclusive Henry Cavendish, as well as a book on colourblindness and its implications for engine drivers and sailors, to which Clerk Maxwell wrote an appendix.

The allegorical title-page shows an angel, the winged Hermes, and chemical apparatus, with a biblical quotation (John, 1:3–4); and the book contains, as well as the biographies, an essay on 'The Chemistry of the Stars' that raises the then-popular topic of extraterrestrial life. William Whewell (against) and David Brewster (for) had turned this into a controversial theme involving questions about creation, evolution, and redemption; Wilson was judicious as usual. Three deal more explicitly with our subject: 'Thoughts on the Resurrection', 'Chemical Final Causes', and 'Chemistry and Natural Theology'. He was a man of firm evangelical faith, with somewhat variable denominational loyalties: initially Baptist, when in England Anglican, and then later Congregational. On the resurrection of the dead, Wilson went for bodily resurrection, from a few of our actual particles, with personal identity conserved. He did not, as he might have done having suffered amputation, ponder at what age and in what state we might be resurrected. On final causes, he looked like Fownes particularly at the components of living organisms: 'no creature is a fortuitous concourse of atoms' (Wilson 1862: 114). There is an endless flux of particles in a stable organism, 'a temple always complete, and yet always under repair' (121) in an amazing concatenation of processes that maintain life. While he declared that we go wrong if we make teleology, the search for final causes, the chief object of scientific inquiry, we cannot seriously doubt that the study of the chemistry of living organisms directs us to God. And thus the contemplation of final causes gives us a foretaste of heaven (164).

Much more original and interesting was his examination of natural theology, which took the form of a kind of essay-review of the books by Prout and Fownes. He began in the traditional manner, in this case looking at the atmosphere, the mix of active oxygen and inert nitrogen being just right for living beings: if the Earth is our mother, the atmosphere could be called our foster-mother. This theme was to be taken up by Cooke, in lectures published in 1864 (Cooke 1864). But then Wilson asked whether we do in fact see unthwarted benevolence. The atmosphere goes also with lung-diseases, and with the miasmas that bring plagues; while other chemical elements and compounds, all too common, go with poisons and death. Prout and Fownes, like other writers on natural theology, have too often ignored 'the *dark* side' (Wilson 1862: 26). They blandly, vaguely and unsatisfactorily allude to the greater good: Men, and women even more, need something better. Women, Wilson noted, scarcely read natural theology, because it was full of 'intricate and unfeminine science' and failed to lift 'the dark veil' (31). They especially could not avoid or turn away from pain, suffering, and death, from disease and bereavement, and from natural disasters that befall humans, and that both now and in the remote past revealed in the fossil record have overtaken animals. Moreover, though we are constantly under repair, we do not remain as good as new: we age, and wonder why. Looking briefly outside chemistry, Wilson noted that carnivores were 'made to destroy': 'God has been very kind to the shark' (43). Agony, pain, and suffering are no '*transient,* incidental, occasional thing', but must be part of our world-view.

Chemistry, he added, cannot weigh pain against happiness in some kind of utilitarian calculation. We may even perhaps be made to wonder whether an evil as well as a good being is at work in the world; but in reality there need be no apprehension of that as a scientific conclusion. But it does all add up to an insoluble problem, an enigma: 'Chemistry can prove that God is light, but not that in him is no darkness at all' (50). The mystery of pain will haunt us through our whole lives; but we can still reasonably hope that while the curtain is indeed thick, the light shines through, and that death will be swallowed up in victory. That is, the promises of revealed religion in the Christian dispensation will console us in a world where benevolence cannot be discerned. We might say that for Wilson the subjective experience of pain, and the miseries he saw around him in the lives of people and animals, revealed the remoteness and thinness of natural theology: the First Cause was not the same as God the Father, who loves and consoles us, and his Son Jesus, the man of sorrows and acquainted with grief.

THE TWENTIETH CENTURY

The Great War (1914–18) was seen as the chemists' war: propellants and high explosives making artillery ever more formidable, poison gases, margarine and other synthetic, ersatz, and inferior products, were its characteristics as bogged-down armies slugged it out. It was hardly possible after that to see chemistry as wholly benign, or pointing directly to God; and its reputation has been equivocal ever since. Earlier than that, by the 1870s there were many formal courses in chemistry, with new textbooks that in the newly secular 'Darwinian' environment made no reference to God; and there was no market any more for popularizations of chemistry in the form of natural theology, though the tradition continued in astronomy and natural history. Moreover, spectroscopy, at first a wonderful analytical tool for discovering new elements, yielded by the end of the century evidence that the chemists' atoms were complex; and by the end of the war, the chemists great taxonomic achievement, the Periodic Table, was being accounted for in terms of the arrangement of protons and electrons. And meanwhile, in the wake of the spectroscope all sorts of other 'physical' instruments were beginning to invade the chemistry laboratory, deskilling those whose instruments of analysis were blowpipes, charcoal blocks, test-tubes, Kipps' apparatus, Bunsen burners, and retorts: the science gradually came to look, feel, and even smell different. Soon elective affinities and chemical bonds were being explained in terms derived from physics. Chemists went on using molecular models made of billiard-balls and wires that go back to the 1860s when they illustrated the latest atomic theory, but their science was no longer seen as fundamental: it had been 'reduced' to physics, and was becoming everybody's service science. The reduction of ores to shining metals is seen as improvement, but the reduction of a science is perceived as downgrading. We might respond that architects and engineers designing buildings and bridges have to conform to the laws of physics, but while their freedom is curtailed by such constraints it would be odd to say that their disciplines were reduced to physics. Structural chemists, making molecules unknown in nature, feel the same: all art is triumph over constraints.

At the end of the twentieth century, a distinguished structural chemist collaborated in a novel kind of natural theology, not based like our other examples on Christianity but on Judaism. In *Old Wine, New Bottles* Roald Hoffmann and Shira Leibowitz Schmidt explore in the form of essays, correspondence, and pictures the relationship of chemistry, the central science, 'the craft, art, business, and finally science of substances and their transformations' to Jewish faith and practice (Hoffmann and Schmidt 1997: 4). They do not try to prove the existence, wisdom, and benevolence of God in the tradition of Prout and Fownes, but to explore religious and scientific findings, fragments of a broken truth, and their connections. Thus they examine how far nature is 'natural' (the natural and the artificial), and look at purity and impurity, at geometry, symmetry, and structures, in a Jewish context of argument, dissent, and struggle to make sense of life. For our times, especially after the chemist's war and the Holocaust, such a tentative linkage through metaphors and practices seems more appropriate as a theology of nature than the kind of legal proof beyond reasonable doubt that Paley and his successors sought to establish by cumulative argument two centuries ago.

CHEMICAL SCIENCES AND NATURAL THEOLOGY?

Alchemists sought to ape and hurry up God's creation, but were concerned about whether artificial gold would be the same as natural gold. Modern chemists too, as they have gone ahead with improving the world through their syntheses of dyes, vitamins, and textiles, have been taxed with producing poor substitutes for the natural and the organic. God's creations are still seen as superior to humans'. Chymists, and notably Boyle, saw in chemistry signs of God's providence, and expected that useful drugs, dyes, and other materials would come from labours in the laboratory. In the age of wonder, Davy presented chemistry as the way to alleviate toil, poverty, and sickness; and sought to refute charges that it was materialistic, supporting vitalism (the idea that living and dead matter obeyed different laws) against what was perceived as the blasphemy of French physiologists. At a time when the word 'creative' was not yet normally applied to humans, Davy saw the chemist exerting:

> On a scale infinitely small a power seeming a sort of shadow or reflection of a creative energy, and which entitles him to the distinction of being made in the image of God and animated by a spark of the divine mind. [Davy 1839–40: IX, 361]

The dream of the God-like chemist led to the career of his fictional disciple, Victor Frankenstein, the victim of his own monster. Davy also saw the attractiveness and inexhaustibility of chemistry at this heroic epoch in its history when it was surging forward in revolutionary vigour, picking up the old metaphor that the greater the circle of light, the greater the circumference of darkness. His vision of mastering nature through chemistry had a macho aspect that has been prominent in science throughout its history; but this did not seem to deter women from coming to his lectures. In the next generation, chemists including Prout and Fownes wrote treatises on natural theology drawing attention to the distribution and small number of elements, the pattern of laws governing their interactions, and the value of chemical remedies to establish God's existence, wisdom, and benevolence beyond reasonable doubt. They met friendly fire from Wilson; and then by the 1870s as chemistry became professional and a secular world view gained strength, their enterprise began to seem absurd: irrelevant to believers, and unconvincing to sceptics. In the twentieth century, chemistry lost its cachet as a fundamental science; but became an increasingly essential part of life in industrial societies, and a science that is still compatible with a theology of nature. We can reasonably expect to see chemists continuing to puzzle out how (or maybe whether) their scientific understanding illuminates their religious and ethical views, perhaps in print as well as in private.

Metaphors from chemistry, impinging on natural theology because they involve materialism or determinism, continue nevertheless to abound; although there has been more and more to learn, the science has not become altogether forbidding, technical, and recondite. Thus it is curious that the ideas behind Goethe's novel continue to resonate. Discussing relationships, people may say that there was no chemistry between us, as though they had no more choice available to them than atoms of copper or chlorine. They may also blame their chemistry for feelings of gloom and inadequacy, or exuberance, attributing depression or elation in a highly simplified way to biochemical imbalance. Less directly exploiting the tension between matter and spirit are metaphors from chemistry that have passed into ordinary usage, or even become clichés. Where would we be without 'catalyst', 'crucible', or 'distillation'? Then there are some chemical terms, like 'flocculant' and 'triturate' that deserve wider currency, and some ordinary words like 'sublime' and 'precipitate' which chemists use in a special sense.

The nature of chemistry has made it a less-obvious science for natural theology like Paley's, but by no means a barren field. The field of 'physico'- and 'astro'-theologies is familiar and widely explored, but to come in through chemistry, taking in some of its promising but unsuccessful developments, like Naturphilosophie and speculations about the unity of matter that did not become the mainstream, could be interesting, revealing distinct intellectual, national, and more local traditions and very varied reasons for pursuing and popularizing the science. After all, it is not obvious why adults should want to spend their lives in curiosity about matter; and natural theology as the search for Design, has long provided an impetus for going into science, giving it a seriousness and importance (going beyond utility) that it might otherwise lack. What might seem to us a thin icing of religion spread upon chemistry, sugar at best to make the medicine go down, was not how it looked to Boyle, sure of the superior excellence of theology, or to Newton. They saw what we call science as the handmaid of religion; and like Faraday later, saw the laboratory as a place of worship. Those concerned with the history, philosophy, and public understanding of chemistry might after all do well to ponder its connection with theologies of nature.

REFERENCES

Brock, W. H. (1992). *The Fontana History of Chemistry*. London: Fontana.

Brooke, J. H. and G. Cantor (1998). *Reconstructing Nature: The Engagement of Science and Religion*. Edinburgh: T. & T. Clark.

Comte, A. (1853). *The Positive Philosophy*. Edited and translated from French by H. Martineau. London: Chapman.

Cooke, J. B. (1864). *Religion and Chemistry, or Proofs of God's Plan in the Atmosphere and its Elements*. New York: Scribner's.

Davy, H. (1839–40). *Collected Works*. Edited by J. Davy. London: Smith, Elder.

Debus, A. (2001). *Chemistry and Medical Debate: van Helmont to Paracelsus*. Nantucket MA: Science History Publications.

—— (2006). *The Chemical Promise: Experiment and Mysticism in the Chemical Philosophy 1550–1800. Selected Essays*. Sagamore Beach MA: Science History Publications.

Faraday, M. (1829). *Chemical Manipulation*. 3rd edn. London: Murray.

—— (1844). *Experimental Researches in Electricity*. Vol. II. London: Taylor.

Fownes, G. (1844). *Chemistry, as Exemplifying the Wisdom and Beneficence of God*. London: Churchill.

Goethe, J. W. (1971 [1809]). *Elective Affinities*. Translated from German by R. J. Hollingdale. London: Penguin.

Herbert, George (1967). *A Choice of George Herbert's Verse*. Edited by R. S. Thomas. London: Faber.

Hoffmann, R. and S. L. Schmidt. (1997). *Old Wine, New Flasks: Reflections on Science and the Jewish Tradition*. New York: Freeman.

Hunter, M., ed. (2003). *Robert Boyle Reconsidered*. 2nd edn. Cambridge: Cambridge University Press.

—— (2009). *Boyle: Between God and Science*. New Haven: Yale University Press.

Johnston, J. F. W. (1855). *The Chemistry of Common Life*. Edinburgh: Blackwood.

Knight, D. M. (1998). *Humphry Davy: Science and Power*. 2nd edn. Cambridge: Cambridge University Press.

Liebig, J. (1851). *Familiar Letters on Chemistry*. 3rd edn. London: Taylor, Walton & Moberly.

Newton, I. (1952 [1730]). *Opticks*. New York: Dover.

—— (1958). *Isaac Newton's Papers and Letters on Natural Philosophy*. Edited by I. B. Cohen. Cambridge: Cambridge University Press.

Parkes, S. (1808). *The Chemical Catechism with Notes, Illustrations and Experiments*. 3rd edn. London: Lackington Allen.

Priestley, J. (1966 [1775]). *The History and Present State of Electricity*. New York: Johnson.

Prout, W. (1834). *Chemistry, Meteorology, and the Function of Digestion, considered with Reference to Natural Theology*. London: Pickering.

Shelley, M. (1999 [1818]). *Frankenstein: or, the Modern Prometheus*. Edited by D. L. Macdonald and K. Scherf. 2nd edn. Peterborough, Ontario: Broadview.

Topham, J. R. (1998). 'Beyond the Common Context: The Production and Reading of the Bridgewater Treatises'. *Isis* 89: 233–62.

Wilson, G. (1862). *Religio Chemici: Essays*. Edited by J. Wilson. London: Macmillan.

CHAPTER 28

··

MATHEMATICS AND
NATURAL THEOLOGY

··

JOHN POLKINGHORNE

NATURAL theology is the attempt to learn something about God from a consideration of the general character of knowledge and experience. It seems clear that the insights of the physical and biological sciences may be expected to make an influential contribution to this endeavour, since they represent important sectors of human exploration of the way things actually are. The discerned deep order of the physical universe, and the observed rich fertility of the living world, are aspects of reality that will surely have to be taken into account and evaluated in a discussion of natural theology. But what could be the role of mathematics in relation to natural theology? Is not that subject too abstract to be part of an attempted correlation of the nature of the world with a claim for the existence of God as its creator? Certainly the contribution that mathematics might make to natural theology may be expected to be more modest and oblique than that which comes from the experimental sciences. Rather than presenting a range of specific observational results, offered for assessment in the light of theological insight and with a view to influencing theological understanding, the role of mathematics may be expected to take the form of an influence on the general tone of discourse concerning the scope and nature of reality. The point being made can be illustrated by passing directly to the fundamental issue of the status of mathematics itself. Is it just a form of mental gymnastics in which the adepts exhibit their intellectual skill by solving fiendishly puzzling problems of their own devising? Or is mathematics something much deeper than that, the exploration of a noetic realm of reality, existing independently of human contrivance? Mathematicians have certainly emerged in the course of hominid evolution, but what about mathematics itself? Was it not always 'there', long before there were any hominids, or even life itself? How we answer these questions will constrain the character of our metaphysical convictions, which in turn will constrain the scope of possible theological belief that we are inclined to entertain.

MATHEMATICAL REALITY

Many mathematicians are convinced that their discipline is more than a form of sophisticated intellectual play. It is an activity that is very much more serious than that. In their view, mathematics is discovered and not simply invented. This testimony needs to be accorded serious respect, arising as it does from lifelong engagement with the subject. Players often know more about the game than the spectators can be aware of, and this is especially liable to be true of a highly technical activity like mathematics. The distinguished mathematical analyst, G. H. Hardy—who certainly cannot be suspected of having had a hidden religious agenda in his thinking—wrote:

> I will state my own position dogmatically... I believe that mathematical reality lies outside us, that our function is to discover and observe it, and that the theorems that we prove, and which we describe grandiloquently as our 'creations', are simply our notes of our observations. [Hardy 1967: 123–4]

Roger Penrose (1989: 95) refers to the Mandelbrot set, a mathematical entity whose character of rich and endlessly proliferating complexity arises from a deceptively simple-seeming definition, by saying that 'Like Everest, the Mandelbrot set is just *there*'. It did not come into being when Benoit Mandelbrot first began to work with that definition, but it was already there, waiting to be discovered. This leads Penrose to say later, 'There is something absolute and "God given" about mathematical truth' (112).

Of course this almost Platonic concept of the nature of mathematics is not without its deniers also. A good opportunity for exploring the issues raised is presented by an extended conversation between two distinguished French savants, Jean-Pierre Changeux, a molecular neurobiologist and a resolute materialist, and Alain Connes, a mathematician who is a firm believer in mathematical realism (Changeux and Connes 1995). For Changeux the only reality is the physical, understood in a strongly reductionist sense, and so he asserts that the existence of mathematical ideas is 'in the neurons and synapses of the mathematician who produces them' (12). For him, all thought, including mathematical thinking, is simply an epiphenomenon of the material.

Connes utterly rejects this reductionist view. He even claims to find in the world of mathematics 'a more stable reality than the material reality that surrounds us' (12). His defence of his position rests on three principal lines of argument. The first is that our mathematical experience displays a consistency of perception and mutual coherence of account to a degree that is at least as impressive as that which characterizes our interaction with the physical world:

> What proves [in fact, too strong a word; 'motivates belief in' would be better] the reality of the natural world, apart from our brain's perception of it? Chiefly the coherence of our perceptions and their permanence... And so it is with mathematical reality: a calculation carried out in several different ways gives the same result whether it is done by one person or several. [22]

The second argument appeals to the great richness of what is encountered, seeing this as a sign that one is in touch with an independent reality. At the beginning of the twentieth century, there was a movement, inspired by the great German mathematician David Hilbert and most powerfully articulated in the *Principia Mathematica* by Bertrand Russell and Alfred North Whitehead, to reduce mathematics to the outworking of logic. Had this succeeded, it would have seemed to imply that mathematics was no more than a monstrous collection of tautologies. However this logical programme received a death blow from Kurt Gödel's discovery of his incompleteness theorem. This showed that an axiomatized system sufficiently complex to include the integers (a modest requirement) was either inconsistent or incomplete, the latter meaning that it contained true propositions which nevertheless could not be proved within the confines of the system. This astonishing discovery had two extremely significant implications. First, it showed that a mathematical system cannot establish its own consistency. While not many people will worry about the consistency of arithmetic, belief in that consistency requires something like an act of faith on the part of the mathematician. Secondly, given that commitment of belief, there will still be truths in arithmetic that cannot be proved from its basic axioms. In other words, even in mathematics truth exceeds what one might call theoremhood. There is an inexhaustible richness present in mathematical reality.

The way in which an apparently unending depth of rational structure and relationship is revealed through the physicists' investigation of level after level of the physical world, is often taken to constitute a powerful argument in persuading us that they are indeed exploring an independent realm of physical reality. In an analogous way, Connes invokes Goedel's theorem in defence of mathematical reality. He says that the inexhaustible character of mathematical systems that is implied by the incompleteness theorem means, for example, that 'the quantity of information contained in the set of all true propositions about the positive integers is infinite', going on to say 'I ask you: isn't *that* the distinguishing feature of a reality independent of all human creation?' (160).

A third line of argument also draws on an analogy with the physical sciences. A persuasive support for realist beliefs in physics derives from the way in which the physical world is frequently found to resist our prior expectation, surprising us by the unexpected character that it displays and forcing on the physicist previously unfamiliar ways of thinking. This stubborn idiosyncrasy encourages the belief that we are encountering a reality independent of us. The paradigm example of this behaviour is quantum theory, with its many counterintuitive properties, such as wave–particle duality. A comparable measure of surprise also occurs in mathematical discovery. Connes's favourite example is drawn from the area of mathematics called group theory (see du Sautoy 2008). Its concern is with the mathematical expression of symmetry properties. A particular part of the theory relates to what are called finite simple groups and the aim is to give a complete account of what their character might be. Almost all finite simple groups fall into certain large generic classes whose nature is readily understandable. However, there are also just twenty-six 'sporadic' groups which defy incorporation in this neat classification scheme and whose existence is odd and surprising. An example of mathematical surprise that may be more accessible to the general reader is the Mandelbrot set, whose infinitely proliferating complexity has been made familiar by its appearance in many psychedelic posters. Yet the set derives from a comparatively simple definition that can be written down in just a few lines.

Two further considerations can be advanced in support of belief in mathematical realism. Despite its apparently austerely logical character, there is a role in creative mathematical thinking for intuitive perception and even unconscious activity. Something is happening which is much more profound than the somewhat banal idea of relentless computation. There are well-documented cases in which, after a long but fruitless conscious engagement with a problem has failed to yield a solution, a period of fallow disengagement may be followed by a moment of sudden illumination in which the answer emerges fully fledged, with only some technical labour needed to complete its details. A celebrated example involves the famous nineteenth-century mathematician, Henri Poincaré. He made no progress with a deep problem that had engaged him and eventually he decided to take a rest from struggling with it. As he was about to step onto a bus to take him away for a while, the complete solution came into his mind unbidden. So sure was he of the validity of his idea that he continued his journey, content to postpone the task of mopping up the technical details until he returned. A further example of the power of intuition in mathematics, even more striking in its nature because of its sustained character, is afforded by Hardy's Indian colleague, Srinivasan Ramanujan. This self-taught genius displayed an astonishing ability to write down profound theorems in number theory which he discovered by the exercise of a tacit intuitive skill, rather than by explicit rational argument. These examples seem most readily intelligible as manifestations of an ability to gain direct access to an existing noetic world, rather than as fortuitous freaks of neural organization.

The final argument to be presented in defence of mathematical realism relates to the evolution of human mathematical ability. One can see that in terms of survival capacity it would be an advantage for hominid brains to have been shaped by evolutionary process so as to gain access to simple arithmetic and simple geometrical ideas. Yet whence has come the human ability to study non-commutative algebras and to prove Fermat's last theorem? These powers surely greatly exceed anything needed for survival advantage, or anything that could plausibly be supposed to be a happy spin-off from such a necessity. In evolutionary explanation it is as vital to have an adequate understanding of the environmental context as it is to get the genetic factors right. I have suggested that pure Darwinian thinking, based on a purely physico-biological account of context, is inadequate to explain the development of sophisticated human mathematical abilities (Polkinghorne 2005: Ch. 3). However, if there is indeed a noetic realm of mathematical truth, it has always been there and it formed part a part of the context of hominid evolution within which mathematical ability would eventually emerge. Survival necessity no doubt led to the initial development of a brain structure capable of access to limited arithmetical and geometrical thinking, but once this modest degree of contact with mathematical reality had been established, new factors would have come into play. Intellectual satisfaction and delight would then have drawn our ancestors into further exploration of that noetic world. The epigenetic plasticity of the human brain, much of whose structure derives from response to experience rather than being genetically predetermined, together with the Lamarckian process of cultural transmission from one generation to the next, would have fostered the growth of human mathematical powers. Belief in the reality of mathematics makes intelligible the human ability to be mathematicians, a capacity which otherwise would seem inexplicably gratuitous.

The insights just rehearsed offer powerful support for a belief in mathematical reality. However, such arguments can never have a force that amounts to being logically coercive, as if only a fool could disagree. (Naturally, the same is true of the contrary belief.) Metaphysical convictions about the nature of reality can be well-motivated, but they will always ultimately require also an act of metaphysical decision and commitment. This is, of course, true for all world-views. Changeux says that he adopts 'a naturalist position that makes no reference whatsoever to metaphysical assumptions' (Changeux and Connes 1995: 213). How hard it is to see ourselves as others see us! His assertion of materialism is a metaphysical assumption as much as any other position. It certainly does not derive from science alone. The test of a metaphysical belief is surely the economy and naturalness with which it can accommodate and make intelligible the widest possible range of experience. The case for mathematical realism can make a strong claim to fulfil this criterion.

NATURAL THEOLOGY

What significance could this understanding of mathematics be thought to have for theology? It has already been acknowledged that the connection must be expected to be oblique rather than direct. A connection may be found in the encouragement that mathematical realism gives to the scientist, as well as to others, to countenance the existence of a non-physical dimension of reality. The possibility—one might claim the great likelihood—of a metaphysics with categories beyond the energetic and material is brought onto the agenda. A significant breach is made in the defences of an assertive physicalist reductionism, an opening made through appeal to experience of a kind that, in particular, is familiar to many scientists. Even staunch physicalists can feel uneasy about this. The philosopher Willard van Orman Quine took a resolutely naturalistic view of reality, but he was moved to declare that his ontology was 'materialism, bluntly monistic except for the abstract objects of mathematics' (Quine 1995: 14), although he declined to elaborate the nature of the exception that he admitted in relation to the character of mathematical reality. Many theists have maintained that mathematical entities, together with aesthetic and ethical ideals, exist in the Mind of God.

The existence of an independent noetic realm of mathematics should indeed encourage an openness to the possibility of further metaphysical riches to be explored. Engagement with mathematics is only a part of our mental experience. In itself it can give no more than a hint of what might be meant by the spiritual. The realm of the divine is yet more distant still, but just as arithmetic may have led our ancestors to begin an exploration that would eventually lead them into the riches of higher mathematics, so taking mathematical reality seriously might be the start of a journey that will lead to greater discoveries about the scope and nature of reality. In this way, mathematics has a modest preparatory part to play in the approach to natural theology.

'Unreasonable Effectiveness'

There is a further way in which mathematics may contribute to natural theology through the manner in which it plays a role as a component in a more complex form of encounter with reality. If the world is indeed multilayered in its character, while yet being fundamentally a unified reality, then its different levels can be expected to have a degree of interconnection and mutual entanglement. Human nature itself could be taken as an illustration of the point. A philosophy of dual-aspect monism sees the human encounter with reality as manifesting both mental and material characteristics present in our experience, while at the same time human beings are understood to constitute integrated unities (see Nagel 1986). On this view, the mental and the material are intimately related as complementary aspects of a single reality. The noetic realm of mathematics should not be thought of simply as an isolated domain, but it may be expected to have subtle connections with other dimensions of the real. Just such a connection is found to be the case in the role that mathematics plays in thinking about the structure of the physical world. At the beginning of modern science, Galileo had already asserted that the Book of Nature was written in the language of mathematics. It was a prophetic utterance on his part.

Time and again it has proved to be a fertile technique of discovery in fundamental physics to seek theories that are formulated in terms of equations possessing the unmistakable character of mathematical beauty. This beauty is a rather rarefied form of aesthetic experience and, like most forms of beauty, it is easier to perceive than to describe. Nevertheless, it is a property whose presence the mathematicians are able recognize and, significantly, to agree about. Involved are qualities such as elegance and economy and the property of being 'deep', that is to say when extensive and surprisingly fruitful consequences are found to flow from an apparently simple starting point (think again of the Mandelbrot set). The physicists' quest for mathematical beauty is no mere aesthetic indulgence on their part, but a heuristic strategy that time and again has proved its worth in the four-century history of modern theoretical physics. It has turned out that it is just such beautiful equations that have also been the ones that manifested the long-term fertility of explanation that persuades us that they really do represent an aspect of physical reality. The greatest British theoretical physicist of the twentieth century, Paul Dirac, made his remarkable discoveries by a life-long and relentless quest for mathematical beauty. His most famous achievement was writing down the relativistic equation of the electron, which he discovered simply through seeking an elegant way in which to combine quantum theory and relativity. Immediately Dirac found that his equation unexpectedly implied a strange feature of the electron's magnetic properties, already known but not hitherto explained. Two years later, the same equation led him to predict the existence of antimatter. Such remarkable fertility was strongly persuasive that contact had been made with a new element in physical reality, and mathematics had provided the gateway.

Dirac once said that it is more important to have beauty in your equations than to have them fit experiment! Of course he did not mean that empirical adequacy was ultimately dispensable. No physicist could think that. If you had solved the equations of your new theory and found that the answers did not appear to agree with experiment, that was undoubtedly a setback. However, it was not necessarily absolutely fatal. No doubt you had had to have recourse to some approximation scheme in getting your answer and maybe you had just made an inappropriate approximation. Or maybe the experiments were wrong—we have known that happen more than once in physics. So there could still be at least a residual degree of hope. But if your equations were ugly... there was no hope. The whole history of physics testified against them.

Dirac had a brother-in-law, Eugene Wigner, who also won a Nobel Prize for physics. He once called this remarkable ability of the abstract subject of mathematics to unlock the secrets of the physical universe 'the unreasonable effectiveness of mathematics'. Why are some of the most beautiful patterns discovered by the mathematicians in their studies, actually found to occur in the structure of the world around us? What links together the reason within (the mathematical thoughts of our minds) to the reason without (the order of the universe)? Wigner said that this was a gift that we neither deserved nor understood.

Physicists are happy to exploit the wonderful opportunities that this gift confers, whether they deserve it or not, but simply as scientists they are not able to understand its origin. Yet it would surely be intolerably intellectually lazy just to treat the unreasonable effectiveness of mathematics as simply a fortunate brute fact—a bit of good luck for those who are good at maths. The instinct of the scientist is to seek understanding as completely as possible. Yet if science's success in the quest for intelligibility is itself to be made intelligible, that will necessarily take us outside the narrow self-defined confines of unaided science, for which questions of the origin and nature of values, such as mathematical beauty, are bracketed out. The role of mathematics in physics could be summarized as the discovery that the structure of the physical world, in its rational transparency and beauty, is shot through with signs of mind. The natural theologian can respond that this is the case because the mind of the creator is reflected in the character of creation. The reason within and the reason without fit together because they have a common origin in the rationality of God. Science is possible in the deep way that it is because the universe is a creation and scientists, to use a powerful and ancient phrase, are creatures made in the image of their creator.

There is a kind of cosmic religiosity, often tacit rather than explicit, that is quite natural to those who work in fundamental physics. It is reflected, I believe, in the way that physicists often use 'mind of God' language when they write for the general reader (for example, Hawking 1988; God is in the text but not in the index). Of course, at best this line of thought can lead to no more than a conception of deity as the Cosmic Mathematician. This limitation is characteristic in varying degrees of all discourse in natural theology. Appeal to limited forms of experience can only yield a limited degree of insight.

ORDER AND DISORDER

One further matter requires our attention. It relates to a theology of nature rather than natural theology itself. That is to say, its concern is not to argue from nature to God but to reflect on the character of nature understood in the light of the belief that it is a divine creation. The world as we discern it appears to be characterized both by the presence of order and by the presence of sheer contingency. The understanding of the evolutionary process as an interplay between chance and necessity would be a striking example of this mixed character. The word 'chance' is a slippery one, for it might carry a number of different meanings: an epistemic uncertainty due to ignorance of determining fine detail (as in the toss of a coin), or simply accident (the coincidence of apparently uncorrelated trains of events), or an ontologically intrinsic uncertainty (as most physicists believe to be the case in quantum events such as radioactive decay). It is quite often claimed that the role of contingency in evolutionary process subverts the theological claim of a divine purpose at work in the history of the world.

These issues have been carefully and helpfully explored in a theologically aware discussion by the statistician, David Bartholomew (1984, 2008). His arguments are illustrated by many examples drawn from the natural and the social sciences. Our concern here can only be with the common mathematical insights that underlie the analysis of particular examples. Two points arise, which need to be emphasized, concerning which any theological discussion of the matter needs to be aware.

The first fundamental point is that order and disorder may interlace and the character of what is discerned will depend upon the level of complexity at which the system is sampled. The toss of a single coin seems purely random, with a fifty-fifty chance of obtaining either heads or tails. Yet, if 1,000 tosses are made in sequence, then the number that are heads will be reliably close to 500. Chance fluctuations often tend to cancel out in an aggregation of individual events. To take another example, the heights present in an adult population will appear to vary randomly between individuals, but if the population as a whole is considered the distribution of heights will be found to fall on the familiar bell curve of a Gaussian distribution. These simple examples illustrate the fact that disorder at one level may generate reliable order at a higher level. The statistical laws of physics make the same point. The most celebrated example is the second law of thermodynamics, which states that entropy (the measure of disorder) will not decrease in an isolated system. This is due the fact that there are overwhelmingly more ways of being disorderly than there are of being orderly, so that in the end disorder always wins. Yet, the second law is statistical in character and not absolute. The spontaneous regeneration of order is not absolutely ruled out, but it is almost infinitely unlikely.

Equally, it is possible for order to give rise to apparent disorder. The paradigm example here is provided by chaos theory (see Gleick 1988). Simple and perfectly deterministic non-linear equations are found in certain well-defined circumstances to yield solutions that are so exquisitely sensitive to the finest detail of their defining initial conditions that the future behaviour implied by them is effectively unpredictable. The sensitivity of the discussion is further illustrated by the fact that in the case of dissipative chaotic systems their future behaviour is not completely random, but there is a subtle order contained within the apparent disorder, for the actual solutions are in fact confined to a complexly structured range of possibility, called a strange attractor.

The interweaving of order and disorder has an interesting connection with the fundamental scientific insight that the regimes in which genuinely novel structures can emerge are always found to be 'at the edge of chaos'. If things were too orderly, they would be too rigid for more than a shuffling of already existent elements to be possible; if they were too disorderly, things would be too haphazard for any novelty that emerged to persist. Just the right mixture of regularity and contingency, order and disorder, is necessary for the generation of the truly new.

The second point that needs to be made is that it is perfectly possible for random processes to lead eventually to determinate consequences, either uniquely specified or restricted to be contained within a narrow range of possibility. Bartholomew (1984: 81) illustrates the point by a simple mathematical game. Ten digits lying between 1 and 10 are randomly selected and the total number found to lie between 1 and 5 is called the current score. The process is then repeated and a new current score is defined as the number of digits that lie between 1 and the old current score. This process is then repeated as often as desired. Although each stage is perfectly random, it is easy to see that the series must eventually converge either to 0 or to 10. Whichever score is realized then becomes the stable outcome of any further repetitions. This model may, perhaps, strike one as a rather artificial example, but it provides a simple illustration of a more general mathematical insight. Despite the randomness of the process, it does not lead to an arbitrary end result, simply lying somewhere in an apparently unrestricted 'possibility space' (any number from 0 to 10), or to convergence on the mean possibility (5). Instead it is certain to lead to one of two specific end points, which a mathematician would call 'attractors'. Which of these is actually reached on a given occasion is not predictable beforehand, for it is 'path dependent', that is to say it depends on the details of the sequence of random processes leading to it. There is, therefore, both an ultimate ordered convergence and a degree of contingency in this randomly generated process.

More detailed exploration of these ideas would require further specification and analysis of the models to which the mathematics was being applied, but enough has been said to make the point that mathematical insight does not at all encourage a simplistic equation of contingency and meaninglessness, as if asserting a role for chance carries a necessary implication of complete and arbitrary purposelessness. Evolutionary exploration neither necessarily implies a kind of random walk through unlimited possibilities, with a completely arbitrary outcome, nor convergence on a totally foreseeable result.

Instead, there can be openness to a limited portfolio of possible final results. Bartholomew (2008: 3) summarizes his theological conclusion by saying that 'chance must be seen as lying *within* the providence of God and not outside it'.

REFERENCES

Bartholomew, D. (1984). *God of Chance*. London: SCM Press.
—— (2008). *God, Chance and Purpose*. Cambridge: Cambridge University Press.
Changeux, J.-P. and A. Connes (1995). *Conversations on Mind, Matter and Mathematics*. Princeton: Princeton University Press.
Gleick, J. (1988). *Chaos*. London: Heinemann.
Hardy, G. H. (1967). *A Mathematician's Apology*. Cambridge: Cambridge University Press.
Hawking, S. H. (1988). *A Brief History of Time*. London: Bantam.
Nagel, T. (1986). *The View from Nowhere*. Oxford: Oxford University Press.
Penrose, R. (1989). *The Emperor's New Mind*. Oxford: Oxford University Press.
Polkinghorne, J. C. (2005). *Exploring Reality*. London: SPCK.
Quine, W. V. O. (1995). *From Stimulus to Science*. Cambridge, MA: Harvard University Press.
Sautoy, M. du (2008). *Finding Moonshine*. London: Fourth Estate.

CHAPTER 29

NATURAL THEOLOGY AND ECOLOGY

CHRISTOPHER SOUTHGATE

INTRODUCTION

ECOLOGY may be understood as the study of the dynamics of the network of relationships by which a diversity of biological organisms is enabled to coexist in any given environment. It therefore involves the insights of Darwinian schemes of evolution by natural selection, but with a particular emphasis on the evolution of mechanisms of cooperation and symbiosis between organisms.

I shall accept, for the purposes of this chapter, the telling criticisms offered by David Hume against versions of natural theology that seek to argue simply from the character of the natural world to the existence and character of God the creator. Hume was right to point to the difficulty in arguing conclusively from nature, with all its apparent imperfection and suffering, to a single benevolent and omnipotent creator (for a recent summary and evaluation of Hume see Sennett and Groothuis 2005: 21–104). The form of natural theology pursued here will be the more modest one of beginning with a conviction as to the existence and character of the God revealed in the Christian Scriptures and understood within the Christian tradition, and then asking what further might be understood of the ways of that God within the world on the basis of the contemplation of creatures, and the systems within which they live. This goes rather beyond Alister McGrath's perspective when he writes: 'natural theology is better to be understood as a demonstration, from the standpoint of faith, of the consonance between that faith and the structures of the world...The search for order in nature is therefore not intended to demonstrate that God exists, but to reinforce the plausibility of an already existing belief' (McGrath 2001: 266–7). My own approach is more exploratory, less apologetic in emphasis, more in tune with this from John Macquarrie, citing John Wisdom:

> The theist goes over the details of his world, tracing and emphasizing patterns and connections that support his conviction, and presumably also trying to explain the

gaps and recalcitrant facts that count against his belief. The very conviction from which he begins perhaps causes him to notice connections that would not otherwise have been noted, or to be painfully aware at other points of a seeming lack of connections. In the long run, the picture must be acknowledged to be ambiguous, in the sense that no finally conclusive proof in support of his conviction can be offered by the theist, or, for that matter, by the atheist who has been calling attention to other elements in the picture. [Macquarrie 1977: 55. For an analysis of Macquarrie on natural theology see Morley 2003]

THE IMPACT OF DARWINISM

It is noteworthy that the now so-familiar term 'ecology', with all its connotations of the natural world as an *oikoumene* consisting of a whole series of interdependent relationships which allow a great diversity of creatures to survive, was coined by Ernst Haeckel as late as 1866. But the huge and decisive development in our understanding of the biological world was that engendered by Darwin's understanding of evolution by natural selection, which emerged seven years earlier with the publication of *The Origin of Species* (Darwin 1859). Darwin's closing image of the 'tangled bank' and of the niches that creatures can explore, in almost every case made possible in their turn by the activities of other creatures, reinforces both the sense of this intricate interrelationship, and also the incessant competition for resources and reproductive opportunities that drives the evolutionary process (489–90). Darwin himself was aware of the two types of natural theology that could be done from this picture. He wrote:

  (i) 'what a book a devil's chaplain might write on the clumsy, wasteful, blundering, low and horridly cruel works of nature' (Darwin 1856)

but also, in concluding the 'tangled bank' paragraph:

  (ii) 'Thus, from the war of nature, from famine and death, the most exalted object which we are capable of conceiving, namely, the production of the higher animals, directly follows. There is grandeur in this view of life, with its several powers, having been originally breathed into a few forms or into one; and that, whilst this planet has gone cycling on according to the fixed law of gravity, from so simple a beginning endless forms most beautiful and most wonderful have been, and are being, evolved' (Darwin 1859: 490).

The distinguished American environmental philosopher and theologian Holmes Rolston III confirms this ambiguous verdict on the creation, writing of it as:

  random, contingent, blind, disastrous, wasteful, indifferent, selfish, cruel, clumsy, ugly, full of suffering, and, ultimately, death [but also] orderly, prolific, efficient, selecting for adaptive fit, exuberant, complex, diverse, regenerating life generation after generation. [Rolston 1994a: 213]

I will return to Rolston's approach below.

There are, then, grave problems in simply making inferences of type (ii)—that the biosphere reflects the work of a God of a grand design, which through the operation of laws gives rise to 'endless forms most beautiful', in the light of the data of type (i). Hume already knew of the apparent imperfection of creation. Darwin's work allows us to go beyond Hume by understanding:

1. the intrinsic connection between the competition between creatures and the refinement of their characteristics (cf. Rolston 1992). *The same process*—evolution by natural selection—engenders both. It is *through* 'war' and 'famine and death' that the 'grandeur' emerges. Therefore, inferences to the ingenuity of a creator God cannot ignore that God's involvement in creaturely suffering.

2. that cooperation in nature can be, indeed would be expected to be, self-interested. Indeed what might at first appear altruistic can often be explained in terms of evolutionary advantage to that individual or lineage. So very intricate networks of cooperative behaviour are perfectly compatible with a strongly Darwinian reading of the world. Therefore, observation of the extent of cooperation in the biosphere cannot be attributed to the loving design of the creator without reference to competition between creatures.

3. that *imperfections* in biological forms are to be expected—if their evolution is driven by the operation of natural selection on spontaneous variation, then it will be contingent on its particular history—it may contain 'frozen accidents', parasitic symbionts, even 'junk' that selection pressure has not been sufficient to remove. Incidentally, the proposals in intelligent design offered by for instance Michael Behe, in which the evolutionary process is periodically supplemented by special divine action to insert irreducibly complex modules of biological machinery (Behe 1996), seem to vitiate the force of natural-theological inferences of type (ii), by making the 'laws' incompetent to give rise to all that makes biological organisms work, while intensifying the problems posed by inferences of type (i).

In recent work I have striven to show that inferences of type (ii) cannot by themselves wholly counter the problems for the Christian theologian raised by inferences of type (i). In other words, the overall beauty and fecundity of the 'package deal' of nature is not adequate to address the problem of the suffering of the individual creature. The problem is well illustrated by an example used by Rolston, that of the second, 'insurance' chick hatched by the white pelican. Typically this chick is displaced from the nest by its elder sibling, and then ignored by the parent birds. It has only a 10 per cent chance of fledging (Rolston 2006: 137–9). For most such chicks, then, life consists of nothing but suffering. I have argued that if God is to be conceived of as having love and care for the individual creature, as opposed to just making consequentialist calculations about the overall system, then to understand the ways of God with such a world means positing that God must suffer with all creaturely suffering, and indeed supposing the existence of some sort of 'pelican heaven' (Southgate 2008: 78–91; cf. McDaniel 1989).

Possibilities for a Natural Theology of the Biosphere

David Fergusson has recently proposed five varieties of natural theology that might be attempted:

1. a strong deist conviction that natural theology is a more reliable and less parochial form of knowledge than revealed religion;
2. a necessary preliminary (establishing, for example, the existence of a deity) on which the claims of revealed religion can be founded;
3. the conviction (following Aquinas) that truths known through Scripture can also be reached by reason;
4. natural theology as apologetic against certain forms of anti-Christian position—Fergusson calls this 'defeating the defeaters', and gives as example the refuting of the deniers of free will;
5. an acknowledgement that the claims of revelation can coexist with the claims of other disciplines. (Fergusson 2006)

The profound (and much under-explored) problem of non-human creaturely suffering in evolution suggests a very cautious approach, one that concentrates on point number 5 rather than attempting 4, let alone 1–3. The profound ambiguity of biological systems, as reflected in the quotations from Darwin and Rolston above, does not easily suggest an inference to a loving creator God. Nor does theological reflection on evolutionary biology offer opportunities to knock down such 'defeaters' as Richard Dawkins—rather it is inclined to agree with Dawkins when he writes that 'if there is no other generalization that can be made about life all around the Universe, I am betting that it will always be recognizable as Darwinian life' (Dawkins 1995: 133). Within the territory of option 5, however, are interesting methodological questions about how 'coexistence' between theology and the sciences is to be managed, as I show below.

I now turn to the work of three authors who in their recent work, and in contrasting ways, have wrestled honestly with the difficulty of doing this type of theology, in which the claims of biological and ecological science are brought into conversation with the Christian revelation.

My first source is Neil Messer, who in his *Selfish Genes and Christian Ethics* (2007), and his contribution to the important collection *Theology after Darwin* (2009), attempts to reconcile the theology of creation with the extent of natural evil I have noted above. The hermeneutical 'lens' from which Messer approaches the natural world is that of the 'peaceable kingdom' in the vision of Isaiah 11:6–9 (cf. also Isaiah 65:25). His eschatology therefore controls his contemplation of the natural world. And as he admits: 'Only revelation can tell us about the peace of creation and final fulfilment; evolutionary biology certainly cannot' (Messer 2009: 148). So the narratives of theology and the sciences are forced apart. This leads to his making what to my mind is an immensely problematic move in terms of natural theology mode 5. Messer endeavours to dissect out, theologically, elements of the scientific picture that he concedes are not scientifically separable (Messer 2009: 149). He imposes, on the grounds that the peaceable kingdom is what God desires, a dualism in which the disvalues of 'scarcity, competition and violence' in biological systems stem not from the divine creative process but from the malign influence of what Karl Barth called *Das Nichtige*, the nothingness that constantly threatens creation (Messer 2009: 148–51). This is, to say the least, difficult—it seems to imply, for example, that God would have liked to create straw-eating lions but was unable to do so (see Southgate 2010).

The enterprise of natural theology in mode 5 has to work through the cautious and critical appropriation of all that is most robust in our understandings of the world, especially those of the natural sciences, bringing it into juxtaposition with Christian theology in ways that respect the integrity of both narratives. Messer himself has contrasted approaches in which the 'shape of the account' is determined by science, as in (he claims) the work of Arthur Peacocke, with approaches in which the shape is determined by Christian doctrine (Messer 2007: 49–62). However, much depends on which doctrine is allowed what shaping influence. Messer privileges the doctrine of the goodness of God, as understood through a vision of God's ultimate redeeming transformation of creatures, over concern for God's sovereignty in creation.

It is, necessarily, the theology of *creation* that has to be held in particularly attentive register with scientific accounts of the cosmos, and other forms of contemplation of its current state. The theology of redemption, central though it is to the Christian confession, rests on a prolepsis, a now-but-not-yet, for which—as Messer and I would agree—science offers no parallels. Likewise Christian eschatology involves a profound measure of discontinuity with the present era, as well as a measure of continuity (Polkinghorne 2002). Its potential to inform natural theology will therefore be limited. Put another way, the great strength of natural theology is that it engages fully with the world as it is, and all that every type of human wisdom can tell of it—its great limitation is that it of necessity finds it hard to speak of the world as God will transform it. Indeed the eschatological vision of Christianity is greatly at variance with the predictions of cosmology in particular (see Russell 2008).

Messer's approach, which involves both prioritizing the Christian doctrine of redemption over that of creation, and over the coherence of the scientific narrative, and adopting a hermeneutical lens derived from eschatology, therefore places him, in my view, at the very edge of what natural theology might attempt. For these reasons it is not surprising that Barth, a thinker notorious for his rejection of natural theology, is Messer's chosen doctrinal ally, and that his reading of Barth leads him eventually to dissect out the scientific narrative in the way I indicate above. To my mind, fruitful theological conversation with scientific descriptions of the world fractures at that point. The world-as-it-should-be is allowed too much dominance over contemplation of the world-as-it-is.

My second source, if anything, errs on the other side of the debate. Holmes Rolston's immensely distinguished work in environmental ethics is accompanied by rather cautious ventures into the theology of nature (Rolston 2006 [1987], 1994a, 2003). Rolston, as

I indicated above, has been at pains to stress the integrity of the ecological narrative—the same processes that give rise to diversity and exuberance also give rise to ugliness and a world full of suffering. Moreover, he offers a naturalized understanding of redemption. The creation is 'groaning', to borrow Paul's language in Romans 8:22, indeed for Rolston it is 'cruciform' (Rolston 2006: 144), yet it does not stand in need of redemption (Rolston 1994a), in that the very processes of the inter-conversion of values that shape ecological systems are taken by Rolston to constitute the redemption of creatures.

I consider that this is not enough to constitute redemption (Southgate 2008: 44–7). It is not enough to say to the pelican chick that its suffering serves the greater good, that that suffering is like 'the slaughter of the innocents' (Rolston 2006: 144), or that its being is reconstituted through microbial digestion and the operation of the food-chains so that it one day may become part of another pelican. Nor is it faithful to the Christian vision of the love of God to conclude that 'if God watches the sparrows fall, he does so from a very great distance' (Rolston 2006: 19; cf. McDaniel 1989: 19).

The problems of an approach like that of Rolston, then, are the exact complement of those of Messer. The latter's insistence that eschatological vision must shape the reading of the world leads him to compromise the integrity of the scientific narrative. Rolston preserves the integrity of the science of ecosystems and illustrates it tellingly with a wide variety of examples. But he reads the Christian narrative too easily out of the world of evolution. The effect is to attenuate the great Christian motifs of redemption and cruciformity, rather than enriching them. The world-as-it-is is being read too easily as the world-as-it-should-be.

My third source of ecological natural theology is the work of the eco-feminist Anne Primavesi in her *Sacred Gaia* (2000) and *Gaia's Gift* (2003). Primavesi points to the decentring effect of Copernicanism on Christian cosmology—when the heliocentric solar system is envisioned as just a tiny part of a vast universe, the central significance of human beings comes into question. (Copernicus knew the universe must be vast because stellar parallax was too tiny to be observed, so even the nearest stars must be at an enormous distance from Earth.) Likewise Darwin's realization of the relatedness of humans to other species diluted our sense of our specialness. And with the coming of Lovelock's Gaia Hypothesis, and the sense that the Earth is an enormously complex and ancient self-regulating system (Lovelock 1979, 1988), humans seem like irritant latecomers, rather than the pre-eminent species.

Science, then, for Primavesi, operates to counter human hubris and sense of specialness, and to reinforce our absolute dependence on the ecological systems of our planet. However, she then presses her reading of our planetary situation further, in ways that will trouble most Christian thinkers. She claims that Christian thought is at fault in stressing that our true home is heaven. Death, she points out, is the driver of the whole evolutionary process—why then should humans assume that they alone have an option to escape it into another non-Gaian life? Here we see natural theology pressed to a new purpose, namely to reframe Christian cosmology in ways that might enable us to live more appropriately on the Earth. This project of Primavesi's resembles that of Sallie McFague in *The Body of God* (1993), who called for a 'remythologisation' of 'the doctrines of God and human beings' with 'ethical or pragmatic concern' (McFague 1993: 81). The similarity is strengthened when Primavesi writes of 'living as if' (2003: 70–1, 82–6). We are to live as if Earth were a self-regulating organism, rather as McFague writes of our living as if the world were the body of God.

This is ecological natural theology written with palpable ethical designs upon us as readers. A very creative element of these books of Primavesi's is her emphasis on gift and gift exchange (2000: 154–79; 2003: 112–35). But most Christian readers will be surprised to learn that she does not want to focus on God as giver. Rather 'we lack intuitions about God' (Primavesi 2003: 133) and we do wrong to transfer 'our gratitude for what earth freely gives' onto 'other people or on to God' (2003: 134). Not only humans, but also God, seem decentred in this theology. It seems a pity that the Earth (on which we are agreed to be absolutely dependent for our embodied lives) is not seen here as the medium of gift exchange, gift and givenness being derived from God as creator and sustainer. There might then have been helpful links with Rolston's emphasis on ecosystems as having systemic value because they permit the exchange of value between entities with intrinsic value (Rolston 1994b).

As it is, Primavesi seems—in a way analogous to Messer though with very different results—to privilege one doctrinal conviction over others. Her emphasis on our physical, mortal embodiment, and on our identity as one creature among many, leads her to stress the sustaining matrix of Gaia (cf. Ruether 1992) at the expense of classical Christian understandings of life after death, and the life of heaven. Indeed it is a characteristic of natural theology mode 5 that its application, its reading of the world of nature, will depend very much on the hermeneutical and doctrinal lenses through which the reading is effected. This is no bad thing as long as the lensing is acknowledged (see Horrell, Hunt, and Southgate 2010 on this process of lensing, also the work of Ernst Conradie cited therein).

Before coming to my own approach in this area of theology I want to indicate a potentially very important area of development. Sarah Coakley, working with the Harvard mathematician Martin Nowak, has been reflecting on recent work that shows how deeply embedded in the evolutionary process strategies of cooperation may be. For a scientific account of these see Nowak 2006. Coakley's analysis is characteristically judicious. She is not attempting an old-style proof of God, a natural theology mode 1 or 2. She writes:

> no one can compel an assent to belief in God: it is a subtle matter of many cumulative factors—spiritual and emotional as well as intellectual. But the intellectual aspects do count, and they often combine with the others.

And she goes on:

> The news about cooperation in evolutionary processes is not...a warm, fuzzy riposte to the story of evolutionary competitiveness or selfishness. What it does show us is that the whole evolutionary struggle has a sacrificial accompaniment, which in certain conditions creatively recurs and forms a vital part of the dynamism of evolutionary development. As this strategy is observed higher up the evolutionary

scale, we start to find accompaniments to its manifestation which are truly intriguing—the widespread sacrificial activities of social insects, for instance, or the practice of a school of dolphins in surrounding a dying companion, even at great risk to themselves.

These phenomena may suggest that cooperation (as mathematically understood) provides a sort of evolutionary preparation for a higher and fully intentional human altruism that can arise only when the cultural and linguistic realm is reached. In other words, ethical tendencies to self-sacrificial and forgiving behaviors, themselves productive and creative within populations, may have their preliminary roots in forms of life much lower than the human.

And that is a very remarkable discovery indeed. If there is a god—even a trinitarian God of compassion, providential involvement and sacrificial love—this is the sort of evolutionary process he might well have made. [Coakley 2009]

There are hints here, and in Simon Conway Morris's work on convergent evolution, that the radically contingent picture of the Darwinian world made famous in particular in the work of Stephen Jay Gould (1991) may be starting to unravel. Conway Morris (2003) would have us believe that once an Earth-like planet had come into being, the evolution of intelligent life was almost inevitable. Coakley wants to imply in effect that—to borrow language from other writers—the universe may indeed be fine tuned for gift-giving, even for sacrifice. It is too soon to evaluate these developments within evolutionary science, and no natural theologian should underrate the power and flexibility of naturalistic explanations. As John Polkinghorne has written, somewhat plaintively:

If the evolution of life is seen to be almost inevitable. the atheists say that naturalism reigns and there is no need for a Creator, while the theists say that God has so beautifully ordained the order of nature that creation is indeed able to make itself. If life is so rare as to make its occurrence on Earth seem a fortuitous event, the atheists say that it shows that humans have emerged by chance in a world devoid of significance, while theists are encouraged to see the hand of God behind so fruitful but unpredictable an occurrence. [Polkinghorne, 1998: 79]

It is, then, a necessary corollary of doing natural theology in mode 5 that different readings of the natural world, stemming from different presuppositions, will continue to coexist with the Christian account of creation. 'Defeaters' may, in this mode, be made to look tawdry or reductive, but they are not 'defeated'. Any effort to expand natural theology into modes 3 and 4 will still face the enormous force of the problem of evolutionary suffering. I simply note here a sense that the balance within Darwinism between competition and cooperation, and between contingency and constraint, may be shifting.

My own approach to reading the ecological world theologically involves—with Rolston—stressing the integrity of the scientific account, and hence the ambiguity of ecosystems, shot through as they are with value accompanied by disvalue (Southgate 2008: 1–17; Rolston 2003). It involves—like Messer—taking very seriously some of the few scriptural passages that seem to offer clues about the eschatological relationships between God, humans, and the non-human creation (Southgate 2008: 82, 92–6; Horrell, Hunt and Southgate 2010). It involves—like Primavesi—developing a theology of gift.

My emphasis here is on the potential for human self-giving in response to divine self-giving love, though I also infer (in a way consonant with Coakley's work described above) that the capacity for self-transcendence is common to the whole created order, and I postulate that this is something God longs for and in which God delights (Southgate 2008: 60–71). This language of self-transcendence could be mapped creatively onto Primavesi's language of gift, providing one could avoid her seeming tendency not to distinguish adequately the source of gift in the all-transcending love of the creator.

CONTEMPLATION AND PRAISE

My approach also involves fusing, as much as possible, scientific insights with those of poets and other contemplatives. To return to Macquarrie's understanding of the enterprise of natural theology, he writes that: 'this descriptive type of philosophical or natural theology does not *prove* anything, but it *lets us see*, for it brings out into the light the basic situation in which faith is rooted, so that we can then see what its claims are' (Macquarrie 1977: 56, emphases in original). The natural sciences help to bring out into the light in very powerful ways the basic situation in which our faith is rooted. Biology and ecology show us the extraordinary beauty and intricacy of that world. They tell us (albeit provisionally, since their depictions are always moving on) things beyond all ordinary seeing—how the light-utilizing properties of certain photosynthetic pigments maintain an oxygen atmosphere on Earth unlike that of any other known planet, how the salt-avoiding strategies of certain marine organisms cause the recycling of sulphur, which land-based organisms vitally require, how in Rolston's memorable phrase 'the cougar's fang has carved the limbs of the fleet-footed deer, and vice versa' (Rolston 2006: 134). Biology and ecology also prevent us from escaping the ambiguity of that world—it makes us confront the conclusion that that same process of 'carving' is founded on the inevitability of suffering. The fawn that is too slow to learn to run is cougar-meat; the lamed cougar starves. Also that the biosphere we have now in a sense rests on a vast history of extinction—as many as 99 per cent of all species that have ever existed are now lost.

However, as has often been claimed in recent years, science by itself tends to 'disenchant' the world, to give rise to reductive ways of seeing that do not do full justice to the human imagination, or necessarily promote human cherishing of the non-human world (cf. McGrath 2002). To put it baldly, science may give us facts, it may even promote wonder (on this McGrath and Dawkins are agreed (McGrath 2002: 171–8)) but it cannot by itself make us see glory.

For an approach to natural theology that used the science of the day to aid seeing, and brought religiously informed poetic observation of the natural world to a pitch that, arguably, has never since been equalled, I turn to the work of Gerard Manley Hopkins. He developed an approach to creation based on his concepts of 'inscape' and 'instress'. As I wrote recently:

the inscape of an entity may be considered to contain what sort of thing it is scientifically—what patterns and regularities govern its existence—but also its particularity, its 'thisness'...every creature has both its pattern of life and membership of its species, and also its particularity as an individual creature. The scientific account of an organism is based on trends, regularities, patterns, over a range of individuals—the perception of the particularity of a specific creature, its 'thisness', is more the preserve of the poet and contemplative.

Hopkins has another, related term—'instress'—which is still more difficult to pin down than 'inscape'. The poet seems to use 'instress' for: i) the cohesive energy that binds individual entities into the Whole, ii) the impact the inscape of entities makes on the observer, and iii) the observer's will to receive that impact...The value of this odd terminology is that it gives full value to descriptions of entities in scientific terms, as being examples of whatever class of entities they belong to, but also acknowledges their particularity and createdness. [Southgate 2008: 97–8]

Hopkins was keenly interested in the sort of description of the world we now call science (cf. Brown 2000). But W. H. Gardner says of him that he would have parted company with the (scientific) rationalists in saying that 'the human spirit must be nourished by the spurting fountains of supra-rational instress, by that "deep poetry" which is nothing less than intuitive ontology—the knowledge of the essence and being of all things' (Gardner 1958: 350).

One of Hopkins's most remarkable observations in his Notebooks—themselves an outstanding training ground for any poet of nature—goes as follows:

I do not think I have seen anything more beautiful than the bluebell I have been looking at. I know the beauty of our Lord by it. It[s inscape] is [mixed of] strength and grace, like an ash [tree]. [Hopkins 1953: 122]

This makes clear just how far beyond ordinary seeing this instressing, at its most intense, can take us. It took Hopkins to *knowledge* of the beauty of God—it might therefore be said to be natural theology at its purest and most direct. But note what lay behind it—a deep schooling in Christian philosophical theology, an intense appreciation of the developments of the science of the time, and an extraordinary openness to the natural world. The same intensity of holy contemplation is advocated by Bonaventure when he writes of 'the second way of seeing' that:

The supreme power, wisdom and goodness of the Creator shine forth in created things in so far as the bodily senses inform the interior senses... In the first way of seeing, the observer considers things in themselves...the observer can rise, as from a vestige, to the knowledge of the immense power, wisdom and goodness of the Creator. In the second way of seeing, the way of faith...we understand that the world was fashioned by the Word of God. [quoted in Deane-Drummond 2006: 57]

Deane-Drummond quotes a further passage from Bonaventure indicating that to be able to develop this way of seeing, the contemplative must:

bring the natural powers of the soul under the influence of grace, which reforms them, and this he does through prayer; he must submit them to the purifying influence of justice, and this in his daily acts; he must subject them to the influence of enlightening knowledge, and this, in meditation; and finally he must hand them over to the influence of the perfecting power of wisdom, and this in contemplation. For just as no one arrives at wisdom except through grace, justice and knowledge, so it is that no one arrives at contemplation except through penetrating meditation, holy living and devout prayer. [quoted in Deane-Drummond 2006: 57]

One of the great problems of natural theology is to wrestle with the problem of sin, and its possibly distorting effects on our ability to learn truly from the creation. So it is significant that Bonaventure so strongly stresses the importance of prayer to contemplation—what T. S. Eliot called 'the purification of the motive in the ground of our beseeching' (Eliot 1969: 196). Moreover, the emphasis in the quotation from Bonaventure not just on prayer but on right living as a necessity for right contemplation is very striking. To adapt Hopkins once again, 'The just man justices' (Hopkins 1953: 51) and in doing so becomes able not just to tell out what lies deep within his being, but to draw in truly the way the created world speaks of God.

In her own work Deane-Drummond is attracted to the work of another poetic contemplative who engaged boldly with the science of his time, Thomas Traherne (Deane-Drummond 2006: 62–3; Traherne's work is also an inspiration in Peacocke 2005: 75–6, 88–90). Traherne found the world 'an Unlimited field of Variety and Beauty' (quoted in Peacocke 2005: 89). But, again, a post-Darwinian aesthetic will read that world rather differently, seeing beauty even in the midst of ugliness—in the hunting patterns of orcas and hyenas, and even, conceivably, in the parasitic strategy of the anopheles mosquito, despite the hideous creaturely suffering these can cause. Such an aesthetic of contemplation is difficult to arrive at and maintain. Faced with the ugliness, as good an observer as Annie Dillard wants to 'shake her fist at creation'; Rolston responds that he would rather 'raise both hands and cheer' (Rolston 2003: 82). Wesley Wildman sees the beauty and the ambiguity, and abandons his belief in the benevolence of God. He writes that suffering in nature is 'neither evil nor a byproduct of the good. It is part of the wellspring of divine creativity in nature, flowing up and out of the abysmal divine depths like molten rock from the yawning mouth of a volcano' (Wildman 2007: 294). God here is the ground of being, but neither loving, nor indeed malevolent, rather the author of 'weal and woe alike' (Isaiah 45:7) But here, I consider, Wildman has parted company with the natural theology I have been discussing—for now Christian doctrine as usually conceived is no longer providing the framework within which the world is to be seen.

The sort of contemplation of which I have been writing very much involves the effort to discern creation's praise of God, of which there are many hints in the Psalms (especially at Psalm 19:1–4), though also a sense, at least in some translations of Psalm 19:3–4, that this is a music we can never properly hear. For further development of this theme of creaturely praise see Bauckham (2002). In a remarkable passage Barth suggests that perhaps creation praises God most intensely in what he called its 'shadowy side'. He writes:

creation and creature are good even in the fact that all that is exists in this contrast and antithesis. In all this, far from being null, it praises its Creator even on its shadowy side, even in the negative aspect in which it is so near to nothingness . . . For all we can tell, may not His creatures praise Him more mightily in humiliation than in exaltation, in need than in plenty, in fear than in joy, on the frontier of nothingness than when wholly orientated on God. [Barth 1960: 297]

INTERPRETATION AND QUALITY

All living things interpret their environments. Indeed in other work Andrew Robinson and I have maintained that this is an under-explored characteristic of life, and a potentially important diagnostic of possible proto-living entities (Southgate and Robinson 2010). Responding to the environment in ways that favour the organism and/or its lineage is a vital part of 'autopoiesis', in Primavesi's term, how organisms become and maintain themselves (Primavesi 2000: 2–4). But the human capacity for interpretation goes far beyond that of other creatures, not least in our capacity to instress their createdness, and hence to discern something of God through encountering them.

For the Christian the human being is in the image and likeness of God (Genesis 1:26), and is called to grow into the likeness of Christ, 'the image of the invisible God' (Colossians 1:15). One way to understand the divine image in the human is as the capacity to respond to an initiative of self-giving love (Southgate 2010). The human vocation, after the example of Christ, is to become the self-given self, the self broken and poured out in love for others (cf. Southgate 2008: 71–3; 2010). While this insight finds its principal expression in terms of behaviour, it can be applied also to perception.

There is a sense in which to see an entity truly, to instress it, is to give oneself to it, to give one's whole sympathy and attention, as we see Hopkins doing with the bluebell. Hans Urs von Balthasar famously noted that 'there is no seeing without being caught up' (1989: 24). True seeing, then, the seeing that gives the self away in sympathy, allows that self to be caught up in the reality of the creature that is seen. And because that creature *is* created, participation in its inscape means participation in the life of the creator who made it.

Natural theology pursued along these lines, then, is very far from the effort to inspect the natural world from a neutral standpoint to find there evidence for God. It is dynamic, participative, existential, it recognizes knowing as involving the whole self. It both relies on faith and informs faith.

Robinson and I have recently made some proposals about the development of the interpretation of signs in human evolution (Robinson and Southgate 2010). Part of our proposal is that many depictions of this evolutionary process overstress the development of symbolic capacity, culminating in language, at the expense of consideration of other types of sign use. If however we bring into consideration the seeming importance of cave-art for the enhancement of human capacities, a richer picture starts to emerge. Perhaps in depicting and contemplating these images humans were engaging with what C. S Peirce called 'qualisigns', signs that depict nothing but the sheer quality of the entity depicted (cf. Short 2007: 209). I myself have never seen the European bison, but looking at the paintings in the Grottes de Niaux I felt I understood bisonness, *felt* bison, as I had never dreamed of doing. In Hopkins's terms I had received from the prehistoric painter the full charge of instress of bison. Recent work has suggested too that the function of cave-art may well have been 'spiritual'—not 'just' a matter of expressing and then seeing the quality of bisonness, but in some way seeking to participate in that inscape, in 'the deep poetry of the world' and thus to make contact with the spiritual world lying within the material.

David Lewis-Williams holds that the paintings are not art in the sense we would understand it, but part of a mystical shamanic encounter with the spirit world, for which the interior of caves was both symbol and catalyst (Lewis-Williams 2002). That accords with my sense that the Magdalenians 'instressed' bison in a heightened, spiritual sense that went beyond mere depiction. As J. Wentzel van Huyssteen says, 'human mental life [from the Upper Paleolithic onwards] includes biologically unprecedented ways of experiencing and understanding the world, from aesthetic experiences to spiritual contemplation' (Van Huyssteen 2006: 239). It may be that the contemplation of qualities, and through that the striving to participate in the deep reality of the world, goes back to the earliest phase of modern human cognition.

The Hebrew word *kavod*, which principally underlies the concept of glory in the Bible, has a root meaning connoting weight. Hence the glory of an entity may be thought of as its weight of reality, its participation in that which is most truly real (Horrell, Hunt, and Southgate 2010: 177, 264, n.48; cf. Deane-Drummond 2010). The natural theology I am proposing here supposes that human perception, at its truest and most generous, is able to recognize not only facts about the world but also, in direct apprehension of the qualities of created things, the glory that lies in their creatureliness. As was implied above, there is often nothing pretty to this glory. The deep reality of created things is full of paradox, of ugliness and violence put to ingenious ends, of subtlety of ecological cooperation even amid apparently ruthless competition, of creaturely praise amidst intensity of suffering.

As T. S. Eliot famously held (in one of the few lines he used twice) 'human kind cannot bear very much reality' (Eliot 1969: 172, 271). This is particularly evidently true when it comes to the complexity of relationships across the whole biosphere. We find it very difficult to conceive of how our industrial activity, energy generation, and ceaseless travel is distorting the atmosphere and hence the climate that the next generation will have to face. Humans are not incapable of global action to avert an unseen threat, as the Montreal Protocol on chlorofluorocarbons demonstrates. But our ability to instress the world truly and respond to it appropriately is held back by our aspiration to autonomy, and the relentless drivers of our appetite and acquisitiveness (Southgate 2008: 101–3); also, arguably, by our evolutionary inheritance, which is one of cooperating in relatively small groups, and of being willing to alter environments to suit the immediate needs of the tribe. (See also Northcott 2007 for another analysis of why our response to the threat of climate change is relatively limited and half-hearted.)

So the generous, self-giving engagement with the ecological world to which I am pointing is not merely an exercise in refining a doctrine of God for academic and apologetic purposes. It has powerful, indeed urgent implications for praxis. Hopkins saw the world as 'charged with the grandeur of God', with a glory that 'will flame out, like shining from shook foil' (Hopkins 1953: 27). One hundred and thirty-three years after that poem was written we instress a world in which science helps us to understand what enormously powerful natural forces are at work. The Indian Ocean tsunami of 2004, triggered by the release, at a subducting fault, of energy equivalent to 10,000 atomic bombs, is the most vivid recent example. On a much more minor level, the blighting of air travel in 2010 by the erupting volcanoes of Iceland is another reminder of our utter inability to influence the huge events that affect the world's crust. So much might still speak of the grandeur of God, the smallness of human capacity. At same time, the rapid onset of anthropogenic climate change seems to speak of the vulnerability of God's 'project' of creation—to borrow the language of Colin Gunton (1998). There is for the first time the possibility that even the peacetime activity of human beings could trigger a major extinction event. The Stern Report on the economics of climate change calmly notes possible levels of mammalian extinction of 25–60 per cent at a mean temperature rise of 3 degrees C (Stern 2007: 66). Higher extents of mean temperature rise could lead to much more profound losses of habitat (Lynas 2007).

The approach I am advocating recognizes, therefore, that reflection on the natural world will consist of both scientific analysis and the reception of epiphanies, and that it is the fusion of these two, brought in turn into hermeneutically sensitive dialogue with the classic theological resources of scripture and doctrine, that characterizes the richest and most creative approach to natural theology. Given the profound ambiguities that we observe in evolved ecosystems, and the urgency of rightly instressing their character and our impact upon them, nothing less than this richness of methodological perichoresis will do.

CONCLUSION

I have shown what type of natural theology I consider appropriate to the reading of ecosystems, and given a number of examples of such an approach. The difficulty of the subject centres on the problem of creaturely suffering in evolution, though it is compounded by the sometimes unacknowledged hermeneutical and doctrinal presuppositions of those working in this area. I have suggested some interesting respects in which the debate is shifting, and offered an approach of my own which draws on the methods both of the scientist and of the contemplative.

REFERENCES

Balthasar, H. U. von (1989, German original 1969). *The Glory of the Lord: A Theological Aesthetics*. Vol. VII: *Theology: The New Covenant*. San Francisco: Ignatius Press.

Barth, K. (1960). *The Church Dogmatics III/3—The Doctrine of Creation*. Edited by G. W. Bromiley and T. F. Torrance. Translated by G. W. Bromiley and R. J. Ehrlich. Edinburgh: T&T Clark.

Bauckham, R. J. (2002). 'Joining Creation's Praise of God'. *Ecotheology* 7: 42–59.

Behe, M. J. (1996). *Darwin's Black Box: The Biochemical Challenge to Evolution*. New York: Free Press.

Brown, D. (2000). 'Victorian Poetry and Science' in *The Cambridge Companion to Victorian Poetry*. Edited by J. Bristow. Cambridge: Cambridge University Press: pp. 137–58.

Coakley, S. (2009). 'Evolution and Sacrifice: Cooperation as a Scientific Principle' in *The Christian Century*, 20 October.

Conway Morris, S. (2003). *Life's Solution: Inevitable Humans in a Lonely Universe*. Cambridge: Cambridge University Press.

Darwin, C. (1856). 'Letter to J. D. Hooker of July 13 1856' available through www.darwinproject.ac.uk (catalogued as Letter No. 1924).

—— (1859). *On the Origin of Species by Means of Natural Selection, or the Preservation of Favoured Races in the Struggle for Life*. London: John Murray.

Dawkins, R. (1995). *River Out of Eden: A Darwinian View of Life*. London: Weidenfeld and Nicolson.

Deane-Drummond, C. (2006). *Wonder and Wisdom: Conversations in Science, Spirituality and Theology*. London: Darton, Longman and Todd.

—— (2010). 'The Breadth of Glory: A Trinitarian Eschatology for the Earth through Engagement with Hans Urs von Balthasar'. *International Journal of Systematic Theology* 12/1: 46–64.

Eliot, T. S. (1969). *Collected Poems and Plays*. London: Faber and Faber.

Fergusson, D. (2006). 'Types of Natural Theology' in *The Evolution of Rationality: Interdisciplinary Essays in Honor of J. Wentzel Van Huyssteen*. Edited by F. Le Ron Shults Grand Rapids: Eerdmans: pp. 380–93.

Gardner, W. H. (1958 [1949]). *Gerard Manley Hopkins: A Study of Poetic Idiosyncrasy in Relation to Poetic Tradition*. Vol. II. London: Oxford University Press.

Gould, S. J. (1991 [1989]). *Wonderful Life: The Burgess Shale and the Nature of History*. Harmondsworth: Penguin

Gunton, C. (1998). *The Triune Creator: A Historical and Systematic Study*. Edinburgh: Edinburgh University Press.

Hopkins, G. M. (1953). *Poems and Prose of Gerard Manley Hopkins*. Edited by W. H. Gardner. Harmondsworth: Penguin.

Horrell, D. G., C. Hunt, and C. Southgate (2010). *Greening Paul: Re-reading the Apostle in a time of Ecological Crisis*. Waco, TX: Baylor University Press.

Huyssteen, J. W. van (2006). *Alone in the World: Human Uniqueness in Science and Theology*. Grand Rapids, MI and Cambridge: Eerdmans.

Lewis-Williams, D. (2002). *The Mind in the Cave*. London: Thames and Hudson.

Lovelock, J. (1979). *Gaia: A New Look at Life on Earth*. Oxford: Oxford University Press.

—— (1988). *The Ages of Gaia: A Biography of our Living Earth*. Oxford: Oxford University Press.

Lynas, M. (2007). *Six Degrees: Our Future on a Hotter Planet*. London: Fourth Estate.

McDaniel, J. (1989). *Of God and Pelicans: A Theology of Reverence for Life*. Louisville, KY: Westminster John Knox Press.

McFague, S. (1993). *The Body of God: An Ecological Theology*. London: SCM Press.

McGrath, Alister E. (2001). *A Scientific Theology*. Vol. I: *Nature*. Edinburgh: T&T Clark.

—— (2002). *The Re-enchantment of Nature: Science, Religion and the Human Sense of Wonder*. London: Hodder and Stoughton.

Macquarrie, J. (1977). *Principles of Christian Theology*. London: SCM Press.

Messer, N. (2007). *Selfish Genes and Christian Ethics: Theological Reflections on Evolutionary Biology*. London: SCM Press.

—— (2009). 'Natural Evil after Darwin' in *Theology after Darwin*. Edited by M. Northcott and R. J. Berry. Milton Keynes: Paternoster.

Morley, G. (2003). *John Macquarrie's Natural Theology: The Grace of Being*. Aldershot: Ashgate.

Northcott, M. (2007). *A Moral Climate: The Ethics of Global Warming*. London: Darton, Longman and Todd.

Nowak, M. (2006).'Five Rules for the Evolution of Co-operation'. *Science* 314: 1560–3.

Peacocke, A. (2005). *The Palace of Glory: God's World and Science*. Adelaide: ATF Press.

Polkinghorne, J. (1998). *Science and Theology: An Introduction*. London: SPCK.

—— (2002). *The God of Hope and the End of the World*. London: SPCK.

Primavesi, A. (2000). *Sacred Gaia: Holistic Theology and Earth System Science*. London: Routledge.

—— (2003). *Gaia's Gift: Earth, Ourselves and God after Copernicus*. London: Routledge.

Robinson, A. and C. Southgate (2010). 'Semiotics as a Metaphysical Framework for Christian Theology'. *Zygon* 45/3: 689–712.

Rolston, H, III (1992). 'Disvalues in Nature'. *The Monist* 75: 250–78

—— (1994a). 'Does Evolution Need to be Redeemed?'. *Zygon* 29/2: 205–29.

—— (1994b). *Conserving Natural Value*. New York: Columbia University Press.

—— (2003). 'Naturalizing and Systematizing Evil' in *Is Nature ever Evil?: Religion, Science and Value*. Edited by Willem B. Drees. London: Routledge: pp. 67–86.

—— (2006 [1987]). *Science and Religion: A Critical Survey*. Philadelphia and London: Templeton Foundation Press.

Ruether, R. R. (1992). *Gaia and God: An Ecofeminist Theology of Earth Healing*. London: SCM Press.

Russell, R. J. (2008) *Cosmology: from Alpha to Omega*. Minneapolis, MN: Fortress Press.

Sennett, J. F. and D. Groothuis, eds. (2005). *In Defense of Natural Theology: A Post-Humean Assessment*. Downers Grove, IL: Inter-Varsity Press.

Short, T. L. (2007). *Peirce's Theory of Signs*. Cambridge: Cambridge University Press.

Southgate, C. (2008). *The Groaning of Creation: God, Evolution and the Problem of Evil*. Louisville, KY: Westminster John Knox Press.

—— (2010). *Ecological Hermeneutics*. London: Continuum.

Southgate, C. and A. Robinson (2010). 'Interpretation and the Origin of Life'. *Zygon* 45/2: 345–60.

Stern, N. (2007). *The Economics of Climate Change: The Stern Review*. Cambridge: Cambridge University Press.

Wildman, W. J. (2007). 'Incongruous Goodness, Perilous Beauty, Disconcerting Truth: Ultimate Reality and Suffering in Nature' in *Physics and Cosmology: Scientific Perspectives on the Problem of Evil in Nature*. Edited by Nancey Murphy, Robert J. Russell, and William Stoeger. S. J. Berkeley, CA: CTNS; Vatican City: Vatican Observatory: pp. 267–94.

CHAPTER 30

NATURAL THEOLOGY AND THE MIND SCIENCES

FRASER WATTS

JUST as there is a natural theology of nature in general, so there is a more specific natural theology of human nature. Just as there are aspects of nature in general that lend themselves to interpretations in terms of the purposes of God, so there are aspects of human nature that invite such interpretation. Further, just as general natural theology has been enhanced in recent centuries by natural science, natural theology of human nature can potentially be enriched by the scientific study of human beings. That is the focus of this chapter: how the mind sciences can be used in natural theology.

There are two aspects of human mental functioning to consider from a theological point of view. First, there is the theological significance of the general capacity for advanced mental functioning found in humans. Secondly, there is the theological significance of particular human capacities such as religion (though the theological significance of the human capacity for morality and relationships might also be considered).

NATURAL THEOLOGY AND SCIENCE

Natural theology does not depend on science. There is, for example, a natural theology in the Old Testament that is pre-scientific (Barr 1993). However, the historical development of natural theology makes it clear how much it has been enriched by science. Natural theology blossomed alongside the 'scientific revolution' of the seventeenth century. The twentieth century, especially in its last few decades, saw a rich development of the mind sciences, which can now be used in a distinctive strand of natural theology.

Sometimes theology has seemed to regard itself as offering an alternative explanation to science of certain natural phenomena, but I regard that as a mistake. I see theology and science as answering different kinds of questions, and theology as offering more an interpretation of natural phenomena than an explanation of them. Rather than theology being an alternative to science, I see science as providing an increasingly rich understanding of the phenomena that theology can then interpret. In that sense, theology feeds off science, rather than providing an alternative to it. Natural theology is often an interpretation of scientific findings. Richard Swinburne has made a similar point:

> I am not postulating a 'God of the gaps', a God merely to explain the things which science has not yet explained. I am postulating a God to explain what science explains; I do not deny that science explains but I postulate God to explain why science explains. The very success of science in showing us how deeply orderly the natural world is provides strong grounds for believing that there is an even deeper cause of that order. [Swinburne, 1996: 68]

There has so far been very little natural theology of human nature, compared to the natural theology arising from cosmology or from biology. Indeed, there has been much less work on the interface of theology and the mind sciences than most other areas of science, though exceptions include Brown, Murphy, and Maloney (1998); Barbour (2002); Watts (2002); Peterson (2003); Jeeves (2006); Seybold (2007); and Jeeves and Brown (2009). Why should natural theology have made less use of the mind sciences? Is there any real problem that makes a natural theology of mind difficult or inappropriate; or is it just theologians perseverating with one particular form of natural theology, and not noticing other possibilities? It may be partly explained in terms of the historical fact that the scientific study of human nature did not really get going until the hey-day of natural theology was over. If so, the development of psychology, cognitive science, and neuroscience may offer richer opportunities for natural theology of mind now than previously. It is hard to see any other reason for not developing a natural theology of mind; indeed it seems potentially a very fertile project.

Natural Theology, Theology of Nature, and Revealed Theology

I shall not be making any sharp distinction between a natural theology of mind and a more general theological interpretation of the significance of mind. The difference between natural theology and theology of nature is always a subtle one. Natural theology has typically been concerned with the case for interpreting phenomena in theological terms, namely with whether, on the balance of evidence, a theological interpretation is appropriate, or even required. A theology of nature, in contrast, is more concerned with exactly how to formulate a theological interpretation, on the assumption that this is an appropriate thing to attempt.

How sharp a distinction is drawn between natural theology and theology of nature depends on how natural theology is approached. Some natural theology operates within a broader framework of revealed theology, making the presuppositions of faith.

Among contemporary natural theologians, Alister McGrath is a strong advocate of that approach. Other forms of natural theology try to avoid theological presuppositions and start with a relatively neutral and detached view of phenomena. They then try to show that it is not really possible to do without a theological interpretation altogether, or at least that it is more reasonable to adopt a theological interpretation than to do without one. Among contemporary practitioners of natural theology, Richard Swinburne is in that tradition of natural theology.

However, I will follow here an approach to natural theology similar to that advocated by John Polkinghorne (1988), in which natural theology is not independent of revealed theology, or separate from it; but neither is it so dependent on the context of revealed theology that it is unable to operate at all without the presuppositions of faith. Rather natural theology is a distinct and coherent enterprise, but not a self-contained one. It is a distinct mode of theology, but one that operates in dialogue with other areas of theology.

MIND AND NATURE: SPECIAL CREATION OR EMERGENTISM

There are two very different ways in which a natural theology can proceed (whether of mind or any other phenomena). One is to claim that mind (or whatever phenomenon is under consideration) could not have arisen naturally and therefore could only have arisen as the result of special creation or intervention by God. The existence of mind thus becomes the basis of an argument for the existence of God. That argument has a long history. It can be found, for example in John Locke's *Essay Concerning Human Understanding* (2008, first published 1690). He assumes that matter on its own could never have produced thought, so thought must have come from an eternal 'cogitative' being, namely God.

In recent times, a similar argument has been put forward by Richard Swinburne (1979), who sets it out more rigorously and carefully than anyone else has done. He allows that there are correlations between brain states and mind states, but argues that there is no direct, publically observable data about the latter, that the correlations are not lawful in the way that is required, and that there are no adequate grounds for interpreting mind–brain correlations in causal terms. It is a serious and careful argument that makes some good points, but I think it would be fair to say that it has not been widely accepted. It seems to me that it makes the mistake of setting the bar too high, and concerning itself too much with whether causal affects of brain on mind can be proved, rather than (more modestly) with what it is reasonable to conclude. It also fails to consider the important role of data arising from the naturalistic scientific 'experiment' provided by head injury.

This line of argument trades on the *un*naturalness of mind (or whatever phenomenon is under consideration), in the sense that it is argued that there is no natural explanation for it. There is an alternative natural theology of mind that turns things round and assumes that mind does arise from nature. This might be called an 'emergentist' natural theology (using that term rather loosely for any theory that does not postulate special creation). Such emergentism becomes the basis for a religious attitude of wonder and awe at nature. We see this kind of natural theology in Charles Kingsley's remark that it is a 'loftier thought' to believe that God 'created primal forms capable of self development...as to believe that He required a fresh act of intervention to supply the lacunas which He Himself had made' (Kingsley 1992).

The same could be said about mind; it could be seen as a 'loftier thought' to suggest that God had created a natural world capable of producing mind than to suggest that mind had to be supplied by God in some more direct way. This kind of natural theology provides a basis for an attitude of reverence towards nature and/or God. It can be the basis for an argument that the natural world has the characteristics that would be expected on the assumption that it was created by God, and so tends to support that assumption. However, it stops short of trying to argue that the natural world is inexplicable without the assumption of a creator God.

With mind, as with other phenomena, it seems to me that the latter form of natural theology is preferable, on both theological and scientific grounds. Theologically, it does not seem satisfactory to assume that God would create a world incapable of recognizing his existence or of having any kind of conscious relationship with him, unless its deficiencies were remedied by some further intervention or addition. Scientifically, it also seems unwise to assume that mind is inexplicable. Admittedly, explaining the origin of the kind of reflective mind found in humans is one of the tougher challenges facing contemporary science. However, there are plausible ideas about the neural basis of consciousness that are worth exploring, such as Francis Crick's (1994) theory of synchronized brain rhythms. There are also increasingly precise theories, about the evolutionary context that led to the development of conscious mind (Barnard et al. 2007). It can never be proved that a phenomenon such as the human mind is inexplicable and could not have arisen from nature, and it is best not to make that assumption.

THE DISTINCTIVENESS OF HUMAN MIND

My focus here will be on *human* mind, because mental functioning is much more highly developed in humans than elsewhere in the natural world. Obviously, there are important issues lurking here about human distinctiveness, and about the universality of mind (that is, panpsychism). I will not go deeply into these issues, but I will assume that:

1. Mind has evolved gradually, and that the human mind emerges from a long process of evolutionary development, and that almost every aspect of human mental functioning can be found in embryonic form in other species.
2. Mind is much more highly developed in humans than in any other species, and I will present a theoretical position about the distinctiveness of human mind.

There is no serious scientific dispute about the distinctiveness of the human mind. The only points for serious discussion are (i) how radically different human mind is from the minds of other species such as chimps, and (ii) what are the fundamental distinctive features of the human mind. There is a long list of potential candidates for the latter, including language, tools/instruments, signs/signals, dynamic concepts, aesthetic sense, metarepresentation, algorithmic capacity, categorization/organization, theory of mind, and anticipatory planning (Amati and Shallice, 2007). It is possible to make a case for almost any of these being the crucial distinctive feature of the human mind, but equally it is difficult to make a knock-down argument in favour of any of them.

I suggest that this is an unfruitful debate, on the grounds that it is focussed at the wrong level. I submit that you need to go down a level to find what is distinctive about the human mind; the answer is best framed in terms of what is distinctive about the human cognitive architecture, rather than in terms of what is distinctive about human cognitive accomplishments. The wide range of distinctive cognitive accomplishments can then all be seen as the consequence of a distinctive human architecture.

There has been an impressive degree of agreement that the key feature of human cognition is that there are two distinct levels that interact with one another. At present, there are various different ways of formulating this distinction, though there is substantial convergence between them. The most rigorous formulation is probably that found in the Interacting Cognitive Subsystems (ICS) theory of Philip Barnard (e.g. Teasdale and Barnard 1993). It is an approach that has the particular advantage, for present purposes, of having been applied to the evolution of cognition, and including a well-specified view of what is distinctive about human cognition. According to ICS, only humans have a nine-subsystem architecture, whereas our primate ancestors had no more than an eight-subsystem architecture. The crucial difference is that humans have two meaning subsystems, where our primate ancestors had only one. What is new and distinctive about humans is the propositional subsystem, the meanings of which are amenable to articulation. This is distinct from the phylogenetically older 'implicational' subsystem that operates with more schematic, tacit meanings. Other psychological traditions have formulated a similar distinction on other terms, for example the psychodynamic distinction between symbolic and sub-symbolic meanings (Bucci 1997)

Another defensible approach to human distinctiveness is to push down yet another level to what is distinctive about the human brain. The human brain is not particularly large in absolute terms, but it is relatively large compared to body size. The ratio of brain to body seems more important for cognitive performance than absolute brain size. However, there are probably two other features of the brain that are even more important for the human mind. One is that there is greater hemispheric specialization in the human brain than in any other species, as a result of language being subserved largely by just one hemisphere. That introduces a unique complementarity in humans between the dominant (linguistic) and non-dominant hemispheres. The other key feature of the human brain is the relative size of the frontal lobes, which are crucial to planning, symbolic functioning, and self-regulation.

THEOLOGICAL INTERPRETATION
OF HUMAN MIND

It is not difficult to argue that the wide range of distinctive accomplishments found in humans, made possible by our distinctive cognitive architecture and brain structure serve God's purposes (rather as in cosmological natural theology it might be argued that the value of the basic physical forces serve God's purposes). It is a presupposition about God that God wishes to reveal himself to his creation and to draw creatures into relationship with Godself. For that to be possible, there must be creatures who have the cognitive capacities to receive God's revelation and to relate to God.

There has been a tendency since early post-Darwinian thought about distinctive human accomplishments (Illingworth 1890) to formulate a theology of gradual evolutionary progress towards human achievements. However, there are good reasons for eschewing the idea of progress. It is an idea that has largely been discredited in evolutionary theorizing. If theologians use it, a tension (and an unnecessary one) arises between theology and science. However, there are also theological objections to the idea of evolutionary progress towards humanity if it is taken to imply that humans are *better* than other species. As sociobiologists such as E. O. Wilson like to point out, insects are generally better at social cooperation. The key point is that humans are manifestly not better morally. They have more advanced capacities, but those are morally neutral.

The distinctive cognitive capacities of humans give them distinctive capacities for both good and evil. There is a distinctive kind of human altruism that Sober and Wilson (1998) call 'psychological altruism' that is more self-conscious, deliberate, and principled than the social cooperation found in other species, which is more limited to reciprocal altruism and kin altruism. However, humans also have a distinctive capacity for evil; we are capable of vastly greater destructiveness than other species, and evil behaviour is often supported by the belief that it is proper and justified (Baumeister 1996). There may be 'progress' (or at least 'directional change' in Ayala's cautious terminology) towards greater cognitive capacities in humans (Ayala 1988) but humans certainly do not represent a pinnacle of moral perfection. There may be cognitive progress without moral progress.

It would tend to support a natural theology of the development of human cognition if it could be argued that it was not an accidental development, but one that was inherent in the evolutionary process and always destined to emerge. One issue here is how 'natural' (i.e. inherent in nature) human cognition is; natural theology always tends to focus on the theological interpretation of what is inherent in nature. The other point is that the theological interpretation of the emergence of human cognition in terms of the purposes of God will be more convincing if it can be argued to be predictable. Though chance process can certainly be argued to play a role in the unfolding of God's purposes (Watts 2008), it is difficult to argue that a completely random and unpredictable development represents the fulfilment of God's purposes.

So how predictable is the emergence of human cognition? There are at least two lines of argument that support its predictability. First, an argument can be advanced that human cognition is a natural culmination of a process of development that was good for survival, and so had the power of natural selection to drive it forward. Among those who support the view that there evolution shows a direction, there are various ideas about exactly what the direction is. One early idea was that it was movement towards greater complexity; however, I suggest that it is more plausible that the direction was towards increasing powers of information processing. It is self-evident that organisms that are good at processing information about their environment will survive better. To that, we only need to add the assumption that the trend towards increasingly good information processing provides the basis from which human cognition emerges. However, that is probably not the whole story. There has been a growing recognition that the transition to human cognitive capacities was closely intertwined with the transition to more complex forms of social organization. This seems to have been a two-way process, in which cognitive developments made possible more complex forms of social organization, and the advantages of social organization provided the impetus for the development of the cognitive capacities that they required.

The Naturalness of Religion: Empirical Evidence

In the second part of this chapter, I will turn to a new natural theology built on the religiousness of humanity. Human religiousness is potentially a stronger basis for a contemporary natural theology arising from the mind sciences, though it is a territory that is much disputed. There are two key questions. First, there is the question of whether humanity is naturally religious. Secondly, there is the question of what can be inferred from that in terms of the existence of God or the truth of religious belief. In recent literature, there has been widespread acceptance of the naturalness of religion, though a variety of non-theistic interpretations of that have been offered.

Religion is ubiquitous among humanity, though not universal. It is estimated that 85 per cent of contemporary humanity is religious (Barrett, Kurian, and Johnson 2001). On the face of things, that looks quite a strong basis for assuming the 'naturalness' of religion. However, the case is weakened by clear evidence of cultural variability. In Europe, the percentage of people who are religious is much lower. Europe may well be the exception (Davie 2002) but the fact that there is such an exception at all significantly weakens the statistical case for assuming humanity to be naturally religious.

However, at this point, it is important to note the complexity of the concept of religion, which includes a variety of aspects that are not well correlated with one another. It seems likely that religious attendance is the most culturally variable aspect of religion, and the one on which Europe is most different from the rest of the world. Davie (1994) has argued that, at least in the UK, that there is more 'believing' than 'belonging' (though that probably depends on exactly how believing is defined). There is much interesting current discussion on how to reconcile the presumed naturalness of religion with cultural variation (Geertz and Markusson 2009; Bering 2010; Barrett 2010).

It is a serious hypothesis, and one that deserves further investigation, that spiritual experience is the aspect of religion that is least dependent on cultural variation. We do not have good international data, but it looks as though the frequency of spiritual experiences may be quite similar in the US and UK, despite striking differences in frequency of church attendance. What is really needed is a cross-cultural study using exactly the same methodology in different cultures. However, responses to the Greeley question (Have you ever felt as though you were close to a powerful spiritual force the seemed to lift you out of yourself?) seem to be very similar in the US (35 per cent, Davis and Smith, cited by Hood, Hill, and Spilka 2009: 345) and UK (36 per cent, Hay and Morisy 1978), despite the well-known differences in religious affiliation. There are other kinds of evidence relevant to claims for the naturalness of religion, and I will briefly consider genetic, neuropsychological, archaeological, and developmental evidence.

Evidence for genetic influence on religiousness is increasingly strong. Comparisons of identical and fraternal twins indicate that about half the variance in religious attitudes is influenced by genes, a finding that has been replicated in different studies in different countries (Waller at al. 1990; Eaves at al. 1999). Though that basic fact is now quite well established, it is hard to know how to interpret it, or what the mechanism of genetic influence might be. It is hard to imagine that there is a gene that controls religiousness directly, and hard to say what the mediation of such influence might be. Until we have made more progress with such questions, it is hard to take this genetic evidence as establishing that it is religion, specifically, that is natural.

There has also been much talk about the brain being 'hard-wired' for religion. This claim has been advanced largely on the basis of brain scanning studies showing brain activity in religious practices such as meditation. Of course, it is no surprise that there is brain activity during religious practices. That is presumably true of all mental activity and it would be utterly extraordinary if the physical brain were not involved in meditation; so, little can be inferred from the fact that it is. Though there are no doubt areas of the brain, and indeed specific neural circuits, that are characteristically involved in religious practices, it is clear that there is no single religion centre (or 'God spot') in the brain, in the way there is a language centre. There are two key points here. One is that religious activity is very diverse, and many areas of the brain are probably involved in some aspect or other. The other is that there seems to be no area of the brain that is dedicated exclusively to religion, and indeed evidence is growing about which other functions arise from areas of the brain involved in religious practices.

There is also archaeological evidence suggesting that religious activity was a key part of the cultural explosion that took place as *Homo sapiens* emerged from its Neanderthal precursors. The issue here is that the actual evidence is somewhat sparse (despite the huge theoretical interest that has arisen in the 'evolution' of religion). More significantly, it is unclear how justified we are in interpreting the archeological in terms of what can properly be called 'religion'. In essence, there is evidence for cave art, and enriched burial practices that involve the use of grave goods for the first time. It is debatable whether this development (c.30,000–60,000 years ago) marks the beginning of 'religion', or whether that doesn't really happen until the development of settlements c.10,000 years ago. A case for seeing the first of these developments in terms of 'religion' can certainly be made (van Huyssteen 2006), but it inevitably involves a good deal of extrapolation from limited evidence, and the 'religion' of this period probably bears only slight resemblances to what we now call religion.

Finally, there is developmental evidence. This is one of the stronger lines of evidence, and the work of Justin Barrett (2012) on 'childhood theism' is impressive. It seems that infants start with the assumption that agents have the supernatural properties of being all-knowing and all-powerful. Only gradually do children distinguish between natural and supernatural agents, and recognize that the former have more limited powers. There is thus rather compelling evidence that 'religious' assumptions about supernatural agents come naturally to children. However, this is, again, only one aspect of what can properly be called 'religion', and can't be equated with the full package.

Though some lines of evidence and argument for the naturalness of religion are stronger than others, there is overall quite a strong case for regarding religion as 'natural'. My main concern about the argument as it stands at present is the undifferentiated use of the concept of religion. Religion is multifaceted, and some aspects of religion are almost certainly more 'natural' than others.

If we make a simple threefold distinction between (i) religious experience, (ii) religious beliefs, and (iii) public religion (institutional structures and associated public practices), my hypothesis would be that religious experience is the most 'natural', and public religion the least. So, for example, in twin studies I would expect this to be reflected in different concordance rates between identical twins for these three aspects of religion, with highest concordance for religious experience and lowest concordance rates for public religion. I would also expect different degrees of cultural variation for these three aspects, with least variation for religious experience, and most for public religion. However, for the time being, this is no more than a hypothesis that invites further research.

INTERPRETING THE NATURALNESS OF RELIGION

It is striking that there is a reasonable amount of consensus about the naturalness of religion. Indeed, it is intriguing how much agreement there is about this among those who are for and against religion. There is certainly a possibility of building a natural theology around the naturalness of religion. However, intriguingly, it is also possible to build a case for atheism on the naturalness of religion. This suggests that there may be more common ground between natural theology and atheism than is often appreciated. Indeed, atheism can be seen as a kind of inverted natural theology.

The concept of 'natural religion' is largely a product of the Enlightenment, and most books on natural religion were published in the eighteenth and nineteenth centuries. Recent literature on natural religion regards it as a historical tradition to be studied rather than a living tradition to be inhabited. The idea of natural religion assumes that 'religion' is a generic concept, which has various specific manifestations. The twin assumptions that religion is both universal and natural provide support for one another. However, it should be noted that the Enlightenment concepts of 'religion' that is being employed here has been much criticized (Smith 1991; Lash 1996). It exaggerates the similarity between different forms of religion, and takes no account of the fact that this concept or 'religion' is a product of the Enlightenment.

Enthusiasm for natural religion can be found in a variety of quarters in the Enlightenment. Some see it as part of the support for natural theology that, in turn, is seen as providing a foundation for revealed theology and Christian orthodoxy. However, many of those interested in natural religion were deists, as Peter Byrne (1989) has pointed out. Some of those interested in natural religion, like the eighteenth-century philosopher David Hume (2008), saw religion as a purely natural phenomenon, and their interest in natural religion was an important element in their religious scepticism.

The concept of natural religion preceded the scientific study of religion that developed in the latter part of the nineteenth century with Max Müller and others. However, the sciences of religion have considerably enriched work on 'natural religion' (even though that term has gone out of fashion, and is now somewhat dated). There is now the possibility of building a natural theology on assumptions about the naturalness of religion with stronger evidential support than in the era when talk of 'natural religion' was more fashionable.

For example, there is an argument for the existence of God based on religious experience, meaning experiences that the person concerned takes to be experiences of God. Such arguments are discussed carefully by, amongst others, Swinburne (1979) and Wainwright (1981). An important background assumption is that experiences ought to be taken at face value unless there is good reason for not doing so. However, in this particular case, there is unlikely to be agreement about whether or not religious experiences should be taken at face value.

A different kind of argument, of a more general kind, would be based more on a predisposition to religiousness in humanity. Rather than saying that religious experiences are experiences of God that provide evidence for God's existence, the point would just be that the development of religiousness in humans is consistent with what one might expect of a God who wished to reveal himself to humanity and to draw people into relationship with him. The claim would be that 'human religions have existed and do exist everywhere because a God really does actually exist, and many humans... feel a recurrent and deeply compelling "built-in" desire to know and worship, in their various ways, the God who is there' (Smith, 2003: 109).

However, though it is possible to build a natural theology on human religiousness, one can also build atheism on the same assumption. There are modern versions of the alliance seen in David Hume between religious scepticism and assumptions about the naturalness of religion. The prevailing assumption of current cognitive science of religion is that religion is false, but in some sense 'natural' (e.g. Boyer 1994). These twin assumptions are so often linked in current writing that not enough attention is given to whether and how they can be reconciled.

Of course, the presumed naturalness of religion provides an explanation for why it might have become prevalent, despite being assumed to be false. The problem is how to explain why something false should have become natural. Boyer's argument on this point assumes that religion is counterintuitive, which sits somewhat uneasily with his assumption that it is natural. He invokes assumptions about the memorability of minimally counterintuitive ideas to explain why religion has become so pervasive. This is a speculative theory, for which there is some indirect support, but it can hardly be regarded as having been securely established.

Even if the prevailing cognitive science account of the origin of religion is accepted for the sake of argument, it doesn't lead to the atheistic conclusions that it is often taken to support. Murray and Goldberg (2009), among others, have explained the fallacies involved. For one thing it is a version of the genetic fallacy to assume that explaining the origin of religion implies that it is false. For another, giving one explanation of religion doesn't imply that other explanations are false. In sum, explaining religion doesn't explain it away.

It is an interesting scientific question why religion should have developed as pervasively as it has in humans, to which all answers are currently rather speculative.

My own inclination is to look for a common explanation of the range of cultural developments associated with the Upper Paleolithic in terms of general developments in the cognitive architecture, rather than specific explanations that apply only to religions. One specific way of formulating that would be in terms of the distinction that Interacting Cognitive Subsystems theory makes between two distinct meaning subsystems, which provides a plausible account of the religiousness us of humanity (Watts 2002, 2009).

It should perhaps be emphasized again that theological interpretations of the naturalness of religion should not be seen as an alternative to scientific explanations for why religion should have developed as pervasively as it has. It certainly needs to be emphasized that (i) theological interpretation does not depend on the absence of scientific explanation, and (ii) theological interpretations of the naturalness of religion need to be advanced tentatively. Though the facts about natural religion are consistent with theological assumptions, they can also be handled on atheist assumptions. Currently, there is a lack of compelling reasons, either empirical or theological, for preferring one approach rather than the other. The naturalness of religion is entirely consistent with theological assumptions, and invites a theological interpretation, but it doesn't require one.

CONCLUSION

Natural theology, developed in conjunction with the mind sciences, is a neglected field, perhaps because the mind sciences only really developed after the height of Enlightenment natural theology was over. However, it raises interesting and important issues and deserves to have a more central place in natural theology in the future. The exceptional cognitive capacities of humans are consistent with what would be expected from a creator who wished to reveal himself and to draw creatures into relationship with himself. The pervasive religiousness of humans, especially their capacity for religious experience, is also consistent with a creator who wished to reveal himself. It would be a mistake to argue that either of these can only be handled theologically; both are intelligible within a naturalistic framework. However, a theological interpretation can handle them within a big explanatory framework that can also make sense, in an integrative way, of the many other things with which natural theology is concerned.

REFERENCES

Amati, D. and T. Shallice (2007). 'On the Emergence of Modern Humans'. *Cognition* 103: 358–85.

Ayala, F. J. (1988). 'Can "Progress" be Defined as a Biological Concept?' in *Evolutionary Progress*. Edited by M. H. Nitecki. Chicago, IL: University of Chicago Press.

Barbour, I. G. (2002). *Nature, Human Nature and God*. London: SPCK.

Barnard, P. J. et al. (2007). 'Differentiation in Cognitive and Emotional Meanings: An Evolutionary Analysis'. *Cognition and Emotion* 21: 1155–83.

Barr, J. (1993). *Biblical Faith and Natural Theology: The Gifford Lectures for 1991, Delivered in the University of Edinburgh*. Oxford: Clarendon Press.

Barrett, D. B., G. T. Kurian, and T. M. Johnson (2001). *World Christian Encyclopedia: A Comparative Survey of Churches and Religions in the Modern World*. Oxford: Oxford University Press.

Barrett, J. L. (2010). 'The Relative Unnaturalness of Atheism: On Why Geertz and Markússon Are both Right and Wrong'. *Religion* 40: 169–72.

—— (2012). *Born Believers: The Science of Childhood Religion*. New York: Free Press.

Baumeister, R. F. (1996). *Evil: Inside Human Cruelty and Violence*. Basingstoke: W. H. Freeman.

Bering, J. (2010). *The God Instinct: The Psychology of Souls, Destiny and the Meaning of Life*. London: Nicholas Brealey.

Boyer, P. (1994). *The Naturalness of Religious Ideas: A Cognitive Theory of Religion*. Berkeley, CA: University of California Press.

Brown, W. S., N. C. Murphy, and H. N. Malony (1998). *Whatever Happened to the Soul?: Scientific and Theological Portraits of Human Nature*. Minneapolis: Fortress Press.

Bucci, W. (1997). *Psychoanalysis and Cognitive Science: A Multiple Code Theory*. New York: Guilford Press.

Byrne, P. (1989). *Natural Religion and the Nature of Religion: The Legacy of Deism*. London: Routledge.

Crick, F. (1994). *The Astonishing Hypothesis: The Scientific Search for the Soul*. London: Simon & Schuster.

Davie, G. (1994). *Religion in Britain since 1945: Believing without Belonging*. Oxford: Blackwell.

—— (2002). *Europe: The Exceptional Case: Parameters of Faith in the Modern World*. London: Darton Longman & Todd.

Eaves, L. et al. (1999). 'Comparing the Biological and Cultural Inheritance of Personality and Social Attitudes in the Virginia 30,000 Study of Twins and their Relatives'. *Twin Research* 2: 62–80.

Geertz, C. and G. I. Markússon (2009). 'Religion is Natural, Atheism Is Not: On Why Everybody is both Right and Wrong'. *Religion* 40: 152–65.

Hay, D. and A. Morisy (1978). 'Reports of Esctatic, Paranormal, or Religious Experience in Great Britain and the United States: A Comparison of Trends'. *Journal for the Scientific Study of Religion* 17: 255–68.

Hood, R. W., P. C. Hill, and B. Spilka (2009). *The Psychology of Religion: An Empirical Approach*. New York: Guilford.

Hume, D. (2008). *Principal Writings on Religion*. Oxford: Oxford University Press.

Huyssteen, W. van (2006). *Alone in the World? Human Uniqueness in Science and Theology: The Gifford Lectures, the University of Edinburgh, Spring 2004*. Grand Rapids, MI and Cambridge: William B. Eerdmans Pub. Co.

Illingworth, J. R. (1890). 'The Incarnation and Development' in *Lux Mundi: A Series of Studies in the Religion of the Incarnation*. Edited by C. Gore. London: John Murray.

Jeeves, M. A. (2006). *Human Nature: Reflections on the Integration of Psychology and Christianity*. Philadelphia: Templeton Foundation Press.

Jeeves, M. A. and W. S. Brown (2009). *Neuroscience, Psychology, and Religion*. West Conshohocken, PA: Templeton Foundation Press.

Kingsley, C. (1992). Letter to Charles Darwin, 18 November 1859 in *The Correspondence of Charles Darwin*. Vol. VII: *1858–59*. Edited by Frederick Burkhardt and Sydney Smith. Cambridge: Cambridge University Press: pp. 379–80.

Lash, N. (1996). *The Beginning and the end of 'Religion'*. Cambridge: Cambridge University Press.

Locke, J. (2008). *An Essay Concerning Human Understanding*. Oxford: Oxford University Press.

Murray, M. J. and A. Goldberg (2009). 'Evolutionary Accounts of Religion: Explaining Religion Away' in *The Believing Primate; Scientific, Philosophical and Theological Reflections on the Origin of Religion*. Edited by J. Schloss and M. Murray. Oxford: Oxford University Press.

Peterson, G. R. (2003). *Minding God: Theology and the Cognitive Sciences*. Minneapolis: Fortress Press.

Polkinghorne, J. C. (1988). *Science and Creation: The Search for Understanding*. London: SPCK.

Seybold, K. S. (2007). *Explorations in Neuroscience, Psychology, and Religion*. Aldershot: Ashgate.

Smith, C. (2003). *Moral, Believing Animals: Human Personhood and Culture*. Oxford: Oxford University Press.

Smith, W. C. (1991). *The Meaning and End of Religion*. Minneapolis: Fortress Press.

Sober, E. and D. S. Wilson (1998). *Unto Others: The Evolution and Psychology of Unselfish Behavior*. Cambridge, MA and London: Harvard University Press.

Swinburne, R. (1979). *The Existence of God*. Oxford: Clarendon Press.

—— (1996). *Is There a God?* Oxford: Oxford University Press.

Teasdale, J. D. and P. J. Barnard (1993). *Affect, Cognition, and Change: Re-modelling Depressive Thought*. Hove: Erlbaum.

Wainwright, W. J. (1981). *Mysticism: A Study of its Nature, Cognitive Value and Moral Implications*. Brighton: Harvester Press.

Waller, N. G. et al. (1990). 'Genetic and Environmental Influences on Religious Attitudes and Values: A Study of Twins Reared Apart and Together'. *Psychological Studies* 1: 138–42.

Watts, F. N. (2002). *Theology and Psychology*. Aldershot: Ashgate.

—— (2008). *Creation: Law and Probability*. Minneapolis: Fortress Press.

—— (2009). 'Darwin's Gifts to Theology' in *Theology, Evolution and the Mind*. Edited by N. Spurway. Newcastle: Cambridge Scholars.

···

CHAPTER 31

A SOCIOLOGICAL PERSPECTIVE ON NATURAL THEOLOGY

···

RICHARD K. FENN

THE MIRACLE OF EXISTENCE

···

IN discussing natural theology, I am not assuming that there is an essential difference between revealed and natural religion. That distinction is essentially political or theological: political when it is used to allow a particular religious tradition to trump or supersede another form of religion; theological when a religious elite seeks to justify proselytizing a subordinate population or to discredit the beliefs of the laity. The political use of revelation to trump natural religion is familiar enough. People on the periphery of a social system may employ apocalyptic or millennial beliefs to condemn the political or cultural centre, or an elite may use apocalypticism to colonize and suppress the faith of a vulnerable population. An elitist, ideological interest in undermining the soul's sense of its own local, unique, particular agency, even while promising it a recovery of its spiritual agency, is revealed in the strategy of Dutch theologians and missionaries in Indonesia, who, according to the anthropologist Webb Keane, argued that 'only when humans realize the agency that is proper to them, wresting it from the false agents to which they had imputed it, will the many local histories flow into a universal one' (Keane 2007: 145). Similarly, anthropological treatments of indigenous religiosity may also subordinate or compare them to imported or more global systems of belief and practice, as if the indigenous is primarily a preparation for or inferior to the universal: natural, as opposed to revealed.

I argue here that to understand natural theology we have to grasp what Freud referred to as a 'pre-animist' form of religiosity, one that was widespread long before spirits became separate beings which inhabited rocks and trees as well as people, and even longer before spirits became gods with their own character, will, and divinity. Even to call this a religion is a bit anachronistic; rather it is a form of the sacred in which being itself is considered and felt to be miraculous. Belief in the sacred does not necessarily need to have a god who has a particular monopoly on being or who is prototypically Being itself, in relation to whom mortals have only a contingent and derived being that can only be known and experienced as a perennial becoming. In this pre-animist state, the cosmos itself is so permeated with spirit that simply to be is to participate in the miraculous.

That is, natural religion may not really be a religion, if by that term we have in mind a well-developed set of beliefs and practices institutionalized in a specific social context controlled by practitioners, specialists, or virtuosos. Certainly it may not be a religion if we think of religion as necessarily implying a more or less accessible divinity whose very being is somehow distinct from the cosmos, or who dwells in a heaven that is wholly uncoupled from the earth. Even if a natural religion has a god or gods, they may not be the same from one valley or mountaintop to the next. The sacred will inhere in a family of forms that may transcend geographic differences, but the forms may not mean the same thing on every mountain or in every valley. That is, the sacred may inhere in spaces such as Neolithic henges or tombs, or in the basements of Stone Age houses where the bones of the recently deceased share or take the place of the anonymous bones of those long dead, but an anthropologist would be hard put to find a religion in the local culture rather than the sacred in a variety of similar but distinct forms, such as stones shaped by the passage of water and time. A Neolithic stone cupped and shaped to hold water may be sacred, just as a Christian baptismal font hollowed out to hold water may be sacred, but the sacred, in the latter case, has been given sanctuary and supervision by a religious system, whereas a Neolithic stone cupped to hold water, blood, or other libations may be simply sacred.

The Time and Place of the Sacred

For lack of a better starting point, I will consider the sacred as a time and place in which individuals or groups, communities, or even whole societies encounter, if only in symbolic gestures and objects, the crises of death, terror, and the passage of time. Towards the end of this chapter we will return in more detail to the work of a sixth-century Celtic monk and poet, Dallan, who composed a poem in honor of St Columba: *Amra Choluimb Chille*. In Columba his followers had found a model to follow whose light blazed again after death, because the saint had escaped the 'second death' in which the soul is confined to hell. It was Columba who:

> would do no fast which was not the Lord's law,
> that he might not die an eternal death.
> Living his name, living his soul. [Clancy and Markus 1995:111]

Now his still living soul, immune to the second death:

> will protect us in Sion.
> He will urge me past torments.
> May it be easily dark defects go from me.
> He will come to me without delay. [115]

Now the poet has an advocate and a powerful spiritual ally whose presence and aid will guard Dallan himself from the death of the soul. Despite death, then, and despite the evil that seeks the death of the soul, no follower of Columba is expendable; their being matters, as though by virtue of Columba's embodiment of being itself. Note that their universe is not 'enchanted' in Max Weber's sense of the term. It is not mundane or transparent until and unless it is somehow invaded by something from the outside; there is no inside and outside. Similarly there is no sense that in embodying such a cosmic wisdom as Columba's, his followers may be divinizing themselves; there is no divinity whose being, like that of the sun, does not permeate all beings and give them life. The metaphors of being proliferate to include all that is elemental being, and therefore all beings matter ultimately.

Columba, we learn from Dallan, was steeped in the Wisdom tradition. Referring to a passage from the Wisdom of Solomon (7:22–4), John Collins notes that:

> Wisdom is so embedded in the universe that it can be expressed in physical terms- 'manifold, subtile, mobile, clear, unpolluted,' pervading all things by reason of her pureness…In 8.1 Wisdom is quite explicitly the principle or order, which 'reaches mightily from end to end and orders all things well'. [Collins 1977: 125]

In such a universe, I would add, one does not have to worry about running out of time. If Wisdom is the source of universal order and indeed 'orders all things well', whatever happens is an expression of Wisdom itself. Becoming is an unfolding and elaboration of being.

In natural religion more generally, I would argue, and specifically in the Wisdom tradition, the world of everyday life is sacred precisely because it is embedded in a cosmos oriented towards the salvation of the soul, and in that cosmic space the soul finds not only its own embodiment but the transfiguration of time itself. There are voices in the Wisdom tradition that proclaim they have been liberated not only from preoccupation and apprehension with time but from the need to make the most of time itself. Thus to be out of time was a sign of blessedness, as it is for the souls whom the fourteenth-century Dante envisages, at the end of their tour of duty in Purgatory, are neither seeking to undo or make up for the past or to speed their passage into heaven. Because they have become masters of their own souls, they do not mind waiting. Dallan proclaimed: 'I have no time!' Rather than being a shout of despair, his exclamation about having no time was an ode to his joy at having, in the vast ranges of his poem, reflected the vastness of the cosmos and of the heavenly wisdom that was embedded and incarnated in Columba himself. It was as if time had been diffused and expanded into the heavens, where it becomes time without end, indeed eternity. As we shall see, such timelessness was essential both to human nature and its destiny.

Even in the poetry attributed to Columba himself, however, we find the attempt of revelation to trump natural religion. Columba imagined that there was a place in the depths of the earth for those who had been born out of due time and who had therefore died before they could have received the blessings of the advent of Christ. Thus there is a place in the cosmos where souls may not be animated by the cosmic breath, the Wisdom, that gives life to, and constitutes the being of, all souls. Some beings, the blessed recipients of revelation, therefore matter more than others; and some beings exist outside the reach of cosmic sympathy and can run out of time. By the time the Wisdom tradition reached the Celtic periphery via Rome, revelation had begun to trump whatever form of the sacred could be found in natural religion.

Even in Rome, however, the sacred still had a life of its own apart from religious institutions. Indeed, the pre-animist view of the soul and of the cosmos survived in Stoicism's 'concept of cosmic breath or "pneuma" [which is] the physical substrate that pervades the cosmos through and through and that holds it together' (Salles 2009: 8). It is a spiritual form of matter, not matter in the modern sense of the word. Therefore 'the affections experienced by one body may be transmitted, either directly or indirectly, to all the other bodies and to the cosmos as a whole. This takes us to the Stoic doctrine of cosmic sympathy' (8–9). Everyone and everything is related to every other one and every other thing through this cosmic breath, which is the breath of God. Therefore to seek to immunize or insulate oneself from the profound effects of other beings is to lose one's connection with and access to this cosmic breath; it is to die spiritually. That is because 'in the Stoic cosmic chain of causes every body is connected to all the others by breath without, however, acting upon all of them directly' (9). Thus the human being is vulnerable in its core to the presence and essence of other beings, and therefore also to their absence, to their vitality, and to their joy, but also to their suffering and to their death. Our innermost beings thus are subject to being acted upon, and by our very nature we are open to change and fated for transformation. Any attempt to resist change, to live in a closed circle of personal reflection, to become monolithic in one's own being, to avoid the delight of intense mutual connection or the anguish of loss, is therefore fundamentally a denial of the miracle of one's own being and of human nature.

A RADICAL VULNERABILITY

At the core of the sacred, then, I would expect to find an experience in which the terrors of non-being are partially assuaged, at least for a while, by a sense of being profoundly coupled with the cosmos. A sense of connection to the cosmos, and to other souls, however, comes at a price: a radical vulnerability to the spirits, to the very beings, of others. Part of that vulnerability leads to the terror of being hurt by their indifference or by their malice, their greed or their disloyalty. However, some of that terror is caused by the disappearance and the absence of the one who seemed to have a grip on being and who embodied cosmic sympathy. Even Columba was known to have made extraordinary efforts to manage the aspects of the psyche that could pose harm to others and thus sought to minimize their vulnerability.

On the other hand, the same vulnerability had a passive side; in his absence and at his death individuals could lose their primal connection to the cosmos. Columba died and thus abandoned those who relied on him for a sense of their being. Thus a profound sense of being coupled with and at home in the cosmos, along with a sense that one's connection with being itself is tenuous and temporary, underlies a vulnerability to terror at the prospect of losing one's own being in the absence of others, and at their death. One's sense of one's own being in the world, then, was that one is dependent on presences that were fleeting, at best, and may have been burdensome, ominous, or dangerous. As Seneca would have it, only a strong connection with a person whose 'innate ability' has given him a name, like Cicero or Vergil's, which will be written in 'the book of Time' will guarantee that one endures past death in the memory of men; fortune and position will never guarantee this, but only such an enduring connection with the greatest of men (Seneca 1917: 145). It is to manage this constellation of death, terror, and time that the sacred offered companionship and practices, danger and protection.

It is hard to know whether such cultural innovation causes or reflects, conceals or reveals the experience of existential terror. Of all the ways that societies have sought to take comfort in and through nature, perhaps the most successful has been the attempt to couple the earth and its periods of light and darkness, calm and storm, with the heavens. Some have coupled the fate of the earth, and its alternating periods of darkness and light, with the heavens by using rocks that glow in the after-light of the setting sun, or by channelling the sun's rays on the longest night of the year into the depths of a cave or tomb. Still others sensed that the passage of time is somehow embedded in and transcended by the universe itself. If so, we may well understand why they sought the miracle of being in the person of extraordinary souls, whose presence was essential to life itself but whose deaths reopened the trauma of time itself, with all its suggestions that every soul is faced with non-being and darkness, absence and helplessness. We shall spend some time with a poetic elegy written in honor of St Columba, as one had who lived and died for others less endowed than he with the wisdom that links the soul with the cosmos. But even Columba had to undergo spiritual rigours in order to link the innermost thoughts of the heart with the divine soul animating the universe. So did the Stoics. Although natural religion, whether Stoic or in earlier forms of the Wisdom tradition, places human being within the context of a miraculous cosmos, even there the return of the sun and of life-giving light is as much an article of faith as of sight; extraordinary presences give life, but they too depart after having had to face their own inner darkness. The connection with superior or supernatural being is tenuous and impermanent; time is therefore always a problem, even to a soul in spiritual synchrony with the movements of the heavens. Although natural religion places being itself within the context of a miraculous cosmos, periods of darkness connote the passage of time. Especially in a universe permeated with divinity, the return of the sun and of life-giving light is an article of faith rather than of sight. Indeed, to stop the passage of time might therefore as well bring an eternal night as an endless day.

THE DREAD OF TIME

Nonetheless, not even the Wisdom tradition, in its Stoic, early Christian, or Celtic varieties was sufficient to allay the anxieties or the terrors posed by the prospect of non-being and expressed in apprehension over the passage of time. The dread of time runs deeper in the human psyche than perhaps we know. Neolithic peoples placed rocks, scalloped by time, over tombs. These monuments may well signify that these Neolithic peoples had found a way to embed time in space and to master the terror that time would run out or sweep them away. If so, they embody the wisdom of a Stone Age people. However, these same stones may not symbolize the transformation of time into space and the victory of the enduring over transient. Did the terror persist, as Seneca put it, that 'The deep flood of time will roll over us?' (Seneca 1917: 143). Granted that the passage of time has left its trace on rocks shaped over hundreds of years by torrents of water, our Western preoccupation with time and our attempts to master its passage may or may not conceal an underlying terror that time will run out sooner rather than later. Still, in a society that has become inured to deadlines and that prides itself on seizing the moment, the passage of time may only *seem* less threatening than in a Neolithic community society where the setting of the sun on the longest night of the year, for example, caused terror that the light may not return.

In looking for ways of describing and interpreting natural religion, I have chosen to begin with the Wisdom tradition because it was able to defend the sacred from being subsumed into Israelite history or being reduced to being a practical illustration and an application of a divinely revealed and promulgated Law. To be sure, the sacred became a source of ethical and cosmological reflection, as well as a way of grounding both the law and the life of the soul in nature itself. As John Collins has put it:

> The Wisdom of Solomon is obviously in continuity with the Hebrew wisdom tradition,... but it develops the cosmic character of wisdom and describes it in language which is more consistently conceptual and scientific.... The Wisdom of Solomon, however, explains the indwelling of wisdom in the souls of the righteous in accordance with its cosmological conceptions of the physical universe.... Nature fights for the righteous (15:7).... In the earlier wisdom books it was implied in the encyclopedic interests of the sages, but here it is explicitly related to the wisdom that leads to God. History is now also included in the sphere of wisdom.... History, like the cosmos, is an illustration of the workings of wisdom. Finally, the effectiveness of wisdom is not limited to the empirical life of the individual. It also endures beyond death, because wisdom and righteousness are immortal and can make righteous people immortal, too. [Collins 1977: 131]

Despite the cosmic animism of the Stoic view, there has emerged a difference between divinity and matter, and between divine and human being; time therefore has become a medium for existence, a source of contingency, and an occasion for the possible intrusion of the terrors of non-being. The Stoic God permeates nature completely; God can neither be distinguished from, subsumed by, reduced to, nor confused with nature.

God is the passionate soul of nature, in the same way that fire is both sustaining in the form of heat and yet an all-consuming essence (Salles 2009: 5). The Stoic God 'pervades matter by being mixed with it through and through in such a way as to be totally coextended with it. In consequence, god is present everywhere in this mixture' (5). Nonetheless God and matter are bodies that 'form nevertheless an irreducible pair' (6). Here, then, is the philosophic equivalent of the Wisdom tradition's comprehension of a God who permeates but is not reducible to the universe: 'Wisdom is so embedded in the universe that it can be expressed in physical terms' (Collins 1977: 125).

The attempt to anchor time in space could only be partially successful; time kept slipping free of its mooring and running, like the tides or the floods, fast and powerfully enough to carry people away. For the Stoic there is plenty to fear from the passage of time. In addition to catastrophes and the violence we normally might fear from enemies, there are the mundane changes of fortune that bedevil the virtuous fully as much as they punish the wicked: over time the body and the mind age, friends desert, enemies take advantage, illness sets in, and all that is left to comfort us is the soul. As Seneca put it:

> It is likely that some troubles will befall us; but it is not a present fact. How often has the unexpected happened! How often has the expected never come to pass! And even though it is ordained to be, what does it avail to run out to meet your suffering? You will suffer soon enough, when it arrives; so look forward meanwhile to better things. What shall you gain by doing this? Time. [Seneca 1917: 79]

That is why Seneca says 'We must make it our aim already to have lived long enough' (165).

In living as if one did not need more time to enhance or ground one's being in the cosmos, the Stoics could rely on their notion of fate. The parallel between God and matter, the notion of a cosmic breath that pervades all beings and sustains a universal sympathy among all beings, is extended from space into time; time is merely an extension of the causations brought into being by the all pervasive divinity within the cosmos: 'In fact, the Stoic god is identified with fate understood as the chain of causes' (Salles 2009: 7). Stoics claim that 'our actions are governed by our souls. A person's character (a particular tension of her soul) causes her action in the paradigmatic way in which the *logos* of a body is the cause of its activities. But any particular action also has an antecedent cause, the Stoics insist (and in so insisting subsume the action under the thesis of fate)' (88). Therefore the only space and time that are needed by the soul for a sense of its own being are the here and now. Such a conflation of space and time also connotes the mutual interpenetration of heaven and earth that characterizes the Wisdom tradition.

Not only the Stoics but some of the early Christian communities grounded the being of the individual in a similar space-time permeated with divinity. Speaking of the Gospel of Thomas, Stevan Davies writes that 'The dual equation of Jesus with wisdom, and Kingdom with wisdom, is occasionally reflected quite clearly in the sayings in Thomas. According to Thomas 91, some people requested Jesus to "Tell us who you are so that we can believe in you." ' (Davies 1983: 13). Jesus responded, 'You read the face of the heavens and of the earth, yet you have not recognized that which is right in front of you and you do not know how to read this very moment.' From the characteristic viewpoint of the Gospel of Thomas, this question is an invalid Christological query. You ought not look to Jesus as a leader or guide; look instead to what is right in front of you. The present moment, the present world, is the goal of the quest, and the significant act is that of perceiving it properly. Here, in Thomas 91, a question about Jesus is turned around toward an examination of space and time—leading to here and now

OUT OF TIME: THE LIMITS OF NATURAL RELIGION

Whether we are examining the Wisdom literature or aspects of classical Stoicism, we therefore have to ask why natural religion does not work better than it does. If the cosmos is on the side of the soul, and if the passage of time is enshrined within the cosmos itself, what is there, in essence, to fear? As we examine some of our sources for possible answers to this question, we will note that the cosmos itself has its terrors: thunder and lightning, for example, or the floods that symbolized for Seneca the passage of time that obliterates one's being. Why, in other words, has natural religion, with so much time on its side, never been fully proof against the passage of time itself? For Columba himself there was a hell deep within the structure of the earth, and the possibility that some are born out of due time to take advantage of saving revelation. If there is a hell embedded in the earth, as there was for Columba, there is a possibility that time will always remain a problem; those in hell have lost forever their chance to enjoy or embody the miracle being. Even within the Wisdom tradition, they may be imagined as having lost the righteousness that attunes their souls to divine Wisdom. In Stoic terms they may be thought to lack the righteousness that allows the soul to correspond with the divine soul that permeates and animates cosmos. For the Wisdom tradition, whether in its biblical or Stoic variations, it can always, for some, be too late.

Even if the cosmos is on the side of the soul, and its inherent powers of salvation are acquired through wisdom and righteousness, terror emerges from revelations concerning the end of time. Thus some aspects of the Wisdom tradition, and hence of natural religion, became assimilated to eschatological or apocalyptic perspectives that find the heavens as well as the earth so profoundly subject to the passage of time that it is difficult for an observer to distinguish the religious cure from the existential disease. However, I would argue that the sacred is never fully capable of suppressing the terror caused by disappearance or assuaging the terror caused by torment and death. True, time may inevitably free itself from any containment in space and become a force in its own right that will transform the cosmos. Nonetheless, if the apocalyptic is a source of revelation that inevitably and eventually trumps natural religion and evokes the dread of time, I would argue that such a dread is inevitably the result of the partial and tenuous coupling of the one psyche to another, or of one's being to the cosmos. Without becoming involved in questions of genre, which seek to distinguish between various kinds of Wisdom literature, or between the Wisdom tradition and the apocalyptic, for example, we still inevitably face the question of why it is that so much faith in the cosmos becomes displaced by the dread of time.

To transcend the passage of time was the sign of the soul that had achieved or realized its true affinity with the soul that animates the cosmos itself. The task of the soul is to accommodate its innermost thoughts and longings to the rhythms and to the divine voice audible to the wise in the heavens themselves. Rather than being terrified, then, by the passage of time, even when the sun disappears at the winter solstice, the path of wisdom is to know that one's own being is grounded in the cosmos, and even the passage of time will only shape the stones above the tomb or wash the more ephemeral parts of the body away, leaving bones to stand the test of time. Nonetheless, there is still much to dread in the universe, and it is often coded by darkness and lives in the invisible, as do demons themselves. Although time itself may be embedded in the cosmos, so are the souls, according to Columba, whose lives and deaths occurred too early to be present at the time of the Incarnation; it is thus too late for them. For them time consists of an unending spiritual death. Even though the universe itself is oriented towards the wisdom already present in the soul of each person, it is the work of every individual to eliminate all those aspects of the self which are not in accord with that very wisdom and which may destine the soul to the same fate as those who lived and died before the time of salvation. For those who fail to stand the test of time, their chance for salvation may be permanently arrested.

Thus there are many circumstantial answers to our question of why the dread of time reasserts itself and that revelation trumps the sacred in its various forms within natural religion. The Wisdom tradition may wear thin because the young are no longer interested in traditional devotions and loyalties. A society may also run out of time under a variety of conditions: in the midst of calamity, when the wicked prosper, or when many are attracted to novelty or to alien forms of inspiration and authority. Especially when there are no presences who seem sufficiently miraculous to restore faith that one's being is anchored in a cosmos that favours one's own salvation, a society may feel itself to be devoid of an eternal place in the cosmos.

The powers of an alien people or empire may make it obvious that a society's rituals and devotions are not working very well. The ancestors are notoriously unreliable; they may not feel gratified by the sacrifices offered them or they may have other things to do than to assist with fishing or the crops. Worse yet, novelty may trump tradition at any time, especially in the form of a prophet with a new revelation and with powers that border on the miraculous. In traditions that have assimilated the notion of righteousness to some notion of conformity to divine law, the relative prosperity and happiness of the wicked or the sufferings of the righteous themselves may arouse the dread that one's own being is not anchored within the cosmos or that time is not on the side either of the wise or the good. The terrors that come with the cosmos, floods and fires, earthquakes and lightning, like the catastrophes that decimate both the wise and the foolish, or the just and the unjust, may animate the terrors associated with the passage of time as being sinks suddenly and irreversibly into non-being.

IN OUR TIME: THE SACRED
AND THE PRESENT

There are various conditions in modern societies that may raise demands for the sacred whether or not the sacred is accessible within what closely resembles either the Wisdom tradition or Stoicism. The more that individuals are unsure of the ground of their being in the cosmos or of the strength of their connections with others, the more they may doubt and yet seek an existential connection with the cosmos or with persons, like celebrities, whose being seems more durable than their own or larger than life. Conversely, the more individuals are engaged in or seek to seize the present, the less they will dread the page of time. The more they take seriously their own subjectivity regardless of its relevance to or authorization by any social context, the less dependent they will feel on access to the sacred mediated by an institution or an elite. Especially where individuals are free to adopt a wide semantic range in their use of traditional terms for the sacred, or claim to be able to give authoritative accounts of their own personal experience, while drawing on a variety of sources of information about the environment or the cosmos, the more they will feel capable of constructing plausible ideas about their relation to the sacred and to the cosmos.

On the other hand, there may be less demand for the sacred, and for a primal connection to the cosmos, among those who have become inured to temporality. Modern societies tend to embed space in time; that is, even the cosmos, as we examine it, is coming to us from times past; we observe the passage of time as we look into space. Modern societies also intensify time pressures and have foreshortened time-frames within which they either reminisce or plan for the future. The very organization of a modern society is temporal; dividends and reports are quarterly, appointments are defined by the clock; the truth-value of a scientific statement lasts only until a later finding qualifies or invalidates it. Even in the interpretation of artistic genres, stress is placed on the ability of the artist to capture motion or a moment. Impressionist painters, for example, seem to have portrayed surfaces that not only reflect but embody or embed the light in scenes that capture a particular moment.

That said, however, it would be a mistake to assume so great a difference between modern and, say, Neolithic societies. Stone Age peoples also used reflective surfaces like quartz not only to reflect but to hold and embody the light of the sun if only for a moment after sunset. But such a moment shines with an eternal light. Quartz, too, often looked watery, and belonged to the same family of icons as the stones shaped by tides and currents over many years. Such stones are double-coded. That is, they embody fluidity and solidity, the transient and the permanent, time and space. It is as if the stone not only embodied but thus arrested the passage of time.

Precisely because Stone Age peoples went to such lengths to freeze time and to couple their own lives or being with the cosmos, one wonders how deeply and how permanently grounded in the universe they felt themselves to be. Transience was a major theme in the iconography of their tombs and henges. Like bones left behind by streams that had washed away the softer remains of the dead, stones shaped over time by water coded disappearance as well as presence, softness, and vulnerability as well as endurance and permanence. The rocks signified the tracks left by time, but their very presence suggested a victory over the passage of time, as if time had been stopped in its tracks.

Natural religion, on the other hand, turned time into space, or made space a medium for embodying the passage of time. Long after Neolithic peoples embedded the passage of time in heavy stones shaped over eons by torrents of water, the Trobriand islanders seem to have followed Cicero's advice of using objects and space as vehicles for time and aides to memory:

> Location segments the corpus of myth into separate cognitive units and it also serves as a mnemonic for recall of portions of the corpus. Secondly, a precise set of locations may serve as a series producer which organizes the totality of a Trobriand mythology along a temporal axis of logical precedence which is coextensive with the spatial axis of the sequence of locations. Thus the Trobriand narrator and his audience listening to the myth of the origin of mortality may be induced to recall the myth of first emergence which precedes it and the journeys of Tudava, the culture hero, which follow it ... For the listener well versed in his tradition, his mind would be speeded through the whole gamut of his culture from first things to last things aided by the positioning of each section of the narrative in one of a series of locales of a sacred geography. Conversely, we in the Western world emphasize temporality as our predominant mode of series producing. [Harwood 1976: 787]

Note that these spatial references to time concerned 'the origin of mortality', the moment indeed when for everyone time is stopped in its tracks: a notion that persists in the folk image of a clock that has stopped at the moment of a person's death. The use of geography to ground time allows the community to traverse and ground a sense of its own being in time. But the reference to Cicero is revealing. Such a use of space to code time is not incompatible with temporal anxieties nor does it suggest that time would never run out in such a space. Thus the Trobriand islanders locate their myths in particular geographical locations:

> the Kula trading voyages are made from northwest to southeast. These voyages might then be assumed to be a ritual reenactment of the mythological corpus; a pilgrimage replicating the sequence of sacred geography. An analogy could be drawn to the stations of the cross. [Harwood 1976: 787]

Both natural and revealed religion have made time the medium by which one's being becomes created, authorized, tested, or consummated, whether through a founding event, a defining moment or *kairos*, a sacred history, an eschaton, or an apocalypse. Time becomes an object of fear as the medium in which the individual's soul is tested and tried, and death is the punishment for those who fail the test of time. Time, because it is the medium of salvation, becomes the object of dread precisely because one's salvation depends entirely on how one uses the time one has been given, or honours the past, or anticipates and longs for a particular, divinely ordained future. Whether within the scope of a sacred history or an eschatological faith, or in a secular and romantic version of a belief in *kairos*, suffering is caused because such a moment has been missed or, for that matter, not arrived.

In a *kairos*, a crucial moment in which life and death hang in the balance, as do good and evil, or the past and the future, the gap can be closed between heaven and earth, between gods and humans. That is why the god is depicted, with long hair falling over the front of his head, which must be seized in the critical moment. In such a moment time intrudes and penetrates to the core of one's own being. All that one has is action, and one must act immediately, in order to seize time and thus quite literally to stop time in its tracks.

What has been lost in modern societies, I would argue, is the capacity of the sacred in the context of natural religion to embed time within the cosmos itself. In Psalm 19 the believer seeks to realize his or her being by attuning the thoughts or meditations of the heart to the heavenly voices that are audible to the faithful throughout the cosmos, but it is a cosmos that somehow is attuned to and fosters the well-being of the individual. The deepest longings of the individual are part of a nature that is given, and it is the telos of the cosmos to fulfil those longings. Collins would agree that the salvific tendency of the world is explained by the presence of righteousness in the world:

> Neither is there a kingdom of Hades upon earth, for righteousness is immortal... The exhortation to love righteousness is therefore an urging to put oneself in tune with that force in the world which is immortal and leads to immortality. The way in which humanity is related to the salvific forces of the world is further expressed in terms of wisdom. Wisdom is, of course, the human attribute of understanding, but it also has a cosmic dimension. [Collins 1977: 124–5]

Who now would argue or believe that the cosmos is on the side of salvation?

'I HAVE NO TIME': THE WISDOM OF COLUMBA

Precisely because individuals in modern societies have reason to question their connection with the cosmos, we may well doubt that there is a wisdom both in the universe and in their souls that orients and drives them towards a triumph over the terror of non-being. Nonetheless, from a sociological perspective, whether we are trying to understand contemporary islanders who track the passage of time and trace the origins of mortality in the landscape, or we are seeking to grasp an ancient dread of time, we need to place ourselves as closely as possible in the mind and heart of some who have expressed their confidence or apprehension about their being in space and in time. Perhaps our closest access to natural religion can therefore be found in the account of personal anguish by the Celtic monk who, as we have seen, mourns in poetry the death of a saint. For Dallan, Columba had stood between him and various dangers that threaten the soul with death over the course of a lifetime. The ground of one's own being, for ordinary mortals, was never as solid as the foundations of noble and authoritative souls.

In the last judgement, when offences against divine sovereignty are finally punished, the soul perishes eternally; there is no reprieve. To a modern ear accustomed to psychoanalytic interpretations it would be easy to attribute such a death to a cruel and overweening conscience; much of Freud's own work was designed to protect the soul from mortification under the relentless gaze of the superego. In the antique world of punitive emperors or sultans, the disfavour of the sovereign could undermine the last vestiges of the soul's sense of its own inner authority and sovereignty.

Sometimes it was the darkness of one's own inner passions that threatened to consume the soul; no wonder that Dallan prayed that 'dark defects' would 'easily' part from him. In the midst of such threats to the individual's own being, the soul needed a powerful friend who could withstand judgement; Columba was 'one who commits no wrong from which he dies' (Clancy and Markus 1995: 111). The soul needs an ally who can maintain a vital presence in the face of terror; Columba converted 'the fierce ones' (113). Certainly the soul needed an internal guide and authority who could remain in control of its own most destructive passions, and remain substantial in the absence of any presence other than its own. Certainly Columba 'fought a long and noble battle against flesh' (111). So that he would not offend a living soul: 'He destroyed the darkness of envy, / he destroyed the darkness of jealousy' (111). 'Although he body's desire, he destroyed it. He destroyed his meanness' (111). In the absence of the great soul capable of overcoming fear and temptation, immune to the second death, the soul may dissolve or be consumed by its own deepest anxiety; Dallan lamented that after Columba's death 'we do not have the seer who used to keep fears from us' (105). Now who will protect his followers from their fierce enemies, and who will eradicate envy, jealousy, and meanness from the hearts and souls of the people?

It would be too easy to read such a lament as reflecting the loss only of a strong, charismatic leader. Columba's uncanny and superb strength was due only partly to the rigours of his asceticism. Columba's soul was coupled with spiritual essences even more powerful than his own. In the presence of such a soul this life is coupled with the next: 'He reached the apostles, with hosts, with archangels; he reached the land where night is not seen' (107). That is, in Columba we have the answer to terror over being consumed with one's own or others' passions, or by non-being itself. His very life suggests that the antidote to terror is to couple the soul with undying and vital presences far removed in both time and space.

Because he 'used to speak with the apostle', time itself becomes coupled with space, and the heavens reunited with the earth (109). Because 'he spoke with an angel', his very nature was grounded in the supernatural, his earthly existence continuous with the heavenly (113). Being deeply rooted in tradition and conversant with the company of heaven, Columba had triumphed over the death of the soul. Therefore he also was grounded in nature and the ways of the cosmos:

he put together the harmony concerning the course of the moon, the course which
it ran with the rayed sun and the course of the sea. [109]

For those who are interested in whether or not there is something Pelagian about
Columba and Celtic spirituality, these affirmations might cause some apprehension that
Columba felt that there was something that individuals could do to warrant or perfect
their own salvation. In fact, there is enough continuity or resonance between time and
space, the heavenly and the earthly, the supernatural and the natural, that whole-souled
righteousness is itself not only a source but a sign of the coupling of the two worlds of the
spirit. To believers as grounded in the Wisdom tradition as were Columba and his followers, this would pose no problem; what beside their faith might be expected to make
them whole?

Thus also to Stoics whose understanding of the cosmos assured them that it was
animated by a divine soul analogous to their own, the Wisdom tradition was more
like a commonplace than an esoteric revelation. Only those with an ideological
commitment to a revelation of radical transcendence wished to place a barrier
between heaven and earth which no soul, however righteous and faithful, could pass
over. At the very least, then, the elegy for Columba evokes a world of the spirit
in which the soul is defended against the terrors of non-being by being coupled
with ancestors and angels, and with both nature and the supernatural. As Collins
reminds us:

> Wisdom is, of course, the human attribute of understanding, but it also has a cosmic
> dimension... Human beings become wise, and friends of God, by the indwelling of
> the spirit of wisdom, which is also the cosmic principle which holds all things
> together. While Wisd. of Sol. 1.4 implies that the recipient of wisdom must already
> be righteous, Wisd. of Sol. 7.27 suggests that it is wisdom which makes them right-
> eous, but we should not regard these statements as opposed. Rather, wisdom and
> righteousness are inseparable. Neither is found without the other. What is impor-
> tant is that the wisdom and righteousness of an individual is not an isolated rela-
> tionship with God but partakes of an order and purpose which is immanent in the
> universe. [Collins 1977: 125]

Natural religion thus insulates the individual from the terror of non-being by affirming a profound affinity between the depths of her own human nature and the motions
of the cosmos. The soul may be terrified by the sheer absence of another soul com-
mensurate with or corresponding to one's own. In addition, the darkest of human passions threaten to consume the soul from within or from without; passion, our own or
that of another, may deprive a soul of any sense of its own vitality and control. All of
this may assault or destroy the soul even without the added burden of fears of being
sentenced to eternal death. Thus the soul so deeply unsure of its own presence or vitality, integrity, or control, needs to be profoundly connected with someone or something far more enduring and vital than itself if it is ever to recover a sense of its own
being and sovereignty.

Such a coupling may take various forms, such as a belief that every living human being is in the presence of a divine soul which permeates the cosmos; conversely, the divine soul may be incarnated in an extraordinary human being whose spirit unites the living and the dead, the natural and the supernatural, indeed earth with the heavens. Therefore Columba's very absence threatens an uncoupling of heaven with earth, of this life with the next, and in that uncoupling a gap opens up through which fear and terror rush in:

> Great God protect me
> from the fiery wall,
> the long trench of tears. [Clancy and Markus 1995: 105]

Now his followers are left without an advocate for their souls in the face of terror and death:

> Now he is not, nothing is left to us, no relief for a soul, our sage
> …
> The whole world, it was his:
> It is a harp without a key,
> it is a church without an abbot. [105]

A seer or a sage, a priest or a monk, or even an ascetic or a holy warrior, can couple the heavens and the earth only if there is continuity in being at all levels of the cosmos. As John Collins puts it of the central chapters (6–9) of the Wisdom of Solomon, there is an order, which 'reaches mightily from end to end and orders all things well' (Wisdom 8:1) One therefore need not despair in the absence of such a soul as Columba, who is able to unite the social order with nature, and in the society he creates is able to encompass humanity itself, because 'there is an order in the world which is directed to salvation and well-being: "God did not make death and he does not delight in the death of the living. For he created all things that they might exist, and the generative forces of the world are conducive to salvation"' (Collins 1977: 124). That knowledge of the order underlying the cosmos, and of the meaning of time, is embedded in the Wisdom tradition, both in its biblical context and in various forms throughout the ancient Near East.

According to our poet, St Columba was steeped in the Wisdom tradition, specifically the wisdom books of Solomon, but he was also the very embodiment of that tradition, an example and expression of wisdom. He understood—and revealed—the coming together of space and time:

> when Wisdom enters into people, it does not simply make them just. Their transformation is far more than merely moral. As people acquire wisdom, they receive 'an accurate knowledge of the things that are, [and are to come] to know the structure of the world and the working of the elements, the beginning and end and middle of times' [Collins 1977: 125–6].

Thus Columba's knowledge of the ordering of the cosmos was a sign that he possessed the wisdom of which he had long made a study.

TIME OUT

There are really two universes of experience and understanding, only one of which is based on the truth about the soul and its relation to the cosmos. One universe is based on anxiety and terror; the threat of soul-loss is real, situational and yet existential, perennial, and endemic. In the second universe the soul finds its salvation through the desire for instruction that leads to understanding not only its place in the cosmos but also the meaning of the moment in the total span of all time, past, present, and future. With that understanding comes the realization that the soul, however real may be the threat of its loss or destruction, is rooted and grounded in the order of the cosmos itself. It is anchored in space and transcends the passage of time. Its own vital presence is given by the deity but can only be received through wisdom. Therefore the soul's desire and longing for wisdom opens a pathway to righteousness; righteousness is the mark of a soul that has discovered the eternal coupling of the living with the ancestral, the human with the angelic, the earthly with the heavenly. By our very nature we are endowed by the order of the universe with the longing and the capacity for the wisdom and righteousness we seek. Only divine judgement upon the darkness of our own and others' passions, along with the terror of non-being, threatens us with the loss of our souls.

It is only when the heavens are experienced as uncoupled from the earth that the passions appear to rule and, when unassuaged, to destroy the soul from within or without. Therefore the terror of feeling one's soul being consumed by the darkest of passions comes to those who have lost a sense of their original coupling with the ancestral and the angelic. With sufficient light we are able to see the universe as seeking to protect and guide our souls on their way to their original destination. Ontology is on the side of eternal life, and the cosmic order is conducive to salvation. Righteousness is not a moral achievement so much as a way of accepting what is already given. The terror of being alone in the universe and of disappearing into a vacuum of non-being is based on the failure to see what is always and already there. No one needs to dread time. In the end, the Celtic poet who proclaims 'I have no time' and the Stoic who says that, by not dreading the future, one comes to live wholly in the present and thus to have time, may have been saying the same thing.

REFERENCES

Clancy, Thomas Owen and Gilbert Markus, eds. (1995). *Iona: The Earliest Poetry of a Celtic Monastery*. Edinburgh: Edinburgh University Press.

Collins, John J. (1977). 'Cosmos and Salvation: Jewish Wisdom and Apocalyptic in the Hellenistic Age'. *History of Religions* 17/2 (November): 121–42.

Davies, Stevan (1983). 'Thomas: The Fourth Synoptic Gospel'. *The Biblical Archaeologist* 46/1 (Winter): 6–14.

Harwood, Frances (1976). 'Myth, Memory, and the Oral Tradition: Cicero in the Trobriands'. *American Anthropologist*, New Series, 78/4 (December): 783–96.

Keane, Webb (2007). *Christian Moderns: Freedom and Fetish in the Mission Encounter.* Berkeley, CA: University of California Press.

Salles, Ricardo, ed. (2009). *God and Cosmos in Stoicism.* Oxford and New York: Oxford University Press.

Seneca (1917). *Seneca IV Epistolae Morales I. Book I–LXV.* Translated by Richard M. Gummere. Loeb Classical Library. Cambridge, MA and London: Harvard University Press.

CHAPTER 32

SCIENTIFIC CRITIQUES OF NATURAL THEOLOGY

PHILIP CLAYTON

RELIGIOUS believers are as interested in grounding their faith in the present as they were in the hey-day of natural theology in the early modern period. To engage in the project of natural theology in the twenty-first century, however, means something significantly different from what it did in, say, the seventeenth century. Today natural theologians are naturally associated with different allies, have different enemies, and play a different cultural role. In our day, for example, the general public will tend to contrast them with 'new atheists' such as Richard Dawkins and locate them near, or perhaps as participants in, the movement known as 'Intelligent Design'.

Most importantly, I will argue, their relationship to the natural sciences will necessarily be different from what it was in the earlier decades or centuries of natural theology. As the historical, cultural, and scientific context changes, so too does the 'frame' through which the arguments themselves will be interpreted—even when the arguments may look identical on paper. Of course, this fact also applies to the scientific critics of natural theology. Some are tempted to dismiss the scientific critiques as representing dogmatic rejections of metaphysics, religion, faith, or values. Certainly in some cases they are. But in other cases, the scientific critics rightly reflect a changed situation: the growing power of science and technology as the world's only truly international language; the shifting status of sacred scriptures in a globalized world; the increasing acceptability of agnosticism and atheism; and the foreignness of metaphysical language in general, and God-talk in particular, to the conceptual world of universities around the world today.

Perhaps a brief anecdote will help express how influential this 'framing' has become. A few years ago I was participating in a one-day meeting organized by Michael Shermer at Cal Tech in Pasadena, California. The audience members, about 700, were similar to most university-related people today: science-oriented, and mostly agnostic and atheist. The question on the table was, 'Does science make belief in God obsolete?' Three of us— Keith Miller, Nancey Murphy, and I—offered subtle, nuanced arguments (or so I thought) for the answer, 'No, it doesn't.' As the day wore on, I was surprised to see how uninterested the audience was in our carefully honed cases. The real star of that day for them was the Christian apologist Hugh Ross, and it was the session with him that they obviously relished the most. They really wanted someone who would make extremely strong claims about being able to prove the existence of the Christian God directly from scientific results, and Hugh was the perfect grist for their mill. It was as if they were saying, 'Now *that's* natural theology!' When the rest of us sounded like Hugh Ross, the audience got interested. But when we argued that contemporary science is *compatible with* theism, or when we argued that Christian truth claims are *possibly true*, they went to sleep. 'Who cares about mere compatibility? If you think you can prove supernaturalism based on naturalism, we're all ears. But if you don't defend a robust supernaturalism, why should we care? You're just a naturalist like us, except with some rosy-coloured religious poetry thrown in around the edges.'

The point is not that everyone should do natural theology according to the model of Hugh Ross (2001, 2006) or that his arguments are the most persuasive. (At least for the Cal Tech audience they seemed impressively unpersuasive.) What the anecdote shows, I think, is that the expectations that natural theologians encounter today are vastly different from those at other points in history. Of course, the well-heeled natural theologian *may* be able to convince his readers that their interests are misguided or their expectations unreasonable. Still, even if he does, he first has to locate himself along the spectrum of contemporary players—say, Hugh Ross and Josh McDowell to Richard Dawkins and Christopher Hitchens—and make arguments that reflect the plausibility structures of today's scientifically trained audiences. Moreover, he will have to create in his readers a set of questions and interests that (in most cases) they will not already have. In the pages that follow we will see just how steep is the mountain that the aspiring natural theologian of today must climb.

THE CHANGED CONTEXT
AND ITS IMPLICATIONS

There are other reasons why the task of natural theology has become more difficult today than in the past. Many of these are well known: the changed status of theology, the decreased influence and declining membership of the Church, and the massively pluralistic context of belief in which we now live as citizens of the global community.

One change that commentators often fail to recognize, however, is the changed status of the humanities. The humanities are no longer thought leaders in the way that they were when many of today's publishing scholars were trained. Also, being active as a scholar in the humanities tends to make one believe that one's own pond is much larger and more influential than it is, and that the neighboring ocean of the natural sciences is smaller and less influential than *it* is. Everywhere one observes the downsizing of faculties and the closing of departments in the humanities. It is interesting to contrast the dwindling national budgets for education in the humanities with the rapidly rising budgets to support the natural sciences. Around the world, students, businesses, and governments view science and technology as useful and powerful, while the usefulness of the humanities comes increasingly into question. The net result is that a scholarly case for God by a humanities scholar, even a sophisticated one, no longer has the authority, the social and political status, that it once had.

Of course, books like Daniel Matt's *God and the Big Bang* (1996) or Francis Collins's *The Language of God* (2006) may still win an enthusiastic following within the author's specific religious tradition, in this case the Jewish and Christian communities respectively. But this warm response does not translate into a broader cultural authority. Non-believing scientists most often lump all Christian apologetic works—evangelical or liberal, rationalist or fideist—into a single category: non-scientific (the gentle response) or anti-scientific (the more militant or 'new atheist' response). Religion–science books by (say) Christians are most naturally viewed as internal statements of what this or that Christian special interest group is 'into'. To non-believing university audiences they have, perhaps, something like the status of a church brochure or the mission statement of a Christian organization that one might come across on a website.

Here I neither defend nor ridicule this response; we move on to evaluation in a moment. At this point it's enough to note that our topic, assessing the scientific critiques of natural theology, requires understanding their very different valence in the contemporary climate. In the university context, books of natural theology no longer function as arguments in some well-defined, neutral space of discourse. Since that discursive space no longer exists, they tend to be interpreted as personal or communal testimonies, hence as internal documents of one or another community of belief. (It goes without saying that this response runs counter to many of the intentions of the natural theologians who write such books.)

I should add that the standard rhetoric of theologians, religious leaders, and even entire denominations does not help matters. In the United States, major denominations are now hiring consultants and Madison Avenue executives to assist them in 'branding' their particular denomination; carefully constructed advertising campaigns already appear in a number of TV markets. It is perhaps inevitable that the carefully honed arguments of Christian apologists will be (mis-)interpreted in light of marketing campaigns of this sort.

THE EPISTEMOLOGICAL SHIFT

No less crucial for understanding the changed context for natural theology is the epistemological shift. Some fifty years ago Roderick Chisholm and his associates helped to launch a powerful school in epistemology under the banner of *foundationalism*. Today conservative evangelical and fundamentalist authors continue to appeal to foundationalist assumptions, but few others do. As Wentzel van Huyssteen (1998) and others have argued, ours has become a 'post-foundationalist' age. Though most grant this point, commentators are divided on what it means. Many characterize our new context as 'postmodern'; and, although there is a wide range of interpretations of this term and no single definition, one easily recognizes commonalities across the descriptions.

However one may wish to nuance the precise nature of post-foundationalist episte-mology, it seems undeniable that *natural theology in a post-traditionalist, postmodern context is a vastly different enterprise than it was in the era of rationalist and foundation-alist theories of knowledge.* Even when many of the same words and arguments are used, their meaning and status has been transformed. If you do a really good job of teaching the five 'Ways' of Thomas Aquinas to a room full of freshman students or seminarians, they may come to understand the individual premises of the argument in somewhat the same way that Aquinas intended; at least this is what the professor hopes. (If one listens carefully to Thomist scholars, however, one quickly realizes how distant Aquinas' assumptions about the natural world are from those taught at contemporary universi-ties.) Nevertheless, the *status* of the project that is entailed by using these five particular arguments is now radically different. Whether we like it or not, repeating the same sen-tences and voicing the same conclusion has become a different speech act in our context.

The question, then, is not whether natural theologians can still speak and write for a specified religious community; of course they can. In fact, the 'new' atheists and others believe that this is *all* that theologians do when they engage in theological reflection. In their view, theologians are *always* doing apologetics, whether they admit it or not. The hard question is whether (say) Christian apologists can really speak beyond their select communities to the general scientific community. Obviously one can preach to secular scientists. But can one compose arguments that, given the assumptions and plausibility framework of secular science, these scientists *ought* to find persuasive?

Some Uncomfortable Questions and a Sceptical Interim Conclusion

Those who listen to the scientific community will recognize that the entire field of 'reli-gion–science' is today widely seen as existing to serve an apologetic function for reli-gious communities. Virtually all the participants, it is said, are doing natural theology; they do not represent an academic discipline but are writing for the sake of their own religious tradition. By contrast, it is argued, when one does science, the goal is just to do good science—and we possess relatively sophisticated means for distinguishing success-ful from unsuccessful scientific theories.

Is it sufficient for natural theologians to write for their own communities? Is the chief goal to 'encourage the faithful', to shore them up against the seas of doubt? If one accepts that this is now the main, or even the only, task for Christian intellectuals, it becomes urgent to reflect on the implications of this shift for the definition, interpretation, and practice of natural theology. Several questions immediately arise:

- Has it become impossible to persuade across the theistic–atheistic divide or, indeed, even across religious lines?
- Is there no longer a 'shared table' of discourse—the metaphor Habermas repeatedly uses in describing the ideal speech situation—at which people can assemble to hear and evaluate arguments from other traditions?
- Do Christian apologists (for example) do natural theology in bad faith, claiming to offer arguments that non-believers ought to be persuaded by, when in fact they know that 'preaching to the choir' is the best that one can do?

Reflecting on these questions points to an inconvenient truth for natural theology: the present intellectual and cultural situation represents the most hostile climate for discussions between theists and atheists that we have seen in many decades. Those who engage in religion–science discussions in the context of the secular university or, say, the American public square today are intimately acquainted with this environment. If you publish a piece of natural theology, no matter how humble, in the *Huffington Post*, you may easily get 600 comments in response. Of these, 200 will be Christians (and a few Jewish and Muslim voices) writing in support, and 400 will be atheists declaring that you are a throw-back to the Stone Age (or worse).

Perhaps an image will help. Imagine a Venn diagram, with the three circles labelled 'Christian', 'atheist', and 'contemporary intellectual' (where this third term refers to the assumptions, beliefs, and attitudes dominant at universities in Europe and North America today—including, of course, assumptions about the status of science). Assume for a moment that one could measure the amount of common ground between these three and could express it as the percentage of overlap between the three circles in the Venn diagram.

I suggest that the cultural and intellectual situation has evolved in such a way over the last few years that the percentage of overlap between the three circles is smaller than it has been for many decades. Of course there are exceptions—relatively small groups of individuals who manage to find genuine conceptual common ground across these boundaries. But certainly the trend is downward. Atheist and theist philosophers in the 1960s and 1970s shared a variety of assumptions that made it possible to engage in common language games (Clayton 2010b). But one would not find the same common ground between, say, William Craig and Daniel Dennett today.

So how should one approach natural theology in such a hostile climate? I suggest five core guidelines:

1. Our mothers taught us that 'two wrongs don't make a right'. It becomes more urgent to resist the temptation to respond in kind to rhetoric-ridden non-arguments, to fight fire with fire. Given the teaching of their defining figure, Christians must hold to this standard with particular strictness.

2. Expecting that heated rhetoric from the ruling party will bend one's own judgement, one will watch carefully over one's own prose. One will attempt to excise the *ad hominems*, self-congratulatory language, and appeals to the assumptions of one's own compatriots that masquerade as real arguments.

3. Philosophy is about the self-critical pursuit of truth. One can reflect on topics in natural theology as an exploration of the current landscape in science and philosophy, weighing pros and cons solomonically (Clayton 2008: Ch. 3).

4. Natural theology might become a regulative endeavour, in (something like) the Kantian sense. That is, one would write *as if* there were a community of truth-seekers, *as if* rhetoric were not a replacement for argument.

5. Natural theologians can play positive roles in their own religious communities. Instead of fostering false certainty, they can actually model an open and self-critical attitude towards the beliefs of their own tradition. (Note that, to the extent they are successful in reducing dogmatism and over-inflated claims within their own communities, they undercut one of the standard atheist objections to religious belief.)

Scientific Critiques of Natural Theology

We have already considered some of the more general concerns that scientists have about the natural theology project and how they might interpret it. It's now time to consider more specific topics.

Arguments by scientists, and arguments made on behalf of science, tend to fall into three categories. The first and perhaps most dominant category consists of criticisms of religious beliefs and religious believing as such. The thesis is that religion is deeply irrational at best, and at worst inherently anti-scientific. We return to this, perhaps the scientist's deepest concern, in the final section.

The second category focusses on bad arguments made by natural theologians. Of course, criticisms of natural theology could in principle be raised by a wide variety of thinkers, whether or not their primary footing is in science (as the other chapters of this *Handbook* make abundantly clear). Still, it's not surprising that those who are drawn to the 'scientific critiques of natural theology' would be especially keen critics of the arguments of natural theologians. Here advocates of science function not as scientists but, more generically, as philosophers. After all, the second-highest achievement of a philosopher is to put together an internal critique of a position that is universally acknowledged to successfully undercut the arguments on its behalf. (The philosopher's highest achievement is to defend a position in a way that is immune to the criticisms.) Because there is nothing distinctively scientific in these criticisms, and because they are well covered by other authors, I treat them only as they naturally arise in the final category.

The third category consists of what scientists view as the more constructive alternative to metaphysical (theological) beliefs and to religious ways of knowing. It begins by emphasizing the epistemic strengths of science and its view of the world. It then emphasizes science's most distinct contribution to discussions with natural theologians: scientific results. Although I treat this topic under a series of headings, the reader should recognize that for the scientist it represents a single sustained argument, to whit: given their epistemic strength and explanatory power, scientific theories of the universe, the history of life, and the human person offer the best accounts that humans can obtain. The edifice of scientific theory taken as a whole therefore represents a stronger overall approach than its religious competitors. Or so, at any rate, runs the argument.

In what follows, then, I attempt to reconstruct the best arguments.

Scientific Knowledge
and Falsification

A friend quips, 'Humans will believe anything!' One doesn't have to be a specialist in the history of human thought, interview natives on tropical islands, or study abnormal psychology in order to find abundant examples of some pretty crazy belief formation. Strange believing comes in at least two flavours: people who believe pretty outlandish propositions to be true (just look at the headlines of the *National Enquirer*), and people who believe plausible things but with insufficient evidence. This latter category includes believing for bad reasons, believing based on no evidence, and believing in the face of strong evidence against one's belief.

Philosophers may have poked holes in particular doctrines advanced by Karl Popper and his followers under the heading of *falsificationism*, but their core thesis remains plausible. At the heart of being rational, Popper maintained, is holding one's beliefs open to falsifying evidence. Indeed, it is rational to actively seek falsifying evidence for one's own beliefs—especially if one is willing to discard those beliefs when one finds evidence of their inadequacy.

More than any other area of human experience, science is dedicated to the pursuit of falsifiable knowledge. Scientific theories can always be traced back to some specific set of evidence. Science encourages multiple competing hypotheses and clear procedures for deciding among the hypotheses. The case for a given theory must be replicable; any research group should in principle be able to obtain the same results as the original authors. In many cases, successful theories allow for predictions. Since predictions are the riskiest form of knowledge claim, they represent the most rigorous test available. The comparative track record speaks for itself: no form of human knowledge claim has ever done as well at the prediction test as natural scientific theories have done. The amazing and unprecedented growth of scientific knowledge over the last few hundred years provides the strongest recommendation one could find for the power of this means of acquiring knowledge.

Evidence-based Knowledge Claims

Empiricism is a technical school in philosophy. But one can recognize the strengths of an empirical basis for one's knowledge claims without buying into everything that goes under the label of empiricism. It would have been great if everything required for rationalist or a priori argumentation were in fact possible: theory-independent agreement on the meaning of central terms, universal assent to core propositions, and shared agreement about how to translate ordinary-language arguments into formal language and then into syllogistic form. But human abilities at these tasks turned out to be significantly more limited than the rationalists claimed. As a result, humans are much more dependent on empirical testing than the history of philosophy has recognized. The unique strength of science lies in the continuing discipline of empirical evidence and empirical testing.

The commitment of the sciences to *methodological naturalism*, at its most basic, expresses this search for evidence that is sufficient to decide which among competing hypotheses is the most accurate. Theists sometimes take this methodological naturalism as directed against them and their beliefs, but that is a misunderstanding. Science prefers causes in the natural order because only causal histories of this kind can be reconstructed, tested, and summarized in scientific theories. We add the adjective 'methodological' in order to express that this is a defining method for the practice of science. It remains logically possible that there could be causes and explanations of other sorts. But such explanations could not play a role in the natural sciences.

Methodological Naturalism and 'Metaphysical' Naturalism

I have shown how the naturalism that one finds in scientific practice is rooted in the basic methods of data acquisition, data analysis, and reconstruction in the natural sciences. It was important to begin this way because theists sometimes criticize this methodological commitment as if it were a metaphysical prejudice—that is, a random and unjustified attack on theism.

But perhaps there is an argument here as well. I have maintained that empirical science is the most rigorous form of knowledge that we possess and that science presupposes naturalism not only in the way its constructs its knowledge claims but also in the kind of claims that it can construct. If these two claims are true, don't we have some grounds for concluding that the objects, causes, and explanations that exist—at least any that we could know—are a part of this same natural order? That is, don't we have at least a presumptive case for metaphysical naturalism? Of course, this is not to argue that nothing could possibly exist outside of the natural order. Nor does it prove that humans could never have any knowledge of anything that isn't acquired through scientific (and therefore naturalistic) means, although some scientists famously argue this way. But the argument does at least switch the onus onto the supernaturalist; it now becomes her burden to show how it is that other kinds of objects and causes really exist and can be known by human knowers.

Experience shows that theists really don't like this argument. It is standard for natural theologians to acknowledge the role of methodological naturalism in the sciences, and equally standard for them to resist drawing *any* metaphysical conclusions from this fact. If neutral philosophical analysis finally supports such a separation, then one must rest satisfied with this conclusion. But such a sharp division does seem suspect. If our most rigorous means of knowing produce knowledge of a certain kind, namely naturalistic knowledge, then we have at least some reason to suspect that all things that can be rigorously known, objectively known, established in a definitive way, may well be of the same kind—that is, also naturalistic.

ULTIMATE ORIGINS AND SCIENTIFIC ORIGINS

Scientists have overstepped their bounds when they argued that there *could be* nothing prior to the physical universe. The argument of the last three sections requires a rather more humble conclusion: the best known, most likely, most assured, most justified kinds of claims about the origin of the universe will be scientific claims. The door to metaphysics can never be slammed completely shut, for it turns out that the door-slammer engages in metaphysics when he tries to make this argument. The strongest argument against the natural theologians is the argument from the comparative epistemic strength of scientific and metaphysical accounts of the origin of the universe.

An analogous criticism is raised concerning the possibility of miracles: interventions by God that bring about a state of affairs that wouldn't have otherwise occurred and (in its strongest form) an outcome that clashes with natural regularities, as for example in a dead man rising from the grave. Scientists who make the impossibility claim find themselves enmeshed in a thicket of metaphysical difficulties from which they rarely emerge unscathed. But a form of the Humean objection continues to be the most effective counter: it is epistemically more justified to believe that the regular patterns of nature have held in a particular case than to believe that an event has occurred which, from a natural point of view, is immensely improbable. A world in which miracles occur is a world in which it is difficult, and perhaps impossible, to carry out science as we know it, since one could never be sure in advance that there *is* a scientific explanation for an unusual event.

SCIENTIFIC COSMOLOGY

So imagine that we have a cosmos and we are trying to display the things in it. Scientists appeal to physical cosmology: explanations given in terms of fundamental physical laws, physical constants, the four forces, etc. Often the story we tell in one area of physics research, such as quantum mechanics, contributes to, enhances, or supplements another part of the story, such as the evolution of stars or reconstructing the early history of the universe. The convergence of distinct areas of physics into a single, coherent account is a source of great satisfaction, since it provides further evidence that we are on the right track in our explanations.

Natural theologians offer very different kinds of explanations. They seem less interested in the advances in science—that is, in scientific successes—and much more interested in the problems we haven't solved yet. This attitude creates some puzzlement for scientists, since it gives the impression that they are not really allies with the scientific project but are looking for areas where it fails. This is one of those areas where, to scientists, they look very much like the Intelligent Design theorists, who seem to want to bring in a God (they call him the Intelligent Designer) where scientists look for good physics explanations.

The debate about 'fine tuning' provides a good example. Believing and non-believing scientists alike agree that the fundamental laws and physical constants must lie within a very narrow range in order for life as we know it to arise. Natural theologians thus consider the fact that life has arisen as evidence of divine design. Non-believing scientists respond in two ways. Some think that the combination of laws and constants that we in fact observe does not need any explanation outside itself; it just is. Others seem to acknowledge that some other explanation is required if one does not consider the God-explanation to be adequate. These scientists are often the ones who endorse the multiverse explanation, namely, that there exists an infinite ensemble of universes in one multiverse. Alexander Vilenkin (2006) has argued that the mathematics of inflationary Big Bang cosmology suggests the existence of such a multiverse. Other critics, however, are concerned that the scientific grounds for multiverse theory are not adequate for such a huge ontological postulation: an infinity of other universes outside our own. These critics are concerned about multiverse postulations in the way we are concerned about string theory: neither seems to be detectable or testable in a scientific fashion.

But the more general point remains. One can respond to conundrums and paradoxes and unknowns in contemporary physics in two very different ways. The scientific way of responding is to use the inadequacies as an impetus for doing new and better science. The philosophical or natural-theological way of responding wants to use the present incompleteness of science as grounds for introducing another kind of argument altogether, metaphysical or theistic arguments. The wise scientist will not try to argue that metaphysics is impossible in principle, for the reasons already mentioned; such arguments are themselves metaphysical and therefore self-refuting. But the scientist may surely expect natural theologians to understand his puzzlement: whenever one encounters the sorts of puzzles that can induce scientific breakthroughs, the natural theologian wants to leave science altogether.

In closing this section, I should note very briefly that, from a scientific perspective, the end of the universe is not symmetrical with the origin of the universe. Big Bang cosmology does suggest an origin of this universe (although, if the Hartle–Hawking hypothesis is correct, there is no first moment, no $t = 0$). But since the best evidence suggests that there will be no final collapse of the universe into a singularity, there is no predicted end of the universe that might provide an opening for natural theologians analogous to the Big Bang. The standard model suggests a gradual 'heat death' of the universe, a final state of virtually no physical interaction a few degrees above absolute zero.

Theists can of course postulate that God will intervene at some specific point, discard the whole physical universe like a failed experiment, and introduce from above 'a new heaven and a new earth'. But one really must acknowledge that there is nothing in the *physical* evolution of the universe as we know it that would suggest such an event is likely. Hence there is nothing in physics that could explain such an intervention from outside; or, put differently, it is hard to see how one could square this divine intervention with anything that we know or could know from the study of physics.

Biology after Darwin Does Not Work towards a Telos

Imagine that the science–theology discussion *were* a rational discussion among competing interpretations. That is, imagine that there could be at least a modicum of agreement between theists and non-theists on the implications of scientific conclusions: when they are supportive of theism (or of a particular theistic belief), when they undercut it, and when they are neutral or close to neutral. These kinds of discussions do not occur very frequently. But if they did, I suggest that the participants (religious believers or not) might well agree that that an initial singularity, such as in a Big Bang cosmology (in the absence of a multiverse), is the kind of cosmology that would be consistent with the metaphysical hypothesis of theism. The discussants might also agree that the fine tuning of physical constants is likewise consistent with that metaphysical hypothesis.

By contrast, I also suggest that they should agree that a universe in which the process of the development of life is random, such as is defended in the standard model of evolutionary biology today, is uncongenial to theism. The reason for this difference is not difficult to state. A physical singularity by definition cannot be explained by antecedent physical conditions. Thus there is at least an opening for a *meta*-physical explanation. What of biology? Recall that classical theism includes the doctrine of providence, the belief that God continues to have some guiding role in the world subsequent to the moment of creation. One can *imagine* a biology that reflected, or even required, some such continuing divine role. For example, the claim that a soul has to be added to every human sperm and egg in order for a human person to be conceived would fall into this category; perhaps, even, biological evidence that evolution produces more and more perfect organisms, or organisms that become increasingly good on some moral scale, would support belief in continuing divine providence.

But the biology that we actually have is very different. Biology after Darwin includes randomness as a fundamental feature of evolution. The causes of genetic variations (e.g. radiation, replication errors) are not guided by the potential usefulness of the resulting phenotypes—if indeed the mutations produce viable phenotypes at all. Over time, biological evolution selects among populations, and one species may do better than others relative to a given environment. It's not just that the standard view provides no evidence that God tinkers with the genotypes; the theory is *based on* the premise of random variations at the genetic level and ruthless selection at the ecosystem level. Such a theory is not easily integrated with the doctrine of divine providence.

Now of course the standard model in biology could turn out to be wrong. Or perhaps some other kind of phenomenon such as 'convergence' (Conway Morris 2003) will eventually receive widespread biological support, encouraging the integration of theism with biology at another level. But natural theology has to appeal to actually existing science and not the science that one wants to exist or that may some day exist. And the biology that actually exists is non-teleological: mutations are not guided; the fitness of an organism is relative to an environment; and selection determines the growth or extinction of populations.

Of course, there are possible theistic responses. For example, the overall telos of history might be discernible only at a metaphysical level. Or, more simply, perhaps only at the level of the evolution of culture or of human consciousness can the overarching teleological patterns be discerned. Biology as such does not and cannot rule out such more metaphysical possibilities. It limits itself to a rather more specific and, I think, compelling observation: Darwinian biology is non-teleological.

Another response would note that biologists are currently correcting the so-called neo-Darwinian synthesis of the 1930s and 1940s. After many decades of 'teleonomy', many are now arguing that we need teleological language for understanding how individual organisms work. I actually support this rethinking of the study of organisms (Clayton 2010a). But note that this fact does not change the previous points. It could well be that our dominant biological paradigm allows us to talk of the purposes of organisms and their behaviours, without thereby endorsing the language of a directionality to the process as a whole.

EVOLUTIONARY PSYCHOLOGY
AND THE NEUROSCIENCES

Evolutionary psychology and the biology of belief represent a newer challenge to traditional natural theology. Many features of human psychology, including dispositions to act or respond in a particular way, can be well explained in terms of their evolutionary functions. Animal ethology, which explores the parallels with animal behaviour, helps make sense of the origins of these behaviours. Even the tendencies to form certain sorts of beliefs in certain sorts of situations have clear evolutionary roots. One can learn from these sciences without accepting overstated claims that cognition is fully reducible to biological causes. To the degree that the power of evolutionary psychology and the biology of belief increase, the openings for natural theology are decreased.

One should draw the same sort of conclusion from the rapid growth of the neurosciences. It is not necessary to say (with Crick 1994) that humans are 'nothing but a pack of neurons'. We are not reducible to 'wires and chemicals', and fMRI imaging does not tell you everything you need to know about human cognition and self-understanding. But the last years have brought an explosion of neurological data; real-time imaging has allowed non-invasive experimentation that previous generations of scientists could only dream about; and we now possess an impressive list of empirical correlations between conscious experience and neural firings.

It's no longer possible to call consciousness a sheer mystery. Even without the overstated claims of Crick and friends, the strength of neurological explanations demands a much stronger view of the dependence of 'mind' on brains. And there's every prospect that the neurosciences will make significantly more progress on these fronts in the coming years. It is natural to treat mental properties as emergent properties, in the sense that non-reductive physicalists do (Brown, Murphy, and Malony 1998), and even as components in emergent causal systems, as defended in the 'strong emergence' school (Clayton 2004). But these developments undercut claims that conscious life should be treated as a completely different substance that follows completely different principles than the brain, as affirmed by classical dualism (Moreland 2008).

FUNCTIONALISM IN THE SOCIAL SCIENCES

I've argued that neo-Darwinian biology raises the greatest difficulties for natural theology, whereas fine tuning and the initial singularity in physics offer at least an opening for the argument for God. Another area favoured by natural theologians is anthropology. Many attempts have been made to show that humans are 'in the image of God', and hence that it is more plausible to believe that we are the product of divine creative intent. These arguments frequently appeal to data from the social sciences to ground their conclusions.

At least four difficulties stand in the way of using contemporary social sciences (cognitive psychology, social psychology, sociology, economics, biological or cultural anthropology, and religious studies) and contemporary social theory as the basis for natural theology. First, contemporary work in the social sciences is being tied ever more closely to natural scientific theories and data. Natural theologians are drawn to the 'grand theories' of human nature that one associates, for example with the 'philosophische Anthropologie' of the early twentieth century (Helmut Plessner, Arnold Gehlen, Max Scheler), but actual work in social science today stands worlds away from such humanities-style arguments. Secondly, the social sciences are committed to explaining the human construction of social realities (see especially Searle 1995). Rather than opening up a line of argument from human social realities to a divine source, this methodological commitment seems to slam the door on such inferences. The third point is similar: social scientific explanations are *functionalist*; they explain statistically significant correlations in terms of the social (or psychological or economic) functions that a given belief or practice has. But natural theologians don't want religious beliefs reduced to their functions; they want to justify them as truly reflecting the divine nature or divine causal actions in the world.

Finally, cultural anthropology and religious studies reveal the vast diversity in human religious beliefs and cultural practices. This exuberant pluralism of religious beliefs about divine entities does not prove relativism, and hence the falsity of (say) all central Christian beliefs. But it does make it more difficult to substantiate the claim that all religious truth lies in the Scriptures or the beliefs of one single religious tradition.

Conclusion

In these pages I have attempted to lay out the more effective scientific critiques of natural theology. Although scientific developments stood in the foreground, the interpretations were heavily (albeit quietly) influenced by work in the philosophy of science, the kind that is largely directed by the sciences themselves.

I admit that this sort of nuanced discussion is not typical of the scientific critics of today. The more usual vitriolic objections to everything religious may help sell books to those who already think that all religion is stupid. But philosophically flawed arguments of that kind fail to show that the success of science entails the defeat of religion. Instead, readers with genuine philosophical interest should bemoan a cultural situation where high-profile philosophers prefer rhetorical tongue-lashings to sustained and sophisticated arguments (e.g. Dennett 2006). Heated atheist rhetoric tends to confirm the theists' assumption (prejudice?) that atheists don't really have the arguments to make their case, and hence that the atheist position is actually based more on dogmatism than on reason. Many of the arguments by well-known scientists are disappointing, even embarrassing, to those who know anything of the philosophical literature, no matter which side of the debate they may personally favour (one thinks of Dawkins 2006, Stenger 2007, and even Hawking and Mlodinow 2010). And aggression breeds aggression; of the literally dozens of books that have now appeared to answer Dawkins's *The God Delusion*, a significant percentage rely on rhetoric more than argument (Eagleton 2009).

Of course, scientific critiques of natural theology can be used for two vastly different purposes: more effectively to destroy natural theology, or to produce more powerful and credible natural theological arguments. My own work happens to serve the latter goal (Clayton 2008; Clayton and Knapp 2011). In genuinely philosophical discourse, one seeks to assess the quality of each argument, whether the outcome of the process supports one's own pre-existing beliefs or painfully undercuts them. It's not obvious that the recent literature is pervaded by discussions of that sort. One may only hope that natural theology becomes a field where the norm is the pursuit of truth through subtle arguments and trenchant criticisms, rather than a stage on which sabre-rattling, buckshot argumentation, and slash-and-burn warfare prevail.

REFERENCES

Brown, Warren, Nancey Murphy, and H. Newton Malony, eds. (1998). *Whatever Happened to the Soul? Scientific and Theological Portraits of Human Nature*. Minneapolis: Fortress Press.

Clayton, Philip (2004). *Mind and Emergence: From Quantum to Consciousness*. Oxford: Oxford University Press.

—— (2008). *Adventures in the Spirit*. Minneapolis: Fortress.

—— (2010a). 'Critical Afterword to the Biosemiotics Debate'. *Zygon* 45/3: 762–72.

—— (2010b). 'Something New under the Sun: Forty Years of Philosophy of Religion'. *International Journal for Philosophy of Religion* 68: 139–52.

Clayton, Philip and Steven Knapp (2011). *The Predicament of Belief: Science, Philosophy, Faith*. Oxford: Oxford University Press.

Collins, Francis S. (2006). *The Language of God*. New York: Free Press.

Conway Morris, Simon (2003). *Life's Solution: Inevitable Humans in a Lonely Universe*. Cambridge: Cambridge University Press.

Crick, Francis (1994). *The Astonishing Hypothesis: The Scientific Search for the Soul*. New York: Scribner.

Dawkins, Richard (2006). *The God Delusion*. Boston: Houghton Mifflin Co.

Dennett, Daniel C. (2006). *Breaking the Spell: Religion as a Natural Phenomenon*. New York: Viking.

Eagleton, Terry (2009). *Reason, Faith, and Revolution: Reflections on the God Debate*. New Haven, CT: Yale University Press.

Hawking, Stephen and Leonard Mlodinow (2010). *The Grand Design*. New York: Bantam Books.

Hitchens, Christopher (2007). *God is Not Great: How Religion Poisons Everything*. New York: Twelve (Hachette, Warner).

Huyssteen, J. Wentzel van (1998). *Duet or Duel? Theology and Science in a Postmodern World*. Harrisburg, PA: Trinity Press International.

Matt, Daniel (1996). *God and the Big Bang: Discovering Harmony between Science and Spirituality*. Woodstock, VT: Jewish Lights Pub.

Moreland, James Porter (2008). *Consciousness and the Existence of God: A Theistic Argument*. New York: Routledge.

Ross, Hugh (2001). *The Creator and the Cosmos: How the Greatest Scientific Discoveries of the Century Reveal God*. 3rd edn. Colorado Springs, CO: NavPress.

—— (2006). *Creation as Science: A Testable Model Approach to End the Creation/Evolution Wars*. Colorado Springs, CO: NavPress.

Searle, John R. (1995). *The Construction of Social Reality*. New York: Free Press.

Stenger, Victor J. (2007). *God: The Failed Hypothesis: How Science Shows that God Does Not Exist*. Amherst, NY: Prometheus Books.

Vilenkin, Alexander (2006). *Many Worlds in One: The Search for Other Universes*. New York: Hill and Wang.

PART V

PERSPECTIVES ON NATURAL THEOLOGY FROM THE ARTS

....

CHAPTER 33

AESTHETICS AND THE ARTS IN RELATION TO NATURAL THEOLOGY

....

FRANK BURCH BROWN

PROSPECTS

IF one were to imagine a map showing the various regions that natural theology typically wants to explore, one could visualize philosophy and science as sizeable continents. That is because, traditionally, what is 'natural' about natural theology is, first, its reliance on reason and our natural human capacities; and, secondly, its attention to nature. By contrast, aesthetics and the arts might be relatively hard to locate. We need to see why that is so—and why it can be important, nonetheless, to include art and aesthetics in natural theology. After considering, in general terms, some of the possible obstacles, especially related to method, we will look at areas in which scholarship in the arts and aesthetics converges with, and participates in, natural theology. The chapter concludes by considering a newly expanded understanding of natural theology and its relation to alternative approaches to aesthetics and the arts.

PROBLEMS

A great deal of art is located in the part of culture that is explicitly religious—to such an extent that it is hard to imagine a religion without artistic symbolism and expression of some sort. Music, painting, poetry, and architecture, for example, are often found in the immediate service of faith and under the influence of 'revealed theology' in a way that natural science and philosophy are not, at least since the Middle Ages. This active artistic involvement in religion is one thing that can make theological reflection on the arts both inviting and rewarding. But it can also make for complications for a natural theology of the arts, if one accepts a traditional notion of natural theology as providing 'support for religious beliefs by starting from premises that neither are nor presuppose any religious beliefs' (Alston 1991: 289).

One way around this difficulty is essentially to deny that it is an issue. In particular, one might argue that what is theologically relevant (or not) about works of art is much the same whether or not they wear a religious label. Accordingly, one could regard all forms of art and beauty as at least implicitly religious, as some theologians do who see beauty as transcendental or who see all art as expressing ultimate concern. Or one could take the stance of Christian theologians who do not consider any form of human artistry as such, or any earthly beauty, to be inherently 'religious' in a positive sense, but who say that Christian reflection on music or on beauty in general can discern patterns and secular parables conducive to faith when seen in the right light.

For now, we need to note why this way of getting around the religious commitments of some art, while not uncommon, is not entirely problem-free. On the one hand, suppose one claims that art in general is religious, or at least implicitly so. While that allows one to discover religious meaning in secular art, it also makes it difficult to explain why some enjoyable art, despite being aesthetically satisfying, seems no more religious, really, than skate-boarding or ski-jumping, both of which have well-attested aesthetic appeal. It also becomes difficult to explain the opposite phenomenon: why, for instance, people who are otherwise 'unbelievers' often seek out what they identify as spiritual forms of art—such as remarkable church buildings and liturgical music—precisely because they perceive them as having a special depth or a kind of beauty unavailable in much other art, and transcending words and religious doctrine (Wuthnow 2001). And if, alternatively, one is using the eyes of faith to look at art or beauty in general, that could seem unsatisfactory for the 'apologetic' purposes of natural theology because it would typically involve looking for analogies or patterns that it seems only a Christian would see as theologically significant anyway.

A second way for natural theology to circumvent the evident religiosity of certain kinds of art is not to deny that the overtly religious commitments of art can sometimes make a difference to both religion and art but to make a methodological choice to begin by provisionally removing or 'bracketing' any religious markers and by focussing on features common to all art. Again this approach, while rewarding, is not without its limitations, especially when taken as an all-encompassing method. How secular does the starting point need to be in order to be safe for natural theology? And how typical even of secular art is this kind of neutrality? What is one to do about the now well-documented fact that a great many modern and contemporary artists, even in the ostensibly secular avant-garde movements of the previous century, have had hidden but definite metaphysical and spiritual aims for their art (Lipsey 1988)?

All of this suggests that it can be problematical for a natural theology of the arts to rely exclusively on either of two assumptions: either that all art or beauty is basically the same in its relevance to theology or that the difference between secular and religious art is so clear and sharp as to necessitate screening out religious art altogether for the purposes of natural theology.

Beyond such issues, there is the consideration that, whereas natural theology has traditionally claimed to rely on reason, nothing seems less bound to rationality and argument than beauty and artistic imagination. Accordingly, if one is to reflect on art and on natural beauty in a reasonable way, one needs to draw on a discipline designed to allow one to reckon philosophically with such things as beauty, sublimity, taste, creative expression, and imagination. In turn, that means using reason partly to see its relationship to what lies beyond reason. That takes natural theology into the field of aesthetics.

ART AND AESTHETICS ON THE MAP OF NATURAL THEOLOGY

For a considerable period of time, natural theology has been regarded as forbidden or alien terrain from various points of view (see McGrath 2008). Criticisms have come from Barthian neo-orthodoxy and, more recently, radical orthodoxy, and varieties of post-liberal or postmodern theology. Depending on which of these standpoints is adopted, natural theology may be viewed as inherently too liberal or romantic, too secular or unchristian, too rationalist or metaphysical, too empiricist—or simply too apologetic, and thus too willing to employ whatever cultural norms and philosophies are prevalent in a given era. Implicit in these often mutually conflicting critiques of natural theology are various views of reason and revelation, of nature and grace, 'Christ and culture', religion and science, and so forth. That gives us all the more reason to note that natural theology takes many forms (Pailin 1995; McGrath 2008). Some of those forms are newly emerging, including ones that might be acceptable to some theologians otherwise critical. In view of this variety, the following discussion situates scholarship in the arts and aesthetics in relation to different approaches to natural theology. This endeavour is necessarily tentative, not only because the scope is broad but also because not all scholars whose work is relevant make use of the concept of natural theology per se.

AREA 1: THE SEARCH FOR EVIDENCE OF GOD OR TRANSCENDENCE IN EXPERIENCE AND CULTURE

Natural theology is perhaps best known for endeavouring to use reason, unaided by revelation, to provide proofs of, or at least evidence for, the existence of God. Such an approach, which has fallen into disfavour, survives today mainly as modified in various forms of apologetics and philosophical theology that are less concerned with proof than with plausibility and intuitive appeal (Migliore 2004: 354–69; McGrath 2008). That is where our first area of shared interest with aesthetics can be located. And here we begin with theological reflection that follows, but extends in new directions, the thought of Hans Urs von Balthasar, who did not see his own work as focussed on natural theology but as concerned centrally with the beauty of revelation. Richard Viladesau (1999) builds on Balthasar's theological aesthetics and on a rich tradition of thought, both ancient and modern, that sees beauty as a transcendental: that is, as an attribute, in some degree, of everything that so much as exists. Viladesau affirms and develops such a transcendental philosophy and theology of beauty (though not only that, since he acknowledges that beauty in relation to art and criticism does not function simply as a transcendental). The connection with natural theology becomes explicit where Viladesau's analysis claims to be based on aesthetic experience, or the experience of beauty, prior to any religious and theological uses of it—experience that he argues nonetheless supports the judgement of God's existence (1999: 105). Viladesau describes beauty, in a transcendental sense, as the intrinsic relation of intelligible form, truth, and virtue to joy, and specifically to the enjoyment of something's lovability and intrinsic worth. As a transcendental, beauty analogically has its source and goal in God. The experience of beauty, for us, is felt as both a sense of fullness and a longing for a total affirmation of the joy of existence. The condition for the possibility of this experience of beauty, Viladesau argues, is implicitly the ultimate beauty of infinite, divine bliss (1999: 138).

In a similar way, but with respect to the particulars of art rather than the qualities of beauty, Justus George Lawler examines the basic building blocks of poetic language. Employing a 'micropoetics', he wants to demonstrate the ways in which these core elements of poetic language function as miniature 'structures of transcendence', whether or not one assents formally and consciously to a theological understanding of the world. Invoking Heidegger's idea of the poet as shepherd of being, Lawler describes how, on an analogy with music, the figural patterns of a poem communicate something through, over, and beyond the merely lexical statement: a kind of 'central poem' in which all lesser poems find their ultimate meaning. The tropes of poetry, not just metaphor and simile but a whole cornucopia from chiasm to enjambment, provide in some sense true names for the mystery of being and the mystery of beauty situated in a 'paralogical realm' (Lawler 1979: 6–7). This sense of things, which Lawler finds even in poetry of John Donne, but more explicitly in Gerard Manley Hopkins, is one he thinks is at the root of Catholic traditions, Eastern and Western (1979: 91), in contrast to most Protestant traditions.

Lawler's way of going about suggesting the *meaning* of poetic meaning as something transcendent anticipates the work of the literary and cultural critic George Steiner. Like Lawler, Steiner concentrates on the language of literature but believes its secrets are somehow made especially manifest in the mystery of music. Just as Lawler speaks of meaning sacramentally—as present through, over, and beyond the microcosm of poetic figuration—so Steiner, although Jewish, uses the Christian language of sacramental real presence, but in the plural, in his book *Real Presences* (1989). 'The meanings of the meaning of music transcend', he writes, without feeling he can specify the nature of that transcendence with metaphysical or theological certainty. Music 'has long been, it continues to be, the unwritten theology of those who lack or reject any formal creed. Or to put it reciprocally: for many human beings, religion has been the music which they believe in.' Even though for the literalist, the truth-functions of Christianity such as transubstantiation and resurrection are 'narratives of verity', they also carry over into the inexplicability of mythical narration (1989: 229). Steiner is not shy of paradox, referring to the density of God's absence, and the edge of presence in that absence. While there is no way to refute deconstruction on its own terms, Steiner says, he repeatedly presents us with language and music as testimony to an excess of presence (similar to what the philosopher Paul Ricoeur would call a 'surplus of meaning'). Steiner's rhetoric reaches wide, claiming that no 'serious' writer, composer, and painter has ever really doubted for long that the work of art has a bearing on good and evil, on the enhancement or diminution of humanity (1989: 145). Steiner does pay special attention to certain works of religious art, especially Dante's *Divine Comedy*. What Steiner says, however, is intended to apply in many ways to all 'serious' art. Published as *Grammars of Creation* (2001), his Gifford lectures in natural theology continue themes already begun in *Real Presences*. Both works use hints of theology to interpret art, and major works of art to hint at theology, even while putting Jewish and Christian thought in tension and dialogue. While Steiner's work fits best with the form of natural theology that looks for support and evidence (no longer proofs) of transcendence in the phenomena of 'secular' art and culture, it shows more than a little affinity with the correlational theology we will consider later.

As the tentative character of Steiner's metaphysical speculation suggests, metaphysics has fallen on hard times. Yet some thinkers have gone ahead to develop a kind of metaphysical natural theology in which beauty and aesthetic creativity play an integral role. For this purpose, the philosophy of Alfred North Whitehead (1861–1947) has remained an ongoing resource. Whitehead's speculative metaphysics was not metaphysics in the older, foundational sense. Attending to experience at many levels, Whitehead was aware of the limitations as well as the possibilities of language and multiple modes of thought (Whitehead 1929, 1938; Brown 1983). Whitehead found inspiration in the Romantics for their refusal to accept a mechanistic view of nature, their respect for feeling as in part cognitive, and their sense of beauty and imagination as not simply self-contained but as perpetually open to new possibility. That, when combined with the deep influence of Plato, shaped his sense of the possible resources of his own metaphysics, which would, however, strive to be broadly empirical in its rationality, and which in its exposition was highly technical.

Consistent with the idea that for Whitehead creativity is a new transcendental (Fetz 1990), William Dean's theological aesthetic, based on Whitehead, emphasizes how process itself has an aesthetic character of 'coming to' that takes place by way of contrast between past and present, and involves creativity and anticipation, while allowing for an element of play (Dean 1972). God is the ground of novelty, and the experience of the 'lure' of beauty is in a fundamental way an experience of God (or vice versa). Edward Farley, in constructing his more wide-ranging theological aesthetic, makes much of Whitehead as one of the few modern philosophers whose vision of reality is at the same time a vision of beauty, which is both the harmonious synthesis of oppositions and the intense quality of experience that accompanies it (Farley 2001: 24–5). For Farley as well as for Whitehead, truth without beauty loses its interest. Marjorie Suchocki writes in the spirit of Whitehead: 'God's feeling, judgment, and love of the world are for the sake of integrating the world into God's own nature as the final adventure of things in a harmony that continuously surpasses itself, and this is beauty' (Suchocki 1995: 75). More phenomenological in approach, F. David Martin's *Art and the Religious Experience* (1972) combines insights from Whitehead and Heidegger to describe aesthetic experience in the various arts as luring us into participation with the religious dimension of experience. None of these studies, in spite of adventuring into metaphysics, make any claim to rest on absolute foundations. Indeed, they share with postmodernism a chastened awareness of the inevitable inadequacy of any conceptual scheme and of the ambiguity in all thought and representation. At the same time, as one can see, they tend to work with broad notions such as 'the religious' and 'the aesthetic' and to have a relatively undifferentiated concept of beauty or creativity.

AREA 2: NATURE AND THE COSMOS INTERPRETED THEOLOGICALLY AND AESTHETICALLY

Whereas the first kind of natural theology is concerned with looking to our experience of the world and culture for persuasive evidence of, or pointers towards, God's existence or transcendent reality, a second kind of natural theology looks to nature itself, and the order of the cosmos, for such signs or evidence. The classic argument from nature's design has often appealed, at least implicitly, to a sense of the beauty of the created order. In that way the argument has been aesthetic. After all, the design of the world would seem less wondrous, less divine, if it were devoid of beauty. When Augustine and medieval Christians under his influence referred to the biblical Book of Wisdom, and its assertion that God has made all things according to the measure, number, and weight (Wisdom 11:20), they partly had creation's beauty in mind. In their thinking, number and mathematics were not divorced from the other qualities of beauty, such as its harmony and luminosity.

That older vision of a natural theological aesthetic, combining mathematics, cosmology, and theology, was incorporated into the very design of Gothic architecture (von Simson 1956; Ball 2008). And just as the Gothic cathedral can be described as incorporating an astonishingly comprehensive aesthetic theology of nature and the cosmos, so does the theology of Dante's 'cathedral in poetry', the *Divine Comedy*, which Dante daringly invites us to regard as a kind of scripture (Hawkins 1999). In moving down into, and up out of, the grotesque horrors of hell, through the hopeful pains of purgatory, into the heavenly spheres and on to the outer Empyrean and the beatific vision in heaven, Dante begins by following reason, in the form of Virgil, prompted by grace and further informed and later transcended by faith. A theologian of nature will notice how, in Dante, images drawn from daily life, and similes calling to mind the creatures of this very world, continue to the end. Even in the final canto of the *Paradiso*, where Dante finds himself paradoxically beyond space and time, there are references to seeds and blossoms, clouds and snow, as well as to a recollection of an infant suckling at his mother's breast, and a memory of how it feels to wake from a dream. In this sacramental universe, the pilgrim Dante who had lost his way mid-life, having earlier lost his beloved Beatrice in death, is called to respond to the higher love that Beatrice now embodies in paradise. And still the love she evokes and transforms retains colours hinting of eros, however purified and heightened. It is by looking into the eyes of Beatrice in heaven that Dante first sees, reflected, the eternal beauty of God (*Paradiso*: Canto 18). And colours, so earthly in connotation, persist in the bright essence of that divine light, even in the joyful ultimate vision: a different colour for each circle of triune light. One of those circles 'in its very color' is painted with our human likeness, and each of the three circles is reflected by the other, 'as rainbow is by rainbow', the natural wonder of rainbows suffusing this most exalted vision of the love that moves the sun and the other stars (*Paradiso*, Canto 34). Here, in the poetry's aesthetics, one has a theology of the cosmos, a theology of nature, love, and beauty, combined with a theology of revelation. A natural theology in the sense of incorporating a theology of nature, *The Divine Comedy* is certainly not natural theology in the sense of making do without the aid of revelation. At the same time, what that revelation means is itself seen in a new light; Dante's *mimesis* of Scripture is simultaneously *poiesis*, a new act of making that is also a making new.

There are artistic theologies of nature that stay closer to the ground, even if the ground is often mountainous. Barbara Novak in a major study has shown convincingly that American landscape painting of the nineteenth century was in some sense painted theology, reflecting devoutly on nature as God's 'second scripture'. The Hudson River School, the American Luminists, and their successors found divine truths in both the microscopic details of South American flowers and in the grandeur of mountains and most of all in the immanence of God's moods symbolized by light. Thus these landscape painters could 'remind the nation of divine benevolence and of a chosen destiny by keeping before their eyes the mountains, trees, forests, and lakes which revealed the word in each shining image' (Novak 2007: 14).

One has the sense that a certain naive quality to the theology of nature persisted longer in America than in Europe, although the aesthetic side was repressed in pragmatism and the industrial revolution. Natural theology reappeared in a wilder and less orthodox form in the natural religious aesthetics of John Muir and the environmental movement, and again in various eclectic forms of eco-spirituality. The work of a theology of nature is still being carried out in significant ways in American artistic and literary terms, different in tone and spirit from either science in the usual sense or formal theology. American essayists and poets such as Loren Eiseley, Annie Dillard, Kathleen Norris, Belden Lane, and Mary Oliver do not, however, simply infuse a sense of wonder into their often scientifically informed scrutiny of nature and landscapes. Their images, narratives, and metaphors, compared with those of the nineteenth-century

Transcendentalists, differ in reflecting also on the grotesque in nature, the horrible suffering of creatures, and the sheer weirdness of God's ways with the world, sometimes less sublime than appalling.

Christianity is perhaps rightly accused of largely disenchanting the world of nature in favour of a divine preoccupation with humanity and history. A recovery of an appropriately religious sense of relationship to nature may rely in part on aesthetics as well as on eco-theology and science. That, at least, is the conviction underlying Alejandro Garćia-Rivera's *Garden of God* (2009), which blends the cosmology of Teilhard de Chardin with theological aesthetics indebted especially to Balthasar. By contrast, one might observe, the quasi-disappearance of God in the a/theology of postmodernism has been accompanied there by the virtual death of nature, corresponding to the retreat from nature that Suzie Gablik sees in much modern and postmodern art (1995). There is a pronounced tendency in postmodern discourse for everything (even embodiment) to become cultural construction or a kind of writing. As David Bentley Hart has pointed out, the postmodern sublime is simply the immensity of the unrepresentable and the excess of indeterminacy (Hart 2003: 66–7).

AREA 3: OPEN INQUIRY INTO THE NATURE OF RELIGION IN ITS CULTURAL EXPRESSIONS

With that reflection on the turn to culture, we are again reminded that religion itself inhabits human culture even when envisioning nature. That brings us to a third kind of natural theology: philosophical theology or philosophy of religion that is free to approach the arts and aesthetic experience in relation to multiple religions without a sense of obligation to a specific theology or religious tradition. In this connection, James Alfred Martin's *Beauty and Holiness: The Dialogue between Aesthetics and Religion* (1990) provides a groundwork with its historical overview of how religions, philosophers, and theologians have pursued questions of the relationship between beauty and holiness.

The classic modern study in this area is Gerardus van der Leeuw's *Sacred and Profane Beauty: The Holy in Art* (1963). The bulk of the study provides a detailed phenomenological description of arts in many eras and contexts, cultural and religious. Van der Leeuw argues that the arts and religion began in a state of primordial unity, after which each art later achieved its own integrity and autonomy, as did religion. Although that process resulted in tension and rivalry, we can discern within each art—dance, drama, literature, pictorial arts, architecture, and music—a trajectory that reaches through conflict towards mutual dependence and unity with religion. Van der Leeuw's Christian theological position becomes explicit in his concluding theological aesthetic. In this aspect, his approach resembles Christian approaches we will encounter later. Here he employs the doctrines of the Incarnation and divine grace to point to the miracle by which the opposition between religion and art is overcome, eschatologically, and partially in history. Everything of the essence of art considered as such relates to the Holy only by analogy, he says. And yet van der Leeuw can also say that holiness and beauty are already co-present in a primordial way, even if holiness is never exhausted by beauty. Their unity pre-exists, awaiting revelation.

Earle Coleman likewise explores what he calls the 'bonds' between art and religion in *Creativity and Spirituality* (1998). Although he does not see all art as religious, he does sees all religion as having artistic features. And certain artworks, he emphasizes, are indeed mediations, 'avatars' or 'incarnations' that yoke the human and the divine. Coleman takes the stance that, when we speak of art, we are referring to something that originates with humans, rather than with God, and that is always penultimate. Yet Coleman identifies common denominators between art and religion, or between the aesthetic and the spiritual: total response, unique emotions, a sense of self and union, beauty, receptivity, and creativity. Coleman's study exhibits a special sensitivity to Eastern religions as well as Western.

Similar in range is Thomas Martland's *Religion as Art* (1981). Martland understands religion and art as counterparts in the creation of the very frames of perception and meaning by which human beings interpret life and experience. Using speech-act theory and the cultural anthropology of Clifford Geertz, he stresses that both art and religion actually create the experience they interpret, rather than simply making some kind of meaning or beauty out of prior experience. With every major work of art, as in every religious movement, there is innovation beyond anything anticipated.

Brent Plate pushes further in postmodern directions (2005) by meditating on the work of Jewish thinker Walter Benjamin, who assists in rethinking religion through the arts. There is no question here of treating art as something essentially the same from era to era or as a culturally detached object of contemplation; on the contrary, in the modern era—the era of mechanical reproduction—the individual work loses its aura, according to Benjamin. That aura, if it continues (albeit diminished), is passed into the control of the masses who have access to reproductions. It is the work of art, not the artwork, that counts, and today the work of art tends to explode tradition and continuity. Beauty does not suffice, given its identification with the unity of form and content, and its dependence on cultural interpretations of symmetry and harmony. Lament becomes the true form of speech, linked to death and inexpressibility. The breaking point of the lines and limits of history is the site of the origins of art, which at this juncture can be a mode of repairing the world. Benjamin rejects the sheer ambiguity of a totally atheological aesthetics and yet, exhibiting his sympathies with Marxism, he focusses on the religious significance of the very material of the media of art. Plate argues that for Benjamin the sense perceptions of the masses create a new community, and that the awaited Messiah is none other than the aesthetic community potentially created in this way (Plate 2005: 139–40).

Plate sees connections between Benjamin's aesthetics and the a/theological aesthetics proposed by Mark C. Taylor in *Disfiguration* (1992). Yet Taylor would have us give up altogether on 'theoaesthetics' and, accordingly, on any hope of Utopia and any dream of salvation. If we are to 'think the unthinkable Other . . . it is necessary to unthink all we have thought with the name "God", as well as to give up on what Nietzsche describes as the "shadows of God" ' (Taylor 1992: 317, 318). For this demanding task, Taylor looks to developments in modern and postmodern art and architecture, including the disaster-laden and desert-like canvases of Anselm Kiefer. If for other interpreters such as Brown (1989) the tone of Kiefer is still capable of generating something like awe amidst the ruins, and the kind of existential question that a theologian like Paul Tillich finds fundamentally 'religious', that is not true for Taylor, who leaves no discernible room for reverence or a residual sense of the holy.

AREA 4: CREATIVE CHRISTIAN INTERPRETATION OF THE WORLD AND CULTURE

We have come to a border where natural theology in any traditional sense usually ends. In fact, we probably reached that border some time back, having in one way already crossed it from the beginning simply by including art and aesthetics as a source and potential means of natural theology. Up to now, the discussion has considered theological or religious aesthetics, and theories of art, in areas related to three different kinds of natural theology: (1) the search for evidence of God or of transcendence in culture and experience; (2) theological reflection on nature and the cosmos, partly as mediated through culture; and (3) interpretation of the nature of religion(s) and culture, where that has bracketed, either initially or completely, a reliance on religious authority and revelation. We conclude by considering: (4) those approaches that remove the brackets by undertaking natural theology overall on the basis of the Christian tradition.

One way of describing this fourth approach is to say that it intends to look at beauty, culture, and the arts through the eyes of faith, in a manner parallel to the way Dante's poetic theology looked at nature and the cosmos. This is what McGrath advocates in his proposed reformation of natural theology (2008), which is intended, in part, to allow Christianity a more capacious understanding of its implications by interpreting culture and the world as a whole. McGrath casts his net very widely indeed, however. And were we to explore this area fully, we might soon be considering most theological treatments of aesthetics and the arts. That would take us from Augustine to Jonathan Edwards, on to Hans Urs von Balthasar and Karl Barth, and then to Jean-Luc Marion and so forth. For our purposes, however, we will be selecting only from thinkers whose theologies are most invested in art and beauty as part of culture and human experience broadly speaking (including the experience of nature). This excludes those whose focus is primarily on the beauty of revelation or of Christian truth, in the manner of Balthasar and Hart (2003). Because of the historical meanings of the term natural theology, moreover, it is important here that faith, in this sense, retain an openness to discovery. For this reason it would be confusing to include Radical Orthodox approaches, to the extent they are represented by John Milbank's assertion that 'either the *entire* Christian narrative tells us how things truly are, or it does not. If it does, we have no other access to how things truly are, nor any additional means of determining the question' (1997: 141). It seems fair to say that, in spirit, and almost certainly in the intent, Milbank's approach goes against the grain of natural theology.

If faith is seeking understanding by means of theology, which very few would dispute, it must be open to seeing new things, or to seeing the same things differently. That seems a minimal requirement for natural theology. Anthony Monti, citing Moltmann, adopts this premise in his *Natural Theology of the Arts* (2003). Like Moltmann, Monti also sees a range of possibilities for natural theology. Monti draws deftly on a wide range of artistry and aesthetics in order to show that art does expand our understanding of faith. Art can also be a persuasive means of drawing outsiders into the Christian hermeneutical circle and, ultimately, a way of providing imaginative glimpses of truth that can only fully be envisioned eschatologically, and in Christian terms. Monti ends with the hope that the experience of art can lead finally to intuitive apprehension of the triune God who is self-revealed in Christ (2003: 169). Whether such an explicitly Christian and Trinitarian theology really emerges 'naturally' from the largely secular arts he discusses seems open to question, but Monti works with a complex notion of art that creates a sense of multiple possible connections with faith.

Jeremy Begbie, who speaks for himself elsewhere in this *Handbook*, likewise teases out figures and signs from art, particularly music. He is cautious about the risk that art will encroach on exclusively Christian claims. In approaching a theology of music and creation, for instance, he declares that Christ himself 'provides the first and supreme benchmark for any theology of creation that dares call itself Christian' (Begbie 2007: 189). This is not so confining as it might sound at first. In undertaking what we might call a phenomenology of music and time, Begbie examines, among other things, those musical structures that create tension and that delay gratification but in a deeply satisfying way that allows eventually for a special feeling of resolution, of promise leading to fulfillment. This 'prefiguring of resolution in music' can, Begbie says, 'provide a way of exploring the prefiguring of the eschaton in the coming of Christ and the giving of his Spirit'. According to Begbie, this musical sense of time is something that theology can miss when it settles for crudely linear models of time. Thus, musical art offers something fresh to theology. In this veiled and figurative manner, music becomes a resource for exploring particular doctrinal areas. Indeed, this may be one way in which 'music, under the grace of God, appears to have been involved in the very salvific processes of which we have been speaking, in the life, worship and witness of Christians' (Begbie 2000: 127). Begbie ties such musical effects closely to grace and the Christian community. In contrast, Albert Blackwell's probing study *The Sacred in Music* (1999) rather freely employs Christian sacramental language to discuss music without insisting on a close Christological link, and invokes the ancient Greek Pythagorean metaphysics of music and proportion in order to help discern manifestations of transcendence in musical harmony. More ambiguously, James Herbert (2008), influenced by the theology of Jean-Luc Marion, studies the divine and mundane in Western art and music in a postmodern theology of art that highlights the paradoxical and apophatic manner in which works of art and music establish a relation between the divine and human that is necessarily distant even when in proximity to the sacramental.

Paul Tillich's theology of culture is explicitly Christian but also aware of ambiguities and tensions. There is always some risk that the very name Tillich, like the name Barth, will trigger a chain of assumptions that trade on stereotypes untrue to the dialectical complexity of either theologian's work taken as a whole. Although Tillich's theology of culture has been examined in detail may times, Re Manning (2005) has recently been of special help in a study that emphasizes the importance of Tillich's early work, his genuine although secondary affinities with Barth, his conflicted but enduring connection with Romantic theology, and his fruitfullness when placed in dialogue with postmodern theology.

In this context what is needed is to highlight features of Tillich's work that draw together our focal issues in a new way. With Tillich our fourth kind of natural theology, which proceeds from a basis in the Christian tradition, uses a method of correlation in which the analysis of the cultural situation, including the arts, is allowed a distinctive and prominent voice to which theology responds. Tillich tries not to impose theological categories on culture in a heteronomous way but to allow the core religious questions to emerge from the cultural situation.

According to Tillich, religion has no choice but to take cultural form, even though no cultural expression of religion is final or ultimate. While religion has its own specific modes of cultural expression, including works of church architecture, what is far more important theologically, from Tillich's point of view, is the religious dimension that comes to expression in virtually all spheres of culture, and in our day, secular art in particular. Works of art express the ultimate concern of human existence, a concern that is at the root of religion, more immediately and directly than other forms of culture. While less reflective than science or philosophy, art's creativity and symbolism is revelatory in character, since genuine symbols participate in the reality to which they point. In this general sense all art is religious; yet some styles of art serve a religious function in each era more fully than others. In modernity, naturalism and impressionism, for example, reacted against idealism and romanticism, but in a way that tended to settle for self-sufficient finitude instead of breaking through to the eternal, as Tillich puts it, and to the 'unconditioned content of reality which lies beyond the antithesis of subject and object'. Things were different with German expressionism, whose dissolution of natural forms and often harshly expressive colours evoked the 'Abyss of being' (Tillich 1932: 86–7).

The artistic expression of the question of meaning, which is correlated with theology's answer, takes precedence over beauty in Tillich's analysis. It is nonetheless significant that Tillich testifies how, when serving as a chaplain in the First World War, he looked at reproductions of the great paintings of the ages, published in magazines. When the war ended, he hurried to a museum in Berlin to see Botticelli's *Madonna with Singing Angels*. There he gazed up in 'a state approaching ecstasy'. In the beauty of the painting, he says, there was 'Beauty itself', the experience of which affected his whole life and gave him 'the keys for the interpretation of human existence'. Tillich compares this experience to what is usually called religious revelation, although he acknowledges it could not match the moments in which prophets have been grasped with the power of the divine presence (Tillich 1987: 235). For both the prophet and for the beholder of art (in this case), however, the encounter opens up depths experienced 'in no other way'. Since Tillich acknowledges that this particular experience was never repeated, this could hardly be equated with the usual ways in which art expresses religion by expressing ultimate concern. Yet even here Tillich is interested in the power of art to express some aspect of that which concerns us ultimately, in and through aesthetic form. In this account Tillich is perhaps exceptionally unguarded but also exceptionally revealing.

If Tillich seems to allow the very forms of art to shape and colour a vision of both existence and its questions, would that not affect how theology's answers would 'look' and 'sound'? And affect how even the questions might be heard the next time? That would especially be true if one registered how fully culture, including the arts, is an integral part of religion itself and yet speaks in multiple voices, not all consonant with one another (Brown 1989). Culture and the religious situation would then be understood pluralistically, as would theology itself. Certain forms of art might then be seen and heard as 'doing' theology in ways the theologian too easily misses and cannot articulate fully in the conceptual discourse usual for theology. There might also be an opportunity to acknowledge even more clearly than Tillich himself does the importance to religion itself of allowing space for protest and critique from the 'other', and the value of uncommitted free play, where the imagination, for a while, lets even ultimate concerns undergo transformation into sheer possibility.

This is just what certain other theologians of art have feared, of course: that a mutually critical method of correlation would allow art and culture to reshape, somehow, the image and sound, the look and feel, of the substance of faith. Some theologians would, with reason, point out that humans can ask the wrong questions even from the depths of their being, or be confused, or might simply quit looking for depth in a postmodern cultural situation. Then what is a method of correlation to do? Perhaps one function of religion, rightly conceived, is to create the very understandings it needs, the way a radically innovative work of music can do.

Even if that is to some extent true, however, there is also a cultural situation, and a human agent, and neither is purely passive. It remains the case that the mutual interaction between message and form occurs inevitably the moment theology opens its mouth to speak. By the same token, art does not speak in a religious and theological vacuum when theology attends to culture, especially in the form of art: Tillich in company with Botticelli, Schleiermacher (1988) with Handel's *Messiah*, Barth with Mozart, Steiner with Dante, Hart with Bach, Monti with Beethoven, Begbie with musical time transformed. It is not that a religious, let alone 'Christian', experience of such art is inevitable. One can enjoy such artistry without it. But the possibility is there, depending on what one hears in the music, and what 'action' art is allowed to take, since the meaning of art is not simply a function of passive contemplation but also of its interaction with its context and its whole milieu (Wolterstorff 1980; Brown 1989, 2000).

This point can easily be missed in modern aesthetics, with its tendency to isolate art. But it can also be missed in the pre-modern traditions of thought, which many theologians are now eager to retrieve. Although the 'Great Tradition' in aesthetics allows us to see beauty and goodness and truth as interrelated and ultimately unified in God (Bychkov 2010), it has historically privileged moral, spiritual, and intellectual beauty—which can leave the arts on a low rung on the spiritual ladder. And since the transcendentals are mutually convertible, that pre-modern way of thinking about beauty in relation to truth has trouble acknowledging what modern aesthetics actually has insisted on: the intimate way in which form shapes meaning, so that medium and message, in aesthetics, are never fully separable. The truth as expressed beautifully or powerfully in art is never just the same as before, or vice versa.

The non-identity (yet integral connection) between some truth as intuited aesthetically and the corresponding truth as articulated theologically makes a difference to how one interprets theological affirmations of art, and not just Tillich's (Dillenberger 1986: 224–49). It is well known that Karl Barth in his *Church Dogmatics* claimed for Mozart a special place in theology. He believed Mozart knew something about creation in its total goodness that no other theologians or philosophers—or indeed musicians—either know or can express as Mozart did. In Mozart's music, Barth says, light shines all the more brightly because it breaks forth from the shadow. Indeed, this music provides 'clear and convincing proof that it is a slander on creation to charge it with a share in chaos because it includes a Yes and No, as though oriented to God on the one side and nothingness on the other. Mozart causes us to hear that even on the latter side, and therefore in its totality, creation praises its Master.' In the era of the devastating Lisbon earthquake, which so troubled theologians, 'Mozart had the peace of God which far transcends all the critical or speculative reason that praises and reproves [God]' (Barth 1960: 297–9).

Not to be outdone, theologian David Bentley Hart, in one of the few passages of his theological aesthetics in which he discusses art, declares: 'Bach is the greatest of Christian theologians'; that is because 'no one as compellingly demonstrates that the infinite is beauty and that beauty is infinite. It is in Bach's music, as nowhere else, that the potential boundlessness of thematic development becomes manifest' (Hart 2003: 286–7).

Allowing for an element of hyperbole in both Barth and Hart, one notices that they go so far as to use the language of 'proof' and 'demonstration' for music, along with acknowledging such music as 'manifestation' of theologically vital realities that transcend reason. Clearly both Barth and Hart believe that, in using words as theologians, they can contribute something to the interpretation of such music, and can bring something new to light in the process. The theologian need not merely listen, and point, speechlessly. Yet, unless Barth and Hart are prepared to say that we can dispense with Mozart or Bach once the theologian is finished—something Tillich never says of Botticelli or even Van Gogh—we are free to conclude that the theologian's words, whatever they may add logically and conceptually, will not, and cannot, exhaust what the art makes manifest and 'incarnates'. In ongoing dialogue, the aesthetic and metaphorical join with the conceptual and verbal forms of theology, but not simply with one voice—as though singing in absolutely seamless harmony—but often in counterpoint and polyphony.

When a theological truth is embodied or expressed aesthetically in human culture, the very expression of it is invariably a transformation, which is potentially both a veiling and a new revealing. What is special about artistic expression is that aesthetically felt thoughts and artistically imagined feelings give body, inner meaning, and possibly ineffable satisfaction or enjoyment (if not final resolution) to what is important about the truths of theology to begin with (Brown 1989). A natural theology that is serious about the very nature of aesthetic experience and its potential religious and Christian significance has every reason to attend to the arts specifically, and in all their diversity. This ranges from the 'free' beauty (often playful) of pure forms to the fully engaged protests and outcries of tragic and absurdist art. Such art—perhaps paradoxically—can not only disrupt theological responses when they are too easy but also prepare for the kind of ecstatic and revelatory experience afforded to Tillich by Botticelli's *Madonna with Singing Angels*.

REFERENCES

Alston, William P. (1991). *Perceiving God: The Epistemology of Religious Experience*. Ithaca, NY: Cornell University Press.

Ball, Philip (2008). *Universe of Stone: A Biography of Chartres Cathedral*. New York: HarperCollins.

Barth, Karl (1960). *Church Dogmatics*. Vol. 3. Translated by G. T. Thomson. Edinburgh: T&T Clark.

Begbie, Jeremy S. (2000). *Theology, Music, and Time*. Cambridge: Cambridge University Press.

——(2007). *Resounding Truth: Christian Wisdom in the World of Music*. Grand Rapids, MI: Baker.

Blackwell, Albert L. (1999). *The Sacred in Music*. Louisville: Westminster John Knox.

Brown, Frank Burch (1983). *Transfiguration: Poetic Meaning and the Language of Religious Belief*. Chapel Hill: University of North Carolina Press.

——(1989). *Religious Aesthetics: A Theological Study of Making and Meaning*. Princeton: Princeton University Press.

——(2000). *Good Taste, Bad Taste, and Christian Taste: Aesthetics in Religious Life*. New York: Oxford University Press.

Bychkov, Oleg V. (2010). *Aesthetic Revelation: Reading Ancient and Medieval Texts after Hans Urs von Balthasar*. Washington, DC: Catholic University of America Press.

Coleman, Earle J. (1998). *Creativity and Spirituality: Bonds between Art and Religion*. Albany: State University of New York Press.

Dante, Alighieri (2000–7). *Divine Comedy: Inferno, Purgatorio, Paradiso*. 3 vols. Translated by Robert Hollander and Jean Hollander. New York: Doubleday.

Dean, William (1972). *Coming To: A Theological Aesthetic*. Philadelphia: Westminster.

Dillenberger, John (1986). *A Theology of Artistic Sensibilities*. New York Crossroad: 1986.

Farley, Edward (2001). *Faith and Beauty: A Theological Aesthetic*. Aldershot: Ashgate.

Fetz, Reto Luzius (1990). 'Creativity: A New Transcendental?' in *Whitehead's Metaphysics of Creativity*. Edited by Friedrich Rapp and Reiner Wiehl. Albany: State University of New York Press.

Gablik, Suzie (1995). *The Re-enchantment of Art*. New York: Thames and Hudson.

García-Rivera, Alejandro (2009). *The Garden of God: A Theological Cosmology*. Minneapolis: Fortress.

Hart, David Bentley (2003). *The Beauty of the Infinite: The Aesthetics of Christian Truth*. Grand Rapids: Eerdmans.

Hawkins, Peter S. (1999). *Dante's Testaments: Essays in Scriptural Imagination.* Stanford: Stanford University Press.

Herbert, James D. (2008). *Our Distance from God: Studies of the Divine and the Mundane in Western Art and Music.* Berkley, CA and London: University of California Press.

Lawler, Justus George (1979). *Celestial Pantomime: Poetic Structures of Transcendence.* New Haven: Yale University Press.

Lipsey, Roger (1988). *The Spiritual in Twentieth-Century Art.* Repr. 2011 with modified title. New York: Dover.

Martin, F. David (1972). *Art and the Religious Experience: The 'Language' of the Sacred.* Lewisburg, PA: Bucknell University Press.

Martin, James Alfred, Jr (1990). *Beauty and Holiness: The Dialogue between Aesthetics and Religion.* Princeton: Princeton University Press.

Martland, Thomas R. (1981). *Religion as Art.* Albany: State University of New York Press.

McGrath, Alister E. (2008). *The Open Secret: A New Vision for Natural Theology.* Oxford: Blackwell.

Migliore, Daniel L. (2004). *Faith Seeking Understanding: An Introduction to Christian Theology.* 2nd edn with Appendix. Grand Rapids, MI: Eerdmans.

Milbank, John (1997). *The Word Made Strange: Theology, Language, Culture.* Oxford: Blackwell.

Monti, Anthony (2003). *A Natural Theology of the Arts: Imprint of the Spirit.* Aldershot: Ashgate.

Novak, Barbara (2007). *Nature and Culture: American Landscape and Painting, 1825–1875.* 3rd edn. New York: Oxford University Press.

Pailin, David A. (1995). 'Natural Theology' in *Companion Encyclopedia of Theology.* Edited by Peter Byrne and Leslie Houlden. London: Routledge: pp. 389–412.

Plate, S. Brent (2005). *Walter Benjamin, Religion, and Aesthetics: Rethinking Religion through the Arts.* New York: Routledge.

Re Manning, Russell (2005). *Theology at the End of Culture: Paul Tillich's Theology of Culture and Art.* Leuven: Peeters.

Schleiermacher, Friedrich (1988 [1821]). *On Religion: Speeches to its Cultured Despisers.* Translated by Richard Crouter. Cambridge: Cambridge University Press.

Steiner, George (1989). *Real Presences.* Chicago: University of Chicago Press.

—— (2001). *Grammars of Creation.* New Haven: Yale University Press.

Suchocki, Marjorie Hewitt (1995). *The Fall to Violence: Original Sin in Relational Theology.* New York: Continuum.

Taylor, Mark C. (1992). *Disfiguring: Art, Architecture, Religion.* Chicago, University of Chicago Press.

Tillich, Paul (1932). *The Religious Situation.* Repr. edn, 1956. New York: World Publishing.

—— (1987). *On Art and Architecture.* Edited by John Dillenberger. New York: Crossroad.

Viladesau, Richard (1999). *Theological Aesthetics: God in Imagination, Beauty, and Art.* New York: Oxford University Press.

Simson, Otto von (1956). *The Gothic Cathedral.* 3rd edn, 1988. Princeton: Princeton University Press.

Whitehead, Alfred North (1929). *Process and Reality.* Corrected edn, 1978. New York: Free Press, 1958.

—— (1938). *Modes of Thought.* Repr. 1968. New York: Macmillan.

Wolterstorff, Nicholas (1980). *Art in Action: Toward a Christian Aesthetic.* Grand Rapids, MI: Eerdmans.

Wuthnow, Robert (2001). *Creative Spirituality: The Way of the Artist.* Berkeley: University of California Press.

CHAPTER 34

IMAGINATION AND NATURAL THEOLOGY

DOUGLAS HEDLEY

Man can neither pray nor sacrifice to this God. Before the *causa sui*, man can neither fall to his knees in awe nor can he play music and dance before this god.

Martin Heidegger (2002: 72)

The Christian Philosopher must rehabilitate the Christian Imagination. That is, the Christian philosopher must show Christians how they can think about God's active and effective presence in the world along with the natural explanation provided by the methods of the sciences.

Edward H. Henderson (2004: 67)

IMAGINATION and natural theology seem to constitute an unlikely combination. One associates the term 'natural theology' with rational, possibly even deductive, arguments for the existence of God. It suggests the dry and maybe crabbed reasoning of professional schoolmen. The concept 'imagination' is more naturally linked with irrational 'Romantic' or poetic musings. Yet there is a deep and important connection between imagination and natural theology. From classical antiquity to some of the most important exponents of natural theology in recent thought, the endeavour to represent the transcendent in a rational manner has generated reflection about the finite mind's capacity to grasp 'the forms of things unseen', and how this capacity might be related to knowledge of other minds or the appreciation of an artwork. Secondly, we need to distinguish between the ideas and the use of certain concepts. Just as one should not limit 'natural theology' to a narrow subsection of theology with that explicit title, so too we should be wary of failing to see that certain thinkers were discussing the problem of the imagination, even if they were using a remote and unfamiliar vocabulary. Plato does not, for example, discuss myths as an instance of *phantasia*, and yet it is perfectly reasonable to see his work with myth as part of an interest in what we might call 'imagination'.

It is often observed that the noun 'imagination' has a wide range of meanings. There may be no core meaning to the word 'imagination' but rather a family of resemblances. It is not immediately obvious why forming images or forming hypotheses, speculating, or fantasizing should all be linked in any interesting manner. Many 'imaginings', for example do not require any mental images. If one 'imagines' that England might win the Ashes, the supposal does not require any images of English cricketers. Common to all meanings of imagining, however, is an intentional element: imaginings are about items, situations, or actions. As intentionality and consciousness have become much more central in philosophical discussion in the last couple of decades, the context of philosophical reflection upon the concept of imagination has changed radically since the mid-twentieth century and especially the austere behaviourism of Ryle's *The Concept of Mind* (1949).

According to the ancient definition of natural theology, it is opposed to civic or poetic theology. Civic theology meant simply the ritual practices of the state; poetic theology the fantastical productions of the poets: their shocking and lurid tales of the struggles and exploits of the gods. Natural theology meant an intellectual rigorous theology. Yet the imagination, poetic and scientific, has shaped natural theology from its origins in Greek philosophy. In part, the influence was negative. The earliest theologians among the Greek philosophers, like Xenophanes or Parmenides, were determined to avoid the absurdities or cruelties of the Olympians. But by the period of the Stoics or the Neoplatonists an allegorical account of the myths was developed. Through this method, the crudities of myths were removed in favour of an overarching natural theology. Such a natural theology was not necessarily theistic. Indeed, most Stoics defended a pantheistic rational theology.

Traditional natural theology tries to provide rational proof for the existence of God. Much so-called Continental thought has been preoccupied with Heidegger's challenge that traditional Western thought has been in the grips of 'onto-theology'—a tendency both to reify and to deify ultimate being in the form of a *prima causa* or *ens perfectissimum*, some supreme item as the first cause or perfect being (Caputo 2002; Wrathall 2003). In its delineation of the history of metaphysics, Heidegger's account has been subjected to far-reaching critique. It is not at all clear that it applies to anything other than rather crude neo-scholastic versions of natural theology of the kind that proliferated in the hey-day of nineteenth-century scholasticism (Hankey 2004). Nonetheless, some theologians and philosophers of religion have greeted Heidegger's position as an exhortation to Christian theology to avoid the twin evils of theological rationalism and idolatry (Marion 1991).

THE IMAGINATION AND AN UNKNOWABLE GOD?

We must distinguish between the conviction in the incomprehensible divine mystery and the idea of God as unknowable. The first principle is essential for any serious theology. The second means the impossibility of natural theology. If we can know the divine at

all—apart from those appeals to revelation which can hardly be employed by philosophers—then it must be on the principle of imaginative analogy and a belief in the scale of
being. The transcendent God of Western theism is veiled and we are placed at an epistemic distance from his Being. Imagination in its highest sense is the 'awakening to an
invisible world': faith is the substance of things hoped for, the evidence of things not seen.
The role of the imagination in psychology, ethics, and aesthetics provides a good analogy
for thinking about the role of imagination in religious belief. In engaging with the inner
lives of other human agents, with moral values or aesthetic qualities, we are required to
employ imagination: to suppose, form hypotheses, empathize, or imaginatively engage
with alien peoples or worlds. Whether Herodotus or Thucydides, or even Solon or Moses,
we have to try to engage with another mind. There can be no 'scientific' (in the narrow
sense) account of engaging in thoughts and beliefs because of self consciousness. The
self-conscious employment of ideas resists law-like causal explanations. If we want to
understand why Caesar crossed the Rubicon or Hannibal crossed the Alps, there is no
avoiding the beliefs, values, and intentions of the agents. That which, for the purposes of
my argument, I will call 'reason'—νοῦς in Plotinus and *intellectus* in either Augustine or
Nicholas of Cusa—was in the past distinguished from discursive ratiocination (διάνοια
or *ratio*). This reason was not intrinsically opposed to what today we might call imagination. For the ancient or medieval scholar, the contemplation of supreme truth through
reason was distinguished from lower forms of instrumental reason.

The Symbolic

Dante insists that, while God does not have hands or feet, Scripture speaks appropriately
and legitimately through such images of the divine reality. The ancient and medieval
mind dwelt symbolically. Man was envisaged as suspended between two realms: the
earthly and the transcendent. Symbols provided mediation and an iconic channel
between these domains. Light, for example, was a central symbol in the philosophy of
the Neoplatonists, especially Plotinus. The figurative dimension of the symbol was in no
way disconnected from its metaphysical and epistemic dimension. The *metaphysical*
dimension of light was understood as the *lux intelligibilis*: the essential intelligibility of
the universe. The *epistemic* dimension, then, was the process and method of attaining
discernment which was contrasted with ordinary ignorance and confusion, and the
clarity of thought that enables the mind to analyse and combine, to detect real connections in the objects of the world. The two dimensions of light could be further coupled
with the *figurative* dimension, for example metaphors of blindness and sight, awakening
and sleep, etc. An ancient or medieval mind would in all likelihood have understood the
light of the *Hagia Sophia*, the cathedral of Chartres, or the *Commedia* of Dante as encompassing all of these dimensions. The visible levels of light in these works were not merely
representations of a wholly *other* reality but were indeed manifestations of that transcendent reality which they symbolized.

The Cambridge physicist Ernest Rutherford famously quipped that there is only physics or stamp collecting. Has the materialism or physicalism, that has become such a dominant philosophical position in the contemporary world, shut off the traditional symbolism of a world suffused with transcendence? There may be much symbolism in the contemporary world—Plato's image of the cave is a most powerful analogy for our world which is suffused with images of brands through television, cinema, the internet, etc.—but the powers conveyed by such images are not meant to represent superior immaterial powers. Psychoanalysis may explore these images, but it tends to locate the source of these images in the depths and recesses of human consciousness, not beyond it. Freud, in particular, seems particularly sensitive to the pervasive nature of symbolism within human experience, whether normal or pathological, conscious, semi-conscious, or unconscious.

The momentous and remarkable triumphs of natural science do not entitle or equip it to explain all phenomena. The physical description of the world excludes the most important fact about experience: consciousness. And for much conscious experience, imagination is a constituent element. The observation of a person, the viewing of painting, or the listening to a piece of music are all instances of intentional states where consciousness and imagination are virtually synonymous. In all such cases, *awareness* of the person, painted object, or sounds is to interpret these phenomena *as* instances of a familiar friend, a horse, or an aria. Moreover, it is the prerogative of the arts to explore the domain of self-awareness and the anxiety and excitement connected to the existence of the world as we know it.

One decisive form of natural theology, with its most eminent proponents in Plato and Plotinus, argues from anomalies and contradictions in our habitual experience of the phenomenal world in order to drive the finite mind towards the transcendent noetic realm in which these contradictions are resolved. Both thinkers employ sceptical arguments in order to reveal the prima facie solid realm of ordinary experience as transitory and evanescent. The inadequacy of and contingency of this realm of shadows leads to an apprehension of that transcendent and necessary reality that lies beneath and beyond the phenomenal world. Philosophy for such thinkers in the Neoplatonic tradition is an imaginative activity that is at once radical and creative: leading out of the cave of habitual experience up the divided line towards the Good 'beyond being'. For this reason, both Plato and Plotinus (or their modern followers like John N. Findlay or Stephen Clark) will often employ thought experiments or poetic images in order to articulate a rational vision of the nature of the intelligible world (Findlay 1966, 1967, 1970; Clark 1998).

Many contemporary thinkers of diverse provenance such as R. Hepburn or D. Z. Phillips have denied that one can *imagine* a transcendent being at all (Hepburn 1992; Phillips 1976). Theism presupposes a capacity to imagine a transcendent source of the world, and many philosophers deny that imagining the world as an object of inquiry is intelligible. Equally for D. Z. Phillips language about a transcendent agent beyond the world relies upon an egregious misuse of language as such talk of any agent presupposes a community to which the agent belongs, a criteria of identification. Such problems of imagining the world or God as a transcendent agent are related to metaphysical issues of modality.

Obviously, many problems in natural theology are linked implicitly or explicitly with the relation between imagination and conceivability.

The major recent models of natural theology in the Anglo-Saxon world have been Richard Swinburne's cumulative case for God as an inference to best explanation and the rebuttal of evidentialism by advocates of reformed epistemology (Swinburne 1977, 1979; Plantinga and Wolterstorff 1983). The first strategy makes theism too closely akin to a scientific theory; the second seems to immunize theism from any rational critique. A number of recent thinkers have suggested that religious belief is neither immediate nor inferential but indirectly mediated. Here one might consider the work of John Cottingham on religious practice or Mark Wynn on the emotions (Cottingham 2005; Wynn 2005).

THE DOCTRINE OF ANALOGY

The Aristotelian/scholastic tradition is less sympathetic to the poetic as a metaphysical resource and tends to a more decisively conceptual theology. One might consider, however, the doctrine of analogy between the infinite being of God and finite beings as expounded by Thomas Aquinas' theory of divine names being neither equivocal nor univocal but analogical. Despite the ontological gulf between God and man, there is sufficient sameness to warrant the use of the term analogical of talk of God. Aquinas justifies the use of non-literal language in *sacra doctrina* as well as in Scripture.

While Aristotle thinks that the command of metaphor marks off poetic genius, he avoids equivocation in his scientific writings. In the modern period Hobbes famously impugns metaphors and tropes as creating confusion in science proper. The question is whether symbols and metaphors are necessary and useful for knowledge or merely ornamental. Should figurative language be restricted to the poet and excluded from more stringent science? Plato's enigmatic use of myths in his dialogues presents a particular instance of this problem, especially in the *Timaeus* and the *Republic*. In these dialogues myths are employed at crucial parts of the dialogues. How do these myths or likely tales relate to reason or Logos?

Yet too strict a division between poetry and the natural sciences is unsustainable. Poetry and the natural sciences are often perplexing to the quotidian mind. A great imaginative construction in a work of art often challenges and reconstructs our ideas about the world. Yet this re-rebuilding of our view of the world has a law-like quality. In a work of imagination there is an element of rightness. The great poet, for example, cannot be merely whimsical and unpredictable. If his vision is to be compelling it must have a logical and moral consistency and its own internal appropriateness. In Shakespeare's great characters for example, we have changes. Yet these changes are constrained by a need to be 'true to life'.

Philosophy and science work with abstractions that have to be learned. One must acquire a specific vocabulary, largely inherited from the Greeks. But in poetry we are allowed to dwell upon the sense images of our immediate and familiar experience of the world. In this sense, philosophy and science seem abstract, pedantic, and even crabbed when compared to the sensuous immediacy of the poetic image. Plato's hostility to the poets is partly based upon this. Austin Farrer, who consciously fused philosophy and biblical studies, can be seen as a theologian who combined both rational argument with meditation upon the poetic image, especially as found in Scripture (Farrer 1948). David Brown extends Farrer's arguments and integrates intimations of transcendence and experiences of divine immanence through landscape and architecture (Brown 2004).

CRITIQUES OF RELIGION

The traditional critiques of philosophical theism revolve around the concept of imagination. Spinoza and Nietzsche are both trenchant examples of such critiques. Spinoza thinks that theism results from the illegitimate transfer of personal qualities to the impersonal substance that is *deus sive natura*. Nietzsche is a more thoroughgoing critic of religion, and he considers man to be a 'sick animal' through the effect of the religious, in particular the Christian, imaginary in enfeebling his instincts. The denial of free will, evil, teleology, and genuine altruism are linked in both thinkers to a theory of the mind's tendency to project illusions onto another terrifying universe. Freud's theory of religion as wish-fulfilment is indebted to this strand of critiques of religion as an illegitimate outgrowth of a sub-philosophical imagination. In more recent literature, religion has been forcefully presented as a by-product of evolutionary mechanisms. Rather like the employment of the light of a flame by a moth, religion is the case of the failure of an otherwise reliable mechanism. Just as the moth usually employs light from the moon or stars effectively but dies when it flies into a flame, so too human beings project sympathies and intentions upon agents seen and unseen. Religion becomes a special and destructive instance of an otherwise useful evolutionary strategy to imagine more than the eye can see or the ear can hear (Dawkins 2006).

The challenge of reductionist critiques of theism based upon the imagination offers a powerful justification for natural theology. If the critic of religion can appeal to some imaginative projection theory, the theist cannot retreat into religious 'language games' or appeals to authority or experience without *petitio principii*.

CARVING UP NATURE AT THE JOINTS

There is a very significant connection between imaginability and intelligibility. If Plato is correct to see science as 'carving up nature at the joints' and if knowledge emerges not by accident or convention but by penetrating the real essences of the world, we need to consider the world as the kind of arena in which real knowledge is possible. It is hard to imagine science as possible in a world which repeatedly rebuffed any attempt to discover order or meaning within it. For the theist, the intelligibility of the world reinforces the idea of world as created by the divine mind. Thus it is unsurprising that hairless apes can imagine remote and hidden forms of order and thus come to understand the world and have access to universal laws of the universe. In this way the cosmos produces minds that both imagine and mirror its intelligible source. It is routinely suggested that the values of duty, honesty, and sympathy are the product of the evolutionary process. But it is much harder to imagine that an interest in abstract truth emerges through the process of natural selection. It seems far-fetched to connect the concern with theoretical knowledge characteristic of human science with the kind of adaptive modification as evinced in the giraffe's neck. The astonishing capacity of human beings to imagine hidden structures of being, to observe laws and patterns in observable phenomena, suggests that the world is providentially susceptible to systematic intellectual inventions of the finite mind.

THE ROMANTIC CONTRIBUTION

Two modern philosophers have decisively influenced the role of imagination: Vico and Kant. Giambattista Vico (1668–1744) was fascinated by the shift in man from beast to citizen: the shaping of the immediate environment and the transformation of nature into an inhabitable world. Vico's thought was shaped by two main strands: the *Epicureanism* of Pierre Bayle and the *Augustinianism* of the Port Royal. Bayle's *Pensées diverses sur la comète* (1682) presented the Epicurean thesis of functioning atheism: egoists, motivated by their passions rather than reason, could build a society without the aid of providence (Robertson 2006). This was a real challenge for Vico and his claim that there cannot be a functioning atheist society emerges out of these questions. He engages the atheists on their own terms and uses their concepts, but in order to refute them. Vico's answer is to claim that wherever one finds an altar, one will find civilization. Rejecting the idea of a primitive state of nature, Vico emphasized the precariousness of human existence and the importance of institutions for the shift from beast to man. The process of civilization cannot be appreciated apart from the understanding of the poetic dimension of human experience. Knowledge or *Scienza* emerges not out of clear and distinct ideas but from poetic or imaginative universals which are gradually and providentially transformed into reflection. The frontispiece to *The New Science* (1744 edition) depicts a female figure (Metaphysics) on a globe of the Earth, contemplating a luminescent triangle containing the eye of God, or providence. Yet beneath this is a statue of Homer embodying the roots of civilization in 'poetic wisdom'. Vico was little appreciated in his own age but was much admired by Herder and Coleridge. Vico's strong emphasis upon providence places him in the domain of natural theology, while his interest in the irreducibly creative and narratival nature of characteristically human self-understanding has exerted a great influence upon thinkers since. His idea that providence can operate through characteristically human institutions and agency was of particular significance for philosophers worried by the atheistic implications of a Cartesian-mechanical universe that seemed to marginalize the mind or spirit. The shift from the hunter-gatherer—as we might rephrase the phase of barbarism of which Vico speaks—to civilization is indeed a poetic activity. The shaping of a human environment, Vico maintains, is grounded upon a human need to find meaning in the world and thereby make it habitable. The shaping of our world through rituals and institution is the protracted and indirect deposit of the imagination. It is also the work of providence.

Imagination enables the individual mind to relate to objects and thus investigate nature, whether in the limited sense of Hume or the stronger transcendental sense of Kant. We must distinguish between imagination in the generic sense and imagination in the specific sense of the poetic imagination. In traditional discussions from Aristotles' *De Anima* through Alexander of Aphrodisias and the Neoplatonists to the great Muslim commentators such as Al Farabi, Avicenna, and Ibn Arabi, the focus is upon imagination as a mental and epistemological capacity: the *vis imaginationis* or the *vis phantastica* (Cocking 1991). Alongside the epistemological discussion of imagination, we find discussions of aesthetic and theological questions which pertain to the nature and validity of religious language or the relationship between poetry and revelation. Dreams and visions are often discussed from a philosophical and theological perspective (Corbin 1969). But it is with the Romantic fusion of the Kantian insistence upon the synthetic power of subjectivity and renewed interest in the status of art that we find an exaltation of the term 'imagination' as 'reason in its most exalted mood' (Wordsworth 1959: Bk XIV, l. 192). Even if many thinkers in the ancient and medieval West were interested in the idea of imagination, the concept was not prominent until the eighteenth century and the Romantics in particular. When Coleridge speaks of that 'synthetic and magical power, to which we have exclusively appropriated the name of Imagination' (Coleridge 1983: II, 16), he is drawing upon a modern tendency to upgrade the imagination and to distinguish it from some inferior capacity, fancy, or fantasy. John Locke expounds the 'busy and boundless Fancy of Man' (1975: 104) and Hume insists upon the fundamental role of the imagination in organizing our experience of the world. But it is Kant's view of imagination as productive, namely as the ground of the synthetic power of the mind in the construction of the realm of appearances, that gives the term its powerful new currency. Imagination is not merely reproductive in the sense of working upon a given set of experienced realities, but imagination shapes the experience of reality itself. Thus perception of the world is itself a creative and dynamic act.

This Kantian thought about the productive nature of imagination in perception reinforces the idea of the special dignity of the human mind in its freedom from sense stimulus. On this Kantian model, perception is an essentially creative engagement with the environment. Employing the imagination in diverse conscious and explicit ways—such as, for example, day-dreaming or creative perceptions of the physical world or suppositions that the world could be otherwise—presupposes freedom. Imagination is the mind's most distinctive freedom from stimulus and this freedom can be linked to the idea of the image in which the soul is formed.

Coleridge helped consolidate a distinction in the English language between a truthful imagination and an epistemically inferior fancy. It should be noted that his distinction is often misunderstood. Western thought has often distinguished between a positive and negative *vis imaginativa*, depending upon whether directed above or below—to the heavenly or the demonic. Coleridge's contrast between imagination and fancy is more Kantian in inspiration. He distinguishes between the primary and secondary imagination by which he means the difference between the unconscious creative and synthetic activity of the mind in perception and the creative imagination which is employed by the artist. These two forms of imagination—conscious and unconscious—are distinguished from mechanical association of ideas, which he designates as 'fancy'. Coleridge is not denying that the association of ideas is an important mental activity, but he is denying it the foundational status which it occupies in the empiricist philosophies of Hobbes and Hume.

Imagination, Fantasy, and True Fiction

Drama, prose, and poetry can be considered as both creative and truthful. Aristotle is thinking of this when he observes that poetry is more philosophical than history. The great poet is presenting universal truths of the human condition rather than contingent facts. The emotions that the great fictional works generate are of great interest. Why are we moved by the fate of Hecuba or Hamlet? Aristotle famously thought that the emotions aroused by tragedy could be said to have a purging effect. The sense in which we are moved by fiction is intriguing philosophically. Why should we be affected by fictional persons or events? And why should this experience be regarded as valuable or even purifying? There is an important tradition of viewing great aesthetic works as possessing a strong didactic component. This is mirrored in the Christian New Testament by the parables. These are tales or fictions that convey truths. In John 3:1–21 Nicodemus asks Christ how a man can be reborn. The literalist Nicodemus states that a man cannot return into his mother's womb. Christ is emphatic that Nicodemus must use his imagination if he is to understand the true nature of divine regeneration.

The region of philosophy that deals with art is traditionally called aesthetics. But 'aesthetics' is a relatively recent development. Medieval and Western philosophy was primarily concerned with the topic of beauty and was often concerned how this relates to truth and goodness:

> Beauty is truth, truth beauty,—that is all
> Ye know on earth, and all ye need to know [Keats 1978 (1819): 282]

Keats was expressing a view widespread in antiquity that beauty must be related to truth. Equally beauty was thought to be related to goodness. The phrase 'the beauty of holiness' of Psalms 29:2 captures this, where the contrast is between this holy beauty and the ugliness of sin.

But is difficult, however, to articulate a philosophically robust account of the relations between the three. If Hume is correct that morality is essentially utility, that is what is 'useful or agreeable to the person himself or to others', it is hard to see how this utility is related to beauty. It is also puzzling for many philosophers why or how beauty might be related to truth. Yet an appeal to the imagination (as opposed to mere fantasy) could show how beauty and truth may be linked. Consider the creative fictions of great artistic beauty, like the works of Shakespeare. Such works aspire to a certain truthfulness. As we have seen, Romanticism has popularized some distinction between imagination and fantasy or fancy. If we wish to highlight the cognitive capacity of the imagination, it is important to distinguish it from those forms of imagination which can throw light upon the world and fantasies that create a mawkish or cruel make-believe. Our emotions can be deepened or purified by a work of the imagination so that we can gain a clearer understanding of reality, whereas fantasy often indulges and gratifies the emotions without any real challenge. We can inhabit world of fantasy just as we can inhabit a world constructed by the imagination, but we will not be instructed. Man's creativity has a negative side. Selfishness, cruelty, anxiety, and fanaticism can be the offspring of fantasy.

The theistic religions all assume a link between beauty, goodness, and truth since all three have their basis in the transcendent reality of God. This is the foundation of the iconoclasm that all three Abrahamic religions share to a greater or lesser degree. The ban upon images of the divine as idolatrous has its foundation in the conviction in the particular power of art to represent the transcendent truthfully and with reserve and awe for the sacred. If art were merely an organ of ornament or amusement, then there would be little point in the prohibitions and limits placed upon sacred art in the great religious traditions.

If we are haunted by the idea of absolute perfection in a world of manifest imperfection, this is testimony to the power of the imagination to envisage the ultimate unity of value and existence. Beauty is often defined as the unity of a manifold. In architecture or a dramatic work the harmonious ordering of the parts constitutes much of the beauty of the work. A traditional theist cannot admire a work of art as beautiful if its morality is questionable any more than she can admire a work of art if it presents an inherently false or beguiling image of life. The nineteenth-century Oxford philosopher Edward Caird would ridicule talk of that which was deemed 'too good to be true', by retorting that whatever was not true was not good enough (Temple 1924: 14)! For the theist, truth presupposes goodness and through beauty the mind can rise to a vision of transcendent unity. Yet it takes the work of imagination to remove the veil of phenomena of our habitual experience and to habituate the mind to the presence of the transcendent God of theism in the world.

CONCLUSION

The association of imagination and natural theology is only counterintuitive if one sees imagination primarily as the capacity to generate fiction. Since natural theology is concerned with truth (is there a God or a soul?), then natural theology can only be misled by the promptings of the imagination. However, if we see the imaginative encounter with reality as an unavoidable aspect of human cognition, then this *apparent* paradox is resolved. After all, we learn more about evil from the true fiction of *Richard III* than the biographies of the great dictators; more about the conflict of duties from *Antigone* than legal handbooks. This is because our world is neither a collection of neutral facts nor a kaleidoscope of our projected fancies. We need the creative contemplation of the imagination to discern those distinctive realities which cannot be designated as either literal and value-free 'facts' or figurative embellishments. Religion, war, eros, and science itself are distinctively human rituals with an inalienable symbolic component. They remain baffling puzzles for the naturalist; for the theist they are mysteries that point to the spiritual reality that pervades and sustains the physical cosmos.

Since the reality of which theology speaks transcends our normal categories, there is room for imagination in the most apparently recondite metaphysical constructions. Heidegger's famous bon mot about the *causa sui* is a instance of a failure to understand the proper role of imagination in natural theology. Heidegger presents the idea of the *causa sui* as a dry abstraction, the bloodless abstraction of 'metaphysics'. Yet when Plotinus coined the idea in Ennead III 8, he was perfectly aware of the oddity of this language. Indeed, he was deliberately employing *paradoxical* language as part of an imaginative approximation of the pre-eminent transcendent power and dignity of the supreme cause. Many later thinkers, including Proclus and Aquinas rejected the term as unintelligible, but Plotinus was trying to stretch the language of philosophy to its imaginative limit. And if we wish to escape the antinomies and puzzles of the cave, without resorting to sterile scholasticism, such imaginative stretching of philosophical language is unavoidable.

REFERENCES

Brown, David (2004). *God and Enchantment of Place: Reclaiming Human Experience*. Oxford: Oxford University Press.

Caputo, John D., ed. (2002). *The Religious*. Oxford: Blackwell.

Clark, Stephen R. (1998). *God, Religion and Reality*. London: SPCK.

Cocking, J. M. (1991). *Imagination: A Study in the History of Ideas*. London: Routledge.

Coleridge, Samuel Taylor (1983). *Biographia Literaria*. 2 vols. Edited by James Engell and W. Jackson Bate. London: Routledge and Kegan Paul.

Corbin, Henri (1969). *Creative Imagination in the Sufism of Ibn'Arabi*. Princeton: Princeton University Press.

Cottingham, John (2005). *The Spiritual Dimension*. Cambridge: Cambridge University Press.

Dawkins, Richard (2006). *The God Delusion*. London: Bantam Press.

Farrer, Austin (1948). *The Glass of Vision*. Westminster: Dacre Press.

Findlay, John N. (1966). *The Discipline of the Cave*. The Gifford Lectures for 1964–5. London: Allen and Unwin.

—— (1967). *The Transcendence of the Cave*. The Gifford Lectures for 1965–6. London: Allen and Unwin.

—— (1970). *Ascent to the Absolute*. London: Allen and Unwin.

Hankey, Wayne (2004). 'Why Heidegger's "History" of Metaphysics is Dead'. *American Catholic Philosophical Quarterly* 78(3): 425–43.

Heidegger, Martin (2002). *Identity and Difference*. Translated from the German by Joan Stambaugh. Chicago: University of Chicago Press.

Henderson, Edward H. (2004). 'The God Who Undertakes Us' in *Captured by the Crucified: The Practical Theology of Austin Farrer*. Edited by David Hein and Edward H. Henderson. New York: T & T Clark: pp. 66–99.

Hepburn, Ronald W. (1992). 'Religious Imagination'. *Royal Institute of Philosophy Supplement* 32: 127–43.

Keats, John (1978). *Complete Poems*. Edited by Jack Stillinger. Cambridge, MA: Harvard University Press.

Locke, John (1975). *An Essay Concerning Human Understanding*. Edited by Peter H. Nidditch. Oxford: Clarendon Press.

Marion, Jean-Luc (1991). *God Without Being: Hors-Texte*. Chicago: University of Chicago Press.

Phillips, D. Z. (1976). *Religion Without Explanation*. Oxford: Blackwell.

Plantinga, Alvin and Nicholas Wolterstorff, eds. (1983). *Faith and Rationality. Reasons and Belief in God*. South Bend, IN: Notre Dame University Press.

Robertson, John (2006). *The Case for Enlightenment: Scotland and Naples, 1680–1760*. Cambridge: Cambridge University Press.

Ryle, Gilbert (1949). *The Concept of Mind*. Chicago: University of Chicago Press.

Swinburne, Richard (1977). *The Coherence of Theism*. Oxford: Clarendon Press.

—— (1979). *The Existence of God*. Oxford: Clarendon Press.

Temple, W. (1924). *Christus Veritas*. London: Macmillan.

Wrathall, Mark (2003). *Religion After Metaphysics*. Cambridge: Cambridge University Press.

Wordsworth, William (1959). *The Prelude or Growth of a Poet's Mind*. Edited by Ernest de Selincourt. 2nd edn. Revised by Helen Darbishire. Oxford: Clarendon Press.

Wynn, Mark (2005). *Emotional Experience and Religious Understanding*. Cambridge: Cambridge University Press.

CHAPTER 35

NATURAL THEOLOGY AND LITERATURE

GUY BENNETT-HUNTER

A BROAD SENSE OF NATURAL THEOLOGY

IN this chapter, I hope to show, by referring to two specific literary examples, that works of literature can demonstrate the possibility of natural theology and can prompt their readers' thinking along natural theological lines by allowing them to have experiences which mirror the structure of those dealt with by natural theology. First, though, it is necessary to make some remarks on the way in which I shall be interpreting the meaning of the latter term.

The literal meaning of 'theology' is discourse about God and therefore depends on the meaning of the word 'God'. I interpret this latter meaning to be a reference to the concept of ineffability—that is, a reference to the concept of what is in principle resistant to conceptual formulation and therefore literal linguistic articulation. I do so for a combination of philosophical and theological reasons. On the philosophical side, I am persuaded by David Cooper's (2002, 2005, 2009) argument that only this concept of ineffability can, in a non-circular manner, explain the meaning of the world of human 'Life' (i.e. the *Lebenswelt*) and that it can do so by uniquely evoking the *ultimately* real, that which is independent of the human contribution to that world. Interested, and initially repulsed, readers are encouraged to engage with Cooper's argument for themselves but, by way of a very brief sketch, he asks the following question: if the meanings of things, the concepts and values with which we invest them, must be explained in terms of their contribution to human concerns, practices, and projects, and therefore ultimately in terms of their relation of appropriateness to the human perspective, the world of human Life to which those practices and concerns themselves contribute, how can Life itself and as a whole be said to have meaning? The answer is: only by placing it in a relation of appropriateness to what is beyond itself, independent of the human contribution and therefore *ultimately* real. This 'beyond' cannot, without circularity, be invested with the concepts and meanings that constitute Life, which it is invoked to explain; therefore it must be ineffable. This philosophical argument for the ineffability of ultimate reality is complemented by the theological view that only that which explains the meaning of human Life properly deserves the name 'God' (cf. Macquarrie 1984: 167). And to conceive God as anything less than the *ultimately* real (i.e. to pretend that God can be conceived at all), would be to encourage the sin of idolatry. It would be to advocate the worship of an object, a part of the human world, albeit the supreme part, which necessarily owes itself crucially to the human contribution. It would therefore be guilty of the theologically unattractive conceptual idolatry to which all ontotheological conceptions of God (i.e. all *conceptions* of God) contribute. The interpretation of 'God' as a reference to the concept of ineffability, which I espouse for both these reasons, is nicely encapsulated in the dictum attributed to several mainstream theologians (and probably written by at least one of them): *Si comprehendis, non est Deus.*

In an attempt to work out a philosophy of religion on the basis of what turns out to be a very similar view, John Macquarrie pessimistically describes as 'ruinous' the present condition of 'natural theology in the old style' whose purpose he interprets as being 'to supply rational proof of the reality of those matters with which theology deals' (1966: 45, 42, 41). He includes in this interpretation the traditional philosophical arguments for the existence of God with which natural theology has often been associated, if not identified. Macquarrie regards all such attempts at proof to be not only theologically and religiously irrelevant—'[t]he God who is the conclusion of an argument... is not the God who is worshipped in religion' (45)—but also doomed to philosophical failure, owing, not least, to the criticisms perpetrated by Hume and Kant. He consequently believes that natural theology, so construed, should be abandoned— and, on this, I share his opinion. However, Macquarrie also thinks that sole reliance on 'revealed' theology, natural theology's supposed alternative, would be undesirable (48). He believes that it is still necessary for theology to have solid rational foundations in order that it may be reconnected with ordinary experience and protected from illusion and superstition. Fortunately, then, Macquarrie advocates and develops a 'natural theology in the new style' which provides rational support for religious belief by bridging the gap between ordinary experience and faith. It takes over, to that extent, some of old-style natural theology's basic functions but without the attendant weaknesses. Such new-style natural theology as he develops owes itself, therefore, to the phenomenological method. It is descriptive rather than deductive, attending not just to the rational arguments in the abstract but also to the conviction which underlies them. It takes seriously the measure of participation involved in religious belief, a feature which might enable it to be a far more effective apologetic than abstract argument alone. Finally, it is existential rather than purely rational, taking the concrete, lived condition of human existence as its starting point (50–1). Taken together, these features of new-style natural theology actually entail, for Macquarrie (1984: 12–13), the blurring, if not the abandonment, of the old, traditional distinction between 'natural' and 'revealed' kinds of theology. If God is the source of everything, this must include knowledge or experience of himself. Not only, therefore, is there no 'unaided' knowledge or experience of God, so that all theology is in that sense 'revealed', but even all 'revealed' theology must come to us via our human faculties of apprehension and is, to that extent, 'natural'. The resultant conception of natural theology is not of a second route to experience or knowledge of God alongside God's self-revelation; nor does it reflect the desire to undermine the role of rational reflection in critically testing revelatory experience. Rather, it is of an appeal to the general possibility of revelation which is accessible to any being with our human faculties, including, but not limited to, our rational ones. Towards the beginning of his Gifford Lectures, Macquarrie describes this definition of natural theology as broader than the one pejoratively held to by Hume and Kant but as no less consonant with the terms of Lord Gifford's foundation:

> When he says that the subject is to be treated as a 'natural science', he cannot mean that God is to be treated as a phenomenon of nature, but that the enquiry is to be carried out by the natural human faculties that are common to all, without appeal to some special source of knowledge. This is how the word 'natural' was traditionally understood in the expression 'natural theology'. [1984: 12]

In the remainder of this chapter, I shall be appropriating Macquarrie's broad conception of natural theology in a literary connexion. But my focus will be on the possibility and nature of religious experience as opposed to religious knowledge. This is because if God is indeed ineffable (in the non-self-stultifying sense that the word 'God' refers to the concept of ineffability), there can be no question of knowing anything at all about him, if knowledge necessarily involves the application of concepts which can then be literally articulated. My alternative focus on experience is in keeping with the phenomenological approach advocated by Macquarrie and has the added advantage that it is not immediately obvious that the notion of experience has to involve the application of concepts. If, as Cooper (1985: 189, 198) suggests, the dualism between subjective and objective dimensions to the notion of experience is dissolved on account of the fact that it is responsible for the vagueness and ambiguity of the concept and, in any case, was 'badly drawn', the notion of experience can be broadened so that, in a broadly religious context, Wordsworthian 'Tintern Abbey moments' are not required to involve the application of concepts but neither are they 'debarred from counting as, strictly speaking, *experiences*' (Cooper 2009: 54).

Therefore, with two closely related caveats, I define 'natural theology' as discourse about the human experience of the ineffable God. The first caveat is that the word 'God' does not refer to an object or entity of any kind but to the concept of ineffability with which any exhaustive, determinate conceptual content is, by definition, inconsistent. Secondly that, at least in the religious context, the notion of experience does not necessarily involve the application of concepts. I intend the term 'natural theology' to refer to discourse about a kind of non-conceptual, but nonetheless experiential, attunement to the ultimately real, and therefore ineffable, God—one which is in principle available to all human beings. It is natural theology, conceived as just such discourse, which I now want to show being enacted in and through works of literature.

FLATLAND: NEW DIMENSIONS
OF NATURAL THEOLOGY

The novelist and Anglican priest, Edwin A. Abbott, is best known for his satirical novel *Flatland* which, I want to suggest, serves the purpose of illustrating the possibility of natural theology. It does so by suggesting the possibility that there may well be dimensions which lie outside the common course of thought and experience and by attempting acquaint the readers with this possibility via analogy and the stimulation of their imagination.

The novel is set in Flatland, a world limited to two dimensions. The protagonist, a Square, from whose viewpoint the novel is narrated, is visited by the Sphere, a prophet from three-dimensional Spaceland, of which the Square can have only limited experience. Describing his first, severely compromised, perception of the Sphere, the Square says, 'I should have thought it a Circle, only that it seemed to change its size in a manner impossible for a Circle or for any Regular Figure of which I had had experience' (Abbott 2008: 82). The Sphere vainly attempts to describe the third dimension in words but the Square has no understanding of the language of height and depth which, to him, simply refers to Northward and Southward directions across a single plane. He cannot perceive height and depth because his eye is on his perimeter. As the Sphere explains, 'in order to see into Space you ought to have an eye, not on your Perimeter, but on your side, that is, on what you would probably call your inside; but we in Spaceland should call it your side' (85). The Sphere describes his vantage-point on Flatland from the height afforded by the third dimension:

> I lately looked down on your Plane which you call Space forsooth. From that position of vantage I discerned all that you speak of as *solid* (by which you mean 'enclosed on four sides'), your houses, your churches, your very chests and safes, yes even your insides and stomachs, all lying open and exposed to my view. [86]

Having failed to convince the Square with words, the Sphere finally prepares him for an 'ocular demonstration' of the existence of the third dimension with the following explanation:

> When I cut through your plane as I am now doing, I make in your plane a section which you, very rightly, call a circle. For even a Sphere—which is my proper name in my own country—if he manifest himself at all to an inhabitant of Flatland—must needs manifest himself as a Circle. [88]

There is an interesting parallel here between the form in which the Sphere necessarily manifests in Flatland and Macquarrie's suggestion that even divine revelation necessarily comes to us via our limited human faculties of thought and perception. The Sphere's 'ocular demonstration' consists in his rising in space so that his circular section perceptible to the Square becomes smaller 'till it dwindles to a point and finally vanishes' as the Sphere leaves Flatland (88). Though the observable facts are incontrovertible, the Square finds the causes as mysterious as ever, since all he can see is a Circle getting mysteriously smaller before reducing almost to a point and then vanishing, reappearing and finally making himself larger again. This sequence encourages the reader to think analogically about the limitations of her own experience. It prompts the thought that just as there would be realms of experience not fully graspable by a creature limited to two dimensions, so there may be for us human beings limited to three. It supports my understanding of natural theology, informed by Macquarrie, by the suggestion that reality may exceed the limited bounds of ordinary, cognitive experience but might nonetheless be imperfectly or partially manifest within that experience. Consonant with it, too, is the suggestion that even such extraordinary 'revelation' as the Square experiences comes through his ordinary, namely two-dimensional, experiential capabilities. However, since the reality outruns the Square's perceptual limitations, and he therefore cannot comprehend the cause of his extraordinary experience, he remains unconvinced. Even when the Sphere positions himself above the Square and touches his side (which the Square perceives as his 'inside' or his stomach), it only antagonizes him:

> Before I could utter a word of remonstrance, I felt a shooting pain in my inside, and a demoniacal laugh seemed to issue from within me....It seemed intolerable that I should endure existence subject to the arbitrary visitations of a Magician who could thus play tricks with one's very stomach. If only I could in any way manage to pin him against the wall till help came. [93]

It is only a mystical vision of Spaceland that can finally convince the Square. As Abbott has the Square describe this vision, his style comes to mimic that of descriptions of mystical experiences in the Bible and in mystical literature:

> I looked, and, behold, a new world! There stood before me, visibly incorporate, all that I had before inferred, conjectured, dreamed, of perfect Circular beauty. What seemed the centre of the Stranger's form lay open to my view: yet I could see no heart, nor lungs, nor arteries, only a beautiful harmonious Something—for which I had no words; but you, my Readers in Spaceland, would call it the surface of the Sphere. [95]

As he looks down on Flatland he can see in one glance what he formerly thought of as the insides of things, now open to his view. Thus the Square experiences the 'omnividence' attributed by Flatlanders to God alone (97). The Square begins to think by analogy and with the aid of the imagination that just as there was a third dimension, ordinarily imperceptible to him (because, in Flatland, 'we have no eye in our stomachs'), so there may be higher dimensions imperceptible even to the Sphere and (the reader extrapolates) therefore to us, three-dimensional, human beings (104). Although the Sphere refuses to accept that it makes sense to speak of a fourth, or yet higher, dimensions the Square's analogical thought, together with the Sphere's refusal to entertain it, is sustained in the opposite direction by the description of a visit to the solipsistic world of Pointland, the 'Abyss of No Dimensions'. The Sphere shows the Square Pointland's King and sole inhabitant who is himself the limits of his world. He can conceive of nothing other than himself, has no experience or conception of length, breadth, or height, no cognizance of plurality: 'he is himself his One and All being really Nothing'. Yet, though ignorant, the

Point is supremely happy in this supposedly self-sufficient condition. The Square and the Sphere listen together to the Point soliloquizing in the third person about itself, significantly, in the language of religious devotion:

> there arose from the little buzzing creature a tiny, low, monotonous but distinct tinkling…from which I caught these words, 'Infinite beatitude of existence! It is; and there is none else beside It.'…'It fills all Space…and what It fills It is. What It thinks, that It utters; and what It utters, that It hears; and It itself is Thinker, Utterer, Hearer, Thought, Word Audition; it is the One, and yet the All in All. Ah, the happiness, ah, the happiness of Being!' [109]

The Square's attempt to startle the King of Pointland from his complacent self-adoration is in vain because, since the Point cannot conceive anything other than himself, he only takes the Square's words to be his own. The reader is therefore encouraged to compare the Sphere's, and perhaps her own, refusal to entertain the idea of higher realms of being, beyond the limits of ordinary experience, to this agreeable but deluded and solipsistic condition of the King of Pointland. Since one can imagine a creature deluded by its own perceptual, and therefore conceptual, limitations into defining the limits of reality in these terms, one should admit, by analogy, that the limits of one's own ordinary experience do not necessarily constitute the limits of reality. Perhaps, therefore, there is an extraordinary kind of experience, like the one of Spaceland granted to the Square, that can put us in touch with, attune us to, the ineffable divine reality which outruns the limits of cognitive experience.

Towards a Natural Theology
of the Ineffable God

While there are similarities between Abbott's strategy in *Flatland* and that of natural theology as I have been construing it, there is a very major difference. Although that to which *Flatland* attempts, through analogy and imaginative thought, to attune us lies outside the ordinary scope of experience and is evoked in religious terms, it is not ineffable in my sense of what is in principle unconceptualizable and inarticulable. This is shown by a recent attempt to apply Abbott's line of thought in the context of the philosophy of religion. Steven D. Boyer (2007) attempts to reconcile the apparently mutually exclusive theological concepts of mystery and revelatory experience with the aid of a mathematical analogy inspired by Abbott's novel. He asks us to consider a circle, an example of a two-dimensional shape, and the way in which geometry allows us to reason about it (96). If the figure were in fact a three-dimensional cylinder being investigated by a mathematician limited to two dimensions, the mathematician could reason geometrically and thus know everything that is two-dimensional about the cylinder. She would reach the same conclusions about the circular end of the cylinder, and with the same accuracy, as in the case of the two-dimensional circle. But, for this mathematician, there is always 'more' of the cylinder to be discovered: a 'more' which transcends what geometry can understand and describe of the figure but which does not cease to be geometrical in character (97). Such a mystery transcends the normal workings of human reason 'dimensionally': even when the object is known (as a two-dimensional circle) it remains unknown (as a cylinder). It strikes Boyer (99) as an 'eminently sensible and fruitful possibility' that the religious mystery should be construed as:

> one in which reason is appropriate and is legitimately exercised, just as two-dimensional geometry is legitimately applied to the cylinder—yet no ultimate 'clearing up' is expected or hoped for. A dimensional mystery welcomes rational investigation, but expects reason to testify to an unfathomable depth or dimension that it can perhaps investigate or even illuminate but never explain or make clear.

But this concept is inconsistent with the notion of ineffability in terms of which I understand natural theology. Boyer's cylinder is unknown in practice (since the nature of two-dimensional geometry happens to be such that it cannot describe solids) but is in principle knowable (were two-dimensional geometry capable of describing solids, or if we used three-dimensional geometry, it would be apparent that there had always been a solid object there to describe). But he also claims that the cylinder's nature is not something which investigation could ever uncover. Now, this must be true also in practice, rather than in principle, since the cylinder is unknown only in practice (the relevant meaning of 'unknown' here is just 'resistant to being uncovered by investigation'). For Boyer, the religious realities are unknown because our rational faculties and our sense organs are such that we cannot reason about them or directly perceive them. In order to determine whether our notion of ineffability (the unknowable in principle) is involved, the key question is therefore 'Does the way our minds and bodies are constituted determine in practice or in principle whether something is knowable?' Boyer's implicit answer to this question is 'in practice' since his argument allows that, if our faculties of reason or our sense organs were different, we could experience and describe the objects of higher dimensions just as the three-dimensional mathematician could experience and describe the cylinder. It is in this respect that we take after Abbott's (2008: 104) Flatlanders who lament that their inability to experience or comprehend the third dimension is owing to the contingent fact that 'we have no eye in our stomachs'. But if the objects which this argument defends are *unknown in practice* and not *in principle unknowable*, it is not clear just how they are distinct from a mystery that can be revealed or what, as Macquarrie (1973: 87) suspects, is not really a mystery at all. It seems that they are just puzzles which we humans simply happen to lack the relevant powers to solve, powers which, in principle, we could have had and powers which we might, conceivably, one day develop.

The notion of ineffability, by contrast, was defended along different lines, according to which 'unknowable by the human mind' simply means 'unknowable in principle'. Cooper's argument is made from the existential phenomenological perspective, from which 'the world' just is that which is constituted by the mental and bodily possibilities of the human way of being; it is that with which these possibilities are always already engaged. There is no possibility of considering potential ways in which the world might be 'if our minds and bodies were differently constructed', or 'if our geometrical reasoning were different', since, if they were, we would no longer be the kind of beings we are and the world constituted by our way of being would cease to be the same human world. Since, for the existential phenomenologist, reality owes itself crucially to the contribution of the human concepts and values with which it is invested, the ineffable cannot be located within those structures of human conceptualization and evaluation. 'God', construed as ineffable, does not refer to a part of the world, or to another, transcendent world, for the experience and description of which our faculties merely happen, in practice, to be inadequate but rather to what is in principle resistant to comprehension and articulation in these ways. What Boyer's argument, following Abbott, has been trying to defend is a movement by analogy from our conceptualizable world to a supposedly non-conceptualizable world. But when we reach *this* world, we cannot avoid investing it with concepts. If we refrain from so investing it, then it loses its significance as a 'world' or 'dimension' or as anything at all and the point of invoking it as such is apparently lost. But if we do invest it with our concepts, then we turn it into part of our finite, human world like any other.

Thus, although the structure of Abbott's strategy mirrors that of natural theology in important and illuminating ways, the reality to which it attempts to attune us is not ineffable, and therefore ultimately real, but a postulated part of our human world. It is a part which lies beyond the scope of our experience only in part, only in practice, and therefore perhaps only at present. There is nothing ultimately real and therefore deserving of worship or adoration about Abbott's higher dimensions or Boyer's excessive objects. Abbott's crucial contribution to thinking of a natural theological kind, however, lies in his insight that the limits of ordinary experience do not necessarily constitute the limits of reality. Boyer's attempt at the application of this insight to philosophy of religion does not, however, appear to acknowledge a fact which, I have argued, is central to the nature of natural theology, namely that these limits do constitute the limits of the conceptualizable and articulable in principle. For Boyer, the subject matter of religious experience is in principle objective, conceptualizable, and articulable. Therefore the notion of experience with which he is working is still too restricted to be able to accommodate its properly ineffable religious subject matter, the notion of which is inconsistent with all three of these features. It violates my first caveat by being construed as an experience of some object, and the second since the purely cognitive experience of objects in principle admits of the application of concepts. If we are to speak of natural theology as concerning the experience of the ineffable God, then, we shall have to build differently on the foundations with which Abbott's major insight furnishes us.

ARTHUR SCHNITZLER'S 'FLOWERS' AS NATURAL THEOLOGY: ATTUNEMENT TO THE INEFFABLE

In an attempt to go further into what natural theological attunement to the ineffable God does have to be like, therefore, I want to engage with a second work of literature, namely Arthur Schnitzler's short story, 'Flowers', an extraordinary and powerful piece of writing which readers are strongly encouraged to read for themselves. I want to build on Abbott's central insight that ultimate reality outruns the scope of ordinary experience and to examine, with Schnitzler's help, the essential nature of the extraordinary experiential attunement to the *ineffable* ultimate reality in which the subject matter of natural theology properly consists.

'Flowers' is the short and intense story of a man's attempt to come to terms with the death of his estranged lover, written in the first-person form of a diary entry or extracts from a journal spanning many months. It is intimated that their relationship was turbulent, that she was unfaithful, and that, the last time the narrator saw her, there was no final resolution as she took her leave. It is suggested that the lover is desperate for forgiveness and reconciliation but that the narrator denies her this. His motivation is unclear; perhaps he is too hurt to forgive or wants to punish her infidelity. During the time leading up to her death, the narrator's lover has ceased to send 'dozens of tearful plaintive letters begging for forgiveness' and now regularly sends only flowers: 'Reminders of one of our happiest days, they arrived once a month with no note attached, silent humble flowers' (Schnitzler 1999: 23). The narrator initially deals with the news of her death by disassociating himself from reality. It seems that the pain is especially intense for him because he now has to give up the possibility of any reconciliation with his lover and of any opportunity even to bid her farewell. By deliberately dulling all his emotions, he is able to dull the pain of his bereavement. The world begins to seem to him quieter as he comes to think that there is no such thing as the emotions of happiness or anguish, only the 'grimaces' of joy or sorrow, the supposed expressions of these emotions. As he puts it, 'we laugh and cry and invite our souls along' (24). As a result, he no longer feels sadness when he thinks about dead loved ones. He comes to think of death as a friend who walks about among the living with no desire to harm them. The protagonist consequently begins to feel more liberated than he has for weeks, something which is noticed by his present lover, Gretel. Sensing that he is no longer a slave to his melancholy, Gretel remarks to him, '[a]t last, today I've got you back again' (24). But while he sees truth in Gretel's statement, the narrator also realizes that this renewed and liberated condition has come at a cost. He has a vision of himself as entirely cold and hard-hearted, as one who 'could stand beside the grave into which a loved one has been lowered, without a tear, indeed without any capacity for feeling' (24).

But this state of affairs does not last for long:

> Something rather strange happened today...It is the day on which every month she used to send me flowers...And the flowers arrived again today...as though nothing had changed. They arrived by post first thing this morning in a long narrow white box. It was very early and I was still half-asleep. It was not until I was actually opening the box that I fully came to my senses. And then I had a shock...There, neatly held together by a golden thread, lay a bunch of violets and carnations...They lay there as if inside a coffin. And when I picked the flowers up, a shiver ran down my spine.—I know how it came about that they arrived again today. She sensed her illness coming on and perhaps already had some inkling of her approaching death,

but nevertheless put in her usual order at the flower-shop. I was not to forgo this mark of her affection.—Undoubtedly this is how their delivery is to be explained; something wholly natural, even perhaps a little touching…And yet, as I held the flowers in my hand, and they seemed to tremble and incline their heads, against all reason and my own resolve, I could not help finding them a little uncanny, as if they came direct from her, as if this were her greeting…as if even now in death she still wanted to tell me of her love, of her—belated faithfulness. [25]

The flowers not only come to represent or to symbolize, but to body forth, the presence of the protagonist's dead lover. He begins to treat them more tenderly, as if they were his lover's soul, 'as if gripping them too tightly might make them suffer…as if their quiet souls might softly start to weep' and their fragrance comes to embody, for him, the pain of his futile longing for her. He treats the flowers just as he would treat the soul of his lover itself, were it physical in nature, were it still incarnate. But, at the same time, he is well aware of the natural explanation for their presence and of the significance which they have come to embody for him. The tension and conflict between the rational and emotional sides of the narrator's nature is apparent in his contradictory reflections on his attitude to the flowers:

I have no wish to delude myself. They are merely flowers, nothing more. They are a retrospective greeting from the other side…They are not a cry, no, not a cry from within the tomb.—They are merely flowers, and some salesgirl in a flower-shop tied them together quite mechanically, put a bit of wrapping round them, laid them in the white box and then took them to the post. And now they are here, so why am I even bothering to think about it? [25–6]

The protagonist still feels remote from the world, disassociated from reality, but, unable to continue repressing his bereavement, the flowers now become the sole focus of his attention, even to the point of his neglecting Gretel, barely saying a word to her. The only part of reality to which he pays any attention is that part which now embodies for him the presence of his dead lover, the part which enables him to externalize, and thus better to tolerate, his feelings of bereavement. He feels that the flowers are trying to communicate a message to him, perhaps that his lover is trying to communicate through them, and feels himself close to understanding their secret language.

The passage of time is evoked by descriptions of the changing seasons and this external cycle of birth and death is echoed in the decay of the flowers which the narrator obsessively keeps in their slim, green vase. As the petals fall, and they come to take on a deathly significance, they take on something of the sacrosanct and he is able to grieve for the flowers in the way that he was unable to grieve for his lover: 'I never touch them; they would turn to dust between my fingers. It grieves me beyond words that they have withered.…Yesterday evening I wept beside them as one weeps beside a grave, yet without even thinking of the woman who had sent them' (27). As spring begins to break, the narrator's thoughts begin to turn from death to life almost in spite of himself. He feels as though the, now deathly, presence of the flowers in his room is the presence of ghosts, of '[d]ead things playing at being alive' for, 'if wilting flowers smell of mould it is only in memory of the time when they were blossoming and fragrant' (28). An intense conflict between life and death, with a wilful bias towards death, begins to pervade his consciousness, perpetrated by the presence both of lively spring outside, bodied forth by the scent of lilac, and of the deathly 'bare stalks, pitiful and dry' still in his room:

> the spring outside, and the sun streaming brightly across my carpet, and the fresh scent of lilac wafting in from the nearby park, and the people walking past below who mean nothing to me, is all that supposed to be alive? I can let down the curtains and the sun is dead. I decide to have nothing more to do with all these people, and they too are dead. When I close the window, no scent of lilac wafts about me any longer, and the spring is dead. I am mightier than the sun, these people and the spring. But mightier than I is memory, for it comes as it wills and there is no fleeing from it. And these dry stalks in the vase are mightier than any spring or scent of lilac. [28]

The tension is resolved when, one day, Gretel comes over to his desk with a fresh bunch of flowers which she lays in front of him. She reaches out for the withered flowers in the vase (the narrator experiences this as an act of desecration—'I felt as though my heart were being wrung'—and wishes to stop her, but finds himself unable to move or speak) and throws them into the street (29). The vital scent of lilac then becomes the new focus of his attention, now not only entering the room from outside but also from the fresh bunch of lilacs brought by Gretel. She holds out the bouquet for him to smell 'cool white lilac blossoms... Such a fresh healthy fragrance—so soft, so cool; I felt like burying my face in them. Laughing, white, kissing flowers—and I felt haunted no longer' (29). Now feeling free of his mental ghosts, the narrator goes out into the spring evening with Gretel and, having returned home, focusses again on the lilac blossoms in his vase, embodying life which he now finds himself able fully to embrace. As the story ends, the absence of death from his mind is mirrored in the physical absence of the dry stalks from his room: 'Down there in the street—no, no, they are no longer lying there. The wind has long since swept them away in the dust' (29).

The Poetic Bodying Forth of Literature

Apart from being an extraordinarily powerful piece of writing, I think this story can be seen valuably to contribute to our understanding of the nature of the attunement which, I have suggested, concerns natural theology. A key word in the story is the Freudian term 'uncanny' which is notably used by the narrator on his receipt of the flowers. This concept is one in connection with which Freud and Schnitzler clearly influenced one another but the relevant Freudian sense of the term is the following:

> an uncanny effect often arises when the boundary between fantasy and reality is blurred, when we are faced with the reality of something that we have until now considered imaginary, when a symbol takes on the full function of what it symbolizes. [Freud 2003: 150]

As I mentioned before, it is not just that the flowers symbolize the presence of the dead lover; they body forth that presence which is inaccessible in any other way. The flowers are treated as though they *are* the lover. It is only thus that the narrator can properly express his hitherto repressed grief. Freud believes, and here he directly refers to Schnitzler, that the potential for a sense of the uncanny in literature goes far beyond what would be possible in real life because 'the realm of the imagination depends for its validity on its contents being exempt from the reality test' (155). It is irrelevant that there is a natural explanation for the flowers' appearance since this has no effect whatsoever on the narrator's and reader's experience of their meaning. The symbol takes on the full force of what it symbolizes but what is symbolized cannot be experienced without the symbol itself and cannot, without loss, be expressed without reference to that symbol.

Similarly, in a quasi-religious connection, Karl Jaspers speaks of 'ciphers', parts of reality which body forth transcendence or God. Jaspers's definition of God as 'the name and sign which lacks all perceivable content' and his denial that God is an object make his understanding of 'God' identical to mine—as a reference to the concept of ineffability (1969: III, 7; 1959: 57). Thus, in the religious case, there is even more reason to affirm the impossibility of access to God apart from the ciphers which embody his presence, since, unlike the lover in Schnitzler's story, he cannot even in principle be conceptualized, nor his nature be expressed in propositions. *Contra* Freud, Jaspers does not think that term 'symbol' is entirely appropriate here:

> 'Cipher', a word I prefer to the word 'symbol', denotes language, the language of a reality that can be heard and addressed only thus and in no other way—while a symbol stands for something else, even though this may not exist outside the symbol. What we mean by a symbol is the other thing, which thus becomes objective and comes to be present in the symbol, yet symbols may turn into elements of the cipher language. [1967: 95, n. 1]

Unlike some accounts of symbols, notably Tillich's (1961), the experience or 'reading' of the ciphers of the ineffable God is not an experience which requires the application of determinate concepts to something supposedly 'objective'.

And herein lies the deep-rooted connection between natural theology and literature. Both potentially bring about a state of affairs where what is inaccessible to experience in any other way is bodied forth. In our Schnitzlerian example, what is embodied is a significance which is admittedly not ineffable but the literary description of the flowers' significance is far closer to the actual experience of the narrator than the alternative Freudian analysis of his repressed guilt and bereavement. Like the uncanny, religious ciphers are exempt from the reality test because they body forth the ineffable. In Schnitzler's story, analogously, the flowers' uncanny significance is irreducible to the propositions of (Freudian) analysis. Although such propositions may illuminate the nature of the experience, they do not do full justice to its lived nature. And, though the latter experience may not strictly speaking be exempt from the reality test, true verifiable propositions about the flowers and the facts of their arrival are irrelevant to the experience of the significance which they embody in the story for the narrator and for the reader. We know perfectly well, for the narrator is quite explicit about this, that there is a natural explanation not only for the flowers' arrival but also for the narrator's projection of feelings of guilt and bereavement onto them. But, though likely accurate, such explanations are, as a matter of fact, nonetheless incapable of explaining the experience away; the experience is irreducible to such propositions. Unsurprisingly, then, the narrator's own attempts to express the flowers' significance in propositional language are signally confused and abortive. With natural theology it is the ineffable that is significantly embodied in concrete forms or religious ciphers, which constitutes a definitive reason why, in the religious case, the significant embodiment is inaccessible in other ways, least of all in concepts and propositions. Whereas, in the case of literature, the media of embodiment are restricted to linguistic forms, in the case of natural theological thought, a whole range of concrete forms (words, objects, gestures, architecture, music, rituals) has, for centuries, also been available as its potential focus. If we are to think of the ineffable being experienced at all, I suggest, it has to be in irreplaceable and irreducible concrete forms, in just the way that the presence of the narrator's lover was irreplaceably embodied for the fictional narrator in the flowers and, for us, in Schnitzler's literary language about them. It is in this way that Schnitzler's story prompts the reader to natural theological thinking: by allowing him to have an experience which mirrors that which centrally concerns natural theology. In both cases, as with Freud's Uncanny, the concrete embodiment takes on the full force of that which it embodies so that what is embodied is inaccessible without the concrete forms and, partly for that reason, the fact of that experienced embodiment is more or less exempt from the reality test. The experience remains untouched by reductive explanation.

I want to end by drawing attention to a line of thought which confirms this view by suggesting, in the opposite direction, that the nature of all literary (broadly 'poetic') language can only be understood if recourse is had to the kind of embodiment found by the ineffable in the whole range of concrete forms in which natural theology traffics. Gadamer contrasts everyday and poetic language in terms of a differing relationship between 'image' and 'concept' (form and meaning). His suggestion is that, whereas in everyday, prosaic language image is occluded by concept, in poetic language they are identical. Whereas everyday language's determinate meaning occludes its form, the function of such language being to point away from itself towards the intentional meaning, the intentional meaning of 'poetic language' in so far as it is *poetic* is nothing other than the being of the poem itself. It is the sensuous presence, the 'corporeality', of the poetic language, its formal characteristics of rhythm, rhyme, metre, and so on (Gadamer 2004: 153). Gadamer writes, 'poetry does not consist in intending something else. It consists simply in the fact that what is intended and what is said is there in the poem' (Gadamer 1986: 72). He illustrates this point with the aid of a simile:

> Ordinary language resembles a coin that we pass among ourselves in place of something else, whereas poetic language is like gold itself. [67]

Poetic language

> is not a mere pointer that refers to something else, but like the gold coin, it is what it represents. [133]

The most satisfactory model for understanding the experience of literary language, for Gadamer, is a religious one (35). He illustrates the notion, inherited by George Steiner (1989), of 'real presence' in the arts in terms of the Christian idea of transubstantiation (according to which the elements of the Eucharist, bread and wine, 'are' the flesh and blood of Christ and thus manifest or 'incarnate' Christ's Real Presence):

> I am simply making use of this problem of dogma to claim that, if we really want to think about the experience of art, we can, indeed must, think along these lines: the work of art does not simply refer to something, because what it refers to is actually there. We could say that the work of art signifies an increase in being. [Gadamer 1986: 35]

For a natural theologian in the Christian tradition, the Eucharist is what now bodies forth the ineffable God par excellence. Gadamer's argument is that the experience of literature, and even of all art, can only be understood with the conceptual resources of natural theology in a Eucharistic vein. And if this argument is well taken, we shall find in it solid philosophical support for what I have tried to demonstrate in this chapter: that works of literature may prompt us towards thought of a natural theological kind.

REFERENCES

Abbott, Edwin A. (2008 [1884]). *Flatland: A Romance of Many Dimensions*. Oxford: Oxford University Press.

Boyer, Steven D. (2007). 'The Logic of Mystery'. *Religious Studies* 43: 89–102.

Cooper, David E. (1985). 'Ineffability and Religious Experience' in *God: Experience or Origin?* Edited by A. de Nicolás and E. Moutsopoulos. New York: Paragon House.

—— (2002). *The Measure of Things: Humanism, Humility and Mystery*. Oxford: Clarendon.

—— (2005). 'Life and Meaning'. *Ratio* XVIII: 125–37.

—— (2009). 'Mystery, World and Religion' in *Philosophers and God: At the Frontiers of Faith and Reason*. Edited by J. Cornwell and M. McGhee. London: Continuum.

Freud, Sigmund (2003 [1919]). 'The Uncanny' in *The Uncanny*. Translated by D. McLintock. London: Penguin: pp. 121–62.

Gadamer, Hans-Georg (1986). *The Relevance of the Beautiful and Other Essays*. Edited by R. Bernasconi. Cambridge: Cambridge University Press.

—— (2004). *Truth and Method*. Translated by J. Weinsheimer and D. G. Marshall. London: Continuum.

Jaspers, Karl (1959). *Truth and Symbol: From Von der Warheit*. Translated by J. T. Wilde, W. Kluback, and W. Kimmel. London: Vision.

—— (1967). *Philosophical Faith and Revelation*. Translated by E. B. Ashton. New York: Harper and Row.

—— (1969). *Philosophy*. 3 vols. Translated by E. B. Ashton. Chicago: University of Chicago Press.

Macquarrie, John (1966). *Principles of Christian Theology*. London: SCM.

—— (1973). *Mystery and Truth: The 1970 Pere Marquette Theology Lecture*. Milwaukee: Marquette University Theology Department.

—— (1984). *In Search of Deity: An Essay in Dialectical Theism*. London: SCM.

Schnitzler, Arthur (1999 [1894]). 'Flowers' in *Selected Short Fiction*. Translated by J. M. Q. Davies. London: Angel Books.

Steiner, George (1989). *Real Presences*. London: Faber & Faber.

Tillich, Paul (1961). 'The Religious Symbol' in *Religious Experience and Truth: A Symposium*. Edited by S. Hook. New York: New York University Press: pp. 301–21.

CHAPTER 36

NATURAL THEOLOGY AND MUSIC

JEREMY S. BEGBIE

THE PLACE OF THE ARTS IN NATURAL THEOLOGY

WHATEVER the disagreements about the precise meaning of the practice of 'natural theology', among those who advocate it today, certain key concerns are readily identifiable. Three of the commonest are worth highlighting straight away. First, and undoubtedly most prevalent, there is the concern to bear witness 'to the nongodforsakenness of the world even under the conditions of sin' (Hauerwas 2002: 20), to testify to the active presence of God where God is not overtly acknowledged *as* active and present, perhaps even where God is openly refused and denied. Secondly, there can be a concern to do justice to the particularities and integrities of the world—whether of politics, economics, physical and biological processes, or whatever; we must 'let things be themselves', resist the temptation to force theological interpretations prematurely. Thirdly, we also often find an apologetic drive—to render theological truth winsome and compelling to those who for whatever reason find the particular claims of revelation unsupportable and unconvincing.

Amidst the recent resurgence of interest in natural theology, there are signs that the arts are beginning to play an increasingly prominent role, especially when the arts are linked to beauty, and not least with respect to the three concerns we have just outlined. It is argued that the arts can offer ample testimony to the activity of God in the world at large; that their integrity is far better preserved by this form of theologizing than by some more traditional approaches; and that, amid the apologetic demands of late modernity, where the limits of narrowly intellectual approaches are quickly becoming apparent and the need to engage the affective and imaginative dimensions of 'sense-making' is acutely felt, the arts can and should play a crucial role (see e.g. Monti 2003; McGrath 2008: Ch. 11).

Music has been drawn into these discussions, though with nothing like the energy and rigour given to the visual and literary arts. As is well known, music is notoriously difficult to write about—as George Steiner puts it, 'In the face of music, the wonders of language are also its frustrations' (1997: 65)—and the contemporary conversation between music and theology is still in its early stages. Nevertheless, some attempts have been made at incorporating music into projects that might be termed 'natural theology'. In what follows, we will briefly examine two recent examples. We will then go on to ask some theological questions, arising from these attempts, about the project of natural theology, before offering some suggestions as to how music might be part of such a project, albeit somewhat reconceived.

DAVID BROWN

A wide-ranging and immensely ambitious theological project has recently been pioneered by David Brown, formerly of Durham University, and currently at the University of St Andrews. The project includes (indeed, is to a large extent constituted by) what he calls an expanded and transformed 'natural religion' (Brown 2004: 9). Brown distinguishes his own approach from 'natural theology as currently conceived' (9), by which he appears to mean the kind associated with modern analytic philosophy of religion, in which the range of what is to count as theologically significant is (as Brown sees it) relatively restricted. But Brown's is still a 'natural theology' in so far as it attempts to offer theological engagement with phenomena far beyond those spheres in which God is overtly acknowledged, and beyond the walls of any church or official religious institution. Brown urges that theologians and philosophers come to terms with large tracts of 'ordinary' human experience that he believes are redolent of God but have been largely ignored by much traditional theology and philosophical theology: he includes such things as sport, humour, dance, gardens, homes, and, not least, the arts. Indeed, he is quite willing to loosen his terminological strictures and speak of 'natural theology' very broadly; after a section on the artists Mondrian, Kandinsky, and Klee, he writes: 'What in effect they sought was a new form of natural theology, where claims about the spiritual nature of the world could be made.' He continues:

> New and powerful forms of natural theology have been developing throughout the twentieth century without either philosophers or theologians having given them the attention they deserve. [2004: 151]

In fact the arts play a crucial role in Brown's enterprise. In his early book, *Tradition and Imagination*, he urges that tradition and Scripture should not be set against each other but that Christians should learn to 'see the hand of God in a continuing process that accompanies both.' (1999: 1) That tradition is better seen as an ongoing process rather than a fixed deposit is of course a point many others have made. Especially distinctive of Brown, however, is the stress he puts on the arts. It is not only theologians and ecclesiastical councils who lead the way in doctrinal development (through the media of verbal propositions and statements), but painters, story-tellers and other artists—the works of creative imagination are integral and indispensable to the process. So, for example, many paintings of the Nativity have highlighted elements in the biblical story that are perhaps implicit in the text, but which nonetheless need the unique powers of visual art to bring into the open. This results in Brown according the arts an elevated and substantial role in the unveiling of God's purposes, a move not unrelated to his questioning the stress traditionally placed on the normativity of Scripture. He maintains that revelation is to be understood as an historical process entailing works of the human imagination that themselves constitute continuing revelation, that traditions of story-telling and art-making are not self-contained or static but emerge through interaction with their surrounding cultures and other religious traditions, and therefore that Scripture cannot be understood as the locus of revelation to be privileged over Church tradition: the arts can in some cases serve to improve and even correct the biblical texts.

With this goes a strong suspicion of 'instrumental rationality' as applied to the arts, the tendency to take an interest in the arts only in so far as a 'message' or 'programme' can be distilled from them—and for the Christian, that means a *theological* message or programme. Brown writes: 'so deep does instrumental rationality run in our culture that the practice of theology also often reflects that same approach, valuing the arts in their own right but only in so far as they "preach the gospel" ' (2004: 22). He contends we must be careful to attend to them respectfully on their own terms with a view to 'the discovery of God', the ways in which they uniquely mediate the divine, without insisting that they serve some identifiable purely practical end in order to be of any worth.

Music is approached from this perspective. Especially important to him is the combination in music of the 'material' and 'ethereal'—a combination crucial to his 'sacramental' theology as a whole. In his book *God and Grace of Body* Brown includes a substantial section on music, with chapters on classical and pop music, as well as on blues, musicals, and opera. The scope is deliberately wide, ranging far beyond music that is explicitly 'religious'; music does not have to provide overt and specific religious content in order to be religiously significant. In *God and Mystery in Words*, Brown offers extensive chapters on texted music in worship (2008: Chs. 3 and 6).

Speaking of classical music, Brown claims that God can be discerned in a wide range of musical styles: 'in intelligible order and in the sublime, in suffering that expects resurrection and suffering that does not, in hesitant exploration and in the confident assertion of faith, in humour and in solemnity, and in the timeless and the temporal' (2007: 294). Of J. S. Bach, he says that since for the composer all music was a reflection of the divine, more a matter of discovery than invention, he was 'in a sense' engaging in 'a natural theology of music' (254).

If we are to speak of this and other music in such terms, Brown believes, we should be clear that it is not that 'God is being forced upon anyone' but, rather, 'favourable conditions [are] being set under which experience of the divine does at least become a realistic possibility'. This is analogous to the way arguments for the existence of God in traditional philosophy of religion 'open up the individual to certain possibilities'—with the added advantage that here the whole person is being engaged ('body, imagination and emotion no less than the intellect') (293–4). Brown's keenness to find God amidst the unchurched leads him to be critical of much Christian treatment of popular music, where a preoccupation with the artist's lifestyle or convictions obscures the implicit religious dimensions of the music (especially when the musician has no explicit faith or theological interest) (346).

Some will take issue with Brown's treatment of particular forms and pieces of music. But the most pointed questions that Brown's enterprise provokes are methodological and criteriological. While undoubtedly intending a perspective that is at least consonant with Christian orthodoxy, and to honour the incarnation ('the primordial sacrament') as pivotal—for the incarnation is paradigmatic for God's willingness to be revealed in a way that is subject to the culturally conditioned historical process of creativity—Brown is highly suspicious about any approach that would privilege Scripture as exercising a normative or corrective role in relation to subsequent tradition. What is insufficiently recognized is the way in which the mainstream Church has never replaced Scripture with (or subsumed Scripture seamlessly into) post-biblical tradition; rather, in its continual return to the texts, Scripture has de facto functioned normatively over later tradition, even if later tradition is accorded the status of a mediator of revelation. As Kathryn Tanner has put it in a vigorous critique of one of Brown's books, for him 'the incarnation as an endorsement of human creativity is . . . played off against the Bible' (Tanner 2001: 119), but this leaves us far from clear why we should accept the incarnation as critical for the revelation of God and his purposes (or for a theology of creativity), for in principle, this could be set aside in the light of a later tradition that found its presence in Scripture offensive, uncongenial, or contrary to widely held religious experiences. To be sure, Brown discusses nine types of criteria for discerning the truth of imaginative theology: historical, empirical, conceptual, moral, criteria of continuity, Christological, the degree of imaginative engagement, the effectiveness of the analogical construct, and ecclesial criteria (Brown 2000: 390–406), but as he himself admits, much more needs to be said, especially as to their relative strength, source, and grounding (2004: 3). It may well be that Brown's eagerness to relate the Christian faith to such a wide variety of cultural perspectives and to respect the integrity of manifold 'experiences', together with the dominance of general categories such as 'religious experience'/'experience of the divine'/'sacrament' has led him to be less than convincing when it comes to delineating how such key categories are anchored in the distinctive specifics and particularities of Christian faith.

ANTHONY MONTI

The very title of Anthony Monti's book, A Natural Theology of the Arts, will be instantly appealing to those sympathetic to the term 'natural theology', and especially so to those eager to approach the arts, including music, from such a standpoint. Setting his discussion against the background of the postmodern 'crisis in the humanities', he rejects the possibility of the arts being used as part of knock-down demonstrations of theological truth or refutations of nihilism. He advocates a subtler and more indirect enterprise. He believes that the arts by their very nature are theologically loaded, irrespective of their explicit content, and aims to 'set out the epistemological, metaphysical and theological grounds for maintaining that artistic creativity can most adequately be understood as an expression of the "real presence" of God, that this is the ultimate meaning and truth of such activity' (Monti 2003: 6). Further, he wants to show that 'the God who is present in works of art can best be understood in a Trinitarian way' (6). (All three of the typical concerns of 'natural theology' we set out above are thus present.)

Monti believes that such a case can be made with the aid of the epistemology of critical realism, a 'metaphysics of flexible openness', and an understanding of art as centring on the process of metaphor (which serves to link epistemology and metaphysics). His discussion ranges very widely across many disciplines, but his two major conversation partners are John Polkinghorne, with respect to epistemology and cosmology, and Jeremy Begbie, with respect to metaphor in the arts.

He wishes to speak of the arts as (potentially) both a 'natural theology' and 'revelation', in that they provide experiences that fall between, on the one hand, the kind of diffuse awareness (e.g. a sense of contingency or finitude) that forms the subject matter of 'natural theology' as traditionally understood, and on the other hand, the kind of 'pointed' and specific experience typical of quite specific revelations (e.g. a sense of God speaking directly to us).

In the process, Monti offers extensive discussions of music and its potential theological import. Indeed, in music, he holds, 'spiritual truth' is enfleshed 'most fully'. Making use of the work of musicologist Victor Zuckerkandl, he argues that music subverts the assumption that order is only possible in the fixed and static, and presents us with 'the unprecedented spectacle of an order that is wholly flux', a pointer to the ontology of 'flexible openness' characteristic of the created world as viewed through Christian eyes (2003: 82–4). In addition to these general comments, he offers more detailed discussions of, among other pieces, Mozart's *Jupiter* symphony and the late quartets of Beethoven. He remarks on the ease with which metaphysical/religious language is often used of the latter. Especially notable in Monti is the place given to the future, to the eschatological potential of art to prefigure, albeit provisionally, the life of the world to come. Here he draws at length on Jeremy Begbie's work on the relation between music and time, the way in which music's temporal features can serve to embody and disclose something of the eschatological character of the Christian faith (Monti 2003: 139–70). Monti's theology is marked by a temporal, forward-driving character, and is thus able to take rather more seriously than Brown the engagement of God with the temporal and transient, not only with the material and fleshly.

Where Monti is weakest is in clarifying and maintaining certain key distinctions, a symptom, one suspects, of the diverse array of theological witnesses he draws into his argument. In particular, the term 'natural theology' often seems to be used as a synonym for something like 'natural' or 'general revelation' (revelation beyond the history of Israel that culminates in Jesus Christ, as attested in Scripture). However, theology, whatever else it is, entails intellectual deliberation on phenomena, whereas general revelation denotes a disclosure (a quite different category). This makes it somewhat confusing to speak, as he does, of the arts *as* natural theology (2003: 92, 123) (Brown can do the same), even if the arts may well offer experiences of a more diffuse sort that many would claim ought to be the subject matter of 'natural theology'.

Clearly, with Monti we are in more resolutely orthodox territory than Brown. Monti is far more concerned than Brown that his project should serve and strengthen a robust Trinitarian faith; in one place, he writes that his natural theology 'finds its fulfilment in, rather than substitutes itself for, the revelation of the Triune God' (2003: 9). While Brown would probably admit to something similar for his own project, his purpose is less to bolster this or that version of the faith, and far more to make effective theological contact with the sheer breadth of human experience. In any case, with Monti, there is no hint that post-biblical tradition could correct Scripture, though there is ample evidence of such tradition amplifying, applying, particularizing, and embodying Scripture's witness, and in this way functioning as 'revelation'.

On the 'Naturalness' of 'Natural Theology'

Arising out of this brief consideration of Brown and Monti, perhaps the most important question that needs addressing is: what distinguishes 'natural theology' from any other theology? Presuming the answer lies in the word 'natural', our question then becomes: what is 'natural' about 'natural theology'? More pointedly, to what extent is this 'naturalness' *theologically* shaped and conditioned, rather than determined and presumed a priori, in advance of theological considerations?

What needs stressing here is what many would regard as a truism, that the term 'natural' is highly fluid in common usage and historically polyvalent. It is also never ideologically neutral: it would be theologically naive to pretend that such a concept of 'nature' or the 'natural' was available, let alone to attempt to employ such a concept as foundational for theology (see Torrance 1993). We are justified therefore in expecting a measure of clarity about the term if we are to gain any sense of what might be entailed in a 'natural theology' that engages the arts.

Rather than attempt to delineate all the historical construals of 'natural' in 'natural theology' (for a succinct and useful survey of different types of natural theology, see Fergusson 2006: 380–93), I propose to explore its meaning in relation to some basic trajectories in New Testament theology, present in the earliest strands of the texts, which here I am going to have to presume, rather than defend, as being basic to classical Christian orthodoxy. We will relate these trajectories to four very broad senses of 'natural' as commonly found when the expression 'natural theology' is employed in theological discourse today, senses which can and do often overlap. All four are present in both Brown and Monti.

First, theology can be described as 'natural' in that it seeks to attend to *the reality of the physical world, the world explored and examined by the natural sciences*. The perspective from which such attention is appropriate theologically, the perspective enjoined by the New Testament, is that shaped at its profoundest level by what has been disclosed and enacted in Jesus Christ: the Son through whom all things were made has become a creature, submitted to creation's brokenness, and has been raised as an anticipation of an ultimate refashioning of all things. Among other things, this elicits a perception of the cosmos not as brute fact but as the outcome of unconstrained love, fashioned out of nothing, ontologically distinct from yet wholly contingent upon the creator, and oriented to a final recreation.

Secondly, theology can be 'natural' in that it seeks to attend to *what is primordially human*. In this respect, the New Testament texts direct our attention not to a generic 'humanity' but pre-eminently to a specific human person, Jesus Christ, the Last Adam, who, it is claimed, embodies the primordial divine intention for humans, and, in and through this person, to the future, corporate, eschatological fulfilment of the human race.

Thirdly, theology can be 'natural' in that it seeks to attend to *those constructive activities we designate as human 'culture'*. Scripturally, we are pressed to conceive these initially in the light of the vocation given to humans to be image-bearers of God, realized in the person and agency of Christ, the one true *imago Dei*. This vocation is to discover, respect, develop, and heal what we are given in creation, with and for the sake of others (Begbie 2007b: 207–09).

To these three we may add a fourth sense of 'natural', one we have not mentioned so far: theology can be 'natural' in that it seeks to enlist a *properly functioning human reason*. 'Natural' theology then becomes that form of theology which aspires—to be no more precise for the moment—to be rational, and in New Testament terms this would appear to mean one oriented first of all to the reshaping of human rationality, embodied in Christ, and in which humans are invited to participate by the Spirit. From this point of view, the much-cherished belief in a universal rational faculty, purportedly independent of the contingencies of time, space, and culture, immune to corruption and free of tradition, and thus capable of laying down in advance unalterable criteria for what is to count as 'rational' knowledge of, and speech about, God, begins to look distinctly dubious (MacIntyre 1988; Gellner 1992; Murphy 1994; Clouser 2005; McGrath 2001: 55–118). To recognize this need not lead to an approach that involves a theological rejection of reason (*contra rationem*), or an addition to reason (*supra rationem*), but rather one that takes its cue from the redemption of the whole person in Jesus Christ, of which our reasoning powers are but one dimension (Rae 1997: 113; Torrance 2005). The thrust of, say, the Apostle Paul's anthropology suggests that this redemption of our rational capacities is intrinsic to the 'salvation' of which the Christian faith speaks. Indeed, the momentum of God reconciling and recreating his creatures in Christ *includes*, through the Spirit, the gift of being able to apprehend it, and, indeed, *requires* such a gift, for on what theologically legitimate grounds are we to claim that some zone or mode of human reasoning is entirely immune to the distortions and deformations of human sin? (This is not of course to claim that all human reasoning outside the Church is distorted and false—this would be yet another theologically unwarranted a priori assumption—only that all human reasoning is *prone* to the effects of sinful bias, that no quarter of our minds can be cordoned off and claim a sort of diplomatic immunity from prosecution.)

Before returning to music, another formal matter needs to be addressed. Earlier we said that one of the commonest motivations of supporters of natural theology is a concern to do justice to the particularities and integrities of the world. This is especially conspicuous among those at work in theology and the arts, and it may be thought that the kind of theological lines we are opening up here move in the opposite direction. It is imperative, surely, that we *first* 'listen' to the artist, give due 'space' to the witness of music and painting, dance and drama, and only *then* introduce normative theological considerations of the kind we are speaking about. (This, as we saw, is a major concern of David Brown.)

Certainly, the ease with which the Church has stifled the arts in the name of a supposed orthodoxy is one of the more shameful aspects of its history. But it is questionable to suggest—as it often seems to be—that a 'respect for reality' (artistic or otherwise) is best gained by aspiring to a vantage point supposedly free of interpretation (an impossibility in any case), or that if an interpretative stance *is* declared it must be one *other* than that provided by the creator's disclosure of his purposes for created reality in Jesus Christ. If we do choose to adopt an alternative (and by implication, superior) ultimate viewpoint for interpreting and discerning artistic practices, it is incumbent upon us to identify the criteria by which we have made such a decision, and to recognize that in so doing we will have relativized the criteria presented to us as ultimate in the witness of the New Testament.

Having said all this, if we do take our bearings strictly from the orientation of the New Testament—the transformative reconciliation of all things in the person of Christ—it would be disingenuous to dismiss as a matter of principle all proposed candidates for 'natural theology'. Precisely *because* of a commitment to God as the redeeming creator (who self-identifies in Jesus Christ), we are bound to take seriously the concern of many proponents of natural theology we noted at the outset—and evident in numerous texts in Old and New Testament—to bear witness 'to the nongodforsakenness of the world even under the conditions of sin'. If the God of Jesus Christ and the Holy Spirit is indeed the God who is active to reconcile the totality of the space-time continuum to himself, can we do otherwise?

Whether we call this endeavour 'natural theology', or, as I would prefer, one responsibility of a theology of creation, is a matter of debate. It is arguable that a continued attachment to the term 'natural theology' is confusing, in that it will too easily bring with it (or smuggle in) some of the more questionable characteristics of Enlightenment apologetics (McGrath 2008: Ch. 7) or earlier Christian thought (Gunton 1995: Ch. 3), in particular assumptions about what is to count as 'nature' or 'natural' that are insufficiently controlled theologically. In this light, Colin Gunton contrasts natural theology with a 'theology of nature', by which he designates 'an account of what things naturally are, by virtue of their createdness' (1995: 56), or, put differently, an interpretation of creation in the light of the self-revelation of God in Jesus Christ.

In any case, there is much to be said for concurring with Eberhard Jüngel when he calls for a '*more* natural theology': one that moves outward from Christ as creator and redeemer of all things, and is thus more fully oriented towards 'nature' than many traditional forms of 'natural theology'. Such an enterprise will lead us:

> deeper into [creation's] needs and difficulties (*aporiai*), but also deeper into its hidden glories! Deeper...into compassionate solidarity with those who cry *de profundis*...But even deeper into the joy of the unanswered mystery of the fact that we are here and are not rather nothing. Deeper into the joy of being able to see the one and only light of life reflecting in the manifold lights of creation and thus, in its light, being able to see with astonishment creation's own [particular] light. [Jüngel 1992: 28–9]

MUSIC'S 'NATURAL' WITNESS

For the remainder of this chapter, then, bearing in mind the theological orientations we have outlined, we may usefully ask: how might music play a part in the endeavour of theology to bear witness to the nongodforsakenness of creation even under the conditions of sin? We have space to offer only four examples, congruent with the four senses of 'natural' we highlighted earlier.

MUSIC AND THE COSMOS

First, there is music's potential to bear witness to the cosmos *as the creation of the triune God of Jesus Christ*. We can consider here some features of the instrumental music of J. S. Bach (1685–1750). David Bentley Hart has written that 'Bach's is the ultimate Christian music; it reflects as no other human artefact ever has or could the Christian vision of creation' (2003: 283). There may be more than a streak of hyperbole here, but the sentiment is not to be dismissed (and the following owes much to Hart's work). Of special importance is something that Laurence Dreyfus has recently argued was central to Bach's art, namely 'invention' *(inventio)* (2004). Many pianists' first introduction to Bach will be one of his two-part 'inventions'. The composer tells us these were designed to serve as models for 'good inventions' and 'developing the same satisfactorily' (Drefus 2004: 2). The word *inventio* derives from classical rhetoric, and in Bach's time was widely used as a metaphor for the basic musical idea, the unit of music that formed the subject matter of a piece. Not only this, it denoted the process of discovering that fundamental idea. The key for Bach was to find *generative* material, an idea that was capable of being developed in a variety of ways, for 'by crafting a workable idea, one unlocks the door to a complete musical work' (Dreyfus 2004: 2). So the method of finding an invention was inseparable from thinking about its possible development—*elaboratio*, to use the rhetorical term. Hence Bach's concern is to show us models of good inventions *and* of their development. It seems that most of Bach's contemporaries viewed *elaboratio* as among the most unexciting parts of composing and could treat it almost casually. Bach appears to have thought about extensive elaboration even from the start, when choosing the initial material. As Dreyfus puts it:

> One might even be tempted to say that in Bach's works both invention and elaboration are marked by an almost equally intense mental activity...In no other composer of the period does one find such a fanatical zeal directed so often toward what others considered the least interesting parts of a composition. [2004: 22, 24]

Indeed, Bach seems to have had an almost superhuman eye for how relatively simple sets of notes would combine, cohere, and behave in different groupings. The Bach scholar Christoph Wolff writes that the principle of elaboration 'determines like nothing else Bach's art and personal style' (2000: 469).

We can highlight three features of this *elaboratio*. First, the elaboration is governed not chiefly by an external, pre-given logic but first and foremost by the musical material itself. Dreyfus's research has shown that, whatever the precise order in which Bach composed a piece, it is highly inappropriate to envision him starting with a fixed, precise, and unalterable 'form' and then proceeding to fill it with music; rather we would be better understanding him searching for inventions with rich potential, and accordingly finding an appropriate form. In other words, this is an art in which the musical material is not forced into preconceived strict grids but structured according to the shapes that appear to be latent in it and thus apt for it. A fugue, for instance, is more like a texture with conventions than it is a PowerPoint template. This is why genre was far more important than large-scale form for Bach and why so many of Bach's pieces modify and even disrupt traditional forms; 'form was seen...as an occasional feature of a genre, and not the general theoretical category subsuming the genres that it later became' (Dreyfus 2004: 28). Christoph Wolff writes of Bach engaging in 'imaginative research into the harmonic implications of [his] chosen subject-matter' (2000: 468). If we allow this aspect of his music to provoke a vision of creation as God's handiwork possessed of beauty, it is one in which creation is not, so to speak, a text that hides a more basic group of meanings. Rather than theological schemes in which forms are given an eternal status in God's mind, or schemes in which God initially creates ideas or forms and then subsequently creates the world, or schemes in which matter is created first and then shaped into forms, is it not more true to the biblical affirmation of the goodness and integrity of creation (and a Trinitarian account of creation) to affirm that it is created directly out of nothing, such that it has its own appropriate forms, forms that God honours and enables to flourish as intrinsic to the matter itself? Secondly, in this music we hear difference as intrinsic to unity. Bach's skill in deriving so much music from such tiny musical units means that he can offer intense experiences of simultaneous complexity and unity. Even the resolutions in his music rarely neutralize its richness: the reconciliation at the end of the 'Dona Nobis Pacem' at the close of his Mass in B Minor does not compromise any of that piece's immeasurable diversity. Indeed, Bach is adept at helping us perceive rich complexity in the apparently simple (for example, in the reprise at the end of the Goldberg Variations). The diverse particulars of creation are not an elaboration on some more profound, more basic, uniform simplicity, any more than the threefoldness of the creator is the expression of a more basic singularity (as in modalism). In Hart's words, 'The "theme" of creation is the gift of the whole' (2003: 282). And the diverse unity of the whole participates in, and thus is witness to, the differentiated unity of the triune creator. Thirdly, we hear the simultaneous presence of radical contingency and radical consistency. With almost any piece of Bach—although perhaps most of all in the solo instrumental works—the music will sound astonishingly contingent, free of necessity. Not only does Bach constantly adapt and reshape the forms and styles he inherits; even within the constraints he sets for himself for a piece, there is a remarkable contingency—Peter Williams even uses the word 'caprice' of this aspect of the Goldberg Variations (2001: 46). So with the created order, we must surely speak not of the 'closed consonances' of identical repetition, but of the particularizing, proliferating ministry of the Holy Spirit, effecting faithful but contingent improvisations on the harmony achieved in Jesus Christ.

Music and the Human

Secondly, there is music's potential to bear witness to *what is primordially human*—which in this context will be the goal of our human existence, the communally shaped humanity enabled by the Spirit and already actualized *pro nobis* in Jesus Christ by the same Spirit. In this connection, we simply point to one particularly significant feature of music.

The power of music to effect social cohesion is legendary. It has long been known that rhythmic music possesses striking capacities in this respect. In recent years biomusicologists and others have focussed much attention on the phenomena of 'entrainment' (Clayton, Will, and Sager 2004; Cross and Morley 2009: 67–70). We tap our feet, sway, bob our heads to music; and even more so when we are with others who do the same. There is some evidence to suggest this skill is unique to humans, and that it is universal: 'In every culture, there is some form of music with a periodic pulse that affords temporal coordination between performers and elicits synchronised motor responses from listeners' (Patel 2008: 402; see also Drake and Bertrand 2001; McNeill 1995). Visual, auditory, and motor cues combine to create a potent and mutually reinforcing mix. And, given rhythm's connections with emotion, this is one of the quickest ways in which emotion is spread and shared. We only need think of the chanting of a protest march, or mass synchronized movement at a rock concert.

Some argue that entrainment was critical in the evolution of our capacity for communal culture: for rhythmic synchronization makes it possible to experience the world in another's time. This capacity of music goes with another that complements it: what Ian Cross calls its 'floating intentionality' (Cross and Woodruff 2009: 87), its semantic indeterminacy. Unlike language, music is susceptible to a large (though not unlimited) range of interpretations; it struggles to be specific, to denote with reliability and specificity. This flexibility allows the hearer considerable space to develop her own 'reading' and application of the music. Putting these together: music can grant an extraordinary sense of embodied togetherness (through entrainment processes, among other things), *while at the same time* allowing for—even encouraging—a sense of particularity and uniqueness (through its floating intentionality). Many other factors are involved here, of course, but recognizing that these two are operating together in most corporate musical experience can be highly instructive. For example, in some current 'alternative worship' (contemporary forms of experimental worship, employing a variety of non-traditional media), wordless rhythmic music is extensively used, and can engender an intense sense of solidarity, and yet at the same time allow for widely diverse responses and stances on the part of those taking part—which can be highly attractive to those anxious about being enlisted to adhere to specific beliefs, doctrines, goals. No doubt at some stage one will be looking for the higher degree of specificity that Christian worship requires; nonetheless, music of this sort in this context may be witnessing to, and making possible, something of that liberating, differentiated human unity promised in Christ and granted through the Spirit in his body, the Church.

MUSIC AND CULTURE

Thirdly, there is music's potential to bear witness to *felicitous culture*. 'Culture' here is understood as the human vocation to take the materials given to hand and mind, and develop (elaborate), reconfigure, and, indeed, heal them in ways that praise the creator. Again, this finds its realization in the person of Christ, the one in whom creation finds its true human priest, and with whom, by the Spirit, we are now invited into strenuous engagement with creation, to extend and elaborate creation's praise, in anticipation of the recreation of all things that has already been embodied in him.

The dynamics of this can be usefully opened up by briefly returning to Bach. We have already spoken about the possibility of music to witness to the character of the world as created by the triune God, to its own inherent order, thus offering 'insight into the depths of the wisdom of the world' (words used on Bach's behalf) (J. A. Birnbaum, as quoted in Wolff 2000). But if there is truth in this, we should not forget it happens through *an active process of making*: principally through *inventio* and *elaboratio*, both of which (as we have seen) are themselves constructive exercises. Bach's *Well-Tempered Clavier* is indeed an exploration of the twelve-note chromatic scale which is indeed derived from the harmonic series, but the scale Bach used and the slightly differently tuned one we commonly use today are in fact adjustments, 'temperings' of what the physical world gives us. If these pieces *are* derived from the harmonic series, they are constructively derived. In fact, Bach substantially reshaped almost everything he touched: from simple motifs to whole styles and genres. He is one of the least 'passive' composers in history.

What this provokes us to imagine is a subtle relationship between given, physical order and artistic order, the former being the inhabited environment, trusted and respected, in which the latter is born, even if born through sweat and struggle. It is a vision of 'faithful improvisation', of the artist, as physical and embodied, set in the midst of a God-given world vibrant with a dynamic order of its own, not simply 'there' like a brute fact to be escaped or violently abused but there as a gift from a God of overflowing generosity, a gift for us to interact with vigorously, to form and (in the face of distortion) transform, and in this way fashion something as felicitous as the *Goldberg Variations*, art that can anticipate by the Spirit the *shalom* previewed and promised in Jesus Christ (see Begbie 2007a).

I would suggest that an 'improvisatory' model along these lines is considerably more adequate to a trinitarian account of creativity than the more antagonistic (and unitarian) schemes often underlying theologies of creativity, where humans are, if not seen as pitted against each other, envisaged as engaged in some kind of zero-sum game. George Steiner's allusive *Real Presences*, a book frequently alluded to in discussions of natural theology and the arts, can be challenged from this perspective (Steiner 1989; see Begbie 2000: 235–41).

MUSIC AND THE RENEWED MIND

Fourthly, there is music's potential to witness to *the thought-forms appropriate to a renewed rationality*—to that 're-schematizing' of the mind (Romans 12:2) made possible through sharing in the mind of Christ through the Spirit. Here we focus on just one way in which this can happen: the perception of musical space.

Whatever the commonalities between visual perception and aural perception, in one respect at least they are quite distinct: in our visual field, objects occupy bounded locations, and cannot overlap without their integrity being threatened. We are unable to perceive red and yellow in the same place at the same time *as* red and as yellow. By the same token, objects in our visual field cannot occupy more than one place at the same time. However, if we hear a tone, it does not occupy a bounded location in our aural field; it fills the whole of the space we hear. A second tone, added to that tone—say, a major third above—will occupy the same (aural) space, yet (provided it is not too loud or soft) we can hear it as a distinct, irreducibly different tone. The sounds neither merge nor exclude one another, but interpenetrate.

The fruitfulness of this kind of perceptual simultaneity ought to be clear. Arguably, the Christian theological tradition has been hampered by relying exclusively or excessively on visual conceptuality in its struggles to 'think together' discrete and supposedly incommensurable realities—God's freedom and the world's, divine and human agency, interpersonal integrity, the two natures of Christ, and, supremely (perhaps lying behind them all), the oneness and threeness of God. Discussion of these issues typically leads to an oscillation between the extremes of exclusion and merger, an inability to preserve the ontological integrity of disparate particulars. But if the perception of musical tones is allowed to jolt the imagination out of some of its visually dominated defaults, many of these classic *aporiai* are massively alleviated, for we are given a way of thinking unity and particularity together without compromising either.

The fruitfulness is extended further if we consider the phenomenon of 'sympathetic resonance', the way in which one vibrating string enables the vibration of another at a distance from it. Ways of conceiving God's free agency as the means by which the world is freed to be itself begin to open up, avoiding the implication that God's freedom-in-action is the negation of the world's. Likewise, the intra-Trinitarian life of Father, Son, and Spirit, whose very nature is that of other-directed *ecstasis*, is rendered more intellectually accessible when conceived in the light of 'enabling resonance', and would seem far more appropriate than the distinctly limited notions favoured in some Trinitarian theology, especially when such notions inadvertently suggest agents who 'decide' or 'determine' to love or give themselves away. Something analogous applies to human persons in relation, and is strengthened if combined with what we discovered about entrainment, the rhythmic enabling of one person to move 'in sync' with another.

There are undoubtedly numerous other possibilities for music to be associated with a 'natural theology' (appropriately conceived)—we have merely touched on a few. Whether or not theologians today avail themselves of the opportunities music affords, in a climate not always conducive to theology 'outside of the box', remains to be seen.

REFERENCES

Begbie, J. S. (2000). *Theology, Music, and Time*. Cambridge: Cambridge University Press.

—— (2007a). 'Created Beauty: The Witness of J. S. Bach' in *The Beauty of God: Theology and the Arts*. Edited by D. J. Treier, M. Husbands, and R. Lundin. Downers Grove, IL: InterVarsity Press.

—— (2007b). *Resounding Truth: Christian Wisdom in the World of Music*. Grand Rapids: Michigan, Baker.

Brown, D. (1999). *Tradition and Imagination: Revelation and Change*. Oxford: Oxford University Press.

—— (2000). *Discipleship and Imagination: Christian Tradition and Truth*. Oxford: Oxford University Press.

—— (2004). *God and Enchantment of Place: Reclaiming Human Experience*. Oxford: Oxford University Press.

—— (2007). *God and Grace of Body: Sacrament in Ordinary*. Oxford: Oxford University Press.

—— (2008). *God and Mystery in Words: Experience Through Metaphor and Drama*. Oxford: Oxford University Press.

Clayton, M., U. Will, and R. Sager (2004). 'In Time with the Music: The Concept of Entrainment and its Significance for Ethnomusicology'. *ESEM CounterPoint* 1: 1–82.

Clouser, R. A. (2005). *The Myth of Religious Neutrality: An Essay on the Hidden Role of Religious Belief in Theories*. Notre Dame, IN: University of Notre Dame Press.

Cross, I. and I. Morley (2009). 'The Evolution of Music: Theories, Definitions and the Nature of the Evidence' in *Communicative Musicality: Exploring the Basis of Human Companionship*. Edited by S. Malloch and C. Trevarthen. Oxford: Oxford University Press.

Cross, I. and G. E. Woodruff (2009). 'Music as a Communicative Medium' in *The Prehistory of Language*. Edited by R. Botha and C. Knight. Oxford: Oxford University Press.

Drake, C. and D. Bertrand (2001). 'The Quest for Universals in Temporal Processing in Music'. *Annals of the New York Academy of the Sciences* 930: 17–27.

Dreyfus, L. (2004). *Bach and the Patterns of Invention*. Cambridge, MA: Harvard University Press.

Fergusson, D. (2006). 'Types of Natural Theology' in *The Evolution of Rationality: Interdisciplinary Essays in Honor of J. Wentzel van Huyssteen*. Edited by F. L. Shults. Grand Rapids, MI: Eerdmans.

Gellner, E. (1992). *Reason and Culture: The Historic Role of Rationality and Rationalism*. Oxford: Blackwell.

Gunton, C. E. (1995). *A Brief Theology of Revelation*. Edinburgh: T&T Clark.

Hart, D. B. (2003). *The Beauty of the Infinite: The Aesthetics of Christian Truth*. Grand Rapids, MI: Eerdmans.

Hauerwas, S. (2002). *With the Grain of the Universe: The Church's Witness and Natural Theology*. London: SCM.

Jüngel, E. (1992). *Christ, Justice and Peace: Toward a Theology of the State in Dialogue with the Barmen Declaration*. Edinburgh: T&T Clark.

MacIntyre, A. C. (1988). *Whose Justice? Which Rationality?* Notre Dame, IN: University of Notre Dame Press.

McGrath, Alister E. (2001). *A Scientific Theology*. Vol. II: *Reality*. Edinburgh: T&T Clark.

—— (2008). *The Open Secret: A New Vision for Natural Theology*. Oxford: Blackwell.

McNeill, W. H. (1995). *Keeping Together in Time: Dance and Drill in Human History*. Cambridge, MA: Harvard University Press.

Monti, A. (2003). *A Natural Theology of the Arts: Imprint of the Spirit*. Aldershot: Ashgate.

Murphy, R. (1994). *Rationality and Nature: A Sociological Inquiry into a Changing Relationship*. Boulder, CO: Westview Press.

Patel, A. D. (2008). *Music, Language, and the Brain*. Oxford: Oxford University Press.

Rae, M. (1997). *Kierkegaard's Vision of the Incarnation: By Faith Transformed*. Oxford: Clarendon Press.

Steiner, G. (1989). *Real Presences: Is There Anything In What We Say?* London: Faber and Faber.

—— (1997). *Errata: An Examined Life*. London: Phoenix.

Tanner, K. (2001). 'Review of David Brown, *Tradition and Imagination: Revelation and Change* (1999)'. *International Journal of Systematic Theology* 3/1: 118–21.

Torrance, A. J. (1993). 'Response by Alan J. Torrance' in *Christ and Context: The Confrontation between Gospel and Culture*. Edited by H. D. Regan, A. J. Torrance, and A. Wood. Edinburgh: T&T Clark.

—— (2005). '*Auditus Fidei*: Where and How Does God Speak? Faith, Reason, and the Question of Criteria' in *Reason and the Reasons of Faith*. Edited by P. J. Griffiths and R. Hütter. London: T & T Clark.

Williams, P. F. (2001). *Bach: The Goldberg Variations*. Cambridge: Cambridge University Press.

Wolff, C. (2000). *Johann Sebastian Bach: The Learned Musician*. New York and London, Norton.

CHAPTER 37

IMAGES IN NATURAL THEOLOGY

KRISTÓF NYÍRI

INTRODUCTION

THE key background assumption of this chapter is that human thinking has both a verbal and a perceptual dimension, with the perceptual, primarily the visual, dimension being the primordial one (Nyíri 2001, 2006). Twentieth-century philosophy, under the spell of the linguistic turn, gave short shrift to images, mental or physical. And reflecting on the indispensable role of images in human cognition was of course never a characteristic preoccupation for philosophies of religion in the Judeo-Christian tradition. Still, there have been, and are, notable exceptions. Aquinas embraced, and built on, the Aristotelian dictum that 'the soul understands nothing without a phantasm', and I take it that there is a close relationship between Aquinas' notion of phantasmata and our notion of mental images (Kenny 1993: 37; Stump 2003: 257–9). Closer to our age, Cardinal Newman, in his *Grammar of Assent*, first published in 1870, interprets memory images as 'reflections of things in a mental mirror', as 'facsimiles of facts', and points out that mental images possess a psychological power that mere concepts do not have (Newman 1881: 23 f.). The Anglican theologian and philosopher Austin Farrer, in his 1943 book *Finite and Infinite*, taking up the notion of phantasmata construed the 'concrete phantasma' as 'a concrete image, but sketchy', underlining however that 'there are cases in which the image is as explicit as we could make it' (Farrer 1943: 125). Romano Guardini, one of the most influential Catholic intellectuals of the twentieth century, in his 1950 essay *Die Sinne und die religiöse Erkenntnis* ('The Senses and Religious Knowledge'), stresses the role images play in the depths of our subconscious, ready to enter consciousness whenever appropriate external stimuli reach us. 'The innermost core of a human being,' as Guardini puts it, is 'in the end essentially dependent on images' (Guardini 1950: 65). Another leading Catholic thinker, Karl Rahner, in 1983 gave a talk on the theology of images in which, referring back to Aquinas' formula *conversio ad phantasma*, he emphasized that traditional Christian anthropology has always regarded intellectual cognition on the one hand, and sensibility on the other, as forming a unity, so that even for the most sublime knowledge it is sensory experience that provides content (Rahner 1983 2–8; 2009: XXX, 472). The Russian Orthodox theologian Paul Evdokimov, in his 1972 book *The Art of the Icon*, underlined that the 'visual is intimately associated with the intelligible; . . . the word and the image are closely linked' (Evdokimov 1990: 72). On the Lutheran side, Rainer Volp, in his 1980 *Theologische Realenzyklopädie* entry 'The Image as a Fundamental Category of Theology', recalled Schleiermacher's view that 'in all genuine thinking images are contained' (Volp 1980: VI, 558). A recent work with a Lutheran background is Sigurd Bergmann's volume *In the Beginning Is the Icon*, in which Begman maintains that theology 'must learn to understand the uniqueness and autonomy of the visual medium. The image has a unique power vested in its capability of producing inner images with external measures and thus influencing our imaginative abilities and our capability to act in the tension between our internal landscapes and external surroundings' (Bergmann 2009: 99). Finally, in David Gelernter's *Judaism: A Way of Being*, one encounters the following formulation:

> Images are the stuff of thought. . . . we spend much of our mental lives . . . wrapped up in imagery, beyond the reach of language. [Gelernter 2009: 3, 20]

Now Judaism and Christianity are of course religions of the book. One might reasonably expect that the religious feelings and experiences of a believer brought up in a world of sacred texts to be tinged with, and indeed informed by, verbal images; here, visual perceptions and imagery will be necessarily influenced, filtered, and modified by prior textual exposures. By contrast, the primordial religious experience focussed on notably by William James and indeed Calvin's *sensus divinitatis*, 'that simple and primitive knowledge, to which the mere course of nature would have conducted us, had Adam stood upright', should essentially involve mental imagery, specific images of the world surrounding us, and images and statues as artefacts (James 1902; Calvin 2008: Bk 1, Ch. 2). It is the nature and variety of such images, and their role at the level of non-revealed religion, that this chapter will explore. First, however, let me remain in the domain of revealed religions.

IMAGES IN REVEALED RELIGIONS

The role of images in the religions of the book is a well-researched topic in the case of Judaism, and especially so in the case of Christianity, where the two main issues are how the invisible can be represented by the visible—the basic answer being that in Christ God became flesh—and whether pictures can serve as a *biblia pauperum*, that is whether they can convey the scriptural narrative to the unlettered (Freedberg 1989: 402 f., 162 ff.; Nyíri 2003: 183). The literature is vast, and I clearly cannot go into great detail here. However, by way of setting the scene for my main argument, I would like at this stage to point to some specific ramifications of the problem.

First, the perhaps minor observation that even within the religions of the book, and even for the scribes and scholars involved in copying and recreating sacred written texts, the susceptibility to images, the impulse to image, can become overwhelming. As Freedberg, printing examples of Arab calligraphy and of various Jewish manuscripts, puts it: 'Even in...Islam and Judaism...with...an apparent emphasizing of word over image, of the written over the figured, the will to image figuratively—even anthropo-morphically—cannot be suppressed' (Freedberg 1989: 5). Secondly, that generally speaking, as Victoria Harrison has recently put it, religious language 'tends to be replete with images and metaphors' (Harrison 2007: 153). In particular, both the Old and the New Testament abound in images, not merely in the sense of using a rich metaphoric language—metaphors of course function, ultimately, by evoking mental images—but also by conjuring up, directly, lively visual images (Evdokimov 1990: 32). 'Judaism', writes Gelernter:

> is in fact passionately attached to images; they are its favourite means of expression.— Even a quick glance at the Bible makes it plain that Jewish thought luxuriates in vivid imagery....Much of medieval art is a celebration of biblical imagery....The medieval Christian artist translates biblical images directly from words into paint, sculpture, tapestry, glass. [Gelernter 2009: 17]

What Gelernter here says is of course not new. It had been demonstrated extensively by the Lutheran German philosopher and theologian Johann Gottfried Herder towards the end of the eighteenth century, and by Austin Farrer in the mid-twentieth century.

Herder interprets the Bible—and I will here in part rely on English paraphrases provided by von Balthasar's *The Glory of God: A Theological Aesthetics*—as being written in the ' "natural" language of images', a text, then, to be reconstructed precisely 'as a world of images' (von Balthasar 1982: 87, 84). The angel of the Apocalypse, as Herder puts it, 'neither speaks nor conceals, but merely points in images' (*deutet in Bildern an*), so 'the images must, therefore, have had meaning and been intelligible in themselves' (von Balthasar 1982: 85). Farrer, in his 1948 book *The Glass of Vision*—the title is a reference to I Corinthians 13:12—speaks of the 'tremendous images' in the New Testament, without which, as he writes, 'the teaching would not be supernatural revelation, but instruction in piety and morals. It is because the spiritual instruction is related to the great images, that it becomes revealed truth' (Farrer 1948: 42 f., with reference to Hume 2007: 100). A striking disclosure, the convincing exposure of something previously concealed, I understand Farrer to imply, takes more than mere words, it takes images. When Farrer speaks of images, he has, primarily, figurative language in mind; but metaphors and visual images belong, as I indicated, to a single continuum, and one can point to a number of instances where Farrer actually alludes to visual mental imagery, for example when he refers to St John seeing the Son of God as 'a Lamb standing as slaughtered, having seven horns and seven eyes' (Farrer 1948: 48; see also Farrer 2006: 18). Certainly both Edmond Cherbonnier in 1953 and Ian Barbour in 1976 took Farrer's position to be such as to relate to visual imagery in the strict sense of the term. 'Perhaps both philosophers and theologians', writes Barbour, 'in concentrating on verbally stated propositions, have tended to neglect the role of images in human thought' (Barbour 1976: Ch. 2). Barbour cites Farrer as one of the rare laudable exceptions—also referring, in the same context, to H. H. Price. Cherbonnier, by contrast, is sharply critical of Farrer. Analysing Farrer's 'attempt to replace a "theology of the word" with visual images as the primary medium of Christian truth', Cherbonnier draws this conclusion:

> the biblical revelation could be apprehended through images only on one condition—that God had embodied his revelation, not in words, but in a book of pictures. Is the fact that he has not done so only accidental or, on the contrary, is it of the highest significance for the understanding of both man and God that he has in fact revealed himself by his Word? [Cherbonnier 1953: 22]

I will come back to Cherbonnier's argument in the next section of this chapter. The present section I will conclude with a reference to Newman.

In his book *A Grammar of Assent* Newman contrasts religion in devoutly Catholic populations, to whom 'the Supreme Being, our Lord, the Blessed Virgin, Angels and Saints, heaven and hell, are as present as if they were objects of sight', with what he calls the English 'Bible Religion', consisting 'not in rites or creeds, but mainly in having the Bible read in Church, in the family, and in private' (Newman 1881: 55–6). As Newman puts it, '[r]eading, as we do, the Gospels from our youth up, we are in danger of becoming so familiar with them as to be dead to their force, and to view them as a mere history'. Here is where 'the practice of meditation on the Sacred Text...so highly thought of by Catholics' enters (Newman 1881: 79). Meditation is, essentially, a process by which believers develop mental images to accompany, and make more vivid, their verbal representations of sacred events. In his book referred to earlier, David Freedberg provides a wonderful summary of how the pattern of Christian meditation from the Middle Ages to the seventeenth century relied on an interplay of text, written or recited, and image, both mental and physical—woodcuts, etchings, prints (Freedberg 1989: Ch. 8). For Newman, the presence of mental imagery in religious thought, imagery arising spontaneously or as a result of meditation, was the precondition of real belief—of 'real assent', as he termed it.

IMAGES IN NATURAL RELIGION

Images, then, fulfil an essential role in revealed religions. However, images by themselves clearly cannot convey the message of revelation. To those who are not acquainted with, or do not believe, the narrative of the New Testament, Christ on the cross is just the depiction of a suffering human being. As Hans Belting succinctly put it in his *Bild und Kult*: 'The image...is comprehensible only through being recognized from the Scriptures. It reminds us of what the Scriptures narrate' (Belting 1994: 10). Or, as Rahner explained, images are in need of a verbal interpretation in order to be recognized as explicitly Christian by those who look at them. There is, obviously, no visual reality which by itself would disclose its Christian meaning (Rahner 2009: XXX, 481). In his 1802 classic on natural theology, Paley offers a somewhat related, albeit twisted, argument. Towards the end of the book he comes to say that since the contemplation of divine nature 'overwhelms our faculties', we seek 'from painful abstraction...relief in sensible images', and might thereby fall into idolatry, a danger which revelation helps us to avoid: if the authority of the text is observed, 'a condescension to the state of our faculties' can be afforded (Paley 1809: 442). In allotting to images and imagery but an accessory function, Paley is prey to a false philosophy of mind. It is correct to maintain, however, that it is only in the domain of natural religion that images can play a more or less autonomous role. And this is exactly the point Cherbonnier raised in criticizing Farrer. The latter, Cherbonnier wrote, of course conceded that 'the object of faith is...not the images themselves but rather the reality beyond them, to which they point'. But then the question can be asked: 'Is it possible to say anything about this reality, or must we remain content to apprehend it simply by gazing at the images?...if the answer is that the reality behind the images can be expressed in words, then *ipso facto* the spoken word has been reinstated as the basis of revelation, thereby rendering the images unnecessary' (Cherbonnier 1953: 21). Out of this impasse, Cherbonnier writes, Farrer attempted to escape by an appeal to natural theology. This Cherbonnier calls a desperate step (22). From the vantage point of this chapter, however, Farrer made a felicitous move. Let me just focus on the crucial juncture in his argument. Images, Farrer maintains, have an essential function in 'the natural knowledge of God'. As he puts it, in *The Glass of Vision*:

> neither in revelation nor in rational theology can we point away from the image to that which the image signifies: in both we must be content to refer to the reality by understanding what the image tells us. Nevertheless, rational analogies and revealed images concerning God do not function in the same way: the rational analogies are natural images: the revealed figures are not...natural.—The rational analogies are natural...in the sense that they may be, and originally are, spontaneous: unless finite things put themselves upon us as symbols of deity we can have no natural knowledge of God....The stars may seem to speak of a maker, the moral sense of a law-giver: but there is no pattern of being we simply meet, which speaks of Trinity in the Godhead...Rational analogies are natural in a second sense: the analogy which the natural symbol appears to bear to God is founded on a real relation in which it stands towards God....Whereas revealed images are commonly just parables. [Farrer 1948: 93–5]

We encounter images, Farrer suggests, images in nature and images of nature, which by themselves are capable of impressing us with a sense of a higher reality; furthermore, visual images are natural carriers of meaning, since they mean by resembling, whereas figures of speech mean by convention. 'Are those Christian minds really so rare', Farrer asks, 'whose nearest gate into the invisible world is a simple awe at natural fact?' (Farrer 1948: 96). The text that begins the first chapter of *The Glass of Vision* is a quotation from the *Epistle to the Romans*:

> That which may be known of God is manifest among men, for God hath manifested it unto them. For his invisible attributes since the creation of the world are clearly seen, being perceived through the things that are made... [*Romans* 1:19–20]

This scriptural passage, to Farrer, is a guide not to revealed, but to natural theology. 'For the moment', he says in the argument I am here concerned with, 'we are discounting supernatural revelation, and considering natural religion: by which we are, therefore, bound to understand our own apprehensions of God through nature.... Natural theology... provides a canon of interpretation which stands outside the particular matter of revealed truth' (Farrer 1948: 98, 111).

What I am attempting to do in the present chapter—namely to provide a rudimentary overview of the ways in which images function in natural religion—is in a sense a sequel to Farrer's philosophy of sacred images. It is, also, a kind of protest against contemporary work in natural theology, which, as you are no doubt aware, has use neither for images, nor for mental imagery. Aquinas' theory of phantasmata is entirely rejected by Swinburne; the move from phantasmata to imagery is only half-heartedly made by Kretzmann; and the part played by visual images in religious experience is judged to be insignificant by Alston (Swinburne 2007; Kretzmann 1999; Alston 1991). In a more immediate sense, my position is a reaction to George Pattison's 1991 book *Art, Modernity and Faith: Restoring the Image*. While finding Pattison's general approach to visual theology instructive and stimulating, I feel his summary rejection of natural theology is exaggerated. I think it is unfair to suggest, as Pattison does, that the natural theology of Neo-Thomism has been entirely unable to supply a theological vocabulary and framework for dealing with the problem of faith and visuality, and hard to take in, say, his empathetic analysis of Ruskin's work followed by total dismissal (Pattison 1998: 52 f.). 'The overall structure of Ruskin's argument', Pattison writes:

> resembles the familiar pattern of natural theology, for its prevailing assumption is that the works of God in creation provide a timeless and universally accessible testimony to their divine origin. The artist is gifted with the ability to see and to represent in his work a truthful image of that testimony and so to be able to direct the less perceptive to see it for themselves. [Pattison 1998: 54]

I believe one might be sceptical when it comes to the idea of a 'universally accessible testimony', and still endeavour to develop a phenomenology of spontaneous religious sentiments as arising in response to specific visual experiences. It is the outlines of just such a phenomenology I will now venture to sketch.

VISUALIZING THE INVISIBLE

Discussing Aquinas' views on the possibility of there being images of incorporeal things, Kenny writes that at any rate 'the image of a non-bodily thing is not an image of it in virtue of looking like it', adding: 'However, there is good reason to believe that what makes an image of X an image of X is never its resemblance to X, even if X is bodily'(Kenny 1993: 98). This latter comment is clearly an echo of Wittgenstein's remark

'Anything can be a picture of anything, if we extend the concept of picture sufficiently', printed in the *Nachlaß* volume *Philosophical Grammar*, the German text of which Kenny translated into English (Wittgenstein 1974: 163). Certainly the remark does not do full justice to Wittgenstein's views on the issue in *Philosophical Grammar*, and even less to the views that the *Nachlaß* in its entirety suggests (Nyíri 2005). It is not Nelson Goodman that Wittgenstein paved the way for; Ernst Gombrich, with his emphasis on the role of resemblance in pictorial representation, or Richard Wollheim, with his notions 'seeing-as' and 'seeing-in' as explaining our experience of pictorial meaning, can more plausibly be said to be heirs to Wittgenstein (Nyíri 2009a: 3, Wollheim 1980). A variety of the notion of 'seeing-in' appears already in Husserl's early thinking; what we 'see-in' the picture is what Husserl calls the 'image object', and Husserl makes the important point that there is an essential conflict between the 'physical image thing' (say the picture as it hangs on the wall) and the 'image object', the latter characteristically pointing away, as the image thing does not, to the 'image subject'—pointing to what the image depicts, represents (Husserl 2005: xlvi, 37, 40, 584 f., 588 f., Sonesson 1989: 270–6).

There is another aspect under which the issue of the image pointing away from itself can be seen. In his book *Painting and Reality*, Etienne Gilson makes a distinction between 'pictures' and 'images' on the one hand, and 'paintings' on the other. There is, he says, a 'radical difference between a painting, whose meaning is in itself, and a picture, whose function is to point out something else' (Gilson 1957: 267). The essence of 'picturing', as he puts it, 'is to represent, or imitate'. Gilson concedes, indeed emphasizes, that '[i]mages are among the oldest products of the fabricative activity of man', that they are 'inseparable from domestic life', and that '[c]hildren delight in looking at picture books', but he makes it clear that in his view images, even religious images, cannot as it were represent anything sublime (Gilson 1957: 260–2). By contrast, the 'ultimate end' of a painting 'is to achieve a fitting object of contemplation'; 'creative painters...feel that there is still another reality hidden behind the appearances of nature', and so '[a]ll truly creative art is religious in its own right' (Gilson 1957: 266, 296, 294). A rather similar approach was formulated by Hans-Georg Gadamer in his *Wahrheit und Methode*. He set *Bild*—picture, image—against *Abbild*, copy. As he wrote, the 'essence of a copy is to have no other task but to resemble the original... pointing, through the similarity, to what is copied' (Gadamer's favourite examples here are the 'passport photo or a picture in a sales catalogue'). On the other hand, in the case of the picture, it is itself 'what is meant... one is not simply directed away from the picture to what is represented. Rather, the presentation remains essentially connected with what is represented—indeed, belongs to it.' As Gadamer stresses, 'the identity and non-differentiation of picture and pictured... remains essential to all experience of pictures'; and he concludes that it is precisely 'the religious picture [which] displays the full ontological power of the picture' (Gadamer 2004: 133 f., 137).

The idea of the image pointing away from itself is momentously formulated by Rahner. For Rahner 'image' means, just as it did for his teacher Martin Heidegger, both the image as an artefact, and the picture that presents itself to us when looking at our surroundings.

'The expression "image"', Heidegger wrote in *Kant and the Problem of Metaphysics*, 'is to be taken here in its most original sense, according to which we say that the landscape presents a beautiful "image" (look); but the same expression is also used in the sense of likeness, e.g. when we speak of a photograph' (Heidegger 1997: 64, 66; Fehér 1996). At first it could seem, Rahner wrote, 'as if our gaze would not get beyond the immediately viewed and circumscribed object'. However, 'one cannot experience at all the limits and the characteristic features of the directly viewed, unless one's glance also tends to go beyond this limit, targeting the expanse of the unviewed visible [*des ungeschauten Schaubaren*]. Looking... involves a kind of sensory experience of transcendence'. And so 'even a picture that does not have an immediately religious subject can be in principle a religious picture... if its being looked at does, through... a sensory experience of transcendence, stimulate and take part in constituting the essential religious experience of transcendence' (Rahner 2009: XXX, 479 f.).

What, then, we are attempting to describe and to present here, are what one could call transcending images. We expect these images to be capable of suggesting extended meanings additional to, and beyond, their straightforward ones; extended meanings to which they point, but which they do not display. The usual, and of course evident, domain in which to look for such images is the natural world surrounding us. 'All created things of the sensible world', wrote Bonaventure, 'lead the mind of the contemplator and wise man to eternal God.... they are the divinely given signs... set before our... sense-oriented minds, so that by the sensible things which they see they might be transferred to the intelligible which they cannot see' (quoted in Freedberg 1989: 165). This passage, Freedberg comments, is 'an unmystical... attempt to explain the process of ascent from the visible to the invisible... Since all created things lead the meditative mind to God, all pictures of them must do so too' (Freedberg 1989: 166). Or recall Aquinas, who in his natural theology upheld that 'all created things are, in a sense, images of... God', formulating, in *Summa Theologica*, the crucial statement: 'Incorporeal things, of which there are no phantasms, are known to us by comparison with sensible bodies of which there are phantasms' (SCG III.19, ST I.84.7). Alister McGrath builds on a venerable tradition when, in his recent book *A New Vision for Natural Theology*, he speaks of 'nature as a legitimate, authorized, and limited pointer to the divine' (McGrath 2008: 5).

The most conspicuous natural image of the divine is the image of light. In the series of elementary religious conversions William James examines, seeing 'a stream of light' or 'a bright blaze of light', experiencing 'the fullness of the light' or 'rays of light and glory', and so forth and so on, are decisive occurrences (James 1902: 68, 215, 22, 245). The creation of light stands at the beginning of various ancient cosmogonies, including, of course, the Old Testament. In Herder's interpretation of the latter, too, the image of light takes centre stage. 'God's most ancient and most glorious revelation', he wrote, 'appears to you each morning as a fact, as God's great work in nature!... Light is the first thing: his revelation, in which everything else can be seen and understood... The light! Light which, as model [*als Vorbild*], is the most revealing demonstration of God' (Herder, after von Balthasar 1982: 86).

When John Martin's painting 'The Celestial City and River of Bliss' was first shown at the Royal Academy in 1841, it was exhibited with the lines from Milton's Paradise Lost:

> Thee, Author of all being,
> Fountain of Light, thy self invisible [Milton 2008: Bk 3: 379]

Pattison, in his chapter 'Icons of Glory', provides an excellent discussion of the 'theology of light', stressing that from the Eastern Orthodox perspective light 'is not merely a symbol or image of divinity; it is divinity' (Pattison 1998: 126). To recall Gadamer's terminology: what is pointed at as the extended meaning of the image of light is, here, non-differentiated from the image. The source of light in our physical world is the sun. Hume, in his *Natural History of Religion*, sect. 7, refers to the god of the ancient Persians as having 'placed the sun as his image in the visible universe'. And of course in the history of religions there have been, and in contemporary human culture there still are, innumerable varieties of sun worship. Let me here single out a religion: Peru's syncretistic religion, in which, as Bergmann writes, 'Christian-Catholic ideas are integrated into the worldviews of the native peoples, and the native religious belief systems have in turn brought about a new understanding of Christian ideas' (Bergmann 2009: 123). Bergmann tells about a Catholic congregation in a small town high up in the Andes, where two mission sisters have stimulated the members 'to express their faith visually', that is to draw and paint. Bergmann prints some of the resulting images (Bergmann 2009: 124). Two of these he specifically associates with 'Mother Earth', the 'central deity in the Andean religion' (Bergmann 2009: 14). What I am struck by is that in both of them the sun, too, figures conspicuously. Light can also be veiled; indeed the image of the veil has profound religious connotations: just think of Paul speaking of a 'vision of the Lord's splendour with unveiled face' (II Corinthians 3:18). I have no time here to pause and analyse this image, and must restrict myself to just mentioning images of two physical phenomena which tend to veil our sight, or veil the light from us: first, mist and fog, and, secondly, clouds. A famous painting that takes the first as its topic is Caspar David Friedrich's 'The Wanderer above the Mists' (1817–18). The painting shows a lonely figure confronting nature in what appears to be deep reverence. Note that what he sees is not just the mists below, but also the high mountains in the distance. Friedrich's painting figures on the website announcing the 2010 St Andrews Gifford Lectures, titled *The Face of God*, given by Roger Scruton. I think the organizers chose the right image. Another painting by Friedrich, 'Sunrise near Neubrandenburg' (1835) gives a sense of clouds veiling the source of light in a way that suggests that there is something supreme, but invisible, beyond the visible—a suggestion humankind must have experienced since the beginning of time, and artists have conveyed in innumerable images. Such images—paintings, photographs—can be very dramatic indeed, as for instance the one found on the cover of the new edition of Farrer's *The Making of St. John's Apocalypse* (Farrer 2006).

While clouds can suggest transcendence by veiling our vision, mountains do the same by elevating our gaze to unfathomable heights. McGrath points to 'the biblical emphasis upon the importance of mountains in relation to divine revelation', and recalls 'the metaphysical poet Henry Vaughan's frequent use of mountain imagery to denote the human longing for "the world beyond"' (McGrath 2008: 61 f.). Pattison quotes John Baggley commenting on Rublev's 'Old Testament Trinity' as saying that the mountain is 'a symbol of an event of profound significance' (Pattison 1998: 129 with reference to Baggley 1987). Mountains are certainly not absent from James's collection of deep religious experiences; a characteristic report:

> I have on a number of occasions felt that I had enjoyed a period of intimate com-
> munion with the divine. These meetings came unasked and unexpected... Once it
> was when from the summit of a high mountain I looked over a... landscape extend-
> ing to a long convex of ocean that ascended to the horizon, and again from the same
> point when I could see nothing beneath me but a boundless expanse of white
> cloud... What I felt on these occasions was a temporary loss of my own identity,
> accompanied by an illumination which revealed to me a deeper significance than I
> had been wont to attach to life. [James 1902: 69]

Kenny, in his collection of essays *The Unknown God*, pays tribute to 'the greatest of the Victorian mountain writers, John Ruskin'. As Kenny writes, 'Ruskin's love of mountains knew no bounds: for him, all natural beauty, all moral goodness, was to be judged by its proximity to or distance from the ideal serenity of the high peaks. For him the mountains were the great cathedrals of the earth' (Kenny 2004: 156). Kenny notes that 'there were links between the Victorian passion for mountains and the Victorian ambivalence about religion.... Those who gave up belief in the eternal God of Abraham, Isaac and Jacob were glad to retain a sublime object of awe in the everlasting snows of Mont Blanc, Monte Rosa and the Matterhorn.' 'John Tyndall, the agnostic President of the Royal Society', Kenny continues, 'thus describes the view from the summit of the Weisshorn: "An influence seemed to proceed from it direct to the soul; the delight and exultation experienced were not those of Reason or Knowledge, but of BEING: I was part of it and it of me, and in the transcendent glory of Nature I entirely forgot myself as man"' (Kenny 2004: 160 f. In fact Tyndall was President of the Royal Institute).

A painting by Albert Bierstadt, 'Sunrise on the Matterhorn' (1875), brings together a number of our themes: light, mist, and mountains. The foreground of the painting is taken up by a group of trees. Although not as grandiose a symbol as that of the mountain, the image of the tree, too, has transcending aspects. For Baggley, the tree is a symbol of 'life and spiritual growth' (Pattison 1998: 129). Certainly Caspar David Friedrich's 'Oak in the Snow' (1820s) might strike one as such a symbol. On a humbler level, the image of any plant is a symbol of growth. Also, it is a symbol of transience, decay, and rebirth. Heinrich Rombach sees in the basic experience of cultivating plants the fundamental possibility of religion (Rombach 1977: 77). The two Peruvian images discussed a moment ago, the images Bergmann associates with 'Mother Earth', definitely suggest such a connection.

If plants remind one of decay and rebirth, flowers, whether naturalistic or stylized, can create a feeling for the tranquil beauty of the created world. Pattison refers to 'Monet's many series of paintings of his Garden at Giverny.... With each treatment of the subject', Pattison writes:

Monet seems to be moving further and further away from conventional concepts of imitation into the pure play of coloural presences.... These paintings assure us, in an irreducibly pictorial way, that the world is a good place to be, that it is holy ground, that we may trust ourselves to the particularity of our carnal situatedness. [Pattison 1998: 149]

We are back at the idea that all genuine art is religious. For Paul Tillich, Expressionist art 'has a mystical, religious character, quite apart from its choice of subjects. It is not an exaggeration to ascribe more of the quality of sacredness to a stilllife by Cézanne or a tree by Van Gogh than to a picture of Jesus by Uhde' (Tillich 1989: 69; Re Manning 2009). A tree by Van Gogh—or even a shoe by him. There are a number of paintings of pairs of shoes by Van Gogh and Heidegger discusses them. The picture of a pair of empty, unused shoes, Heidegger writes, would tell us very little. Van Gogh's peasant shoes, however, convey a significant message. 'From the dark opening of the worn insides of the shoes the toilsome tread of the worker stares forth.... On the leather lie the dampness and richness of the soil.... In the shoes vibrate the silent call of the earth, its quiet gift of the ripening grain.' But they also cannot but suggest, Heidegger adds, a 'shivering at the surrounding menace of death' (Heidegger 1971:32 f.).

I take Heidegger to say that the worn empty shoes suggest death because of what they do not show: the person to whom they belong, or formerly belonged. They display, to use a phrase by Rombach, 'an image of emptiness' ('ein Bild der Leere') (Rombach 1977: 73). Of course to every image, as we made clear earlier, there belongs the essential tension between what is absent and what is present. And perhaps nowhere is that tension more extreme than in the case of one of the most fundamental of images, or even the primordial transcending image: the death mask made of stone or clay and placed upon the decaying face of the dead, pointing away from its unchanging countenance to the beloved person who in this world is no more (Belting 2001: 17, 37).

CONCLUDING REMARKS

The assumption I have put forward at the beginning of this chapter was, strictly speaking, a simplifying one. We might indeed maintain that in human cognitive development and activity the visual is more basic than the verbal. However, preceding and underlying both, there is the motor dimension—muscular tensions, kinesthetic experiences, bodily movements (Bruner 1966). In his 1954 book *Art and Visual Perception*, Rudolf Arnheim gives a masterly summary of a substantial earlier research tradition which had demonstrated that to muscular sensations there correspond schematic inner images, images of the position of the bodily self in relation to its surroundings (Arnheim 1954; Nyíri 2009b). Among the forerunners of his position Arnheim includes William James, referring to the latter's *The Principles of Psychology* (1890), Chapter VI. He could also have referred to Chapter XV of the same book, the chapter 'The Perception of Time', where James comes to say that it is feelings in the muscles of the eye, the ear, and also muscles in the head, neck, etc., by which we estimate lengths of time. As he puts it, 'muscular feelings can give us the object "time" as well as its measure'. I find it fascinating to compare these views of James with a passage in his *The Varieties of Religious Experience* where he writes of the state of mind, known to religious men, but to no others, in which the will to assert ourselves and hold our own has been displaced by a complete surrender to, and trust in, God:

> In this state of mind, what we most dreaded has become the habitation of our safety... The time for tension in our soul is over, and that of happy relaxation, of calm deep breathing, of an eternal present, with no discordant future to be anxious about, has arrived. [James 1902: 47]

Since the 1980s, conceptual metaphor theory has invited ever more detailed descriptions of how kinesthetic sensations give rise to so-called image schemas (Lakoff and Johnson 1980). Those images in our subconscious that Guardini was speaking about are, it appears, created by unconscious motor experiences.

Among unconscious motor experiences, eye movements are of special importance. By way of conclusion, let me draw attention to a seminal essay by Wallace Chafe, published in 1980, in which the author elaborates a parallel between, on the one hand, vision in general and eye movement in particular, and, on the other hand, verbal processes (Chafe 1980). As Jana Holšánová (2008), following in the footsteps of Chafe, has recently demonstrated in a series of studies, patterns of eye movements and patterns of thinking mirror each other. What Bonaventure said about our 'sense-oriented minds', namely that 'by the sensible things which they see they might be transferred to the intelligible which they cannot see', seems to be entirely borne out by today's cutting-edge cognitive research.

References

Alston, William P. (1993 [1991]). *Perceiving God: The Epistemology of Religious Experience.* Ithaca, NY: Cornell University Press.

Aquinas, Thomas (1947) *Summa Theologica.* Translated from Latin by the Fathers of the English Dominican Province. New York: Benziger Bros.

—— (1991). *Summa Contra Gentiles*, Bk III. Translated from Latin by Vernon J. Bourke. South Bend, IN: University of Notre Dame Press.

Arnheim, Rudolf (1954). *Art and Visual Perception: A Psychology of the Creative Eye.* Berkeley: University of California Press.

Balthasar, Hans Urs von (1982). *The Glory of God: A Theological Aesthetics.* Vol. I: *Seeing the Form.* San Francisco: Ignatius Press; New York: Crossroad Publications.

Barbour, Ian G. (1976). *Myths, Models and Paradigms.* San Francisco: HarperCollins.

Belting, Hans (1994 [1990]). *Likeness and Presence: A History of the Image before the Era of Art.* Translated from German by Edmund Jephcott. Chicago: The University of Chicago Press.

—— (2001). *Bild-Anthropologie: Entwürfe für eine Bildwissenschaft.* Munich: Wilhelm Fink Verlag.

Bergmann, Sigurd (2009 [2003]). *In the Beginning Is the Icon: A Liberative Theology of Images, Visual Arts and Culture.* Translated from Swedish by Anja K. Angelson. London: Equinox.

Bruner, Jerome (1966). 'On Cognitive Growth' in *Studies in Cognitive Growth*. Edited by J. C. Bruner et al. New York: John Wiley & Sons.

Calvin, John (2008 [1559]). *The Institutes of the Christian Religion*. Translated from Latin by Henry Beveridge. Peabody, MA: Henrickson.

Chafe, Wallace L. (1980). 'The Deployment of Consciousness in the Production of a Narrative' in *The Pear Stories: Cognitive, Cultural and Linguistic Aspects of Narrative Production*. Edited by Wallace L. Chafe. Norwood, NJ: Ablex.

Cherbonnier, Edmond La B. (1953). 'The Theology of the Word of God'. *Journal of Religion* XXXIII/1: 16-30.

Evdokimov, Paul (1990 [1972]). *The Art of the Icon: A Theology of Beauty*. Translated from French by Steve Bigham. Redondo Beach, CA: Oakwood Publications.

Farrer, Austin (1943). *Finite and Infinite: A Philosophical Essay*. Westminster: Dacre Press.

—— (1948). *The Glass of Vision*. Westminster: Dacre Press.

—— (2006 [1949]). *A Rebirth of Images: The Making of St. John's Apocalypse*. Eugene, OR: Wipf & Stock.

Fehér, István M. (1996). 'Karl Rahner szellemi gyökereihez: Heidegger és a XX. századi teológia'/'Zu den geistigen Wurzeln Karl Rahners: Heidegger und die Theologie des 20 Jahrhunderts' in *Karl Rahner emlékülés: Az ige meghallója/Der Hörer des Wortes: Karl Rahner*. Edited by István Boros. Szeged: Logos Kiadó.

Freedberg, David (1989). *The Power of Images: Studies in the History and Theory of Response*. Chicago: University of Chicago Press.

Gadamer, Hans Georg (2004). *Truth and Method*. 2nd edn. London: Continuum.

Gelernter, David Hillel (2009). *Judaism: A Way of Being*. New Haven: Yale University Press.

Gilson, Etienne (1957). *Painting and Reality*. New York: Pantheon Books.

Guardini, Romano (1950). *Die Sinne und die religiöse Erkenntnis*. Würzburg: Werkbund-Verlag.

Harrison, Victoria (2007). *Religion and Modern Thought*. London: SCM Press.

Heidegger, Martin (1971). 'The Origin of the Work of Art' in *Poetry, Language, Thought*. Translated from German and introduced by Albert Hofstadter. New York: Harper & Row.

—— (1997). *Kant and the Problem of Metaphysics*. Translated from German by Richard Taft. Bloomington: Indiana University Press.

Holšánová, Jana (2008). *Discourse, Vision, and Cognition*. Amsterdam: John Benjamins.

Hume, David (2007). *Dialogues Concerning Natural Religion and Other Writings*. Edited by Dorothy Coleman. Cambridge: Cambridge University Press.

Husserl, Edmund (2005). *Phantasy, Image Consciousness, and Memory (1898-1925)*. Translated from German by John B. Brough, Dordrecht: Springer.

James, William (1890). *The Principles of Psychology*. Boston:Henry Holt.

—— (1902). *The Varieties of Religious Experience: A Study in Human Nature*. The Gifford Lectures on Natural Religion Delivered at Edinburgh in 1901-1902. London: Longmans, Green & Co.

Kenny, Anthony (1993). *Aquinas on Mind*. London: Routledge.

—— (2004). *The Unknown God: Agnostic Essays*. London: Continuum.

Kretzmann, Norman (1999) *The Metaphysics of Creation: Aquinas's Natural Theology in Summa Contra Gentiles II*. Oxford: Clarendon Press.

Lakoff, George and Mark Johnson (1980). *Metaphors We Live By*. Chicago: University of Chicago Press.

McGrath, Alister E. (2008). *The Open Secret: A New Vision for Natural Theology*. Malden, MA: Blackwell Publishing.

Milton, John (2008). *Pardise Lost*. Edited by William Kerrigan, John Rumrich, and Stephen M. Fallon. New York: The Modern Library.

Newman, John Henry (1881). *An Essay in Aid of a Grammar of Assent*. London: Burns & Oates.

Nyíri, Kristóf (2001). 'The Picture Theory of Reason' in *Rationality and Irrationality*. Edited by Berit Brogaard and Barry Smith. Vienna: öbv-hpt: pp. 242–66.

—— (2003). 'Pictorial Meaning and Mobile Communication' in *Mobile Communication: Essays on Cognition and Community*. Edited by Kristóf Nyíri. Vienna: Passagen Verlag.

—— (2005). 'Wittgenstein's Philosophy of Pictures' in *Wittgenstein: The Philosopher and his Works, Working Papers from the Wittgenstein Archives at the University of Bergen*, no. 17. Edited by Alois Pichler and Simo Säätelä: pp. 281–312.

—— (2009a). 'Gombrich on Image and Time'. *Journal of Art Historiography* 1, 1-KN/1 <http://arthistoriography.files.wordpress.com/2011/02/media_139131_en.pdf>.

—— (2009b). 'Film, Metaphor, and the Reality of Time'. *New Review of Film and Television Studies* 7/2: 109–18.

Paley, William (1809 [1802]). *Natural Theology: Or, Evidences of the Existence and Attributes of the Deity*. 12th edn. London: Printed for J. Faulder.

Pattison, George (1998 [1991]). *Art, Modernity and Faith: Restoring the Image*. 2nd enlarged edn. London: SCM Press.

Rahner, Karl (1983). 'Zur Theologie des Bildes'. *Halbjahreshefte der Deutschen Gesellschaft für christliche Kunst* (München) 3/5: 2–8.

—— (2009). *Sämtliche Werke*. Vol. XXX: *Anstöße systematischer Theologie: Beiträge zur Fundamentalontologie und Dogmatik*. Freiburg: Herder.

Re Manning, Russell (2009). 'Tillich's Theology of Art' in *The Cambridge Companion to Paul Tillich*. Edited by Re Manning. Cambridge: Cambridge University Press: pp. 152–72.

Rombach, Heinrich (1977). *Leben des Geistes: Ein Buch der Bilder zur Fundamentalgeschichte der Menschheit*. Freiburg: Herder.

Sonesson, Göran (1989). *Pictorial Concepts*. Lund: Lund University Press.

Stump, Eleonore (2003). *Aquinas*. London: Routledge.

Swinburne, Richard (2007 [1992]). *Revelation: From Metaphor to Analogy*. 2nd edn. Oxford: Oxford University Press.

Tillich, Paul (1989). *On Art and Architeture*. Edited by John and Joan Dillenberger. New York: Crossroad.

Volp, Rainer (1980). 'Das Bild als Grundkategorie der Theologie' in *Theologische Realenzyklopädie*. Vol. VI. Berlin: de Gruyter: pp. 557–68.

Wittgenstein, Ludwig (1974). *Philosophical Grammar*. Edited by Rush Rhees. Berkeley: University of California Press.

Wollheim, Richard (1980 [1968]). *Art and Its Objects*. 2nd edn. Cambridge: Cambridge University Press.

....

CHAPTER 38

THE FILM VIEWER AND NATURAL THEOLOGY: GOD'S 'PRESENCE' AT THE MOVIES

....

ROBERT K. JOHNSTON

A renewed natural theology might hold the key to the reconnection of discussions and debates that have long gone their separate ways, allowing theology, philosophy, the natural sciences, and the arts to engage in a productive conversation.

[McGrath 2009: 206]

REEL SPIRITUALITY AND NATURAL THEOLOGY

....

THE claim of two of my recent books, *Reel Spirituality* (2006) and *Finding God in the Movies* (co-authored with Catherine Barsotti, 2004) is that God shows up at the movies. Such an assertion is not unique to me. Similar declarations are made by Joel Martin and Conrad Ostwalt Jr in *Screening the Sacred: Religion, Myth, and Ideology in Popular American Film* (1995), Albert J. Bergesen and Andrew M. Greeley in *God in the Movies* (2000), Ken Gire in *Reflections on the Movies: Hearing God in the Unlikeliest of Places* (2000), David Dark in *Everyday Apocalypse: The Sacred Revealed in Radiohead, The Simpsons, and Other Pop Culture Icons* (2002), Gareth Higgins in *How Movies Helped Save My Soul: Finding God's Fingerprints in Culturally Significant Films* (2003), Gerard Loughlin in 'Spirituality and Film' in Philip Sheldrake, ed., *The New SCM Dictionary of Christian Spirituality* (2005), and Craig Detweiler in *Into the Dark: Seeing the Sacred in the Top Films of the 21st Century* (2008), to name only a few. But what exactly does God's 'presence' at the movies mean? How is a 'reel spirituality' described, and how might such an experience relate to natural theology? Such questions are the focus of this chapter.

First, some preliminary remarks. The claim that God can be found in the movies, though ambiguous in its meaning, invites conversation about the present crisis in the Church, where transcendent experiences have too often been replaced by traditional teaching about the transcendent. Ken Gire speaks for many:

> I have experienced [God]…more in movie theaters than I have in churches. Why? I can't say for sure…movies don't always tell the truth, don't always enlighten, don't always inspire. What they do on a fairly consistent basis is give you an experience of transcendence. [Gire 2000: 120]

To say that God can be found at the movies also recognizes that art has become a primary source of spiritual experience for a growing number of contemporary people. After narrating the story of Albert Einstein coming up to the violinist Yehudi Menuhin after a concert and saying, 'Thank you, Mr Menuhin; you have again proved to me that there is a God in heaven', Richard Viladesau reflects:

> Aesthetic experience seems to play a major role—at least for some people—in the exercise of the practical judgment for belief in God—perhaps a great deal more than the traditional 'proofs' of God's existence set forth in apologetic theology. [Viladesau 1999: 104–7]

Lending credence to this observation, sociologist George Barna in a poll taken in 2000 found that 20 per cent of Americans turn to 'media, arts and culture' as their primary means of spiritual expression and growth, and the percentage is projected to grow yearly (Barna 2005: 48–9)

Given our busy lives, many today take scant time to reflect on life's meaning, except in places like the Cineplex. Here, perhaps is a reason for the growing interest in the spirituality of film. As Western society has moved beyond the sterile rationalism of high modernity to embrace a more broadly conceived spirituality, Hollywood itself has mirrored the trend, offering a growing list of spiritually charged movies. As Craig Detweiler and Barry Taylor noted in their book, *A Matrix of Meaning: Finding God in Popular Culture* (2003), 1999 might well have been the year that changed Hollywood. Though the number of films with spiritual significance had begun to increase several years earlier, it was in 1999 that this trend perhaps reached a tipping point. As the millennium turned, *Fight Club*, *The Matrix*, *Run Lola Run*, *Magnolia*, *Dogma*, *The Sixth Sense*, *The Green Mile*, *Keeping the Faith*, *After Life*, *The Blair Witch Project*, *The End of the Affair*, and *American Beauty* all came out, to name only a partial list. Detweiler and Taylor noted that 'each of these movies reveals a belief in the transcendent, in unexplainable phenomena, in the random, the unknown, the wholly Other' (Detweiler and Taylor 2003: 166–7). Their observation about a perceived tipping point has proven true, as the first decade of the new millennium has continued to strongly reflect cinema's interest in the Spiritual/spiritual/religious.

American Beauty (1999) might well be taken as representative of this trend (Johnston 2004: 57–72). The movie tells the story of two generations, both seeking significance for their seemingly meaningless lives. Ricky, a wounded seventeen-year-old, has retreated from life. Inseparable from his video camera, he records the mundane and everyday as his way of connecting with life. When asked by his neighbour Janie, what was 'the most beautiful thing' he had ever filmed, he shows her a scene with a plastic bag dancing in the wind. As viewers see the bag floating suspended in the air, Ricky tells Janie:

> It was one of those days when it's a minute away from snowing. And there's this electricity in the air, you can almost hear it, right? And this bag was just...dancing with me. Like a little kid begging me to play with it. For fifteen minutes. That's the day I realized that there was this entire life behind things, and this incredibly benevolent force that wanted me to know there was no reason to be afraid...ever.

Janie's dad, Lester, is on his own search for that 'plastic bag floating in the wind', something, anything, that would help him reconnect with life. Burned out in his job, trapped in a loveless marriage, unable to communicate with his teenage daughter, he seeks to rediscover life's meaning, joy in the ordinary. And joy does eventually come. As the movie ends, his life flashes before his eyes. We see memories of him lying on his back watching falling leaves and shooting stars, of his grandmother's leathery hands and his brand-new Firebird, of his young daughter at Halloween and his wife laughing at a carnival. Lester realizes anew that his life is to be cherished: 'It's hard to stay mad when there's so much beauty in the world', we hear him say in a voiceover. Given life, he says his 'heart fills up like a balloon that's about to burst...and then I remember to relax and stop trying to hold it, and then it flows through me like rain. And I can't feel anything but gratitude for every single moment of my stupid little life.'

Both Ricky and Lester uncover a (T)transcendent beauty within the ordinary that is transformative. But what is it that they, or we as an audience, discover? A new understanding? An experience of beauty? A sense of the whole? An encounter with that which lies behind and within the beauty of the ordinary? God? The ambiguity of the journey of Lester and Ricky is mirrored in the ambiguity of responses from those who see the movie. Take, for example, these diverse reactions to *American Beauty* taken from the over 2,500 viewer responses posted on the Internet Movie Database (April 2010):

> 'This film changed my life'
> 'One disgusting film.'
> 'There are several parts of this movie where I lose control every time I see it, and none more so than the paper bag scene.'
> 'It's hard not to become more introspective and more honest with yourself after seeing this movie.'
> 'The closer I look, the worse it gets.... This film doesn't know what it wants to say.'
> 'If I'm ever missing the beauty in my own world, this is a great work of art to remind me that I don't have to look very far.'

SPIRITUAL EXPERIENCES AT THE MOVIES

In order to get at the question, 'What does God's presence at the movies mean?', I surveyed the forty-nine students in my theology and film class in the autumn of 2009, asking them to write a two-page reflection paper on one movie that had been spiritually significant to them. All wrote from a Christian perspective. Had viewing this movie proven to be a (T)transcendent experience for them? If so, how and why? The students were to describe the movie briefly, then give their experience spiritually with it, and end with what if anything resulted from their viewing. My question was put in writing so that all were given the same instructions. My question was also purposely left open-ended and ambiguous, with no definition of 'spiritually significant' being provided. While not scientifically rigorous, the poll sought to uncover what if any knowledge/experience/encounter of God the students might have had at/in/through a movie. The results are suggestive as we explore the connection of natural theology to the arts.

Interestingly, the responses fell more or less evenly into three groups, though in some of the descriptions, students moved freely back and forth between these differing meanings:

1. Some described how God's presence had been mediated through/experienced in the cinema. They had had a divine encounter that proved transformative in their lives.
2. Others perceived through their movie-going experience something greater, more, other, or whole. Their spirits were moved, but they did not believe this to be, or were not sure whether it was, a divine encounter. Many described this experience, none-theless, as something God was involved in, and it proved illumining for them.
3. Still others asserted that while they hadn't had any kind of (S)spiritual experience with film, they had watched certain movies from which they had garnered spirit-ual truth. Certain movies, often with religious or quasi-religious themes, had illustrated for them, or deepened, the reality and importance of God in their lives. These movies had been theological parables that proved instructive about God.

ENCOUNTERING GOD

Students who said they encountered God through their film experience spoke forth-rightly about it. Here is a cross-section of responses:

> Though I have had many connections and revelations in my experience with film, I would describe very few of them as transcendent. However there are those few times where something divine takes place and the film going experience changes into a transformational moment. One such moment took place for me the first time I saw the film *There Will Be Blood*.

> While watching this movie [*The Holiday*] in the theater in December, 2006, God came down and touched my heart to say I see your pain, and you are not alone.

> Through the movie *Slumdog Millionaire* I experienced a poverty that far exceeds the degree of poverty here in America. It is in this movie... I see my calling to help even the 'least of these' in our society (Matthew 25)... I encountered the divine in the film... This film invaded my personal space and caused me to critique my own real-ity and how I interact with the poor in my own community and world.

When I watched the film *Lars and the Real Girl*, I experienced a divine encounter and revelation about what integration truly looks like from God's perspective...watching *Lars and the Real Girl* gave me a new sense of hope and vision for how I want to integrate psychology and theology, and allowed me to see the healing power of God's love through his people.

Shawshank Redemption served as a medium that was a transformative experience for my faith. Moreover, it served as a transcendent experience that began to heal my faith.

One of the many movies in which I have had a 'divine encounter' would be *The Ultimate Gift*, based on Jim Stovall's book of the same name.

Of those who said that they truly met God at the movies, the results were often profound. One older student recalled seeing *Easy Rider* three times one Saturday afternoon in 1969 (and remembered in detail the experience some forty years later!). He said that when Captain America (Peter Fonda) spoke of 'blowing it' soon after he and his friends left the hippie commune for the vacuousness of Mardi Gras, he had already concluded the same thing by himself. Though he had never lived in community, my student left the theatre that day determined to do so, and began his search the very next day. Moreover, in the film, those in the commune had clasped hands, praying for 'simple food for our simple tastes'. These 'Jesus hippies' made such an impression on the student, that though he was at the time non-religious, he says his journey towards Jesus began that day. Forty years later, he still lives communally and now is a Christian minister.

Others wrote of a movie that provided divine consolation in helping them through the divorce of their parents (*Now and Then*), or a divine invitation to be reconciled with their father and brother (*Big Fish*). One man wrote of being called into the ministry as he saw *Legends of the Fall*, hearing God say through the Holy Spirit, 'As Tristan's father never gave up on him, but still loved him unconditionally, so I love you.' A woman spoke of the film *Lars and the Real Girl* as causing her to respond to God's call to serve him by helping those, like her brother, who had disabilities. Another was influenced in her decision to work as a psychologist while watching *Braveheart*. A man said that after seeing *The Truman Show* 'I thanked God for his love and prayed that he would give me the strength to continue my walk with Him and not stray away.'

What all these individuals had in common as they watched a wide variety of movies was their clear sense of being in the presence of God, even as they were immersed in the particulars of film. The movie's story merged with their own stories, resulting in a divine encounter that changed their lives.

'SPIRITUAL' INSIGHT

Another group of students had what one described as a profoundly 'human moment'. One spoke of 'tears of identification'; another of the cinematic experience bringing 'personal fulfillment'. What this group of movie viewers seemed to be getting at by their testimonies was an experience at the movies which was extraordinary and illumining, but not necessarily divine. For these viewers, the world and/or their personal lives took on spiritual depth and texture because of the movie they saw. But, they were reticent to say they had actually met God at the movies.

One student, for example, saw *As Good As It Gets*. When Melvin (Jack Nicholson) storms out of the office of the psychiatrist and looking around at the clients in the waiting room, says, 'What if this is as good as it gets?', he heard the line as spoken to him. 'Hearing that line was, in many ways, a wake up call to the fact that my life, at that point, was not as good as it was going to get.' One can imagine someone saying, this was a (T)transcendent moment. But in describing this, he said:

> I think this was a transcendent experience, rather than a Transcendent experience, although one certainly brought about by the Spirit's work in my life. In all honesty, I'm not sure I've ever had a capital "T" transcendent experience with a film. I think that's due mostly to my holding film at arms length, attempting to analyze it as a specimen of sorts (most often), or simply taking it in as escapist entertainment.

More dramatic, surely was the experience of one student who had in high school been addicted to drugs, cigarettes, and alcohol. His friend at the time took him to see *Traffic*. Not knowing the story, he was shocked when the politician's daughter locked herself in the family bathroom to do drugs. He knew the routine, he said. When the father realized what the girl was doing and banged on the door to let him in, the movie, he said, 'became a horror movie for me and I was totally speechless'. This was his greatest fear splayed out before him on the giant screen. He says he doesn't remember the conversation he had afterwards with his friend, 'but I do know what the movie said to me'. The trip to the Cineplex with his friend was his first experience of someone revealing to him that they knew he was doing drugs. Moreover, the movie made him 'totally terrified of continuing (his) substance abuse'. He said that: 'This movie opened a door in my life where I began to see my problems and addictions in a true reality.'

A young woman in the class wrote of going to see *Away We Go* and being 'deeply influenced [in her] views of the importance of relationships, marriage, family, and inner healing'. 'What started off as a relaxing Friday evening', she wrote, 'turned out to fill my soul with so much hope. I remember smiling many days after the viewing and the hope still remains.' Another student was touched 'personally, powerfully, and poignantly' by *End of Days*. A young woman wrote of 'a humanly transcendent experience' she had watching *Save The Last Dance*. It gave her the courage and inspiration to try out for her college's dance team, and the grace to accept the consequence when she was not chosen. The movie *Gattaca* moved another student deeply, giving him courage to push his body to the limits, after growing up afraid because he was 'tall and skinny, not very strong, and too-often sick'. The words of Vincent at the film's climax, 'I never saved anything for the swim back', became a source of ongoing inspiration to him, allowing him to live into a new reality. And it was the movie, *You Are My Sunshine* (in Korean, *You Are My Destiny*) by director Jin-Pyo Park that gave another 'a glimpse of hope when I desperately needed to see it'.

In a large number of these movie experiences, the story on the screen was said to parallel the viewer's own life in one way or another: having moved constantly when a child as the family sought the 'perfect location'; sensing one's life was adrift; giving up dancing when she failed to be chosen for the varsity squad in high school; being frustrated 'in the face of God's silence'. It was in cinematic experiences that connected with such life experiences that these viewers found their spirits deeply affected.

THEOLOGICAL KNOWLEDGE

Lastly, among those who wrote about meaningful spiritual experiences at the movies, there were those who said that their experience of film was edifying because at the Cineplex they occasionally found in film a parable, a visual reminder of Christian theology, a metaphor of Christian truth that proved compelling. One young man said 'I do not think that I can honestly pick a film that has moved me deeply in a spiritual manner . . . [but] there is at least one film that was intellectually, and I believe (in retrospect) spiritually informative and significant for me. That film was *Pan's Labyrinth*.' Another spoke of being 'reminded of the frailty and relative short time allotted to me' by the movie *The Curious Case of Benjamin Button*: 'It highlighted for me the inevitable fact of death', forcing him to consider his own life and 'to consider the fact that it will end'. *Forrest Gump* was seen by another as representative of God's love for us; *A Christmas Carol* reminded another of the saving grace of Christ.

Often the movies mentioned had recognizable Christian-themes—*Lord of the Rings* came up four times. *A Walk to Remember* taught one young woman 'love as I had never experienced or witnessed it in real life'. *The Passion of the Christ*, *For the Bible Tells Me So*, and *The Green Mile* were also named. Typical is this response to *Signs*:

> The primary reason I believe this movie 'worked' for me, and moved me in some spiritual sense, was the authenticity of the characters and seeming believability of the story line. In some sense I was able to vicariously identify with Graham, and was thus moved, as his character was, to re-evaluate and thereby restore my faith in God's sovereignty.

Typical as well is this assessment of *Shawshank Redemption*: 'This movie, while powerful on its own merit, also possessed significant theological value to me.' He goes on to speak of the prison as a metaphor for the world and its power to conform humans into its own image, of the spiritual metaphor of Mozart's music, and of Andy as a Christ-figure.

One student wrote of his experience of the movie, *Lars and the Real Girl*, where a small town in the upper Midwest is asked to accept the radically introverted, emotionally unstable Lars, when he shows up at church pushing in a wheelchair an anatomically correct blow-up doll named Bianca. He says she is a missionary of Brazilian and Danish descent. Throughout the story their relationship remains 'chaste', but can his church community accept this odd 'couple'? The movie asks the question of viewers, how does love respond? The student said the movie '*challenged* me with questions.... It *broadened* my understanding of the complexity of the mind and also the power of pain. It even caused me to *reflect* on my definition of love.' For this student, *Lars* provided him the opportunity to consider the Church as community and to ask, 'What kind of Christian would he have been in that situation?' But this student also writes:

> Regarding the question of transcendence I am left questioning... I cannot truly say that this movie has given me a context to meet with God. However, I can acknowledge that the Word of God dwelling in me is still at work—even when watching movies. This movie has certainly caused me to reflect, but it is only within the context of the Word and Spirit dwelling within that I experience any Transcendence. I find that for me the film gains meaning when integrated with humanity's story and God's story—then Transcendence takes place because reflection moves to response based on reality.

For another student, it was the experience of viewing David Lynch's *The Elephant Man* that allowed him to see more clearly, through eyes filled with tears, the God-given shape of the human. When John Merrick is invited to have tea with Dr Treves and his wife, John tells them he wishes his mother could see him now with his lovely friends: 'Perhaps she could love me as I am. I've tried so hard to be good.' As Mrs Treves begins to cry uncontrollably, so did the student. He writes that every time he sees the scene, he realizes anew that John is a creation of God—that in fact, 'God is found most beautifully in the "grotesque"'. For this student, John Merrick showed him 'a full humanity: in suffering, in faith, in hope, and in love'. Still another student reflected on a movie she saw as a child—*The Land Before Time*. The story is about a brave dinosaur who journeys to the 'Great Valley' with a group of orphaned dinosaurs, fighting danger and gaining confidence as they learn to trust one another. She concludes, 'Christianity became clear to me...I experienced the meaning of Christianity. The movie gave me answers to death, the Christian Journey, and allowed me to picture what the Promised Land would be like.' The movie 'exemplified the journey involved in being a Christian'.

What the student papers suggest is that a transcendent/spiritual experience through film means different things to different people. Some could remember a movie that was Spiritual; others chose to talk about film as being spiritual (lower case 's'); and still others considered some films to be parables of Christian truth already known to them. Not surprisingly, the results of these different experiences also varied—from transforming their lives, to offering a spiritual experience or insight, to providing them theological confidence and support. But whether the movie was thought transcendent, spiritual, or supportive of Christian truth, what stood out to all these students was the fact that film has the capacity to deepen our faith, to open us out to God.

From Film to Natural Theology:
Five Observations

The question now before us is this: could this threefold response by these seminary students to the question concerning how they experienced a 'reel spirituality' be of help as
we reflect on natural theology and the arts, and, more particularly, natural theology and
film? Conversely, could discussions of natural theology help us understand something
of the real differences in these student reflections on film? Is there, for example, the same
plurality of meaning that the student responses suggest as we consider the diverse discussions of natural theology? And what might be some implications for our understanding of natural theology in recognizing this? Let me make five observations.

First, just as with the student's varied responses to their assignment in which they
were to describe a transcendent experience, if any, which they had had through watching a movie, so natural theology can, and does, mean a variety of things to different people. For some, to use T. F. Torrance's felicitous phrase, it should be placed 'under the aegis
of revelation', thus becoming dependent upon God's self-revelation. There are, for those
in the Reformed tradition, 'two books' of revelation—that found in the created order
and that found in Scripture. Thus, film, as part of the created order, can be a 'theatre' or
'mirror' that displays the presence of God. Here is one definition of natural theology. For
others, 'natural theology' carries with it the recognition that humanity has access to a
limited knowledge of God through creation, which is mediated through the creativity of
those made in God's image. To transpose Aquinas' argument in his *Summa contra
Gentiles*, meditation on the works of God's creatures—those created in God's image—
'enables us, at least to some extent, to admire and reflect on God's wisdom ... We are thus
able to infer God's wisdom from reflection upon God's work through his creatures'
(2.2.3–4). Seen from this angle, film elicits feelings of wholeness, fittingness, and well-
being that our reason and imagination can access. Still others, particularly during the
last few centuries, have wanted to replace natural theology's *analogia entis* ('analogy of
being') with an *analogia fidei* (an 'analogy of faith'). All knowledge of God is understood
in terms of God's saving revelation in Jesus Christ. Thus, film can provide analogies,
parables, that are valuable for teaching, but these find their referent and meaning not
first of all by their reference to our stories, but to Christ's story. The echoes and hints
found in creation and creativity find their referent in the full revelation of God in Christ
Jesus.

Secondly, we have too often divided knowledge into two compartments—that which
is gained through reason and that which is accessed through the imagination; that which
is revealed by God, namely supernatural knowledge, and that which is knowable by
humankind, namely natural knowledge; that which is propositional belief and that
which is experiential faith; that which is sacred and that which is secular; that which is
Spiritual and that which is spiritual. Yet, the reality of life is messier than all such polari-
ties would suggest, as the students' testimonies of the power of film in their lives reflect.

A significant number of these students had trouble in their descriptions sorting out the spiritual from the Spiritual, the experiential from the reflective, the sacred from the secular. And this is for good reason. Our conscious experiences of the (T)transcendent within the Immanent are complex, involving reason and imagination, symbol and observation, simultaneously. Having said this, it is also often the case that in certain experiences, one or another of our feelings, sense observations, or symbolic relationships tends to predominate. It is this weighting to their movie experience that caused some to say it was transcendent, others that it was profoundly human, and still others that it taught spiritual truth that invited reflection from a Christian perspective.

For example, some of these students had spiritual experiences through film that allowed them to experience awe and wonder outside the typical theological boundaries of creed and Christian community. These feeling perceptions invited further reflection and reintegration within their existing Christian theology and Church life. But what was agenda-setting was not their prior set of beliefs, or their later theological reflections, but the divine encounter itself.

Harvey Cox, along with many others, has commented that as we move from the modern period into the post-modern, we are also moving from the Age of Belief (where beliefs and creeds take precedence) into the Age of the Spirit (where awe and a recognition of mystery become foundational) (Cox 2009: 1–20). As a result, (S)spiritual experience is no longer considered by many as untrustworthy. It is no longer evidence for theological belief that is sought by many, but exemplars. It is not logical inference that holds power over peoples' lives, but testimony. Here surely is the testimony of a large majority of my students' response to their film-going.

What is viewed as foundational is not so much rational necessity, as meaningfulness; not so much proof, as consistency. It is not that for these students one's 'head' has been replaced by one's 'heart', the objective by merely the subjective, but that authentic personal experiences link head and heart, reason and imagination. The era of 'men without chests' is over, to use C. S. Lewis's well-known phrase from his *The Abolition of Man*. Those who think their reasoning power so advanced (their 'heads' so big), do not realize this is only because there has been a shrivelling up of their sentiment (their 'chest'). Both intuition and deduction, love and logic, reason and imagination, must find their place together.

Thirdly, given our increasing recognition of the importance of both the objective and the subjective, or, better, given our understanding that our personal understanding is neither objective nor subjective but personal, we need no longer be captives in our understanding of 'natural theology' to an Enlightenment understanding which has privileged rationality. On the Roman Catholic side, Vatican I spoke of God being known with certitude by higher reason alone. Not to believe this was 'anathema'. There was the assumption here that when reflecting on nature, or perhaps when observing a work of art, one could move reasonably and with sure footing from the known to the unknown, from the natural to the supernatural. But such certitude is rejected by most today, for human reason is limited. It is perspectival and incomplete. Moreover, one's imaginative experiences often open up vistas to the real that otherwise seem unavailable.

Surely this was the witness of the students' experience with film. In their viewing of a particular movie, the unknown expressed itself within the known.

On the Protestant side, Karl Barth seems also to have been operating with an 'Enlightenment' definition of natural theology when he shouted 'Nein' at Emil Brunner's suggestion that creation is a point of contact with God. If Brunner's natural theology was such an attempt to use non-revelatory sources as the basis for knowing God (which I don't think it was), then Barth was correct. If natural theology is a human construction, if it means the misuse/misunderstanding of nature by self-deifying people, then Barth is surely correct in his vehement rejection. But Barth's understanding of natural theology, grounded perhaps in his lack of connection between nature and grace, seems both extreme and unbiblical. Certainly the spiritual/Spiritual experiences of these students while watching film were not considered by most (though there were a few 'Barthians' in the mix) to be their attempt to know God apart from God's own revelation. Rather, the hesitancy of most who were not sure whether their experience had been spiritual or Spiritual, was exactly the opposite—their humility before the divine, and their unwillingness to presume to assert God's presence. Moreover, the experience of others who said they had had a divine encounter was not the attempt to assert the existence of God by human reason (or by imagination for that matter), but the recognition of God's self-revelation through the filmic experience. Romans 1 and Psalm 19 argue that God makes himself know through creation. Genesis 20 and II Chronicles 36 suggests that God is known through human experiences as well. Creation, and by extension human creativity, can become occasions of divine self-disclosure.

In our natural theology, we must avoid both the idolization of Nature, and its denigration. Such extremes have unfortunately been all too typical in Christian theology for the last few centuries. They also seem to be lurking behind a few of my students' choices and comments. In their search for transcendent meaning in film, some gravitated only to Christian-themed films, limiting their spiritual encounters to what had clear Christian symbolism or analogy. Only these qualified for them as spiritually significant. A few others said that only as their viewing of film was put into conversation with our knowledge of the Son through the Spirit, could one talk about film being Spiritual. Both had predetermined that what was transcendent must be anchored in Christian theology and what was 'natural' could only be the occasion of God's presence as it was brought into conversation with God's revelation in Christ. Both groups found in their movie selection only the confirmation of a theology already believed.

But if one recognizes that all knowledge of God is dependent on God's initiative, including that through creation, conscience, and creativity, then such caution is both counter-productive and theologically mistaken. It unnecessarily cuts Christians off from the full range of authentic experiences of God. Moreover, rather than being neutral, disinterested activity, natural theology rooted in the cinema actually presupposes faith. Another way of saying this is that natural theology shows that faith makes sense within the general wisdom of humankind. Rather than God being understood only in the extraordinary, many of the students' experience with film suggests that God can be understood within the wide range of ordinary human experience, including movie-going. What student after student witnessed to was film's ability to point its audience beyond the fragmentary nature of life and help viewers discover a fuller understanding of themselves, the world, and their God.

Fourthly, Avery Dulles, in his tribute to Karl Rahner, has written perceptively on the similarities between discovery and revelation. Here, perhaps, is a helpful way of describing the interrelationship, even the co-inherence, between those experiences dubbed 'spiritual' and those described as 'Spiritual' by my students. Etymologically, the two words—'discovery' and 'revelation'—are nearly synonymous. While 'discovery' means uncovering, or laying bare, 'revelation' means an unveiling. Both refer to 'the manifestation of something previously hidden.' (Dulles 1980: 2) It is in this overlapping of meaning between these two sources of insight, one thought 'natural' and the other 'supernatural', that confusion becomes apparent. Some students testified to the 'Spiritual' meaning of the film they had seen; others to having a 'spiritual' experience. Some believed something had been revealed to them; others, that they had discovered something (often about themselves). The reality is that just as with the etymologies of 'discovery' and 'revelation', the differences between the Spiritual and the spiritual remain indistinct.

Dulles's reflections on 'discovery', making use of the insights of Michael Polanyi, are particularly interesting here. He quotes Polanyi, the scientist turned philosopher, who probed the nature of the scientific method in order to get at its genius:

> Discovery is defined as an advancement of knowledge that cannot be achieved by any, however diligent, application of explicit modes of inference. Yet the discoverer must labor night and day. For though no labor can make a discovery, no discovery can be made without intense, absorbing, devoted labor. Here we have a paradigm of the Pauline scheme of faith, works, and grace [cf. Philippians 2:12b–13]. The discoverer works in the belief that his labors will prepare his mind to receive a truth from sources over which he has no control. [Polanyi 1961: 246–7]

For discovery to take place according to Dulles and Polanyi, what is required is what Polanyi labels 'a heuristic process', in which (1) a certain set of data arouses curiosity, (2) causing one's attention to become focussed on the point where meaning may be expected to emerge. We then coax our mind to deliver suitable ideas (he calls this the 'tacit dimension'), but we cannot force the evidence to reveal its mystery. (3) Instead, a climatic moment of illumination is grasped (it 'comes into our head', 'strikes us', 'presents itself to us'), and (4) the discovery is confirmed, self-validated. In Polanyi's words, the discovery 'arrives accredited in advance by the heuristic craving which evoked it' (Dulles 1980: 3–10).

Here, in summary, is what many of my students also experienced. They saw a movie, where a certain set of data (the film story) coincided with their own felt need evoking curiosity and focussing their attention. As was the case with the student who was addicted to drugs who saw *Traffic*, their attention was focussed such that new meaning emerged, not by their own effort, but as a moment of illumination. That is, they did not so much grasp meaning, but surrendered to it (in his case, to its 'horror'). And the result was 'accredited . . . by the heuristic craving that evoked it'. The discovery that came from watching *Traffic* was at one and the same time both unexpected and yet anticipated. Being summoned to attention by the movie he was watching, the student became focussed on the need for meaning to emerge, and when a new discovery presented itself, it rang true to his spiritual reality, and he left the theatre both shaken and changed.

What is telling about my student's experience is not how easily his discovery fits Polanyi's paradigm, but that my student also called this experience the work of God in his life. It was 'revelation', not just 'discovery'. Or as Dulles suggests, it may have been both. In its human and phenomenological aspects, the category of discovery may, in fact, be an acceptable way of speaking about what traditionally has been called 'revelation'. What from one perspective is 'a fulfillment of a human heuristic craving' to discern more fully the true meaning of their existence, might be seen from another 'as a gift of God'. That is, something might be both 'spiritual' and 'Spiritual' ('I sought the Lord, and afterwards I knew; I was found by Thee'). Dulles concludes his discussion of Polanyi's understanding of discovery with these words: 'Seen from above, it is God's free act of self-communication; seen from below, it is the self-unfolding of the human spirit in its quest for transcendent truth and meaning' (Dulles 1980: 21).

Fifthly, and finally, a more developed pneumatology seems necessary if we are to understand theologically the spiritual experiences of those at the movies. Though God's revelation is one, for God is one, to focus upon salvation history, as a few of the students did in responding to film, is to bias the discussion towards the Christological, and away from the Spirit. Natural theology, on the other hand, gets us outside the soteriologically charged and opens us to the pneumatological. It can be of real assistance in this regard as we try to understand film's spiritual possibilities. To be sure, natural theology, to be fully grasped, needs the light of God's revelation in Christ Jesus. But to begin Christologically, or to move there too quickly or strongly, risks closing one's ears to the depth-soundings of natural theology, aborting the exploration of God's presence outside the believing community experience of Christ. This is what happened to Karl Barth as creation theology was eclipsed by his Christomonism. Listen as well to C. S. Lewis who though he first met God through experiences of nature and the arts, ends his autobiography *Surprised By Joy* with these words:

> When we are lost in the woods the sight of a signpost is a great matter. He who first sees it cries 'Look!' The whole party gathers round and stares. But when we have found the road and are passing signposts every few miles, we shall not stop and stare. They will encourage us and we shall be grateful for the authority which set them up. But we shall not stop...though their pillars are silver and lettering of gold. [Lewis 1955: 238]

Here is the danger of a soteriological approach.

In his second speech *On Religion*, Friedrich Schleiermacher explores art's ability to 'awaken' religious feeling, to 'open up' and 'direct' individuals to religion, for art 'belongs to' and 'proceeds from' an original religious impulse. Discussing the possibility of a conversion, or awakening, in the hearts of his friends who were 'cultured despisers of religion', Schleiermacher wrote:

> If it is true that there are sudden conversions whereby in men, thinking of nothing less than of lifting themselves above the finite, in a moment, as by an immediate, inward illumination, the sense of the highest comes forth and surprises them by its splendour, I believe that more than anything else the sight of a great and sublime work of art can accomplish this miracle. [Schleiermacher 1988: 138–9]

One thinks of Tillich's experience during a furlough from the horrors of the First World War when he walked into a Berlin museum and looked straight into Botticelli's 'Madonna with Singing Angels'. He called the experience 'revelatory ecstasy.'

Schleiermacher at times seems wrongly to conflate spirit and Spirit, as I would understand him, but his instincts are sound. For him, there not only is 'feeling' (*Gefuhl*), which is the immediate consciousness of the whole of ourselves as it is affected by the existence of all things in and through the infinite, but there is 'intuition' (*Anschauung*), our immediate perception of the divine revealing itself through our lived-experiences. Where *Gefuhl* concerns an inward and subjective awareness, a feeling, *Anschauung* suggests the self-disclosure of an 'Other', an intuition. Religion, that is, must be defined, not only in terms of the Self, but in terms of Another. It is the work of the Spirit in and through our spirits that is the basis of one's (T)transcendent experiences in and through film. Reflecting on the testimonies of my students and drawing on Schleiermacher's insights, I would conclude that many of the spiritual/Spiritual experiences they had were the work of the Spirit active, present, and in conversation with them in and through the affective spaces opened up within the cinematic experience. The filmic event offered these students an occasion whereby God entered their lives.

Conclusion

Although 'natural theology' has traditionally had to do with rational reflection on nature, the concept can be broadened to include not only creation, but creativity; not only reason, but imagination; not only deduction, but intuition. Perhaps Moltmann is correct that the better term would be 'creaturely' theology (Moltmann 2000: 67). Key to any natural, or creaturely, theology through the arts—or more particularly, key to film becoming a spiritual/Spiritual experience for its viewers—is what Sallie McFague has labelled the 'loving eye' rather than the 'arrogant eye' (McFague 1997: 67–117). Here, perhaps, was the difference between some of those students in the third group who used their theological grid to 'judge' the movie they were watching; and those who instead were opened by the movie to first experiencing its story as their own. As one of the students confessed, he most often held 'film at arms length, attempting to analyze it as a specimen of sorts'. Rather than Martin Buber's 'I–Thou' experience, his movie-viewing could be characterized as an 'I–It' experience.

Film, of course, provides a particularly powerful opportunity for 'I–Thou' experiences. As many have observed, the Cineplex functions almost like a cathedral: people come expecting something; the room is darkened; you pay your money; you give over

your attention; you are open to entertaining something new (here is the original meaning of 'entertain-ment'—to entertain new thoughts, experiences, people); the music sets
the mood; your co-participants help direct your emotions by their responses. But for the
Spirit to be present, the first step must be that of 'paying attention'.

McFague, writing about *Super, Natural Christians* (1997), focusses her attention on
how to read 'the Book of Nature'. Hers is an ecological concern. But her comments apply
equally not only to creation, but to creativity; not only to science, but to the arts.
Particularly relevant is McFague's distinguishing between Descartes's 'objectification' of
what you see (holding it disinterestedly at arm's length), and the loving eye's focussing
on the other so absolutely that there is a radical 'objectivity'. In this way, love is actually
the discovery of reality. Enraptured by—that is, in love with—the 'reality' on the big
screen, viewers are able to see more, to discover more. We must reject the artist Frank
Stella's famous, but wrong-headed observation: 'What you see is what you see.' When
you pay attention, there is something more (Monti 2003: 78). And ultimately, as Simone
Weil has recognized, 'absolute unmixed attention is prayer' (Weil 2001).

REFERENCES

Barna, G. (2005). *Revolution!* Wheaton, IL: Tyndale.

Barsotti, Catherine M. and Robert K. Johnston (2004). *Finding God in the Movies: 33 Films of
Reel Faith*. Grand Rapids, MI: Baker.

Bergesen, Albert J. and Andrew M. Greeley (2000). *God in the Movies*. Piscataway, NJ:
Transaction Publishers.

Cox, H. (2009). *The Future of Faith*. New York: HarperCollins, HarperOne.

Dark, David (2002). *Everyday Apocalypse: The Sacred Revealed in Radiohead, The Simpsons,
and Other Pop Culture Icons*. Grand Rapids, IL: Brazos Press.

Detweiler, C. and B. Taylor (2003). *A Matrix of Meaning: Finding God in Pop Culture*. Grand
Rapids: Baker Academic.

Dulles, A. (1980). 'Revelation and Discovery' in *Theology and Discovery: Essays in Honor of
Karl Rahner, S.J.* Edited by William J. Kelly. Milwaukee: Marquette University Press.

Gire, K. (1996). *Windows of the Soul: Experiencing God in New Ways*. Grand Rapids: Zondervan.

—— (2000). *Reflections on the Movies: Hearing God in the Unlikeliest of Places*. Wheaton, IL:
Victor Books.

Higgins, Gareth (2003). *How Movies Helped Save My Soul: Finding God's Fingerprints in
Culturally Significant Films*. Lake Mary, FL: Relevant Books.

Johnston, R. (2004). *Useless Beauty: Ecclesiastes through the Lens of Contemporary Film*. Grand
Rapids: Baker Academic.

—— (2006). *Reel Spirituality: Theology and Film in Dialogue*. Grand Rapids, MI: Baker.

Lewis, C. S. (1955). *Surprised by Joy*. New York: Harcourt, Brace & World.

Loughlin, Gerard (2005). 'Spirituality and Film' in *The New SCM Dictionary of Christian
Spirituality*. Edited by Philip Sheldrake. London: SCM Press: pp. 302–3.

McFague, S. (1997). *Super, Natural Christians: How we should Love Nature*. Minneapolis:
Fortress Press.

McGrath, Alister E. (2009). 'On Secrets, Lilies and Daisies: A Response to Holmes Rolston'.
Conversations in Religion and Theology 7(2): 194–206.

Martin, Joel and Conrad Ostwalt Jr (1995). *Screening the Sacred: Religion, Myth, and Ideology in Popular American Film*. Boulder, CO: Westview Press.

Moltmann, J. (2000). *Experiences in Theology*. Minneapolis: Fortress Press.

Monti, A. (2003). *A Natural Theology of the Arts*. Burlington, VT: Ashgate.

Polanyi, M. (1961). 'Faith and Reason'. *Journal of Religion* 41: 237–47.

Schleiermacher, F. (1988). *On Religion: Speeches to its Cultured Despisers*. New York: Cambridge University Press.

Viladesau, R. (1999). *Theological Aesthetics*. New York: Oxford University Press.

Weil, S. (2001). *Waiting for God*. New York: HarperCollins, Perennial.

Index